In memoriam
Frank, Wilf, Doris and Ron.

maurice barnwell

DESIGN CREATIVITY & CULTURE

AN ORIENTATION TO DESIGN

black dog publishing
london uk

CONTENTS

FUTURES

PROLOGUE

DESIGN IS A CULTURE, NOT A DEPARTMENT
In today's world design is everywhere, or, to be more precise, design awareness is everywhere. In the last decade design has evolved, its application now near universal, its discipline specific practice augmented by interest from an array of areas contiguous to design. *Design, Creativity, and Culture: An Orientation to Design* offers a unique, fresh and innovative approach to assessing the role of design and creativity in human culture. It is objective and free from overt bias, acknowledging design history, design process, cultural studies, media studies, visual culture, political culture, and information technologies. It is inclusive, making reference to the full spectrum of design disciplines from various cultures, providing examples from architecture, interior and product design, fashion and graphic design. Intended for students and practitioners of all design disciplines and for anyone with an interest in the interaction between design and culture. The text provides an exploration of the cultural heritage of design together with future visions on the role of design in the coming decade. It provides an essential orientation to the understanding of design in the twenty-first century.

WHY DESIGN?
Design is a decision-making process, to quote Frank Pick, "design is intelligence made visible".[1] Design matters, it always has. In 40,000 years humankind has progressed from the manufacture of items of survival to items that indicate 'lifestyle'.[2] We have come full circle, in the coming decade design will once more be concerned with human survival.[3]

There is always something to be sold–be it product, ideas or attitude. In the cultural climate of post-Second World War, (addressed in Section Two, "Form") the meaning and role of design changed from activities concerned with personal survival to those reflective of commercial survival. The market-based economy would remain the dominant design reality, proving the cultural context for design for the next 50 years or so until the arrival of digital realties. In the second decade of the twenty-first century design will, by necessity, have more to do with people, ideas and attitudes and, taking advantage of available interconnections, suggest pathways towards a sustainable future, (see Section Three, "Futures".)

WHY CREATIVITY?
Creativity has been an intrinsic component of human survival. It is an essential motivational ingredient to the process of design innovation. It is often the result of team work and is dependent on what is already known. Creativity relies on passionate, inspired, knowledgeable intuition, it is never the result of navel gazing; it is the process of making unusual connections.

Humans have a long and distinguished history in the application of creative thought processes in solving, by design, the challenges presented by living on this planet. Over two and a half million years ago early hominids were using simple stone tools to assist in their survival. For millennia the basic form and utilitarian nature of those tools remained unchanged. There were some refinements of design which produced tools of greater diversity but the basic format remained unchanged. Then about 40,000 years ago there was a dramatic surge in creativity and in the material culture of our ancestors; they began to produce a wide range of tools, began to fabricate dwellings and began to document their lifestyle. The culture of design began.

WHY CULTURE?
We live in culture. As the economist and social critic Thomas Sowell so adroitly explains, it is culture that helps people "cope and aspire amid the realties of life".[4] Unfortunately, all too often, design ideas fail to connect meaningfully or effectively with peoples lives. And it is lives that matter. A designer must be an inquisitive observer of human cultures. To quote Aldous Huxley:

> *To see ourselves as others see us is a most salutary gift. Hardly less important is the capacity to see others as they see themselves.*[5]

Culture is information dependent. Design changes culture and at the same time is shaped by it. The presence of culture and the practice of design exist in a state of symbiosis, providing a network of opportunities to the vigilant practitioner. Culture generates design diversity. Modifications stemming from cultural evolution both reflect and determine developments in design. Cultural beliefs and social practices create and reinforce frames of meaning which, in turn, influence ways of relating to a product or service.[6] These cultural framings impact on how people use or do not use a particular product. Cultural values are often reflected in the form and function of a product, and are integral component parts of lifestyle.[7] It is culture that gives products relevance and provides the rituals within which artefacts are used. Subject to our cultural allegiance and by what we choose to believe, we all process available information in a personal way, creating a unique view of reality.

TELL ME A STORY
There are consequences to everything we do and do not do; our actions are shaped by our understanding of the

world, and that understanding is dependent upon our stories. Designs weave narratives and fantasies that have significant value to the user. The role and significance of the story-telling process in human culture is well documented. In *Design Redux*, Stuart Walker notes that "the stories, mythologies and histories kept alive in oral cultures become compelling, intricate, relevant and profound because they were allowed to evolve over time, were contributed to by many, were changed and adapted to context and, in the process, accumulated layers of meaning and complexity".[8] He sees recent developments in computer applications and in design practice as having "strong parallels" to the story-telling process. "An object without history is fiction and an object which has not moved on from history is retrospective. An authentic product could be seen as a mix of the two."[9]

What story are you going to tell? You have access to an array of highly adaptive and exploratory technologies, from iPods and iPads, from smartphones, through the www, YouTube, Twitter and Facebook. These offer unimagined possibilities in adapting to and utilising the story-telling process in the design process. For the first time in human history design has the very real possibility of being truly inclusive, incorporating voices, ideas and concepts from others to assist in the research based design challenges that lie ahead. A word of caution; be ever vigilant against controls imposed, overtly or covertly, by government agencies or communication monoliths.

DESIGN, CREATIVITY, AND CULTURE: DESIGN ORIENTATION

Culture shapes how humans perceive reality. One of the more significant characteristics of design is its ability to adjust to changing cultural contexts, from the nineteenth century utopian idealism of William Morris through the more egotistical statements of some of the star designers of the latter part of the twentieth century. Design is diverse. It can, to quote John Maeda, "connect deeply to the greater context of life".[10] Or, as Victor Papanek observes, the role of much of the design of the last half of the twentieth century failed to connect to that context. "As long as design concerns itself with confecting trivial 'toys for adults', killing machines with gleaming tail fins, and 'sexed-up' shrouds for typewriters, toasters, telephones, and computers, it has lost all reason to exist."[11] The reality, as is often the case, falls between these polemic disputations. Some design is designed to sell, some to be useful, some to make a statement, some to objectify an argument. If, as is often stated, design is problem solving, then as Koberg and Bagnall explain, "the design process is a problem solving journey".[13] Lets begin the journey.

The opening section, "Matrix", provides a wide ranging overview of design and its place in human culture. The second section, "Form", provides a more detailed assessment of the cross-disciplinary nature of design, from the aftermath of the post-Second World War period up to the present with its emphasis on environmental concerns. The final section, "Futures", is exactly that—an assessment of the changes in the nature of the design process and practice that are required to face up to the encounters ahead as we strive for a sustainable world. Today's designers are faced with a crystal ball of possibilities. *Design, Creativity, and Culture* provides an orientation to design. It shows how previous generations responded to change, presents current concerns, and offers suggestions as to how designers can prepare for their future. Enjoy.

"Would you tell me, please, which way I ought to go from here?"
"That depends a good deal on where you want to get to", said the Cat.
"I don't much care where", said Alice.
"Then it doesn't matter which way you go", said the Cat.
"so long as I get somewhere", Alice added as an explanation.
"Oh, you're sure to do that", said the Cat,
"if you only walk long enough."
Lewis Carroll (Charles Lutwidge Dodgson),
Alice's Adventures in Wonderland, 1865.

MATRIX

Pronunciation:
/ˈmeɪtrɪks/
noun (plural matrices /-siːz/ or matrixes

the cultural, social, or political
environment in which something develops.

Origin:
late middle English (in the sense 'womb'):
from Latin, 'breeding female', later
'womb', from *mater, matr-* 'mother'

Source:
Oxford Dictionaries online

CHAPTER ONE
COSMOS: DESIGN EVOLUTION

Technology becomes interesting when it facilitates new kinds of interaction among teachers, students, and the external world.[1]
John Thackara.

A WAY FORWARD BY DESIGN

After a design heritage stretching back over 30,000 years we seem to have lost our creative way in a maze of technology. A maze always has two principle characteristics, a path (think of this as being your chosen personal design philosophy) and walls (prevailing social conditions and cultural constraints.) The path, forward or backward, is a matter of personal choice. The creative design process can assist in explaining past affairs and in the deciphering of many of the challenges that lie ahead.

First, technology is not the enemy. Stone tools, printing, steam power, electricity, the Internet, all have shaped human culture. All have impacted on the design process. All have generated new problems and areas of concern. All have demanded the application of new ways of seeing and thinking. All have, eventually, enhanced the human condition. A common response to the current multifarious sphere of design is a feeling of being out of control. John Thackara explains;

> Most of us feel far from in control. We're filling up the world with amazing devices and systems—on top of the natural and human ones that were already here—only to discover that these complex systems seem to be out of control: too complex to understand, let alone to shape, or redirect. Things may seem out of control—but they are not out of our hands. Many of the troubling situations in our world are the result of design decisions. Too many of them were bad design decisions.... If we can design our way into difficulty, we can design our way out.[2]

Where to begin?

IN THE BEGINNING

Our story will end around 4.5 billion years from now when our galaxy collides with the giant Andromeda spiral galaxy that is made up of about a trillion stars and lies roughly 2.5 million light years away.[4] Coincidently,

this is approximately the same time that the fuel powering our sun runs out. The sun will blow up into a giant red giant and engulf many of the surrounding planets. As Sir Martin Rees, the Astronomer Royal points out, "Any creatures who witness the sun's demise, here on Earth or far beyond, won't be human. They will be entities as different from us as we are from a bug."[5]

Our story began some 13.7 billion years ago with the Big Bang and the birth of the universe.[6] Much later, around 4.5 billion years ago our Sun and Earth were formed.[7] By about 4.3 billion years ago, the magma had cooled, the continental crust had begun to form and the atmosphere and seas began to form.[8] Between 3.8 and 4.5 billion years ago the Earth suffered a meteorite bombardment that may have introduced the essential genetic ingredients of all known life forms and doubled the amount of water on Earth.[9] The Great Oxidation Event occurred about 2.4 billion years ago and led to a sudden rise of oxygen to levels similar to those experienced today.[10] During the Cambrian explosion around 600 million years ago, vertebrates started to evolve.[11] It took another 250 million years for life to creep out of the sea and onto the beaches and into the giant ferns. 250 million years before the present era the first mammals and dinosaurs had appeared.[12] The long reign of the dinosaurs ended abruptly about 67 million years ago, probably because of a cooling planet and possibly another meteorite or asteroid impact such as the one which created the Chicxulub crater in the Yucatan.[13]

The *cetaceans* (whales, dolphins and porpoises) descendants of land-living mammals, entered the water roughly 50 million years ago. Many millennia later anthropoid apes began to swing from the deciduous trees alongside the herds of grazing animals that roamed the broad savannas of what is now Africa. Monkeys branched off from their ape ancestors between 25 and 30 million years ago. Around seven million years ago our human ancestors diverged from their common chimpanzee line—chimpanzees and soon-to-be humans had parted company—an evolutionary transition had occurred.[14] Only after this evolutionary step did we develop the three significant characteristics that made possible our rapid evolution and global dominance—an upright stance, a large brain, and tool making skills—characteristics that made possible the culture of design.

New discoveries and reinterpretations of human evolution are constantly modifying our view of things, but according to recent research the early upright bipedal hominid put in an appearance around four million years ago, more likely a scavenger than a hunter and probably a vegetarian. *Homo erectus* came onto the scene about two million years ago and remained the most successful species for one and a half million years before disappearing from the fossil record approximately 250,000 years ago.[15]

A computer-assisted reconstruction of a Neanderthal child by a research team at the Anthropological Institute, University of Zürich.[16]

Between 200,000 and 120,000 years ago variants of *Homo sapiens* evolved including *Homo sapiens neanderthalensis* who lived in Europe surviving through some dramatic fluctuations in climate, before dying out 25,000 years ago. What may be regarded as the first traces of modern humans can now be dated to around 100,000 years ago. It would seem that for some time *Homo sapiens* sapiens competed with *Homo sapiens neanderthalensis* for the dominant evolutionary role.[17] *Homo sapiens sapiens* (the sapiens variety of the species *Homo sapiens*) are the only remaining living representative of the family *Homo genus* of bipedal primates in *Hominidae*, the great ape family.[18] We are on our own.

THE INCREDIBLE JOURNEY

Two things are evident—our ancestors propagated and travelled until they populated most of the planet. Recent research indicates that the all modern *Homo sapiens* sapiens, outside of Africa, owe their existence to a single tribe of maybe 200 persons who crossed the Red Sea some 70,000 years ago from the Horn of Africa and into Arabia, a portentous journey of what was then about eight miles. From there they went on to colonise the rest of the world.[19] The $50 million Genographic project is a massive study of DNA samples from a quarter of a million volunteers in different continents that is providing the most precise map yet of humankind's great colonisation of earth showing that the modern day human populations in Europe, Asia, Australia, North America and South America are all descended from these common ancestors.[20] The origins of the modern human species is documented in a recent BBC programme, *The Incredible Human Journey*.[21]

As our ancestors travelled they evolved and developed complex social structures. Our proto-ancestors ritualised actions. Social interactions established social norms. Humans are the only species on earth that build fires, cook their food, clothe themselves, and develop technology, all of which require intelligent observation, analysis, and planned repetition, the basic elements of the design process. Humans have also developed a desire for self-expression; this has led to cultural innovations such as art, literature, music and design. Around 35,000 years ago the first anatomically-modern human had moved into Europe. Our ancestors evolved in their evolutionary niche, developed and used tools and, for us the most revolutionary and significant fact, they found it necessary to codify knowledge and to leave a record of what they knew to be real. The design process began to evolve.[22]

THE WALKING, TALKING, THINKING, DESIGNING HUMANOID

There is much that we still do not know about our beginnings. We do know from the fossil evidence that the evolutionary process was well and truly at work, favouring those with the ability to walk upright, maybe because this posture allowed them to see more of the immediate environment or, far more likely, because it freed the hands to do other things, making them better providers. We know that over a considerable time period, the sophisticated toe control necessary for tree climbing gave way to an increased sensitivity and manipulative ability of the hands. The fingers became even more dexterous. The hip and thigh bone changed to bear the additional weight of walking upright, but it still needs some evolutionary improvement; just think of the thousands of hip replacement operations that happen every year! And of course our feet changed as we developed an instep and arch, all the better to walk with.

The most significant change was in the size of the brain. Despite having bodies only around one-fifth larger than chimpanzees, our brains are around 250 per cent heavier. In the last 3 to 4 million years hominid brain volume has increased from less than 400 ml to roughly 1400 ml. The modern brain is a network of astounding three-dimensional intricacy—it contains close to one hundred billion nerve cells, or neurons. Each of these cells has the capacity for connecting to hundreds or maybe even thousands of other cells through synapses—we may have as many as 100 trillion possible connections—a little like the Internet.[23]

Challenging the brain is thought to help in maintaining existing synaptic connections and may encourage the formation of new connections.[24] Some cultural commentators see the brain as a human based computer that processes information using ordered, logical operations. However, research indicates that brain operates in a random manner, "disorder is essential to the brain's ability to transmit information and solve problems.... Hovering on the edge of chaos provides brains with their amazing capacity to process information and rapidly adapt to our ever-changing environment."[25] Significantly, as John Locke pointed out way back in 1690 in "An Essay Concerning Human Understanding", each human mind is unique, with its own history.[26] More about creativity in Chapter Four, "The Creative Act and the Prepared Mind".

The dramatic increase in brain size paved the way for language, creativity and other unique aspects of human mental capacity.[27] Big brains require lots of energy to operate. The human brain accounts for about two per cent of adult body weight yet it uses 20 per cent of the body's total energy production and consumes around 25 per cent of its oxygen intake.[28] Dietary changes that incorporated the higher calorific content obtained from meat is thought to have provided the energy that the brain required to grow. It had taken around six million years for the pre-human brain to grow enough to allow for thinking patterns linked to communal living, creativity, and the invention and use of tools. Once this leap had taken place and as social interaction developed an even more rapid rate of change occurred, modifying the way our ancestors thought, and establishing the matrix for the beginning of the culture of design.

Like most primates, humans are by nature social beings, but what is it that sets us apart from our primate cousins? Social acts that we now take for granted such as the cooking of food over a fire gave early *Homo sapiens sapiens* distinct advantages.[29] Cooking would have helped break down cellulose in foraged plants which would have made the food more digestible. Cooking meat would have helped kill microbial parasites often found in wild animals. In addition, fire provided some protection from the cold and would have helped keep predators away from camp sites at night. Fire probably also would have been a focal point for social gatherings. It is very tempting to humanise our early ancestors, to visualise an extended family coming together around the fire pit to eat, socialise and maybe plan tomorrows adventure—but that is more fantasy than fact.[30]

THE CREATIVE PRIMATE

What has set us apart from other species on the evolutionary trail is our creative ability. In a very short time we have adapted to live in every climactic region on earth and are now considering extra terrestrial habitations. We have manipulated, by design, every known material and when that was not enough we have invented new ones. From our very beginnings we have found it necessary to give visual form to ideas and concepts. We have considered it essential to codify knowledge and we have found it appropriate to bring order and clarity to our lives, to live a designed life. John Heskett points out that "design, stripped to its essence, can be defined as the human capacity to shape and make our environment in ways without precedent in nature, to serve our needs and give meaning to our lives…. Design matters because, together with language, it is the defining characteristic of what it is to be human."[31]

Handy hand axes—these multipurpose tools that could have been used to chop wood, butcher animals, and make other tools, dominated early human technology for more than a million years. Ancient hand axes have been found in Africa (left), Asia (centre), and Europe (right).

THE TOOL-MAKER

Recent research has pointed to the fact that many other animal species make tools. "Nonetheless, human tool-making has a characteristic that makes it different from animal tool-making. Humans make tools to make tools."[32] The earliest evidence of stone tool-making may date back more than 2.5 million years. The use of Acheulean techniques of tool-making are normally dated from around 1.65 million years ago to about 100,000 years ago. The evolutionary advance in the making of stone tools during this period may have exercised the human brain, paved the way for language development and encouraged advanced social behaviours relating to the division of labour and the associated activity of group hunting. Recent research by a group from the Department of Bioengineering, Imperial College, London, indicates direct links between tool-making and language evolution during the lower Palaeolithic era.[33] "Our study reinforces the idea that tool-making and language evolved together as both required more complex thought, making the end of the lower Palaeolithic a pivotal time in our history. After this period, early humans left Africa and began to colonise other parts of the world."[34]

Between 70,000 and 40,000 years ago things changed dramatically.[35] Tool technology became increasingly sophisticated and changed values and lifestyles; it changed the very pattern of human life. Enhanced tool design made hunting more efficient. Hunting needed to be done in teams, this changed the working day and the menu. As with modern chimpanzees the majority of the day had been taken up with foraging for the fruits and berries to sustain life. Now, a group of tool using hunters could bring home enough food from a single excursion to feed several family groups for days. This relatively simple act, the hunting group, changed social interaction and gave rise to the extended family group with a more secure base and a more permanent sense of society. Our ancestors now had time to develop other skills and activities. These early ancestors laid down the basic mental matrix necessary for thought and reason, language and culture, creative expression and the practice of design. The sequential mind of these modern humans had the power to conceptualise, to envisage something that did not exist. The manufacture of stone tools required the power of serial thinking, the ability to make something bit-by-bit in a very specific order, and to repeat the process. The shape of the tool was now determined by the process rather than the natural shape of the material. Creativity and design changed patterns of culture.

These changes in lifestyle were to impact on our physique. Preciously massive bodies were also reduced as the technology became more advanced, relying on better tools and a switch from thrusting to throwing spears. (Some researchers claim that our ancestors shrank by about six inches—but this is still being debated.) The archaeological remains of these early humans show far less physical stress than Neanderthal. Plus it would seem that these peoples lived longer and exhibited a longer period of dependency, characteristic of today's humans. Longer lives meant that the older generation could instruct the next generation, in this way, the history and culture of the tribal group could be passed on—the beginning of learning. It may not be too fanciful to imagine those travellers of our past surviving and multiplying, continuing their evolutionary march into the present. Motivated by creativity, inspired by their information rich data banks, developing and using the first technology; a technology that changed our physiology, gave us language, encouraged new hunting skills and patterns of social interaction. A technology that was linked to the design process, that helped determine human culture and made us who we are!

Be culturally literate, because if you don't have any understanding of the world you live in and the culture you live in, you're not going to express anything to anybody else.
Paula Scher, Graphic Designer, Partner, Pentagram.

CULTURAL EVOLUTION[36]

There is no consensus as to what constitutes culture. Cultures are a reflection of shared meanings and accepted values. In 1750, Samuel Johnson observed; "We are all prompted by the same motives, all deceived by the same fallacies, all animated by hope, obstructed by danger, entangled by desire, and seduced by pleasure."[37] More recently, writing in 1949, Clyde Kluckhohn concluded that culture refers to "the total way of life of a people", and it is "a way of thinking and believing".[38] And later in "The Study of Culture", he concludes that "A culture refers to the distinctive way of life of a group of people, their complete 'design for living'." In 2002, Steven Pinker adds a more timely explanation. "Culture... is a pool of technological and social innovations that people accumulate to help them live their lives."[39] A view endorsed by Denis Dutton, "The truth of the human situation is that we are biologically determined organism that live in culture. That we are cultural creatures is part of what is determined by our genes."[40]

Culture has made us what we are, it has moulded our patterns of thought, provided us with our values and preferences and has helped furnish us with our social norms. Cultural 'know-how' is obtained through the input of information, and can provide 'tools of understanding', or, to use a phrase of JM Balkin, it can provide each of us with the prerequisite cultural software necessary for our life on earth. "The different beliefs and worldviews that human beings possess are

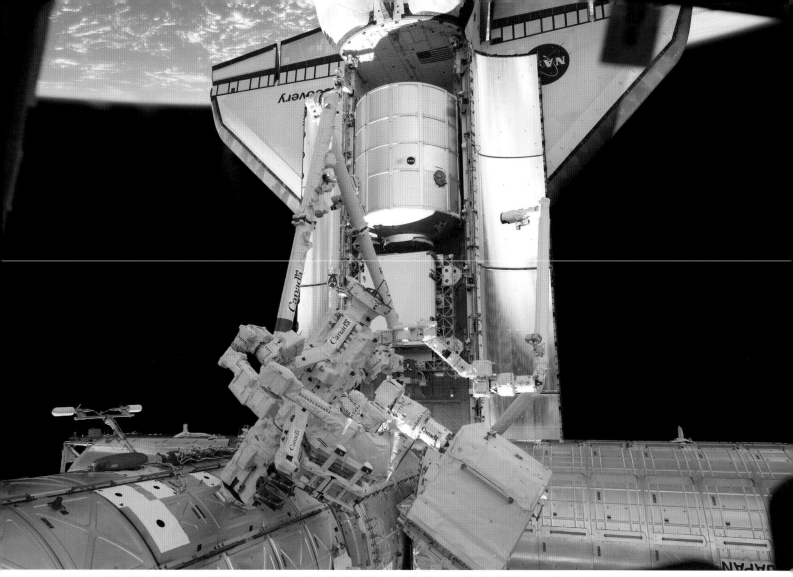

The docked space shuttle Discovery and the Canadian-built Dextre, also known as the Special Purpose Dextrous Manipulator (SPDM), are featured in this image. Photo: STS-133 crew member on the International Space Station. 26 February 2011. NASA.

the product of the evolution of cultural information that is instantiated in human beings and helps make them the unique individuals they are."[41] Human beings living in close proximity need a sense of order, a sense of belonging, and a sense of meaning in their lives. The Canadian archaeologist and anthropologist Bruce Trigger summarises, "Culture is constructed by humans in order to communicate and create community... culture is an assemblage of imaginings and meanings... culture is always transitional, open and unstable."[42]

How do humans learn culture? Balkin offers some suggestions. "Culture is not a top-down network.... It is more like the network of networks called the Internet, which has no centre and in which an astonishing array of diverse information flows from different points simultaneously."[43] Many anthropologists and sociologists accept that human beings have natural social tendencies and that particular human social behaviours have non-genetic causes and dynamics. This approach implies continual cultural change. Culture is never static. Cultures are dynamic and ever-changing and responsive to changes in ways of thinking and meaning.

In some saloons of the Wild West it was customary to check your gun at the entrance. In some of the more enlightened eating establishments of the twenty-first century you are required to check your cell phone on entry—and for much the same reason—the possible interruption of social discourse.

Designers play a decisive role in endowing the products and services of a culture with their significant meaning. We have progressed from an industrial society through a post-industrial society where services and information were more important than industry and goods, to a new, yet to be designated information rich society where sustainability is the defining characteristic. Cultures will change to adapt to the necessary adjustments required to ensure our continued survival. Designers need to be ultra sensitive to the consequences of cultural change.

THE END OF EVOLUTION?

The fossil record makes it very clear that the mystifying Cambrian explosion, often dated as between 520 and 580 million years ago, changed the patterns of life on earth. Some of the finest examples of early life, the diminutive Pikaia, "harkens from the Burgess Shale, a forbidding windswept outcrop in the Canadian Rockies that once, some 520 million years ago, was located at the edge of a tropical, equatorial reef teeming with life".[44] The investigation of this event remains a topic of intense speculation. What is most apparent is that there was a cataclysmic shift in the ecosystem that changed the nature of the atmosphere and biosphere. In our modern world, equally powerful forces are at work which will change the human habitat forever; most of these have political, economic and commercial overtones, many have implications for the design culture.

Technology changes faster than nature. The scientific and technological achievements of the last century are awesome, their implications huge. Today we modify the temperature of our living environment irrespective of outside climate, we can live anywhere on this planet and indeed in extraterrestrial habitations. We can live in illuminated environments 24 hours a day. We have instant access to most, if not all, of human knowledge, and we have ever present interactive forms of communication. We can travel to any place on the globe and return before the end of the week. And yet, and yet....

SOME THINGS NEVER CHANGE

For all our advances we face the same social problems that have plagued humanity for millennia. As Lee McIntyre, summarises;

> We have satellites and fax machines that transmit stories of barbarous cruelty that could have been told by our ancestors. We have ever more sophisticated weaponry of war and yet no true understanding of what causes war in the first place. Terrorism, crime, war, and poverty continue unchecked throughout the world, largely because we lack the understanding to stop them. We are as ignorant of the cause-and-effect relations behind our own behaviour as those who lived in the eighth or ninth centuries once were of those behind disease, famine, eclipses, and natural disasters. We live today in what will someday come to be thought of as the Dark Ages of human thought about social problems.[45]

This view is endorsed by Paul Collier, Professor of Economics, Oxford University, who notes that the least developed countries "coexist with the twenty-first century, but their reality is the fourteenth century; civil war, plague, ignorance".[46]

DESIGN EVOLUTION;
FROM VITRUVIAN MAN TO ASIMO

The human capacity for creativity, expressed as deign, has allowed for the introduction into the world that which was not there before.[47] This is the process of design. What may be regarded as one of the earliest attempts to codify the design process may be found in the writings of Vitruvius and dates from around 80 to 10 BCE. In his *De architectura* (*The Ten Books on Architecture*),Vitruvius establishes the interdisciplinary nature of design theory and practice.[48] He maintains that architects need a liberal education, they should be knowledgeable in both the arts and sciences, he stresses the importance of geometry, optics, mathematics, music and medicine. Architects must have a firm understanding of history and philosophy which renders them "courteous, just, and honest without avariciousness", and capable of presenting visual renditions of their designs while defending their designs in a logical and informed manner. Two millennia later and these observations remain valid—not just to architecture but all design related activities.

Vitruvius is remembered today for his research in what was to become the field of ergonomics. *Vitruvian Man*, produced by Leonardo da Vinci, is an illustration of the human body inscribed in the circle and the square derived from a passage about geometry and human proportions in the writings of Vitruvius. Variations of this initial study of human related proportions and the apparent harmony of the human form is now applied to architecture and all areas of art and design.

Historical applications of standardised measurement were evident during the Middle Ages when architects, builders and craft labourers produced the magnificent majesty of the Gothic cathedrals. Not a blueprint nor architectural drawing in sight! To quote from the BBC web site:

> The Medieval mason was not a monk but a highly skilled lay craftsman who combined the roles of architect, builder, craftsman, designer and engineer. Using only a set of compasses, a set square and a staff or rope marked off in halves, thirds and fifths, the mason was able to construct some of the most amazing structures ever built: Gothic cathedrals. Their awesome size combined with their appearance of lightness and fragility have led people to believe that Medieval masons had some magical secret but this was actually just an understanding of proportion and basic geometry.[49]

That 'understanding' of the Master Mason was stockpiled in his head—just imagine having the ability to construct mental cathedrals. Today, the term anthropometrics is used when referencing the standardised measurement of the human individual for the purposes of understanding human physical variations.[50] In 1955, Henry Dreyfuss, in his *Designing for People*, introduced the design world to Joe and Josephine. These two anthropometric figures "remind us that everything we design is used by people, and that people come in many sizes and have varying physical attributes... Joe and Josephine have numerous allergies, inhibitions, and obsessions.

They react strongly to touch that is uncomfortable or unnatural; they are disturbed by glaring or insufficient light and by offensive colouring; they are sensitive to noise, and they shrink from disagreeable odour.

Our job is to make Joe and Josephine compatible with their environment. The process is known as human engineering."[51] Different environments necessitate different standards of compatibility.

DESIGN PROFILE: SIZE CHINA

SizeChina. Each of the ten head forms was designed using two hundred individual scans.
All images courtesy Size China.

Roger Ball is a Canadian designer and a graduate of the Ontario College of Art & Design and of the Domus Academy, now resident in Hong Kong. After graduation he co-founded Paradox Design and created a wide range of products for major sporting goods clients. In 1998 he received *Business Week* magazine's Award for Best Product for the Skycap Snowboard helmet. Ball relocated to Hong Kong where he serves as Associate Professor at the Hong Kong Polytechnic University and Director of SizeChina.[52]

Always intrigued by human measurement, Ball was puzzled by the poor sales of some North American sporting goods in Asia. His award winning Skycap, the first helmet designed for snowboarders, sold well in North America but not in Japan, the leading snowboard market in Asia. This was more than a matter of price or aesthetic preferences; it was a matter of size—the helmets did not fit. What was needed were reliable ergonomics, based on the Asian head shape, as a functional alternative to the Caucasian model offered by Henry Dreyfuss.

In 2006 Ball established SizeChina,and having secured funding in excess of $5 million Hong Kong from a consortium of government, education and business partners, he and his team embarked on an 18 month research project to compile the first of ergonomic data on the head and face shapes of Chinese populations.[53] The research involved the analysis of over 2,000 individuals in six mainland China locations (Guangzhou, Hanzhou, Lanzhou, Chongging, Beijing and Shenyang) making it one of the largest anthropometric surveys ever undertaken. At each location the research was associated with a university or business partner with prior experience in human factors. Using laser scanning

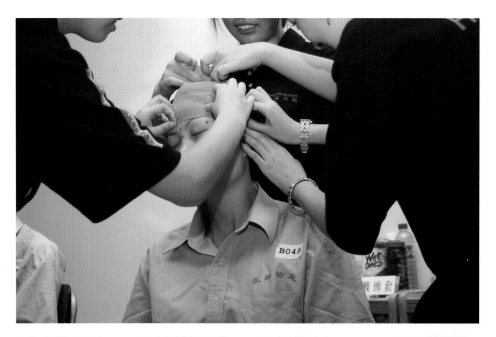

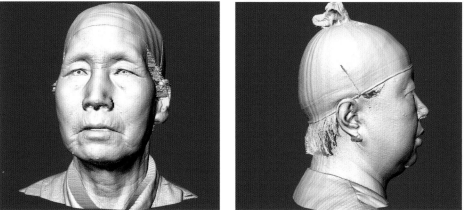

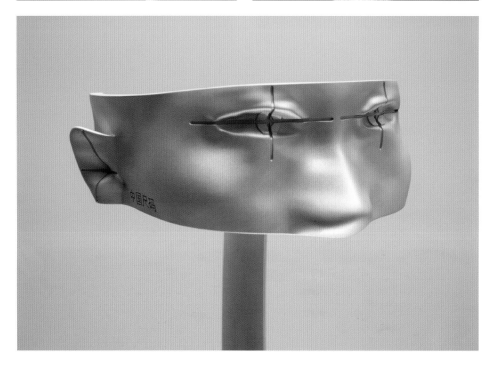

technology and 14 'landmark' facial points the resulting information was made available in a product line of gender neutral, standard head forms (available in solid or electronic formats) summarising measurements of adults between 18 and 70.

One oft-overlooked aspect of anthropometric research is making the results accessible to designers in a language that they can relate to, rather than the stilted language of statistics and physiognomy. To quote Ball, "Most designers don't want to know the 'standard deviation of popliteal height for a 95 percentile female Caucasian sample'. They just want to know how tall to make the chair."[54] The results from the SizeChina project make possible functional ergonomics in a range of areas, from optics, sports, medical, and electronics to communication and entertainment. In the 2008 International Design Excellence Awards, co-sponsored by *Business Week*, SizeChina won the accolade of best in its category and was co-recipient of the Best in Show award—the other co-recipient was the Apple iPhone. In 2009, Roger Ball won the 2009 Presidents Award for Research at the Hong Kong Polytechnic University.[55]

SizeChina is an example of contemporary design creativity that is responsive to a changing cultural dynamic. It is reflective of social innovation where education, business, and government combine to produce a satisfactory solution to a real life problem. That, after all, is what design should be.

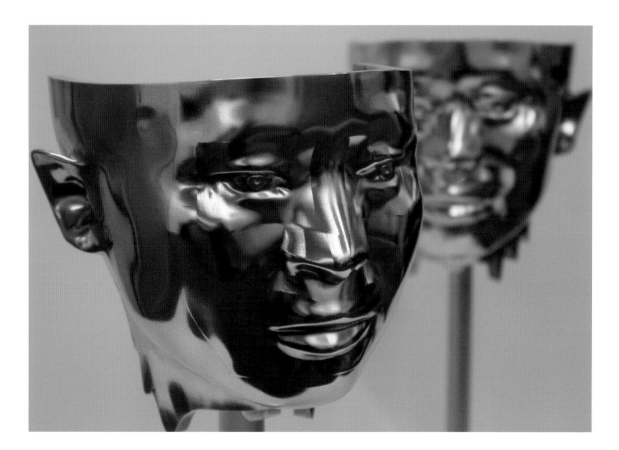

LIFE GOES ON

Up until the nineteenth century most people lived very local unconnected lives. Then, the power of steam changed everything. Steam powered locomotives, steam powered presses, multiplied and reinforced all forms of interconnections. As Claude Shannon and Warren Weaver make clear in their seminal *The Mathematical Theory of Communication*, more interconnected societies appear to be better able to cope with the challenging events of life.[56] The near future is certain to contain many challenging events that will benefit from the enhanced interconnections made possible by technological innovation.

WHO DO YOU KNOW?

Our survival as a species may well depend upon how well we communicate with each other, on the sharing of information. Within the next decade or so, taking advantage of breakthroughs in genetic engineering and advances in intelligence augmentation, "we will have a far greater appreciation of the consequences of our actions".[57] Those actions will be dependent upon the sharing of information. It is that sharing which will mediate the interconnectedness of disparate societies.

In the 1960s, the Harvard psychologist Stanley Milgram, advanced the concept of six degrees of separation, suggesting that everyone is connected to everyone else in six steps or less.[58] How many people do you know? Lets make a conservative estimate of 100. If each of those 100 know 100 and so on, then just five degrees of separation is enough to connect every person on earth. Given that the earth's population is near seven billion this allows for those individuals who may not know 100 others.[59] In 2010, Facebook claimed more than 500 million active users of which 70 per cent were outside the United States. Furthermore, about 50 per cent of users log on every day. The average user having 130 'friends'.[60] While we may not know how many friends share friends, the degrees of separation continue to decrease.

Correcting the information imbalance between ignorance and knowledge is a design challenge. The noted sociologist Manuel Castells claims that the Internet has created a fundamental transformation in the structure of communication.[61] In 1676, Isaac Newton stated that "If I have seen a little further it is by standing on the shoulders of Giants."[62] (This metaphor appears around the edge of the British two pound coin.)

These models assume that all cultures are the same 'height'. In our modern world there are far too many instances of where, fuelled by ignorance and intolerance, an alternative model has evolved resulting in succeeding generations of dwarfs standing on the shoulders of dwarfs.[63]

POST-WAR RECONSTRUCTION

The process of design is first and foremost a creative act. Initial research generates data from a range of resources which is then subject to rigorous analysis and motivated by factors that are often unique to that specific field of enquiry. These range from safety and engineering concerns, process and cost of production, ethics of manufacture and distribution, environmental issues and of course, user appeal. Designers have to consider the characteristics (including ergonomic data) of the 'average' user, producing objects or services that satisfy the demands of the intended market.

In addition to these operational factors a designer must also be conscious of political and socio-economic influences and concerns–the cultural dynamic. Two World Wars resulted in revised attitudes to the role of design, both in terms of manufacturing and distribution and in the more allusive values of national identity. In the aftermath of the Second World War, nations relied on innovative design to re-brand national identities and to secure market share in the emerging global marketplace. This is the focus of Section Two, "Form".

In the late twentieth century, much design thinking abdicates responsibility in the search for market share. Design was overwhelmingly concerned with bottom line justification. Then design became fashionable. We created a star system for designers, endorsing the value of their design by placing them in the hallowed confines of museums and art galleries. Design belongs to the real world, but that world is constantly redefining itself. In the second decade of the twenty-first century, changes in demographics and in the political spectrum are creating a new design reality, a sustainable reality, where solutions aimed at improving the human condition are foremost. Solutions will take advantage of technological developments and information technology and will be responsive to the needs of many who fall outside the privileged ten per cent. Satisfactory design will help people live their lives. (See Chapter Eleven, "Design for the 'Real', Real World".)

WELCOME YOUR NEW PARTNER

Designers, by the very nature of what they do, live in the future and function as future forecasters. In the very near future you may well have a robot as a design partner.[64] NAO is a bilingual ambassador of French advanced technology; it is an is an autonomous, programmable interactive humanoid robot that can see, hear, speak, feel and communicate and has the capability of interacting with other NAOs. Claimed to be the most widely used humanoid robot for academic purposes there are over 1,000 in use in universities and laboratories in over 30 countries. "Educational robots are fun, motivating, challenging and visionary. NAO, as a hands on way of teaching and learning, is helping pave the way for the future of education."[65] As you would expect from a fully active partner, NAO has the ability to browse the Internet and interface with any website to send or retrieve data.

NAO Humanoid Robot, ALDEBARAN Robotics company.
Designed by Thomas Knoll and Erik Arlen.
http://developer.aldebaran-robotics.com.

More about robotics in Chapter Two, "The Nature of the Design Process".

BREAKTHROUGHS—IN THE BUBBLE

NAO may represent a breakthrough—but breakthroughs are notoriously difficult to pinpoint. It would be tempting to identify the Internet, the World Wide Web, text messaging and robotics as breakthroughs. Certainly all of these recent innovations are changing how we think and what we think about; all will be covered in more detail in later chapters. There is much to think about. Design is a matter of mind set. As Thackara explains, "in the bubble" is a phrase used by air traffic controllers to describe their state of mind when faced with a mass of constantly changing information. [66] They need to feel, and to be, in control. The question then is how designers can be in control; how to design your way forward to where humans are once more at the centre of things. [67] Just before we explore who we are and where, in a design sense, we may be going, (Section Three, "Futures") it is necessary to establish just how we got here.

CHAPTER TWO
THE NATURE OF THE DESIGN PROCESS

A designer is an emerging synthesis of artist, inventor, mechanic, objective economist and evolutionary strategist. Richard Buckminster Fuller, American architect, author, designer, inventor, futurist and life long environmentalist.

THE HUMAN ELEMENT

John Heskett makes it abundantly clear: "Design is one of the basic characteristics of what it is to be human, and an essential determinant of the quality of human life. It affects everyone in every detail of every aspect of what they do throughout each day. As such, it matters profoundly."[1] Design is a way of thinking and acting. Design is research based and process developed, it is dependant upon information and formed by cognitive processes. In our modern world design is about interactions and connections.[2] The new technologies are transforming our lives, creating new way of living and working, creating new forms of organisations, new social networks, new connections; our lives will never be the same again. Most of these changes are brought about by design and all too often proffered solutions ignore the human element. Technological culture is not out of control, but out of design.

Some cultural critics foresee a less than satisfying future for human culture, some blame the technological determinism presented by science fiction. "From *The Matrix* to *Enemy of the State*, successful descriptions of the future have an ability to draw us towards them, to command us to make them flesh... the effect of futurist fictions, projections and predictions is to fuel our desire for a technology boom."[3] What is the relevance to design? Designers, by the very nature of what they do, are future forecasters, always concerned with things, events, situations, that have yet to happen. One of the supplementary roles of design is to enrich our world while remaining true to human instinct; at the same time being acutely aware of the environmental dangers that threaten our continued existence on this planet. Design has been, is, and will be, a process, a matter of informed choice and knowledgeable selection.

THE MATRIX—THE NATURE OF DESIGN

Design is a state of mind. *The Matrix* is a 1999 futuristic film directed by Larry and Andy Wachowski which references *Simulacra and Simulation,* the philosophical treatise by Jean Baudrillard[4] in which he discusses the interaction between reality, symbols and society.[5] (Which, it may be argued, provide the environs for design.) Early in *The Matrix*, Morpheus, the dream master, offers Neo (anagram of "one") two pills. The red pill will answer the question "what is the Matrix?" and the blue pill will allow life to carry on as before.

The question then is not about pills, but what they stand for in these circumstances. The question is asking us whether reality, truth, is worth pursuing. The blue pill will leave us as we are, in a life consisting of habit, of things we believe we know. We are comfortable, we do not need truth to live. The blue pill symbolises commuting to work every day, or brushing your teeth. The red pill is an unknown quantity. We are told that it can help us to find the truth. We don't know what that truth is, or even that the pill will help us to find it. The red pill symbolises risk, doubt and questioning. In order to answer the question, you can gamble your whole life and world on a reality you have never experienced.[6]

There are tangential similarities to the practice of design. The design matrix allows for the creative interaction between numerous disconnected 'bits' in the search for a designed solution.[7] You have choices. Do you continue along the well trodden path of familiarity (which most design does) or do you apply a creative design process to produce results that will change the very fabric of human culture?—as both stone tools and the web have done. Take the red pill.

DESIGN PROCESS

Too much modern design is concerned with 'spin', a process of making the unacceptable acceptable. The most obvious examples being the greenwash acquired by most major oil companies and car manufacturers; there are, unfortunately, far too many other examples of design transgressions. It is time to place emphasis on the ethical and moral ramifications of design—to design without spin and refocus emphasis on the human element.

In the comic science fiction, *The Hitchhiker's Guide to the Galaxy*, the super computer Deep Thought takes seven and a half million years to compute an answer to the meaning of life, which turns out to be 42.[8] Somewhat more prophetically, the noted mythologist Joseph Campbell observes that "what people seek is not the meaning of life but the experience of being alive".[9] This is where the design process comes in.

Matrix is Latin for womb; an enclosure within which something originates or develops. The two design chromosomes are creativity and innovation. According to Bill Moggridge, the co-founder of IDEO, innovation has more to do with development and creativity more to do with discovery.[10] He stresses the value of a team approach and how crucial it is to incorporate the potential user at an early stage of the design process. He cautions designers to remember that they are not designing for themselves and emphasises how essential it is to fully understand the complete cultural context of the potential design. However, it would be circumspect to remember that the design process is not a colour coded two-dimensional schematic of independent boxes—the 'boxes' are variable, adaptable, forever changing their form and possessing 'fuzzy' edges. In the creative design process the range of conceivable possibilities do not 'add up', they multiply.[11] Inconsistency rules!

> *It takes all the running you can do, to keep in the same place. If you want to get somewhere else, you must run at least twice as fast as that!*[12]
> Lewis Carroll, *Through the Looking-Glass, and What Alice Found There*, 1871.

We are all under continuous pressure to do more, and with increased speed. While the fastest track from A to B may well be a straight line, the results may be less than spectacular. If on that journey, and taking advantage of all available technologies, you venture off to an array of side venues you are far more likely to acquire unusual connections that will result in a more engaging design solution. John Wood explains: "This is because a less centralised alternative offers more opportunities for increasing the level of synergies within, and across the social, political, cultural and industrial domains.... It may mean persuading producers to accept rewards that place less emphasis on income, and more on an enhanced quality of life."[13]

From our very beginnings we have continually developed solutions to the challenges of human subsistence and development; those discoveries have always taken place within specific cultural contexts. Once upon a time we were only aware of our own cultural context. Modern day designers have to recognise the multitude of contexts that exist. The intended user will, more often than not, be different to themselves. Maybe older, maybe younger, maybe more active, less active, maybe with a different cultural heritage. What used to be termed "human factors" just does not cover the full spectrum of human characteristics. Designers need a more comprehensive, inclusive multi-faceted orientation to culture and the design process.

WHAT IS DESIGN?
A MATTER OF CHOICE AND POWER

"Design is what human beings do."[14] Humans have designed the world in which they exist and, by design, humans will have influence over the shape and form of future existence. Every generation believes that it is at a cross-road, and most of the time that is true. Designers today are faced with a

multiplicity of choices in a cultural context that often appears to be without direction and where the results of their actions can have unforeseen consequences. They are in need of new creative methods to make sense of the world, to assist in giving form and meaning to modern culture. Designers need design orientation.

From the advent of stone tools up until the introduction of transistors, the form of an object has signified its function. By applying diligent creativity we have been able to reveal all. Even those monstrous steam driven gargantuan goliaths of the nineteenth century fascinated and intrigued by their outward display of power and potentiality. We are now facing a situation where the most powerful and transforming aspects of our technological life are invisible. On the local highway we can see the difference between a bicycle and an 18 wheel rig and react accordingly. Intel recently announced the first microchip that contains more than two billion transistors.[15] In 2009, a collaboration between IBM and the Los Alamos National Laboratory resulted in the world's fastest supercomputer. Roadrunner can run at speeds above the "petaflop barrier" of 1,000 trillion operations per second and requires 57 miles of fibre optic cable to link its 10,000 connections.[16] Do these developments have meaning to you? Can you visualise their significance? Can we really imagine how these technological developments will change our lives? They will most certainly have an affect upon us and on our cultural environment. Larry Hickman makes the most valid observation. "No longer does any aspect of the food we eat, the clothes we wear, the goods and services we produce, the means in which we organise ourselves socially and politically, remain untouched by complex technological factors."[17]

It has been suggested that during our life we come into contact with over 30,000 designed 'things', each of which we have to learn to use.[18] Often the developed use is far removed from the original concept. Alexander Graham Bell designed the telephone as a method to record the transitory spoken word; it was never his intention to begin a revolution in the nature of communication, to provide every individual with a personal, transportable icon such as the smartphone. In a technologically inspired future you will need to be prepared for the unexpected and able to recognise and develop potentiality. But first you must be able to judge what is 'good'.

IS IT GOOD?

As Samovar *et al* state; "Perception is the means by which you make sense of your physical and social world."[19] Perception influences your understanding of 'good'. Do you perceive good design as emphasising aesthetics, form, function, profitability, and/or responsibility? The March 2009 issue of *Metropolis* provided an assessment of what constitutes 'good design'; examples range from Philippe Starck's dysfunctional Juicy Salif lemon squeezer, through the 'purity' of Dieter Rams designs to the Jonathan Ives iPod. To quote Peter Hall; "The iPod may seem like an innocuous music-playing device, but in fact it is an argument about how we should navigate, purchase, download, and listen to sound... design is not just about how a thing looks or how it works; it is also about the assumptions on which it rests." The article concludes that:

> Good Is Sustainable
> Good Is Accessible
> Good Is Functional
> Good Is Well Made
> Good Is Emotionally Resonant
> Good Is Enduring
> Good Is Socially Beneficial
> Good Is Beautiful
> Good Is Ergonomic
> Good Is Affordable.[20]

One of the major barriers to assessing how well design performs is the divorce of content from context. In the modern world design is an intrinsic part of manufacturing industrial capitalism with fundamental connections to current economic theory, business practice and the changing dynamics of global culture. It is reflective of current values, belief systems and moral standards. It provides a means of focus with contemporary concerns such as personal safety and the environment. How do we know what's good design? How do we evaluate design, how do we determine its cultural value?

It is courting disaster to remove a designed object from its home environment, stick a 'good design' label on it and inject it into the pristine and potentially hostile environment of those cultural zoos we call art galleries and museums. Even more absurd is the misguided attempt to legitimise design by utilising similar judgmental criteria as are applied to the so called "fine arts". Certainly one reason that this has happened is the insecurity of design critics who are ever fearful of being considered second class cousins to their more erudite fine art colleagues. Plus there is the perceived necessity of promoting design as physical evidence of national pride and character in the global marketplace. And herein lies one of the problems— the apparent conflict between the popular taste of the market place, where consumer driven sales are seen as the prime criteria of success, and the elitist cul-de-sac of 'good design' where judgmental criteria often appear to be in empathy with philosophical ideals that are far removed from reality. Have you noticed how the labels and tags in design museums provide information on the designer, materials and maybe even the process of manufacture but none that I am aware of ever indicate success in the market place where the real critics live.

Success and acceptance in the 'real' world has always been the way that the populace has passed judgement. Historically such success has been designated as vernacular design or "unselfconscious" design to use the phrase popularised by Christopher Alexander.[21] We have depended upon successful design to feed us, clothe us and shelter us. We have depended on design to define ourselves culturally and to communicate to others who it is we think we are. Successful design has depended on the intelligent use of available materials and processes of manufacture. Design solutions are subject to prevailing cultural values and acceptance by the intended market. In such design models the human element is front and centre.

FOOD, SHELTER, FIRE, AND A BROADBAND CONNECTION

Humans have a basic need for food, shelter and fire, all of which demand the application of the design process in one form or another. Traditionally these innovations have had intimate connections to the human element and to our ability to communicate, to record and pass on what we know.

All design communicates. "We are all designers" is more than a catch phrase: it is a truism. If you were to stop 100 people on the street and ask them what design means you would probably get 100 different responses. Depending upon their personal context, design may mean high fashion and designer boutiques, uncomfortable furniture and antiseptic interiors, colour coded signs in the local supermarket, gadgets at the local museum store or one of a kind items at a craft fair. If any of those 100 streetwalkers did identify design with manufactured product then it would probably be as the superficial wrapping of product in nice shapes and friendly colours. None would consider that design was essential to our cultural survival. You know different.

Bread-making is an activity of survival shared by many cultures. Each process is culturally specific and the means of production reflective of available technology. The assessment process is based on how well the produced object conforms to established

Bread makers in Afghanistan, 1980.

guidelines, there is no reward for originality. This staple commodity is revered for its adherence to preestablished norms which are supportive of the cultural group and provide well recognised models. Content is controlled. Various rising agents are used, some bread is leavened, some unleavened, some has salt, some does not. The form is an essential characteristic—be it a bagel, baguette, pita or roti. The satisfactory form indicating the "goodness of fit" resulting from

an unself-conscious design process.[22] The rules for production are not codified (modern cookery books aside) but are often complex and rigidly maintained, protected by ritual and or supplication; today we rely on copyright. Traditionally the bread of a people helped define the culture of that group.[23] We still demand marks of identity in our foodstuffs, but in our complex world, most are bought, most the result of a very self conscious design process.

DESIGN PROFILE: DOMESTIC SHELTER. HOT AND COLD

Construction of an Inuit igloo, Arctic region of Canada. Photo: Laurnet Magnin.

AT HOME IN A COLD CLIMATE

Take the ten top engineers and architects in the world, give them the very latest super computer and all the software available and I doubt that they could improve on the design of the igloo.[24] The igloo is an iconic structure with strong associations to Inuit culture. It is functional, strong, simple in form, complex in its engineering, and demonstrates an ingenious and innovative use of available materials and process of production. Victor Papanek regarded the Inuit as the best designers in the world.[25] The design 'fits'. No longer a common form of shelter, these structures ranged in size from small, overnight shelters for one or two persons to relatively large complexes of joined igloos.

The construction secret is the spiral form of the dome which resembles a parabolic arch. The blocks of snow, ranging from approximately 15 to 30 centimetres in width, making them easy to handle, are cut using a snow knife; usually some form of animal bone such as a caribou antler.[26] The blocks are then layered in a single spiral to form a half circle; they are angled in slightly, resulting in the dome form. As with all domes it is the final key block which is the most important, consolidating the strength of nature's strongest form. Exposed to the elements, both internal and external, the surface will melt and re-freeze thereby adding to its strength. The igloo exploits both structural forces of compression and tension. The combined weight of the snow blocks compresses the snow crystals producing a structure that holds up well under compression. It has been reported that the form is so strong that it can withstand the weight of a marauding polar bear. (I have no documentation to support this claim which may well be a rural myth.) Under tension the same block of snow can be penetrated with very little force.

Ventilation is an important design feature of the igloo, both to let fresh air in and keep cold air out by way of the cold air trap positioned just below the entrance. Internal light and heat is provided by a single soapstone blubber oil lamp with a moss wick. Add the natural heat from the body and even when it is minus 40 degrees outside, the internal temperature will be a little above freezing. Although environmental issues were never a contributing factor to the design, the igloo is built from readily renewable resources resulting in no carbon footprint. The igloo remains an outstanding example of the unselfconscious design process, producing a design that 'fits' while making use of available materials and production processes.

Bedouin style tent made from black goat hair, Saudi-Arabia, 2011.
http://imagesofsaudi.blogspot.com

AT HOME IN A HOT CLIMATE

The very word Bedouin translates as "man of the tent". The Bedouin of the Arabian Desert use a black tent known as the *beit al-sha'r*, or "house of hair". The design of the Bedouin tent is determined by function, materials at hand, the available process of production plus the load capacity of their pack animals.[27] Loaded on the back of a male camel, this easily transportable shelter made possible the nomadic ventures of legend, journeys that stretched from the Atlantic coast of Africa, through the Middle East and on through middle Asia to the borders of Tibet. The design challenge remains that of transportable domestic shelter. The primary design consideration is heat. In addition to shade, the tent must provide protection against wind, sand, and dust. In a climate where daytime temperatures can exceed 120 degrees, the pitched tent can bring that temperature down to around 95 degrees. The design process is unselfconscious, but the solution is different to that of the Inuit, responding to a different set of cultural controls.

As with the Inuit, these groups are nomadic; but they are not hunters; they are herdsman. How does this influence the design? The design, manufacture and construction of the Black tent is tied in to the domestication of goats and sheep. These animals provided evidence of tribal wealth while providing the raw materials for the fabric of the tent. The herd is precious, far too valuable to slaughter just for hides. But these animals have expendable, replaceable, recyclable body fibres. The fibres are woven together on mobile horizontal ground looms that provide narrow strips of material.[28] These are sewn together, edge to edge, to provide the basic tent material. The Black tent is one of the earliest examples of sustainable modular architecture. It is made up of rectangles of fabric, each panel being about seven to eight centimetres in width and around seven to eight metres long. New panels can be added to increase the size of the tent. Each year new sections are added to the middle so that by the time a panel is worn (between five to six years) it has reached the outer rim where it can be pierced to accept the necessary ties and where it can be easily removed, recycled and reused. The average tent length is around six to nine metres with a shallow depth of three metres and a height of one and a half to two metres.

These woollen strips are heavy and supported on short vertical wooden poles and anchored with hemp ropes, two affixed to each vertical pole, and three at each side of the tent. The rope-ends are then pegged to the ground or tied to large clumps of brushwood and buried beneath the surface of the sand, acting as a sand anchor. The resulting low profile and shallow slope make it resilient to desert winds and sand storms. Technically the Black tent is a very efficient tension structure, requiring the minimum of supporting framing. The loose weave allowed hot air to escape through the fabric. An added bonus (discovered no doubt by 'experience' or 'communal sense') was the advantage presented by the natural lanolin in the unprocessed fibres. When wet the fabric swells to close up and provides just enough protection against the occasional short sharp shower. But more importantly, the constant friction of erecting and dismantling caused the fibres to bond together (like rubbing a wool sweater). This felting provided the very necessary protection against the more regular desert sand storms

Over generations, each tribal group developed its own distinctive style—providing the necessary identification from a safe distance. Those groups that tended to travel in more mountainous terrain raised the pitch of the roof to shed rain, closed the sides to improve insulation. Desert Nomads flattened their roofs and opened up the sides. The Black tents are among the most sophisticated types of temporary shelter ever developed.[29]

TRADITION IS THE ENEMY OF PROGRESS
PROGRESS IS THE ENEMY OF TRADITION[30]

In summary, (and referencing Alexander) in the unselfconscious design process there is little thought or social reward for design innovation. The relative success of an unselfconscious design is decided by how close it comes to the primary model and upon its acceptance by the intended market. There is most definitely a 'right way' to produce the artefact. There is little division of labour or reliance on specialists. The information is inherited and shared by most members of the group. There is no codification of knowledge, no blueprints, no working drawings. In those cultural groups that emphasise the unselfconscious design process, the established social patterns, favour inherited rather than acquired knowledge. Actions are governed by habit, design decisions are made according to custom. Ritual and taboos discourage innovation. In our modern world most of us use the same

browser and communication software to acquire what we know. What the unselfconscious design process requires is the ability to recognise failure and to make the appropriate correction. The success of the process does not depend on any one person but on the solidarity of their culture (collective intelligence?). And there is no rush—generations of minor refinements lead to a satisfactory solution for all.

Do not assume that the unselfconscious design process means old, outdated or inefficient. The design process is a natural activity of all humankind. We need design to get through the day and to tell us who we think we are and where we think we belong. In a design sense we are motivated by what we learn (which can be seen as the more self-conscious side of our design process) and by what we believe (which is more reflective of the unselfconscious part of our design process). Make absolutely no mistake, to function as a satisfactory designer we need to be aware of the cultural value of both. With the advent of new communication technologies we are close to being able to collapse the time delay associated with the 'unselfconscious' practice and integrate that practice into a reinvigorated design process.

FIRE

The control of fire was a primal technology for humankind. It assisted in the processing of food which enhanced the diet; it provided artificial warmth which allowed for habitation in colder climes, thereby assisting in the global migration of our species; it provided a source of artificial light, lengthening the work day and making access possible into dark interiors; it was a source of protection against other predators; it permitted the hardening of wooden and stone tools and eventually permitted the transmutation of matter. For around one million years the fire pit provided the place for community gatherings and may have assisted in the development of social bonding. Fire was, above all else, a source of power.[31] The most significant source of power in our world is the computer, the origins of which can be found in Victorian Britain, and it all began with steam.

Combine water and fire and you get steam. The first practical steam-powered 'engine' was a water pump, developed in England by Thomas Savery, who patented his devise on 2 July 1698. Savery demonstrated it to the Royal Society in London on 14 June 1699.[32] Around 1710, an ironmonger and Baptist lay preacher, Thomas Newcomen, refined these first faltering steps to develop a pump to remove water from the mineshaft's of England.[33] This was

Richard Trevithick's London Railway and Locomotive of 1808. WJ Welch.

followed in 1769 by the engineering brilliance of Scottish inventor James Watt, combined with the entrepreneurial vision of Birmingham born Matthew Boulton, whose combined efforts produced the reciprocating steam engine that provided the basic invention from which all steam powered rotary movement, including the railway engine, takes off.[34] Both Watt and Bolton were members of the Birmingham based Lunar Society.[35]

It was the eccentric Cornish strong-man and steam engine pioneer, Richard Trevithick Jr who developed the first successful railway when, in 1808, he built and ran the engine called "Catch me who Can" on a circular track near Torrington Square, just south of London's Euston Station. His father, Richard Trevithick Sr had been in direct competition with James Watt to produce steam engines for use in Cornish mines. Richard Trevithick Jr's undertaking in London failed economically and there is an unsubstantiated story that he had to borrow his stage coach fare home from a young engineering apprentice, George Stephenson.[36]

Stephenson designed his first locomotive in 1814. In 1821, a parliamentary bill was passed to allow the building of the Stockton and Darlington Railway. George Stephenson, with the help of some local backers, and assisted by his 18 year old son Robert, established a company to manufacture the steam engines and construction of the line began. Not all were believers—in the prestigious *Quarterly Review* of March 1825, the editorial had this to say; "What can be more absurd and ridiculous than the prospect held out of locomotives travelling twice as fast as stagecoaches."[37] By November 1829 George and Robert Stephenson had perfected their steam engine, The Rocket, which won the famous Rainhill Trials.[38] The age of rail began when, in 1830, the engine was used to power the first modern railway that linked the cotton manufacturing town of Manchester with the developing port of Liverpool. Within 20 years a network of railway lines criss-crossed Britain. By the time of the Great Exhibition of 1851 a network of 7,000 miles of track linked London with the manufacturing towns of the Midlands and the North of England.[39]

With the introduction of timetables people became aware of the need to be on time. This phenomenon was forever immortalised in *Bradshaw's Railway Companion*, introduced in 1840.[40] But what time is it? In mid-nineteenth century America there were 144 official time zones. It was the Scottish born Canadian engineer, Sandford Fleming, chief engineer of the Canadian Pacific Railway, who, in 1884, proposed worldwide standard time zones, although it was to be 1929 before all the major countries of the world accepted this innovation.[41] Sandford Fleming was multi-dimensional in his creativity, designing the Threepenny Beaver, the first Canadian postage stamp in 1851.

The late nineteenth century witnessed a social fascination with rail travel, resulting in world breaking secular structures such as bridges, viaducts, tunnels and stations. Indeed, the railway station offered a totally new kind of public space within the urban landscape of nineteenth century Europe. Their size, grandeur and technological brilliance rivalled that of the cathedrals of the Medieval era. The station, and its associated hotel, became fixtures; both in the real everyday world of commerce and transportation and in the fictionalised accounts by such divers writers as Arthur Conan Doyle, Charles Dickens, Thomas Mann, Marcel Proust, Leo Tolstoy and Emile Zola, all of whom used the site of the railway station and hotel to stage their dialogues of social interchange.[42] These writers realised that for all its originality, it was not train travel that was significant, it was the congregated people that represented the crux of change. Culture before design.

Renovated roof, train shed, St Pancras rail station, 2010. Original design by William Henry Barlow, 1863–1866. The canopy spans 240 feet (73m) across the platforms without intermediate support—then the widest of its kind in the world.

The train shed at St Pancras Station in London was designed by William Barlow in 1863 and construction began in 1866. The arch spans 243 feet and is over 100 feet high at its apex and 689 feet long. It was completed in 1868 and remains the largest enclosed train station covering in the world. The station is fronted by the Midland Grand Hotel, a marvellous gothic style fantasy designed by Sir George Gilbert Scott and built between 1868 and 1876. The station opened on 1 October, 1867. The first train, an express for Manchester, ran non-stop from Kentish Town to Leicester, a distance of some 97 miles (156 km) and was the longest non-stop run in the world. The hotel opened to customers on the 5 May 1873 and closed in 1935. It survived the bombings of the Second World War only to be threatened by demolition in the 1960s. Following an £800 million (about $1.2 billion) restoration project, St Pancras is now the London terminus to the cross-channel rail link, allowing travel from the heart of London to Paris in just two hours and 20 minutes.

In 1861, Alexander James Berefesord Hope provided a contemporary assessment of changing values:

> The railway station, with its fluctuating thousands, has replaced the sulky booking-office, Gloucester Coffee-house, or Elephant and Castle. The long train stands in the place of the compact stage coach; great central hotels, with their machinery of lifts and their array of coffee-rooms, are gradually encroaching on the tavern and lodging house.[43]

The editors of the *Building News* concurred. "Railway termini and hotels are to the nineteenth century what monasteries and cathedrals were to the thirteenth century. They are truly the only real representative building we possess."[44] These symbols of modernity were not for the select few to marvel at in museums and galleries, but, in every real sense, to be entered into by the travelling public.

The railway stations were indeed the cathedrals of nineteenth century society. These huge constructions were new and exciting, nothing like them had ever been seen before; they signified new wealth; the prominence of the middle classes; and the shifting power base in society with the increasing power of the industrial Midlands and North of England. The steam powered railways demonstrated a new way of thinking about the world. In manufacturing, the introduction of these massive power sources demanded a new economic theory. New business equations began to replace their 'natural' forerunners. It became necessary to calculate the relationship between energy expended and potential profit, part of that relationship was 'time' related.

The nineteenth century was seen as the Golden Age of Steam. Steam power dramatically increased productivity, made possible human mobility on an unprecedented scale and "set in motion a series of feed back loops that increased city populations, productivity, and consumption".[45] Railway travel changed many aspects of everyday life in Victorian Britain. People could travel with ease to the next town or community, they could now marry outside their home village, thereby strengthening the gene pool; travel helped to break down regional insularities, creating a new sense of nationalism. There were three classes of travel, each with its own fare structure, ensuring that all classes could travel in varying states of comfort. Leisure travel was a totally new phenomenon, with town workers being able to travel to the countryside or seaside on their day off. Goods could travel–wholesale and retail markets were established to handle out-of-town commodities–fresh fish and milk became staple commodities to land locked towns. It was the railways that changed attitudes to time. The influence of steam power continued to dominate many aspects of Victorian society. At the end of the century, steam power seemed much more promising than the newly invented gasoline driven internal combustion engine for automobiles.[46] One can only wonder how the world would be now had we focussed on steam rather than oil as a primary energy source for our personal transportation devices.[47]

BROADBAND CONNECTION

Pax Britannica refers to a period of British imperialism which followed victory at the 1815 Battle of Waterloo and lasted for a hundred years until the outbreak of the First World War.[48] In the aftermath of the Napoleonic Wars, Great Britain was the most powerful country in the world. With her trade routes protected by the Royal Navy, Britain's economic and strategic strength was assured. The quiet Industrial Revolution consolidated the factory system which, in turn, depended upon the flow of raw materials from around the world. British shipping dominated the worlds seas and oceans, often however subject to the vagaries of time and tide. What was needed were more reliable tide charts along with a system for rapid calculation.

The digital revolution began in nineteenth century England. In 1821 Charles Babbage, aided by Augusta Ada Byron, Countess of Lovelace–the daughter of the poet Lord Byron–attempted to produce the worlds first programmable computer to calculate tide tables; essential information when fortunes relied on accurate and timely navigation. Babbage, a mathematics professor at Cambridge University, produced two types of mechanical computer. The Difference Engine, conceived in 1812, of which a small model was produced in 1822. Work began on a working full scale model in 1823, the intent being to do arithmetic "without any mental attention once the given numbers had been put into the machine".[50] The objective being to compute and print mathematical and navigational tables of latitude and longitude. A portion of this first Difference Engine, part of its calculating mechanism, was built in 1832 but work was halted after £17,000 of public monies had been spent.[51] In 1833 Babbage transferred his energy to a new and

A masterpiece of engineering, this two-century old Jacquard loom wove intricate patterns into cloth and carpets following programmed instructions, stored on 'punch cards'.

improved model–a general purpose, fully programmable automatic digital computer which he called an Analytical Engine, a general symbol manipulator that could perform any type of calculation. Babbage acquired sponsorship from the British government who foresaw the military advantage of such calculations. It was inspired by the productive and automated Jacquard silk looms of France, which used punch cards to control a sequence of operations.[52] Ada Lovelace saw the possibilities that existed in merging what we know with what we see–or to use her words, "We may say most aptly that the Analytical Engine weaves algebraically patterns just as the Jacquard loom weaves leaves and flowers."[53] She was the first person to realise that if you are dealing with an automated machine then the process handles all information, whether visual or textual, in the same manner. Ada Lovelace contributed many of the ideas for programming the machine which included the concepts of the programming loop and the subroutine. Her extensive notes include step-by-step instructions on programming the engine; "this contribution has since led the computing industry to recognise her as the world's first programmer".[54] Indeed she was the only programmer prior to the computer revolution in the last half of the twentieth century. The United States Department of Defense Programming Language ADA is named in her memory.

The Analytical Engine had all the elements considered prime in a computer: an input devise, a control unit, a processor, storage facility and an output devise. It was designed to be steam powered, requiring the services of one attendant.[55] The Analytical Engine was never completed, the tolerances required by the brass cogs and wheels of their machine was beyond the available level of technology. Realisation of the concept had to wait for the age of the transistor (introduced to total industry indifference in 1948 by a team of researchers at Bell Labs in New Jersey) and the micro-processor. We had to wait about 120 years for the first commercial working model of a computer. The personal computer age began in January 1975 when *Popular Electronics* ran a cover story on a machine called the Altair 8800. It was a do-it-yourself machine that you could assemble at home. The Altair kit cost $397, a fully assembled version was available for $498.[56] Nearly 40 years on and some observers are suggesting the arrival of a computer generated third culture. Individuals "are born into their first culture, their ethnic culture. They are raised in their second culture, their civic culture. And they work and play in their third culture, the global communication culture."[57] There are new partnerships in the third culture.

THREE LAWS OF ROBOTICS[58]

1. A robot may not injure a human being or, through inaction, allow a human being to come to harm.
2. A robot must obey orders given to it by human beings, except where such orders would conflict with the First Law.
3. A robot must protect its own existence as long as such protection does not conflict with the First or Second Law.

Robots made their fictional debut in 1921 in the Czech author Karel Capek's play *RUR (Rossum's Universal Robots)* which featured machines created to simulate human beings.

In 1927, Fritz Lang introduced the robotic gynoid Maria to the screen in his classic, *Metropolis*.[59] Set in 2026, this movie initiated our pessimism about the relationship between humans and robots. That attitude was reinforced in 1948, when Norbert Wiener, professor of mathematics at MIT, coined the word "cybernetics".[60] In a 1950 address to the Society for the Advancement of Management, Wiener foresaw a third world war where tens of thousands of men would be required to fight, and where they would be replaced on the home front by "mechanical men". These would prove to be more efficient and more economic than humans thereby creating massive unemployment and an unstable society.[61] His assertion also showing the dangers inherent in future forecasting, (see Section Three, "Futures").

In the real fictitious future, robots were endowed with personality. "Fictional robots always have a personality: Marvin[62] was paranoid, C-3PO[63] was fussy and HAL 9000[64] was murderous. But reality is disappointingly different. Sophisticated enough to assemble cars and assist during complex surgery, modern robots are dumb automatons, incapable of striking up relationships with their human operators."[65] But that could soon change. As robots begin to play a more decisive role in society, the new machines will need a way to interact with humans. This begs the question of what sort of properties does a synthetic companion need so that the human partner does not feel divorced from or inhibited by the robot? Robots will need personalities. This could be a problem in those societies that do not recognise that animate and inanimate objects are governed by the laws of ecology.[66] We may have to acquire a more holistic view where everything is connected to everything else.

AN APPLE A DAY

From those initial attempts in our ancestral caves, human beings have made sense of their world through the processing of a range of sensory signals. Developments in robotics and associated technologies continues that process. Robotics will transform all areas of design—architecture, interior, product, graphic and fashion design, multi-media and interactive—all areas of design. These transformations will occur in your working life. You have a choice, you can hide you head in the sand and hope that it will go away. Alternatively you can begin to prepare, begin to think how your area of interest can adapt to benefit all.

The early signs of that transformation are evident in what are the most pressing challenges facing many societies, the rapid increase in the numbers of elderly and their associated needs. Robots in healthcare are already a reality. Telephones, computers and iPods have shown how people can develop relationships with electronic objects. The next generation of digital companions will intensify these relationships. Put aside your preconceptions, disable the rear view mirror and think objectively how the use of robots can humanise design by amplifying the human element.[67]

Many counties including Britain, most European countries, Japan, the United States and Canada, face the challenge presented by people living longer, (see Chapter Ten, "Design for the 'Real', Real World"). An aging population has specific requirements that need to be addressed. Extensive research and innovative design is being undertaken by institutions and research centres worldwide into the integration of robotics into the healthcare system. To meet this challenge, some health and local authority services plan to place greater emphasis on community care and the effective use of robotic technology. Robots can be programmed and re-programmed in response to need, they are less prone

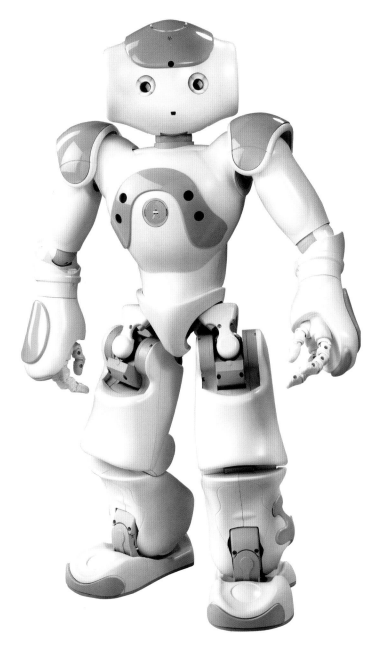

NAO NAO is a bilingual ambassador of French advanced technology; it is an autonomous, programmable interactive humanoid robot that can see, hear, speak, feel and communicate and has the capability of interacting with other NAOs.

to mistakes and their function unaffected by performing necessary repetitive tasks. Wisely utilised, they can be user friendly companions, allowing for longer periods of independence, which is one of the most important objectives of elder life.

IS THE ROBOT IN?

LIREC is a European funded research project exploring the design challenge of building of long-term relationships between human and artificial companions.[68]

LIREC aims to establish a multi-faceted theory of artificial long-term companions (including memory,

emotions, cognition, communication, learning, etc.), embody this theory in robust and innovative technology and experimentally verify both the theory and technology in real social environments. Whether as robots, social toys or graphical and mobile synthetic characters, interactive and sociable technology is advancing rapidly. However, the social, psychological and cognitive foundations and consequences of such technological artefacts entering our daily lives–at work, or in the home–are less well understood.[69] Current research hopes to increase our understanding.

ROBOTS IN NORTH AMERICA

There is considerable and wide ranging research into the use of robots in the American health system. Researchers at the Massachusetts Institute of Technology believe that robotics will one day handle complex jobs in healthcare, agriculture, and product production. "People underestimate the long-term effects of robotics on society", states Rod Brooks, cofounder of robotics company iRobot and director of the MIT Computer Science and Artificial Intelligence laboratory. "Robots are getting closer to people. We need to see how robots and people interact."[70] Another American institution, Georgia Tech, is exploring the area of how domestic robots can help the physically impaired.[71] One of the more exciting use of robots in North America is Robonaut 2, which travelled to the international space station in November 2010 and will, for the next decade or so, assist in a range of activities from undertaking scientific research to the performance of mundane 'domestic' chores.[72]

ROBOT CARE IN JAPAN

Japan's population is the most rapidly ageing in the world; 30 million people, about 25 per cent of the population, are over the age of 65, (see Chapter Ten, "Design for the 'Real', Real World"). Fortunately, Japan has about 44 per cent of the world's industrial robots and is applying that expertise to healthcare. Honda's ASIMO (standing for Advanced Step in Innovative MObility) is one of the most advanced bipedal robots in the world.[73] When deployed in healthcare it could assist nursing staff in the performance of tasks requiring lifting and transportation. It could also be programmed to address cognitive decline, reminding patients to drink, eat, take medication, remind them of appointments and generally assist in these essential, repetitive but often overlooked tasks. The robot could provide 24 hour monitoring of life signs, triggering immediate emergency response when needed. Domestic versions could assist in household chores, extending independent living options. Parallel developments are underway at Toyota who have their very own Robot band. Toyota is also exploring the field of domestic robots capable of caring for people,

An example from the Intelligent Robotics Laboratory of Osaka University. This image is of a female android and her real life model. The researchers also plan to test her ability to put hospital patients at ease.

assisting in domestic duties, providing basic healthcare and assist in short distance human transport.[74]

ROBOTS AND CULTURE IN JAPAN

Waseda University, Tokyo, has a Humanoid Robotics Institute that has developed a robot flutist capable of playing the challenging "Flight of the Bumblebee".[75] The Ishikawa Komuro Laboratory at the University of Tokyo has developed a three fingered robot that utilises parallel processing of information to explore real world interactions, the result being amazing dexterity allowing the robot to catch a baseball pitched at high speed.[76] Tomotaka Takahashi at Kyoto University has developed ROPID, a bipedal robot capable of running and even jumping.[77]

Robots have also made an appearance in education where they are being introduced into primary schools. The world's first robot teacher, Saya, has been in development for the past 15 years by Professor Hiroshi Kobayashi at the department of mechanical engineering at Tokyo University of Science. Saya was tested in a real classroom of fifth and sixth graders. "Robots that look human tend to be a big hit with young children and the elderly."[78] Robots are also a hit

with the fashion cognoscenti. In 2009, Fashion designer Yumi Katsura showed her collection of wedding dresses in Osaka including one paraded by the HRP-4C gynoid, the Japanese government's newly developed 'cybernetic human.' Japan's National Institute of Advanced Industrial Science and Technology (AIST) created 4C to work in the 'entertainment industry'.[79]

Acting robots have made their debut on the Japanese stage. Osaka University have developed an Actroid, a humanoid robot with strong visual human likeness.[80] In 2008, the playwright Oriza Hirata introduced the first robot-human theatre on stage at Osaka University. The play, called *Hataraku Watashi* ("I, Worker"), is set in the near future. One of two featured robots loses its desire to work; the play raises questions about the relationship between humanity and animate technology. On a somewhat lighter vein is the Robot Football World Cup or RoboCup which attracts the best robot teams from all over the world. Their stated aim is that "by the year 2050, develop a team of fully autonomous humanoid robots that can play and win against the human world champion soccer team".[81] This tantalising forecast offers a post-Beckham entertainment reality!

DESIGN PROFILE: JŌRURI AND BUNRAKU

Niugyo Jōruri, puppet theatre, Tokushima Prefectural Government, Japan. The play *Keisei Awa no Naruto* was first staged in June of 1769 at the Takemoto Theatre in Osaka in commemoration of its re-opening. It is one of the most popular pieces in the Bunraku repertoire. This image depicts the mother meeting the daughter she had been forced to abandon as an infant ten years earlier.

Living with artificial life forms is not new. The magical world of Japanese puppets was established in the sixteenth century, and was popularly known as Joruri.[82] It existed without imperial patronage; it depended for its success on popular support. Towards the end of the eighteenth century the art form was in decline. It was revived some 150 years ago by Uemura Bunrakken who introduced his form of puppet theatre in Osaka. Today we know that theatrical from as Bunraku.[83]

The dolls of Bunraku are animated by three visible men; all are dressed in black. The white faced puppet master (*omozukai*) controls the top of the doll and its right arm. The two assistants have a veil of cloth covering their faces. The *hidarizukai* wears gloves but with the thumb visible, he moves the dolls left arm. The third member of the troupe (*ashizukai*) crawls around offering support to the body, making it walk. All must breathe as one to bring life to the doll. "It is traditionally taught that a puppeteer needs ten years to learn how to operate the feet, another ten to learn the movements of the left arm, and ten years to learn how to operate the head and right arm—a total of 30 years before he is allowed to perform a leading role."[84] These performers are supported by musicians playing the *samisen*—a long—necked string instrument—and a chanter (*tayu*). It takes around five years for the combined team to function as a single unity. Team work is all.

Many non-Japanese have found fascination in this unique theatrical form, including Roland Barthes, the noted French literary critic, social theorist, philosopher, semiotician and a frequent visitor to Japan which he described as "the empire of signs".[85] In 1976 he wrote a short piece on "The Dolls of Bunraku".[86] In this he claims that, "Bunraku does not aim to 'animate' an inanimate object in such a way as to make a piece of the body live, a shred of a man, all the while retaining its vocation as 'a part'. It isn't the simulation of a body which is sought, but rather, if we may say so, its palpable abstraction."[87] In a very lengthy but most informative and revealing article, the actor and writer Christopher A Bolton offers parallel assessment of Bunraku and Japanese animation (*anime*).[88] His explorations range from the works of the eighteenth century playwright Chikamatsu Monzaemon to the "uncanny parallels" with the recent *anime* form such as the 1995 *Ghost in the Shell*, directed by Mamoru Oshii. Bolton claims that "The human-machine hybrid known as the cyborg has been invoked by many authors and critics to test the boundaries that define human subjects, but it remains an ambivalent figure."[89]

Manga represents a 481 billion yen market in Japan.[90] With a pre-war heritage, modern manga developed during the period of Occupation, 1945–1952, and may have been influenced by American popular culture and images that derived from comics and film, in particular Disney cartoons.[91] Susan J Napier, Mitsubishi Professor of Japanese Studies at the University of Texas, Austin observes that:

> Manga are often described as comic books, but they are quite different from what Americans would think of as comic books. More like graphic novels, they are thick (sometimes telephone-book-sized) volumes, which depict anything and everything–from mystery stories to etiquette lessons–and are read by almost all the Japanese population from childhood through at least middle age. In many cases manga are the direct sources for Japanese animation (anime) and many of the most popular anime narratives also exist in parallel manga form.[92]

One of the most telling and informative manga series are those by Keiji Nakazawa. Entitled *The Barefoot General*, they tell in a most personal manner, of the after effects of the atomic bombing of Hiroshima.[93] In Britain, *SelfMade Hero*, winner of the UK Young Publisher of the Year 2008 award, publishes *Manga Shakespeare*. These series of graphic novel adaptations of William Shakespeare's plays are presented as a fusion of classic Shakespeare with manga visuals.[94] Kyoto Seika University has established a Faculty of Manga which "systematically teaches its essence" to around 600 undergraduate students.[95]

DESIGNED TO COMPUTE

In the West, the narrative construct developed differently, emphasising text over image. 'Cartoons' are seen as childish pursuits, unworthy of attention or study. This is somewhat perverse considering that we live in such a visually dominated culture. Lets step aside from ambivalence, messages of bodily transcendence, cyborgs, animation and manga–but keeping them all in mind lets think of robotics and design.

Todays designers are technologically smart, adapt at eye hand coordination, skilled in computer use and very comfortable with concepts of cyberspace and virtual reality. Books (even this one) just don't cut it. The youth of today are image conscious, concerned with what they wear, what objects that buy, what music they listen to, what videos they watch–all these combined provide a cultural uniform that is acceptable to their relevant group. What if we were to pay as much attention to the inside image. What if we could converge the technological brilliance of robotics with the "palpable abstraction" of Bunraku, and add the allure of manga, all contained within the friendly form of a 'pal' computer. The designers of tomorrow would show little hesitation in allowing such creative and transforming technology into their culture. Better by design.

A decade ago, Ray Kurzweil, the author, scientist and futurist, predicated that by 2018, 1013 bits of computer memory, roughly the equivalent of the memory space in a single human brain will cost $1,000 and "will be millions of times faster than the electromechanical memory process used in the human brain and thus will be far more effective".[96] He goes one step further, predicting that by 2029, a $1,000 personal computer will be 1,000 times more powerful than the human brain. How are you going to handle all that power? Along with personal empowerment comes personal responsibility. Think first, act second.[97]

We will return to technology and the culture of design in Section Three. Now lets consider where, in terms of design, we are, and how we got here. The next two chapters offer additional thoughts about the form of the design matrix. Section Two, "Form", provides an overview of modern design, with an emphasis on creativity, the design process and the cultural context of design. Section Three, "Futures" is exactly that, as assessment of the near future and how you can prepare for the fascinating and callenging times ahead.

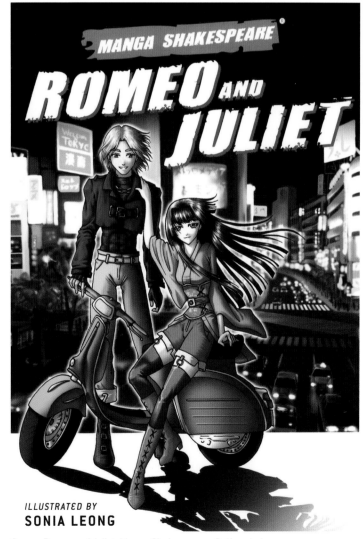

Cover, *Romeo and Juliet*, Manga Shakespeare. Selfmade hero.

CHAPTER THREE
WORD, TEXT AND IMAGE —FROM CAVE WALL TO TWITTER

Words are, of course, the most powerful drug used by mankind.
Rudyard Kipling, 1923.[1]

I TOLD YOU SO

Language is the primary expressive vehicle for thought and is essential in the transfer of information. In *Decoding Reality*, Vlatko Vedral asserts that information is the most profound concept of modern science. "The Universe and everything in it can be understood in terms of information. We are information."[2] The transfer of information between people is the most basic, critical and challenging aspect of the design process.

It seems somewhat obvious to assert that communication depends on literacy, a very recent acquisition in human evolutionary history.[3] Equally obvious is the fact that people in non-literate cultures use language in a variety of creative ways to communicate, to tell stories, to prefabricate histories, all of which are systems of oral communication.[4] Writing is a cultural technological adaptation that extends and codifies universal innate human communication skills. Printing and the Internet are more recent technological adjustments to cultural change and *vice-versa*. The smart phone and text messaging have revitalised the oral connection and a new media ecosystem of 'real-time stream' of always-on data is emerging.[5] Changes in patterns of communication are ongoing.

We are much better designers when we are more knowledgeable about ourselves and about others, ever respectful of the diversity that makes the human species so dynamic. The process of information transfer is first and foremost a cultural practice that is fundamental to human development. Information is multi-dimensional in character. Any message can mean different things to different groups dependent on the cultural context of the sender and the recipient.[6] The one contextual commonality being that the possession of information places the receiver in a position of influence.

Information is power. In *The Revolution Will Not Be Televised: Democracy, the Internet, and the Overthrow of Everything*, Joe Trippi observes that, "The power is shifting from institutions that have always been run top down, hoarding information at the top, telling us how to run our lives, to a new paradigm of power that is democratically distributed and shared by all of us."[7]

THE FIRST SCREEN

All users of information depend on symbol recognition.[8] Around 35,000 to 40,000 years ago, for reasons we can still only guess at, our ancestors began to find it necessary to give symbols concrete form. In our ancestral shelters outlines of hands, drawings of bison, horses and woolly rhinoceros began to appear on the cave walls. These early creations have less to do with what we call 'art' and far more to do with information and the transfer of knowledge.

In the Cantabrian Mountains region that straddles south-western France and northern Spain are around 200 caves that contain inscriptions from the Upper Palaeolithic period. These are radiocarbon dated from 32,410 years ago at Chauvet to 11,600 at Le Portel. The Grotto Chauvet, hidden and perfectly preserved due to a prehistoric landslide, was discovered in December 1994. This grotto features inscriptions that include hand stencils, complex finger markings, panels filled with dots and representations of numerous animals including stags, horses, bears, panther, an ibex a mammoth and even a rhinoceros.[9] Collectively, these inscriptions are the largest body of evidence we have of humanity's creative, cognitive and cultural beginnings. As Stephen Gould indicates, there are far more signs than animal figures and therefore

Hand stencil in the Chauvet-Pont-d'Arc Cave. (Vallon-Pont-d'Arc, Ardèche, France). French Ministry of Culture and Communication, Regional Board for Cultural Affairs, Rhône-Alpes Region, Regional Department of Archaeology.

the signs may be considered to be of more importance.[10] We have no way of knowing why these signs and images were produced. It is dangerous to apply the cultural values of our contemporary context to a contextual situation that is beyond our understanding. What is evident is that these images represent a huge leap in consciousness. At a time when the acquisition of food and defence against marauding predators would have been a dominant concern, we can only wonder why our ancestors devoted so much time to the production and maintenance of these images. It is very difficult to accept some form of aesthetic relief.

In our day, art has acquired cultural status; in the last half century or so its acquisition has turned artwork into the ultimate consumer durable, the most expensive toy in the box.[11] This belief in the high cultural value of art preconditions us to 'see' aesthetic value in these inscriptions. We may be overlooking their communication value.[12] Robert Sternberg explains:

> The load of cultural information pressing down on even more complicated networks of band societies, where people could not yet read or write, opened new opportunities for people adept at drawing; the underground sanctuaries at places like Lascaux became 'socialisation machines' in whose bowels rhythmic ceremony, sensory deprivation, and exposure to 'virtual worlds' compellingly rendered on the cavern walls helped ingrain band norms and wisdom.[13]

Or, borrowing a concept from Umberto Eco, these inscriptions may have been a shopping list of their observable world, an attempt to grasp the incomprehensible.[14] These graphic signs may have been a demonstration of a 'story' activated by the existing synaptic neural connections.[15] Theories aside, there is no explanation for the sudden appearance of these images. As of yet there are no precursory images that would indicate an increasing sophistication of representation —and as has been observed many times, why are what may seem to be images of humans lacking the visual 'aesthetic' that were applied to the depiction of animals. There are many unanswered questions regarding their origin and purpose; what is beyond question is their communication role, even accepting that what we perceive as 'communication' changes with our cultural context.

FROM WEDGE TO WEBB

If, as Rudolf Arnheim asserted over half a century ago, we organise visual material according to specific psychological premises, then how do we organise words into symbols with meaning?[16] Words are symbols that can be arbitrary, ambiguous and abstract.[17] In the beginning there was the spoken word; oral language always precedes written language. The oral tradition has limitations, it is subject to the personal editing and cultural accent of each individual involved in the process of transfer. In many pre-writing societies the process of transfer itself was a speciality assigned to story-tellers or tribal elders; a form of information hierarchy developed. In the earliest of societies the people with the most power were those who had been entrusted with the memory of the tribe. Very often these early power merchants relied on tricks of memory to recall, or at least trigger recall, of blocks of information. Verse is a mnemonic aid.[18] Daily rites and rituals are mnemonic devices—there were many other forms including material objects. These mnemonic memory devices were used to recall tribal myths, histories, medicinal cures and legends of the tribe, they were used during oral presentations of information, and may have added a degree of authenticity.[19]

The next logical step was to record the sound of language. Writing, the second communication revolution, made the spoken word and the associated thought permanent. It was a true and thorough revolution in human culture, providing a means to record information and allowing for the sharing of that information. It made possible the establishment of a database of human knowledge. But here, a word of caution; writing can tell the truth but with equal aplomb it can lie.

Despite all the research, the origins of writing remain a mystery. It may have been an example of cultural polygenesis, occurring to different cultural groups around the same time, probably motivated by trade. What we currently believe to be the earliest examples of writing were developed by the Sumerians in what was then Mesopotamia. The area between the Tigris and Euphrates rivers was a very verdant and productive agricultural environment and provided a stopping place for our nomadic ancestors. It was here, in what is now Iraq and the area around the Persian Gulf, that the first urban cultures emerged. Well, urban may be somewhat of an exaggeration. Starting with relatively small village-like communities these early urbanites quite literally put down roots, began an agricultural existence, domesticated animals, practised crafts and developed the first complex societies. These early settlements often came into being at the junction of trade routes and as a result it became necessary to have a record of transactions. What was required were materials to record with and a method to register that record. Clay was readily available as were reed like plants—these provided the elements necessary for incising wedge-like marks into the clay. The resulting incisions being the beginnings of a cuneiform writing system, a system that was in use for more than 5,000 years.[20] Think of it as being texting with clay.

DESIGN PROFILE: EPIC OF GILGAMESH
ENJOY THE MOMENT

Designers are always operating in the future, that is part of the nature of the design process. Many writers have been fascinated by the forecasting of future events and in the search for human immortality, from *Gilgamesh* to *2001: A Space Odyssey*, more recent explorations include *The Matrix* and *Avatar*. Around 4,500 years ago, an unknown poet produced the *Epic of Gilgamesh* written in cuneiform script, a script which had developed from being an accounting *aide-mémoire* to a sophisticated writing system capable of recording creative literary compositions.[21]

This first known literary epic tells of the life and desires of Gilgamesh, an early ruler of the Mesopotamian city of Uruk (modern day Iraq) about 2750 BCE. He is devastated by the death of a close friend, Enkidu. Gilgamesh, wishing to escape the inevitability of death, embarks on a journey of self-discovery to the end of the earth in search of eternal life. Along the way he meets a divinity, Uta-napishtim, who reminds him of the limits of being human.

Composed nearly 5,000 years ago, this sage advice still resonates through the millennia. What I find amazing is that this epic tale was produced to be viewed by a very small number of persons, a few hundred at most, and that now, thanks to the Internet, it is known by hundreds of thousands the world over. The story has somewhat ironic modern parallels. On his epic journey, Gilgamesh discovered that friendship can bring peace to a whole city and that a pre-emptive attack on a monster may have dire consequences.

> Humans are born, they live, then they die, this is the order that the gods have decreed. But until the end comes, enjoy your life, spend it in happiness, not despair. Savour your food, make each of your days a delight, bathe and anoint yourself, wear bright clothes that are sparkling clean, let music and dancing fill your house, love the child who holds you by the hand, and give your wife pleasure in your embrace. This is the best way for a man to live.[22]

Cuneiform script tablet recording the allocation of beer, probably from southern Iraq, Late Prehistoric period, about 3100–3000 BCE, The British Museum.

KEEPING TABS

In room 56 of The British Museum is a small, 5,000 year old tablet which represents, in cuneiform script, the records of a local administrator, recording the allocation of beer to workers.[23] This tablet has both pictograms and five different shaped impressions, which may represent numbers. When fully developed, this cuneiform system of symbol recognition was made up of some 1,200 characters representing numerals, names and objects. The Sumerians were the most sophisticated cultural group of that time, and they needed an improved form of recording temple-based business transactions. Increased trade meant increased cultural interaction and the ideas and concepts associated with the Sumerians travelled throughout their sphere of influence. This early form of cross cultural design may be evident in the sudden appearance of hieroglyphic script in Egypt around 3100 BCE, although this is a matter of continuing debate.

Writing made the cultural values and social ideals of that culture available to future generations. One other point of interest that divides oral transfer from written transfer is that written forms of communication emphasise social divisions—the division between the illiterate and the literate. In our modern world there is so much information, much of which is transitory in nature and visual in form. We may be in need of a new interpretation as to what constitutes literacy.

LIGHT THE WAY

In early Medieval Europe few could read and write. There was a very limited amount of written content, what little there was tended to be remembered by heart with the 'script' acting as a mnemonic devise. The earliest examples of continuous writing have no punctuation or even separation between the words. It is probable that the process of reading was dependant upon speaking the words out loud in order to untangle the continuous lines of characters into words with meaning. A question worth pondering—when we read we know where the end of words are, how do we recognise the end of words in spoken speech? [24]

In Medieval Europe, the majority of manuscript production was carried out in monasteries and so the very act of production was considered an act of devotion. The labour would often be divided between a scribe for the text and lay artists for the illumination. During the Dark Ages[25] the knowledge gained by the scholars of the Classical age was lost and life was governed by superstitions and fears fuelled by ignorance.[26] In Europe, isolated monastic centres salvaged what little remained of Ancient knowledge. One essential point—in the West, what was recorded and copied focussed on past events—following the dictate that everything that could be known, was known. There was no encouragement for original comment or contemporary content (the exception being the personal glosses that sometimes appeared in the margins) and very little control over accuracy. Robert Harrison points out, "Practically all the writings that have come down to us from the Middle Ages are what scholars call 'composites', and represent the combined efforts of the author and every scribe who got his hands on the work."[27] One thing that these magnificent objects were definitely not, was a literal, objective account of reality.

It was a financing scheme of the established church that created the conditions for the next major revolution in the culture of communication, the standardisation of text. The concept of an indulgence is based on the medieval doctrine that sinners must not only repent of sins that they have committed, they must also pay some sort of retribution. Given the post-Black Death revelry, the Medieval booming mercantile economy and the accompanying change from a barter to a money based economy, the conditions existed for social acts requiring retribution. A reformation of secular economics and church finances created the context for the 'indulgence'. Market demand for these proclamations of penance added to the massive surge in the need for documentation, scribes could not scribble fast enough. What was needed was a method to automate and accelerate the process of production.

THE PRINTED WORD

Trade drove the economy of the ancient Roman Republic (509–27 BCE.) and the import of papyrus scrolls from Egypt provided the necessary material for the commercial production of books. The Republic was followed by the Roman Empire.

The process of commercial production alters with the closing of the Roman book trade in the sixth century and its replacement by the monastic *scriptorium*. It alters again in the late twelfth century in Italy, and at the beginning of the thirteenth century in northern Europe, with the passage of production into lay hands in the Medieval city and the gradual closing of the monastic scriptoria. The process alters yet again with the revitalising of scriptoria among house of the *devotio moderna* in the fifteenth century and the increase in production associated with Italian humanism.[28]

In the Medieval world, the transfer of knowledge was limited by the means of production. It could take a year to copy a manuscript and use the hides of up to 200 sheep, making the recording of information a very laborious and expensive proposition.[29] The result of this labour was valued as much, if not more, for its symbolic presence than for its actual content. Copies varied and were subject to the vagaries of the monastic *scriptoria*. The development of printing in the West during the mid-fifteenth century standardised product and was to have the most far-reaching effect on humankind. Printing changed for ever the way that we access and process information, changed the established power base by extending the number of people having access to content; personalised interpretation and thereby empowered a much greater percentage of the populace. But don't be misled, the transfer to a literate, more knowledgeable society took centuries to achieve; indeed the transfer is ongoing.

Information has conferred power on those in the population who had access and who were in a position to be able to make use of it. In pre-printing Europe a very small percentage of the population were literate, maybe less than two per cent.[30] After printing, the percentage increased substantially and now, thanks to the new technologies, it is, or at least could be, universal and at the same time personal. Printing changed the nature of knowledge itself. The Internet is about to create an equally cataclysmic change to the nature of knowledge. But nothing comes for free. Personal empowerment, then and now, has associated cultural costs.

THUS HAVE I HEARD[31]

The economic and cultural conditions were in place in fifteenth century Europe for the rapid advancement of knowledge and information. What was needed was some form of automated writing system to aid in the transfer of information. Such a system had been tried before. As early as the ninth century the Chinese had been producing printed books using the block technique.[32] The oldest dated piece of printed ephemera still in existence is the Chinese translation

of the *Diamond Sutra*, just seven pages pasted together to form a scroll nearly five metres long and just over 30 centimetres high.[33] The date is equivalent in the Western calendar to 11 May, 868CE. The obvious high standard would seem to indicate that the craft of printing had been around for some time. In the eleventh century the Chinese were printing with movable type. Instead of cutting one block for one unit of text Bì Sheng is credited with the development of a system whereby each individual character was cut in clay and fired.[34] The resulting porcelain unit was movable and reusable. An iron base was brushed with a mixture of pine resin, wax and ash. The characters would then be set and the plate heated gently to soften the mixture. A flat board was pressed down over the characters to ensure an even height—and now you were ready to print. Afterwards it was merely a matter of reheating the mixture, loosening the characters, cleaning them with some form of solvent and putting them back into their circular, revolving character case. This process was in active use a good 400 years before printing with movable type was introduced into Europe.[35]

Let us be clear what Gutenberg did and did not do. Johannes Gutenberg did not invent printing. The process of printing emerged in ninth century China. He did not invent printing with movable type; the Chinese printer Bì Sheng did that around 1040 using ceramic pieces of type. Gutenberg did not even invent printing with movable metal type. The Korean Royal Court did that in the fourteenth century, the oldest extant movable metal print book is the Jikji Simche Yogol, which was produced in the Heug Duck Sa Buddhist temple in Chungjoo, Korea in 1377.[36] What Gutenberg devised was a very efficient process of printing with movable type that took advantage of available knowledge and exploited existing cultural conditions. He did formulate a more appropriate alloy, a mix of lead, tin and antimony for the cast letters and he perfected a punch and mould system which allowed the mass production of the individual letter forms.[37] He did design a new kind of press, based on those used to squeeze olives. The press employed a large screw that applied pressure on the printing surface and the new metal type was able to withstand the force and produce clear, precise impressions on the imported hand-made paper from Italy. And he did concoct a smudge resistant ink of lamp black, turpentine and linseed oil necessary for the faster production process. And above all, he did have the drive and tenacity to see that his idea was realised.

Nothing is actually known of Gutenberg's early life until his mercenary actions resulted in legal proceedings. It is thought that he was born around 1398 in the city of Mainz and that his family were goldsmiths and coin minters, thereby proving the necessary 'craft' background and technical knowledge. In 1434, while living in Strasbourg, there is a record of proceedings that he brought against the City of Mainz for non-payment of some form of annuity resulting from the death of his mother. In 1439 there are further records of his dealings with two disgruntled former partners.[38] Not to put too much of a spin on things, Gutenberg was definitely not motivated by philanthropic ideals. He had no intent to transform society nor to change the Medieval world. His actions were not altruistic, all he wanted to do was make a fortune. Many of his early attempts failed, including one quite spectacular venture to sell devotional mirrors to the pilgrims at a local pilgrimage fair at Aachen when he got the date of the fair wrong.[39] Then he had a gem of an idea.

Page from Johannes Gutenberg's famed 42-line Bible, the first document to be printed with moveable type in the Western world.

TYPEFACE[40]

When a new technology challenges an existing technology there is a period of adjustment—a time when the expectations of the audience influence the form of the new technology. To print you need type. Gutenberg faced the challenge of acceptance and so made the typeface of his printed bible look as close to a hand scripted manuscript as possible. It has been suggested that some of the Gutenberg bibles were sold as the product of monastic *scriptoriums*. The modern Latin alphabet consists of 52 letters, including both upper and lower case, plus ten numerals, punctuation marks and a variety of other symbols. In the fifteenth century, the characters and marks of the popular *Gothic Littera Bastarda* family of book hands, formed from the hybridisation of *Gothic textura* with cursive scripts, were far more numerous.[41] There are over 300 separate letter forms used in the font of the Gutenberg bible and it is estimated that between 50,000 and 100,000 types would have been cast to meet the needs of the team of 12 printers involved in the two year production process, making the whole venture a very expensive endeavour.[42]

> *Beware the man of one book.*
> St Thomas Aquinas (Scholastic philosopher and theologian, 1225–1274).

The new printed books increased the amount of available information but people had to be trained how to access this overload. Design innovations such as paragraphs, chapters, page numbering and most innovative of all, indexing, were introduced, not all at once but over time. (We are still waiting for similar design innovations to help with the current information overload.) Printing made it possible to compile authoritative texts in vernacular languages, from scattered and often corrupted Latin manuscripts. The era of reliance on manuscripts was over. Within 50 years printing shops were in existence in over 250 cities throughout Europe. These shops provide a meeting place for all involved in production—the writer, the printer, the bookseller—adding a new element to urban civil culture during the onset of the Renaissance. Within another 20 years the Reformation brought into existence the cheap, mass produced pamphlet type book and with it the concept of propaganda. Printing turned the Bible from a specialist manuscript for devout theologians into a best seller. Printing rekindled interest into long forgotten or suppressed ancient texts. Printing provided guides to success in the secular world with maps and tables and descriptions of production processes. Printing introduced new ideas as publishers were ever anxious to find new titles. Printing allowed people to think for themselves. Printing changed attitudes to knowledge.[43]

Étienne Jules Marey, Flight of a gull, bronze, 1887. Sculpture by Marey, cast in bronze in Naples. (Décomposition du vol d'un goéland, sculpture en bronze. 1997, dépôt du Collège de France en 1977, Musee Marey, Beaune, France. Photo: JC Couval.)

A NEGATIVE VIEW

Western cultures came to accept the printed word as the hallmark of what distinguished them from pre-literate societies and to see printed words as 'containing' the meaning; "it must be true, I read it" became a popular vindication of print. Photography has taught us a revised visual code. Photographs change, modify and enlarge our ideas of what is worth looking at. There is a grammar and ethics of seeing. We are told that a picture is worth a thousand words.[44] Unlike video, television or film images, which are all transitory, the photograph has itself a physical presence. The printed word is abstract, the photographed image is, at least momentarily, an image of reality. It can also be seen as an unequivocal matter of fact—and, like print, it can lie.[45]

The origins of the photographic process may be found at the very beginning of the nineteenth century, and, not surprisingly, are tied into the world of manufacturing capitalism. In 1802, Josiah Wedgwood, the quintessential industrial capitalist, wrote an article entitled, "Description of a procedure for copying paintings onto glass and for making silhouettes by the effect of light on silver nitrate".[46] Using paper coated with silver chloride, he succeeded in producing images of paintings, silhouettes of leaves, and human profiles which he used as a merchandising tool. However, because the entire surface of the paper blackened after exposure to light, these images were not permanent. Wedgwood never capitalised on the process.

Some 15 years later, in France, Joseph Niépce, who had just learned the lithographic process for creating images, tried to automate the process for copying and reproduction initially by using the camera obscura.[47] He soon realised that he could copy from real life and produced the first 'photograph' around 1826/1827.

Frustrated by his inadequate drawing skills, the Englishman Henry Fox Talbot[48] attempted to draw with the aid of both a camera obscura and a camera lucida.[49] Early in 1834 he began experimenting with silver nitrate treated surfaces as had Wedgwood and Niépce before him. This resulted in the first 'negative'. The earliest surviving paper negative is of the Oriel window in the South Gallery at Lacock Abbey, Wiltshire, in England. It is dated August, 1835.[50]

TELL THE TRUTH

Photography provides visual evidence of the world seen, but not seen, as demonstrated in the sequential photographs of Eadweard Muybridge and Étienne Jules Marey.[51] Marey sought to make sense of, and record, what he saw. This resulted in a life long quest to visualise motion, to reveal just how bodies, human and animal, move. The subject had fascinated other researchers; Leonardo da Vinci bought birds in the marketplace and released them, giving him a few precious seconds to observe their mechanics. His range of experiments and observations are faithfully recorded in his *Codex on the Flight of Birds*, 1490–1505.[52] Marey invented a 'photogun', that shot a rapid series of pictures.[53] This 'gun' was able to take advantage of 'stripping films' developed by George Eastman in 1884.[54] Marey produced a three-dimensional model of his research and had it cast in bronze by a foundry in Naples.

Eadweard Muybridge was born in Kingston-upon-Thames, near London, England in 1830. His family were attracted by the lure of the 1849 gold rush and moved to America; following a stage coach accident in 1860 he returned to Britain. He made a return visit to America in 1866 and a little later directed a photographic survey of the Pacific coast. In 1872 the railway magnate and racehorse owner Leland Stanford commissioned Muybridge to settle a bet to prove that when a horse galloped there is a stage in its gait when all four legs are simultaneously off the ground at the same time. Muybridge designed an elaborate system of batteries of about 24 cameras, all with fast shutter mechanisms. Attached strings stretched across the race track were broken by the passing horse tripping the shutters. Leland Stanford won his bet. Muybridge produced the first successful sequential photographs of rapidly moving objects that are still used to study motion.

In very general terms, a photograph is a two-dimensional representation of a three-dimensional world. A photograph is concerned with things that are present to the senses, you cannot photograph a dream, which is presumably why dream-like photographs have always seemed to intrigue photographers. A successful photograph is concerned with either information, aesthetics or emotion; a very successful photograph combines all three. There is a duality concerned with photographs. On the one hand they promise truthfulness and honesty and on the other they are seen as being in the domain of the arts, and more recently as being an integral part of multi-media pieces where they are subject to a whole range of software manipulation.[55] Today, image manipulation is commonplace. Adobe Photoshop Elements 8 offers the ability to "create the perfect group shot" allowing the user to "easily combine the best facial expressions and body language from a series of group shots to create a single perfect composite". Adobe Photoshop Elements 9 has amplified the ability to "create the perfect photo your camera couldn't capture". Telling the truth has never been more problematic.

The persuasive power of photography is based largely upon our preconception of what a photograph is. We accept a photograph as a record of reality captured by a dispassionate machine and we learn to interpret what we see. Despite all the research, little is known about how precisely we 'read' a photograph. There is competition between logic and feeling. Logically we know that a photograph is no more than an image printed onto a sheet of coated paper. In one sense, for all our sophistication and worldliness, photographs still hold a magic and mystery for us. We are afraid to throw away the photograph of someone we love, especially if that person is far away or dead. We have built a cultural barrier against defacing a photograph of a family member—could you take a photograph of any loved one and poke the eyes out? However, we may not be as 'protective' when those images are stored on iPhoto or a USB. Photography only shows one view of reality, and even then it tends to be one person's view of one reality at one point in time. It can be argued that the frozen visual image is less flexible

than the written word; we tend to be more free in our creative reinterpretation of text than photographs, indeed we often rely on photographs to remind us of how things were while text can suggest how things may be.

One other point, within the Western liberal tradition, humanism demands that it is the victim/loser that is shown. The danger is that we experience the 'unbelievable' things that happen in our world in the comfort and familiarity of our own home. We scan the illustrations in our magazines, we passively take in the TV images or the PC download and often the unbelievable becomes tinged with the concept of beauty (we use what we know to interpret what we see), and this charm leads to acceptance and eventual boredom. Unfortunately sometimes the connections get crossed, poverty and starvation are very photogenic.

In todays pixilated world we are exposed to so many visual images that we train ourselves to react in a very specific way to certain signals. The camera catches us in the very act of being human; it exposes all our values and foibles, helps us tell the truth, helps us to lie; we even have popular software to assists in the manipulation of images. Peter Plagens, suggests that photography, "the last art form to be tethered to realism, its factual validity has lately been manipulated and pixelated to the point of extinction".[56] This observation becomes of prime importance when evaluating the visual form and content of computer mediated communication. In our pixilated age, the process of image reproduction is itself never ending, never static, never the same two days running. More about that in the final chapter.

THE MOVING IMAGE

Mitchell Stephens, in the opening paragraph in the preface to his book *The Rise of the Image the Fall of the Word*, has this to say:

> In much of the developed world the last third of the twentieth century has been characterised by relative peace and prosperity, yet it has been filled with a kind of despair. There is a sense of exhaustion in philosophy, politics and the arts. We worry that vanity, materialism and cynicism reign unchecked; that our civic life has eroded; that we have lost touch with basic values, with what is real... these phenomena can be explained in part by the transition from a culture dominated by the printed word to one dominated by moving images. [57]

That is an innovative and all encompassing claim. And it all began in France. It was not long before innovative minds found a way to make the still image appear to move.[58] The first were the French brothers Louis Lumière (1864–1948) and Auguste Lumière (1862–1954) who, on 28 December, 1895, projected the first public showing of a selection of ten of their single-reel films to a paying audience in the Grand Cafes Salon Indien on the Boulevard des Capucines in Paris. The cost of entrance was high at one franc, which is about $5 in todays value. The show lasted for about 20 minutes (a series of brief shorts, most were about 40 seconds long) and the audience were witness to the first public demonstration of film which included clips of workers leaving the Lumière studio in Lyon and a train arriving at the Lyon station; the arrival of the train was so convincing that some of the audience fled the 'cinema' in horror, believing the image of the train speeding towards them was real; and so began our fascination with the artificially constructed 'reel' world of the movie.[59]

50 years later, following the end of the Second World War, the combatant nations were engaged in re-branding campaigns, very necessary for economic survival in the post-war world, (see Section Two, "Form"). In many instances, film played an essential role in the restructuring of cultural values. Film was the most persuasive and popular of all forms of communication. It was almost universal while being intimate, requiring active participation in the form of a modern day pilgrimage. The tribe watched the cave wall come alive with motion, sound and eventually, colour.

Each nation had a different cultural agenda, different values and different genres. Much post-1945 Japanese film promoted a pre-modern, indigenous national identity.[60] British film culture focussed on past achievements and historical pageants.[61] French film received active government support as it reclaimed its historic role as the initiator of film culture.[62] The French recognised earlier than most the importance of cultivating a national image—"une certaine idée de la France",[63] as postulated by Charles de Gaulle; this was considered essential to counter the advances of Hollywood and the American "rendezvous with destiny".[64] Certainly American film was a formidable force in propagating North American values.[65] Film remained site specific, the audience came to the screen, prepared to enter into an artificially created environment of the imagination. Admission was often subject to societal guidelines referencing age and film content was subject to classification with legal ramifications to transgressors. Then came television.

SPONSORED INFORMATION

Television personalised and domesticated the reception of the moving image. Recent research indicates that by the time the average person reaches age 70, they will have spent the equivalent of seven to ten years watching television.[66] Constantin Perskyi made the first known use of the word "television" at the 1900 World's Fair in Paris.[67] Numerous claims are made as to being the inventor of television. Several inventors, including the

Englishman A A Campbell-Swinton and the Russian scientist Boris Rosing, attempted to build electronic television systems based on the cathode ray tube. Between 1924/1925, the American Charles Jenkins and John Baird from Scotland, each demonstrated the mechanical transmissions of images over wire circuits. 12 months later Baird operated a television system with 30 lines of resolution running at five frames per second. In 1928, the Federal Radio Commission issues the first television station license—W3XK—to Charles Jenkins and in 1930 he broadcast the first TV commercial.[68] A two station network began broadcasting in America in 1939 but all network broadcasting was halted during the Second World War. In 1946, the three station NBC network resumed broadcasting. By 1951, 17 million television sets had been sold in North America. We had to wait until 1956 for Robert Adler to invent the first practical remote control called the Zenith Space Commander.[69]

During the 1950s, the nuclear family was captivated by television as it became the dominant mass medium.[70] The young spent almost as much time watching television as in the classroom and acquired broadcast values.[71] It is worth quoting one of the more well known of Marshall McLuhan's probes. McLuhan considered the effects of the electronic revolution on the individual, on culture and on our global society. He considered past examples of technological intrusion and postulated that

> *Societies have always been shaped more by the nature of the media by which men communicate than by the content of the communication.*[72]
> *The Medium is the Massage,* 1967.[73]

What was unique to North America, and bearing the McLuhan quote in mind, is the way in which television was (and is) financed. Up until very recently, in most European countries, television was 'controlled' in one way or another by the state, usually through some sort of licensing arrangement and with the government having tight control over the form and content of the medium. Television was seen as primarily educational. In North America the production of television programmes was market driven, paid for by advertisers. From the onset, the content of North American television covered the full spectrum of popular culture. Appropriately called 'soaps' provided the sponsored vehicle of promotion for many domestic products, products which otherwise had no individual identity.[74] Programmes presented images of the ideal family, living in an ideal unreal, world, sustained and identified by what was consumed. The reality was so convincing that the audience often sent congratulatory messages on programmed births and weddings and condolences over deaths. The essential reality for television moguls was not to sell programmes to audiences, but to sell audiences to advertisers.[75]

This remains the raison d'être for most North American television.

No other medium, not print, not computers, not the Internet, penetrated into North American homes at such an amazing rate. It took over 70 years for the telephone to make its way into 50 per cent of North American homes. In 1946 there were around seven thousand television sets in America.[76] A survey of junior high school students in 1949 showed that 50 per cent had television set in their home.[77] At the end of the 1950s, television had entered into over 87 per cent of all homes in America.[78] Apple sold its first all-in-one personal computer in 1977. By 2000, the computer has entered into about 40 per cent of North American homes.[79] According to a 2008 Research and Markets report about 80 per cent of American homes currently have a desktop or notebook computer.

In 1962 when AT&T and NASA collaborated on the launch of the first communication satellite I doubt that they realised that they were providing the means for the first live reporting from a war front. The advent of the Vietnam War—the first to be experienced live via television by the general public—was also the first war to be terminated by resulting public pressure, a fact not lost on the American administration who have never allowed uncontrolled, uncensored coverage of any later confrontations, preferring to 'embed' media.[80]

More recently it has become not only socially acceptable, but also often a requirement of group membership, to criticise television. These range from the innocuous knocks of reference—the boob tube, the dumb black box—to the description by Mark Frost, co-creator of *Twin Peaks* that "in this country, television is used primarily as a narcotic to prepare people for the commercials".[81] It is perhaps a sad commentary of the medium and an endorsement of the observation that television has not yet developed from its initial stage, that many of the most memorable televised moments are 'commercial'.

DESIGN PROFILE: COCA-COLA

Coca-Cola was initially brewed up by Dr John Styth Pemberton in Atlanta during 1886 and sold as a brain tonic. The brand name was penned by Pemberton's book-keeper, Frank M Robinson. His flowing cursive script became one of the most recognised logo's on earth. All good things come to an end.[82] The popular "Things go Better With Coke" campaign of the 1960s (devised by McCann-Erickson) along with the radio jingle (recorded by The Limelighters in 1963), had run its course. On 18 January 1971, Bill Backer, the McCann-Erickson creative director of the Coca-Cola account had to overnight at Shannon Airport due to fog on the flight to London. In the morning the passengers were reminiscing over a few bottles of Coke and Backer realised that Coke was "a little bit of commonality between all peoples". On his eventual arrival in London he meet with two songwriters, Billy Davis and Roger Cook to prepare a new song to be recorded by the New Seekers. Backer said that he did not know how the song should start but he did have the last line—"I'd like to buy the world a Coke and keep it company".[83] And so was born one of the most famous of all commercial songs. It was recorded by the New Seekers and promptly flopped. The bottlers in the US treated it with disdain refusing to buy air time to broadcast this message of commonality.

Backer and McCann-Erickson managed to convince the executives at Coca-Cola that the song needed to be seen as well as heard. The company agreed and budgeted $250,000 to produce a television commercial. Locations were scouted in the UK, production moved to Italy, and after several false starts the commercial was shot partly on a hillside outside Rome with the close-ups being filmed at a local race track. The actors held a Coke bottle labelled in the language of his or her native country. None of the hillside actors actually sang, they all lip synched to the New Seekers radio version of the commercial. The commercial was broadcast across America in July, 1971. By November, Coca-Cola had received over 100,000 thousand letters about the commercial, the majority of which were very positive. Two versions of the song were released, one by the New Seekers and a more country and western style version by the Hillside Singers. Both versions made it into the pop music charts. Nearly 40 years after the initial release the sheet music continues to sell and the "I'd Like to Buy the World a Coke" commercial has become legend.[84]

But just before you jump on the anti-television bandwagon ask yourself if the collective "we" know more now than "we" did 50 years ago.[85] I think that there is no doubt that because of mass media and technological advances in the means of communication, we have an increased awareness of world events than did almost anyone half a century ago. Mass media has contributed to a change in cultural values. We may not be better people than our grandparents but we are certainly better informed. The hope for television lies in the new technologies, in computer mediated information and the Internet. With the increasing fragmentation of the audience and with the convergence of the supporting technological infrastructure, brought about by satellite and cable; digital and high definition technology; liquid crystal, plasma and flat screens; with projected holographic displays, and a 2,000 channel multi-verse just a short step away, change, quite literally, is in the air. There is very obvious discontinuity and fragmentation of the medium; it will reform and reformat, becoming more reflective of the cultural mores of the era. Give it time.

In the Medieval world it took a year to copy one manuscript. Prior to 1450 there were no printed books in existence in Europe. By 1500, it is estimated that there were some 20 million books in 35,000 editions; roughly one printed book in existence for every five Europeans.[86] In our modern world, Paolo Cherchi Usai estimates that nine billion hours of moving image media are being generated annually.[87] "Add to this photographs, print, web sites, e-mails, let alone conversation, and the information produced in any one year is beyond the reach not just of any one scholar, but of the whole community of media historians."[88] We need help.

NETWORKS

At no other time in human development have conditions been more exciting, at no time has the design environment been more pregnant with possibilities. As we hurtle through the infinity of space and time towards an unknown and totally unimaginable future it is the designers on this planet that have the responsibility of communicating changing values to the general human population. I have read most of the books, heard the speakers from Bill Gates to Nicholas Negroponte, but have never been able to formulate a satisfactory explanation of the Internet. Then I came across a book by Salman Rushdie, *Haroun and the Sea of Stories*, published in 1990. Unintentionally, Rushdie provides a most convincing description of the Internet. A brief quote from *Haroun and the Sea of Stories*:

> Iff, the Water Genie told Haroun about the Ocean of the Streams of Story, and even though he was full of a sense of hopelessness and failure the magic of the Ocean began to have an effect on Haroun. He looked into the water and saw that it was made up of a thousand thousand thousand and one different currents, each one a different colour, weaving

in and out of one another like a liquid tapestry of breathtaking complexity; and Iff explained that these were the Streams of Story, that each coloured strand represented and contained a single tale. Different parts of the Ocean contained different sorts of stories, and as all the stories that had ever been told and many that were still in the process of being invented could be found here, the Ocean of the Streams of Story was in fact the biggest library in the universe. And because the stories were held here in fluid form, they retained the ability to change, to become new versions of themselves, to join up with other stories and so become yet other stories so that unlike a library of books, the Ocean of the Streams of Story was much more than a storeroom of yarns. It was not dead but alive. [89]

The Internet came into being on 29 October, 1969, when the first two nodes of what would become the ARPANET were interconnected between UCLA and SRI International in Menlo Park, California. The World Wide Web, based on research and development by the British scientist Tim Berners-Lee[90] and Belgian born Robert Cailliau,[91] was created on 6 August, 1991, when the European Organization for Nuclear Research (CERN) posted the first few pages. On 30 April 1993, CERN announced that the web could be used by anyone without charge, thereby ensuring that the web would indeed become worldwide.

The International Telecommunications Union reports that in 2010, the number of Internet users will surpass two billion. According to Internet World Stats, of these over 41 per cent are in Asia, with North America accounting for 15.7 per cent of total users.[92] Two thirds of global Internet users are non-English speakers enhancing the cross-cultural context of the Internet.[93]

Close to two billion users and unknown trillions of packets of information encourage the perception that we are struggling with information overload. Max Bruisma makes the point, "In a world that is so saturated with media, undifferentiated information threatens, by its overwhelming bulk, to swamp real meaning. In such a context, it become vital, rather than giving the individual message an arresting form, to embed the message in meaningful associations with other messages."[94] Satisfactory, sustainable design demands a network of meaningful connections. The journey may be of more import than either the points of departure or arrival. It is not so much a matter of being what you know, but how you learn.

INFORMATION IS PHYSICAL[95]

More than 2,200 years ago, Archimedes of Syracuse was charged by King Gelos II to calculate the number of grains of sand required to fill the Universe. Using some inspired reckoning Archimedes calculated that it would take 10^{63}

grains of sand. Vlatko Vedral suggests that "If... we take a grain of sand as analogous to a bit of information, then this is a pretty good guess of the Universe's information carrying capacity."[96]

A recent issue of *Discover* magazine posed the quintessential question, How much does the Internet weigh on any given day? On the Internet everything, text, visuals, video, everything is made up of a stream of binary digits. Mathematical they may be but they are also tangible, embodied as voltages in electronic circuits, and therefore they have mass. *Discover* concluded that everything on the Internet weighed roughly the same as the smallest possible grain of sand, one measuring just two-thousandths of an inch across. Leading them to conclude that in the stanza penned by William Blake in 1803 "he was being more prophetic than he could have ever known". [97]

> *To see a world in a grain of sand*
> *And a heaven in a wild flower,*
> *Hold infinity in the palm of your hand*
> *And eternity in an hour.*
> "Auguries of Innocence", William Blake, 1803.

Technological innovation is a major force in cultural and behavioural change, from developing an etiquette for a mobile society to changing the form of communication, where a new phonetic form of writing based on symbols and abbreviations is changing language itself.[98] To be effective communicators, the language that we use must be adaptable and suited to communication in the digital age. We need to more fully understand how the new forms of messaging are generating new associations and new meaning. Matt Warman, the technology editor of the *Telegraph* asserts; "Technology will infiltrate every aspect of our lives—the mobile phone will become a gateway to global communications, and link seamlessly to the web and every screen in homes and offices."[99] Biz Stone, the founder of Twitter has, not surprisingly, a similar vision. "There are now three times more mobile phone subscribers than Internet users. In the decade ahead, mobile and web will collide to fulfil the promise of technology: helping people help themselves. The open exchange of information will lead to a more informed, engaged, and more empathetic global citizenry."[100] A report by an agency of the UN showed that mobile phone use, rather than the Internet, is a far more important and relevant means of communication to people of the poorest developing countries.[101]

ALL THUMBS

Wireless networks are the fastest growing communications technology. Users have generated a most creative response both to image and to language, but as with any new technology there are concerns about application. The 1 June cover of *The New Yorker* was created by Jorge Colombo using the iPhone app 'Brushes' to capture the image of the hot dog stand outside Madame Tussauds on 42nd Street in New York City.[102] The 'Brushes' app costs less than $5, providing all smartphone users with an affordable creative tool.

The mobile network society offers innovative and restructured means of communicating human thought in a cross-cultural context. Not surprisingly it is the young that are in the process of actively exploring this phenomenon. The new range of smartphones make possible an extensive array of applications that can enliven and enhance the educational process, yet some schools remain opposed to these devices, seeing them as disruptive elements to the classic stilted environment. The more enlightened schools realise that as with all other technological advances, it is how it is used that is key. As one senior administrator points out, "Cell phones aren't going away. Mobile technology isn't going away.... Right now, what we are telling kids is 'You go home and use whatever technology you want, but when you get to school, we're going to ask you to step back in time.' It doesn't make any sense."[103] The youth culture is an 'always on' culture where the fear of not being part of the loop is ever present, and where the participants have absorbed text messaging as an integral part of their culture, and in so doing are in the process of developing a new flexible language of communication adapted to the immediacy and compactness of the media form, even if at times it is, "hrd 2 rd".[104]

The new youth culture redefines the relationship between communication, technology, and society. Misuko Ito is a cultural anthropologist who is interested in how digital media are changing relationships, identities, and communities; she researches new media and mobile phone use at Keio University and the University of Southern California's Annenberg Center for Communication. She states that it "makes peer-to-peer networks the backbone of an alternative way of life, with its own language, based on texting and multimodal communication, and its own set of values... to not have a *keitai* (cell phone) is to be walking blind, disconnected from just-in-time information on where and when you are in the social network of time and space".[105] These are rapidly forming and constantly changing communities based on personal values and interests, where the network dynamic generates a fluidity of meaning.

ALL OF A TWITTER

Smartphones and Blackberries have given rise to new formats. In 2003 an unidentified man using the pseudonym "yoshi" 'published' the first cell phone novel (*keitai shousetsu*). Five of the best selling novels in Japan in 2007 were originally cell phone novels.[106] Each novel is between 200 and 500 pages, with each page containing about 500 Japanese characters.[107] Twitter is a form of story-telling limited to 140 characters. The company was founded in March 2006 and in October 2009 the company was valued at one billion dollars.[108] Twitter is a mobile social software that allows the broadcast and reception of short messages within a social network; its use has exploded to over three million users. For the latest user figures see: http://blog.comscore.com. Twitter provides a never-ending stream of presence messages providing the illusion of a fragmented experience of opinions, events, news, ideas and feedback. It allows thousands of users to enter into conversations conducted among multiple users at any point.

The very nature of the medium means that exact numbers are difficult to obtain and are forever changing. As a guide, Nielsen Mobile reported in late 2008 that North American teenagers with cellphones received on average, 2,272 'tweets' a year.[109] There are no available figures to show how many hand written letters the average teenager composed in a year.[110] Kevin Weil of Twitter claims in his blog that Twitter users were writing 5,000 'tweets' per day in 2007, 300,000 per day in 2008 and 2.5 million per day in 2009.[111] In July 2010 Twitter, has had its 20 billionth message posted. A study undertaken in 2010 indicated that texting had overtaken the mobile phone as the preferred method of communication among teenagers in North America, with more than 30 per cent of teens sending more than 100 texts a day.[112] Many social commentators still 'see' this generation as being incapable of meaningful communication—who learns from whom?

The immediacy of tweets has not been lost on the world of business and commerce with many major companies operating their own Twitter sites. Twitter is the latest mechanism for politicians to get themselves in the public consciousness. Twitter is restructuring language, or at least the language of immediate use. It is growing in use by job seekers and what has emerged is an effective method to 'twitter' a resume.[113] It is also changing how we write; according to Caroline Tagg, a British linguist, texting is closer to speech than the written word.[114] But there are still limitations. The anthropologist Edward T Hall identified what he termed the Silent Language, forms of non-verbal communication that influence meaning.[115] These characteristics include body language, eye movements, the use of silence and other expressive behaviours, all of which fall outside the operating parameters of Twitter with its reliance on text-dependent messages.

CONNECTIONS

With the vast expansion of available information in our post-industrial world and where the digital images and text stand front and centre in shaping our expectations of things to come, the process of communication will be very different. In an information rich environment the ability to distinguish between fact and fiction may be less important than discovering new connections; it may well be that 'links' are of more importance than content, that the journey is more informative than the venue. Few of us realise the extent to which our patterns of communication are changing. While previous generations navigated the oceans and discovered new land masses to colonise, we are discovering that information is space that can be navigated and, perhaps, one day inhabited.

We will need to learn new disciplines of use, a revised communication etiquette. It was not all that long ago that the use of the telephone required entry into some form of box like container to ensure privacy. Now, individuals broadcast their messages to all and sundry, often failing to recognise that they are, indeed, broadcasting. The accumulation of devices of communication and the often associated "continuous partial attention", has resulted in some organisations having 'topless' meetings where all communication devices and laptops are banned. [116]

There are many critics of the new communication reality, many suggest that the Web, Twitter and Google are encouraging a mass attention-deficit culture. Tyler Cowen, the American economist and academic offers an alternative view.

> The arrival of virtually every new cultural medium has been greeted with the charge that it truncates attention spans and represents the beginning of cultural collapse—the novel (in the eighteenth century), the comic book, rock 'n' roll, television, and now the Web. In fact, there has never been a golden age of all-wise, all-attentive readers. But that's not to say that nothing has changed. The mass migration of intellectual activity from print to the Web has brought one important development: We have begun paying more attention to information. Overall, that's a big plus for the new world order.[117]

Soothsayers have always delighted in finding connections between technological innovation and moral decline. Currently it is the new media that attracts their attention; we are informed that search engines lower our levels of intelligence and that social networks reduce our attention spans. The reality is at odds with these pessimistic views. Steven Pinker, a Professor of Psychology at Harvard, and the author of *The Blank Slate* and *The Stuff of Thought*, clarifies the situation.

> The new media have caught on for a reason. Knowledge is increasing exponentially; human brainpower and waking hours are not. Fortunately, the Internet and information technologies are helping us manage, search and retrieve our collective intellectual output at different scales, from Twitter and previews to e-books and online encyclopaedias. Far from making us stupid, these technologies are the only things that will keep us smart.[118]

The last century has witnessed several false communication promises attributed to technology. In the immediate post-Second World War environment, social scientists welcomed the arrival of television, seeing in it a force for international understanding and as a way of arousing and stimulating the pursuance of knowledge by the young. Instead it has become a very effective demographic tool, a way of selling audiences to advertisers, a near perfect medium for product placement.[119] These are a few of the ever changing forms of information access and retrieval. Apple are on target to sell 25 million iPads in 2011. Ignore at your peril.

Along with many other academics I saw the arrival of the Internet as offering new hope for the moribund fields of academia where administration rules. Instead the Internet has become the e-commerce net. Maybe, just maybe, mobile communications will be different, and live up to its potential promise, maybe it will promote and encourage the creative communication of human thought in a cross-cultural context. Certainly, technology generated communication has produced new disciplines, encouraged new ways of thinking about the world and created new social hierarchies. In the very near future we will expand those hierarchies to include intelligent machines, robots, cyborgs and other technology inspired constructs, all of which will present new communication challenges which will demand creative responses.[120] You have the power, it us up to you to acquire the knowledge to use it wisely. Designers need to be prepared today for tomorrow's design realities. Designers need a new orientation to design.

TELL ME A STORY!

Telling stories is as old as language itself. Psychologists inform us that we all develop a "theory of mind" around the age of four.[121] This enables us to understand each other. It helps us understand those people we know and those that exist in narrative form. Sam Leith observes that "Story-telling is a way of trying out situations imaginatively, of preserving knowledge and social value, of attesting to a commonality of experience. Stories are central to how we think about the world: from the individual to the wide sweep of history. The ability to put yourself in another's shoes is the foundation-stone of all morality."[122] It is also intrinsic to the design process. To re-quote Stuart Walker from the prologue: "An object without history is fiction and an object which has not moved on from history is retrospective. An authentic product could be seen as a mix of the two."[123] Both stories and design are collaborative, both assist in making sense of the world.

Common Ground Publishing is an assembly of sites and blogs which discuss and explore the meaning and purpose of 'design'. The following is an extract from their *Design Principles and Practices*:

> Design is also an act, a manifestation of agency, a process of transformation. The narrative of design runs like this: take the available designs in the world (inherent to found objects, architectures, landscapes, processes, human relationships, cultures). Then engage in the act of designing, or rework and revoice these designs. This is never just a business of reproduction and replication. It always involves an injection of the designer's social interests and cultural experiences—their subjectivity and identity, no less. The residue, as the narrative draws to a momentary close, is the world transformed, no matter in how small a way. But the world is never quite the same again, and the redesigned is returned to the world, becoming traces of transformation that join the repertoire of available designs—new openings to new design narratives.[124]

At the very beginning of *Alice's Adventures in Wonderland Alice* offers the observation, "what is the use of a book… without pictures or conversations".[125] Most of the story of Alice's adventures is told through a dialogue which creates rich original verbal views and observations. Add pictures, make them move and you get to film. Once upon a time we went to the cinema and focussed on a single screen—a cave wall but with movement - and the movies of the time reflected that singularity.[126] Then came television and we began to have a choice over which screen we watched. With the profusion of channels came channel surfing, but still on a single screen. With computers came 'windows'. Now we absorb information from a multiplicity of sources at the same time and from a variety of devices from computers, television and smartphones to the omnipresent BlackBerry, iPod and iPad, keeping several windows up and running. This is discontinuous fragmentation. Using the available technologies we construct our own stories (views of the world) which remain fluid and ever changing. What we are still waiting for, like Alice, is to pass through the looking glass.[127]

CHAPTER FOUR
THE CREATIVE ACT AND THE PREPARED MIND

Alice laughed: "There's no use trying", she said;
"one can't believe impossible things."
"I daresay you haven't had much practice", said the Queen.
"When I was younger, I always did it for half an hour a
day. Why, sometimes I've believed as many as six impossible
things before breakfast."
Lewis Carroll, *Alice's Adventures in Wonderland.*

IMPOSSIBLE THINGS

The last chapter provided an overview of the development of language and its role in the process of communication. One result of the move from script to print in Western Europe was manifest in the Enlightenment of the eighteenth century when reason and logic were seen as paramount. By the nineteenth century the expressive nature of the English language was in need of a creative approach that challenged existing boundaries of use and meaning. The verbal nonsense of Edward Lear's verse served as inspiration to English usage.[1] The words and logical conundrums of Lewis Carroll encouraged a creative attitude to logical concepts at a time when the Victorian's believed they were witness to The Age of Improvement.[2] At the start of the twentieth century it was time for a more comprehensive look at the role of creativity in cultural development.

From our very beginnings we have depended upon creativity to make our way in the world. The human creative ability is not so much the result of adaptation by evolution but of the advanced intellectual potential that is uniquely human, a potential which endows humans with the full power of independent action expressed through behavioural features such as design.[3] There is a vast amount of information available regarding creativity —hundreds of books, thousands of articles and papers, not to mention innumerable web sites dedicated to the subject of creativity. (See the "Design Profile: A Select 'Creative' Bibliography" at the end of this chapter.)

Creativity is a 'hot' topic in the arts and in business. Creativity is used to excuse the lack of skill in visual rendition and as a come-on in the commercial world, encouraging financial investment in 'creative workshops'. In our information rich world of design, creativity is concerned with connections between the objective descriptions and values associated with science and technology and the often subjective values attributed to aesthetics, ethics and social responsibility; this is the arena for design, for the exercise of the prepared mind. In the near future one area where we will need to be very creative is in the resolution of environmental challenges to our continued existence as a species. We will need to believe impossible things, (see Chapter Twelve, "Design Futures: A Matter of Questions".)

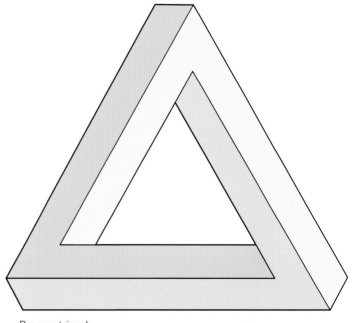

Penrose triangle.

The Penrose triangle is a perceptual paradox, an example of an impossible figure; logically it cannot exist in three dimensions and yet visually it seems to make sense. It challenges our visual imagination which responds by making assumptions about the form and what we think we see. Non-triangular three armed forms do not normally exists in our 'real' world, and so our processing abilities cannot see them. In a design sense, creativity is seeing those 'connections' that do not normally exist in our world. As with the Penrose triangle, sometimes we have to change our viewpoint to see things as they really are.[4]

THE CREATIVE PROCESS

One of the earliest working models of the creative process is attributed to Graham Wallas, the English social psychologist, teacher, and one time leader of the socialist Fabian Society. In his seminal work, *The Art Of Thought*, published in 1926 and now unfortunately out of print, he outlines his comprehension of the creative process.[5] Wallas proposed that creative thinking proceeds through four phases:

Preparation, define, observe, study. Nothing comes from nothing. Know your field of study, be familiar with the current cultural ethos. Be prepared.

Incubation—allow time for ideas to develop. Wallas noticed that many great ideas came only after a period of time was spent away from the problem, usually after engaging in other activities. Put the problem aside and get on with the rest of your life. Incubation can last minutes, weeks, or even years.

Illumination—the light goes on! The "Eureka" phenomenon. Wallas was intrigued by how the moment of revelation followed on from the period of incubation. It seems that the mind at rest suddenly makes all those unusual connections that generate the new concept. Illumination is not confined to solitary endeavours, often the 'flash' comes amidst group discussion.

Verification—check it out, make it work. Good ideas are ten-a-penny; it is perseverance and dedication that makes the difference. Does the solution fit the problem—if not how can it be made to do so?

The model outlined by Wallas remains the basis for most creative thinking programmes available today.[6] Recent brain imaging studies have added weight to Wallas' intuitive understanding of the creative process.[7] Creative thinkers are less likely to be contemplators of navels and more likely to be practised in observation skills, seeing things that others miss, capable of putting aside blinkers and preconceptions and able to make unusual connections. However, as the noted American social scientist, Donald T Campbell cautions, creative thinkers must be alert to the inherent dangers of false knowledge, those biases and prejudices often 'protected' by those with vested interest. As Campbell explains; "The total creative process requires a drive to action and the implementation of ideas. We must do more than simply imagine new things, we must work to make them concrete realities."[8]

We have an intrinsic picture of the creative process being an act of private contemplation resulting in some form of revealing revelation. More often than not (at least in terms of design) the most satisfactory and inspiring results emerge from joint thinking sessions and passionate, thoughtful discourse.[9] True, individual reflective time is needed to work out the details, but as Robert Weisburg, Director of the Brain, Behavior, and Cognition Cluster at Temple University emphasises, people who produce creative solutions are not geniuses. They use the same thought processes as everyone else. What sets them apart is their application of knowledge, motivation, and dedication.[10]

IT'S ALL IN THE MEMES—MAYBE!
The design culture is a social activity that demands creative behaviour.[11] Paradoxical in nature, creativity is an idiosyncratic activity that thrives on networking. And, like many things in life, the earlier the values of networking are learnt, the better. Koberg and Bagnall explain: "Life is a continual sequence of encounters. Some are unavoidable; to be enjoyed or suffered by choice. Others

can be controlled consciously. Creative problem-solving is a process of dealing intelligently with those situations that can be controlled."[12]

There is no single definition nor explanation of creativity; no way to quantify, no way to measure nor calculate. The process of creativity has been variously attributed to divine intervention, the cognitive process and cultural conditioning. A renowned neuroscientist sees "creativity as a reflection of selectional neural systems".[13] It is, in all probability, a mix of reasoning, intuition and perception. Creativity may be partly genetic, maybe memes play a part. One researcher supporting the gene-centric view of human evolution suggests that a meme is a unit of human cultural evolution correspondent to the gene.[14] A meme is any idea, mode of behaviour, or skill that can be transferred from one person to another by imitation and repetition, for example by way of tribal stories, clothing codes, technological inventions—how to bake a cake, throw a baseball or make a stone tool. The memes are then passed on from generation to generation, in a way that we do not as yet fully understand, helping to ensure that future generations are in some way preconditioned/pre-wired to facilitate cultural evolution by way of creative endeavours.

ACT CREATIVE
Creativity is not discipline specific, often associated with the arts it is fundamental to scientific enquiry, technological innovation, engineering, architecture, business, economics, design and every aspect of human endeavour. Tantalizingly difficult to define it is the most basic human trait—more than anything else, it is creativity that makes us human. Gerald Edelman observes: "If our scientific description of the world is concerned with nature, our creativity reflects the ability of our brain to give rise to a second nature."[15]

The design process demands creative behaviour from its participants. Creativity is not an ability that only the chosen few posses—every person on this planet, including your parents and grandparents, are creative—we have to be in order to survive and prosper in the ever changing cultural context. And that brings us to one of the major hurdles to continued creativity, the boredom that accompanies unthinking repetitive action.

Boredom is a pattern not a reality, so change the pattern. Take a new way home, rearrange your kitchen and bathroom cupboards. Better still, do something this weekend that you have never experienced before; go to a classical concert, ballet or poetry reading; if you are not a sports enthusiast go to game; take a hike, bake a cake; spend 30 minutes browsing your thesaurus, expand your cultural repertoire, increase your knowledge of your culture and of other cultures; act creative, experience all that life has to offer, a designer can do no less!

LATERAL THINKING

Creative acts brings us to the lateral thinking guru, Edward de Bono who introduced the term in the title of his book *The Use of Lateral Thinking*, published in 1967. "Lateral Thinking is for changing concepts and changing perceptions. Lateral thinking is concerned with the perception part of thinking. This is where we organise the external world into the pieces we can then process."[16] Lateral thinking looks at a problem from a different perspective, as de Bono suggests, its not a matter of digging a hole deeper but digging in a new place. Trying harder in the same direction may not be as useful as changing direction.[17] But as we all know, changing direction is hard, it often means letting go of cherished beliefs, opinions and attitudes. Often we need help.

One of de Bono's most impressive books was written in 1972, *Children Solving Problems* in which he asked young children, aged five to seven, some complex questions—complex to adults that is—the kids had no problem with such problems as "how to stop a cat and dog from fighting"; "how to improve the human body"; "design a bicycle for a postman", and my personal favourite, "how to weigh an elephant". All the solutions that the children produced were innovative. They do not, however, prove that young children are great inventors or problem solvers; they do show that young minds, with very limited life experience, can, quite naturally, use all the information that they have acquired in their short lives to address complex problems using outbursts of free association. One of the most innovative and creative responses to the weighing an elephant problem was produced by five year old Michael Clemmetsen who suggested placing a bathroom scale under each of the elephants feet and adding up the four weights. Brilliant! I often wonder what career path Michael Clemmetsen followed.[18]

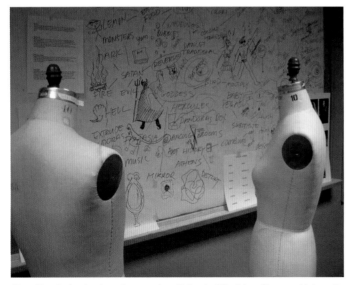

Results of a brain storming session, School of Fashion, Ryerson University, Toronto, 2009.

I DON'T KNOW ABOUT THAT

One of the main barriers to lateral thinking and the creative process is not, as you may suppose, what you don't know, but rather what you do know, a priori knowledge. Let me explain. We live disciplined lives. Every time that we access a piece of information we categorise it; is it history, is it geography, is it three-dimensional form, colour, etc., then we place it in the appropriate file box in our memory. Our file boxes are different, dependent upon life experience and personal environment. Regardless, over time they become overloaded. Given the pressure of modern life, when we are required to access the file we tend to choose the well trodden path of experience, accessing the top of the box. The "it worked last time" approach. Lateral thinking is a way of accessing all the knowledge that you know, not just the top of each file. "Creativity, it has been said, consists largely of re-arranging what we know in order to find out what we do not know. Hence, to think creatively, we must be able to look afresh at what we normally take for granted", so states George Kneller, Professor of Philosophy at Columbia University.[19]

BRAINSTORMING

There are various methods to encourage the use of what we know, these include brain storming techniques. Many of these activities appear at first sight to be artificial but after you have used them a few times they tend to become more natural, like riding a bicycle. One of the best introductions to the creative process is *The All New Universal Traveller*, by Don Koberg and Jim Bagnall; check it out for explanations and suggestions, and for detailed examples of exercises to work out your creative potential. Their emphasis is on various approaches to brainstorming creative solutions. And as they say, "Practised creative behaviour breeds automatic creative behaviour."[20] Neurologically this is called "use dependent plasticity".[21]

Another barrier to creativity is the non thinking pre-conditioned response. You all have experienced that family member or friend who, after you have told them what you are studying responds, "Well I don't know much about art but I know what I like." What they are really saying of course is "I don't know much about art but I like what I know." We all feel safe with that with which we are familiar; it is difficult to let go. So much for the academic approach, now to some examples of creativity in action.

It is seen that the Moon is most evidently not at all of an even, smooth and regular surface, as a great many people believe of it and of the other heavenly bodies, but on the contrary it is rough and unequal. In short, it is shown to be such that sane reasoning cannot conclude otherwise than that it is full of prominences and cavities similar, but much larger, to the mountains and valleys spread over the Earth's surface.
Galileo Galilei, letter dated 7 January, 1610.[22]

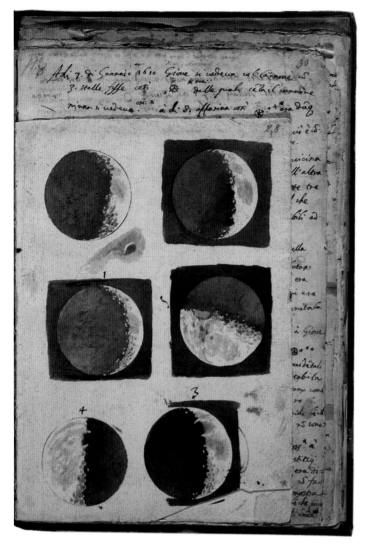

Drawings by Galileo of his observations as seen through his telescope, 1610.

year old Galileo Galilei turned his gaze skywards and on 25 August 1609 he demonstrated his first telescope to Venetian lawmakers who foresaw commercial rather than astronomical profit in the invention. Galileo published his initial telescopic observations in March 1610 in a short treatise entitled *Sidereus Nuncius* (*Starry Messenger*) allowing us to expand our view of the world and its place in the cosmos.[26] This event was to shatter long held assumptions, and resulted in dire consequences for Galileo. Lee McIntyre explains:

> Single-handedly Galileo discovered four moons of Jupiter, craters and mountains on the moon, sunspots, and the phases of Venus. Each of these discoveries in its own way was devastating for the Ptolemaic/Aristotelian system then favoured by the church, which supposed not only that the earth was at the centre of the universe but also that the heavens were perfect.[27]

Conflict with the established knowledge base in the form of the Catholic Church resulted in charges of heresy, an appearance before the Roman Inquisition, a Papal ban on his books (which remained in effect until 1835) followed by a forced recantation by Galileo and house arrest. There is often a social cost to being creative. Galileo died on 8 January, 1642.[28]

CAREFUL HOW YOU TREAD

Concerned by rapid industrial advancement in Germany, Great Britain responded by staging a massive piece of showmanship. The Great Exhibition of the Works of Industry of All Nations of 1851 was a self-financing undertaking intended to reinforce British industrial prestige. It was the defining event for nineteenth century Great Britain; the designer/architect of the principle

DO YOU SEE WHAT I SEE?

Presbyopia (diminished ability of the eye to focus on near objects) was an affliction that affected many over 40s in Medieval Europe. The Franciscan friar, Roger Bacon, noted in his *Opus Maius* of 1267 that sections of glass spheres could be placed over material to magnify the image. By the end of the thirteenth century Italian craftsmen had managed to flatten out the sections and set the resulting lens in frames to be placed over the eyes. In 1466, Duke Galeazzo Maria Sforza of Milan ordered 200 pairs of spectacles from a spectacle maker in Florence.[23] In 1585, an Augustinian monk, Tommaso Garzoni provided in his encyclopaedia of over four hundred professions, an entry on glass makers which included brief details on the manufacture and grinding of lenses.[24] What is quite amazing is that in the intervening years no one thought about the joint magnifying effect of two lenses before Hans Lippershey applied for a patent for the telescope in 1608.[25] Shortly afterwards, the 45

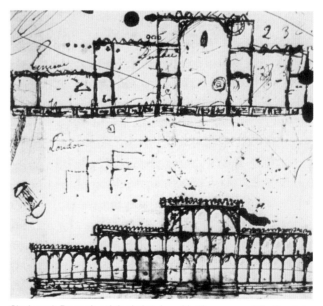

Sir Joseph Paxton's original sketch on blotting paper of the Crystal Palace, 11 June 1850.

structure personified the ideal Victorian self-made man. Born in 1803, the seventh son of a seventh son, Joseph Paxton became a gardener at the Horticultural Society's Chiswick Gardens in London. William Cavendish, Sixth Duke of Devonshire, impressed with Paxton's horticultural skill offered Paxton the position of Head Gardener at Chatsworth, the ancestral home in Derbyshire. Chatsworth was reputed to possess one of the finest landscaped gardens of the time. The 23 year old Paxton arrived at 4.30 am on 9 May, 1826. "By breakfast at 9:00 am he had inspected the grounds, set men to work, had the famous water works demonstrated, met and fallen in love with his future wife."[29] His wife to be was Sara Bown, a niece to the Housekeeper at Chatsworth. Sara and Paxton were married on 20 February, 1827.

In 1836 the Royal Botanical gardens at Kew had acquired from the reaches of the Amazon a giant water lily which was named, Victoria Regia, to honour the Queen. However, they could not induce the plant to flower. Paxton acquired a sample took it back to Chatsworth, designed and built a special iron and glass structure which contained a tank with constantly flowing water and achieved blossom!

The Duke was delighted to show off this achievement to his guests and Paxton provided another highlight when one of his six daughters, seven year old Annie, walked across the lily leaf. For most of us that would have been success enough but Paxton's enquiring mind wanted to know how a leaf could support a child. He studied the underside of the leaf and was intrigued by its undergrid organic structure which he is reported to have said was "like transverse girders and supports".[30] Some time later, in 1850, while chairing a meeting of the Midland Railway in Derby, Paxton recalled this lily and produced the famed blotting paper sketch for the revolutionary modular, prefabricated design of what was to be called The Crystal Palace, home of the 1851 exhibition.[31] This unique structure, some 1,848 feet long, by 408 feet wide, with a transept of 72 feet and a height of 108 feet, encompassing 33 million cubic feet, was built in less than eight months. Paxton headed the Opening Day procession, received an additional honorarium of £5,000 from the profits generated by the exhibition and was knighted by Queen Victoria at the closing of the exhibition. Sometimes creativity can be rewarding.

DESIGN PROFILE:
FRAGMENTED IMAGE—A NEW WORLD VIEW

Arcades of Paris—Passage des Panoramas, renovated in 1830s.

Arcades of Paris—Passage des Panoramas.

Pablo Picasso first visited Paris sometime in 1900 when the work of the 19 year old was included in the exhibition of Spanish art at the *Exposition Universelle*.[32] (It was at this exhibition that *Campbell's Soup* was awarded a gold medal, an image of which still appears on its label.) The work of Picasso attracted the attention of Ambroise Vollard who gave Picasso his first one man show in Paris in 1901. In April of 1904 Picasso finally left Barcelona to live in Paris and join the avant-garde circle of writers and artists, including Modigliani, Braque, Max Jacob and Apollinaire, who lived in and around the famed, decrepit *bateau lavoir* (the laundry boat) at 13 Rue Ravignan, Montmartre. (The original structure was destroyed by fire in 1970; the present structure was rebuilt in 1978.) "Number 13 was a ramshackle building made mostly of wood, zinc, and dirty glass."[33] It was without gas and electricity, had one toilet and one water tap to service the 20 or so studios. It was, surprisingly, quite new, having been originally constructed around 1867 (the year of Canadian Confederation) and was initially 'home' to a Canadian fur trapper.[34] The structure was 'renovated' by a somewhat eccentric architect, Paul Vasseur in 1889. Picasso was to live in this sparse environment for five years, until 1909.

At the start of the twentieth century Paris had that magnificent and tantalising mix of the new and the old, and seemed always to be prepared for the future. The work of Cézanne and the post-Impressionist painters Van Gogh, Seurat and Gauguin were on display in the galleries and Salons. The cafes were home to the emerging Fauvists and Cubists with the soon to be Futurists, aided and abetted by Filippo Tommaso Emilio Marinetti, loitering in the wings. The venerable cultural institutions were celebrating France's colonial possessions with shows of exotic treasures from Africa and Southeast Asia. Writers and critics such as Max Jacob, Guillaume Apollinaire, and Gertrude Stein were providing the material for the extensive supporting media infrastructure that was centred on Paris. The world watched.

1906 was a crucial year for the ambitious 24 year old Picasso. He visited an exhibition of pre-Roman Iberian sculpture at the Louvre. Maybe suffering from a few pangs of home-sickness in the Summer he journeys back to the remote Catalan village of Gósol in the Spanish Pyrenees accompanied by one of his models, Fernande Olivier. This journey reawakened his Catalan heritage.[35] Around the end of that year there was an exhibition of African and Oceanic Art at the Trocadéro in Paris. Here Picasso was able to study at first hand masks and carvings from the French colonies of the Ivory Coast, the French Congo and New Caledonia. On 22 October 1906, just three days before Picasso's 25th birthday, the 67 year old Paul Cézanne, considered by many critics of the day as the greatest living painter, died at Aix en Provence, thereby creating a vacuum for some aggressive creative individual with a prepared mind to fill.

The ambitious Picasso invested in a very large, best quality canvas, had it especially lined for extra permanence and began a series of preparatory sketches on the topic of sexually transmitted disease; prostitutes and brothels were a popular late nineteenth century genre. Benefiting from his creative ability to see the world from a different perspective, Picasso, while alluding to the Spanish master El Greco, dispenses with all the old visual trickery of Western painting; no false perspective, no phony modelling, no single light source or viewpoint. To the artistic heritage, Picasso added the present, represented by the culture of Africa and Oceania. The cafes of the Parisian arcades provided the cues of visual reality and of the reflections and refractions of fragmented perception.[36] The creative mind of Picasso assembled the component parts of what many regard as the first truly modern painting. His creative brilliance being able to translate a kinetic, three-dimensional montage into a static, two-dimensional work of art. The creative process that preceded the production of *Les Demoiselles d'Avignon* is well documented in 16 sketchbooks and numerous preliminary studies.[37]

When, in 1907, he showed some of his closest friends his latest, unfinished and very large canvas, which only much later became known as *Les Demoiselles d'Avignon*, (Picasso referred to this work as "*mon bordel, my brothel*") he did not declare that he had invented Cubism. Indeed the first documented use of the term dates from the Summer of 1908 in a review by Louis Vauxcelles of a show at Kahnweiler's gallery at 28 rue Vignon, Paris, which included the work of Braque. Vauxcelles made reference to Braque's way of reducing "everything—sites, figures, and houses—to geometric outlines, to cubes". And so the descriptive tag was born.

Picasso did realise that with the death of Cezanne it was time to act if he were to make his mark in the Parisian art world. He did know that quite consciously he was creating something new, dangerous and possibly wrong. The fear of failure is a strong deterrent to innovative creativity. Thomas Edison, is reported to have said, "I have not failed 10,000 times. I have successfully found 10,000 ways that will not work."[38] Picasso's fragmented view of our world worked.

UP IN THE AIR

The creative process can generate the concept, but often persistent tenacity is required to develop that concept into reality. Once we accepted the fact that the Earth was round, we were fascinated by the challenge of circumnavigation by sea,[39] land[40] and air. In 1863 the 25 year old Ferdinand Graf von Zeppelin travelled from his home in Germany to be an observer on the side of the Union during the American Civil War. It was here that he 'observed' a tethered reconnaissance balloon. On his return to Germany he was inspired to research the practicality of travel by "ships of the air". In 1894, Count Zeppelin's first plans for an airship were considered impractical. Undeterred he produced new designs along with the realisation that it was also necessary that he raised the necessary capital to see that his designs were realised.

Appropriately enough the new phase in aviation history began at the very start of the twentieth century when on 2 July 1900, the prototype Zeppelin took to the air on a flight that lasted less than 20 minutes around Lake Constance in southern Germany. The investors were not impressed and lost faith in the enterprise and the Zeppelin company was forced into liquidation in December 1900. New investors and a new director, Dr Hugo Eckener saw production resume and new flights took place in 1905 and 1906. More financial input was required and Count Zeppelin was allowed to use a lottery to raise the required funds. In spite of numerous mishaps, public enthusiasm for airships remained high in Germany. In addition to responding to the consumer market further design innovation was spurred by the advent of the First Word War which witnessed airships being used by the German Army and Navy.[41]

Charles Goodyear was born in 1800 in New Haven, Connecticut. In 1834 he invented a rubber valve for life preservers. For the next decade or so he experimented mixing rubber with various materials in his attempts to fully popularise this unique material. His quest resulted in financial ruin for his family and time in debtor's prison for himself. His activities provoked commercial enemies who were determined to find commercial profit in this unique substance. An accident in his workshop in 1838 resulted in Goodyear developing a process to vulcanise rubber. More funds were required to continue his research; by 1843 he was in debt to the tune of $50,000 and had failed to secure patents for his process in Britain or in France.

Entry 378 in the 1851 *Official Catalogue of the Great Exhibition of the Works of All Nations* is for The Goodyear Rubber company of New Haven, Connecticut, for India rubber goods. Goodyear invested over $30,000 to display his manufactured objects in the Goodyear Vulcanite Court within the American section. There was a hard rubber desk with gilt edges on display alongside an array of object which ranged from waterproof maps, medical instruments, walking sticks, dolls heads, and

a rubber pontoon, but it was his India Rubber flute that received "Honourable Mention" in the musical instrument section. During his life he took out an assortment of patents for various applications of his vulcanising process, yet overlooked the one that was to be the most profitable, car tyres. Charles Goodyear died in 1860 leaving debts of nearly $200,000. However, the company continued.[42]

In 1911 the Goodyear company began its research into lighter-than-air craft and produced its first balloon in 1912. It was a Goodyear balloon that won the first international balloon race from Paris to England in 1913. With the advent of the First World War Goodyear technicians applied their skills to producing around 1,000 balloons for the American army and navy. The developing balloon and airship technology had its fair share of problems. In 1924 Goodyear acquired the American rights and patents for the Zeppelin and the Goodyear-Zeppelin company was established in Arkon, Ohio to construct American airships. There were numerous crashes and mishaps and this venture failed to produce a reliable form of air transportation.

Meanwhile the concept of airship travel remained popular in Germany, so much so that in 1928, an appeal by Hugo Eckener, the director of Luftschiffbau Zeppelin for public donations resulted in a fund to construct the LZ 127 Graf Zeppelin. Ever conscious of the need for both financial and popular support, Eckener searched for sponsors for a "Round-the-World" flight. This promotional opportunity caught the attention of one of America's most successful tycoons, William Randolph Hearst, who requested that the flight officially start at Lakehurst Naval Air Station, New Jersey. Hearst placed a reporter, Grace Marguerite Hay Drummond-Hay, on board who thereby became the first woman to circumnavigate the globe by air.

The German LZ127 Graf Zeppelin left Lakehurst on 8 August 1929 and flew back across the Atlantic to Friedrichshafen to refuel before continuing on 15 August across Siberia to the Kasumigaura Naval Air Station Tokyo, a nonstop leg of 6,988 miles (11,246 km), arriving three days later on 18 August. After staying in Tokyo for five days, on 23 August the Graf Zeppelin continued across the Pacific to Los Angeles, California for the first ever nonstop flight of any kind across the Pacific Ocean. Continuing across the United States the Graf Zeppelin landed back at Lakehurst on 29 August, The entire voyage took 21 days, five hours and 31 minutes during which time the airship travelled 30,831 miles (49,618 km).[43] The Graf Zeppelin went on to make 144 trans Atlantic flights flying more than one million miles without any accident.

It had taken 66 years to progress from seeing the concept afforded by the reconnaissance balloon to realising an air circumnavigation of the Earth. Just 20 years later, in 1949, The Lucky Lady II, a B-50A of the US Air Force, with a crew of 14 commanded by Captain James Gallagher, became the first aeroplane to circle the world nonstop. The aircraft was refuelled four times in flight and the journey of 23,452 miles took 94 hours and one minute.[44] As Graham Wallas had pointed out, perseverance and dedication are often required to bring a creative endeavour to fruition.

UNDERGROUND

A laid off electrical engineer is responsible for the most innovative example of graphic design of the twentieth century. Frank Pick was Design Director of London Transport in the 1930s and responsible for creating an overall image for the very diversified units that made up London Transport. (It was Pick who provided what remains one of the most expressive descriptions of design; "design is intelligence made visible".) One design aspect that Pick almost overlooked was the necessity of a clearly informative map until electrical engineer designed and drew a schematic map of the underground system in his own time while laid off from his job at London Transport. Utilising *a priori* knowledge of electrical wiring diagrams and circuitry, in 1933, Henry (Harry) C Beck provided the prototype for modern urban transportation maps. What Beck realised was that underground there are no visible landmarks, views and perceptions change. Geographic accuracy of location or scale are irrelevant; what is required is a clear picture of how to get from A to B and where to make the appropriate connections.[45] Beck provides, incidentally, an example of reversal of attributes, a creative exercise that can be revealing. Some of the more usual attributes relate to physical form, psychological meaning and social affiliation. It can be of value to reverse logically developed attributes— make small large, hard soft, change monochromatic to technicoloured, turn outside inside, or, as Beck did, change surface to underground.

None of the above individuals had access to privileged information. What they did have was an open mind, prepared and ready to recognise and take advantage of any situation that presented itself. As Louis Pasteur stated in a lecture at the University of Lille, on 7 December 1851, *Dans les champs de l'observation le hasard ne favorise que les esprits préparés.* ("In the fields of observation chance favours only the prepared mind.")[46]

THE PREPARED MIND—COPY IT RIGHT

A mind is prepared by the acquisition of information. Creativity is a process of reassembling things that are known in innovative ways; you can not use what you do not have and, in the field of design, this reality conflicts with attitudes to copyright. None of the Ancients relied on copyright to get their message across, Newton did not copyright gravity nor Einstein $E = mc2$.[47] Picasso and Braque had no copyright on Cubism and Andy Warhol freely appropriated images used in

his 'factory' productions.[48] In our modern culture the world of publishing, music and film have developed stringent copyright protection attitudes backed up by international law. The world of graphic design and fashion design has more lenient attitudes towards derivation and appropriation.[49] We live in an information intense society, check any media source and see the huge number of positions advertised in the Information Technology sector, often abbreviated to the acronym IT. Our design reality may be to copy IT right.[50]

Creativity is a very fragile commodity. It does not take much to stifle it, to send it into a state of hibernation, to re-emerge in some later or different society. The creative process does not flourish when subject to overt guidance or other cultural pressure. Creativity will not be officially cajoled, it will not obey 'traffic signs' such as "this avenue of exploration is closed until further notice". There is a significant cultural cost to restricting human creative potential.

There is no pleasure to me without communication: there is not so much as a sprightly thought comes into my mind that it does not grieve me to have produced alone, and that I have no one to tell it to.
Michel Eyquem De Montaigne, c. 1580.[51]

SEE, THINK, DO

Information is having or obtaining knowledge about facts and events; communication is the transfer of that information between people. Submerged in a cacophony of multimedia communication any design must posses spatial drama. On the street we require that design makes the message legible. The street signs in our urban world mediate contact with the environment, without them we would be lost. We live in a world of communication, constantly sending, receiving, analysing, synthesising what we access but, unfortunately, as the cell phone and personal web pages testify, all too often we have very little of any value to say. The successful designer will always have something of value to say.

Perhaps the most significant thing that design does is to give a richness of meaning to life—it can enliven and enrich the audiences experience—it can instruct, it can delight, it can motivate and, unfortunately, all too often it can bore! Put away your cell phones, disable your web pages and instead, read, go to the theatre, go camping, watch dance, hear some music, travel, get out there and experience the real world. Become familiar with the cultural signs of your time. I can think of no greater condemnation of modern culture, no greater proof of the emptiness of so many lives, than so-called reality TV, where millions of couch viewers will watch other people living there choreographed lives instead of getting out there and living. I repeat, all designers need to 'live' every moment of every day.

Street signs, New York City.

THE CREATIVE EDGE

The creative process is comparable to language ability —it is something that all humans possess and it can be developed—and just like language ability some humans become more proficient than others. But make no mistake, the creative process as expressed through design has always been, is, and will continue to be a dominant, essential characteristic of humankind. It is not an exaggeration to say that the creative process has given humankind the evolutionary edge over all the other species on this particular planet. It is possible to see creative design as expressing and, more importantly, as transmitting human knowledge. We can derive from design insights into human experience past, present and future and through those insights we can determine what were, and are the prevailing human values, and hopefully, derive a relevant future focus.

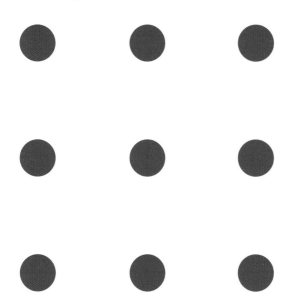

Nine dots in three lines of three.

EVERYWHERE, ALL THE TIME

In our childhood we joined the dots to make pictures make sense. (Using the schematic above, connect all nine dots, using just one line going in one continuous direction—for the solution see the endnote.)[52] Today we need to join discontinuous bits of information into meaningful associations. We have been conditioned for the last 500 years or so (since the introduction of printing in the West) to process information in a very disciplined way. One major challenge of the creative problem solving process is how to overcome any pre-constructed roadblocks to the creative application of what it is that we already know. Unprecedented changes in forms of communication made possible by the computer and other related technologies have given new impetus to cross-disciplinary dialogue within a global context. "There is nothing new about machines that do things that humans

cannot. Throughout history, mechanical replacements for humans in processing and communicating information, such as the alphabet, writing, print, and the telegraph, have driven society to evolve, to differentiate, and fragment. This process generated new disciplines, new ways of thinking about the world, and new cut-and-control social hierarchies."[53] So wrote James Burke a decade or so ago.

One of the greatest acts of cultural vandalism occurred in 47BCE when the marauding troops of Julius Caesar ravaged the great library of Alexandria.[54] Tens of thousands of scrolls composed by nine generations of scholars were assigned to oblivion. We have no way of knowing the amount and wealth of information lost by this barbaric act. We do know that the library at Alexandria was perhaps the first attempt to collect all the worlds knowledge under one roof. Now you have access to all (most at the moment, but all later) the worlds knowledge without leaving home. What you elect to do or not do with that information is very much up to you.

HOW DO I KNOW WHAT TO FIND, AND HOW DO I RECOGNISE IT WHEN I'VE FOUND IT?

Imagine that you have to prepare a three page appraisal of Art Nouveau by 9:00am tomorrow. You could head off to the nearest library and check out their holdings on Art Nouveau. The result will be predictable and in all probability less than revealing; in the process you will have learnt very little. Now, think of an alterative approach. Ignore the Library of Congress, Dewey/Nippon/Korean Decimal or any other classification system; ignore the discipline controlled distribution of the books on the stacks. Go to the furthest volume and look up Art Nouveau in the book index. Do that to every book in the collection. My local university library has a collection of four million books. Allowing for 30 seconds per book, an eight hour search day, and a five day search week, it would take you just over 16 years to complete your search, just a little late for your 9:00 am deadline.[55] The latest IBM super computer is capable of 280 trillion actions per second.[56] If all the information were in place you could, at least in theory, access the index of every book in seconds, look for unusual connections and generate unique knowledge—now you are learning!

Lets go one step further, and remember that we are talking about near science fact not science fiction. Place yourself outside that library. Imagine every book; strip off the covers (with all the preconditioning index information); think of every page in every book; now think about every paragraph on every page in every book —merge them all. Now add every image ever recorded, every photo, every video, every TV programme, every film, in every language; add every sound ever recorded; give a good shake and mix. Making sense of all that information, determining relevance and value, that, at least in theory, is the challenge that you will have within your working life.

According to William Horton, "The 545 miles of shelves in the Library of Congress hold over 100 million pieces of literature, including 27 million books, 1,200 newspapers on file, 100,000 films, 80,000 television and 500,000 radio broadcasts, and one million other sound recordings.... Every day of the year a 1,000 new book titles are added."[57] The University of California's Berkeley's School of Information Management and Systems undertook a research survey to determine how much new information is created each year. Their summary concluded that "Print, film, magnetic, and optical storage media produced about five exabytes of new information in 2002... five exabytes of information is equivalent in size to the information contained in 37,000 new libraries the size of the Library of Congress book collections."[58]

The Library of Babel, (*La biblioteca de Babel*) composed by Jorge Luis Borges in 1939 and first published in English in 1962.[59] The short story introduces the concept of the universal library where past, present and future are linked through a network of connections, similar to the World Wide Web. The story contains a number of mathematical ideas which provide insight into the unimaginable. The opening paragraph provides a dynamic visual sketch of an eternal cosmic library with apparently infinite hallways spiral staircases and bookshelves (a far less complicated variant features in the Harry Potter movies); "Each wall of each hexagon is furnished with five bookshelves; each bookshelf holds 32 books identical in format; each book contains 410 pages; each page 40 lines; each line, approximately 80 black letters. (Twitter's 140 characters?) There are also letters on the front cover of each book; those letters neither indicate nor prefigure what the pages inside will say."[60] Each book is interpolated with every book written or that will be written.

The reality is that the current information output is estimated to be growing by around 30 per cent per year. You are going to need considerable assistance from future hardware and intelligent software to gain maximum value from all existing human knowledge, why should you settle for less?

SEE THE WORDS, READ THE IMAGE

"How can I tell what I think till I see what I say?"[61] The new design environment calls for a multi-skilled approach, traditional design tactics are not enough. When considering a viable, creative form of design we need to remind ourselves that all forms of media and representation continue to evolve in significant ways after their initial introduction. The invention of the printing press in the West depended on a coming together of cultural change and technological innovation, both of which continued to modify the process well after Gutenberg's death. Printing gave modern languages their form and structure, made possible the codification of information, and changed the way that we thought about the world and our place in it. As late as the seventeenth and eighteenth centuries, printing was still viewed by many intellectuals and thinkers within the "perspective" of their past and seen as injurious to the culture of the day.[62]

Now that most information is received by way of a moving image, be it a film, video, web or phone screen, we can no longer apply old standards. We may ask for instance why so-called national rates of literacy still rely only on the processing of words and not of images. "In coming years literacy will mean knowing how to choose between print, image, video, sound, and all the potential combinations they could create to make a particular point with a specific audience", says Bronwyn Williams, associate professor of English at the University of Louisville; "What will not change is the necessity of an individual to be able to find a purpose, correctly analyse an audience, and communicate to that audience with information and in a tone that the audience will find persuasive, engaging, and intelligent." [63]

YKWIM[64]

The mobile network society is the latest arrival on the communication scene, making wireless networks the fastest growing communications technology in history, one that offers innovative and restructured means of communicating human thought in a cross-cultural context. Professor Manuel Castells explains that "Because communication is at the heart of human activity in all spheres of life, the advent of this technology... raises a wide range of fundamental question."[65] Many of those questions are design related. Castells concludes, "wireless communication technology does have powerful social effects by generalising and furthering the networking logic that defines human experiences in our time".[66]

Wireless communication technology has inadvertently created a new language of communication. This creative means of communication has been expanded to include non-standard abbreviations and symbols. In a very short time span, co-operating, creative minds have incorporated these designed notations into a new language. Figures are hard to come by and constantly changing but reportedly more than 30 billion e-mail messages and five billion text messages are exchanged every day. This is a clear indicator of how technology is emphasising the value of reading, both as an economic reality and as a social activity. It is possible to go further and suggest that these new communication constructs are redefining what it means to be literate. The simple form of text messaging (SMS) has been supplanted by a multimedia message system (MMS) where text, images and streaming video combine to extend peer-to-peer communication, and, in so doing, make meaning more fluid. MMS offers the tantalising concept of perpetual contact and perpetual change, maybe the age old search for perpetual motion is at hand, at least in an ethereal form.

WHAT IS OR WHAT MAYBE

Culture snobs often deride the 'common audience' because of their perceived ignorance and lack of sophistication. Works of merit are protected and isolated in those cultural theme parks we call galleries and museums. However, the 'common audience' has practical familiarity and access to photography, television, video, computers, iPod's and smartphones. In the twenty-first century, even these visual and audio stimulations will not be enough; we must understand what we see and feel, pro-actively react to prevent problems from emerging. Cast aside simplistic fundamentalism in all its forms and search for new creative connections. The world of tomorrow needs design today. The new culture of design has generated new disciplines, encouraged new ways of thinking about the world and created new social hierarchies. "Technology has now created the possibility and even the likelihood of a global culture. The Internet, fax machines, satellites, and cable TV are sweeping away cultural boundaries."[67] In the very near future we will expand those hierarchies to include intelligent machines, cyborgs, robots and other technology-inspired constructs, all of whom will become our partners in our creative endeavours. Anyone likely to be involved in design culture will need to be prepared today for tomorrows design realities and above all else will need to be in a constant state of creativity. We must begin to think about the new culture of design from the perspective of what maybe rather than what is. But first, in Section Two "Form", a more comprehensive look at the role of design within the cultural context of the twentieth century.

A SELECT "CREATIVE" BIBLIOGRAPHY

Boden, M, *The Creative Mind: Myth and Mechanisms*, New York: Routledge, 2004.

Edelman, Gerald M, "Creativity", in *Second Nature. Brain Science and Human Knowledge*, New Haven and London, Yale University Press, 2006, pp. 98–105.

Fung, Alex, Alice Lo, Mamata N Rao, *Creative Tools*, Hong Kong, Hong Kong Polytechnic University, 2005, 2007.

Hodder, Ian, "Creativity as a social process", in *Creativity in Human Evolution and Prehistory*, Steven J, ed., London: Routledge, 1998, pp. 62–64.

Human Development Report 2004, Cultural Liberty in Today's Diverse World, Geneva: United Nations Development Programme, 2004.

Kelly, Tom, Jonathan Littman, *The Art of Innovation*, New York: Random House, 2001.

Koberg, Don, Jim, Bagnall, *The Universal Traveller: A Soft-Systems Guide to Creativity, Problem-Solving, and the Process of Reaching Goals*, Menlo Park, CA: Thomson Crisp Learning, 1972, 2003.

Merrill, Peter, *Innovation Generation: Creating an Innovation Process and an Innovative Culture*, Milwaukee, WI: ASQ Quality Press, 2008.

Roy, Robin, *Creativity and Concept Design*, Milton Keynes, Open University, 2004.

Sternberg, Robert J, ed., *Handbook of Creativity*, Cambridge: Cambridge University Press, 1999.

Thackara, John, *In the Bubble. Designing in a Complex World*, Cambridge, MA: MIT Press, 2006.

Wallas, Graham, *The Art of Thought*, London: Jonathan Cape, 1926.

Weiner, Robert Paul, *Creativity and Beyond: Cultures, Values, and Change*, Albany, NY: State University of New York Press, 2000.

Weisberg, Robert W, *Creativity: Beyond the Myth of Genius*, New York: WH Freeman, 1993. *Creativity. Understanding Innovation in Problem Solving, Science, Invention, and the Arts*, Hoboken, NJ: John Wiley, 2000.

FORM

CHAPTER FIVE
REVOLUTION, WAR AND DESIGN

The habit of calling a finished product a Design is convenient but wrong.
Design is what you do, not what you've done.
Bruce Archer, Professor, Department of Design Research, Royal College of Art.[1]

Household potato-peeler.[2]

DESIGN EXPERIENCE

Every designed object in this world represents something that someone was able to think about, that is the future forecast part of design, and was able to make, that is the available materials and technology part of the equation. The designer is very aware of the perceived possibilities and limitations of materials and those perceptions are controlled by the cultural values that each designer submits to. Much of what we think we know about materials is derived from personal experience. We know, just by looking, how we think an object will feel, how heavy the visible mass will be and even what odour is likely to be associated with the object. Based on experience we know what the result and sound will be if we drop, flex or in some other way try to manipulate the object. But that knowledge, that field of expectations, is dependent upon what values we have pre-assigned to that object and to the materials of which it is made.[3] The very cultural history of humankind on this planet is based on collective experiences, various forms of acquired knowledge, different forms of perception, all these provide the controls we accept and use in our interpretation of the real world. Design by experience.

Both the hand axe and the potato peeler are respectful of ergonomics. The hand axe is considered the oldest artifact that demonstrates both functional and aesthetic sensibilities. The knapping of *Acheulian bifaces* requires great skill and precision. The symmetrical form is worked well beyond that required by function alone. It is though to have been produced by *Homo*

A hand axe made from banded ironstone, from the site of Kathu Pan 1 in the Northern Cape, South Africa. Its association with fossilised tooth plates of the extinct elephant, *Elephas recki recki*, suggest a minimum age of c. 600 000 years. Photo: McGregor Museum, Kimberley, South Africa.

ergaster (*Homo Erectus* in Africa) around about 750,000 years before the present (BP). While it is unlikely that the *Pleistocene* hunter consciously set out to design the banded ironstone hand-axe tool, as the industrial designer responsible for the peeler no doubt did, both are responding to similar design parameters.

Life to our ancestors was a daily battle for survival, and that survival included the hunting of game as large, if not larger than modern elephants. Modern re-enactments have shown that it is possible to skin and butcher over 45kg of meat in about one hour using these hand tools (it could take around one hundred hours to butcher an entire carcass).[4] Speed was essential; presumably those early hunters did not want to be hanging about exposed to other scavengers for any longer than was absolutely necessary.[5] The range of objects manufactured by these early humans was made from homogeneous materials, removed from nature and subjected to simple transformations in order to utilise intrinsic mechanical performances. In other words they made use of the available materials of their particular environment. The potato peeler is a self conscious design, based on learnt rather than inherited knowledge, and produced for mass impersonal use utilising the manufacturing processes of an industrial society. Context is all.

The distinction between the past, present and future is only a stubbornly persistent illusion.[6]
Albert Einstein.

THE AGES OF DESIGN

The first recognisable stone tools date from about 2.5 million years ago. In the intervening years, the world has undergone around 25 changes between glacial and interglacial conditions.[7] The last Ice Age began about 110,000 years ago ended relatively recently, about 12,000 years ago, providing a changing context for design.[8] Around 6,000 years ago people from north-west Europe introduced domestic livestock,[9] seed corn[10] and primitive farming techniques into their lifestyle. The farming groups were now tribal rather than family in nature. They settled near a water source with access to well-drained and easily cleared soil—the beginnings of agriculture. The primitive Emmer wheat was harvested with the help of manufactured sickles.[11] There existed a very real and immediate connection between the user, the material and the process of production. The users technical knowledge was made up of a deep familiarity, in both the physical sense and in the perceptual sense, with the material used. Further, although there is no way we can be certain, we can surmise that each cultural group had a developed and shared set of values by which they interpreted these early products.

The first cities appeared in Mesopotamia around 4000 BCE.[12] The resulting increase in population size resulted in the establishment of new social groupings, the associated manufactured products took advantage of local conditions that resulted in design variations.[13] Excess in food production may have initiated early trade endeavours as these cities became the hub of trans-continental trade routes and centres of information exchange. Connections ruled.

IRON AGE

"A little less than 3,000 years ago the sky's of Tuscany in western Italy were heavy with the smoke from the great Etruscan iron works."[14] The ore came from the island of Elba, just off shore and the richest source of iron ore in ancient Italy. Each smelting furnace was small, less than two metres high, and was fired daily. Workers poured baskets of charcoal and ore into the furnace, added a little limestone and used bellows made of animal skins to raise the heat to 1100 centigrade. Droplets of iron formed into a bloom which are removed, reheated and beaten to drive out the slag. Experts believe that up to ten million kilos of ore

were produced annually for more than 400 years. It was a very real iron age.[15]

TIME FOR A CHANGE

The expansive and productive period in Europe was succeeded by the early Middle Ages.[16] Gradually, Europe emerged into the modern age. A fragmented assortment of states emphasising regional differences. Peter Jay explains:

The Renaissance and the Reformation challenged and partially overthrew traditional moral and intellectual authorities based on the church. Growing commercial, financial and manufacturing sophistication matured to the point from which the Industrial Revolution was launched.[17]

As James Burke eloquently explains, it is difficult for us to realise that things have not always been as they are today. We tend to think that our cultural values, our knowledge, our common sense, our way of thinking have always been the way of the world. Burke asserts that we still live, love and die, Summer still follows Spring and people still make use of their available knowledge to better their lot in life. We work to earn money to spend on commodities and services provided by others. We obey the clock rather than the sun. We defend by force and legislation that which we regard as ours.

In this democracy of possessions what we possess is inalienably ours, private property protected by strict legislation from appropriation by any other individual or by the state. Most of us have the right to free speech. Each of us, at least in the Western world, has the right to life, liberty and the pursuit of happiness.[18]

Ways of the world change. In Europe, up until 1720, changing weather patterns and the success of the crop regulated population size. The cycle of abundance and famine, occasionally modulated by plague, repeated itself endlessly. The most devastating Medieval plague was the so-called "Black Death" which may have decimated up to 50 per cent of the population of Europe between 1348–1349.[19] The last recorded outbreak of the bubonic plague in Europe was in Marseilles during the Summer of 1720 when a reported 50,000 people died.

The eighteenth century witnessed new discoveries and inventions, revised social structures, new attitudes to education, religion and government, new forms of entertainments, new patterns of trade and enhanced procedures of industrial production.[20] It was indeed a time of enlightenment and reform.[21] During the eighteenth century Britain colonised much of east coast America then lost her colonies in the ensuing American Revolution.[22] Economic policies changed eighteenth century culture, creating revised social attitudes and new opportunities for design. Different attitudes towards the role of design in society became evident in the Old World and the New World.

THE AGRICULTURAL REVOLUTION

In eighteenth century London, businessmen and merchants could sip the new exotic elixir, coffee, in any one of the 2,000 coffee-houses that had opened in the metropolis. One additional service provided was the provision of newspapers for the perusal of their clientele. "The rise of the coffee-house thus spurred the emergence of the metropolis as the media centre."[23] More news, more ideas. The eighteenth century witnessed a dramatic increase in British agricultural productivity. Jethro Tull's seed drill, 1701, Joseph Foijambe's Rotherham iron plough, 1730, and Andrew Meikle's threshing machine, 1786, combined with three-field crop rotation and selective breeding of livestock generated significant surpluses of foodstuff.[24] The changing context supported dramatic increases in population, creating even more mouths to feed and hands to employ. An agricultural revolution transformed agrarian practices, provided the surplices that paved the way for the Industrial Revolution.[25]

By 1776, when Adam Smith wrote *The Wealth of Nations*, Great Britain was established as a major commercial power, but political power was still with the landowners. In agriculture new field legume crops, such as peas and beans built up nitrate in the soil, enriching it and making it ready for cereals. This led to the new practice of four field crop rotation. New root crops such as carrots and turnips provided Winter foodstuffs. Turnips in particular enabled livestock to be fed throughout the Winter, where previously most animals had to be slaughtered in the Autumn.[26] Bigger harvests, bigger profits. Large landowners and ambitious recruits from the work-a-day world of business, for whom ownership of land conferred the right to vote, bought out the smaller landowners, who in their turn had money to spend in other areas, including industrial manufacture.[27] Even the working poor, who made up about 90 per cent of the British population, were better off. They had excess money to spend on such luxuries as tea, sugar, cocoa, tobacco, the newly available cotton underclothes and even books.[28] Most of the raw materials were imported, with the British merchant fleet protected by the might of the British navy.

TRADE TRIANGLE

As far as the merchants were concerned there was just one hole that needed to be filled in the patterns of trade.[29] Textiles from the English mills and newly manufactured goods filled the holds of the ships as they sailed from the west coast British ports of Bristol and Liverpool to the new markets opening up in Africa, India and beyond. Cotton, tobacco, sugar and other raw materials from the American colonies provided the necessary cargo to fuel the Industrial Revolution back home; but what could fill the holds from Africa to America. Slaves provided a pertinent cargo; they could be sold in the West Indies and the Southern American Colonies for five times the

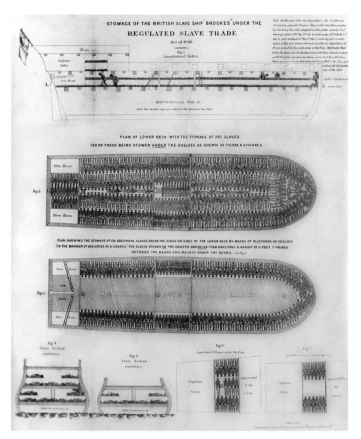

"Stowage of the British Slave Ship 'Brookes' under the Regulated Slave Trade, Act of 1788", shows each deck and cross-sections of decks and "tight packing" of captives. After the 1788 Regulation Act, the 'Brookes' was allowed to carry 454 slaves, the approximate number shown in this illustration, allowing a space of 6ft by 1ft 4in to each man; 5ft 10in by 1ft 4in to each woman and 5ft by 1ft 2in to each boy. However, in four earlier voyages (1781–1786), the 'Brookes' carried between 609 and 740 slaves in conditions far worse than those illustrated.

price paid to the Black and Arab slave traders in Africa.[30] Even if, as often happened, up to one fifth of the cargo was lost through disease and starvation, the remainder still assured a substantial profit. The British East India Company made about half a million pounds sterling profit each year from insidious slaving, a staggering amount in the 1700s.[31] Slaving remained part of British commerce until, thanks to the campaigning work of the Quakers, Charles Fox and William Wilberforce, anti-slaving legislation was accepted in the House of Commons, being carried by a vote of 114 to 15. It become the law of the land on 25 March 1807. The bill made it unlawful for any British subject to capture and transport slaves.

Political *laissez-faire*, the original policy of free trade, competition in slaving, imperial protection of the sources of raw material, all combined to provide financial might to Great Britain's silent revolution. The westward looking ports of Liverpool and Bristol became the major ports of export and the immediate hinterland prospered; the cotton mills of Lancashire[32] were within easy access to the port of Liverpool; the iron industry of Coalbrookdale[33] in Shropshire used the River Seven to get manufactured goods to Bristol. Design played an integral role in all of these developments as did economics. In the world of finance, speculation was rampant.

1720—THE YEAR THE BUBBLE BURST

The infamous South Sea Bubble fiasco took place in 1720, the precursor of contemporary forays into the world of greed and unrealistic expectations which, in more recent times, culminated in the financial meltdown of 2008.[34] The South Sea company was established in 1711 and, following England's war with Spain, the company was granted exclusive trading rights in Spanish South America. Britain's war debt of around ten million pounds sterling would be financed in return for six per cent interest.[35] Everyone was convinced that they could make profit out of the exploitation of others. Isaac Newton lost over £20,000 of his fortune in the South Sea Bubble adventure. As a result of this crisis, he is reported to have stated, "I can calculate the motions of heavenly bodies, but not the madness of people." Jonathan Swift, who also lost a fortune, was inspired to write *Gulliver's Travels*, 1726, which is a shamming satire about British society and the infinite human capacity for self delusion. He presented his observations in the form of a novel which has since been reassigned to the genre of children's literature.[36]

"WITH HATCHET, PIKE AND GUN"[37]

Throughout the eighteenth century, domestic British industry prospered, particularly those concerned with the manufacturing processes that used the readably available raw materials and the new source of power, steam.[38] By the mid-nineteenth century two very different patterns of relationships were evident in the old world and in the new. In both locations there was an ongoing debate about the relationship between design and the process of mechanisation. The question tended to polarise responses. In Great Britain, for example, there was a surplus of labour; this tended to justify a continuation of craft-type production processes and generate opposition to the machine. Indeed those traditional industries that tried to introduce mechanisation were hit by a series of machine breaking confrontations by those people displaced by the machine. The Luddites, named after their mythical leader, Ned Ludd, were a group of skilled textile workers in early nineteenth century Britain who tried to prevent the industrialisation of the textile industry during the initial phase of the factory system. Luddites blamed mechanisation for increased unemployment, poverty, and hunger in the industrial centres of the North of England.[39] In our modern world, the displaced hand loom weaver has been replaced by the displaced industrial conglomerate. Change is all.

Stanley Mill, Kings Stanley, Gloucestershire, was built in 1813 on the site of a Tudor mill. There is a record of working mills on this site from 1565 until the current mill ceased production in 1989. Built for the manufacture of woolen cloth, the main building was one of the first in England of "fireproof" construction, with galleries of cast iron columns spaced according to the width of a loom. It is currently slated for re-development.

> *"The rich man in his castle,*
> *The poor man at his gate,*
> *God made them, high or lowly,*
> *And order'd their estate."*[40]
> Victorian Hymn, 1848.

KNOW YOUR PLACE

By the middle of the nineteenth century, at the time of the Great Exhibition of the Works of Industry of all Nations in 1851, steam driven machines could cut and form just about any material faster and with greater accuracy and reliability than any hand process.[41] Steam powered printing presses were making the world's news and views available to all; relative high literacy rates ensured that the populace was better informed than ever before. Not everyone was thrilled by these apparent advances. A small but influential group were horrified by what they saw and by the transition that they observed in the relationship between the worker, the place of work, and the ownership of the means and tools of production. These reform minded individuals believed that machine production meant the demise of both individuality and the time honoured social role of the local craftsman and threatened the established social hierarchy. They called for honesty, in design and in the process of manufacture. The most articulate opponents of this industrialisation of the work process were John Ruskin[42] and William Morris.[43]

Morris was a craftsman, poet, writer, designer and one of the founders of the Socialist Party in London. His writings and designs gave rise to the Arts and Crafts Movement in the latter half of the nineteenth century. Affronted by the conditions of industrial production, the solution offered by Morris, was to re-create a system of manufacture where the worker could benefit from the joy of participating in the process of production and where the end-user would somehow derive psychological benefit from using a product that had been created with love and skill. "A thing of beauty is a joy forever",[44] summarised this belief. A prolific writer, Morris provides many design related quotes, perhaps his most endearing being, "If you want a golden rule that will fit everybody, this is it: Have nothing in your houses that you do not know to be useful, or believe to be beautiful."[45] Morris' ideas were both naive and impractical. The inevitable advancement of machine production would not be halted, nor would public 'good taste' become more holistic through the very limited productions of craft type cottage industries.

In 1878 Morris discovered political action. In the 1870s the "Firm" (Morris, Marshall, Faulkner and Company) was threatened with bankruptcy and Morris had been forced to adopt a more commercial approach. The frustration and disillusionment that he felt coincided with the emergence of a new political ideology, Socialism. Rejecting the principles of industrial capitalism with what Morris perceived as its exploitative philosophy, and seeing Liberalism as an ethic for the middle class fence sitters, he turned to Socialism. In 1885 with Eleanor Marx, the wife of Karl, Morris helped to start the Socialist League. From then on almost everything that he did revolved around the ongoing class struggle. In a letter written by Morris in 1883 to Andreas Scheu, co-founder of the Scottish Land and Labour League, he explained how he arrived at Socialism:

> In spite of all the success that I have had, I have not failed to be conscious that the art I have been helping to produce would fall with the death of a few of us who really care about it, that a reform in art which is founded on individualism must perish with the individuals who have set it going... art cannot have a real life under the present system of commercialism and profit mongering. I have tried to develop this view, which is in fact Socialism seen through the eyes of an artist.[46]

In America things were very different. Despite a doubling of the population base there was a labour shortage and the machine was given a more enthusiastic welcome. The idea of a labour saving machine seemed to be the answer to many of the problems that beset the developing economy. One other significant design influence was that, despite its physical size, the American market was far more homogeneous than that of any European nation. In America mass production and standardisation meant that every day object such as guns, farm machinery, bicycles, typewriters and, later, sewing machines were produced as a result of what was called the American system of production, what we would call mass production.[47]

THE WAR TO END ALL WARS

The first Hague Convention on the peaceful resolution of international conflicts was negotiated in 1899 and came into force on 4 September 1900.[48] The negotiated declaration, signed by 26 countries, banned the use of some modern technology such as bombing from the air and chemical warfare. It was widely believed that war was a major impediment to commercial and industrial progress. The reality was that technologically assisted mass violence, not peace, was to be the forging feature of the twentieth century.

On 28 June 1914, Gavrilo Princip, a Bosnian Serb student, assassinated Archduke Franz Ferdinand, heir to the Austro-Hungarian throne, in Sarajevo, providing the pretext for war.[49] The First World War began in August 1914. In April 1917, the United States entered the war against Germany and the Austro-Hungarian empire.[50] The Federal Government immediately began to mobilise society to meet the demands of total war. Millions volunteered for, or were drafted into, military service. Government worked with business, labour, and agriculture to increase weapon and food production. War also quickened the pace of social change. Millions moved from the land to cities to work in war industries. Mobilisation placed women in jobs previously closed to them and their contribution to the war effort helped promote suffrage and win women the right to vote.[51]

The First World War lasted for four years and three months, ending on 11 November 1918. It involved 60 sovereign states, resulted in the demise of four Empires (the German Empire, the Hapsburg Empire, the Ottoman Empire, the Russian Empire), gave birth to seven new nations, and resulted in the death of ten million combatants, with another 30 million wounded. Michael Howard elucidates; "That its course should have been so terrible, and its consequences so catastrophic, was the result not so much of its global scale as a combination of military technology and the culture of the people who fought it."[52]

AFTER ARMAGEDDON

Victory on the battlefields of France, it was hoped, would be followed by a new era of peace, political stability, economic growth and affluence. These optimistic hopes failed to materialise; emerging democracies were supplanted by authoritarian regimes; affluence was replaced by depression, and within 20 years Europe and North America were involved in another world war.

In America, the 1920s started out as an era of hope, affluence, jazz and flappers, components of the celebrated "Roaring Twenties".[53] There were major changes in the cultural context. The 1920 National Census revealed that for the first time more people lived in cities than on farms in America. New-found prosperity, technological innovation and advertising created the world's first mass-consumption economy. Consumer goods such as radios, automobiles, washing machines, and refrigerators became affordable; sports and movies became big business; businessmen and inventors became celebrities. In the 1920s, culture became popular.[54]

DESIGN IN FRANCE —THE BIRTH OF MODERNISM

The post-war designer had new attitudes towards design and on the responsibility of the designer; these attitudes were expressed in a range of design movements, from the excesses of art deco, through the radical reassessment of the Bauhaus[55] up to the onset of consumerism.[56] The term "Art Deco" has only been around since the late 1960s–it is a contraction of the name of the defining exhibition that was held in Paris in 1925–the *Exposition Internationale des Arts Décoratifs et Industriels Modernes*.[57] In 1912, the French Chamber of Deputies endorsed the plan for an exhibition, partly in response to exhibitions held in Austria at the Vienna Secession during the *fin de siècle*; in Brussels (The Brussels International Exhibition,1910); London (The Japan British Exhibition,1910) and Turin (International Exhibition of Industry and Trade,1911). The date set for the French Exhibition was 1915, but these plans were interrupted by the First World War. The project was revived in 1918 and the new date set for 1922, later postponed until 1924 and finally approved for 1925.

This government sponsored exhibition was regarded as being of major political importance. Paris had demonstrated its cultural superiority through most of the nineteenth century, it was now seen as crucial to lay claims to the twentieth century. The exhibition would clearly demonstrate the post-First World War survival of French cultural values and the continuing superiority of French craftsmanship. It was also intended to be a physical statement of Allied solidarity. Late in 1924 France even issued an invitation to Russia to participate. Of the Allies, only America turned down the opportunity to take part, although the Department of Commerce did send an official commission to observe and report on the exhibition.

The report, published in 1926, stated that America had completely misunderstood the French definition of 'modernism' and that participation in the exhibition would have been an appropriate gesture of solidarity with the Allies.[58] Any form of participation by Germany in the Exhibition was of course totally rejected. France had re-occupied the Ruhr mining area in 1923, causing rampant inflation and laying one of the foundation stones for the Second World War. As the 1925 exhibition date approached those commercial concerns that stood to gain financially from the exhibition began to add their support. The 'department store' was a new urban fixture which promoted an awareness of design to a larger public. The four major department stores in Paris, Le Bon Marché, Galeries Lafayette, Printemps and Grands Magasins du Louvre (closed in 1974) were given prime positions in the French section of the exhibition.[59]

IT'S ALL ABOUT SURFACE

Unlike some of the Modernist art movements of the time, with their philosophies of reform and incendiary manifestos, Art Deco was a celebration of craft technique and surface decoration, which combined resulted in an exuberant display of luxury. Simultaneous design developments in North America which promoted industrial manufacturing techniques, with forms empathetic to mass manufacture, and materials suited to processes of mass production, ran counter to the underlying format of Art Deco, providing another foundation to modernism.

While not rejecting the past, all participants in the Exposition had to comply with published guidelines and detailed regulations that were published by the organising committee in 1922.

> The Exposition… is open to all manufacturers whose produce is artistic in character and shows clearly modern tendencies.… That is to say that all copies or counterfeits of historical style will be banned; that is to say also that any manufacturer is eligible since everyday objects are as capable of being beautiful as the most exclusive objects.
>
> All industrialists, artists and artisans, in whatever material they specialise, wood, stone, ceramic, glass, paper, fabric etc., in whatever form they use it, and for whatever purpose, can and should be modern, just as their illustrious ancestors were in their time, in giving each object a logical, well proportioned, and perfectly executed form fit for the conditions of modern life.
>
> Today the public is responding: it is realising, more or less clearly, that in an age of railways, automobiles, aeroplanes, electricity, there should be furniture more appropriate than that of the past, however beautiful it may be. The real way to be modern is to find the form which best fits the function, taking into account the material, which should be used to the utmost, and that is all.[60]

There was an Admission Committee to oversee and regulate the kind and quality of work on display. The organisers also insisted that all pieces should be shown "in Context", that is, as part of an organised room ensemble.

Visitors to the 1925 Exposition could see the work of such noted designers as Émile-Jacques Ruhlmann (furniture and interiors), Jean Dunand (lacquerware), Edward McKnight-Kauffer (graphics), Paul Colin (graphics), Paul Poiret (fashion), Sonia Delaunay (fashion), René Lalique (glass, jewellery), Edgar Brandt (metalwork), Jean Puiforcat (silverware), Demetre Chiparus (sculpture) and the ineffable Romain de Tirtoff, better known by the French pronunciation of his initials, Erté.[61] The magazines of the time gave prominence to coverage of the Exposition with *Gazette du bon ton* considered the most innovative illustrated fashion magazine of the period.[62] Collectively these designers celebrated surface and decoration, craft technique and hand production. These characteristics provided clear demonstration of the continuing superiority of French craft production–but in a 'modern' context. This was defiantly not an exploration of mass industrial production.

French design of this period developed a modern method of expression almost entirely within the craft tradition. Two of the most notable expressions of this sophistication of craft technique being veneering and lacquering. Veneering, (*placage*) is the process of covering a solid base, normally wood, with a thin sheet of precious or rare timber, usually chosen for its surface characteristics.[63] The surface could be further enhanced by using inlays of precious materials such as silver, ivory and mother of pearl. The French colonies provided a rich source of exotic wood including, ebony, calamander and rosewood from Madagascar; purple heart, satiné rouge and tulipwood from French Guiana. These woods could be used on their own as solid components or as thin veneers over less expensive foundations. Most of these exotic woods are now on protected species lists.

The prime advantage of veneering is that it allows the structure of a piece of furniture to be disguised, so giving the appearance of one continuous surface. This means two things–first, the technique of veneering is predisposed to more simplified forms, and secondly, it can be used to cover up less skilled craftsmanship or shoddy materials. Almost by accident this meant that simple bold forms that relied on veneering for decorative effect replaced carved or intricate forms. The result of all this is the production of pieces of furniture which look as though they have been formed out of a single piece of material.

Lacquer is the generic term applied to a range of substances derived from insect and plant sources.[64] The more refined, a version of shellac, is the by-product of an insect cocoon found on various trees indigenous to Indochina Vietnam, Laos, China, and Japan. The insect (*Laccifer lacca*) consumes the sap of the tree, its exudation producing the encasing resin. When the insect dies, the larvae hatch and migrate to another tree.

The remaining cocoon is dissolved in an alcohol base sealed in airtight containers and allowed to separate into differing layers of density over several months. The substance was used by craftsmen to achieve a high gloss surface finish to furniture and other *objects d'art*.

THE PROCESS

The preferred wood for lacquer work was pine or other woods with an even and soft grain. The surface was meticulously prepared. It was sanded and rubbed down to remove surface irregularities and to eliminate any surface interruptions such as those caused by knots and joints. A first coat of lacquer was applied to fill the surface pores. This was followed by the priming process of one or two coats of a material made up of lacquer mixed with finely ground burnt clay. During the hardening process each layer of lacquer must be cured in an environment with controlled levels of high humidity. The hardened lacquer is then pumiced and polished smooth before the next layer can be applied. Each layer would have to be left at least 24 hours and in some cases as long as three weeks before it could be rubbed down with pumice again, ready for the next coat. The last layers could be further enhanced by the application of a layer of fine hemp, linen, paper or silk. A wide, shorthaired brush applied the final layers of lacquer. Some designers such as Jean Dunand could use up to 40 coats on a single piece with most pieces taking months to produce.[65] Definitely not mass production.

Art Deco was a style of the 'New Rich'. Emile Jacques Ruhlmann's "Pavilion of a Wealthy Collector" was undoubtedly the most popular of all the pavilions at the Exposition. Ruhlmann was almost entirely self-taught. He operated as both a furniture designer and as an interior designer, becoming the most noted of all the *assembliers*. His forms are often simple, always elegant; the materials always luxurious and the craftsmanship superb. Ruhlmann's designs attracted the support of an extremely rich clientele. His designs and his design philosophy personify French design of the 1920s. Unlike latter-day Arts and Crafts practitioners, Ruhlmann was free from any philanthropic ideas of bringing art and design to the masses; his views were unashamedly elitist:

> We must make *de luxe* furniture. I know that it is regrettably contrary to those generous beliefs for which I respect my colleagues. It would be preferable to educate the masses, but it is necessary to proceed otherwise. We are forced to work for the rich because the rich never imitate the middle classes. In all periods craftsmen have followed the leaders whose work is addressed to the rich. And the rich, without grudging it, are lavish with the money– and time–necessary for the solution of problems. It is the elite that launches fashion and determines its direction. Let us produce, therefore, for them. The *nouveau-riche* is prepared to pay a fantastic sum for his *commode de style*. But the rich client wants to own furniture which he can be sure he will not find in the homes of those less rich than himself. That is one of the reasons why, in the past, he sought out antiques. But now, with the proliferation of more or less successful *pastiches*, his taste for antiques is gradually disappearing. When he discovers that for

The apartment of Madame Mathieu-Levy, rue de Lotta, Paris, designed by Eileen Grey. 1924–1925. The interior features a Serpent chair, two of her Bibendum leather chairs, and her famed Black lacquered screen just visible in the doorway. Image courtesy the National Museum of Ireland.

50 *louis* one can acquire a passable imitation of the Neoclassical sofa for which he paid 10,000 francs, he will decide that from now on he will buy nothing but exclusive modern furniture.[66]

The image represented by Ruhlmann's furniture was what 'modern' design was all about in France in the 1920s. Unfortunately, this encouraged designers to think narrowly, to think of design in isolation from the reality of modern, post-First World War society. French designers could not return to the past but they could, very self-consciously, by 'design', manufacture a new tradition. Collectively these designers celebrated surface and decoration, craft technique, hand production, and catered to the luxury market. Their products had little in common with similar stylistic developments in North America that highlighted new materials, mass production techniques with products intended for the mass market.

One figure who provided the determining link from the past to the future, from Art Deco to modernism, was Eileen Gray, a seminal figure of modernism.[67] She mastered the 9,000 year old ancient Japanese technique of *Urushi*[68] (lacquerware) and produced some outstanding examples such as the famed lacquered wood and metal screen produced in 1924,[69] an array of innovative furniture designs including the famed Bibendum Chair, one of the most recognisable furniture designs of the 1920s. The chair, unlike some of its modernist counterparts, is very much for lounging in, for being comfortable in. The Beachwood frame is carried on

polished, chromium plated stainless steel tube legs; the seat is supported by rubber webbing to improve personal comfort; two semi-circular padded tubes, encased in soft, supple leather, seem to embrace the body; the whole design providing comfortable, informal, stylistic elegance. Eileen named the chair, Bibendum, after the iconic "Michelin Man" mascot that the tyre company had introduced at the Lyon Exhibition of 1894 and which, by the 1920s, had become *the* commercial symbol of France.

Bibendum (aka the Michelin Man) c.1930.

DESIGN PROFILE: CHARLES EDOUARD JEANNERET

Une maison est une machine-à-habiter.

"The house is a machine for living in", is one of most famous of Le Corbusier's affirmations. Wearing a black suit, a black bowler hat, exactly circular, horn-rimmed glasses, he was an idiosyncratic figure cycling along the streets of the Latin Quarter to his studio at 35 rue de Sèvres, close to Le Bon Marché, one of the world's first department stores. His birth name was Charles Edouard Jeanneret, he was born in 1887 into a bourgeois family in the Swiss watch making town of La Chaux-de-Fonds, a few miles from the French border. In 1920, for reasons that are far from clear, he adopted the pseudonym Le Corbusier. He trained not as an architect but as an engraver.

As a teenager Le Corbusier travelled widely throughout Europe. He travelled to Vienna in 1907 to meet with Josef Hoffmann, then in 1908/1909 he worked for 14 months in the architectural office of Auguste and Gustave Perret in Paris. Here he learnt the down to earth business of an architectural practice and the technical sophistication of reinforced concrete construction.[70] He also attended classes at the Sorbonne and the Écoles des Beaux-Arts. He left the office of the Perret brothers in November 1909. In 1910, Le Corbusier travelled to Germany, first to Munich then to Berlin and to the office of Peter Behrens. This is where he came into contact with the other disciples of the Modern Movement, Walter Gropius and Ludwig Mies van der Rohe. His letters home indicate his dissatisfaction with the Behrens office routine—seeing it as an example of how success can bring in commissions but reduce personal input.[71] From this practice he learned the practicality of dealing with large corporate clients and became increasingly interested in machine processes and the world of industrial design, becoming convinced that pure geometrical shapes were the most appropriate forms for industrial production.

Lyndos, Rhodes.

During 1911–1912 Le Corbusier took his voyage of discovery through the southern Mediterranean and Adriatic, travelling through the Balkans, Greece and Turkey. This he claimed, was the journey that had the longest lasting influence on his design philosophy. He discovered the small white cubes of Mediterranean vernacular architecture and was intrigued by their visual interaction with sunlight, with the sky and nature in general which provided a kinetic *chiaroscuro* of light and shadow. This is where he discovered the interplay between forms, rhythms, and light which gave rise to one of his descriptive maxims.

> Architecture is the skilful, exact, and magnificent play of volumes assembled in light. Our eyes are designed to see forms in light; shadow and light reveal forms; cubes, cones, spheres, cylinders, and pyramids are the great primary forms so well revealed by light; their image is exact and tangible, free of all ambiguities. This is why they are beautiful, the most beautiful forms. Everyone agrees on this point, children, primitives and metaphysicians. It is a prerequisite of plastic art.[72]

He stayed in Monasteries and was impressed by their discipline and community organisation. He spent one month in Athens, visiting and sketching the Parthenon every day. (When you visit the Parthenon, leave your camera behind and draw what you see, you will learn a lot more!)

Le Courbusier, like many European's, believed that the First World War would be over very quickly, and that there would be much to be rebuilt. In preparation he designed, in 1914, a system for the rapid construction of inexpensive houses, his Dom-ino house. The house relied on standardised concrete framing and made use of factory produced windows, doors and fixtures. The system was never utilised, but in 1925 he was able to take the next step when he was commissioned to design a pavilion for the *Exposition Internationale des Arts Décoratifs et Industriels Modernes* in Paris, the so called Art Deco Exposition. Le Corbusier explored a radical new construction technique using a steel frame and reinforced concrete, producing a standardised, practical and habitable 'cell,' designed to suit the modern context. It was furnished with ready made, mass produced furniture (including Thonet bentwood chairs) and industrial fittings. It is here that he was able to demonstrate that a house is a machine for living in.

His *Pavillon de l'Esprit Nouveau (Pavilion of the New Spirit)* was intended as a head-on attack on the very principles that the Exposition stood for, handcrafted, individualistic design, surface decoration and unbridled luxury. Instead Le Corbusier offers a more complete vision of what constitutes architecture; he affirms that architecture is about space not style; that design extends from concern and attention to every detail, from door handles and hinges to the ceramics of the kitchen and bathroom. He explores the possibilities offered by what he termed natural industrial selection, where the logic and requirements of the production line are expressed in standardised parts, showing that their use does not have to translate into standardised thinking.[73]

Between 1920 and 1925 he wrote a series of articles for the magazine *L'Esprit Nouveau*, a magazine which he and Amedee Ozenfant and Paul Dermèe had founded in Paris in 1921. While it primarily served as a vehicle to spread architectural theories and enhance the public image of Le Corbusier, it "was part of an exchange network with avant-garde magazines such as *MA, Stavba, De Stijl, Veshch/Gegenstand/Object, Disk,* and others".[74] It ran to 28 issues over a five year period; these were later collected and published in four books that became associated with the emerging 'International Style'. The most famous book—*Towards a New Architecture* was published in 1923, which drew accolades from his peers but did not influence the selection jury for the 1927 competition to design a League of Nations headquarters in Geneva, his functional proposal was flatly rejected, the stated reason being that the entry was not drawn in India Ink as specified in the entry rules of the competition.

This rebuff was answered in typical style. He relocated to La Sarrez in Switzerland and founded in 1928, the Internal Congress of Modern Architecture (CIAM) which, over the next decade or so, went on to formulate many of the basic principles of modern architecture.

And that brings us to his pre-Second World War masterpiece, which in many ways provided the monument to what the mature International Style had become. It is also the supreme example of how, according to Le Corbusier, a building interacts with its surroundings. The Savoye family commissioned Le Corbusier to create a country home in Poissy, 30km to the north-west of Paris. The Villa Savoye, 1928–1929, is a house built on *piloti*. It is a steel and concrete structure with stucco walls and steel-framed windows that hang from the infrastructure. During the Second World War, the occupying Nazi forces used it as a local headquarters. After 1945 the Savoye family sold it to the local authorities and it fell into disuse. In the 1950s it was rescued from oblivion by the French Minister of Culture, André Malraux, who initiated having the structure listed as a *bâtiment civil* in 1964 and as a historic monument in 1965.

Villa Savoye, Poissy, Le Corbusier, 1928–1929.

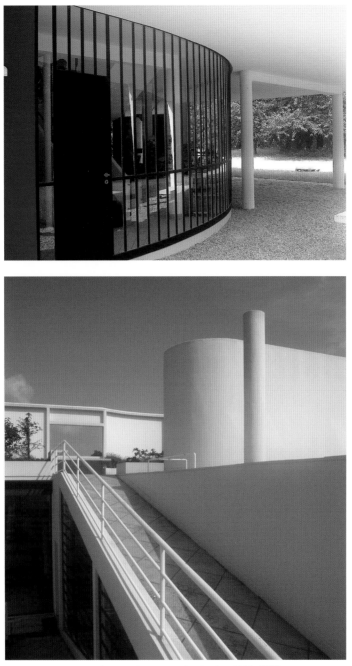

Villa Savoye, Poissy, Le Corbusier, 1928–1929.

The Summer retreat was situated in a rural site on the hill outside of Poisy. Le Corbusier outlined his overall design concept:

Site: a magnificent property consisting of an enormous pasturage and orchard forming a cupola surrounded by a girdle of high hedges. The house must have no 'front'; situated at the summit of the cupola, it must be open to all four horizons. The habitation floor, with its hanging garden, will be raised on pilotis allowing views all the way to the horizon.[75]

The Villa Savoye fulfilled the principles of the five "Points of a New Architecture" Le Corbusier and Pierre Jeanneret had formulated: The pilotis (columns which raised the house above the ground), free plan (due to free-standing walls there are no restraints upon the division of interior space), free facades (the exterior walls are no longer load-bearing), flat roof with

Sharp Design Centre, Ontario College of Art and Design, Toronto. Will Alsop, 2004.
Photo: Tiffany Barnikis.

roof garden (replacing land "lost" underneath the building), and ribbon windows. Frank Lloyd Wright characterised the 'solid cubes' of Le Corbusier, which appear to rest precariously on thin supporting poles, as "big boxes on sticks".[76] The "big box on sticks" model is still in use. For example see the Sharp Centre for Design, Ontario College of Art and Design, Toronto, designed by Will Alsop and completed in 2004.

In 1929, Le Corbusier made his first visit to South America, travelling by train to Bordeaux, then aboard the MS Massilia, which he described as "a miracle of modern construction and organisation".[77] He delivered a series of lectures in Buenos Aires, Montevideo, Rio de Janeiro and Sao Paulo. In November, on his return aboard the ocean liner Lutétia he re-established contact with the legendary 23 year old Josephine Baker whom he had met in Buenos Aires and with whom he had become enamoured.[78] Baker had had a previous relationship with another prominent architect, Adolf Loos who had designed a house for him in 1927; unfortunately this black and white boldly stripped building was never built.[79] The productive sea voyage resulted in a book, *Precisions on the Present State of Architecture and City Planning*, 1930. Soon after his return, Le Corbusier married Yvonne Gallis, a dressmaker and fashion model. She died in 1957.[80] On 27 August, 1965, Le Corbusier went for a swim in the Mediterranean Sea at *Roquebrune-Cap-Martin*, just beneath Eileen Gray's E-1027 house. It is assumed that he had a heart attack and died. He was 78.

Once I built a railroad, I made it run, made it race against time.
Once I built a railroad; now it's done. Brother, can you spare a dime?
Once I built a tower, up to the sun, brick, and rivet, and lime;
Once I built a tower; now it's done. Brother, can you spare a dime?[82]

THE BIRTH OF MODERNISM IN AMERICA

In France, Art Deco was well conceived, well thought out, well planned, and carefully promoted by French designers and critics alike. It was, almost instantly, criticised by the functionalist architects and some avant-garde thinkers of the time. There is absolutely no doubt that its form and iconography, its materials and process of production, firmly upheld French tradition, craftsmanship, and confirmed the 'rightness' of the *status quo*. The Art Deco style was a response to the conflicting forces unleashed by the process of industrialisation, compounded by the social, political and economic upheavals of the time–the cultural context–and that context was very different in America. In the 1930s, design in America responded to the cultural forces of mass consumption and mass culture, oblivious to the political forces that would serve as a prelude to world war.

In America, the "Roaring Twenties" started out as a decade of victory, exuberance and hope. There may have been prohibition but there was jazz and flappers and a general feeling that 'good times' were here to stay. For many this was a decade of boom. People were attracted to the speculative return on investments offered by stocks and shares, if they did not have funds immediately available they could invest using borrowed money. The boom ended, dramatically and suddenly for most, on Black Tuesday, 29 October, 1929, the day that the New York Stock Exchange closed its doors. Panic sale of stocks on the New York stock exchange reached enormous and unimagined proportions as investors clamoured to get what was left of their money. By the end of the day, the Exchange had lost four billion dollars and by the end of that year stock values had dropped by 15 billion dollars. And so began a decade of depression which lasted until 1941 with America's entry into the Second World War.[83]

> *The movement will undoubtedly reach our shores in the near future. As a nation, we now live artistically on warmed-over dishes.*
> Charles Richards, Chairman of the American Committee of the Commerce Department at the 1925 Exposition.

In North America, the 1930s were a decade of market driven mass production and mass retailing to service the mass market. It was an era of the pioneering industrial designers who helped to forge the form and character of the Machine Age as it catered to the immigrant enhanced urban communities of the period. It was proactive design that gave the competitive edge to those businesses struggling to survive the Depression.

Émile-Jacques Ruhlmann died in November 1933. He was regarded as the last of the French *Ébéniste* and the acknowledged master of luxury and elegance in early twentieth century French design. His philosophy was evident in the massive and elegant SS Normandie, the Queen of the French Line, Compagnie Générale Transatlantique, which was launched in October 1932 although it was to be 29 May 1935 before she set out on her maiden crossing to New York. Pierre Patout had collaborated with Ruhlmann on the design of L'Hotel d'un Collectionneur at the 1925 Exposition Internationale des Arts Décoratifs et Industriels Modernes in Paris and now took the lead in designing the opulent interior of the Normandie. Their collective mark was evident in this floating advertisement to the exclusive luxury of Art Deco. Between May 1935 and August 1939 the Normandie carried 848 first class, 670 second class passengers and a crew of 1,345 on 139 trans-Atlantic crossings 'in style'. The day of luxurious ocean travel was about to be overtaken by technology in the distinctive shape of the DC-3.[84] The craft based processes associated with Art Deco in France were responding to the requirements of a luxury intense market. Not so in America where the move to modernity was based on mass production for mass markets; where exotic woods and precious materials were replaced by industrially produced materials suited to mass production such as the extended range of plastics and chromium plated steel plus the innovative mass utilisation of materials such as aluminium foil and linoleum.[85]

The rural electrification programme brought power to 44 millions radios in American homes by 1940; many of those radios were tuned in to hear President Roosevelt's "Fireside Chats".[86] The printed word still held sway with the *Saturday Evening Post* and *Colliers* catering to the general interest audience; *Fortune* spoke to business while *Time* and *Life* took the message to the general populace, ratifying the concept that a picture is worth 1,000 words.

The exclusivity of the SS Normandie was supplanted by the diesel-powered Zephyr with its array of technological advances: shot-welded stainless steel, a General Motors diesel engine with aerodynamic design, air- conditioning, and recessed fluorescent lighting in the passenger cars. Other notable trains included the 20th Century Limited designed by Henry Dreyfuss and Raymond Loewy's Broadway Limited. Hundreds may have sailed across the Atlantic but in America millions took the train. The height for rail travel in terms of passenger numbers was reached in 1920, when 1.2 billion passengers traveled America by train; by 1939 that figure had been reduced by around 50 per cent. Rail gave right-of-way to the car.

On the ever increasing highways the visual standardisation of Texaco's service stations under the red star banner by Walter Dorwin Teague was far more comprehensive than any of the programmes

Life Magazine, November 23, 1936, Time Inc, used under licence. First *Life* cover features a photograph of the construction of Fort Peck Dam, Montana, by Margaret Bourke-White. Completed in 1940, the dam began generating electricity in July, 1943.[88]

devised by Cassandre or Paul Colin. At home many could afford the Kodak's Baby Brownie also designed by Walter Dorwin Teague and Russel Wright's American Modern dinnerware graced many a table, becoming the most popular wedding gift of the period. The kitchen had its own 'star' appliance; Raymond Loewy's Coldspot refrigerator for Sears being far more culturally significant than any elite piece of furniture by Ruhlmann. The Coldspot's simplified form was more symbolic of the modern world and, most crucial of all, far more widely promoted by the infrastructure of mass media and advertising than any comparable product in France. The practice of design changed, from iconoclastic individual to the team approach; "by 1941, products for whose design Loewy's Fifth Avenue, 60-employee office was responsible, grossed $750 million, rising in 1946 to $900 million".[87] Now, that is progress. There was a political component to design and culture in the 1930s in America where Roosevelt and his New Deal programme represented the future. The development was reflected on the pages of the new and visually exciting photo magazines such as *Life* and business magazines such as *Fortune*. Culture was transformed.

COVER STORY

In the early 1930s, the American populace had access to over 4,500 magazines. By 1939, despite a depressed decade, that number had grown to over 6,000 titles. It was a competitive world. Think for a moment, its 1936, unemployment hovers around 25 per cent; seven depressed years have resulted in a malaise of the general public. You decide to launch a new magazine that features photographs; what do you select for the cover of the 23 November inaugural issue? Maybe a movie star; Charlie Chaplin and his social protest film, *Modern Times*, the last great silent movie would be a worthy contender; or maybe what is regarded as the best film of 1936, *The Great Ziegfeld*, a lavish dance spectacular, very representative of Hollywood; or maybe a sports personality such as Jessie Owens, a black sharecropper's son from Alabama and an alumni of Ohio State University. Owens won three individual gold medals plus a fourth team gold medal in the 1936 Olympics in Berlin. The publisher, Henry Luce,[89] chose none of these, opting instead for a photograph by Margaret Bourke-White of the Fort Peck Dam in Montana shot during construction–and he was right–the image proved to be empathetic to the mores of the time; by the end of 1937 circulation of *Life* had reached around 1.5 million.[90]

Life was to prove to be the most influential and popular magazine in America and its impact on the consciousness of middle class public opinion in America was immense. It was Luce, who in a special issue of *Life*, published on 7 February 1941, defined the twentieth century as "the American century". In the country at large, there was a positive attitude to new technology accompanied by belief in a better world of tomorrow. This optimistic posture was possible for a few short years before the manufactured mayhem of the Second World War.

> *Rich fellas come up an' they die an' their kids ain't no good, an' they die out. But we keep a-comin'. We're the people that live. They can't wipe us out. They can't lick us. And we'll go on forever, Pa... 'cause... we're the people.*
> Ma's (Jane Darwell) final soliloquy in John Ford's *Grapes of Wrath*, 1940.

The 1930s was an era when advertising became a fundamental characteristic of life in modern North America.[91] Advertising helped to promote and popularise the iconography of the modern age through the objects associated with a commercial consumer culture. For those unable to participate in the consumer revolution there was always the artificial world of film. In this decade of depression the local cinema provided a place of refuge from the omnipresent depression.[92] Two of the outstanding films of the period were set in the Depression; the musical *42nd Street*, directed by Lloyd Bacon with choreography by Busby Berkeley was nominated for the Academy Award for Best Picture in 1934; the gritty social commentary of John Fords 1940 film of John Steinbeck's *Grapes of Wrath* garnered seven Academy Award nominations.

A BETTER TOMORROW

America was a magnet for creative individuals escaping the cultural intolerances which were to become manifest in the generated horrors of the Second World War. But America is not Europe. While European design seemed to be obsessed with theory and was highly structured, American design was more pragmatic, more overtly commercial, more concerned with making profit.[93] However, to quote OB Hardison Jr, "During this period of retrenchment, art was summoned to the barricades by ideologues of all persuasions.... American popular culture welcomed the new aesthetic as presented in advertisements, graphics, poster art, and design. Whatever its detractors might claim, the new art communicated.[94]

Reading the magazines and newspapers of the time, it becomes obvious that there was a developing, commonly held belief that if everyone pulled together it would be possible to achieve a better tomorrow. From this cultural consensus came modified belief systems and adjusted value systems that resulted in a re-branding of America. The magazines created a respect for machines that most people did not come into contact with but that affected their daily lives; machines such as turbines and hydro-electric dams and power stations. These same magazines, through their editorial and advertising pages, promoted new domestic machines and household appliances that

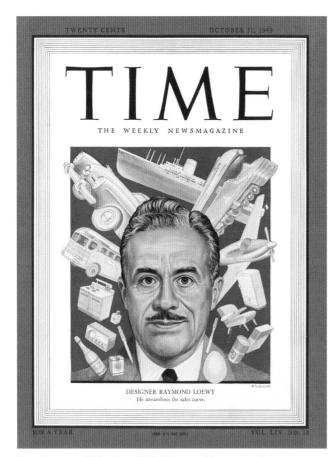

Time Magazine, 31 October 1949, Time Inc. Used under license.

were becoming available through mass retail outlets and mail-order catalogues. The consumer became familiar with new materials such as Formica and an expanded range of plastics. This new age also meant new processes of production, distribution and marketing.

In 1932, Norman Bel Geddes, writing in his book *Horizons*, said;

> Art in the coming generations will have less to do with frames, pedestals, museums, books and concert halls and more to do with people and life....When automobiles, railway cars, airships, steamships or other objects of an industrial nature stimulate you in the same way that you are stimulated when you look at the Parthenon, at the windows of Chartres, at the *Moses* of Michelangelo, or the frescoes of Giotto, you will have every right to speak to them as works of art. Just as surely as the artists of the fourteenth century are remembered by their cathedrals, so will those of the twentieth be remembered by their factories and the products of those factories.[95]

A NEW WORLD DISCIPLINE

One result of the Depression in North America was the competition it created as manufacturers developed increasingly sophisticated skills to secure their share of a decreasing market. One newly available skill was the

services offered by the new industrial design studios. This new breed of designer needed a developed visual literacy and an understanding of the competitive business climate in North America. So the mix of industrial competition, economic reality and commercial acumen were responsible for creating the new profession of the industrial designer in a society that up to then had paid very little attention to the phenomenon of design. It is equally perverse that despite all the lip service and intense discussion that had gone on for decades in Europe regarding design and its relationship with industry and people, the European's were unable, or unwilling, to develop the professional industrial designer. Design was the most legitimate creative activity of the twentieth century, and people such as Norman Bel Geddes, Raymond Loewy, Henry Drefuss and Walter Dorwin Teague were among its early stars; Raymond Loewy even made the cover of *Time* on 31 October 1949. Many of the other designers of the period were media stars in their own right, and became living symbols of the new age.

The very economic strength of North America lay in what were then pioneer industries. An editorial in *Fortune*, of February 1934 explains; "Now it is the turn of washing machines, furnaces, switchboards and locomotives. Who is going to design them?" The individuals who did design them made it their business to keep up with developments in science and technology and although they may have established similar studio practices and similar persuasive arguments about the commercial necessity of design, each worked from a very different base. Raymond Loewy, was a former engineer turned fashion illustrator; Walter Dorwin Teague was a typographer and illustrator; Henry Drefuss and Norman Bel Geddes were recruits from the theatrical world. Collectively they attracted clients by offering a range of services that they had basically invented; improved visual dynamics and consumer appeal, superior ergonomics, less expensive methods of production which resulted in reduced unit cost and most importantly, increased sales and a better profit line. The majority preferred the role of consultant to that of the in-house designer, they were generalist in the design sense rather than specialist, they acted as the intermediary between the client and other specialists such as engineers, model makers and market researchers.

DESIGN FOR PEOPLE

Streamlining, for all its quirks, hit people where they lived; it gave them improved vehicles of public and private transportation; it provided far more satisfactory household appliances and in a way, the consumer became the client, they may not have commissioned the designer but they did pass judgment in the court of the marketplace. Streamlining, or to give its original name, "stream forming" was the first design movement to deal with matters according to their practical significance. It brought down to earth the high minded assumptions and theories of the

Life Magazine, 15 February 1937, Time Inc. Used under licence. The article appeared on page 9 and featured a photograph by Margaret Bourke-White, which was also used on the cover.

Internationalists. To the dynamics of mass production and mass distribution had been added the previously unfathomable dynamic of mass taste. Hand in hand with the productions of that other dream factory, Hollywood, North American design of the 1930s provided a drama, excitement, and romance to a general public struggling with unemployment and lost hope. The market conditions, the technological innovations and the improved production capabilities gave birth to the first design movement that was responsive to the needs of the people, and the professional designers were its protagonists.

Between 1933 and 1935, President Franklin D Roosevelt introduced The New Deal, a package of economic reforms designed to lift America out of the Depression. The popular media and social critics of the day recognised that the programmes focussed on the three "Rs"; "Relief", "Reform", and "Recovery".[96] The New Deal was selective, the vast social discrepancies recorded for all time in the descriptive photograph shot by Margaret Bourke White and used as the lead article in *Life Magazine*, 15 February 1937.[97] Proof of "The World's Highest Standard of Living", symbolically portrayed by the white middle class family, secure in the ownership of their new car, confident that "There's no way like the American Way." Meanwhile the ongoing

depression is advertised by the refugees from the Louisville flood which had left almost a million persons homeless along the Ohio and Mississippi rivers. The editorial page is juxtaposed on the facing page with a photostrip advertisement for Heinz Aristocratic tomato products from "the Good Green Earth" of Bowling Green, Ohio.[98]

Prevailing economic conditions were worsened by the governments hands off policy and an adherence to the gold standard—all of which led to reduced levels of market demand and hence of production, resulting in high unemployment.[99] What was needed was a concerted effort to break the depression, to counter the acceptance of defeatism with a dream of what could be—and that takes us up to the New York Worlds Fair of 1939. The Fair opened on 30 April 1939; the unemployment rate was 26 per cent with around 11 million American's out of work.

The eyes of the Fair are on the future—not in the sense of peering into the unknown and predicting the shape of things a century hence—but in the sense of presenting a new and clearer view of today in preparation for tomorrow.
Official Guide Book of the New York World's Fair, 1939.

THE WORLD OF TOMORROW

Grover Whalen was a prominent politician and businessman in New York City during the 1930s and 1940s. His first major political assignment was as chief of police. Later he was appointed by Fiorello La Guardia as New York's official greeter. In 1935 he became president of the New York World Fair Corporation, charged with selling the concept of the Fair to sponsors and to the general public. Grover Whalen and his colleagues aimed to make it; "a world's fair that will be easy to see, easy to understand, easy to like, easy to get to".[100]

The theme of the 1939 New York World's Fair was "Building the World of Tomorrow"—providing a post-Depression, futuristic view of America as it would be in 1960.[101] More than 60 nations were represented at the Fair, each with its own pavilion.[102] The nation most conspicuously absent from The World of Tomorrow was Germany. The Fair was a colossal undertaking, covering 1,267 acres in Flushing Meadows, Queens; it would attract over 60 million visitors. At a time when the cost of a subway ride was five cents, admission to the Fair was 75 cents, making it an expensive venue. However, visitors did get a tantalising glance of what might be and learnt some new definitions. The central landmarks of the Fair were the Trylon and Perisphere (the largest globe ever made up to that time,) they were connected by the Heliciine, the world's longest escalator. The Perisphere housed a diorama called "Democracity" which, in keeping with the Fair's theme, depicted a utopian city-of-the-future.

The Fair was motivated by politics but it was a commercial undertaking, attracting major industrial sponsors intent on enhancing their brand awareness, none more so than Westinghouse who produced a 50 minute, full-colour "infomercial" which was shown on movie screens throughout America. This corporate propaganda film follows the exploits of a typical American family, the Middleton's.[103] (Mom, Dad, 'Bud' the young son and his elder sister, Babs, all fresh from Indiana.) The family are visiting the family home in New York to see the wonders of the World's Fair at Flushing Meadows, Long Island. Once at the Fair the family never leave the Westinghouse Pavilion where they are confronted by an array of futuristic appliances, including Elektro, the Westinghouse Motoman and his dog Sparky. While the men of the family explore television, the women marvel at a 'Dream Kitchen' which features a dishwashing contest in which Mrs Modern washes her dishes with a Westinghouse washing machine, while Mrs Drudge does hers by hand. Not surprisingly, Mrs Modern wins hands down. The Middleton's provided role models for the consumer culture deemed necessary for the prosperity of the Nation, providing clear guidelines on what, how, and why to buy.

I HAVE SEEN THE FUTURE

The Fair provided a venue for industrial designers such as Bel Geddes, Henry Dreyfuss, Walter Dorwin Teague, and Raymond Loewy to give the general public an optimistic view of the future while selling their professional services to business moguls.[104] The Fair's futurist concept provided an ideal occasion for the introduction and use of aerodynamic forms which became indicative of the era. The streamline aesthetic was popularised by Norman Bel Geddes but based on sound engineering research undertaken by the Hungarian Paul Jaray (1889–1974), who designed and tested streamlined automobiles in the wind tunnel of the German Zeppelin works in Friedrichshafen in the early 1930s.[105]

The Fair was divided into thematic areas, with the Transportation area being the most popular. It was dominated by the auto industry, but travel by air, sea, and rail also made their futuristic appeal. Noticeably absent were plans for urban public transportation systems. Norman Bel Geddes was responsible for the hit exhibit of the World's Fair, the one exhibit that everyone wanted to see, Futurama, sponsored by General Motors at a cost of $7 million, with a $200,000 design fee going to Bel Geddes. Thousands stood in line, at times reported to be a mile long, to experience Futurama.[106] This was the exhibit that took people on a 15 minute journey across America. Sitting in velvety upholstered armchairs they experienced "a magic Aladdin-like flight through time and space" across Bel Geddes' vision of St Louis as it would be in 1960. The city was complete with skyscrapers, placed so that none could cast a shadow on its neighbour, pedestrian walkways high above the street traffic, a huge centrally located dirigible hanger floating on a pool of oil, and seductive 14 lane highways for all those cars General Motors was intent on selling. The model highways were filled with 10,000 scale model cars, all moving at three prescribed speeds. Radio beams at front and back of each car maintained a safe distance between vehicles, and at dusk, light strips which were embedded in the edge of the road were tripped on and off as each car passed, eliminating the need for headlights. When visitors left the Futurama exhibit they were given a small blue and white lapel pin which contained the phrase "I Have Seen the Future". Bel Geddes touched a responsive nerve in visitors to the Fair; instead of showing production lines and bombarding people with dry facts, he mirrored other areas of popular culture and emphasised entertainment in his innovative stage set.

The most significant achievement of the Fair was that it offered, for a vey brief period, an optimistic outlook for the future. On 24 April 1939, just before the Fair opened, *The New York Times* best-seller list included John Steinbeck's *Grapes of Wrath*, that classic novel of the Depression. The non-fiction list featured the pirated English translation of Hitler's *Mein Kampf*.[107] The Fair opened on a balmy sunny Sunday, 30 April 1939. On 1 September, Germany invaded Poland; on 3 September, France, Great Britain and most of the countries of the British Empire and Commonwealth declared war on Germany. The dream of tomorrow beame a nightmare.

GM Pavilion ("Highways and Horizons" and "Futurama"), designed by Norman Bel Geddes and Albert Kahn, New York Worlds Fair, 1939. Courtesy General Motors LLC. Used with permission, GM Media Archives. Futurama was the most popular attraction at the fair, it received over 25 million visitors over two seasons.

CHAPTER SIX
DESIGN AND POST-WAR RE-BRANDING

Following on from the 1945 unconditional surrender of the axis powers,[1] the world was split into three ideologically and economically defined groups, North America, Western Europe, Australasia and Japan made up the so called "Free World"; the Soviet Union, Eastern Europe and China made up the Communist Bloc and the under-developed, developing, or less developed were branded as the "Third World". The next half century would see many refinements and changes to these groupings as, aided by design, nations sought to redefine themselves.[2]

A NEW WORLD ORDER

The great cities of Europe and Asia that were destroyed in the outrageous bombing of the Second World War, Rotterdam and Warsaw; Dresden and Coventry; Stalingrad and Hiroshima lay in ruins; the architectural heritage obliterated and the cultures shattered; but they also became symbols of hope for a more peaceful and fulfilling future. That hope failed to materialise. War and revolution remained defining characteristics of culture throughout the 1950s into the 1960s; the Cold War, the Korean War, and decolonisation emphasised that the world order had changed; the United States and the USSR became super powers.

European culture from the end of the Second World War up until the mid 1970s is defined both in North America and in Europe, by three principle features; an unprecedented increase in living standards; the emergence of a music driven youth culture and by the development of the concept of a consumer society. These distinct trends tend to dominate the evolution of the design process during this period. It was the period when culture became popular, when the attitudes and belief systems of society were shaped by the new realities of a post-war culture, largely as defined in film and television. The post-war period's material culture, its lifestyle, its patterns of consumption, and its preferred leisure activities reflected these changing times. Before we explore the 1960s it may be judicious to see how some of the prominent players prepared for the age of design.

BRITISH UTILITY

War changes everything; visual reinforcements of change were evident in the homes and on the street of major urban centres in Britain.[4] Utility ruled. Reuse and recycle

This 1945 file photo shows August Schreitmueller's sandstone sculpture *The Goodness* from the Rathausturm (Town Hall Tower) overlooking the destroyed city of Dresden in the aftermath of the bombings of February 13–14, 1945.[3] Photo: Richard Peter.

were economic necessities rather than aspects of social awareness. Prevailing social conditions changed the role of women and the associated clothing codes. In the UK, the functional turban and the wedge heeled shoe, born of factory work, became common marks of the modern woman. Women wearing trousers became a more frequent sight on city streets.

During the war, publicity was largely replaced by propaganda, what little advertising was allowed supported the utilitarian cause; new reasons to purchase were provided. The Ministry of Food, under the tag line "Dig for Victory", encouraged people to eat domestically produced foodstuffs. Potatoes and carrots were easy to get hold of, flour for bread had to be imported. An ingenuous form of food control witnessed an advertising campaign that introduced the characters of Potato Pete and Dr Carrot; even a traditional nursery rhyme was adapted to give mealtime a Potato Pete theme:

There was an old woman who lived in a shoe.
She had so many children she didn't know what to do.
She gave them potatoes instead of some bread,
And the children were happy and very well fed.[5]

There were thousands to be re-housed and fed. The distribution of food and clothing was controlled by a ration system. More immediate concerns were the effects of bombing and the shortage of timber. Furniture presented a particular challenge to those trying to control both consumption and production. The Board of Trade produced 'Utility' specifications that outlined the amount and quality of materials for making everyday goods.[6]

New furniture was available to those who could prove immediate need. Price was easy to control, standards of manufacture more difficult. The answer was to establish enforceable standards of design, regulating both form and quality in such a way as to make standards easy to check before bestowing the utility mark of approval. The CC41 'Utility' sign quickly became recognised as an endorsement of quality. Responsive to wartime conditions, a revised social ethic accepted that what little there was should be shared equally across all the various strata of society. Gordon Russell is traditionally seen as the driving force behind the Utility furniture design programme, the exact nature of his role remains a matter of ongoing research.[7] However, the chance to impose 'good design' on the population as a whole was grasped with some enthusiasm by design reformers who focussed their passions on creating a new Great Britain by design.[8]

British wartime street scene.

MAKE DO AND MEND

To guide the general public through these trying times, the government issued numerous leaflets including Make Do and Mend.[9] This included advice on how best to utilise available clothing and textile resources. Recycling was encouraged, a post-*Gone with the Wind* suggestion

being to transform old curtains into dresses and sheets into underwear. Father's trousers could be transformed into skirts for his daughters. With many men away on war duty there is a section entitled, "Men's Clothing into Women's". Indicative of the clothing codes of the era was the suggestion that "Plus-fours would make two pairs of shorts for a schoolboy". Scavenged parachute silk became the most prized possession of all, providing a touch of romance with a hint of danger to the recycled blouses and nightwear.[10] Dresses for women had to be free from any use of excess material, skirts were knee length, no elastic waist bands or fancy belts and shoes had a maximum heel height of 5 cm. Cosmetics and stockings were almost non existent. Some women would draw a line down the back of each leg to mimic the seam of stockings. Others used gravy browning to colour their legs–but with undesired side effects, the organic based browning was attractive to flies and insects and was not water repellent.[11] Design guidelines were imposed on men's clothing styles; fake jacket pockets were required on men's suits, and trousers had a designated maximum length of 48 cm, with no turn-ups.[12]

In October 1942, *Vogue* magazine wrote approvingly about the Utility Scheme for clothing. "All women have the equal chance to buy beautifully designed clothes suitable to their lives and incomes. It is a revolutionary scheme and a heartening thought. It is, in fact, an outstanding example of applied democracy."[13] Eight top designers in the London fashion world (including Hardy Amies, Norman Hartnell, Charles Creed and the House of Worth) had been asked to submit designs for Utility wear for women. Their designs were put into mass production, and were in the shops in the Spring of 1943.[14] Second-hand clothing was free from any rationing restrictions with jumble sales and market stalls providing a valuable source of supply. There was an active black market, clothes that had been looted from bombed out shops, warehouses and private homes found there way back into circulation.[15]

DESIGN BY DECREE

'Victorious' British troops returned to a country ravaged by war, with rationing of most commodities including food, clothes and furniture and with reams of restrictions and 'guide lines' to cope with. Bombing had decimated many homes, the best accommodation that the victors could expect was in one of the emergency prefabricated houses produced; half a million had been planned, but only 156,623 were built. Many of these used an aluminum construction system and were manufactured in former aircraft factories. The most innovative element of the design being a factory manufactured 'back-to-back' kitchen/bathroom unit with built in fixtures. These single-storey, 600 square foot homes were designed as a temporary measure, despite their asbestos panelling many remained in use into the 1980s.[16]

The Design Research Unit (DRU) was one of the first generation of British design consultancies combining expertise in architecture, graphics and industrial design. It was founded in 1943 by the managing director of Stuart's Advertising Agency, Marcus Brumwell with designers Misha Black and Milner Gray and the poet and art critic Herbert Read. The DRU was responsible for the wartime Ministry of Information, the Council of Industrial Design's Britain Can Make It (1946) and they made a major contribution to the Festival of Britain (1951). The illustration shows examples of their work-ranging from street signage, work from the London Transport network and the British Rail Logo (1965). The DRU became part of Scott Brownrigg in August 2004. Illustration courtesy of Scott Brownrigg.

In 1943, during the war, The Ministry of Information established the Design Research Unit, intended as the UK's first design consultancy. The DRU was founded by the head of an advertising agency and staffed by an art critic, an architect and a graphic designer, the results of their work can still be seen on the streets of London.[17] As the end of the war approached the British Government could see that if the country were to play a role in the post-war industrial world, then Britain would need to move away from the idealism and mentality of Arts and Crafts production to a realisation of the essential role of design in mass manufacturing. It was obvious that design would play a vital role in any post-war regeneration of industry. In December,1944, several months before the end of the war, the government created the Council of Industrial Design, (CoID) its original declared objective being "to promote by all practicable means the improvement of design in the products of British industry".[18]

BRITAIN CAN'T HAVE IT

One major post-war step in reaching this goal was the promotion of the Britain Can Make It exhibition of 1946, held between September and November at the Victoria and Albert Museum (V&A), in South Kensington, London.[19] This featured the products of a reconstructed British industry and drew an audience of 1.5 million–no mean achievement just one year after the end of the war. The main theme of the exhibition was the transition from war to peace, with examples of the consumer goods that would soon be available to the British public. The CoID thought it critical to convince manufacturers, retailers, and the general public that design was of prime importance in the new industrial world.

The exhibition was nicknamed "Britain Can't Have It" by the British press because most of the items on show were for export; a very necessary activity to obtain the funds to pay for the war, in particular to the USA for all the equipment and to Canada for all the food that was consumed during the war. It was only in December 2006 that the final instalment of £11.6 million (about $19 million) was paid of the £600 million borrowed from Canada. On 31 December, 2006, the UK made a payment of about £45.5 million (about $72 million) to the US to discharge the last of its loans from the Second World War. Over a period of 56 years, Britain repaid more than $6.3 billion to the United States.[20] As they say, nothing, particularly war, comes for free.

There was some remarkable examples of design innovation among the 5,000 objects on display. In the section, "Designs of the Future", visitors were introduced to aluminum sewing machines, the kitchen of tomorrow, a toboggan shaped, air-conditioned bed and a "Bicycle of the Future".[21] This streamlined, prototype electric bicycle designed by Benjamin

George Bowden featured a reversible electric motor/dynamo in the rear wheel hub which stores energy while the bicycle is travelling downhill and releases it on uphill gradients. Other design innovations included a shaft drive, which eliminated the cumbersome chain drive, an instrument panel and even an optional radio. The design was intended to show the developments likely to occur in the next 20 years. As Paul Clark notes, there are "similarities between Bowden's ideas and those of a contemporary engineer, Corradino d'Ascanio, whose designs for Piaggio in Italy resulted in the Vespa scooter".[22]

The aluminum prototype of this futuristic bicycle was handmade by the MG Auto Company in England in 1946. It proved to be far too expensive for consumer production and so this initial venture ended. Undeterred, and after an abortive venture to South Africa, in 1960 Bowden contracted Bomard Industries in Michigan, USA, to produce a more mechanically conventional, one-speed version of the dynamic, organic design. Built in headlight and tail lights were added and the resulting model was produced using a fibreglass frame. Bomard was beset with financial and administrative problems and went out of business having produced just 522 examples of this 'Bicycle of the Future".[23]

DESIGN IS GOOD FOR YOU

The 1950s were a time to rebuild. Over 750,000 homes had been destroyed by bombs and rockets. It was a time for social reform; a time for a national health service; a time for the nationalisation of industry (1,500 British collieries were nationalised in 1947, followed by the iron and steel industries in 1948/49). In the work-a-day world of post-war Europe there was, initially, a degree of consumer resistance to design and products associated with Germany and Japan. There was a continuing preference to the perceived humanism and friendly natural materials associated with Scandinavian design. The 1950s witnessed a new found interest in art which was to establish art as the most commercially successful post-war cultural phenomenon. Designers in particular were attracted to the free flowing biomorphic forms associated with Surrealism–these were seen as a viable alternative to machine like, technological forms reminiscent of the more stark wartime realities. Meanwhile the general market were discovering the attractions of conspicuous consumption as 'advertised' in imported American film and television shows.

By the mid 1950s everyday British life had been transformed from 'make do and mend' to a lifestyle more in keeping with the beginnings of conspicuous consumption. A domestic economic mini-boom provided the market for newly available consumer products; clothes and even frozen food were welcomed to the High Street of a British nation reconstructing itself. In 1949, the British pound was devalued by 30.5 per cent against the dollar (from $4.03 to $2.80) making imports more expensive. One immediate affect being the increase in the cost of bread by 50 per cent, from 4d to 6d per loaf. 26 other nations followed Britain's devaluation lead, reinforcing the fact that America was now the world's dominant economy.[24]

Aware of the impending commercial competition that more freely available American and European products may provide, the Design Council in Great Britain attempted to educate the domestic audience through a variety of exhibitions and publications. These were seen as necessary to help differentiate between 'good' and 'bad' design; 'Good design', naturally, being British. The associated motto was that "good design means good business". The Council recognised that there could be a boom in design and wanted to help prepare the context that would give prominence to British designers. The journal *Design* was first published in 1949. The Festival of Britain was staged in 1951.

On a rainy 4 May 1951 the Festival of Britain was opened by King George VI.[25] It was located on London's South Bank just across the Thames from Charing Cross station. Four years in the planning, at a cost of 11 million pounds of badly needed public funds, the Festival was planned to be a country wide celebration of Britain's victory, reinforcing Britain's history, achievements and culture. It was also viewed as a proclamation of its economic recovery. Coincidental references to the centennial celebration of the Great Exhibition of 1851 were to be an added element. The Festival planners were overwhelmingly middle class who saw a degree of moral responsibility in defining the design characteristics of a 'reconstructed' Great Britain. The Festival was the first exposure many people in the post-war period had to bright colours, new materials, new technology and of course, new design. By the time the Festival opened it had lost much of its original intent–it was no longer 'international', it had lost most references to the necessity of trade, and there was virtually no mention of the Great Exhibition of 1851. It had become a nationalistic moral booster; in the words of Gerald Barry, the Festival Director, it became, "a tonic to the Nation".[26]

The Festival of Britain was open for five months and over 8.5 million people visited the South Bank site (considerably more than visited London's ill fated Millennium Dome some 50 years later.) Two of the Festival's main attractions were the 300 foot Skylon which, some quipped, like Great Britain at the time, had no visible means of support,[27] and the aluminum clad Dome of Discovery, the largest dome in the world at the time, designed by Ralph Tubbs.[28] This revolutionary looking structure contained all the celebrated scientific and technological breakthroughs of the era. The structure was designed to be dissembled and rebuilt on another site after the exhibition ended (reminiscent of the relocation of Paxton's Crystal Palace from Hyde Park to Sydenham)–instead this magnificent and adventurous structure was shamefully sold for scrap by the incoming Conservative government of 1952.

The Festival was a celebration of Nation, the most prominent statement of which was the Lion and Unicorn

300 foot high, post-tensioned cable, Skylon, braced steel panels covered in satin aluminium louvers. Designed by Philip Powell, Hildago Moya and the engineer Felix Samuely. Festival of Britain, 3 May–30 September 1951.

Pavilion. Here those heraldic symbols of nationalism and patriotism, the Englishness of which had been recently re-established by George Orwell in his 1941 essay, "The Lion and the Unicorn: Socialism and the English Genius", are parodied into large corn dollies.[29] They were over flown by a flight of doves suspended from the ceiling–a devise that has found contemporary parallels.

There were also new things to see and new ways of seeing on view. The Canadian Wells Coates designed the Telekinema and the Television Cinema pavilion which provided many of the visitors with their first experience of television. The Telekinema seated over 400 people and could project film as well as full-screen closed-circuit television. Visitors could watch stereoscopic films with multiple sound tracks and by wearing special polarised glasses they could experience the illusion of three-dimensional space 60 years before *Avatar*.[30] The Telekinema later became the National Film Theatre and in 1957 was relocated to its present site in the Southbank Centre.

The Festival catalogue *Design in the Festival* sold 95,000 copies (at five shillings, making it quite expensive) and was to have a profound affect on design thinking in Great Britain throughout the

Dome of Discovery, 365 foot diameter, concrete and extruded aluminum, Ralph Tubbs.

people reported seeing UFOs. These widely reported brushes with extra-terrestrials created a mind set that was responsive to crystal patterns, rocket references and symbols of atoms and space. On a more material level there was Perspex, Formica and other plastics, plus a range of synthetic fibres which provided a new tactile feel to the decade.

The contemporary design style of the 1950s highlighted the gap that had developed between the 'educated' values of the Council of Industrial Design and their designers with the values of the general British public. There were some highly successful examples of design innovation; in 1947, Kenneth Wood introduced a new domestic appliance, the Kenwood Chef which 'revolutionised' British kitchens. However, the high minded, moralising tones of the Council and its publications were at odds with the voice of the general public—a significant number of whom were now under 25. A class and age based dichotomy emerged in British design and was to prevail throughout the next decades. To the general public debates over design were less important than the availability of goods in the local shop—which gave rise to the battle of the brands in the 1960s.

In retrospect, what was surprising was that after the most destructive war in human history, after rockets and atom bombs, there was a huge discrepancy between the obvious vital significance of technology in the post-war society, and in the insignificant role that it played in the ideological design debates of the day. This is even more surprising when you consider that this was the decade when wartime technologies were put to peaceful use, "In 1945, Britain had 22 aircraft companies, nine engine manufacturers and a support network of R&D laboratories."[33] There was the first public appearance of the jet engine and its use in medium-and long-range commercial aircraft. The American Boeing 707, with an interior designed in part by Walter Dorwin Teague, was the first jet to be offered to commercial airlines; the British Comet, was the first commercial jet to reach production but problems with metal fatigue and poor window installation technology delayed its entry into regular service. The redesigned Comet 4 series was in

1950s and into the 1960s. The Festival organisers intended that the Festival should tell "a new sort of narrative about Britain: an Exhibition designed to tell a story through the medium, not of words, but of tangible things".[31] In 2010, Neil MacGregor, Director of the British Museum, was a little more adventurous. In a 100-part series for Radio 4, he explored world history from two million years ago to the present in 100 objects.[32]

The 1950s was the decade of the first nuclear power station; the first satellite was launched and many

Doves, Plaster, Lion and Unicorn Pavilion, Festival of Britain, 1951.

Flight Stop, a flock of 60 geese in flight, Michael Snow, Toronto Eaton Centre, fibreglass, 1977. Photo: Tiffany Barnikis.

general use for over 30 years; and the French Caravel (an amazing angle of assent) had a commercial life of close to 50 years–all these jets made their inaugural flights in the 1950s.

TIME FOR A CHANGE

Sometimes overlooked was the ongoing influence of American popular culture on post-war cultural attitudes in Britain. Popular media, in the form of comics and magazines infiltrated into the lifestyle of the young–their advertisements introducing such essential consumer products as Tootsie Rolls and chewing gum. The advent of commercial television, introduced in September 1955, featured American programming; shows such as *Maverick, Dragnet* and the effervescent sitcom *I Love Lucy* familiarising British youth with views of a promoted paradise, removed from the utilitarian reality of life in Britain.[34]

One other very noticeable transition of the 1950s was the emergence of a youth culture, most evident in their clothing codes and music preferences. In the 1940s 'nice' boys and girls dressed like their parents. By the mid-1950s there were Teddy Boys, DA haircuts and rock and roll. Within a decade the orchestrated foxtrot of Victor Silvester had given way to the imported beat of Bill Haley and His Comets. In December 1954, their version of "Shake, Rattle and Roll" had reached number four in the British charts. In 1956 the movie *Rock Around the Clock*, featuring Bill Haley was released in Britain with the group playing in several British cities, generating the first youth based skirmishes with authority.[35] British youth was dancing to a very different tune.

An influential study by the sociologist Mark Abrams, entitled, "The Teenage Consumer", revealed that 90 per cent of the money spent by British youths between 13 and 25 came out of the pockets of working class teenagers.[36] This was a major revelation to manufactures and retailers. But designers, who were mostly middle class, were less than enthusiastic to take this social fact into account. To many, the prevailing cultural stereotypes and underlying class aspirations were completely foreign. So-called "contemporary design", promoted by the Design Council was pitched to the values and tastes of the middle class. This Council-approved approach was a homogenised, comfortable variation of the modernist aesthetic–totally out of keeping with the prevailing cultural context. To use the words of David Kynaston, there was a "profound cultural mismatch between progressive activators and the millions acted upon".[37] Many of the old cultural conventions that had seemed to be so descriptive of British life began to crumble. New cultural forms such as cinema and pop music began to play their role in determining the cultural context for

design. Four million British teens found themselves in a position of power. Rates of unemployment were low and they had money in their pockets. Professional designers practised selective hearing, but the mass market listened and provided what was required.

NEVER HAD IT SO GOOD

After the 'Utility' period of rationing and shortages, the 1950s marked a period of relative affluence in Britain.[38]

> Between October 1951 and October 1963 wages were estimated to have risen by 72 per cent, prices by 45 per cent. There was full employment, and the availability and consumption of pleasurable possessions such as cars, washing machines, record players and television sets testified to the expansion of the 'affluent society'.[39]

Rationing was coming to an end and many of the old divisive social and cultural structures began to be challenged, particularly by the young. The old class-based distinctions between high and mass culture seemed irrelevant to youth intent on leaving their mark on the new Britain. On 20 July 1957, the British Prime Minister, Harold Macmillan, assured his faithful supporters at a rally in Bedford that "most of our people have never had it so good".[40] He was mimicking the line of the US Democratic Party which used "You never had it so good" as a slogan in the 1952 US election campaign.

It was not just political jargon that made it across the Atlantic, Hollywood movies, television, glossy magazines, and consumer goods proved an instant hit with the youth of Britain. Films in particular provided a few hours of escape, time to fantasise about the dream cities of America where even the rebels had their own cars and motorbikes. One film that proved very popular was *Rebel Without a Cause*, 1955, starring James Dean as a bored teenager lost in an affluent middle class lifestyle. Jim Stark (aka James Dean) had access to his own large car, his family lives in a home filled with luxury consumer goods, yet something is missing. Dean's character portrays an anguished, identity-seeking teen seeking some form of redemption - epitomised in the films most famous line; "You're tearing me apart!" Jim's cry was felt by many a British teen as, lost in the darkened interior of the local Odeon they fought the same battles.

> *From a tight knot of streets between Piccadilly and Regent Street, the suit has conquered the planet.*
> *The Economist*, 16 December, 2010.

THE SUIT

The mans suit has become the conforming uniform of capitalism. An article in *The Economist* notes that: "When Barack Obama first visited Hu Jintao, paramount leader of the People's Republic of China, the men were clad in near-identical dark blue suits, white shirts and red spotted ties."

Suit, designed and manufactured by Brioni, Italy and sold through Cecil Gee, London. The late 1950s, Brioni's stylistic silhouettes was marked by a longer, tighter-fitting coat, slightly accentuated shoulders and bolder colours and patterns. These became the model for later Mod suits of the 1960s. Photo: Brioni Spa.

The origin of the suit can be traced back to King Charles II of England, who in October 1666 'reformed' men's court dress as a precaution against any further fall-out from the plague outbreak of 1655. Samuel Pepys records in his diary that: "The King hath yesterday in Council declared his resolution of setting a fashion in clothes which he will never alter."[41] Indeed it was the King's declared intent to create a national costume that remains unchanged, at least among aristocratic Englishman. This new style of dress resulted in a coat and vest of equal length, (the inner garment was later reduced in length to become the appropriately named, waistcoat); these were worn over narrow breeches. Eventually over the next two centuries, this would evolve into the three-piece suit.[42]

Beau Brummell was the model 'Dandy' in early nineteenth century British sartorial society.[43] His very sober attire was in marked contrast to some of the exuberance of Regency fashion. Brummell dressed in dark blue long coats during the day, and black in the evening. These were worn over tight-fitting pantaloons and white linen shirt like undergarments. He fully realised that the real power base of British society was at Court. He bought a commission in the tenth Light Dragoons and thereby into the echelons of Regency high society. The term Dandy came into use to describe a member of the lower classes who challenged the stylistic accoutrements of fashionable aristocratic society.

More than a century later Mayfair and Belgravia rapidly reverted to their pre-war status as home to the most affluent members of London society. In the 1950s Saville Row tailors catered to the needs of their aristocratic male clientele with the introduction of the Edwardian suit.[44] Jackets in the Edwardian style were single-breasted, long, fitted and often featured velvet trim on the collars and cuffs. The suit introduced the morning coat effect with long narrow lapels, narrow trousers, white shirt with cut away collars, all set off with a fancy waistcoat (pronounced wes-ket,) and topped by a narrow brimmed bowler hat. Whatever the weather, a furled umbrella was the essential artefact of status.[45] Sometime in 1953 the lads south of the Thames began to mimic the style, adapting certain elements and making it their own so that by the end of 1953 what emerged was the fully fledged Teddy Boy Suit.

TEDS

Britain produced the first Teddy Boys.[46] These urban, unskilled working class boys, established an identity through their clothes and music preferences. The Teds first appeared in the hard core working class areas of south and east London in the early 1950s as Britain was coming to the end of post-war austerity. They represented the face of a British youth culture who could for the first time afford new clothes and indulge in personal forms of entertainment.[47] The Teds reached their peak in 1956 and died out after the race riots in the Summer of 1958. Though short-lived, their influence was immense. They transformed the working class wardrobe, which up until that time consisted of week day work clothes and 'Sunday best'. They established the commercial reality of a teenage market[48] and made it acceptable to dress for show.[49] All this was done while some clothes rationing was still in effect. In *Subculture: The Meaning of Style*, Dick Hebdige argues that:

> Far from being a casual response to 'easy money' the extravagant sartorial display of the Ted required careful financial planning and was remarkably self-conscious—a going against the grain, as it were, of a life which in all other respects was, in all likelihood, relatively cheerless and poorly rewarded.[50]

Even their music preferences were rationed. The fastidious British Broadcasting Corporation (BBC) who, in the 1950s had a monopoly on broadcasting, only allowed 22 hours per week for the broadcast of popular music.[51] This limit on 'needle-time' was in response to an agreement with the musicians union to protect the livelihood of professional musicians—an additional control being that only every third musical item could feature a vocal.[52]

The clothing that the Teddy Boys wore was designed to shock their parents' generation. The Teds modified the Edwardian suit of fashionable Belgravia; they wore drip dry, non-iron, poplin shirts to replace the custom made cotton genre; Slim-Jim or boot-lace ties instead of the old school version; thick crepe shoes rather than the bespoke variety; drainpipe trousers without turn ups, worn short enough to reveal florescent socks; single button, finger tip length drape jacket, often adorned with velvet collars and turned back cuffs. They discarded the rolled umbrella in favour of the more practical comb which became as essential Ted sartorial ornament. The trademark drape jacket was not as impractical as it seems. Not only did it act as a badge of recognition but, as it was made of woollen cloth with deep pockets; it kept its wearer warm as he hung around on the street and was also good at concealing weapons and alcohol. The boys tried a number of experimental hairstyles. Hair was heavily creased and combed on top into a high forward set wave. The hair on the side was swept back and behind the ears; the final 'stroke' was to run the comb up through the hair to create a division referred to as a DA (duck's arse).

Teddy girls adopted a clothing style to supplement the boys dress code. They added their own touches with pencil skirts, later adopting the American fashions of tight toreador pants and voluminous circle skirts. If the boys could ape Edwardian style fashions then the girls could spoof Dior's 'new look'. Their 'look' was completed with ballet slippers and with hair worn in ponytails.

The dress of the Teddy Boys was a real world expression of their social frustrations with the class ridden aspects of British society, it indicated their subliminal social aspirations to gain acceptance in the new, "never had it so good", urban environment. At the beginning of the 1960s the Teddy Boy look was replaced by an Italian-inspired, fashion conscious Mod style. The British media did not differentiate, Ted or Mod, both were regarded as symbols of a nation in moral decline. Two new descriptive terms appeared around this time— teenager and juvenile delinquent—for most of the social commentators of the day the terms were synonymous. A phrase favoured by the social scientists of the day, "moral panic", was used when discussing youth culture, subcultures and style.[53]

MODS

The Mods started in London's East End.[54] Being a Mod required revised attitudes to life, the adoption of a mind-set with loyalties to different modes of fashion and musical styles. The first wave of Mods were generally lower middle class, and were obsessed with new fashions, including slim-cut Italian styled, three buttoned mohair suits. Depending upon availability and economics, these were either custom made from Cecil Gee who imported the Italian brands Canali and Brioni, or tailored from a local bespoke tailor such as Lew Rose in Romford. Fashion and style became vitally important, as was the attention to detail. One week a six inch jacket vent was required, next week it could be an eight inch vent. Shoe styles changed, reflecting what was available at Raoul's, near the Flamingo in Wardour Street or at the Ivy Shop in Richmond. These changes, unnoticeable to the uninitiated, were essential elements to being 'sharp'.

The Vespa and Lambretta scooters were the required forms of personal transportation.[55] Legally, one wing mirror was required for all motorcycles and scooters. The Mods exceeded specifications by adding up to 30 mirrors, further enhanced by an array of headlights, crash bars, whip-style aerials and other paraphernalia. The pop artists of the day may have appropriated images from the commercial world, the Mods made appropriation mobile.

Initially, the preferred music was modern jazz and rhythm and blues. The original Mods gathered at all-night clubs such as The Scene, The Flamingo and The Marquee in London to demonstrate their dancing prowess and sartorial style.[56] Their all-night urban social lifestyle was fuelled, in part, by amphetamines. Within a very short time the music preference changed from an imported "Blue Beat" to the home grown sounds of British rock bands, including the Small Faces and a group from Acton called the High Numbers, better known by their later name, The Who.[57] *Quadrophenia*, a double rock opera album released by The Who in October 1973, is regarded by cognoscente as the finest rock LP ever.[58] A film version was released in 1979 where the Brighton riots of May 1964 (see below) were immortalised as the centrepiece of this soon-to-be cult film and partly inspired a Mod revival in the UK in the late 1970s which was in part a reaction to the Punk revolution which debuted with the arrival of The Sex Pistols in 1976, (see Chapter Nine).

Whaddya rebellin' against, Johnny?
Wha'ya got?'
Johnny in *The Wild One*.

ROCKERS

Rockers preferred beer to amphetamines and motor bikes rather than scooters to get them to their transport cafe rendezvous, the most famous being the Ace Cafe on London's North Circular road. Prior to the 1960s they were referred to as "Ton-up Boys", "ton-up" being the English euphemism for exceeding 100 mph. The Rocker subculture drew on the working class for membership. Their role model was the leather clad "Johnny" (aka Marlon Brando) the star of the 1953 Columbia Pictures movie *The Wild One*. Like Johnny they wore metal stud decorated leather motorcycle jackets with patches and pin badges. Riding necessitated aviator style goggles, a white silk scarf was the only allowed decorative affectation. Leather trousers and tall motorcycle boots completed the uniform. The essential hairstyle was kept in place with Brylcreem a pomade formulated from an emulsion of water and mineral oil stabilised with beeswax.[59] Rockers became defined as the antitheses of their scooter-riding, drug dependent Mods.[60] Tribal conflict was inevitable. Clashes occurring during British Bank Holiday's at the southern English holiday resorts of Clacton, Margate and Brighton, the most infamous being on the 18 May 1964 where more than 1,000 teens converged on Hastings. The resulting mayhem was avidly recorded in the popular media of the day. [61]

The subculture genre has been extensively explored and analysed. A common phrase used to encompass Ted, Mod and Rocker was "resistance through ritual", part of that resistance was the appropriation of consumer durables which were subject to modification expressive of feelings and values that were only recognised by fellow initiates.[62] Dick Hebdige qualifies: "These 'humble objects' can be magically appropriated; 'stolen' by subordinate groups and made to carry 'secret' meanings: meanings which express, in code, a form of resistance to the order which guarantees their continued subordination."[63]

Ted, Mod or Rocker, all relied on clothing style and selected artefacts to give meaning and substance to their image; none had even the slightest connection to the cannon of 'good design' being preached by the design profession who had no empathy nor understanding of the role of popular culture in the life of a nation; that was about to change. The distinctive nature of Teds, Mods and Rockers disappeared, overwhelmed by the highly commercialised era of the "Swinging Sixties" and the elevation of London's Carnaby Street as the new arbiter of fashion and style, (see Chapter Eight). The cultural revolution brought about by British youth in the 1950s was to have a delayed but extremely strong influence on the youth of Europe in the 1960s and possessed very 'popular' connections to North American culture.

The rapid rate of change in the cultural dynamic is exemplified by changes to music preferences and clothing codes that emphasised the symbolic power of the young. The 1956 movie *Rock Around the Clock*, featuring Bill Haley introduced rock and roll, new clothing codes, and new idioms of language.[64] In the 1964 film *A Hard Day's Night* the Mod dressed Beatles initiated a new range of cultural associations. The Provocative clothing and confrontational behaviour of The Sex Pistols was revealed to the British television audience on 1 December 1976. To dismiss these developments over a 20 year period as a form of subculture tends to minimise their affect on the general cultural mores of the time.

THE TIMES THEY ARE A-CHANGIN [65]

In post-Second World War America it was a time of economic and social transformation. Returning GI's bypassed the family farm in favour of urban centres. The GI Bill made it possible for a high percentage of men to get a college education. Women had to give up their jobs to the returning male dominated workforce, but they had had their first taste of job equality. The 1950s began with another war. The Korean conflict began on 25 June 1950 and paused with an armistice signed 27 July 1953.[66] The first American 'advisors' were sent to South Vietnam in July 1950, supported by $15 million in military aid to the reinstated French Colonial forces.

During the 1950s in America, consumers were introduced to an array of "new and improved" products, including Play-Doh, Special K cereal, Crest fluoride toothpaste, and Quaker Instant Oatmeal. On 15 April 1955, Ray Kroc opened the first McDonald's franchise in Des Plaines, Illinois, and the first day's take was $366.12; in April 1955, Dr Jonas Salk's polio vaccine was declared "safe, effective and potent", and millions of school children were given polio shots. Most significantly of all, on 1 December 1955, Rosa Parks refused to give up her bus seat to a white man, in defiance of Alabama law. Albert Einstein and James Dean died. Bill Gates, Steve Jobs, and Tim Berners-Lee were born. The social and political upheaval that characterised the 1960s lay ahead.

> At the opening of the decade, the United States found itself in the enviable position of being far and away the most powerful nation on earth. Its industrial base, undamaged and immeasurably strengthened by the Second World War, manufactured over half of all the world's products, along with producing raw material like steel and oil in prodigious quantities.[67]

Materially, the 1950s was a time of Orlon, Dacron and Tuperware, when the grey flannel suit epitomised the status quo in fashion and lifestyle. It was a time when surface triumphed over substance, Naugahyde was used as an alternative to leather and Decro-Wall panelling, a vacuum formed vinyl sheet masquerading as brick or stone, decorated dens and family rooms. It was a time of motels, drive-ins, shopping malls and amusement parks. A time for Hula hoops, 3-D movies, tail finned Cadillac's, Barbie dolls, pony-tails and poodle skirts, Coke and Burma Shave signs.[68]

In the halcyon days of the 1950s it became evident that science and technology could be put to 'domestic' use, promising a high tech future free from restrictive inconveniences imposed by war. The resulting lifestyle of self-indulgence made not only consumption conspicuous but the model to aim for. This fundamental cultural transformation was reflected on magazine covers; Norman Rockwell's folksy *Freedom from Want* (*The*

Saturday Evening Post, 6 March 1943) replaced by the Coca-Cola cover of *Time*, 15 May 1950, the first commercial product to appear on the cover of a mass circulation magazine. During the 1950s Coca-Cola successfully colonised the worldwide soft drink market.[69]

The developing 'American Lifestyle' was first exhibited abroad at the 1958 Universal Exposition in Brussels. The designer Winston Spriet pointed out, "The most complete example of 1950s decoration at the fair is without doubt the American pavilion... where everything is laid-back; no machines, no statistics... just drugstores, hi-fi's, soda fountains, ice cream and ultra modern design; everything there is soft and seductive. Toasters and colour television sets are on display. The visitor falls into a delicious consumer trap. The main attraction is the circarama, on whose circular screen all of America is laid out before ones eyes."[70] The pavilion also included car simulators, a robotic arm, and a daily fashion show.

One other significant design phenomenon of the 1950s was Barbie. Originally 'modelled' on the film star Jane Mansfield, who at the time, was married to the President of Mattel. Barbie was 'born' on 9 March 1959, in Los Angels. This 11" model of WASP America, with her platinum blond hair, blue eyes and blinking eyelashes very quickly became accepted as a 'star' in her own rite. Now, often deconstructed and ridiculed, Barbie became a significant phenomenon of late 1950s mass culture. Designed to appeal to a vast range of individuals regardless of their social class or profession. She is the perfect stereotype for the conspicuous consumption of glamour, her commercial importance enhanced by the necessity of additional purchases.[71] To date, well over 650 million Barbie's have been marketed worldwide.

AMERICAN POPULUXE

The term "Populuxe" is a contraction of populism, popularity and luxury—the "e" being a linguistic affectation.[72] It was given its present definition by the historian and critic Thomas Hine in the 1980s to cover the range of consumer durables that appeared in America after the end of the Second World War. Two essential components in the spread of Populuxe were both offshoots of that war, the ability to mass produce and the commercial opportunities afforded by the media of mass communication. The production lines produced the product and the media, in particular the movies and television, delivered the market. Consumption patterns changed, the family ethic that had frowned on indebtedness was cast aside in favour of credit cards; Diner's Club made an appearance in 1950 followed by American Express in 1958 and Visa in 1959 (originally the Bank of Americard).[73]

Two individuals, one an immigrant and the other born to recent immigrants, responded to prevailing conditions and gave America what it wanted, one in the form of product, the other in the guise of entertainment. Both Walt Disney[74] and Raymond Loewy[75] reputably started out with around $50 in their pockets. Raymond Loewy arrived from France in 1919, an ambitious 26 year old, he had lost both parents in the influenza epidemic of 1918–1919. Over the next several decades he became the most well-known designer in America, providing many of the iconic symbols of the age, from the streamlined Greyhound buses and Coca-Cola bottles, to the ever present pack of Lucky Strike cigarettes and the logos for Shell, Nabisco and Exxon. He established new parameters for industrial production with his 1935 Coldspot Super Six refrigerator for Sears, revolutionised ideas about public transportation with the locomotives he designed for the Pennsylvania Railroad (1934 GG-1 locomotive, the 1936 K4S, and the 1938 S-1 and T-1); revitalised the auto design industry with the elegant 1953 Starliner model for Studebaker and the idiosyncratic and much underrated 1962 Avanti.

M.I.C.K.E.Y.M.O.U.S.E.

In the post-war era, new forms of entertainment were devised by Disney. Walt Disney's ancestors had emigrated from County Kilkenny in Ireland. His father Elias Disney had moved to the United States after failing at farming in Canada. Walter Elias Disney was born on 5 December 1901 in Chicago. In the Fall of 1918, Disney attempted to enlist for military service but he was rejected because he was under age. Undeterred, he joined the Red Cross and was sent overseas to France. On his return to America he spent time in Kansas (the family had moved there from Chicago) started a company called Laugh-O-Grams which produced *The Alice Comedies*, his first inroads into animation. These stories featured a real girl and her adventures in an animated world. The company went bankrupt and so ended this first foray into the world of animation. Disney packed his bags and headed to California to join his brother Roy O. When Disney arrived in Los Angeles he had an unfinished cartoon in his suitcase. Mickey Mouse was born in 1928 on that train journey to LA. The significance of these ventures into the unreal were not lost on the greatest cultural critic of the age, Walter Benjamin who argued in his often quoted essay of 1936, "The Works of Art in the Age of its Technological Reproducibility", that film and cartoons were a means for humanity to come to terms with the increasing dominance of technology on human culture.[76]

In the 1950s Disney had four of the top ten films released in the United States. *Sleeping Beauty*, 1959, was listed at number six, *Cinderella*, 1950, was reported to be number three in box office grosses, *Peter Pan*, 1953, came in at number two and the number one film of the 1950s was *Lady and the Tramp*, 1955. In the 1950s Disney productions won 23 Oscars and the Mickey Mouse Club aired five days a week. In 1955 Disneyland opens in Anaheim, California. Animated culture had arrived.

THE FIN IS IN!

After the war it was Harley J Earl, an automotive stylist, engineer and industrial designer and a Vice President of General Motors that took the next step. Harley Earl is regarded as the father of the "Fin". When talking about his Dream Cars in 1956 he had this to say. "Of all the useful and beautiful products designed by stylists, the best known and most appreciated is the American automobile, which ranks second only to fashion in the attention given to changing and improving appearance."[77] Earl was the first car design director to hire women as designers and stylists, variously reported in the press as "Designing Women" and "Damsels of Design". The 1953 Corvette was one of the most successful designs to come out of Harley Earl's GM design studios.[78]

PLASTIC FORM

In post-war North America, design became an established part of contemporary business practice. It had grown from strong, indigenous roots, and was relatively free from overt European theoretical purism. Plus the more aggressive business attitude tended to exploit available technologies. Some of that technology transformed our lives; television, transistors, automation, nuclear power and new plastic materials, all had a significant impact on the changing cultural context. The 1950s were without doubt the Age of Plastics.[79] PVC (Polyvinyl chloride) was one of the most widely used. It was possible to use PVC to create cheap artificial leathers and copies of other expensive materials. These new plastics could produce almost any desired shape and colour, it was to be another 20 years or so until they were allowed entry, in their own right, into domestic interiors.

NATIONAL SOAP

Some of the most adventurous and original designs in plastic were to be found in the array of radios that became available. The cost of radio ownership had decreased dramatically as the numbers produced increased to keep pace with market demand so that by the 1930s radios were on sale for under $10. What made the North American radio audience different from the emerging European audience was advertising. North American radio, was in the main, sponsored radio, with most shows being dependent on major advertisers, who in turn found in radio a unique method of spreading the word and creating market demand for the new products and services of the consumer society.[80] Radio soaps were the most profitable of all, aimed very specifically at the house-bound wife in the 25 to 34 year age category. Proctor and Gamble became the largest single sponsor of daytime radio programming.[81] But it was the productions of Hollywood that impacted both domestic and international culture. By

the end of the 1930s, colour was added to sound and more than 100 million tickets to the movies were sold each week in America. Then came television.

CHANNEL VISION

It took a little more than a decade for television to move from the field of science fiction to providing a field of dreams in the domestic environment. In the late 1920s, Richard Buckminster (Bucky) Fuller, philosopher/inventor/designer and lifelong conservationist developed the aluminum Dymaxion House in response to the inability of existing home building techniques to provide economic habitation. Exploiting all the knowledge of production line assembly that American industry had acquired, the house was designed for factory manufacture. It was to be produced in kit form, designed for ease of transportation and on-site assembly. Exploiting all the economies and quality controls of factory production would eliminate the handcraft tradition of construction with all its vagaries of imprudent assembly. Buckminster Fuller was fond of comparing the handcraft system of house building with the production line technique of car manufacture. (One of the many things that continue to amaze me is that in the twenty-first century we still build houses by hand.) The earliest known example of the Dymaxion House made an appearance in 1929 at Marshall Field's Chicago department store. It was a Marshall Field advertising executive who is reputed to have come up with the term "Dymaxion", using parts from three of Fuller's most often used words; dynamic, maximum, and tension. The house was climate controlled and had many of the component parts, such as wiring and plumbing, pre-installed. Plus it had one other innovation. In the "go-ahead-with-life" room there was a radio, a phonograph, some office machines and a 'television'.[83] Introduced just before the war, all television broadcasting was suspended during the war, broadcasting began again in 1945. Millions of homes were faced with the same design decision—where to place the TV. More than 60 years later and we are still unsure where to put the television in our home environment. In 1990, *The New York Times* was still debating the question in its design notebook section.[84] It is also fascinating to consider how we differentiate between the placing and use of a television screen and a computer screen.

In 1951, *Home* magazine instructed homeowners about proper "televiewing" distance and how to light a room. Motorola went so far as to advertise "a TV set for every decorating scheme, introducing 'furniture-styled' cabinets that would go with everything from Mexican Peasant to Swedish Modern. "Emboldened by swivel furniture, living rooms were rearranged so that every member of the family had a view. As befits a luxury item that purported to nurture family togetherness, the monumental box was nearly always positioned in the living room."[85] In 1946 there were around 7,000 television sets in American homes. By 1960, that number had increased to over 50 million. The 'Golden Age of Television' provided "a lush jungle of messages, lessons, cues, and instructions on living in the material world".[86] With an industrial base in tact, America produced half of all the manufactured products in the world including more than two-thirds of the worlds motor vehicles. By 1980 that percentage had dropped to less than one fifth. Cultures evolve.

CHARLES AND RAY EAMES

Charles Eames (1907–1978) and Ray Eames (1912–1988) gave shape to America's twentieth century. Their lives and work represented the nation's defining social movements: the West Coast's coming-of-age, the economy's shift from making goods to producing information, and the global expansion of American culture. The Eames' embraced the era's visionary concept of modern design as an agent of social change, elevating it to a national agenda. Their evolution from furniture designers to cultural ambassadors demonstrated their boundless talents and the overlap of their interests with those of their country. In a rare era of shared objectives, the Eames' partnered with the federal government and the country's top businesses to lead the charge to modernise post-war America.[87]

While still in high school, Charles began working in the local steel mill and became interested in engineering and architecture. In 1924 he received a scholarship to study architecture at Washington State University. In 1929, when he 22 years old, he visits Europe to see at first hand the Weissenhof Seidliung exhibition in Stuttgart, and he makes it his business to visit the architectural creations of Ludwig Mies van der Rohe, Le Corbusier and Walter Gropius. (These voyages of discovery remain essential for all interested in design.)

Charles returned to America early in 1930, just after the Stock Market crash and set up an architectural practise in St Louis. The depression was not the best of times to start a new business and the next few years were tough for Charles. In 1934 he decided to try his luck in Mexico and existed by doing some house painting and odd jobs. He returned to St Louis in 1935 and sets up his second design practise–this time things began to happen. In 1937 he met Eero Saarinen who had just returned to St Louis after working with Norman Bell Geddes. Charles also accepted a position as Head of Experimental Design at the Cranbrook Art Institute and began to collaborate with Saarinen on several architectural projects and on a joint entry for the 1940 Organic Design Competition sponsored by the Museum of Modern Art during the early days of the Second World War, before American involvement. Charles and Eero Saarinen won the competition for their chairs made with a seat of moulded plywood with a compound curve. The competition also resulted in a

Charles and Ray Eames. Plywood Chair, 1945–1946. Manufacturer: Evans Company. This version is a Vitra product.

new-found collaboration with Harry Bertoia[88] and, later, Ray Kaiser who became his second wife and lifelong design partner.[89] The Eames' later innovations in curved plywood exploited the new technologies of mass produced furniture designed to set new standards in domestic and office furniture.[90]

We are told that 'design' is problem solving–the design team of Charles and Ray Eames solve problems by making connections.[91] The design process sketch outlines the Eames' process of problem solving. The first area of concern identifies the interests and concerns of the design office. The second area represents the area of genuine interest to the client. The third indicates the concerns of society as a whole. Area four indicates an area of overlapping interests and concerns, and it is here that the designer can work with conviction and enthusiasm. As Eames clearly indicates, these areas are not static, they grow and develop as each one influences the other.

Charles and Ray Eames have a deservedly cult-like reputation among architects and designers; they were certainly all rounder's responsible for designing some of the most outstanding chairs of the twentieth century, along with ingenious children's toys, exhibitions (see Chapter Seven on their participation in the American Pavilion for the 1958 Moscow State Fair), and films. One of their most innovative films was produced in 1977, the original concept sketch was produced in

1968. *The Power of Ten*, is a nine minute stop-motion animation explanation of the continuity of matter, from individual atoms to the environs of the solar system.[92] They also produced iconic mid-twentieth century house designs in Los Angeles, including their own home in Pacific Palisades.

I can think of no finer example of the uniqueness of North American design in the late 1940s than Charles and Ray's own house at Pacific Palisades, constructed between 1948–1949. Designed for their own use, conforming to their own personal design philosophy, this house illustrates the balance between industrial production and individual humanism. Initially the house was to be constructed at a beach front location and the site was to be landscaped. Charles and Ray had second thoughts and re-located the house at the rear of the lot so as to conserve the beach environment.

With most of their money spent on buying the lot there was not very much left to pay for construction. The house is constructed largely from standard industrial components and structural members with the steel decking, steel walls, steel joists and steel framed windows bought straight out of a builder's catalogue. This is not a system, not industrially produced, but an assembly of freely available component parts–put together by design–creativity in action. The steel frame has opaque, translucent panels which defines the maximum volume without physically enclosing the space. It is of course reflective of the temperate climate in California, allowing for the blending of interior and exterior space. As a structure it remains, definitely, defiantly, West Coast American.

THE "RITE" WAY TO DESIGN

The home relates superbly to use and to its owners' personality and the local environment. Their way of seeing, thinking and designing was appropriate for both time and place. Gerrit Rietveld, Le Corbusier and Charles and Ray Eames all possessed the skills necessary to adjust their designs to accommodate the appropriate rites of domestic life. The Eames house became almost as famous as their chair designs and was featured in several glossy and trade publications. The house appeared in the September 1950 issue of *Architectural Forum*, the article was headed "Life in a Chinese Kite: Standard industrial products assembled in a spacious wonderland".[93]

Ray in particular was insistent that a sense of magic was essential to domestic interiors. Rather than design the magic in, Ray concentrates on designing a flexible space in which magic is likely to happen. In such an interior you bring your personal magic with you. After all, we construct our own icons and totems; these become the magical decorations that identify our space, not to be tidied up and put away when visitors come, but to be enjoyed; magical decoration made functional. Ray was well aware of and sensitive to the concept

that objects have an identity, they can trigger memory, have character, texture, patterns, can 'speak', they are decidedly not inanimate. An empathetic selection of objects, most found, some designed, allows for the construction of humanistic household alters, providing an appropriate personal place.[94]

With its use of ready made, industrially produced components the Eames house became a demonstration of an 'attitude' to design–a mind set that resulted in a very humane environment. If the work of Mies and Gropius belong to the technical sphere, then the Eames house provides the sphere of the cultural place–and most certainly an alterative to the entrenched North American attitude of 'organic' concrete architecture so beloved of Frank Lloyd Wright.[95] In the Eames house there is a commitment to technology, but that commitment is tempered by a personal morality, a sociological commitment to domestic ritual, from baking bread to decorating Christmas trees.

And for one final thought on the magic of personal space, on the essential nature of domestic rites and on a satisfactory design process, I quote from Antoine De Saint-Exupery, the famed French airman and writer, chiefly remembered today for his children's story *The Little Prince*, first published in 1943. Here is part of the conversation between the fox and the Little Prince:

> "One only understands the things that one domesticates", said the fox.
> "Men have no more time to understand anything. They buy things already made at the shops. But there is no shop anywhere where one can buy friendship, and so we have no friends any more. If you want a friend, domesticate me...."
> "What must I do, to domesticate you?" asked the little prince.
> "One must observe the proper rites", replied the fox.
> "What is a rite?" asked the little prince.
> "It is an act too often neglected", said the fox. "It means to establish ties."
> "They are what makes one day different from the other days, one hour from other hours."[96]

That is what successful and satisfactory design should be; establishing the appropriate social environment for the practice of the "proper rites" of our culture. Charles and Ray Eames understood that and, what is even more important, practised it.

CHAPTER SEVEN
STYLE AND ECONOMICS: POST-WAR RECONSTRUCTION, FRANCE, ITALY, AND GERMANY

Good design is as little design as possible.
Dieter Rams.

CULTURAL REVIVAL

Design played its part in redefining the restructured nations in the post-war period. While nations were keen to demonstrate the values and virtues of their particular brand of design, some aspects of culture remained unchanged, providing a mark of national distinction in the increasingly competitive global market. France had to resolve political disjunction and cultural scission as the wartime realities of occupation, collaboration, resistance and the stigma associated with Vichy France were resolved. There remained the threat of ongoing hostilities as France, guided by Charles de Gaulle, clashed with the Allies, in particular with President Roosevelt. America had its own idea on the political shape of liberated France, preferring an American military administration[1] as opposed to a reinstated 'liberated' French government, called for by General De Gaulle in his memorable Liberation Day address from the balcony of the Hotel de Ville, Paris, 25 August 1944.

> *Paris ! Paris outragé! Paris brisé! Paris martyrisé! mais Paris libéré ! libéré par lui-même, libéré par son peuple avec le concours des armées de la France, avec l'appui et le concours de la France tout entière, de la France qui se bat, de la seule France, de la vraie France, de la France éternelle. [2]*

Paris! Paris outraged! Paris broken! Paris martyred! But Paris liberated! released by itself, liberated by its people with the help of the armies of France, with support and help of all France, France which is fighting for France alone, the real France, eternal France.

This antagonism would sour post-war relationships. During these turbulent times the overriding reality was that if France was to avoid civil war and take its place in the post-war world then there would need to be an aggressive economic reconstruction; that reconstruction would be founded on traditional industries, such as fashion, where France had an unassailable reputation and on the emerging engineering technologies that had been developed during the war, now applied to the manufacture of aircraft and cars for the domestic and export market. Additionally, the post-war market was very different to that that had proceeded the war. Thinking of the young in the post-war era, Nicholas Hewitt observes:

> Their culture would soon be made more of images than ideas, of images conveyed through artistic media—music and film in particular—and readily diffused more and more by television. Their way of thinking would have to be structured according to a new grammar required by the new technologies.[3]

The Second World War began with the invasion of Poland on 17 September 1939. After an inglorious campaign, France formally surrendered to Germany on 25 June 1940. Jean-Paul Sartre, Coco Chanel, Dior, Yves Montand, Maurice Chevalier, Picasso, and Albert Camus were among those who lived and worked in Paris during the German Occupation. After the end of hostilities in 1945, it did not take long for Paris to re-establish itself as a leader in Haute Couture fashion.[4] Magazines such as *Marie-Claire* (founded in 1937) and *Elle* (1945) were just two of the near 200 fashion magazines that provided the very necessary supporting media infrastructure. In 1947, it was Christian Dior who re-established the invincibility of French fashion and French Haute Couture. Dior was born in 1905 in Granville, on the Normandy coast.[5] In the late 1920s, with family support, he ran an art gallery, Galerie Jacques Bonjean, featuring the works of Georges Braque, Pablo Picasso, and Jean Cocteau. The death of his mother and an elder brother brought an end to the gallery and to the family firm. The Design Museum web site summarises Dior's activities during the German occupation of Paris.

> When the Second World War began in 1939, Dior served as an officer for the year until France's surrender. He joined his father and a sister on a farm in Provence until he was offered a job in Paris by the couturier Lucien Lelong who was lobbying the Germans to revive the couture trade.[6] Dior spent the rest of the war dressing the wives of Nazi officers and French collaborators.[7]

Meanwhile, his sister Cathérine, who was a member of the French Resistance was incarcerated in the Revensbrück concentration camp. Fortunately she survived and was liberated by the Russians at war's end.

After the war, Dior was invited by Georges Vigouroux, a childhood friend from Granville to revive Philippe et Gaston, a struggling couture house owned by

Marcel Boussac, the "King of Cotton" who had a business empire of racing stables, newspapers and textile mills. This is where connections come into play. Dior's first encounter with the Boussac empire was through Henri Fayol, designated as Boussac's right-hand man. Henri's wife, Nadine was a champion of Dior. After a visit to the workshops of Philippe et Gaston, Dior rejected the idea of joining the house as their designer. Following a meeting with his favourite clairvoyant, Madame Delahaye in Paris (Dior was extremely superstitious) and much negotiating with Boussac, Dior changed his mind. The final negotiated contract gave him a salary, a third of all profits and most importantly, the new venture bore the name, Christian Dior Limited.[8] On 16 December 1946, Dior was able to open his couture house at 30 Avenue Montaigne, Paris. The assembled team consisted of Dior, Raymonde Zehnacker ("Madame Raymonde") from Lelong who was appointed head of the design studio; Madame Bricard from Molyneux, Marguerite Carré from Patou accompanied by 30 of her seamstresses; Jacques Rouët was installed by Boussac as business manager; the final team member was a 20 year old tailor, Pierre Cardin. Dior's first couture show was held at the height of the worst Winter in France since 1870 with France still suffering from wartime shortages. Benjamin Schwarz explains:

> On an icy mid-morning in February 1947, after seven seedy years of privation and shame, Paris and its most important industry came exuberantly back to life. In what remains the most famous fashion show in history, the new House of Dior presented its inaugural collection in its Louis XVI salon. In steady tempo, model after model swirled in dresses and suits in neutrals and luscious colours with tight bodices and wasp waists, their long, profligately full, elaborately pleated skirts scattering the audience's cigarette ashes as they flared open. Adopting the silhouette and requiring the intricate dressmaking art—and layers of underpinnings—of the *Belle Epoque*, the "New Look", as Carmel Snow, the editor of *Harper's Bazaar*, dubbed it on the spot, was in fact a defiant anachronism.[9]

Dior had christened his new collection the Corelle line because of the form of the skirts which seemed to blossom from stem like waists. It was Carmel Snow, who is reported to have said, "Your dresses have such a new look"–the market forget Corelle and fixed on the New Look. The New Look was not all that new. More a revival of the *Belle Époque* era of Dior's childhood and a reassertion of classic French couture skills.[10]

The House of Dior faced competition from The House of Chanel, founded in 1919. Chanel's celebrated two-and three-piece suit was introduced in 1923 and her signature cardigan jacket in 1925, creating a new uniform for the initiated. Her famed 'little black dress' made its appearance in 1926. In the Spring of 1934, the streets of Paris witnessed demonstrations by the extreme right wing *L'Action française*, and the left leaning *Le Front Populaire*. Gabrielle 'Coco' Chanel decided to leave the Faubourg and accompanied by the illustrator and designer Paul Iribe, moved into the Ritz Hotel. The couple planned to spend their Summers at a villa on the Riviera. During the Summer of 1935, just before a game of tennis, Iribe collapsed with a heart attack and died soon afterwards. At the age of 52 Coco was once more alone, she returned to Paris in the Autumn to immerse herself in work.

During the occupation of Paris, Coco began a relationship with Hans Gunther von Dincklage, a French speaking, half English, half German intelligence officer who was 13 years younger than the 56 year old Coco. Much earlier, in 1919, Chanel had introduced her then lover, the Grand Duke Dmitri Pavlovich Romanov to the Russian born French perfumer Ernest Beaux. Discussions pursued, the result being the development of Chanel No. 5, the most celebrated perfume in the world. When Galeries Lafayette decided to stock the fragrance Chanel had to expand production. She entered into an agreement with an established cosmetics company, Bourjois, co-owned by Pierre Wertheimer. The deal gave Wertheimer 70 per cent, Théophile Bader, the founder of Galeries Lafayette, received 20 per cent with Chanel owning the remaining ten per cent.[11]

During the occupation Chanel denounced the Wertheimer brothers to the Nazis. The brothers, anticipating such a move, had fled to America and had signed over their 70 per cent holding to a business associate, Félix Amiot. Amiot collaborated with the Germany military—he owned an airplane propeller company—returning Les Parfums Chanel to the Wertheimer brothers after the liberation of Paris. "Coco Chanel was arrested immediately after the liberation of France and charged with abetting the Germans but Churchill intervened on her behalf and she was released."[12] Chanel and von Dincklage left France for Switzerland where Coco lived in self-imposed exile in upper Lausanne on the shores of Lake Geneva until 1953, returning to Paris when she was 70 years old. There would appear to be very little information on just what Chanel did do during her eight years in exile. Returning to Paris, she took up residence once again at the Ritz and at table 11 at *Angélina*, 226, rue de Rivoli. Here the Gitanes smoking Coco surveyed her reflective world in the mirrored walls of the most celebrated *salon du thé* in Paris. She reopened her salon on the Rue Cambon and on 5 February 1954 Chanel showed her first collection for 15 years. Her foray into the post-war fashion scene was ridiculed in the French and British press but praised in America where Grace Kelly, Elizabeth Taylor and Rita Hayworth all wore Chanel.[13]

The Citroën DS19 made its debut at the 1955 Paris car show. Photo: Citroën Communication.

A long harangue with the Wertheimer brothers over the rights to manufacture her perfumes was finally resolved in 1947, giving Coco a two per cent royalty on gross sales worldwide, at that time this represented around one million dollars per year. Gabrielle 'Coco' Chanel died on 10 January 1971 in her apartment at the Ritz Hotel. She was 87 years old. She had just three outfits in her wardrobe and a fashion empire that brought in over $160 million a year. In many ways she was true to her epitaph, "I was a rebellious child, a rebellious lover, and a rebellious *couturière*—a real devil."[14]

FRENCH INDUSTRIAL DESIGN

The political and social culture of France in the 1950s remains under-researched. France had the post-occupation reality to adjust to; wars and revolutions associated with the decolonisation realties in Algeria and Indochina impacted the cultural context. In terms of design, the *SS Normandie*, (see Chapter Five) regarded as the outstanding example of twentieth century French design was commandeered by the US while in New York harbour in 1942; converted into a troopship, the *USS Lafayette*, caught fire, sank and was eventually scrapped in October 1946.

In the immediate post-war era in France, there were significant examples of the connection forged between technology, design excellence, and exports. French post-war advances in the area of industrial design are evident in the previously mentioned Caravelle, the mid-range jet aircraft, designed and assembled in Toulouse by Sud-Aviation, a nationalised aeronautics company. The most revolutionary aspect of the design being that it was the first commercial jet to have rear mounted engines, this aspect of aviation design is now commonplace. During the late 1950s the Caravelle became a very real symbol of French

design expertise, it entered service with Air France in 1959 and many of the 280 planes manufactured were sold abroad. The superiority of the French aeronautic industry is indicated in sales figures—through December 1965, the French Caravelle was in fourth place with 212 aircraft sold as opposed to 319 of the DC-8; 428 Boeing 727, and in top place, Boeing 707/720 with 598 aircraft sold. By the mid-1960s "the Caravelle accounted for 77 per cent of all jet traffic in Europe".[15] In 1962, BAC/ Aérospatiale Concorde entered into an agreement to construct the worlds first (and to-date only) supersonic domestic aircraft.[16] Only 16 were ever built, the reason for its demise still debated—what is beyond debate is that the majority of the design elements originated in France.[17]

Germany had the peoples car, France had the 'peasant's car', the rear engine powered Renault 4CV and the utilitarian Citroën 2CV which achieved 58 mpg/4.8 litres per 100 km. The 2CV had a production life of 42 years during which time nearly four million were produced. Citroën also produced one of the most elegant cars of the 1950s, the luxury DS19, designed by the Italian sculptor and industrial designer, Flaminio Bertoni in collaboration with the French aeronautical engineer André Lefèbvre. The DS19 was introduced into the market at the 1956 Paris Motor Show. Spoken phonetically in French, the initials "DS" mean "a goddess".[18] The 'goddess' displayed a very modernistic, verging on space age form; the wheels are partially hidden and the headlights, mirrors and indicators all integrated into the body shell. Roland Barthes, the revered semiotician, saw the DS19 as "a superlative object", an "exaltation of glass", whose elements are held together "by sole virtue of their wondrous shape". Barthes equated the technical magnificence of the DS19 with the magic inherent in the Gothic cathedrals.

I think that cars today are almost the exact equivalent of the great Gothic cathedrals: I mean the supreme creation of an era, conceived with passion by unknown artists, and consumed in image if not in usage by a whole population which appropriates them as a purely magical object: "The New Citroen" by Roland Barthes, an essay in *Mythologies*, 1957.[19]

It is difficult to think of any other single car model that introduced so many technological innovations. The most innovative characteristic being the *Citro-Matic*, the world's first central hydraulic system, referred to as an air-oil system providing power steering, brakes, clutch and transmission; an air-oil suspension system which allowed the body to float on compressed air, providing an automatic levelling system and a variable ground clearance, which allowed the driver to select one of five heights, two of which allowed for the changing of a wheel as the DS19 did not have a jack.[20] Additional innovative design features to this front wheel drive vehicle include an aluminum cylinder head; an engine that is mounted on rubber blocks to absorb vibration so that there is no metallic contact between the engine and body; Nylon engine fan, safety-no-spoke steering wheel, two radiators to provide independent heating to front and rear compartments, all topped off with a fibreglass roof panel.

PLANNED SALVATION
America did not succeed in imposing a military administration on post-war France; it did succeed in restructuring the education system in Italy, Cristina Allemann-Ghionda summarises;

> After the end of the Second World War, Italy was the first Axis country (followed by Germany and Japan), to undergo a process of "reeducation" by the allied troops, focussing initially on the education system. Under the direction of American scholars and school innovators, school syllabi and textbooks were rewritten in order to replace the ideological indoctrination exerted by the Fascist regime from 1923 to 1943 with democratic ideas.[21]

In Europe, the Marshall Plan, the American financial insurance against the spread of Communism, provided the necessary economic support for the rebuilding of the manufacturing base—in particular in those countries on the losing side, and therefore seen to be most at risk—notably Germany and Italy.[22] With small-time manufacturing such a dominant part of the Italian industrial scene—in addition to the country's art and design heritage—Italian industrialists who were empathetic to the role of design were placed in a preeminent position in post-war Europe.

Aided by the Marshall Plan, the immediate post-war Italian economy made an impressive recovery. In the decade between 1951 and 1962, British exports increased by a very modest 29 per cent, those of France increased by 86 per cent, West Germany's by 247 per cent and Italy's by a massive 259 per cent.[23] Italy was brand conscious, the post-war, post-Fascist Republic needed to identify, by design, the new social and cultural environment and showcase independent design as an expression of the new democratic Italy. Magazines such as *Domus*, *Abitare* and *Stile* were integral in the re-branding of Italian design.

ITALIAN STYLE
The American influenced Italian election of 1948 was in reality a propaganda battle at the start of the Cold War. Funded by the CIA the Christian Democracy ran a vitriolic campaign and defeated the parties of the left (Popular Democratic Front and the Italian Socialist Party), forming a government that excluded the Communists.[24] The election of 1948 resulted in, a move, to use the words of Jonathan Woodham, "towards a more style-conscious aesthetic, geared to the pockets of the more affluent sectors of society".[25]

Writing in June 1949, *The New York Times* correspondent, Michael L Hoffman observed:

> Italian industrialists have never shown much interest in the job of adapting their products to the mass market, with the result that the scale of their operations remains small and their costs high. The idea of persuading the low income consumer to feel the need for something he's never had, using advertising, and then give it to him at a price he can afford, could be Marshall Plan's biggest contribution to Italy—if it gets anywhere.[26]

During the 1950s and 1960s Italian design became "fashionable" obtaining a reputation for style and sophistication.[27] This was in part due to the work of Gio Ponti.[28] Born in 1891 in Milan, Ponti enrols for an architecture degree at the Milan Polytechnic, graduating in 1921. In 1923, instead of practising as an architect, he became Artistic Director of Richard Ginoria, a ceramics manufacturer for whom he wins the 'grand prix' at the 1925 *Exposition Internationale des Arts Décoratifs et Industriels Modernes* in Paris. Over the next decade he turns the company into a role model of industrial design excellence by decorating simple ceramic forms with elegant neoclassical motifs. In 1928 Ponti founds *Domus*, which he establishes as Europe's most influential architecture and design magazine. He retains control until 1941 when he switches to found another magazine *Stile*. In 1947 Ponti leaves *Stile* to resume the editorship of *Domus* in 1948.

DESIGN PROFILE: THE WASP

Early 1950s. Vespa assembly line in Pontedera factory. Courtesy, Archivio Piaggio "Antonella Bechi Piaggio".

THE BUZZ WORD

American influence, the Marshall Plan, politics, all come together with the Vespa. Italy had been rather late entering into the industrialised world and in the immediate post-war period this proved to be an advantage. The majority of Italian manufacturing companies (outside the giants of Fiat, Olivetti, etc.) were relatively small, possessing a craft mentality to production. They were highly flexible and therefore able to quickly respond to changing conditions. The Vespa scooter was the first self-consciously designed product conceived for both utilitarian function and visual appeal to roll of the rebuilt post-war Italian production lines. It was however, just one of 16 lightweight mopeds and motorcycles on show in Milan in 1946.[29] As Davide Mazzanti explains, Piaggio, the manufacture of the Vespa, was "a shipbuilding company that became a railway engineering company, banking on hopes of post-war revival and an odd-looking vehicle designed by the man who invented the helicopter".[30]

The name Vespa means "wasp" in Italian and refers to the original body shape of the well-known scooter line. In 1945, Enrico Piaggio, an aeronautical engineer by training, the son of Piaggio's founder Rinaldo Piaggio who established the company in Pontedera, Italy in 1884, was faced with the challenge of converting military production facilities into domestic use.[31] The Piaggio factory had produced the Pontedera fighter plane and had been decimated by allied bombing. Enrico decided to leave the aeronautical field in order to address Italy's urgent need for a modern and affordable mode of urban transportation for the masses. He began by exploring a scooter called the "Paperino" that had appeared on the streets of Turin in 1940 well before the end of the war. There was just too much market resistance—from traditional motorcyclists who looked on the scooter with macho disdain, to the general public who were not prepared to put their lives at risk on such a small vehicle. After the war things were different, the context had changed, now the general public were prepared to accept any form of available personal transportation, providing it was available at the right price, and providing it looked modern.

Enrico Piaggio engaged the services of the aeronautical engineer Corradino d'Ascanio (who had joined Piaggio in 1933 to work on the design of helicopters) to research the production of a two-wheeled vehicle that would be extremely simple and economical, both to manufacture and to use and would respond to the need for innovative forms of urban mass mobility.[32] Women were seen as part of the initial target market for this new unisex product. It was envisaged that the scooter would provide them with safe and economical urban transportation that was easy to mount while wearing a dress or skirt and did not require any special form of clothing. Stylistic acknowledgement was made to developments in America, in particular to the work of Harley Earl and other Detroit car stylists, who were producing the heavily chromed streamlined roadsters of the day.

The Vespa was constructed by a variety of appropriated techniques from the aeronautic and car industry. It had a forward single tube fork, a wheel suspension borrowed from aircraft production; the body was moulded and welded from sheet steel and was based on car production technology. The almost instant success of the Vespa was to a large extent due to the fact that it anticipated an evolution in values and modes of living, in particular the emerging women's movement. Its unisex design inspired confidence, and unlike the motorcycle with its more aggressive and macho image, it was discreet, light, comfortable, and because the engine was totally enclosed it was possible for drivers and passengers to wear stylish street clothes. At a time when dresses and skirts were de rigeur, and trousers were defiantly a socially unacceptable form of attire for Italian women, they could take advantage of the flat floorboard and maintain their grace and fashionable elegance.

How successful was the Vespa? It received very important visual endorsement when it was featured in William Wyler's, Oscar winning *Roman Holiday*, of 1953.[33] The two major American movie stars of the day, Audrey Hepburn and Gregory Peck, were featured riding through the streets of Rome on a Vespa. A decade or so later, the Vespa became a popular symbol of the youth culture in Great Britain, in particular for the Mod's of the 1960s—an intriguing study in semiotics and cultural transfer. (This was addressed in the last chapter). In 1956, its tenth anniversary, sales of the Vespa reached the million mark. Overall, the Vespa has sold over 16 million units to date.

A SEAT IS A SEAT IS A SEAT

During the 1960s, Italian designers separated themselves from the wave of functionalist theory and the sterility of the latter day Internationalists that beset much European 'good design'. Italian free thinkers such as Ettore Sottsass Jr and Joe Columbo embraced the new materials and new methods of production to produce moulded expressions of revitalised design mediations. Italian style was now the fashionable rage and, almost overnight, Italy replaced the sagging public image of Scandinavia as the provider of well designed products, notably in the shape of domestic and office furniture. One major difference however was that Italian design and manufacture was free of the socially reforming zeal of Scandinavian design. Italy provide furniture that appealed to the design conscious aficionado, rather than the socially aware user.

Before 'design', humankind sat, squat, worked and meditated oblivious to the need of any artificial means of pelvic support.[34] Design changed all that. Material innovation provided seats and psychological development provided the appropriate archetypal rationale. All seats must acknowledge the central

Peoples Park, Shanghai, 1980s.

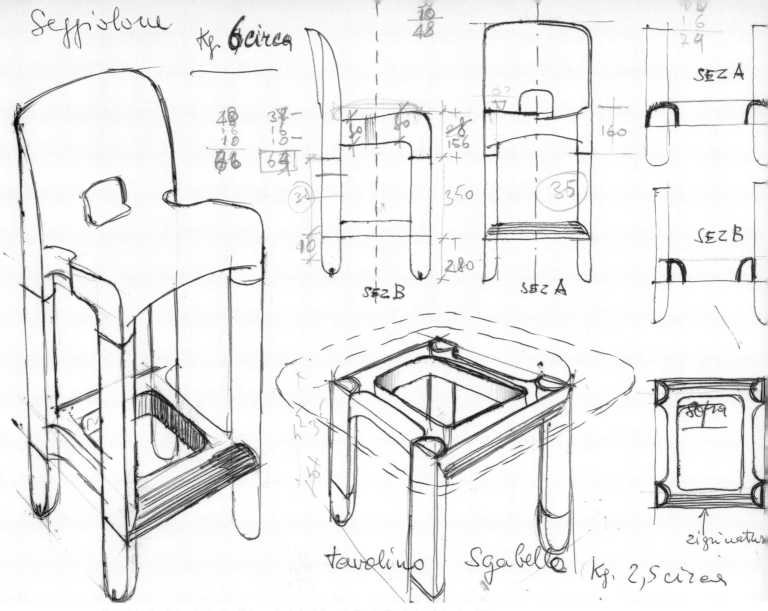

Sketch by Joe Colombo for the Universale chair. © Ignazia Favata Studio Joe Colombo, Milan.

truth of the biophysical nature of the human form, and all seats should serve that truth, providing ergonomically correct forms that are comfortable, that fit. Amazingly, many 'design' seats do not; they may respond to prevailing design aesthetics but often disregard anthropometrics and the domestic environment. Our domestic context has individual character and descriptive features, it is the focus for our personal psychological and social dramas. Design should assist in providing the location for our personal possessions, generating a place where we can become ourselves, in comfort.

Post-war Italy had the advantage of an existing strong craft tradition but was also committed to the use of new materials. The Italian designers of the late 1950s and early 1960s concentrated on developing a unique response to the changing times. Advances in material technology and the development of synthetic plastics and the associated production processes had a marked impact on the designed form. Carl Alviani notes on the Core77 website:

In many cases, plastic substitutes were superior to their predecessors in wood, metal, ceramic or cloth. Simply because there were so many of them, materials could be fine-tuned to fit the function of the product. In many more cases, though, it was a matter of efficiency: a moulded part uses only as much material as it needs, and no more.[35]

PVC (Polyvinyl chloride) made an appearance in 1933, polyethylene and nylon in 1939, and PET (Polyethylene terephthalate) in 1941. Currently, PET is the third most common synthetic polymer in global use, fundamental in the manufacture of beverage, food and other liquid containers. Injection moulding is a manufacturing process for producing high volume parts from both thermoplastic and thermosetting plastic materials. The material cost is small but major investment is required in the machinery of production and in the preparation of the essential moulds. Successful manufacturing is dependent upon the design of mouldable parts that are empathetic to the process.

Universale stacking chair. Joe Columbo. 1965. © Ignazia Favata Studio Joe Colombo, Milan.

The Swiss-based, Danish designer, Verner Panton became one of the foremost, adventurous designers in Europe, obtaining international respect for his meticulous design research. In the 1960s, he designed an inflatable chair for a hotel in Norway; a single piece, cantilevered plywood chair and the worlds first functional one-piece plastic chair. Although designed in 1959–1960, it required considered technical assistance from the German-based Vitra furniture manufacturing company, (the company was producing under license from Herman Miller chairs designed by Charles and Ray Eames, including the Lounge Chair and Ottoman from 1956 and the Aluminum Group from 1958). Panton's iconic stacking side chair in polyurethane plastic eventually reached production in 1968.

In 1965–1967, 'Joe' Cesare Columbo's[36] Universale stacking chair produced by Kartell in injection moulded polypropylene and rubber was initially intended to be a single unit chair cast in aluminum. The challenges were considerable and so, instead, it was produced in plastic sections, including interchangeable legs of two heights that can be unscrewed and replaced, plus a base unit that can further adjust the chairs height making it suitable to bar installations. The design of the individual component parts reflects Colombo's pursuit of purposeful production, it is designed to facilitate rapid manufacture and easy removal from the mould. Born in Milan in 1930, Joe Colombo was originally a fine artist before taking over his fathers electrical equipment company in 1959 and opening his own design studio in Milan in 1962. Colombo was a design prophet who saw his role as the "creator of the environment of the future". He embraced change and the role that new production technologies could play in the design process. In his tragically short life his declared ambition was to create inexpensive, well designed products, that took full advantage of all the latest production processes.

THE NEW DOMESTIC LANDSCAPE

Post-war design advances in Italy were summarised in a memorable exhibition curated by Emilo Ambasz, entitled, Italy: The New Domestic Landscape, staged at the Museum of Modern Art in New York from 26 May to 11 September 1972.[37] The show explored the complexity of the design culture in Italy in the early 1970s.

> To organise the exhibit, Ambasz first distinguished between Objects and Environments, and divided the latter into three groups: design as postulation, design as commentary, and counterdesign as postulation. In a cunning reversal, the Objects section was installed in the comparatively natural environment of MoMA's sculpture garden, while the Environments were placed within the more conventional space of the galleries. It was this sequence of environments that we found particularly revealing within the context of the era's experimental architecture.[38]

Radical groups such as Superstudio were able to voice their views alongside the recognised design virtuosos such as Gae Aulenti, Ettore Sottsass, Jr and Joe Colombo. Colombo enthusiastically endorsed the use of modern technology and the recently available synthetic materials of the era. Characteristically these were interpreted in a very individual and innovative fashion. The vast majority of us live in boxes of various sizes and shapes. Forget the restriction of wall irregularities, concentrate on the most practical and innovative use of the space. For the MOMA show, Joe Colombo designed a pioneering, multifunctional, space-saving, "Total Furnishing Unit". This infinity adjustable module incorporates 'blocks' for kitchen, wardrobe, bathroom, and sleeping accommodation, all of which combined the use of about 28 square metres. This was to be his posthumous exploration of portability and efficiency in a new domestic landscape. Joe Colombo died in 1971, before the MOMA show opened.

DESIGN PROFILE: THE COLOUR OF YOUR MONEY

Newborn Baby Girl, Benetton, September, 1991. The campaign was "an attempt on the part of the company to feature images from the real world which have some social and universal relevance, in order to break through the barrier of indifference which often surrounds these isues.[43]

The Italian fashion industry is built on a rich cultural heritage combined with a distinctive aesthetic and an awareness of the value of promotion. And none understand that better than Benetton. According to *Business Week* we each receive over 3,000 commercial messages per day, many of which make claims to enhance our sense of well-being "But as emotional beings we engage in desire and fantasy; we have psychological needs for love and acceptance... and it is these forces that makes advertising appeal to us."[39] For advertisers, getting noticed becomes paramount, it is after all what they pay for. Some advertising campaigns have succeeded in being both outstanding from creative and conceptual points of view and censorious from a more sociological view-point.

In the world of fashion, Manufacturers and retailers use advertising to appeal to far more than peoples functional need for clothes. In the 1950s the Benetton family business was in a very sorry state.[40] The founding father had died, leaving a very young son, Luciano, and daughter, Giuliani to carry on. By 1963 the family firm had recuperated and established a factory for the production of knitted sweaters in a small village near Treviso in northern Italy. The company is now international in scope with a franchised network of more than 5,000 stores around the world. Benetton subcontracts over 90 per cent of its production to over 200 small producers, this gives the company a great deal of flexibility in responding to market dictates.[41] Benetton dedicate about four per cent of their annual profits to enhance the brand identity—but this is exceeded by the amount of 'free' publicity in magazines, television and other media generated by controversial campaigns.

In 1982, the company appointed the photographer Oliviero Toscani to mastermind their image. In 1984 the company began to advertise its range of fairly conservative products beyond Italy and France. Their first global campaign, which ran in 14 countries started to focus on multi-racial groups of young people. From the very beginning this approach was controversial, and nowhere more so than in South Africa where the campaign was promptly banned. Over the next decade or so Toscani, steered campaigns through a series of similar, universal themes, which he considered to be "signs of the times".

A photograph has the ability to arouse interest, to shock, to gain attention in the way that text cannot. The target audience for Benetton is upwardly mobile, young women in the 14 to 24 age bracket. A group seen collectively as being socially conscious consumers. The multi-cultural harmony campaign used staged photographs—the "Reality" campaign of 1991/1992 made use of previously published news photographs including the one that drew most attention—the photograph of AIDS victim David Kirby on his death bed in May 1990 (the advertisement ran in 1992). The photograph was taken by a young Ohio University student, Therese Frare, as part of a photographic documentary on the lives of clients and caregivers in a hospice at Ohio State University for people with AIDS. The photograph was published in *Life* magazine in November 1990. It won the Budapest Award and claimed second place in the prestigious World Press photo contest in 1991. This "fame" brought it to the attention of executives at Benetton. Therese Frare had been shooting in the Pater Noster hospice in Columbus, Ohio where Kirby was spending his last weeks of life. Kirby's parents gave permission to Benetton to use the image believing that it would raise local AIDS awareness—many local residents had panicked at the thought of David returning home to die in their midst. Benetton donated $50,000 to the Pater Noster hospice. In 2003, the photograph was included in *Life* magazine's "100 Photos that Changed the World."[42] Another controversial image from 1991 showed a new born baby girl, Giusy, covered in vernix with her uncut umbilical cord clearly on view it "became one of the most censured visuals in the history of Benetton ads". Appearing as part of the Reality campaign, this image was banned in several counties including America and Canada. Universally it created unprecedented argument, with some finding the image obscene. At the same time, however, the image was exhibited in a Flemish museum as part of a show celebrating motherhood. Obscenity, it would appear, is in the mind of the beholder.[44]

To quote Toscani "We don't imagine that we are able to resolve human problems, but nor do we want to pretend that they don't exist. We believe advertising can be used to say something besides selling a product—something more useful." A noble statement—but of course the campaign is very consciously constructed, and aimed at their prime target market—ever wonder why there are seldom any clothes in these Benetton campaigns? These series of advertisements made use of documentary photographs (sometimes doctored) placed within an ambiguous context which, or so it is suggested, increase the audience's deeper engagement with the communication process. Benetton have steered their corporate campaigns back to the familiar world of "ambiguous context" with their series of death row portraits.[45] In 2000, Benetton's Sentenced to Death initiative about inmates photographed on death row proved to be the most controversial ever, resulting in the resignation of Toscani. However, the 'story' was extensively covered by the world's media and increased domestic debate on the ethics of capital punishment.

In the early 1990s Toscani co-founded the magazine *Colors* (also owned by Benetton) with American graphic designer Tibor Kalman. The editorial content and structure was again supportive of socially conscious consumers. *Colors*, which is published in seven editions and eight languages, is essentially a compendium of hardcore, in-your-face reality with no advertising and little if any commentary—just the stark reality of a world many of us do not want to acknowledge, let alone live in—or design for.[46]

The dancer Elisbeth Boeklen, and a Mercedes-Benz 8/38 hp, Stuttgart type 200 roadster, in front of a house by Le Corbusier, reinforced concrete, steel frame and piloti. Weissenhofsiedlung, Stuttgart, 1927. Courtesy Daimler AG.

GERMAN DESIGN HERITAGE

Post-war design in Germany exemplifies the connections between design, culture, politics and national identity.[47] Coal was an essential source for the generation of power needed to rebuild the European industrial base. The German Ruhr was a prolific source of coal. There was much political manoeuvrings to achieve a viable solution that benefited all European nations; understandably, France was sensitive to the provision of any advantage to Germany.[48] Another German resource to be 'shared' by the victors was German technical, industrial, and scientific information—and the people who were familiar with the application of that information.[49]

The November 1989 fall of the Berlin Wall and subsequent political events have allowed for a more informed assessment of post-war design in Germany. There has been, quite understandably, an emphasis on the rational design process and the accompanying machine aesthetic which developed in the inter-war period in Germany, most notably at the Bauhaus. This is often followed by the assertion that with the rise of Fascism in Italy and the emergence of the Nazi regime in Germany, following Adolf Hitler's claim to the Chancellorship in 1933, an end came to German support for creative experimentation, replaced by an avowedly anti-modernist aesthetic. While there is a degree of validity in this observation it does however neglect the extremely strong rational engineering facet in German culture and the accompanying expertise in mass production, and mass consumption of everyday, domestic objects.[50] In the inter-war period, there was the outstanding example set by the *Weissenhofsiedlung* experimental housing exhibition of 1927, held just outside Stuttgart. This "ideal suburb" included 33 house and 63 apartments designed by 17 international architects for the organising Deutsche Werkbund.[51]

Germany had its own manufactured icons of modernity, including the streamlined elegance of the Flying Hamburg diesel-electric train which entered service in 1933 operating between Berlin and Hamburg, with a top speed of 165 km/h it was the fastest scheduled passenger train in the world. The massive autobahn system of roads conceived during the days of the Weimar Republic, and inaugurated in 1931 when the first stretch between Cologne and Bonn was opened by Konrad Adenauer on 6 August—this became the model for many later highway systems. The Graf Zeppelin LZ127 airship was the marvel of the age and circumnavigated the globe in 1929. It inaugurated transatlantic passenger service and was subsequently joined by the Hindenburg LZ129. From Germany they made regularly scheduled flights to both Brazil and the United States, reducing considerably the time of trans-Atlantic travel. The Hindenburg died in flames at Lakehurst, New Jersey on 6 May 1937, bringing to an end this initial stage of mass air transportation.[52]

Further peaceful developments were ended by the start of the Second World War in 1939 which witnessed the transfer of technology, engineering and design expertise to the manufacture of the arms and armaments of mass destruction. As a measure of how fast that development was, when the war began in 1939, 75 mm cannon were still horse-drawn.[53] Just six years later when the war ended, there were five German manufactures of rocket-style jet engines.[54]

Most design histories seem to side-step design related developments made during wartime and the impact that those have upon the succeeding cultural context. Towards the end of the Second World War, rockets entered into the lives and consciousness of the general public. The notorious V-2 rocket, (*Vergeltungswaffen Zwei*), in reality a long-range ballistic missile,[55] was manufactured using slave labour at the Mittelwerk factory at Thuringia.[56] The rocket had its test flight in Peenemünde on 3 October 1942. On 8 September 1944 the offensive use of the V-2 began, over 3,000 rockets were launched against Britain and Belgium during "Operation Penguin". The lead scientist was Werner von Braun, whose thesis, *Construction, Theoretical, and Experimental Solution to the Problem of the Liquid Propellant Rocket* (dated 16 April 1934), was kept classified by the German authorities until 1960.

As the war ended, von Braun, a commissioned SS (*Schutzstaffel*) officer, accompanied by 126 of the principal designers and engineers associated with the V-2 along with 300 trainloads of V-2s and parts were transferred to the United States. (In his book *My Father's Son*, Canadian author Farley Mowat, then a member of the Canadian Army, claims to have obtained a V-2 rocket in 1945 and shipped it back to Canada, where it is reported to have been on display in the 1947 Canadian National Exhibition in Toronto).[57] Other researchers from the V-2 programme ended up in Russia. The two super powers gained access to the scientists, engineers and designs associated with the V-2 through Operation Paperclip (United States) and Operation Osoaviakhim (USSR). The V-2 programme was the progenitor of the United States and Soviet Union space programmes.

It was Wernher von Braun's team that launched the V-2 in New Mexico and developed the rocket to carry the first US satellite into space.[58]

POST-WAR DESIGN CULTURE IN GERMANY —THE ECONOMIC MIRACLE

The destruction of the greater part of Germany's industrial base in the war made the path clear for a radical reassessment after the war. The period between 1946 and 1964 is often referred to as the time of the economic miracle. During this period Germany's gross national product rose at a spectacular rate. Between 1949 and 1950, West German foreign trade doubled, and between 1954 and 1964 it tripled. This surge in foreign trade was accompanied by a parallel increase in domestic consumer demand (at least in West Germany) and the development of a new industrial base to produce the objects for both foreign and domestic markets.[59]

THE BUG

After the war, some wartime symbols remained. Ferdinand Porsche was born in 1875 in the German-speaking part of Bohemia in the Austro-Hungarian Empire.[60] He started his automotive career designing electric cars in Vienna. He created a sensation, still by the way waiting to be repeated, at the Paris Universal Exposition of 1900 when he exhibited a car equipped with electric motors installed in the hubs of the wheels thus providing amazing flexibility in navigating and parking on urban streets. Porsche also took advantage of the pioneering work on streamlining and aerodynamics undertaken by the Hungarian Paul Jaray, begun in 1919 and patented in 1927.[61] By 1930 he had established his own design consultancy and began to do concept development work on a *Volksauto*, a "peoples car". Various associations, mostly with manufactures of motor bikes, came to nothing. He began producing prototypes of the *Volksauto* in the 1930s including the experimental V3 that was put through a 30,000 kilometre trial in October of 1936.[62]

In 1934 he decided to take his plans to the new authorities in Berlin. The plans came to the attention of the new Chancellor, Adolf Hitler who, at the 1937 Berlin Motor Exhibition, announced his support for the production of a state-sponsored peoples car. The Beetle was seen as a possible solution to Hitler's declared aim to produce a small, inexpensive vehicle that was suitable for the new autobahns. In 1936 three prototypes were produced, and it became very obvious that this was indeed a revolutionary vehicle. The four cylinder, air-cooled engine was situated in the rear of the car. Each of the four wheels had independent suspension. Between 1936 and 1938, 60 preliminary vehicles were built in a factory in Stuttgart. During the war various versions were produced including the amphibian Schwimmwagen, and a utilitarian military version, the *Kübelwagen*. The manufacturing plant at Wolfsburg was heavily damaged during the war, but it was about four kilometres inside the British Occupation Zone. The production line started up again in 1945. This time, thanks to the Marshall Plan, the mass production methods at the Wolfsburg plant were of American origin. The 1,000th Volkswagen came off the production line in March, 1946. By 1958, Volkswagen were producing 2.5 million cars and selling 100,000 of them in the US. By 1972, the Volkswagen passed the record set by Henry Ford's "Model T", becoming the world's most popular car.[63]

There was a post-war fascination in Germany for all things American. Henry Ford's autobiography sold more than 200,000 copies. In the 1950s American magazines such as *Business Week* and *Time* were avidly sought on the black market. Furthermore, thanks mostly to the Marshall Plan which provided a great deal of start up finance, over 500 significant German companies were controlled by American capital. American films promoted the American way of life—consume and live! Coca-Cola, which had been produced in the interwar period in Germany was re-launched in 1949. By the mid-1950s there were 96 bottling plants in Germany. In the immediate pre-war era Germany had not taken to streamlining, considering the philosophy of streamlining products in the name of increased sales as being dishonest and irresponsible. After the war they were not quite so sure. The 1952 translation of Raymond Loewy's *Never Leave Well Enough Alone* was a best-seller among the design fraternity.

POST-BAUHAUS DOGMA

The post-war design culture in Germany was undeniably influenced by attitudes and concepts developed during the halcyon days of the Bauhaus.[64] At the very start of this book I placed emphasis on choice, on how what we choose to believe has an influence on how we see past, present and future. Our view of the Bauhaus illustrates changing beliefs. Design museums, publications, website's, not to mention numerous commercial publications, often talk about Bauhaus style. It was never the intention of its founder, Walter Gropius, to develop a style, just thinking designers. Students were subjected to a diverse range of thoughts on process, theory and practice from a collection of the most avant-garde artists of the interwar period—not a designer on staff. The teachers included many of the pioneers of the modern movement, Josef Albers, Marianne Brandt, Wassily Kandinsky, Johannes Itten, Paul Klee, László Moholy-Nagy, Ludwig Mies van der Rohe, and Oskar Schlemmer. The Bauhaus was small and ran for only 14 years, from 1919 to 1933, yet its educational imprint remains on just about every design programme on earth.

Germany had its own domestic design heroes. Wilhelm Wagenfeld, one of the stars of the rationalised Bauhaus, was regarded as the paragon of design virtue. His collection of essays on design *Wesen und Gestalt: Der Dinge um uns (Essence and Form: The things around us)* was published in Potsdam in 1948, alas now out of print, it was hailed as the way forward. Let us not forget that Germany was divided between East and West and during the period of the Cold War design was used to promote a strong positive image of West Germany where it was used, along with the consumer ethic, as a measure of the divide between the two nations. Wagenfeld was one of the few designers who regularly moved between the two Germany's, at least until the construction of the Berlin Wall in 1961. Paul Betts notes that:

the post-war period gave rise to a unique West German 'design culture' comprising a vast network of diverse interests, including the state and industry, architects and designers, consumer groups and museums, and educators and women's organisations. What united them all was the identification of design as a vital means of domestic recovery, cultural reform, and even moral regeneration.[65]

GOOD DESIGN IS...

Inspired by post-Bauhaus dogma, "functionalist" designers in Germany continued the belief that "design is good for you", producing objects for some mythical, ideal society. The rational purity of Braun, under the directorship of the last of the Bauhaus disciples, Dieter Rams, personified this approach.[66] Rams designed or oversaw the design of over 500 products from audio equipment and kitchen appliances to the Oral-B toothbrush. Over the years he has amassed an impressive number of awards and accolades. The Royal College of Art in London appointed him a "Royal Designer for Industry", and awarded him an honorary doctorate; the Industrial Designer Society of America presented him with a "World Design Medal"; and his work has found its way into the permanent collections of design museums including the MoMA in New York, the V&A in London and the Stedelijk Museum in Amsterdam.

Born in 1932 in Wiesbaden, Germany, Dieter Rams learned about the principles of rational design in his grandfather's carpentry workshop. He saw how the skilful use of appropriate materials and utilitarian form could produce simple but functional design. These childhood influences created an appreciation for simple forms bereft of all unnecessary clutter. They were oft expounded by him in his "less is better" mantra which was the hallmark of his design philosophy. In 1953 he graduated from the architecture/interior design programme at *Werkkunstschule* in Wiesbaden. After college Rams worked first as an architect, and it was as an architect that he got a job at Braun in 1955 which led to him being appointed Design Director in 1962, a position he maintained until 1995.

Braun was founded in 1921 by Max Braun, the inventor of a revolutionary electrical shaving system, as an electrical goods company. The business expanded in the 1930s and produced a range of radio components. After the war, it resumed production and added kitchen mixers to the product range. The Marshal Plan had provided the financial underpinning for the revival of Germany's electronics industry, but it was now facing intense competition from Japan where companies such as Sony, exploiting the newly acquired transistor technology, were focussing on the production of cheap,

personal radios and other electronic goods. Germany could not compete on price. Design gave German products the competitive edge.

When Max died in 1951 the company was headed by his two sons who obtained the assistance of Dieter Rams in establishing a new, more "modern" attitude and outlook for their products. Collectively, Braun products are seen as optimising a concern for function while emphasising form and style as symbolic factors in the design. While other nations sought identification through architecture and furniture, Germany favoured the technology of home and office. It was Rams who domesticated modern electrical goods, giving them a readable identifiable form that was indicative of the electronic age, German rational purity with a Japanese accent.

The first real success for Rams came with the 1956 design of the Phonosuper SK4 radio and record player (designed in cooperation with Hans Gugelot of the Ulm Institute) which Rams viewed not so much as a radio but as a mobile sound machine. There were some technical innovations such as detaching the loudspeakers from the body so as to reduce interference, but the real innovation was in the language of design. Rams spoke to the new generation of post-war baby boomers who's musical taste was more likely to favour modern jazz than classical swing. The SK4's innovative plexiglass lid allowed visual access—there is something visually fascinating about a continuously circulating object—and earned the unit its nickname of "Snow White's Coffin". All the surface complexities were controlled by an invisible grid, with controls and function clearly viable. At a time when most radios were encased in wooden cabinets this was a risky path—however, a sufficient percentage of the market was supportive of the clean, crisp look of Braun products to assure market growth and add to the prosperity of Braun which became respected for its design as well as its technical performance.

This same rigid approach was applied to kitchen appliances such as juicers. Rams often described his kitchen appliances as being like "a good English butler"—there when you needed him and melting into the background when you did not. This revised, post-Bauhaus rational aesthetic was to dominate the "good design" idiom of the late 1950s and extended into the 1960s. It provided an acceptable model for nations such as Germany and Japan for whom increased productivity was to be so essential in the new international markets of the age.

KITCHEN DEBATE

This was the era when design acquired political overtones and was used in the ongoing Cold War, forever immortalised in the so-called "kitchen debate" between Soviet Premier Nikita Khrushchev and US

Vice President Richard M Nixon at the 24 July opening of the American pavilion at the 1959 Moscow Fair in Sokolniki Park. The "debate" ranged over the relative values of washing machines, the role of women and the cost of housing. The debate resolved nothing, but it did polarise attitudes, and it did motivate close to three million Soviet citizens to visit the American pavilion and see for themselves the range of consumer durables on display alongside frozen foods and colour television sets.[67] Some fortunate visitors were given plastic Tupperware bowls as gifts. Inside, visitors could see a multi-screen presentation designed by Charles and Ray Eames, entitled *Glimpses of the USA*, which projected over 2,200 images onto seven 20 by 30 foot screens which were hung from the ceiling of Buckminster Fuller's 200 foot Kaiser aluminum dome with its gold anodised surface. Within two years the difference in values and attitudes were given concrete form when, on 13 August 1961, the wall was constructed to divide the German Democratic Republic from the Federal Republic of Germany.[68] For the next 30 years 'design' played a significant part in establishing the 'brand' of West Germany.

By the 1960s, "Good German Design" even made it into the realm of popular culture. "In 1967 the artist Richard Hamilton created a print called *Toaster* that was based on his reverence for Dieter Rams' designs for Braun. This started a fruitful relationship that culminated in an exhibition of Dieter Rams' work, together with Hamilton's, at the International Design Centre in Berlin in 1980. Hamilton opened the exhibition and wrote: "My admiration for the work of Dieter Rams is intense and I have, for many years, been uniquely attracted towards his design sensibility; so much so that his consumer products have come to occupy a place in my heart and my consciousness that the Mont Saint-Victoire did in Cezanne's."[69] In 2008, the print was re-issued in a *Toaster Deluxe* series.

Over the years, Dieter Rams has shown the strength of his convictions, stressing integrity, rejecting superficial styling, believing in the long-term use of products and rejecting all aspects of planned obsolescence and the throw-away society. He and his team had a clearly defined design process that resulted in a rational purity and functionality in the designs.[70]

He prefers long-term relationships with his products and clients, refining over time, adjusting to fit the changing cultural context.

Design isn't marketing, but more and more companies are treating it like that... there should be an absolute commitment to design and technology, and they have to go together. When I started at Braun there were difficulties between the designers and engineers, as there are in many companies, but I noticed that the engineers liked to have a brandy, so I'd buy a bottle of good cognac to share with them. To be a good designer, you have to be half-psychologist.[71]

Comparisons have been made between the design philosophy that powered Braun to greatness and the more recent phenomenon of Apple under the design leadership of Jonathan Ive. Ive is Senior Vice President of Industrial Design at Apple and the principal designer of the iMac, iPod, iPad and the iPhone. Both product ranges made use of available technological advances, both used design to gain a competitive edge in the marketplace. A mark of differentiation may be that while Dieter Rams SK4 radio and record player may still be revered and used, an iPod becomes technologically obsolete and discarded to join the mountain of cell phones and related devices. Difficult to envisage a sustainable iPod or cell phone.

One variant in determining success is sales. Alice Rawsthorn explains in an article in *The New York Times*; none of the exquisitely logical products developed by Dieter Rams and the rest of Braun's design team were the bestsellers in their sectors. Yet the purity and intelligence of their design made Braun a byword for quality and touched many more people than those who actually bought its radios and shavers.[72] Not so with Apple. Figures are hard to substantiate, a general consensus is that by the Spring, 2011, Apple had sold 8.25 million units of its iPad and 304 million iPods.

Speaking in 2007, Rams was expressed concern over the nature of design. "Now, more than ever, when industrial design as a discipline seems to have lost touch with a clarity of purpose and focus, it is time to perhaps get back to a core of principles and strip away the superfluous once again."[73] Concerned by the visual cacophony on display in all major retail outlets and celebrated on the pages of the Design press, Rams re-thought and codified his approach to design which he summarised as "Ten Commandments on Design".[74]

DESIGN PROFILE:
TEN COMMANDMENTS ON DESIGN—DIETER RAMS

GOOD DESIGN IS INNOVATIVE
It does not copy existing product forms, nor does it produce any kind of novelty just for the sake of it. The essence of innovation must be clearly seen in all of a product's functions. Current technological development keeps offering new chances for innovative solutions.

GOOD DESIGN MAKES A PRODUCT USEFUL
The product is bought or used in order to be used. It must serve a defined purpose—in both primary and additional functions. The most important task of design is to optimise the utility of a product's usability.

GOOD DESIGN IS AESTHETIC
The aesthetic quality of a product is integral to its usefulness because products we use every day affect our well-being. But only well-executed objects can be beautiful.

GOOD DESIGN HELPS US TO UNDERSTAND A PRODUCT
It clarifies the product's structure. Better still, it can make the product talk. At best, it is self-explanatory.

GOOD DESIGN IS UNOBTRUSIVE
Products fulfilling a purpose are like tools. They are neither decorative objects nor works of art. Their design should therefore be both neutral and restrained, to leave room for the user's self-expression.

GOOD DESIGN IS HONEST
It does not make a product more innovative, powerful or valuable than it normally is. It does not attempt to manipulate the consumer with promises that cannot be kept.

GOOD DESIGN HAS LONGEVITY
It does not follow trends that become outdated after a short time. Well designed products differ significantly from short-lived trivial products in today's throw-away society.

GOOD DESIGN IS CONSEQUENT TO THE LAST DETAIL
Nothing must be arbitrary. Thoroughness and accuracy in the design process shows respect toward the user.

GOOD DESIGN IS CONCERNED WITH THE ENVIRONMENT
Design must make contributions toward a stable environment and sensible raw material situation. This does not only include actual pollution, but also visual pollution and destruction of our environment.

GOOD DESIGN IS AS LITTLE DESIGN AS POSSIBLE
Less is better—because it concentrates on the essential aspects and the products are not burdened with non-essentials. Back to purity, back to simplicity!

CHAPTER EIGHT
DESIGN, SOCIAL PROTEST AND POPULAR CULTURE

All we are saying, is Give Peace a Chance.[1]
John Lennon.

PEACE FOR OUR TIME[2]

War and cultural revolution were characteristics of the 1960s.[3] It was also the decade when the disfranchised found their voice. It was a time of social experimentation, of civil rights, of free love, flower power, and pop music. Permissiveness and liberalisation changed attitudes to censorship, sex and contraception. Design became a commodity. The existing cultural format was revitalised by the young, but it was not purely hedonistic. Both in Europe and North America the young found their political voice.

One of the most widely known symbols in the world is the Nuclear Disarmament logo which is now used universally as a symbol of Peace. In 1957 the ruling Labour government ceased to advocate unilateral disarmament for Britain. On 2 November 1957, "Britain and the Nuclear Bombs", by JB Priestley was published in the *New Statesman*. The article generated numerous letters of support from British intelligentsia resulting in the formation of the Campaign for Nuclear Disarmament (CND) which held its inaugural public meeting on 17 February 1958. Several independent groups came into being around this time including the Direct Action Committee against nuclear war (DAC), formed to protest British H-Bomb tests on Christmas Island in the Indian Ocean between 15 May and 19 June, 1957–an incident that is not mentioned on the Islands current website.

The original Peace symbol was for the DAC.[4] It was designed in 1958 by Gerald Holtom, a graduate of the Royal College of Arts.[5] He showed his preliminary sketches to a small group of people in the *Peace News* office in North London. The DAC were planning the first major anti-nuclear march from London to Aldermaston during the 1958 Easter weekend; that is where the symbol made its public debut.[6] In subsequent years the route of the march was reversed,

The first public appearance of the symbol on the first march from London to Aldermaston, 1958.

Banner used on the annual march from London to Aldermaston, 1958. 21 x 26 cm, cloth. Painted by Kenneth Hockney (the father of David). Courtesy Estate of Roger Rawlinson & the Peace Museum, Bradford, UK.

the organisers realised that there wasn't much point in ending up in Aldermaston with almost no one around except the marchers, so they changed the direction to end in a rally at Trafalgar Square. In later years the final venue was moved to Hyde Park to accommodate the increased number of marchers. The media coverage of the march gave cultural prominence to the Peace symbol and it was adopted by the DAC and used in all their subsequent literature and publicity.

The power of this symbol is emphasised by the fact that various far right and fundamentalist groups have considered banning it, regarding it as having satanic associations. Ignorance rules. For the Aldermaston march, about 500 signs were produced, half were black on white and half white on green. The displayed sign was designed to change, mirroring the church's liturgical colour change, "from Winter to Spring, from Death to Life". Black and white would be displayed on Good Friday and Saturday, green and white on Easter Sunday and Monday.[7]

What does it mean? What were the influences behind the design of one of the worlds most recognised symbols? There is an unfounded urban myth that links the design to weapon silos–there is no truth in this. Gerald Holtom, a conscientious objector, had worked on a farm in Norfolk during the Second World War; he explained that the symbol incorporated the semaphore letters N(uclear) and D(isarmament.) When these two are joined together they create the line down and through the circle and the two arms pointing downwards on either side complete the logo. Although designed for the CND movement the symbol has quite deliberately never been copyrighted–it is free for all to use–an example of copy-IT-right. The original four drawings on three sheets of paper can be seen in the Special Collections at the University of Bradford. The Peace Museum, Bradford, has high quality facsimiles on show.[8] Unfortunately the symbol is also open to misuse. Tiffany & Co has produced a platinum and diamond peace sign with 4.8 carats of round-cut diamonds set into platinum. The Tiffany pendant has a price tag of $4,750.[9] Peace at a price.

DESIGN PROFILE: COME THE REVOLUTION!

LA COUBRE

At 3:10 on the afternoon of 4 March, 1960, an explosion rocked Havana's eastern waterfront. The 4,3 tonnes freighter, *La Coubre*, operated by the Compagnie Générale Transatlantique of France and transporting in its holds 76 tonnes of Belgian artillery shells, grenades and small arms ammunition from the port of Antwerp, exploded.[10] Exact figures are hard to come by, but it is estimated that between 75 and 100 persons were killed and over 200 injured. Ernesto Guevara de la Serna, better known as Che Guevara[11] had been appointed head of Cuba's National Bank and was attending a meeting in the nearby INRA[12] building. Che had studied medicine at the University of Buenos Aires and had worked as a doctor and spent the next several hours attending to the wounded. The next day Fidel Castro mounts a massive show of sympathy for the victims. The funeral cortège made its way along the Maleçon seafront boulevard and past a stand on which stood Fidel, Jean-Paul Sartre, the French existentialist philosopher and Simone de Beauvoir, the French philosopher and author of *The Second Sex*, the seminal writing of contemporary feminism. They had been invited to Cuba by Che Guevara as witnesses to history.

THE BIRTH OF AN ICON

From the very beginning, Fidel Castro recognised the essential role of photography in recording history. He had selected a group of photographers to record and tell the story of the Cuban revolution. Alberto Diaz Guttiérez, known as Alberto Korda, a former fashion photographer, had been appointed Fidel Castro's personal photographer. Korda was on assignment from the newspaper *Revolucion*, and he dutifully recorded the event.[13] He took photos of Fidel and his two guests. Standing a little back, in a zippered jacket, was Che Guevara. Describing how he came to take the picture, Korda said: "I decided to watch from the crowd and used my Leica with its medium telephoto lens. I panned the podium and suddenly Che moved forward into my camera. I made a picture, and immediately thinking for a cover of our newspaper, turned the camera vertical, made another—and the moment had gone."[14] The shot was taken at 11.20 am, on 5 March 1960, using a 90 millimetre lens. It never made it on to the front page, instead it was relegated to an inside page. The original print hung on the wall of Korda's studio, unnoticed for the next year.

An ubiquitous image based on *Guerrillero Heroico* (the heroic fighter), Jim Fitzpatrick, 1968, from a
photograph by Alberto Korda, 5 March 1960.

REBEL WITH A CAUSE

Korda recalls being moved by the intensity of Che's expression, which he described as
being *encabronado y dolente* (angry and sad). In the original horizontal frame, Che stands
between a man and palm fronds, but in the process of printing the photo, Korda removed
the strands and the anonymous profile and isolates Che. With a military one-star beret
perched on his head, his leather jacket zipped up to his neck, hair blown by the wind
and with dark eyes staring into the distance, he provides the iconic image of a rebel
with a very specific cause. The image has been commandeered by freedom fighters and
revolutionaries around the world, it adorns many a dorm room and it used to sell everything
from ice cream to cigarettes. "It is perhaps the most reproduced, recycled and ripped off
image of the twentieth Century."[15]

Che was murdered in a schoolhouse in La Higuera, Bolivia on 9 October 1967, by a burst
from a M2 carbine fired by Warrant Officer Mario Terán of the Bolivian Second Rangers
Battalion who were trained, equipped and guided by US Green Beret and CIA operatives.

The hands of Che were hacked off and he was buried in an unmarked grave. In 1997, a team of forensic scientists from Argentina and Cuba found and identified the corpse of the man with no hands. 30 years after his death, the remains of Ernesto 'Che' Guevara were finally returned to Cuba and interred in a mausoleum in the suburbs of the city of Santa Clara.[16]

HEROIC FIGHTER

The first time that the Korda image appeared in print was in April 1961, about one year after the photograph was taken, when it was used in the pages of *Revolucion*, to promote a conference where Che was the featured speaker. In 1967, when Che was fighting his final guerrilla campaign in Bolivia, the Korda photograph appeared outside of Cuba for the first time. It was used in an article in *Paris Match* written by French journalist Jean Lartéguy about the guerrilla movements in Latin America.[17] Two months later, in October, Che was captured in the hilly scrub of eastern Bolivia and shot on the orders of Colonel Zenteno of the Bolivian high command.[18] A few days later, Castro addressed a huge memorial rally at the Plaza de la Revolucion in Havana. The facade of the Ministry of the Interior building featured a five-storey blown up image of the *Guerrillero Heroico* (heroic fighter) which helped hide this monstrous piece of Soviet-inspired modernist architecture. The worlds press and news agencies covered the event, most featured the image, and the vital connection between the Che image and revolutionary movements was established.

Jim Fitzpatrick, an Irish artist/designer created the iconic two-tone portrait of Che Guevara in 1968, based on the photo shot by Alberto Korda. Fitzpatrick first came across it in the German weekly, *Stern*. "One of the images was Korda's but it was so tiny that when I blew it up all I got was a dot matrix pattern. From this I did a quasi-psychedelic, sea-weedy version of Che." Only later, when he finally got his hands on a larger version of the photograph, from Provo, a Dutch underground movement, was he able to produce the iconic image. It is rumoured, but far from proven, that Provo had been given the image by Jean-Paul Sartre, who was present at the Havana funeral when it was taken. Recognising the image's ubiquitous nature and wide appeal, the Maryland Institute College of Art called this picture "the most famous photograph in the world and a symbol of the twentieth century". London's V&A Museum also proclaims that it is "considered to be the most reproduced image in the history of photography".[19]

Fitzpatrick was incensed by both the murder of Che and the dismemberment of his body. In response he produced numerous copies of the print, sending them off to left-wing political activist groups across Europe. "I deliberately designed it to breed like rabbits", he says of his image, which removes the original photograph's shadows and volume to create a stark and emblematic graphic portrait. "The way they killed him, there was to be no memorial, no place of pilgrimage, nothing. I was determined that the image should receive the broadest possible circulation." He adds, "His image will never die, his name will never die."[20] Nor, or so it would appear, will the commercialisation of the image, "He has become a global brand."[21] Andy Warhol included images of Che in his highly commercial pantheon of pop cultural and media celebrities produced at his 'factory'. The appropriation of the image reached new levels of debasement when Madonna dressed up as Che for the cover of her 2003 single *American Life*.

A SOCIETY OF ABUNDANCE

The 1960s provided an enriched social context for design; culture became commercial; Mad Men ruled. The prevailing economic order in North America and Europe supported private benefit and the accumulation of personal wealth. The cultural historian, Thomas Frank, observes, "Mainstream culture was tepid, mechanical, and uniform; the revolt of the young against it was a joyous and even a glorious cultural flowering, though it quickly became mainstream itself."[22] The established grey flannel culture was challenged by a counter culture. What is sometimes overlooked is the commercial revolution that occurred as the world of commerce changed the way it operated and its business practices. Business discovered "market segmentation" and "demographics", both of which impacted design, both of which will have major impact on the design process in the coming decade. The corporate world recognised the value of brand image and its interaction with consumer identity, perhaps the best example being the cola wars between Coca-Cola and Pepsi.[23] As Richard Tedlow, Professor of Business Administration at the Harvard Business School, points out, "There was no such thing as the Pepsi Generation until Pepsi created it."[24] Overall, the 1960s witnessed a consumer revolution and the emergence of a 'pop' culture which encompassed all areas of design and all aspects of visual culture; all these changes were amplified by an expanding communications infrastructure of glossy magazines and a profusion of television channels. The vast array of commercial announcements installed the consumer as the new arbiter of choice—but how to choose?

Designers were as confused as everyone else. 1960 saw the reissue of Nickolaus Pevsner's *Pioneers of Modern Design: From William Morris to Walter Gropius*. Originally published in 1936, amidst all the emerging bias' prevalent at that time, this was the first defence of the machine aesthetic as the appropriate style for the modern age. Pevsner put forward a perception of design history as linear, as a steady, academically proven progression from the Medieval inspired historicisms of William Morris and the Arts and Crafts Movement to the "machine aesthetic" of Walter Gropius and the Modern Movement. Reyner Banham's *Theory and Design in the First Machine Age* was also published in 1960. This tempered the objective idealism promoted by Pevsner with an enhanced world view of design, adding Italy and America to the overall mix, but still reinforcing many of the objects, people and ways of seeing proffered by Pevsner, while remaining faithful to the traditional class distinctions that riddled British society. Both publications offered views and opinions that were removed from the reality of contemporary developments in the culture of design. However,

Banham did indicate a way forward, commenting that; "It is time for them (the Establishment) to try to face up to pop as the basic cultural stream of mechanised urban culture."[25] Banham may have endorsed pop but for him postmodernism had "the same relation to architecture as female impersonation to femininity. It is not architecture, but building in drag."[26]

In our world, considerable discussion takes place over our affluent lifestyle. In the immediate post-war period most observers of culture endorsed the concept of popular prosperity. There were the critics, foremost of which was John K Galbraith who, in 1958, published *The Affluent Society* which attacks advertising, consumer opulence, and environmental degradation.[27] Vance Packard, the American journalist and social critic achieved popular acclaim with his million selling book of 1957, *The Hidden Persuaders*,[28] in which he purports to show how advertisers in particular made use of psychological techniques to manipulate expectations and induce desire. The Korean war had ended just five years earlier and the mass media had informed the general public how the attitudes and beliefs of detainees could be changed, often overriding prior beliefs and values. The journalistic tag of "brain washing" was applied to this process of unconscious re-learning and was popularised in John Frankenheimer's political thriller of 1962, *The Manchurian Candidate*. Packard made reference to mind control in *The Hidden Persuaders*, opposing the covert manipulation of consumers through the use of subliminal techniques.

IF I CAN'T SEE IT, IT MUST BE TRUE

One of the most enduring of all urban myths came into being during the 1960s, its unparalleled acceptance being at least in part due to the belief that we are far too smart and sophisticated to be influenced by advertising. If advertising works, therefore it must be by surreptitious means—it must be subliminal.[29] The stalwart work of Galbraith and the popularised pronouncements of Packard were soon followed by less than stellar, verging on fictitious, works, eager to cash in on this 'new' phenomenon.

In 1957 James Vickary undertook an elaborate hoax to promote his market research company. The local movie theatre in Fort Lee, New Jersey, was showing the very popular 1955 movie *Picnic*, starring William Holden and Kim Novak. This film, appropriately enough, covers a 24 hour period in a typical Mid-Western town. Vickary claimed that over a six week period, using a tachistoscope, (a super fast strobe light developed by the Eastman Kodak company) he projected images for a specific amount of time; "eat popcorn" and "drink Coca-Cola" were flashed for 3/1,000s of a second once every five seconds. According to Vickary, this very brief projection ensured that the motivational message was not consciously perceived. Vickary claimed that sales of popcorn rose 57 per cent and sales of Coca-Cola rose by 18.1 per cent. His 'research' was accepted as fact. The popular press endorsed the belief.

The New Yorker, Newsday, and the Saturday Review, among others, deplored the subconscious sell, the most alarming invention since the atomic bomb, according to Newsday. Representative William Dawson of Utah said subliminal advertising was "made to order for the establishment and maintenance of a totalitarian government if put to political purposes". The National Association of Radio and Television Broadcasters banned the use of subliminals by its members. And the New York State Senate unanimously passed a bill outlawing the technique.[30]

In their rush to vilify, the press, the professional associations and government all failed the general public by this act of unsubstantiated endorsement. No detailed description of Vickary's research has ever been published, no independent evidence to support the concept has been undertaken. In an interview with Advertising Age in 1962, Vickary stated that the original study was a total fabrication, a ploy used to promote his Subliminal Projection Company.[31]

In 1974, almost two decades after the Vickary deception, Canadian professor Wilson Bryan Key published Subliminal Seduction.[32] This is a speculative, highly personal, account of subliminal messages supposedly embedded in advertisements. Unhindered by established research parameters Keys saw SEX wherever he looked, and he did a lot of looking. "In a single whiskey ad, Key found a volcano, a mouse, a skull, scorpions, three wolf faces, the head of a rat, a lizard, a shark, a white bird, various masks, fish, a swan, a cat, and dozens of sex's."[33] Key's epitomises the confusion between research and the search for justification. His work lacks positive, objective historical evidence and relies on personal judgement—and that judgement ignores the reality of art production in the pre-Photoshop age where the time consuming air brushing of images was often out-sourced. Mass printing in the 1960s and 1970s was nowhere near as sophisticated as it is today, many of Key's 'images' could be accounted for by the process of colour separation and flaws in the printing process. Key's revealing assessments conveniently ignores all these. In a moment of near-lucidity, Key says of his own work, "the author has frequently believed, while researching this book, that he might be off on a paranoiac delusion of some sort".[34] Well put. Key would have found it more beneficial to look at the clouds or into a camp fire— or even better still research the psychological phenomenon of Pareidolia where a type of eternal stimulus is misperceived and regarded as significant, producing an illusion.[35]

As with Hidden Persuaders, Subliminal Seduction ignited a media frenzy. Government officials, religious leaders and intelligentsia spoke out against this perceived conspiracy. Politicians introduced legislation and government agencies established policies against subliminal selling. This rush to judgement emphasises the three most important facets of the design process— research, research, research! For the record, neither the American Psychological Association nor the American Sociological Association have found any scientific merit in theories of mind control; and yet the myth lingers on.

WORDS MATTER

We live in a consumer culture, and advertising is central to that culture. A few thoughts about advertising and design in the modern world. There are some organisations who depend for their 'reality' on the communication process to create and establish their identity—the process of communication is substantially more significant than the product. This is particularly true of products that do not themselves have any recognisable identity; soft drinks and laundry detergents come to mind. Fast moving consumer brands are given an identity largely created and consistently reinforced through product promotion and advertising on an immense scale. During the last few decades, design has been subject to the overt concerns of the bottom line. In today's market research-driven advertising industry, intuitive instinct has all but been replaced by input from focus groups, market analysts and spin doctors—and in an age when conglomerates rule and one or two points in market share can make the difference between substantial profit and bankruptcy protection, no one is inclined to rock the boat.

Copywriters were sovereign in the 1960s. Whatever the age, there is little doubt in the essential role of the copywriter in cutting through the verbal excess and getting to the point. One of the very best, and regarded as the enfant terrible of American advertising in the 1960s was George Lois.[36] Born in 1931 of Greek immigrant parents in the upper Bronx area of New York, fascinated by drawing and with a vocabulary resplendent with words drawn from schoolyards, baseball lingo, comic strips, Daily News headlines, Marx Brothers movies, popular songs and the mass culture of New York city, Lois was ready for some early training at Parsons. This was followed by a short period with Bill Golden at CBS records and, after the Korean War, a position with Doyle Dane and Bernback. It was the DDB agency that gave birth to "Big Idea Thinking", the basis of much advertising in the 1960s. "I always understood the concept", says Lois, who felt at home at DDB, where the art director was king. Combining shrewdly shot visuals with irreverent text, Lois and his colleagues came up with such seminal advertising moments as the Volkswagen "Think Small" campaign. "If it's a product, you have to understand its competitors, what it's all about; you have to understand the culture and world history. Then you've got to create a big idea."[37]

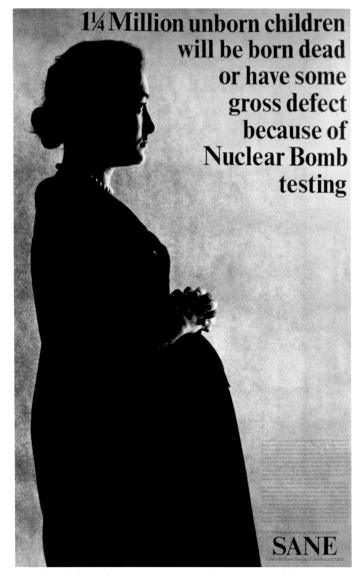

Committee for Sane Nuclear Policy, George Lois, Art Director and Designer, 1962.

In 1960, aged 28, Lois left DDB to become co-founder of Papert, Koenig, Lois, whose billings in seven years went from zero to $40 million. In 1962 it became the first ad agency to go public. In spite of his commercial success, Lois remained committed to helping causes that he believed in, as with his poster for the *Committee for Sane Nuclear Policy* (SANE). 1961 was a year of dangerous confrontations in post-Sputnik Cold War hostilities.[38] There was a nationwide fear that satellite based missiles were a threat to America. This paranoia spawned support for building a nuclear arsenal. Overlooked was the human cost of the testing of nuclear weapons. SANE was initiated to inform the general public of potential hazards of atmosphere

nuclear testing, which as the official documents indicated, could result in "1 1/4 million unborn children will be born dead or have some gross defect because of Nuclear Bomb testing". In 1961 Lois was contacted by Dr Benjamin Spock, best known for his best-selling book *Baby and Child Care*, he was also a major social activist and a board member of SANE. Spock asked George Lois to produce a poster for SANE for use on the New York subway. The woman featured in the poster was Lois' secretary and the copy came straight from official government sources. The commanding image forces the audience to reflect on the potential horror of this particular woman's child being born with a birth defect.

> I did the SANE poster for Dr Spock in 1961. The woman we photographed was my then very pregnant secretary. I wanted to photograph her naked (backlit to form a silhouette with some light on her face), but Dr Spock asked me not to. And besides, in 1961, I'm sure the New York Subway authorities would have rejected it, with the excuse that it would have invited graffiti…. As it turned out, in those days of McCarthyism, the fully clothed image on the posters were covered with tons of 'pinko commie–go back to Russia' graffiti.[39]

COVER STORY

In 1962 the magazine *Esquire*, challenged by more revealing men's magazines, was in financial trouble and potentially two issues away from folding. The insightful editor, Harold Hayes, hired Lois to save the magazine giving him *carte blanche*. Lois claims he never designed a cover.

> Designed work has no place on a magazines face. A design is a harmony of elements. A cover is a statement. It should provoke, challenge, interest, entice, snare, grab, arouse, titillate, excite, shock, infuriate, seduce, motivate. It should give the reader an irresistible taste of the magazine's spirit. It should captivate the reader.[40]

The cover of a magazine must communicate to the potential reader; it must be far more than eye-candy. It sits there soliciting action by potential purchasers; when inspected it must engage. Lois used the covers of *Esquire* to provoke debate on many of the most controversial issues facing America from racism and feminism to the Vietnam War. Working in collaboration with photographer Carl Fisher, Lois designed 92 covers which sold over 150 million copies. When he began work on Esquire it was in the red. Over the next four years, Esquire made over $3 million in profit as annual circulation rose from 500,000 to 2.5 million. As Lois says his covers didn't hurt.[41]

The March 1964 cover is an example of one idea that didn't work. As a concept it sounds great. For an upcoming series on the American Indian, Lois phoned the Indian Affairs Bureau to find out who had posed for the Indian on the American nickel, designed by the sculptor James Earl Fisher in 1912. The image was in fact a composite made up from three Seneca Nation chiefs; Iron Tail, Two Moons and John Big Tree. This was 51 years after the event, but they managed to locate the 87 year old Chief John Big Tree, (birth name: Isaac Johnny John) still living on a reservation just outside Syracuse. He was flown to the photographers studio in NYC. The 87 year old, six foot two Chief arrived resplendent in the prerequisite grey business suit and with a crew-cut. This was not the image that Lois had in mind. The studio dressed John Big Tree up with a black wig, padded out his toothless mouth with cotton and shot his historic profile. Chief Johnny Big Tree then flew back, via Mohawk airlines to Syracuse. He died on 6 July 1967, in the Onondaga Indian Reservation, New York.

In 1967 Cassius Clay converted to the Islamic religion and became Mohamed Ali and a Black Muslim minister. He refused military service as a conscientious objector. A federal jury didn't believe his rational and sentenced him to five years in jail. The boxing commission stripped him of his title and the general public condemned him as a draft dodger and even labelled him a traitor. The April 1968 cover of *Esquire* was modelled after a famous fifteenth century masterpiece, *The Martyrdom of St Sebastian*, by Andrea Mantegna.[42] *Esquire* had a sensational cover, it was reproduced and sold as a protest poster, and three years later, Ali had his conviction squashed.

One of the most controversial *Esquire* covers was from October 1966. The lead story was by John Sack, *Esquire*'s war correspondent in Vietnam. This story preceded the My Lai massacre of 16 March 1968, and at 33,000 words, was and still is, the longest ever published in *Esquire*.[43] Lois produced the cover with the inscription, "Oh My God—We hit a little girl" and set it starkly in white against a funereal black background. "When I asked Harold how badly we would piss off America, he said, 'If they don't like what's on our cover, they can always buy *Vogue*, Sweetheart.'" That was 1966, a premature time for indicting what became America's longest and wrongest war (until now)."[44] An observation endorsed by Mark Kurlansky who notes that: "At the height of the 1968 fighting, the US military was killing every week the same number of people or more as died in the 11 September, 2001 World Trade Center attack."[45]

Many sociologists agree that American culture, in general, is based not on any historic model as is often the case in Europe and Asia and other older societies, but on modern myths. In 1963 the myths of the Kennedy dynasty, the Wild West and the right to bear arms, all came together on television. On 24 November, Jack Ruby shot Lee Harvey Oswald dead, live, in front of millions of TV viewers of all ages, classes, and sects, providing a television event broadcast throughout North America. Lois recreates the moment in a more broad, abstract and insightful manner. Here the all-American kid, sitting on the statutory rag rug in the comfort of his home den, grows up instantly, confronted by 'live' violence surrounded by the modern day icons of Coke and hamburger.

Chief Johnny Big Tree, George Lois, Art Director and Designer. Cover for *Esquire Magazine*, issue no 364, March 1964.

"Oh my God—we hit a little girl.", George Lois, Art Director and Designer. Cover for *Esquire Magazine*, issue no 395, October 1966.

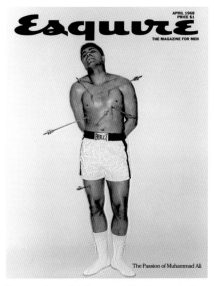

The passion of Muhammad Ali. George Lois, Art Director and Designer. Cover for *Esquire Magazine*, Issue no 413, April 1968.

Why Jack Ruby killed Lee Oswald... an untold story. George Lois, Art Director and Designer. Cover for *Esquire magazine*, issue no 402, May 1967.

CULTURAL PROFILE: CULTURAL EVENTS OF THE 1960S

"We were—waist deep in the Big Muddy,
But the big fool said to push on."
Pete Seeger, 1967.[46]

1955–30 April 1975 Vietnam War (Second Indochina War).

1957–1969 The Soviet Union and the US were involved in the space race which began after the Soviet launch of Sputnik 1 on 4 October 1957. This was followed by the Soviet cosmonaut Yuri Gagarin, aboard the spacecraft Vostok I, becoming the first man in space on 12 April 1961. The race was ultimately over when Neil Armstrong became the first human to step onto the Moon on 21 July 1969.

1961 13 August, East German border guards begin construction of Berlin Wall that physically separated East Germany and West Germany. It was dismantled in 1989.

1962 The first computer video game, *Spacewar!* programmed by Steve Russell is released.

1962 Rachel Carson's, *Silent Spring*, marked the start of the worldwide environmental movement.

1962 Bay of Pigs invasion of Cuba by the US fails.

1963 Touch-tone telephones introduced by AT&T.

1963 Dylan and Pete Seeger perform duet rendition of "We Shall Overcome" at Newport Jazz Festival, which became the anthem of the age.

1963 22 November, President John F Kennedy is assassinated.

1964 The Beatles journey to America, spearheading the first British Invasion. They release the seminal concept album *Sgt. Pepper's Lonely Hearts Club Band* in June 1967, which included "Lucy in the Sky with Diamonds".

1965 On 17 April, the first student protest against the war in Vietnam. 35,000 march on Washington.

1965 Malcolm X assassinated.

1966 *The International Times* was launched at London's Roundhouse on 14 October with a gig headlined by Pink Floyd.[47]

1967 15 January, The first Super Bowl is held in Los Angeles Coliseum, Green Bay Packers defeat the Kansas City Chiefs, 35–10.

1967 Summer of Love in San Francisco saw as many as 100,000 young people converge on the Haight-Ashbury neighbourhood of San Francisco, a very physical and visual reinforcement of the cultural and political rebellion of the decade. "Happenings" were announced in the Haight-Ashbury's own psychedelic newspaper, *The San Francisco Oracle*.

1967 Canada celebrated its 100th anniversary of Confederation by hosting the World's Fair in Montreal, Quebec (Expo 67) where the new film format Imax was demonstrated. "Expo" provided a home to a Buckminster Fuller Geodesic Dome.[48]

1967 *2001: A Space Odyssey*, directed by Stanley Kubrick, written by Kubrick and Arthur C Clarke.[49]

1968 31 January, The Viet Cong launched the Tet Offensive. 1 February 1968, Saigon, Vietnam: Chief Brigadier General Nguyen Ngoc Loan, of the South Vietnamese national police, executes a Vietcong officer with a single pistol shot to the head.

1968 4 April, The assassination of civil rights leader Martin Luther King Jr.

1968 6 June, The assassination of presidential candidate Senator Robert F Kennedy.

1968 October, The Jimi Hendrix Experience release the highly influential third album *Electric Ladyland*. This is often cited as one of the greatest rock albums of all time.

1968 Christmas Eve, the first Earthrise to be witnessed by a human. (Frank Borman and the crew aboard Apollo 8 who became the first astronauts to leave Earth's orbit.)

1969 15 August to 18 August, Woodstock Festival, Bethel, New York, 500,000 people gathered for three days of music and a celebration of peace that changed the world.[50]

1969 15 November, over half a million people march in Washington DC, making it the largest anti-war rally in American history.

1970 4 May, Students at Kent State University protest the American invasion of Cambodia. The Ohio National Guard were called in, shooting into the student crowd, killing four students and injuring nine.

Now is the Winter of our discontent.
William Shakespeare, 1594, *Richard The Third*,
Act 1, scene 1.

1968 was a very violent year.[51] It was a year of
cataclysmic change, political, social and cultural, across
the globe. The year saw riots and anti-war marches
across the US, student unrest in Mexico, Britain,
Pakistan, Japan and the US, and a mass uprising in
Czechoslovakia.[52] From Paris to Prague, to Chicago,
Mexico City, Rawalpindi, Tokyo and London,
'popular' struggles erupted on the streets and were
seen as a threat to the established regimes.[53] Although
the various concerns may have been local, the desire to
rebel was global, fuelled by alienation at the established
order—be it communist or capitalist, freely elected or
imposed—the ogre was authoritarianism in all its forms.

I REBEL—THEREFORE WE EXIST

Revolution, both social and physical, has been an
ongoing reality of European culture. It resurfaced
once again in Paris during the hot Summer of 1968.
Every culture has its distinguishing characteristics;
in the French academic system there has always been
a heavy emphasis on politics and philosophy. The
philosophy of discontent had attracted some supporters
of note, including Albert Camus, the French-Algerian
author, philosopher, and journalist who was awarded
the Nobel Prize for Literature in 1957. In his *The
Rebel: An Essay on Man in Revolt*, the classic essay
on revolution, is the famous quote, "Rebellion is the
common ground on which every man bases his first
values. I rebel—therefore we exist."[54] What today has
the ring of a cliché was, in the 1960s, an incendiary
precept, a call to arms.

TO THE BARRICADES!

In May 1968 a series of protests and general strikes
caused the eventual collapse of the De Gaulle
government in France.[55] Many saw the events as an
opportunity to shake up the old society and the protests
centred on social aspects and traditional cultural
values, focussing especially on the education system
and employment. The struggle began in March on the
campus of the new purpose built institution of Nanterre
University. Situated in the western suburb of Nanterre,
near La Défense, the business district of Paris, as an
extension of the Sorbonne, it claims Nicolas Sarkozy,
President of France, as one of its more famous alumni.
In 1968, it was Danny Cohn-Bendit, known because
of his political orientation and his mop of red hair, as
'Danny the Red', who achieved fame. Then a sociology
student, currently Co-President of the group European
Greens-European Free Alliance in the European
Parliament, he led a group of eight students who took

over the Dean's office on 22 March to protest at the
recent arrest of six members of the National Vietnam
Committee. The unrest spread. What began as a series
of student strikes at a number of universities and lycées
in Paris, developed into all out confrontations with
university administrators and street battles with the
police in the Latin Quarter. Many French workers with
concerns of their own, empathised with the student
cause and joined them on the streets of Paris, forming
what Mark Kurlansky astutely observes, "an alliance of
temporary convenience".[56] These demonstrations were
followed by a general strike by students and workers
throughout France. At the peak of the disturbances,
ten million French workers, roughly two-thirds of the
French workforce were on strike.

On Friday 3 May a meeting was called in Paris'
Sorbonne University to protest against the closure of
Nanterre University the day before. The Sorbonne's
administrators called in police forces who appeared in
full riot gear, armed with tear gas. They surrounded
the University and arrested 527 students as they
attempt to leave the campus. On 6 May more than
20,000 students march to the Sorbonne and the
first significant battle begins with students erecting
barricades and launching volleys of paving stones
and other missiles at the police. At the height of their
influence the students of Paris gathered close to
130,000 people to demonstrate on the streets of the
capital. These were far from being social malcontents.
"The male students wore jackets and ties or neat
jumpers and short hair and well-pressed trousers. The
women had long hair and sensible skirts and hair-
bands. There were few jeans or sandals or beards."[57]
On 16 May 1968, after two weeks of sporadic street
fighting in Paris, President Charles de Gaulle dissolved
the National Assembly and called new elections for
23 June 1968.[58] Do not be misled, this was not the
voice of disfranchised working class youth, it was the
disaffected voice of the young middle class rebelling
against the status quo.

"Soyez réaliste, demandez l'impossible." (Be
realistic, demand the impossible.)[59] In terms of
visual communication, the students produced very
powerful, very immediate, and very topical images
which appeared as hand bills on the streets of Paris.
Using easy to comprehend symbols, plus a fresh
vibrant style, these images were intended to be easily
accessible. Most were produced by the *Atelier Populaire*,
comprised of students from the *Ecole des Beaux-Arts*.
Their technique was mostly silkscreen, sometimes the
less sophisticated lino-cuts. In all cases these designs
were produced under time constraints. Ever wary of
fifth columnists, the location of the 'press' was a closely
guarded secret. The economy of image was indeed the
strength of the campaign. Slogans often originated in the

Student posters from the Atelier Populaire, Paris, May 1968.
"Sois jeune et tais toi" (Be young and shut up).

defiant war cries from the street, chalked on blackboards back at headquarters, they were refined and simplified by committee and became the basis for about 300 designs that made up this campaign of protest.

During this period Cohn-Bendit was declared an undesirable alien and barred from living in France. There may have been associated elements of anti-Semitism. In his support, hand bills were produced featuring an image of Danny with the proclamation *"Nous sommes tous indesirables"* ("We are all undesirables"). The images and words, like the campaign, left no room for inflection—these are immediate signs, demanding immediate action. Not surprisingly the event was recorded in the popular music of the day.[60] The Rolling Stones issued their *Street Fighting Man* album and The Beatles recorded their first version of "Revolution" as the B-side of the "Hey Jude" single, released in late August 1968.

> *Picture yourself in a boat on a river*
> *With tangerine trees and marmalade skies*
> *Somebody calls you, you answer quite slowly*
> *A girl with kaleidoscope eyes.*
> Lucy In The Sky With Diamonds,
> Lennon/McCartney, 1967.

ROBBY, ADS AND POP

To find the origin of the term "Pop" we have to go back to London in the 1950s and to the Independent Group of artists and writers that included the architect James Stirling, Theo Crosby, editor of *Architectural Design*, the writer and critic Reyner Banham, and artists Eduardo Paolozzi, Victor Passmore and Richard Hamilton. They held, what is now regarded as the iconic exhibition, This is Tomorrow, at the Whitechapel Gallery, London, between 9 August and 9 September 1956.[61] Participants were divided into 12 cross-disciplinary teams and required to construct "a display that reflected in some way their view of the contemporary environment".[62]

Visitors were welcomed by a 12-foot tall image of Robby the Robot, star of the Hollywood film of 1956, *Forbidden Planet* and the odour of strawberry air freshener. The show included an American Jukebox playing the latest pop music from the US; a cut out of Marilyn Monroe from *The Seven Year Itch*, 1955, and a very small collage, just 26 x 25 cm, entitled *Just What is it That Makes Today's Home so Different, so Appealing?* by Richard Hamilton. This first "pop" collage tabulated the emergence of the icons of pop culture, "Man, Woman, Humanity, History, Food, Newspapers, Cinema, Telephone, Comics (picture information,) Words (textual information,) Cars, Domestic appliances, Space."[63] The architectural team of Alison and Peter Smithson,[64] who were participants in the exhibition, stated in an essay published in November 1956: "Gropius wrote a book on grain silos, Le Corbusier one on aeroplanes, and Charlotte Perriand brought a new object to the office every morning; but today we collect ads."[65] And so Pop was born. The term was coined to describe the Hamilton collage but was later applied to almost everything having to do with the popular culture of the period.

POP GOES THE EASEL

According to Tilman Osterwold, "Pop is entirely a Western cultural phenomenon, born under capitalist, technological conditions in an industrial society. Its programmatic epicentre was America."[66] Pop art generated the question, "Is it Art?" American pop artists discovered the icons that adorned the supermarkets and featured in popular culture, hot dogs and hamburgers, cola, Campbell soup cans, and the idols of Hollywood.[67] They turned advertising into art. None was better prepared for this transformation than Andy Warhol. Following a period of study at Pittsburgh's Carnegie Institute of Technology he worked as a window display artists in a Pittsburgh department store. By 1950 he had moved to New York where he undertook graphic work for magazines such as *Vogue* and *Harper's Bazaar*. By 1959 Warhol had achieved considerable success in the advertising world, "earning an annual average of $65,000 accompanied by almost annual art directors medals and other awards of professional recognition".[68]

His transfer to the world of fine art was consolidated in 1962 when he participated in the 'New Realists' exhibition at the Sidney Janis Gallery in New York. Also in 1962 Warhol produced the first of the *Campbell's Soup Cans* and the *Marilyn* Diptych. All the images of Marilyn Monroe originate from a single clipped black and white still from the 1953 film *Niagara*. Warhol was attracted to the dot screen mechanical imperfections of cheap printing processes and out of register colour separations, which combined, he believed provided individuality to multiple copies. His technique of exploiting photographic images and reproducing them with the repetitiveness of advertising produced common icons which found ready acceptance in the marketplace—he was, after all, using a visual language that all could read, and some could wear. The 'Souper Dress' was produced in 1967 for a marketing campaign by Campbell's Soup. In keeping with the mores of the time this A-line mini-dress is disposable. Made of a blend of wood pulp (80 per cent) and cotton the dress was lightweight, intended to be worn a few times then thrown away. It cost $1 plus two soup labels. In recent auctions examples of this dress fetch upwards of $2,000 making it a prime example of the convergence of design, culture and commerce.

CULTURAL REVOLUTION OR CULTURAL REVOLUTION?

Cultural Revolutions occur when there is a paradigm shift in the way people live and where the results are quantifiable and evidence is manifest in every strata of society. The Industrial Revolution, the Russian Revolution and Mao Zedong's Cultural Revolution provide emblematic examples. The other form of cultural revolution is where, rather than a fundamental change, there is a demonstrated shift in cultural values that tend to be associated with a specific group; and it is this latter descriptive form that is applied here. In Britain, the 1960s was a decade of relative affluence. The young had money to invest in the support of a chosen lifestyle. The market responded and a new generation of designers consciously made use of what was to become termed, the Pop aesthetic, in their designs. One of the first outward signs of this was in the area of fashion, or to be more precise, the emerging dress of street culture.[69]

The French couture designer André Courrèges was the first fashion designer to recognise the cultural reality of the youth market. An expert tailor who had trained with the Spanish designer Balenciaga, Courrèges had been presenting his own collections since 1961. It was his Spring collection of 1964 that introduced *la mini-jupe* in a show where he launched his Moon Girl Collection, which contained thigh high skirts in white and silver colours and geometric shapes. Even more revolutionary, was the footwear. Low broad heeled, calf high boots made of white vinyl with cut-out slots near the top. This was the origin of the 'Go-go' boot which was quickly adopted by dancers on American TV shows, *Hullabaloo* (1965–1966) and *Shindig* (1964–1966). Further endorsements were provided by Nancy Sinatra's 1966 number-one pop hit "These Boots Are Made for Walkin" while the more erotic associations were displayed by Jane Fonda in the 1968 science fiction film *Barbarella*.

POP SHOPS[70]

Swinging London was about style and image. It was Mary Quant who popularised and promoted the mini-skirt in London when she opened her famed Bazaar in the King's Road, Chelsea in November 1955, and introduced the world to the mini-skirt in the 1960s.[71] Always innovative she embraced the newly available plastics and foresaw the fashion applications by introducing plastic boots, skirts, and accessories. She also made use of the Op Art imagery popularised by Bridget Riley the artist and designer whose work was widely used in dress and fabric designs. The tag "Op-Art" was used in an article in the 23 October 1964 issue of *Time Magazine*.[72] This accidental descriptive appellative became a cliché of the era.

Fashion design responds to a wide range of influences which feedback into society in unforeseen ways. The mini-skirt had political and economic implications. In Britain the tax system classified skirts under 24 inches long as 'children's clothing' and therefore free from the 12.5 per cent sales tax. Given that many minis were around ten to 12 inches long, on 5 November 1965, the British government brought in new Customs and Excise rules to prevent women avoiding taxes by buying children's sized skirts.

Barbara Hulanicki, in partnership with Stephen Fitz-Simon, established Biba in 1964, opening their first shop in Abingdon Road, Kensington. By 1965 the business had expanded so much that they had to move to larger premises in Kensington Church Street. In September 1969, they moved to even larger premises, a former grocery store in Kensington High Street. But even this was not large enough. With new backers and finance Biba moved into the 400,000 square foot, Art Deco Derry and Tom's department store on Kensington High Street where they were getting up to 100,000 customers a week.[73] Biba stocked the 'total look' in which shoes, tights, and other accessories coordinated with the clothes providing inexpensive distinctive clothing to suited to the urban

Time Magazine, 10 April 1966, Time Inc. Used under licence.

environment.[74] She included rubberised raincoats, floppy hats and rugby shirts into her range. The latter were dyed and worn as mini-dresses. Biba closed its door in 1976. After several years in the world of Brazilian fashion, she returned to London in 1980 and explored fashion photography and fashion illustration. In 1990 Barbara Hulanicki established an interior design business in Miami.

SWINGING BOUTIQUES

Merchandising and commerce were essential to the promotion and success of Swinging London. Shops became 'boutiques' and thrived in the consumer enclaves along the King's Road in Chelsea and Carnaby Street in Soho.[75] Offering affordable fashionable clothing in a relaxed informal self-serve environment, they became places to be and to be seen in. Most sported exotic names. Mr Fish offered psychedelic inspired clothes. At 488 Kings Road, there was Granny Takes a Trip, 1965, owned by John Pearse and Nigel Weymouth it catered to the sartorial needs of Jimi Hendrix, Bob Dylan, and The Beatles. John Pearse had apprenticed with Hawkes and Curtis, bespoke gentlemen's tailors of Saville Row. Fashion and music were co-dependent.

The UFO Club at 31 Tottenham Court Road was for a short time in the late 1960s, one of the most famous clubs in London. The house group at the UFO Club was Pink Floyd. The psychedelic inspired graphics for the UFO were designed by Hapshash and the Coloured Coat, a design partnership between Michael English and Nigel Weymouth. These innovative communication pieces were a world removed from the good design establishment. In their own words, they "felt sidelined by the art establishment, the art world and the galleries, so we thought that we would make the streets our gallery and the poster is the perfect medium to do that".[76]

Close to very fashionable Sloan Square in Cale Street, was Hung on You which provided a showcase for vintage American clothing. This venue was favoured by The Rolling Stones.[77] In 1967 Hung on You moved to 430 King's Road, Worlds End, where fashionable Chelsea meets working class Fulham. This location became Mr Freedom in 1969 and Paradise Garage in 1970. In 1971 it was the birthplace of Punk when Malcolm McLaren (aka, Malcolm Robert Andrew Edwards) and Vivienne Westwood opened their first shop at 430 King's Road, called Let It Rock, conceived as a shrine to the Teddy Boy culture of the 1950s.[78] The role of McLaren and Westwood in designing Punk is covered in more detail in Chapter Nine, "Postmodern, Post-Pop, Post-Punk, Post-Green".

John Stephen was the king of Carnaby Street and leader of the 1960s male peacock revolution.[79] Aged 18 he came to London from Glasgow in 1952. Within four years he had opened his first shop, His Clothes, on the first floor of a not very impressive location in Beak Street. A year later, he moved round the corner to number 5 Carnaby Street where he produced his very individual creations in a workroom at the back of the shop. Within a very short space of time, he had 15 separate shops spread along the length of the street under various names, and branches in other trendy parts of London.

Other designers appropriated popular images into their designs. Union Jacks in various guises and discarded uniforms were available at *I was Lord Kitcheners Valet*. Originally located at 293 Portobello Road in Notting Hill, success among the weekend traders of London's most famous street market led to branches opening in Carnaby Court in Soho and King's Road in Chelsea. These shops specialised in vintage clothing, surplus costumes from the film industry, and old military style uniforms. Regular customers included Eric Clapton, The Who, and Jimi Hendrix, who purchased his famous braided military coat here. It is said that Peter Blake, who designed the album cover for *Sgt Pepper's Lonely Hearts Club Band*, got the idea for The Beatles costumes from *I was Lord Kitcheners Valet*.[80]

Carnaby Street became synonymous with the idea of Swinging London. Relying on traditional skills from the Soho based 'rag trade' amplified by the entrepreneurial skills of the young fashion specialists the shops offered trend driven merchandise at attractive prices. At its peak, Carnaby Street was a physical reflection of contemporary changes in society and culture. Today it is a gaudy, gimmick laden tourist trap.

INSTANT GOOD TASTE...
FOR SWITCHED ON PEOPLE

Terence Conran, a graduate of the Central School of Arts and Crafts, was responsible for introducing 'design' into the Swinging London scene. Although now known as a restaurateur and writer, it was Conran who with his Habitat stores added a design dimension to 'pop'. He opened his first Habitat store at 77 Fulham Road in May 1964, concentrating on modern furniture and home accessories. Through adapt utilisation of the new colour supplements offered by the main Sunday newspapers, Conran spread the word that good, Habitat-sponsored design, is good for you. According to the promotional material the store offered "a pre-selected shopping programme... instant good taste... for switched on people".[81] Despite its location the fashionable set patronised Habitat and made it a desirable venue on those 'consuming' Saturday promenades.

The Habitat chain had, by 1985, expanded to 42 stores in Britain. Conran "has probably done more than anyone else, or any other agency, to bring design and its importance into the consciousness of the British public".[82] He went on to establish the Conran Foundation which in 1989 initiated the founding of the Design Museum[83] located at Shad Thames, just across the river from the Tower of London. Opened by the Prime Minister, Margaret Thatcher, in 1989, the Design Museum was a development of the earlier, 1982–1987, Boilerhouse project at the V&A. The Habitat chain was sold to IKANO (the owner of IKEA) and then in 2009 to Hilco a restructuring specialist. Terence Conran was knighted in 1983. Design evolves.

DESIGN CULTURE—LITERARY RELEVANCE

Habitat moderated the pop excesses of the 1960s and made design relevant to a wider audience. The literature of the day added another dimension to those designers sensitive to design relevance. Connections between consumerism and environmentalism were highlighted by Rachel Carson in *Silent Spring*, 1962, which first appeared in serial form in *The New Yorker*.[84] Carson set in motion a popular movement demanding government imposed controls to protect the fragile environment. *The Feminine Mystique*[85] by Betty Friedan, published in 1963, demonstrated that women have a right to education, to personal fulfilment in the wider world and to an identity of their own. In 1965, Ralph Nadar produced *Unsafe at Any Speed*, a condemnation of business and design practices by the major American auto makers.[86] Nadar claimed that these design inefficiencies resulted in vehicles that could cause serious injury even in low speed crashes. While these publications may not have appeared on many required reading lists of design courses in the 1960s they were instrumental in the re-evaluation of the culture of design that occurred in the 1970s and 1980s.

CHAPTER NINE
POST-POP, POSTMODERN, POST-PUNK, POST-GREEN

THE WALL

The last 30 years of the twentieth century witnessed continuing wars and revolutions. It was a time when everything, war, revolution, politics, sport, culture and design, went global. Communication went global, *CNN* and *Al Jazeera* began offering 24 hour news coverage. Cities became global with the newly available forms of communication allowing for the examination of meaningful communication between all of Earth's inhabitants.[1] Conflicts such as the ten year Russian occupation of Afghanistan, the 1979 Iranian Revolution and the Sri Lankan Civil War which began in 1983, all received extensive media coverage—none moreso than the 4 June, 1989 suppression by the Chinese army of the communal Tiananmen Square uprising in Beijing.[2] The climax of these decades of discontent came with the opening of the Berlin Wall on 9 November 1989 which received global coverage.[3] It seemed that with the end of the Cold War, the 1990s would be a time of cultural renewal and design revitalisation. Philip Meggs, clarifies: "A period of international dialogue had begun… conceptual innovation and visual invention spread like wildfire. An international culture embracing the fine arts, performing arts, and design spans national boundaries, extending from traditional centres to every corner of the globe."[4]

END OF MODERNITY

By the 1970s the word "design" had entered into the common lexicon, everybody was a designer. The architectural design language of the 1970s was dominated by a latterday International Style, which was, to paraphrase Frank Lloyd Wright, flat-chested glass monoliths masquerading as architecture.[5] It was also a reflection of the structural crisis in the global economy, a crisis made of stagflation and rampant militarisation which resulted in structures designed as economic space containers rather than cultural landmarks.[6] It was time to reassess the sterile modernity of 'good design'. The end of 'Modernity' was prefaced by the good design movement.

By the 1970s it was very obvious that the high-minded idealism and grandiosity associated with the rhetoric of 'good design' was not going to solve real world problems. Those 'real' problems were highlighted by the oil crisis of 1973 which was not so much a result of resource shortages rather than a strategy of resource management designed by OAPEC during the Fourth Middle East War.[7] The resulting downturn in the global marketplace had a significant impact on the shape of the world heading into the final decades of the twentieth century, and tangentially, on the culture of design.

In terms of design, contemporary material culture was made abundantly aware of where its material came from and the subsequent environmental cost of materialism. The designer generation of the 1970s were cognisant of the fact that the utopia envisaged by the Modernists had not come to pass. They were living in a post-industrial society enamoured by the forces of consumption. Sometimes left out of the equation of evaluation is the role that consumption and the world of commerce had upon design.[8] We were to see that the growth of consumerism would not in fact lead to a more egalitarian society, but to a more violent and less equitable one.

THE DAY MODERN ARCHITECTURE DIED

Designers found (or, to be more precise, re-found) culture, which was postmodern. It is generally accepted that it was Charles Jencks in his 1977 book *The Language of Post-Modern Architecture* that provided a name and an identity to the diverse movement.[9] He even provided an exact time and date for the end of Modernism; 3:32 pm, on 16 March 1972, that was when the much lauded and professionally praised Pruitt Igoe housing development in St Louis, Missouri was dynamited as uninhabitable.[10] It had been a prize-winning complex designed for low income people by Leinweber, Yamasaki & Hellmith and built just 20 years earlier.[11] Following in the theological steps of Walter Gropius, Ludwig Mies van der Rohe and Le Corbusier, it was viewed as a logical development of the "machine to live in" concept. But reality had overtaken theory.

The complex of 33, identical 11-storey apartment buildings was located in the De Soto-Carr neighbourhood, an extremely poor section of St Louis. These sterile towers provided 2,870 'homes'. Cost-cutting measures by the St Louis Housing Authority wrecked intended caring elements and eliminated any remaining hint of humanitarian design. There was little in this maligned environment to celebrate, resulting in a general malaise and a total lack of any sense of community. Tenants were marooned by faulty lifts; lonely old people died unnoticed and unattended; children's play area's were remote and unsafe, their fields of concrete and tarmac more suited to the requirements of pushers and pimps. Overall problems of vandalism resulted in a complete breakdown of the functionality of the complex; architectural Modernism had totally isolated itself from its public.

FRAGMENTED POSTMODERNISM

As we saw in Chapter Four, the fragmented image that Picasso provided in his exploratory paintings, now referred to as Cubism, were in keeping with the cultural context of Paris during the first decades of the twentieth century. At century's end it was time to rethink fragmentation. The world had changed, the process of communication had been revolutionised; there was a multi-channel television universe complete, thanks to video, VCR and CD-ROMs, with personal storage and access facilities. Then came the wonderful world of the personal computer, the WWW and the Internet, providing access to a massive fragmented collage of images and associations. In his 1996 edition of *What is Post-Modernism?*, Charles Jencks puts it this way: "the globe has been irreversibly united by current technologies into an instantaneous, 24 hour information world".[12] If modernism had negated the information component of design, then postmodernism demands that the audience be literate in the semiotic value of historical style. Postmodernism can be seen as a transitional movement which relished the fragmentation of the major design categories of the past, and then expressed them in revitalised and vibrant ways.

SURFACE: LEARNING FROM ART DECO

While the great majority of designers are more than happy to tread the safe and fairly happy path of convention, sustaining rather than challenging the design status quo, some, such as Robert Venturi and Denise Scott Brown, have realised and exploited the cultural interconnections, they have consciously tried to give expression to this linkage in their work. This husband and wife team were instrumental in giving a human dimension to postmodernism. It all began with their influential books, *Complexity and Contradiction in Architecture*, 1966, and *Learning From Las Vegas*, 1972, which heralded the introduction of postmodernism. They then applied their ideas concerning "the postmodern complex and contradictory" forces to furniture design.[13] Combining traditional moulded plywood [14] construction with plastic laminate surfaces, the collection share a similar silhouette in profile. From the front, through jig-sawed and fretted backs, enlivened by silkscreen appliqué decorative plastic laminates, the chairs communicate a variety of historical styles; Chippendale, Queen Anne, Empire, Hepplewhite, Sheraton, Biedermeier, Gothic Revival, Art Nouveau, and Art Deco. Venturi refutes Miesian maxims with his own observations. "I am for richness of meaning rather than clarity of meaning; ... I prefer 'both-and' to 'either-or', ... More is not less.... Less is a bore."[15] The range was designed in 1979 but not produced by Knoll until 1984.

The high priest of postmodernism in North America, Michael Graves, has 'targeted' attention from architecture to the more commercially viable areas of product and furniture design. Graves makes sophisticated, and some say elitist, references to past classical styles where the emphasis is on content rather than form; where symbolism replaces rationality and where multiple meanings are preferred over single interpretations. His now famous kettle was designed in 1985 and mass produced by Alessi, selling over 40,000 in its first year. It is made of stainless steel with a blue handle and a whistle in the shape of a red bird. Forget about function—in order to remove the whistle you have to immerse your hand in the steam generated from the boiling! There remains the basic question as to why you would pay up to $200 for this non-electric kettle when you can get a perfectly good electric version for $20 Totems can be expensive.

PRELUDE TO MEMPHIS

The 1980s were conspicuous by consumption. Demographics changed. Hippies were replaced by Yuppies (young urban professionals) and Dinkies (double income no kids). In the USA, Ronald and Nancy Reagan made full use of fashionable conspicuous clothes to demonstrate American affluence to a global market. In Britain, Margaret Thatcher, the Iron Lady, maybe taking a lead from John Molloy's *Women: Dress For Success*, popularised the elegantly tailored suit.[16] Power dressing was in.

Time Magazine, May 14, 1979, Time Inc. Used under licence.

Philosophical debates over the function of design were replaced by the more easily recognisable designer label made all the more accessible by the increasing use of credit cards.

Indicative of the 1980s approach to design was the initiative by the British government who, in 1983 and in conjunction with the Design Council, launched a 'Design for Profit' campaign. The Design Council even went as far as to produce a 40 page guide with the grandly stated title, *Design and the Economy: the role of design and innovation in the prosperity of industrial companies*.[17] In an earlier publication, *Profit by Design*, the point was emphasised; "to put it simply, the design process is a planning exercise to maximise sales and profits".[18] This then was official 'good design'. Not a mention of environmental concerns nor sustainability. Then came Memphis, described by the Design Museum as "a Milan-based collective of young furniture and product designers led by the veteran Ettore Sottsass. After its 1981 debut, Memphis dominated the early 1980s design scene with its postmodernist style."[19]

Kevin Coffee explains the role of museums in providing a necessary impetus to the culture of design in the emerging industrial reality of the twentieth century:

> Very diverse cultural practices develop within sufficiently large polities, in response to, and contributing to, a matrix of social relationships. Museums play a formative role in defining and reproducing those relationships through their policies and narrative practices. As importantly, how museums are construed, who uses them, and how they use them, are also defined within this web of relationships.[20]

Around mid-century, the "web of relationships" included design. The Machine Art show of 1934 at the Museum of Modern Art in New York was the first to give voice to the new design reality. This was followed by the 1940 Organic Design in Home Furnishings competition which was won jointly by Charles and Ray Eames, and Eero Saarinen with their chairs made with a seat of moulded plywood with a compound curve[21], (see Chapter Six). In 1972 the MoMA staged, Italy: The New Domestic Landscape (see Chapter Seven). 20 years earlier, Olivetti: Design in Industry, had introduced North America to the work of Ettore Sottsass and other prominent Italian designers. According to the accompanying *Bulletin*, "The Olivetti company, may critics agree, is the leading corporation in the Western world in the field of design."[22]

QWERTY

Olivetti was founded in 1908 by Camillo Olivetti who began to manufacture his first typewriter at a factory just outside Turin in Northern Italy.[23] His son, Adriano, took over the company in the 1930s, and in co-operation with Marcello Nizzoli, founded the formal design policy of Olivetti. Nizzoli remained the chief in-house designer until the late 1960s. Olivetti's commitment to design permeated the entire company, from the workplace to corporate promotion; from graphics to the frequent sponsorship of exhibitions. In 2003 Olivetti was absorbed into the Telecom Italia group.

Ettore Sottsass designed the iconic, symbolically named Valentine portable typewriter, for Olivetti, which went on sale, as you would expect, on 14 February 1969.[24] Sottsass claimed that it was the "anti-machine machine". He wanted to reinvent the way people used typewriters, bringing them out of the office onto the street and into the boutique, the cafe or the disco. The red was significant to this counter-culture classic. It is, the designer said, "the colour of the Communist flag, the colour that makes a surgeon move faster and the colour of passion". The Valentine became the ultimate fashion accessory for the "girl-about-town" of that era.[25] Fashionable it may well have been, but it had a deplorable habit of shaking and rattling during use and a had short commercial life. As a product its price was not competitive, the technology outdated and any further development was made unlikely by the rising price of oil–and hence of plastics. In 2007, Sottsass said that it was the Valentine that made him reconsider his position as a designer, encouraging him to turn his back on industrial production and take the more exploratory path that led to Memphis.[26]

ON THE ROAD AGAIN

That path was by way of visits to North and South America, to India and other locations around the world. In India he appreciated the sacred nature of objects. In America he became intrigued with the Beat generation.[27] Sottsass was fascinated by the perceived status of objects, by the cultural and social meaning of objects, (a fascination that he shared with Ray Eames–see Chapter Six). His personal repertoire of influences overpowered beliefs in consumerism and provided the launching pad for a voyage of imaginative self-discovery. "I believe that the future only begins when the past has been completely dismantled, its logic reduced to dust and nostalgia is all that remains", (see Chapter Twelve, "Déjà Vu is everywhere",). Sottsass rejected the popular rationalist doctrine, favouring a different approach. "When I was young, all we ever heard about was functionalism, functionalism, functionalism.... It's not enough. Design should also be sensual and exciting."[28]

MEMPHIS

By the late 1970s, Sottsass was working with Studio Alchimia, established in 1976 as a group of avant-garde furniture designers including Alessandro Mendini and Andrea Branzi. Then in his 60s, he left Studio Alchima to form a new collective, Memphis. The group was founded on 11 December 1980, at a meeting at Sottsass' Milan house and at the nearby trattoria. The name arrived, it is said, because Sottsass was playing a record of Bob Dylan's

"Stuck inside of Mobile with the Memphis Blues Again", over and over again. After a few bottles of wine, Memphis seemed to sum up exactly the feel the group was aiming at. As Barbara Radice (Sottsass' then partner and future artistic director of Memphis) put it in 1984, it was all to do with the "blues, Tennessee, rock 'n' roll, the American suburbs, the capital of the Egyptian pharaohs, and the sacred city of the God Ptah".[29] (Ptah is a god of creation and the patron of architects, artists, and sculptors. His cult centre is Memphis, Egypt). These characteristics may not seem very Italian, not very modernist, not very rational either–but certainly sensual and exciting, that's the true context of Memphis.

The group, which eventually counted among its members Michele de Lucchi, Matteo Thun, Javier Mariscal, Marco Zanini, Aldo Cibic, Andrea Branzi, Barbara Radice, Martine Bedin, George J Sowden and Nathalie du Pasquier, was a reaction against the post-Bauhaus 'black box' designs of the 1970s and had a sense of humour that was lacking at the time in design. Memphis was prepared to mix twentieth century styles, colours and materials in a way that pristine 'good design' could or would not, "The results were presented in Milan on the 18 September 1981: 31 furniture objects, three clocks, ten lamps, and 11 ceramic objects were euphorically acclaimed by 2,500 visitors."[30]

TO THE BARRICADES—AGAIN

The bastions that Memphis attacked were the old ones, the same as those that had provoked the avant-garde designers from the times of Art Nouveau on; the status quo, tradition, and what in design had become the monster inhibitor to creativity, "good taste" now enshrined in design museums around the world, complete with appropriate labels, defined and analysed by erudite and near incomprehensible rambling's in magazines and journals that catered to the design intelligentsia. The market wanted some fun and colour in its life.

> Memphis embodied the themes with which Sottsass had been experimenting since his mid-1960s 'superboxes': bright colours, kitsch suburban motifs and cheap materials like plastic laminates.... For the young designers of the era, it was an intellectual lightning rod which liberated them from the dry rationalism they had been taught at college and enabled them to adopt a more fluid, conceptual approach to design. The Memphis collective's work was exhibited all over the world, until Sottsass quit in early 1985.[31]

In 1988 Sottsass dismantled the group and the brand name was sold–so do not think for one moment that all that 'Memphis' material on sale in museum shops has anything to do with the original movement–it does, reflective of its context, demonstrate the sales potential of a design brand.

The groups activities and exhibitions were to provide a well promoted outlet for experimental design for the next decade. It can be seen as the initiator of a new global style in the culture of the 1990s. Initially the group was seen as a big put on, as a kind of designer kitsch for those who wanted to thumb their collective noses at the bourgeois designer culture of the 1980s. Some saw that in fact the group were asking some fundamental questions about form and function and about cultural preconceptions, in particular as related to materials. One of their most important innovations was, to use the true and tested phrase of William Morris, to question the "honest use of materials". Plastic laminates had been around for over 30 years, but always masquerading as something else, more often than not, wood. Memphis used decorated laminates that revel in being plastic and that explore the characteristics of plastic laminate. Memphis, quite literally took plastic laminates out of the closet and kitchen and proudly displayed them in living rooms and the more formal status areas of the home.

Memphis explored the range of materials available in our institutionalised culture, materials that culture has pre-assigned specific identities and values to and tried to free materials from those associations. Among the materials favoured were printed glass, zinc-plated and textured metals, Celluloid's, industrial paints and finishes, neon tubes and of course plastic laminates–but the plastic laminates associated with the American consumer culture, suburban coffee shops and soda fountains. Plus the Sottsass design process reawakened cultural interest in ancient civilisations, established cultural associations with materials, all forms of surface decoration and of course, colour. The real significance of Memphis was the way in which all these elements coalesced into a whole, reminiscent of the Uruguayan-born French poet, Comte de Lautréamont famed description of Surrealism as; "The chance encounter of a sewing machine and an umbrella on a dissection table."[32] Memphis enthusiastically embraced the meeting of cheap and expensive, ancient and modern, mass and high culture, new colours, new forms. Many of their pieces function as modern-day totems.

The *Carlton Bookcase*, designed by Sottsass in 1981 is one of the most representative and totemic items. Functionally it is a combined bookcase and room divider, the wood infrastructure covered with a plastic laminate *Bacterio* which Sottsass had designed in 1978. This piece promotes image over function and celebrates the need for sensory expression in design. As Barbara Radice wrote in 1984:

> Memphis, like fashion, works on the fabric of contemporaneity, and contemporaneity means computers, electronics, video games, science-fiction comics, *Blade Runner*, *Space Shuttle*, bio-genetics, laser bombs, a new awareness of the body, exotic diets and banquets, mass exercise and tourism. Mobility

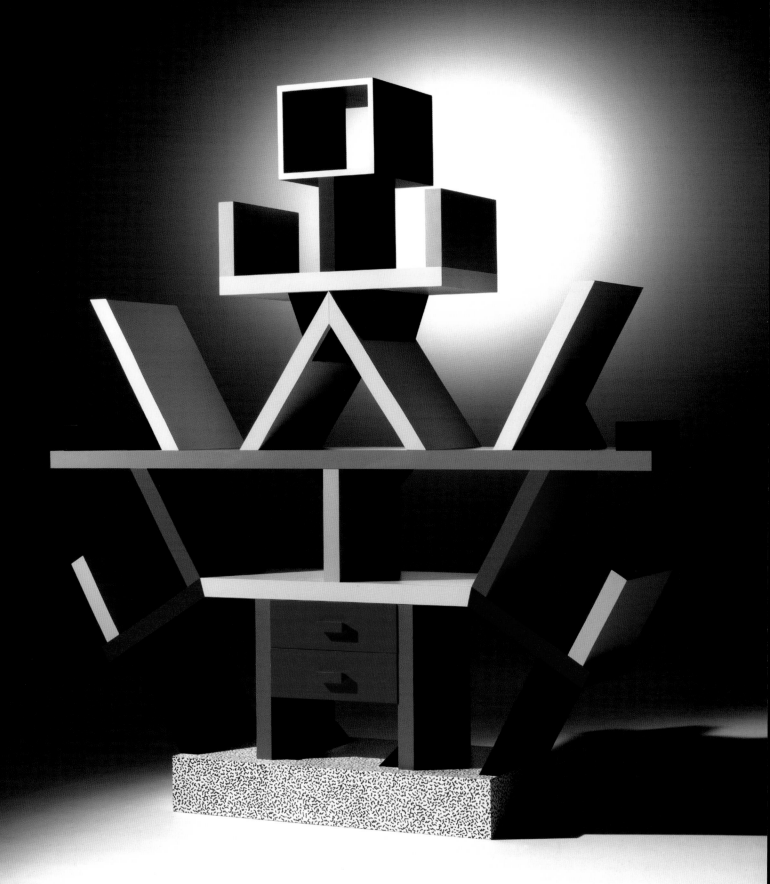

"Carlton" by Ettore Sottsass, Memphis Milano Collection, Room divider in plastic laminate, sizes 190 x 40 x 196 cm, 1981.
Photo: Aldo Balloo. Courtesy Memphis srl.

is perhaps the most macroscopic novelty of this culture. Not only physical mobility but also above all mobility of hierarchies and values; and mobility of interpretations which has liquefied the contours and solidity of things, shrinking the long, lazy waves of our "spirit of the times" to increasingly high frequencies until they burst and evaporate in a dust of hypotheses, in a world of events. What matters to us is not their substance but their appearance, their virtual image.[33]

The influence of Memphis was considerable. They were responsible for developing a new language of design at a time when the old one was no longer appropriate or capable of matching the dynamic changes in the cultural context. Memphis lasted just three years, the company was bought out by an industrialist who continues to produce design trivia under the Memphis label. The greatest contribution that Memphis made to the stagnant design of the 1980s was in the generation of new energies. It started an opposition to the tired and conservative culturally heavy values of official "good" design. Yes it was elitist, yes it was geographic specific, and yes it found its market in the wealthy museum-type shops in Europe and North America. But it did question traditional values, it did question the assertions of our material culture and, perhaps most notable of all, it brought back fun to design. In today's world, Memphis, Tennessee is where FedEx's 12 square mile SuperHub uses the latest logistical technologies to help power the global economy.[34] They really should have a statuette of the god Ptah in their entrance lobby which should be resplendent in Memphis furniture—a true synthesis of past, present and future.

PUNK

The relationship between design and culture is complex and ever changing. We live in a pluralistic society where diverse political ideologies, economic policies and alternative cultural values find their way into the design process. The designed object can be seen, at least in part, as a tangible expression of those varied influences. And that brings us to the safety pin. The 1970s witnessed industrial unrest in Europe, North America, Japan and Australasia. 1973 was the year of the first major oil crisis. In 1975 Punk arrived, the BBC website explains:

> In July 1975, Britain was in recession. Unemployment figures were the worst since the Second World War, with school leavers least likely to find work. Public spending had risen to 45 per cent of national income and the optimism of the 1960s had faded away. Tabloid newspapers initiated scares about vandalism, education, pornography and sexuality in general, pointing to 1960s 'permissiveness' as the cause. The IRA had begun a mainland bombing campaign in 1974. Margaret Thatcher had become leader of the Conservative Party in February 1975 and had begun formulating her own brand of Tory policy.

Many of the young people who became Punks in the next few years were from impoverished working class inner-city backgrounds. The social and political climate in which they had been growing up resulted in a feeling that was a mixture of frustration, boredom and poorly focussed anger. It was inevitable that this would cause a tide of teenage resentment that would find a voice and, coupled with the increasing disillusionment with the complacency of established rock bands, it is not surprising that what emerged became what is now known as 'Punk'.[35]

Punk was very much a designed confrontation. It was born out of the fractured social discontent of Malcolm Edwards (aka McLaren)[36] and Vivienne Westwood.[37] Malcolm McLaren, poignantly described by Christopher Lindner as a "university drop-out, rock enthusiast, politicised malcontent, and budding entrepreneur... rivetted by the radical ideas of the Situationists International, an avant-garde political and artistic movement with revolutionary aspirations of debilitating consumer society and eliminating its everyday forms of alienation".[38] The Situationists were a group of around 70 would-be-revolutionaries who were based in Paris and reached their zenith during the hot Summer of French student rebellion in 1968[39] (see Chapter Eight).

In 1971, McLaren and Westwood opened Let it Rock, the first of their retail outlets at 430 King's Road. In 1973 they visit New York and immersed themselves in village life; Andy Warhol and his factory of Pop, and the hard rock of cross-dressing The New York Dolls. Motivated by this "research", in 1974 they transformed 430 King's Road into its most radical phase, SEX.

McLaren and Westwood saw their creations as a way to politicise fashion, as a 'style' of destabilisation, "to sell music, clothing, art, jewellery, and other fashion accessories all expressively designed... to subvert the *status quo*".[40] Their revitalised store commercialised the darker underside of sex, pornography, fetish, and S&M, by providing inflatable rubber masks, whips and chains, and bondage type street clothes. They also introduced the one distinctive object that would serve as the trademark of Punk, the safety pin. All these goods displayed behind the new bright pink logo, SEX. "We decided we needed mannequins to model our clothes and so we invented The Sex Pistols", said McLaren. "Fashion was much more important than music. Punk was the sound of our fashion."[41]

ROTTEN PUNK

Following another visit to New York underground scene in 1975 McLaren decides to 'manage' an abrasive group of musical wannabe's known variously as The Strand, and The Swankers, who had taken up near residence status in the back of 430 King's Road, into a confrontational cohort. After a four week crash course in music technique, The Sex Pistols fronted by vocalist John Lyndon (aka Johnny Rotten) emerged to confront the British public. The group played its first gig on 6 November 1975, at St Martin's School of Art, London, to an audience of about 40 persons who had come to hear the featured pub rock group, Bazooka Joe.[42]

The initial set ended when members of Bazooka Joe quite literally, pulled the plug on The Sex Pistols, an act which resulted in a physical altercation between members of the two bands on stage. What began, maybe accidentally, became a staged occurrence at most later performances. Their club notoriety aided and abetted by confrontational behaviour, resulted in EMI signing the band to a two year contract on 8 October 1976. The Sex Pistols first recorded single, "Anarchy in the UK", was released on 26 November 1976. The associated publicity secured them an interview on 1 December with Bill Grundy on *Thames Today*, a evening show on local London television. Bill Grundy lost no time in goading the inebriated group into a profanity laden barrage which outraged the British public and provided the media with a field day, The newspapers were unanimous in condemning the anti-social behaviour and cultural attitudes of Punk, accusing them of corrupting their peers and wrecking the morals of the whole nation.[43] Some went as far as predicting the end of British culture. One of the more memorable headlines stemming from the *Daily Mirror* of 2 December, describing The Sex Pistols as "The Filth and the Fury".[44] The headline was reused as the title of a Sex Pistols documentary released in 2000. One other immediate response was that EMI recalled all copies of "Anarchy in the UK", had them destroyed and cancelled their contract with The Sex Pistols.[45] On 9 March 1977, A&M signed The Sex Pistols and dropped the band within a week and the 25,000 copies of the "God Save the Queen" that had already been pressed were destroyed. Virgin records finally released the single on 27 May 1977. By the late 1980s, images of Punks were appearing on London postcards promoting Punk as a tourist attraction.

REVOLUTIONARY TO ICON

By the 1990s things had evolved, former revolutionaries became icons. During the 1980s Malcolm McLaren pursued a career in music. In 1989, working in collaboration with the Greek composer Yanni, McLaren rearranged "The Flower Duet" into a work called "Aria" which featured in British Airways' World's favourite Airline global campaign of the 1980s and 1990s.[46] The original 90 second commercial was shot in Utah in 1984 and, along with the Apple commercial, "1984", (see below) ranks as one of the greatest television commercials ever produced. In 2008, Johnny Rotten, the lead singer of The Sex Pistols, was used to establish the brand awareness of *British Country Life Butter*. He appeared in press advertisements and in a television commercial, where dressed in country tweeds he announced, "It's not about Great Britain, it's about Great Butter."[47]

A memorable cover for the April 1989 issue of the magazine, *Tatler*, had Vivienne Westwood masquerading as Margaret Thatcher. (Margaret Thatcher, who as Prime Minister of the United Kingdom from 1979 to 1990 oversaw a tumultuous decade of social and political revolution.)[48] With a tag line of, "This woman was once a Punk", and using fanzine popularised torn newsprint typography this cover took *Tatler* into new fields of association. In 1992 Vivienne Westwood received the Order of the British Empire (OBE) from the Queen and Vivienne delighted the assembled photographers by twirling to show that she was *sans culottes*. In 2004, she was rewarded for her life-long innovative commitment to British fashion with a major retrospective at the prestigious V&A in London. In 2006 Vivienne Westwood was installed as a Dame of the British Empire for services to fashion. A Punk no more.

ABOUT FACE

During the 1970s, much mainstream graphic design was traumatised by the principle of 'good design' and the Swiss grid. Punk graphics changed that. Fanzines were in some ways a pre-Twitter form of social networking. Fans and groupies began to assemble their own instruments of communication. Among the more adventurous were *Panache*, 1976–1992; *Chainsaw*, 1977–1985; *Ripped & Torn*, 1976–1979 and acknowledged as the first and in may ways the preeminent fanzine, *Sniffin' Glue*, 1976–1977. In "Scissors and Glue: Punk Fanzines and the Creation of a DIY aesthetic", Teal Triggs explains:

> A4, stapled and photocopied fanzines of the late 1970s fostered the 'do-it-yourself' (DIY) production techniques of cut-and-paste letterforms, photocopied and collaged images, hand-scrawled and typewritten texts, to create a recognisable graphic design aesthetic.... This was a period of substantial cultural, social and political change where Punk reacted against the 'modern world' and the adsorption of 'hippy culture' into the mainstream.... Punk also reacted against the mid-1970s 'hit parade' rock music scene.... Punk music was seen as an alternative to the mainstream music industry and provided something new and liberating through its independent and 'do-it-yourself' approach.[49]

The most famous catch-phrase associated with Punk, "this is a chord, this is another, this is a third. Now form a band", originally appeared in the December 1976 issue of the fanzine *Sideburns* and was later reproduced in The Stranglers fanzine *Strangled* early in 1977.[50]

Jamie Reid had been a fellow student with Malcolm McLaren at Croydon Art College in 1968. They shared an interest in the writings of Marshall McLuhan and in the pronouncements of The Situationists. Reid produced the graphic content for six issues of *Suburban Press*, a magazine that included texts by the Situationists in its critique of modern society. He achieved notoriety with a series of bumper stickers that included phrases such as "Save

Petrol, burn cars" and "Special Offer. This store welcomes shoplifters." In 1976 he was invited by McLaren to help in the promotion of The Sex Pistols and was responsible for the design of the covers for *Anarchy in the UK* and *God Save the Queen*, which were evidence of this commitment to arresting visual imagery. There were the inevitable brushes with the establishment. His cover for *Never Mind the Bollocks: Here's The Sex Pistols* resulted in legal action on charges of obscenity. However, a Professor of English at Nottingham University documented the 1,000 year history of the Anglo-Saxon term, "bollocks" and charges were dropped.[51] Reid and McLaren were equally aware that the visual packaging and presentation of The Sex Pistols were vital to their success.

Neville Brody was disillusioned by his student days at Hornsey College of Art in 1975 and at the London College of Printing in 1976. He turned his attention to the youth subculture, in particular the graphics and imagery associated with Punk. Design stints with Rocking Russian, Stiff Records and Fetish Records were followed by a defining period as Art Director of *The Face,* 1981–1986, and a major show at the V&A in 1989. Brody was a founding force of Fontworks in 1990. *The Graphic Language of Neville Brody* by Jon Wozencroft, is reported to be the world's best-selling graphic design book.[52]

Terry Jones began his training at the West of England College of Art at Bristol. Design assignments at *Good Housekeeping* and *Vanity Fair* were followed in 1980 by his launch of the street fashion magazine *i-D* which began life as a home-produced fanzine, another example of 'do-it-yourself' (DIY) production techniques. Its success resulted in its evolution into yet another glossy style mag.[53] *The Face* did not fare much better. Launched in May 1980, within a short period of time it became recognised as the "fashion bible of the 80s".[54] Neville Brody was Art Director from 1981 through 1986. In the 1990s the magazine lost its distinguishing character. Increasing competition and an expensive libel case resulted in the magazine losing its appeal. It ceased publication in May, 2004. The appropriation of Punk graphics and ideology by mainstream design is an example of how a counter-culture becomes absorbed into the mainstream, representing a viable market segment in a rapidly fragmenting marketplace. Reid, Brody and Jones changed the face of graphic communication designs and its relationship with postmodernism.[55]

FASHION AND CULTURAL TRANSFORMATION —THE JAPANESE SENSIBILITY

In the 1960s Rei Kawakubo worked as a stylist for fashion related shoots for several Japanese magazines. When she could not find clothes to match her styling needs she started designing and making her own range, establishing Commes des Garçons (like the boys) in Tokyo in 1969. In 1970, Kenzo Takada introduced his

distinctive collection in Paris and so began the Japanese invasion of international fashion. The revolution began much earlier on the campuses of several Japanese universities. Kenzo is a graduate of Bunka College of Fashion; Issey Miyake is a graduate of the Graphic Design Programme at Tama Art University and acquired much of his personal design philosophy while a student at Tama. Yohji Yamamoto graduated with a law degree from Keio University before studying fashion at Bunka Fashion College. Rei Kawakubo is a philosophy graduate of Keio University. If there is one unifying perception to the breadth of creativity of this group then it is their dedication to see clothing as concept.[56]

By the early 1980s many people associated with fashion were questioning the traditional belief that clothing should express wealth and status. The trend began in Japan with the unsettling clothes of Yohji Yamamoto and Rei Kawakubo. These clothes were usually black and often intensely torn or ragged. The trend gathered momentum and was reflected in the Paris showings of the Winter 1983/1984 collections when a contingent of Japanese designers emerged and presented a totally new concept in dressing. They transformed elements of Punk into an art form, legitimising the look by strutting it on the Parisian runways, their overriding message being that clothes should interact with the persona.[57]

Reactions to the collections were mixed. Depending on whom you chose to believe, the Japanese movement was the most exciting and innovative thing to happen to fashion in decades or, conversely, an outrage, a travesty of what clothes are supposed to be about. The evidence of this 'travesty' was expressed in clothing items such as sweaters, coats and dresses which sprouted holes and more than the occasional slash.[58] Hems that were uneven, seams that were made visible, fur used with the pile going in the "wrong" direction, sleeves that encompassed the hands and, at times, came four to the garment. Rejecting stereotypes, these designs became the hallmarks for a new way of seeing, a new sensibility, one that was individual and interactive, one that merged the clothes with the character of the wearer. What started out as a fashion trend became a lifestyle. Every Sunday the young and some not-so-young took to the streets around Yoyogi Park in Tokyo. This was deconstruction and reconstruction in action. There was music, street performance and of course fashion. There were references to influences from the East and from the West, all magnificently and provocatively displayed on a stage that became an entry into a more global sensibility to design and fashion.[59]

Yohji Yamamoto, Rei Kawakubo and Issey Miyake were among the first designers to broadcast the new Japanese sensibility in fashion. Collectively, their designs explored the tension that exists between Western inspiration and the perpetuation of traditional Japanese values.[60] Although Kawakudo objects to being classified as a 'Japanese' designer; she refutes ethnic boundaries, seeing her work and her aesthetic as being transnational.

An interesting collaboration with Jamie Reid, the creative force behind The Sex Pistols, Comme des Garçons Homme Plus launched an Autumn/Winter 2008 menswear collection entitled "Time For Magic". This featured the images and text-based works of Jamie Reid from 1972 to the present and reinforced Kawakubo's assertion of the transnational character of her designs. Reid's political attitude combined with Rei Kawakubo's innovative vision provided a timeline summary of fashion's divergence from Haute Couture to that of influential brand management. In a January 2011 article in *Hyperbeast*, Edward Chu suggested that the 1981 Paris show of Rei Kawakubo "ended the French Fashion Syndicate's influence in the fashion industry and sparked off a new era of creation and brand management".[61] The new look had moved to Tokyo.

There was another genesis to the Japanese fashion scene. In 1964 Tokyo was host to the Olympic Games. After the games, the IOC awarded the Olympic Cup to the City of Tokyo for its perfect organisation of the games and the Olympic Diploma of Merit to Kenzo Tange for his design of the National Gymnasium.[62] It was Tange, a resident of Hiroshima, who won the 1949 competition to design the Hiroshima Peace Memorial Park; (in 1990, The 1st Hiroshima Art Prize was awarded to Issey Miyake, see Chapter Eleven).

By wars end, around 80 per cent of buildings in Tokyo were destroyed. The 1960 census reported a population base of nearly ten million existing with limited water supplies, (compounded by a three month drought in 1964), accompanying food shortages and with a devastated transportation infrastructure. The Games were expected to attract two million visitors. The stadium, sports facilities, accommodation for athletes were all additional challenges. Tokyo responded by undertaking one of the most spectacular urban reconstruction programmes of the twentieth century. The city was, quite literally, reborn at a cost of $2.8 billion.[63]

The Olympic Village was constructed in Yoyogi in an area known as Washington Heights, a former compound for families of the American forces of occupation. The site was adjacent to Takeshita-dori. After the games ended and the athletes moved out some of Tokyo's youth moved into the area, establishing what was to become the renowned area of Harajuku resplendent with Tokyo's first boutiques and bars and restaurants geared to the needs of the young *Harajuku-zoko*. The Harajuku tribe prowled Takeshita-dori adjacent to the foot of Omotesando where the Tokyo fashion *fricandeaus* promenaded.[64] During the economic realignment of the 1980s, Haute Couture was augmented by casual street fashion, Shibuya joined Harajuku as initiators of what was to become the mainstream fashion trend in Tokyo. In the English abstract of *Rethinking 'Shibu-Kaji'* Professor Nanba Koji of Kwansei Gakuin University makes an astute assessment:

> In 1988, some teenagers made a practice of gathering in the Shibuya area with their friends. Their style was casual, but their clothes were not so cheap. Basically, they had wealthy parents, lived in middle class areas and went to schools attached to private universities. Their style was called *Shibu-Kaji* (abbreviation of Shibuya casual), and they were called *Shibu-kaji zoku*. At first, they were only loitering in the Shibuya area as a group, especially on the *Center-Gai* (centre street). They were represented in fashion magazines as stylish urban boys and girls. They were trendsetters for young people of the same age. It was said that they belonged to the generation of *Dankai Jr* (Japanese second baby boomer). In the beginning of the 1990s, they came to be regarded by the media as delinquent youth. *Shibu-kaji zoku* was the last one of the major youth subcultures which had a suffix *-zoku*. It was the turning point of youth sub-cultures, from *-zoku* to *-kei*. This means that the focus of youth sub-cultures in Japan was transferred from deviance to taste.[65]

Postmodernism, Pop and Punk shared at least one common characteristic—consumerism was required to define and justify these various means of expression. There were significant changes in the methods of production and distribution allied to what was becoming an increasingly fragmented market. Changes in the available processes of communication prompted changes in the business of design. David Raizman summarises:

> Late capitalism signifies investment directed towards increasingly segmented (rather than collective) audiences, and a readiness of business to design, manufacture, and market products with increasing speed, responsiveness and sophistication in a highly competitive environment, stimulated even further by an accelerated interactivity between design, manufacture, and marketing through the use of digital technology.[66]

There is an increasing emphasis on research in the design process. And it must be research, not a search for justification. The ergonomic research of SizeChina mentioned in Chapter One is an example of innovative research that recognises the needs of the user, takes advantage of sophisticated technological developments to go far beyond what used to be termed 'human-factors' and create a database of information with a multiplicity of uses. Design is no longer restricted to the product or service; it now encompasses the use to which that product or service is put, and the cultural context of its use. One developing term to cover this reorientation of design is, "service design". The Core77 website provides a succinct assessment of the role of service design.

Time for Magic, Jamie Reid for Comme des Garçons Hommes Plus, Winter 2008, Tokyo.

The job of an industrial designer is to consider the end-user's experience. Once upon a time that was as basic as making a chair supportive in the right places, making a handle chunky enough to grab or asking the graphics guys to make the numbers bigger for legibility. Nowadays it's getting more complicated.

A modern product like an iPhone works... not only because of its inherent industrial and interface design, but because of the ecosystem in which it 'lives'. In the case of the iPhone that ecosystem has been carefully designed, in the form of the iTunes Music/App Store, (among other things); providing consumers with an easy way to buy and use music and apps increases the phone's utility, improves the customer experience, and creates wealth for the record labels, musicians, and software companies. In other words, as well-designed as the iPhone is as an individual object, it is the design of the services around it that makes it a game-changer.[67]

Times change, so do people, so does design. Global communication initiates an awareness of change, helping people to learn fast, to adjust to changing cultural dynamics, to adopt new attitudes and learn new aptitudes. A few decades ago a mouse was no more than a domestic pest and a mackintosh a nineteenth century type of rainwear. To communicate by telephone we searched for an isolated box like container to protect our 'privacy'. We had knowledge of our culture while remaining ignorant of others. We ignored time zones and planned all our activities in local time. We rarely read labels in the supermarket and green was no more than a colour with supposed calming capabilities. How the world has changed.

Some things don't change. We still have a long way to go to make this world of ours more 'user friendly' to more people. As explained by Lee McIntyre in Chapter One, we still lack any real understanding of the cause of war, terrorism, famine and poverty, we still live in the "Dark Ages of human thought about social problems".

Harajuku.

In terms of design we still build houses by hand, we may
keep our cars for a few more years, we sort our garbage,
we profess a concern for our environment but dispose of
cell phones with an alarming disregard for sustainability.
Our experiences of material characteristics and processes
of manufacture are likely to be derived from 'virtual'
environments rather than the real world. We need to
consider the real world.

CHAPTER TEN
DESIGN FOR THE 'REAL', REAL WORLD

The main trouble with design schools seems to be that they teach too much design and not enough about the ecological, social, economic, and political environment in which design takes place.
Victor Papanek, *Design for the Real World*.

TO THE ABYSS AND BACK

Our real world problems began to emerge over 60 years ago and it will require transformative change to solve, or at least come to terms with, the challenges ahead. But do not be disheartened, we have been here before. A sense of melancholy gripped Europe at the end of the first millennium. From around 950, many were convinced that the world would end on 31 December 1999. Charles van Doren explains. "There was a dearth of ingenuity and invention. Many problems seemed to be insoluble. People tried to hang on, hoping that life would not get even worse. They seem to have given up hope that it would get any better."[1] But get better it did. "New solutions of old problems became obvious. Why had no one thought of them before? Imaginative political and social arrangements were tested and were often found to work. Artists made new kinds of art, poets wrote new kinds of verse, and philosophers were surprised to discover that there were all kinds of new ideas to be thought."[2] There were cathedrals to be built, water mills to be put to use to increase production, silk and wool to be woven, mechanical clocks to be used, ships to sail, new worlds to find, discoveries to be made and a renaissance to prepare for.[3] Once more our world is on the cusp.

THE REAL WORLD c. 2012

Certainly our world is faced by unprecedented challenges. There are no simple solutions. Solutions are likely to be as complex, fluid and diverse as are the challenges. However, you can, and should, make a difference. John Thackara points out, "The world contains its share of selfish and incurious designers, of course. But no designer that I have ever met set out to wreck our planet, force us to eat fast food, or make life miserable. Our dilemma is that small design actions can have big effects—often unexpectedly—and

designers have only recently been told, with the rest of us, how incredibly sensitive we need to be to the possible consequences of any design steps we take."[4] It is estimated that upwards of "80–90 per cent of the cost of a typical product and some 80 per cent of its environmental impact, is determined at the design stage".[5] This then would seem to be the logical place to start rethinking design for the real 'real' world. First a little background. Today all forms of media point out the damage caused by catering exclusively to the top ten per cent of the worlds most affluent population, these impairments range from degradation of the environment to continuing social inequalities.

THE BUSINESS OF DESIGN

Back in the 1950s, affluence was not only good it was the model to aim for. Wartime sacrifices and memories of the Great Depression were still fresh in peoples minds. The period from the late 1940s through to the early 1970s, was the golden era of American style capitalism. In Europe and North America the economy boomed.[6] Enhanced patterns of consumption were seen as one way of overcoming class conflict and as an assurance against international conflict.[7] In 1947, J Gordon Lippincott, wrote his highly influential book, *Design for Business*, which praises the values of consumerism.[8] Into this context, in 1958, the Canadian economist John Kenneth Galbraith launched *The Affluent Society*,[9] his polemic against conspicuous consumption and his support for capital expenditure in transportation infrastructure and education.[10] Nearly half a century later, in 1996 he provided a prospective assessment of "The Environment" within *The Good Society: the Humane Agenda*.

> The Good Society has three closely related economic requirements, each of which is of independent force. There is the need to supply the requisite consumer goods and services. There is the need to ensure that this production and its use and consumption do not have adverse effect on the current well-being of the public at large. And there is the need to ensure that they do not adversely affect the lives and well-being of generations yet to come.[11]

Galbraith's three requirements apply to design and each presents its own set of interconnected challenges to design. First, who determines what are exactly, the "requisite consumer goods and services"? Do all of Earths near seven billion inhabitants have claim to the same range of goods and services that the privileged ten per cent in the affluent developed world have? If so, then we need to find at least two other Earth like planets to provide the necessary raw materials to meet the demand. Secondly, who establishes the level of "current well-being"? Lastly, the future focus of most elected governments is on the next election—will voters agree in sufficient numbers to concern themselves with "generations yet to come".

We may not have all the answers, we may see these as apparently insurmountable obstacles. In this context, design does matter and designers can make a difference. However, Dr Paul Polak, makes the valid point: "The majority of the world's designers focus all their efforts on developing products and services exclusively for the richest ten per cent of the world's customers. Nothing less than a revolution in design is needed to reach the other 90 per cent."[12] His newest project is D-REV, a non-profit venture that seeks "to create a design revolution by enlisting the best designers in the world to develop products and ideas that will benefit the 90 per cent of the people on earth who are poor, in order to help them earn their way out of poverty".[13] A revolution needs a manifesto.

DESIGN PROFILE: RULES OF ENGAGEMENT

In 2006, John Thackara proposed eight "Rules of Engagement" that should feature in a design process when facing up to some of the sustainable design challenges ahead.

RULE ONE: Look near as well as far. There is a lot of work to be done nearby as well as far away. It is easier to enhance the human resources, culture, heritage, traditions, know-how and skills of a local culture than that of a distant one.

RULE TWO: Work for actual people, not for categories. Be on your guard whenever you read the words "the poor" or "the elderly" or "the blind" or "the disabled". These casual (and widespread) habits of language disembody and dehumanise people. (If you don't believe me, ask a blind person).

RULE THREE: Respect what's already there. Designers are trained to change things for the better—not to leave well alone. The good news is that visiting designers can act like mirrors, reflecting positive things about a situation that local people no longer notice or value.

RULE FOUR: Empower local people. Any design action that rearranges places and relationships is an exercise of power. A good test for the sensitivity of incoming designers is whether they enable people to increase control over their own territory and resources.

RULE FIVE: Commit long-term. When Sergio Palleroni offered the support of design students to communities in New Orleans, he committed to a minimum of three years' engagement. It takes time to understand a situation, time to listen to local people and gain their trust, time for appropriate solutions to emerge.

RULE SIX: Small is not small. Small design actions can have big consequences, many of them positive ones. If someone builds a bus stop in an urban slum, a vibrant community can sprout and grow around it. Such is the power of small interventions into complex urban situations. Read *Small Change*, by Nabeel Hamdi for more inspiring examples of the power of thinking small.[14]

RULE SEVEN: Think whole systems. Aspen project leader Paul Polak reckons the design and technology of a device, such as a pump, or sprinkler system, is not much more than ten per cent of the complete solution. The other 90 per cent involves distribution, training, maintenance and service arrangements, partnership and business models. He and Jim Pattel at Stanford Business School get students to plan whole business solutions to development opportunities.

RULE EIGHT: Hands-on or hands-off. Hungry people need posters and campaigns less than they need food to eat.[15]

PEOPLE ARE THE REAL WEALTH OF A NATION

After more than two millennia of development, the population of Earth in 1930 was estimated to be two billion. Today, it is estimated to be seven billion. By 2050 the number could reach in excess of ten billion—a five-fold increase in just 120 years. The January 2011 issue of *National Geographic* paints a worrying picture:

With the population still growing by about 80 million each year, it's hard not to be alarmed. Right now on Earth, water tables are falling, soil is eroding, glaciers are melting, and fish stocks are vanishing. Close to a billion people go hungry each day. Decades from now, there will likely be two billion more mouths to feed, mostly in poor countries. There will be billions more people wanting and deserving to boost themselves out of poverty. If they follow the path blazed by wealthy countries–clearing forests, burning coal and oil, freely scattering fertilisers and pesticides–they too will be stepping hard on the planet's natural resources. How exactly is this going to work?[17]

You may well ask. In terms of design there are two segment areas to consider; the fortunate ten per cent for whom present production and consumption patterns have increasingly been shown to be unsustainable; and the less fortunate 90 per cent who, as Angharad Thomas pointed out in 2006, "do not constitute a market for designed or designer goods".[18] But they do constitute a market for design. Far too many of this worlds seven billion inhabitants live in overcrowded, unstable and dangerous environments without access to safe drinking water or adequate sewage systems and where the lack of electricity compounds problems of personal safety. In some communities health problems such as the impact of HIV/AIDS encourage exclusion.

Design is about and for people, all people. Design is also about context. The designed product or service must function within the constraints of local economic, political, manufacturing and cultural constraints. Solutions that choose to ignore these constraints' are likely to prove irrelevant. Paul Polak's blog provides a sobering example.

> More than 160 million people in India are considered 'Untouchable'–people tainted by their birth into an irrational caste system that defines them as impure and less than human. Ghandi called them Harijans, or 'children of God' and launched campaigns to improve their lives, but in spite of his efforts, Untouchables in India are still not allowed to drink from the same wells as upper class Hindus, or attend the same temples, or drink from the same cups in tea stalls. They spend their lives doing menial jobs like cleaning toilets, and are frequent victims of violence.[19]

A small village of 120 families in Orissa obtained their safe drinking water from a local shopkeeper. Customers provide their own cans to refill. One member of the Harijan community inadvertently touched the tap on the 3,000-litre storage tank. A Brahmin family complained and the shopkeeper was forced to drain his tank and 'purify' it. The solution to this culturally specific problem was to arrange a bicycle home delivery system. The illogic of the situation was that you now had higher caste labourers delivering water to lower caste Harijam. Illogical it may be but the 'service' is acceptable to the cultural context of use.

Design can assist in the provision of an environment for people to enjoy long, healthy, safe and creative lives, free from poverty, inequality and social exclusion. The United Nations Development Programme publishes the Human Development Report (HDR) annually. The report for 2010 makes it clear that the past cannot be used as an indicator of things to come. New problems require new means of redress:

> First, we cannot assume that future development will mimic past advances: opportunities today and in the future are greater in many respects. Second, varied experiences and specific contexts preclude overarching policy prescriptions and point towards more general principles and guidelines. Third, major new challenges must be addressed–most prominently, climate change. [20]

SOCIAL INJUSTICE

The 2008 report by the World Health Organisation claims that a "toxic combination of bad policies, economics and politics is in large measure responsible for the fact that a majority of people in the world do not enjoy the good health that is biologically possible. Social injustice is killing on a grand scale."[21] The world is in need of design led, innovative solutions that address poverty, education, health, ageing, and the environment;[22] (environmental issues are covered in more detail in Chapter Thirteen, "Design Futures: A Matter of Questions").

POVERTY

Today, most designers are encouraged to design for the marketplace. It is time to design for real people in the real world. Poverty as a word slips nicely off the tongue but, for many, lacks definition. Poverty is a state of depravation of the common necessities required to live a humane life. These include the provision of adequate food, clothing, safe drinking water, a place to sleep, a place to learn and a place to work. According to figures from the World Bank, in 2004, over 20 per cent of the global population existed on less than $1 a day. The highest rates of poverty being in South Asia (30.84 per cent of the population) and Sub-Saharan Africa (41.09 per cent).[23] More specifically, India is home to 41 per cent of the worlds poor, and despite its post "Olympic" face, China has 22 per cent of the worlds poor.[24] More than 80 per cent of the world's population lives in countries where income differentials are widening.[25]

Poverty is not restricted to the developing world. As Douglas Kellner of the University of Texas points out, "contemporary capitalist societies and cultures... are in a situation of seemingly permanent crisis with deteriorating social conditions increasing human suffering".[26] Paul Harris of *The Observer* provides a North American focus: "A shocking 37 million Americans live in poverty. That is 12.7 per cent of the population–the highest percentage in the developed world".[27] Most damning of all is, as Marilyn French points out, in 1988, "the nations of the world spent over $110 for each man, woman, and child on military expenses–overwhelmingly more than on food, water, shelter, health, education, or protecting the ecosystem".[28] There is no indication that things have changed over the last two decades.

THREE GREAT POVERTY ERADICATION MYTHS

The social innovator and writer Paul Polak is critical of the "Three Great Poverty Eradication Myths". First, that poverty may be alleviated by generous and well intentioned donations. Donations alone will not bring about an end to poverty. Second, the much lauded increase in national economic growth is often at significant cost to the poor; and lastly, investment injection by global multinationals will provide jobs and eradicate poverty. Polak shows that approaches based on these approaches have, in general, failed. In some areas where these approaches have been tried, such as sub-Saharan Africa, poverty rates have actually gone up. These observations are supported by the 2008 report from Care International which shows that despite spending billions of dollars a year on emergency feeding programmes for the hungry the numbers of people without food is increasing. "In the last two years another 100 million people have been pushed into hunger and can no longer afford food."[29]

Microeconomics is an approach that works. It helps the poor finance their own endeavours.[30] Unexploited market opportunities do exist for the desperately poor. Social innovators have identified these opportunities and have developed innovative, low-cost tools that have helped impoverished rural farmers use the market to improve their lot in life.[31] A parallel path is suggested by Dambisa Moyo, a Zambian born economist, who argues for the elimination of all aid within five years. She sees this as a vital step towards economic sustainability for Africa. "Despite one trillion dollars in western aid over the last 60 years, the economic lot of the average African has only gotten worse."[32] Moyo is an advocate of micro-finance and her rational is endorsed by Bangladeshi Nobel laureate Muhammad Yunus the founder of the Grameen bank which offers micro-credit schemes as part of a poverty reduction programme.[33] A basic income programme pioneered by German aid workers has helped alleviate poverty in a Namibian village; The plan, funded by a coalition of aid agencies, provides a basic income of around $13 for each of the 1,000 inhabitants of the village of Otjivero—no strings attached. It is up to the individual to use the money to better their lot in life.[34] Microeconomics work.

Design can play a vital role in fighting poverty, but it will require approaching the challenge in a creative way. We know the problem. What to do? The first thing is to get to where the action is needed. Designers need to recognise that communities in both developed and developing societies cannot be understood through standard social research methods or second-hand data. It is difficult to comprehend hunger if you have never been hungry, or the insecurity that accompanies homelessness if you have a secure place to sleep.[35] Jeffrey Sachs serves as the Director of the Earth Institute at Columbia University and has written extensively on poverty. He calls for global co-operative commitments to achieve the collective aspirations of the world for a more peaceful, prosperous, and sustainable new millennium. This is very much an operational setting for design. "I believe that the design community, and all of the rest of us (in economics, engineering, the arts, public health and more) should take our cue from the shared global commitments. If we all act to add our part to shared global goals, we can achieve what we've promised even if our governments are woefully inadequate."[36]

EDUCATION[37]

Imagine how challenging life would be if you had never gone to school. Lacking the most basic literacy skills you could not read signs, labels, fill in forms, apply for assistance—buying or selling in the local marketplace would be difficult without at least a grounding in simple math. "All children around the world have the right to an education. Investing in education is not just the right thing to do; it's the smart thing to do… education gives people the skills they need to help themselves out of poverty and into prosperity."[38] There are 900 million people in the world today who cannot read and write. Two-thirds of them are women. 98 per cent of the worlds illiterate live in developing countries. An estimated 400 million children will never get the chance to have an education.[39] In many countries, the traditional role assigned to women and girls militates against their enrolment in school.

In far too many countries child labour is rife. According to the International Labour Organization (a specialised agency of the UN), around 186 million children between five and 15 years of age have to work.[40] Increasing partisan conflicts and the misuse of enforced child conscription add further to continuing rates of illiteracy. Less than one per cent of what the world spent every year on weapons was needed to put every child into school by the year 2000 and yet it didn't happen.[41] If it did, think of the design opportunities—all those millions have to be clothed, all need textbooks and teaching aids, all need a secure and safe place to learn—and all of these need to be designed for local production taking advantage of locally available materials and production processes. (Rule Three and Four, "Rules of Engagement".)

HEALTH

Healthcare is one area where design can make a very real and immediate difference and where John Thackara's "Rules of Engagement" should be considered in all design proposals. While not minimising the necessity for improved medical care, design can help in other ways, in particular with regard to the provision of safe drinking water and in improving interior air quality. The problem is an old one, and there have been some significant attempts (mostly ignored by the "professional" design community) to mollify the situation. A Canadian university with financial help from a government agency was respectful of Thackara's rule one: "look near as well as far" in designing one highly satisfactory response to the need for local reliable water availability.

Waterloo Water Pump, Malaysia. I.D.R.C. Ottawa. Developed by Dr Alan Plumtree and his team at the University of Waterloo.

In 1978, the Canadian International Development Research Centre (IDRC) asked researchers at Waterloo University to design a hand pump that would be inexpensive enough for poorer countries to afford, durable enough to stand up to 18 hours a day of continuous use, yet simple enough for villagers to maintain and repair themselves. The pumps would also have to be designed so that they could be manufactured within the developing countries, creating jobs for local populations and making spare parts readily available.[42]

The researchers, led by Dr Alan Plumtree, started in their local Mennonite community where farmers had been using practical, reliable hand pump technology for generations. This Mennonite pump became the basis for the researchers' design. Some of the underground sections of the revised design were made of polyvinyl chloride (PVC) which is readily available in most countries. PVC is rust resistant, and does not contaminate the taste—an 'iron' taste and odour is often associated with the more traditional cast iron pumps. Over the years there have been some interesting design adjustments made. In Malawi, carnivorous hyenas associated the white coloured plastic spigots with bone and gnawed and chewed on them. The colour of the spigots was changed to black and the associated problem solved. Sri Lankan villagers ran out of replacement plastic rings and

substituted hand made leather ones—a twist now used by several communities. The basic Waterloo design has been adapted for different conditions around the world. The University of Malaya co-ordinated the design and manufacture of the related Unimade pumps in 13 countries. There are tens of thousands of these pumps in daily use worldwide.[43]

From a Mennonite farm in Ontario, through a Canadian university laboratory to villages throughout the developing world, the spread of the Waterloo hand pump is an outstanding example of co-operative, sustainable design. Despite its more than 30 year success record, despite helping tens of thousands of people in many locations around the world, this innovative design is ignored by all the worlds design museums and collections, it does not even appear in Toronto's own Design Exchange. Canapés before commitment.

Solar powered water heater, near Lhasa, Tibet. Given the high altitude the kettle will reach boiling point in about 20 minutes.

INTERIOR TOXIC AIR

The air we breath can kill us. Indoor air pollution, including smoke and other products of incomplete combustion arising from solid fuel cooking stoves, is a major environmental risk factor, usually ranking behind lack of clean water, poor sanitation and malnutrition as a cause of death arising from environmental factors— many of which can be alleviated by design. Half of the world's population and approximately 80 per cent of rural households in developing countries cook with solid fuels like wood, coal, crop residues and dung. The toxic laden smoke causes cancer, pneumonia and obstructive pulmonary disease. According to the World Health Organization (WHO), smoke from burning solid fuels is estimated to be responsible for 1.6 million deaths each year in the world's poorest countries.[44] That's a staggering death every 20 seconds, the time it took you to read this paragraph.

The challenge is easily stated—develop a fuel-efficient biomass stove that reduces environmental impact; that improves domestic air quality and improves the health and hygiene of users—which in the vast percentage of cases will be women. Numerous studies reinforces the challenge. Developing solutions that are functional and respective of prevailing cultural conditions are not as easy.

In some areas of the rural floodplain areas of Bangladesh the mud built cooking stove is still prevalent. Danesh Miah of Kookmin University, Seoul, estimates that the use of an improved cooking stove would result in a saving of about two-thirds in the annual fuel-wood consumption while having significant benefit to the domestic interior and the health of women and children.[45] All too often, designed solutions ignore local cultural values and preferences. "In India the government subsidised 50 per cent of the cost of eight million stoves that it distributed. Initially, the programme encountered some difficulties because the stove design was not appropriate for the tools and food used by the population."[46] An extensive and well documented research brief from RTI identifies the challenges associated with the design, manufacture and use of an improved cooking stove (IPS) that will reduce indoor air pollution (IAP).[47] The ANAGi is an improved cooking stove designed for use in Sri Lanka. It consists of a single clay stove capable of holding two pots developed to suit the cooking habits and food preferences prevalent in Sri Lanka. It can use a variety of available biomass material including coconut shells and the fronds and leaves of local plants. It is reported to be twice as efficient as traditional three stone pots. Initially introduced in 1986 there are reported to be more than 300,000 in use throughout rural Sri Lanka. The United Nations Foundation has established the Global Alliance for Clean Cookstoves with a stated goal of enabling one hundred million homes to adopt clean and efficient stoves and fuels by 2020.[48]

AGEING[49]

Over the next 50 years, the age composition of nearly every country is expected to move to one in which the old outnumber the young. (There are differing suggestions as to what age the term 'elderly' applies.) A US census report, *An Aging World: 2008*, studies the demographic and socioeconomic trends that accompany ageing. The report shows that, globally, within ten years, older people will outnumber children under five for the first time. It forecasts that over the next 30 years the number of over-65s is expected to almost double, from 506 million in 2008 to 1.3 billion. Already, the number of people in the world 65 and over is increasing at an average of 870,000 each month. The oldest old, people aged 80 and older, are the fastest growing

portion of the total population in many countries.[50] "By 2040, when China's median age will rise to 44 years, the ratio of elderly to youth will be a remarkable two to one."[51] Various countries are at different stages in their demographic realignment. The most advanced being Japan.[52] Within the next decade there will be three seniors for every child under 15 in Japan. One in six will be over 80; Japanese women have the highest life expectancy on earth at 86.44 years; the Japanese government is predicting that by 2055 seniors will make up around half the population.

A report in the British medical journal, *The Lancet*, concurs, "stating that most babies born since 2000 in France, Germany, Italy, the UK, the USA, Canada, Japan... will celebrate their 100th birthdays".[53] This massive shift in demographics provides exciting and rewarding opportunities for design intervention. However, to be effective, all resolutions must utilise a user centric approach to ensure familiarity with the challenges and the production of satisfactory solutions. (See Rules of Engagement, Two, Three & Four.) Solutions will have an immediate positive effect but will also have a secondary economic consequence by making welfare costs sustainable.

Jizo-dori, Sugamo, Tokyo. Automated external defibrillator (AED) devices are located at about 100 metre intervals.

THE JAPANESE MODEL

Already caring for the elderly accounts for half of the Japanese health budget. Healthcare reform aside, this change in demographics has profound implications for design—the senior segment of Japanese society control around half of the country's wealth. This has created an economy sensitive to the needs of the over 60s, an economy that will encompass medical care and treatment and the provision of health facilities. Change is evident in the integration of robotics into the care of the elderly and is becoming evident in the future design plans of corporate Japan who have introduced robotic pets,[54] intelligent toilets,[55] custom designed cars, cybernetic suits[56] and even graveyard webcams into this brave new world. The new economy will also focus on the cultural needs and social aspirations of the elderly, a dynamic group who are fashioning their own cultural space.

In the developed world, increasing numbers of over 60s have sufficient disposable income to impact the market. Many urban centres cater to the young, some of the more enlightened communities are providing services and facilities aimed at the senior market.

The district of Sugamo in Tokyo, for example, is now a vibrant area for the over-60s, rivalling the cities more famous Harajuku District, which caters to Tokyo's teens and pre-teens. Sugamo Station is on the Yamanote line (the same line that serves Harajuku). The stations facilities are designed with the elderly in mind—its walkways and stairs are wide enough to cater to the physically challenged and those who need to use a wheelchair or a cane.[57]

Sugamo is home to the *Togenuki Jizo* temple. *Jizo* is the wise *Bodhisattva* who protects the weak and innocent and is said to have the ability to lengthen life. Elderly from all Japan travel to *Jizo dori* to worship and shop. In Sugamo, *Jizo dori* is a popular shopping street where many of its shops offer goods and services aimed specifically towards the needs and preferences of the older generation. As you would expect, the stores offer a range of traditional products and foodstuffs, including *shio-daifuku* (salty rice cakes), Jizo soba buckwheat noodles and rice crackers. There a few unusual items, including the famed lucky red underwear, believed to promote vigour in the wearer.

There is a clearly demonstrated human need for the camaraderie afforded by being part of a congenial social circle within a compatible environment. This social conception benefits from policy innovation, both local and national, and by the support of motivated business concerns. Most fundamental is the supporting participation of the users. The Sugamo neighbourhood allows for a celebration of life while accepting the reality of death—a cultural space that is part performance, part solemnisation, and part commemoration—a cultural space that befits from inclusive design and social innovation.[58]

'REAL' CURRENT DESIGN PRACTICE

There are many young designers and social entrepreneurs who are sufficiently motivated to face up to challenges of the *Millennium Development Goals* outlined earlier in this chapter. More concerned with social injustice than designer labels these young revolutionaries explore the potential offered by creative design intervention. The suggested readings mentioned in the endnotes provide factual information on some current concerns and no doubt many of you have your own areas of interest. With current design practices in mind I would like to present a few

examples or material, product, and process that you may not be so familiar with.

MATERIAL: BAMBOO, THE MIRACLE GRASS

First let me quote from *A Yankee on the Yangtze* written by William Edgar Geil in 1904.

> A man can sit in a bamboo house under a bamboo roof, on a bamboo chair at a bamboo table, with a bamboo hat on his head and bamboo sandals on his feet. He can at the same time hold in one hand a bamboo bowl, in the other hand bamboo chopsticks and eat bamboo sprouts. When through with his meal, which has been cooked over a bamboo fire, the table may be washed with a bamboo cloth, and he can fan himself with a bamboo fan, take a siesta on a bamboo bed, lying on a bamboo mat with his head resting on a bamboo pillow. His child might be lying in a bamboo cradle, playing with a bamboo toy. On rising he would smoke a bamboo pipe and taking a bamboo pen, write on bamboo paper, or carry his articles in bamboo baskets suspended from a bamboo pole, with a bamboo umbrella over his head. He might then take a walk over a bamboo suspension bridge, drink water from a bamboo ladle, and scrape himself with a bamboo scraper.[59]

Global rates of deforestation accompanied by increased CO_2 emissions threaten the earth's biodiversity and the quality of the very air we breathe. Reports from the UN estimate that 60 acres of tropical forest are felled worldwide every minute. Some of the most extreme examples of deforestation are recorded in the developing world. "Nigeria, which lost an estimated 15 million acres between 1990 and 2005, or about one-third of its entire forest area, and has one of the world's highest deforestation rates."[60] Official government data from Brazil's National Institute for Space Research reported that around 3,145 square miles were wiped out between August 2007 and August 2008, that is a deforestation jump of 65 per cent over a 12 month period.[61] The rapid global increase in food prices is cited as the main cause in encouraging the destruction of 'natural' rainforest in favour of land to cultivate cash crop such as soy and provide grazing land for cattle barons.

There is no one solution to the consequences of deforestation, but amazingly, the simple bamboo plant can make a dramatic positive impact. Bamboo provided the first 'greening' of Hiroshima after the 1945 atomic apocalypse. It can provide the fastest growing canopy for the re-greening of degraded lands; stands of bamboo release 35 per cent more oxygen back into the environment than equivalent stands of trees. There are about 1,200 species of bamboo which thrive in diverse terrain from sea level to 12,000 feet on every continent expect the polar regions, making it one of the most widely used plants on earth. Bamboo has a tensile strength superior to mild steel (withstands up to 52,000 pounds of pressure psi) and a weight-to-strength ratio surpassing that of graphite.[62] Bamboo is the fastest growing plant in the world and has been measured growing at a rate

Bamboo forest, *Meigetsu-in* temple, Kamakura, Japan.

of three feet per day although three to six inches is more the norm. Bamboo is naturally pest-resistant and can actually help rebuild eroded soil. It can be grown without any chemical fertilisers or pesticides. Yet, bamboo is not actually a wood at all, but a hollow grass that renews itself in three to seven years. Bamboo is truly a miracle grass.[63]

PRODUCT: WHAT TO WEAR

Material diversity has been a major part of the clothing industry. Up until very recently all materials were 'natural' or, at least; derived from nature. All fibres were obtained from either animal or biological sources such as silk, cotton, flax (linen) and hemp. The first recorded manufactured fibre dates from 1799, it was known as artificial silk and was obtained from plant cellulose.[64] Cellulose acetate appeared in 1865, Rayon in 1924, all were plant based. Nylon, the first true synthetic fibre, came to market in 1939. It was offered as a replacement to silk. The needs of war produced nylon parachutes and Wartime rationing provided the market for nylon stockings.[65]

> *With fingers weary and worn,*
> *With eyelids heavy and red,*
> *A woman sat, in unwomanly rags,*
> *Plying her needle and thread –*
> *Stitch! stitch! stitch!*[66]
> *The Song of the Shirt*, Thomas Hood, 1843.

ETHICALLY MADE

Sustainable fashion is not just about materials and processes of production, it is about human rights, codes of conduct and labour conditions, particularly in the developing world.[67] The production of fabric and clothing has always been closely related to social conditions and cultural values. The mills of industrial Victorian England provided the cultural symbol of working class suffering that was to inspire the 24 year old Friedrich Engels to compose "The Condition of the Working Class in England".[68] Written in 1844, following his two year stay in Manchester, it is contemporary with "The Song of the Shirt", the vilifying and sorrowful poem about sweatshop labour penned by Thomas Hood in 1843.

That five dollar tee shirt and those blue jeans you are wearing have substantial environmental cost. Cotton is not the most ethical fabric. Just 2.5 per cent of farm land worldwide is used to grow cotton, yet it accounts for ten per cent of all chemical pesticide use, and 22 per cent of insecticide use. Seven of the top 15 pesticides used on US cotton crops are deemed by the EPA to be potential or known human carcinogens.[69] The cultivation of cotton consumes vast amounts of water. Cotton represents nearly half the fibre used to make clothes and other textiles worldwide[70] According to the World Wildlife Fund (WWF), conventional cotton consumes more water than any other agricultural commodity. It can take more than 11,000 litres of water to produce one kg of cotton.[71] In our modern world most cotton continues to generate problems connected with its cultivation, processing and use in the infamous manufacturing 'sweat shops' which are often associated with developing countries. The accompanied exploitation of labour and the environmental impact of dying and finishing are rationalised and sanitised by designer brand labels in the malls and retail outlets of the developed world. Recent estimates conclude that the worldwide jeans market (the essential uniform of youth and responsible for significant cotton usage) is around $50 billion annually. That is a lot of jeans.

The Central Asian Republic of Uzbekistan is the sixth largest producer of cotton in the world, the government of which makes an estimated one billion US dollars from the annual sale of cotton, much of which has been picked by hand by women and children. The Aral Sea in Uzbekistan, which was once the worlds fourth largest inland body of water is reduced to about 15 per cent of its former volume– all this environmental plunder in the name of cotton.[72] Then there is the human rights issue. The annual crop of around 800,000 tonnes is not harvested by machine but by people. "Every Autumn when the crop is ready, the government shuts down schools and forces children as young as seven into the fields, with strict quotas to meet and expulsion threatening them if they don't make the grade."[73] You need to know the origin of the cotton of your jeans, but you are unlikely to find that information on the label.

SUSTAINABLE TEXTILES

In *Sustainable Fashion and Textiles*, Kate Fletcher observes "Though everyone from Barneys to Target sells clothes that claim to be green, there is no one standard for Earth-friendliness."[74] There are many options regarding fibre and fabric, and the associated information diverse and often confusing. Choices are difficult to make As with almost all design decisions there are trade offs to consider. It us up to you to undertake the prerequisite research before making your own informed decision, always remembering that small steps can have significant impact.[75]

World fibre demand in 2005 was recorded as being 59.54 million tons of which 25.76 was natural fibres with the remainder being manufactured fibres, mostly polyester. Any consideration regarding sustainable fashion must begin with a working knowledge of the characteristics of materials. When, in the 1980s, design became 'green', focus moved from artificial fibres to natural fibres. In the 1990s an array of 'sustainable' fibres and fabrics were on offer. Into the 2000s and fair trade became of prime concern as did the ethics of manufacture. Just what is it that makes fashion sustainable is open to much debate. Recent searches have resulted in sustainable claims made in the name of recycled materials, fair trade, cruelty free wool, and organic cotton—all of which warrant your consideration.[76] Thanks to a very active PR and promotion campaign the most successful 'alternative' fibre is organic cotton.[77]

Although renewable resource based fibres such as soya bean have been available for may years, none have managed to obtain any significant share of the fibre market.[78] In 1929, Henry Ford established a research laboratory to explore the extraction of chemicals from crops. A friend introduced Ford to the soy bean and he became intrigued by its potential. The first recorded soybean fabric dates back to 1941 when the researchers at Ford's Soy Laboratory produced a soybean fabric which was used in a suit for Henry Ford. He began using soy based materials in automobile production, eventually even making a prototype soy based car body.[79]

One other fibre deserving of consideration is bamboo. However, "claims made about bamboo fabric need to be carefully studied. The clothing fibre is made of cellulose obtained by processing raw bamboo. There is little factual information ava ilable on the production process but it may not be that 'sustainable'."[80] Promoted for its strength, soft texture, hypoallergenic[81] nature and unrivalled moisture management capabilities, bamboo fabrics have become a fashionable sustainable fashion item.[82]

PROCESS: DRESS TO IMPRESS

The operating parameters of fashion design are expanding in direct relationship to the explosion of available information and with regard to emerging cultural concerns, in particular those related to environmental and humanitarian concerns. Consumers are integrating new concerns into their purchase decisions; questioning how are the garments made—by whom, in what conditions, by what process, and from what material.[83] Knowledgeable consumers are informed about appropriate fabric finishing concerns including the affect of colour (darker, more heavy metals, more pollution, etc.) and materials, both traditional and alternatives, and the process of manufacture.[84] One New Zealand manufacturer of merino wool products allows the consumer to type in a *Baacode* and trace back the wool used in a garment to the originating sheep station where the merino fibre was produced.[85]

Many urban areas have garment drop boxes—ostensibly an example of re-use, but not necessarily by local residents. The contents of some of these boxes are sold by weight to countries in the developing world where they

Temple bell production, recycling scrap metal. Chiang Mai, Thailand.

re-emerge in local markets.[86] All these concerns can, with a creative refocus, generate original solutions. We all make our own mark in our own way. The design challenge is how to embrace past, present and future and produce proactive design statements.

That synthesis of time, place and technology is evident in temple bell production that is a feature of a temple complex just outside Chaing Mai in Northern Thailand. The production technique is a variation of the lost wax process and more traditional sand-casting techiques; the material is 'appropriated' from the immediate surrounding area; the Monk in charge of casting relies on eye and experience to mix the various metals in the smelting process; and, because the mix varies, each bell has a unique 'voice'. The design is subject to cultural specific parameters. The bell is usually proportioned so that the height and width at the base are equal. The pitch of the bell rises as its surface are decreases or as the thickness of the casing increases. [87]

> Once, when Kang XI, the second emperor of the Qing Dynasty was a crown prince he went to Wu Tai Mountain to meditate. He usually practiced Chan (Zen). One day, as he was taking a walk around the temple gounds, he heard an evening bell toll. Suddenly, the ringing no longer came from the bell, but it peacefully resonated from deep within his mind.... According to Master Baek, hearing the sound of the bell as the sound of one's mind is a hard level to achieve for a spiritual; practitioner because it means that one's ego has melted away.[88]

Women's self help group Laos.

Sustainability has both a local and global focus; it is empathetic to other millennium development goals such as promoting gender equality and the empowerment of women. Design cannot do it all, nor does it have all the answers, but enlightened, intervention design can improve people's lives and assist in bringing an end to poverty and a fairer use of available resources. These utopian aims are achievable. Robert Davies explains:

> The challenge is to stop paternalistic top-down aid from undermining the self-help capacity of the poor, enable them to access affordable design and technology and facilitate traditional market mechanisms that empower local people as entrepreneurs and distributors. There is a quiet revolution now going on, led by designers, architects, social entrepreneurs, NGOs, micro-finance intermediaries and socially committed small firms, that business can partner to make a massive potential impact on poverty and sustainability.[89]

The recent travelling exhibition Design for the other 90 per cent which originated at New York's Cooper-Hewitt Museum demonstrated that simple and effective products can help respond to challenges in the field of Shelter, Health, Water, Education, Energy and Transport.[90]

Enlightened, creative self-help programmes can be very successful. In the tiny village of Gudda in north-western India, the 500 residents have seen the light, and it is solar powered.[91] The nearby Barefoot College has, for the last 35 years, been a training ground for some of the most disenfranchised persons in India.[92] More recently a group of women have established the Women Solar Engineers Association of Hyderabad. All had previously worked as stone crushers, after a six month training programme they now install solar powered panels that benefit local rural communities.[93]

SWADESHI

Maybe what the other 90 per cent require are more barefoot designers. This concept is hardly new. During India's struggle for independence from Great Britain, Mahatma Gandhi instigated *swadeshi* as part of his ideology.[94] In literal translation the phrase means "belonging to one's own country". Gandhi applied this concept to support locally produced goods that utilised indigenous skills and locally available materials.[95] The concept did not originate with Gandhi, nor is it restricted to India. It may be time to relook at how the concept may be applied within the context of the twenty-first century. Working Villages International is dedicated to establishing self-sufficient, environmentally sustainable villages around the world.[96] They have an impressive record, however a more active 'design' input may further increase their achievements.

Indian foreign secretary Nirupama Rao foresees that the two dominant forces in the coming decades will be India and China.[97] Currently China has the edge.

> One of the great ironies revealed by the global recession that began in 2008 is that Communist Party-ruled China may be doing a better job managing capitalism's crisis than the democratically elected US government. Beijing's stimulus spending was larger, infinitely more effective at overcoming the slowdown and directed at laying the infrastructural tracks for further economic expansion.[98]

During the last half of the twentieth century the relationship between India and China was marked more by antagonism than by cooperation; the most notable example being the opposing attitudes regarding Tibet. However, both nations have an extensive cultural heritage stretching back to the start of the first millennium. It was the transmission of Buddhism from India to China and later to Japan that was to prove a unifying element to these cultures.[99] Time to consider the cultural heritage of China and Japan.

CHAPTER ELEVEN
THE PHOENIX RISES: DESIGN AND THE CULTURAL HERITAGE OF ASIA

On the scales
Kyoto and Edo balanced
in this Spring of a thousand years.
tenbin ya/kyo edo kakete/chiyo no haru
Matsuo Basho, 1644–1694.[1]

IN 1,000 YEARS TIME...

Design is a universal human characteristic. The creative design act can be hindered or amplified by the prevailing cultural context. Contexts change. Step back 1,000 years, suppose it is the year 1012, imagine that you are engaged in a philosophical debate concerning the future of humankind.[2] You are asked to consider which nation will be the most influential force in the world in one thousand years time. Which nations would be the top contenders?[3]

Regarded by some historians as the oldest living civilisation of Earth, India, with a population of 80 million by AD1000, would be worthy of consideration.[4] Despite its remoteness from Europe, a few adventurous travellers reported to the rest of the world news of India's impressive heritage of art, architecture, science, astronomy, philosophy, and particularly, the 1,000 year history of mathematics. The classical period of Indian mathematics ranged from AD400 to 1200. "The best known achievement of Hindu mathematics is our present decimal position system."[5] The number zero as we know it was conceived by the Hindus around AD650.[6] Arab traders brought the concept of zero with them from India to Europe. Your digital world is totally dependent upon the digits zero and one.

The vast Islamic empire reached from North Africa to Southeast Asia and encompassed most of Spain and Northern India and Persia. Persia (modern day Iran,) one of the world's oldest continuous major civilisations with urban settlements dating back to 4000 BCE. Medieval Arab intellectual life was far brighter than in any European city and certainly their medical knowledge and standards of personal hygiene exceeded any European standards, with the possible exception of Islamic Spain.[7] In the old Islamic world, knowledge was sacred. Cordoba's library held over 400,000 volumes, all of which of course were hand scripted manuscripts, one of a kind items.[8] Drawing on translations of ancient Greek texts aided by Jewish scholars, Arab intellectuals broke new ground in medicine, mathematics, physics and optics. At the start of the millennium the Persian philosopher and physician Ibn-Sina discovered that tuberculosis was contagious, but his teachings would not reach Europe for centuries.[9] Early in the eleventh century, Ibn al-Haytham, (AD965–1039), regarded as one of the first scientists, developed the first law of motion nearly 500 years before Galileo.[10] In his *Kitab al-Manazir (Book of Optics)* a seven-volume treatise on optics, physics, mathematics, anatomy and psychology he outlines his experiments using light; these were later explored by Isaac Newton in the late seventeenth century,[11] and al-Haytham provides the first accurate descriptions of the camera obscura, a precursor to the modern camera.[12]

The Islamic world was also absorbing ideas from a formidable neighbour, China, the best organised and most technologically advanced society of the time. The Song dynasty (960–1279) is referred to as the Chinese Renaissance, it was a period of both consolidation and transformation in all aspects of Chinese culture including innovations in the arts, technology and philosophy. Three inventions that were to have a significant affect upon human cultural development date from the Song dynasty; printing with moveable type, gunpowder and the compass. During this period Chinese life, both economic and personal, was transformed. A booming economy necessitated the minting of bronze coins and, around 1100, the printing of the world's first paper money. Trade flourished, a market economy linked together the coastal port cities with those of the interior. An organised civil bureaucracy promoted productivity in almost every aspect of life. China's civil service fanned out from the centres of power to administer almost one hundred million people; the component bureaucracy provided an avenue of upward mobility. Education flourished. Most villages had elementary schools, and one student in 20 went on to higher education. Education was life long, it was not unusual to find persons of 18 and 80 sitting side-by-side taking common civil service examinations.[13] The curriculum was liberal, including the "Five Studies"; military strategy; civil law, revenue and taxation; agriculture and geography; and the Confucian classics. The required examinations are regarded by most historians as the first standardised tests based on merit.[14] Successful candidates were awarded degrees accompanied by special privileges of dress and enhanced social position. Collectively this group became the scholar-gentry class who assisted in local government and in the propagation of the Confucian moral code.

The obvious question must be why did these extremely sophisticated cultures relinquish their cultural prominence? The highly centralised nature of Islamic society made innovative thinking possible but strictly controlled its application. The same was true to a different degree in China which produced the most advanced scientific and technological thinking of the day, but their chosen lifestyle did not encourage adoption or expansion. The state controlled all activity; all individual activity was subordinate to the common good, a common good defined by bureaucrats. Confucian thought kept tight constraints on the active, free-thinking, analytical mind. The Mandarins believed that the most powerful tool for social management was classification and record keeping. The result was that although education and the acquisition of knowledge was held in high esteem, there was little social reward or benefit for the application of creative endeavours.

Cultures are never static. For a complex weave of interconnected reasons having to do with trade, in particular the trade in textiles and spices, and with the recognition of secular power, humanistic thought began to influence patterns of social behaviour in Mediaeval European liberal thinking. This liberalisation of knowledge would lead, in a few centuries to the European Renaissance —and we have been living in that shadow ever since.[15]

Now, project forward a thousand years or so, who will be the dominant cultural group around 3012? For make no mistake, no single cultural group has claims on the future; what we do, and more importantly, what we do not do, will have influential effect on the design context of AD3012. A recent report by the National Intelligence Council indicates that the dominating influence of the US is over, the centre of global influence is moving firmly to the east.[16]

SILK, INCENSE, AND SPICE

WH McNeill, argues that, around AD1000, it was the growth of commerce and trade in China that "tipped a critical balance in world history".[17] In the first millennium, trade was global, with commercial activity flourishing along legendary trade routes. It was trade along the Silk Road and Spice Route that provided the finance, in the form of taxes and duties, for the development of cities, towns and ports where merchants and traders, and local craft producers could practice their skills.[18] Infrastructures developed to support these commercial undertakings, methods of finance were established, transportation arrangements made, supporting manufacturing facilities developed to process some of the commodities, and of course all the traders, merchants and their cohorts needed to be fed and accommodated.[19] Among the most desirable commodities of trade were silk, incense and spice.

SILK ROAD

The silk road was in fact not a single road, but a series of interlocking trade routes that criss-crossed Eurasia, stretching from Japan, through Korea, China, Central Asia, India, the Middle East, Turkey and on to Venice and the rest of Europe. Well established by the start of the first millennium AD these roads carried not only silk and other precious commodities but ideas, culture, music and art, connecting cultures from central Asia through to Europe.[20] A northern road linked Xi'an to the western borders of the Roman Empire.

> For more than a thousand years this northern Silk Road provided a route for caravans that brought to China, dates, saffron powder and pistachio nuts from Persia; frankincense, aloes and myrrh from Somalia; sandalwood from India; glass bottles from Egypt, and many other expensive and desirable goods from other parts of the world. And the caravans went home with their camels and horses loaded down by bolts of silk brocade and boxes filled with lacquer ware and porcelains. [21]

Once they learnt how to cultivate and process silk for themselves, some European nations developed their own silk manufacturing industries. By the thirteenth century, Italian manufactured silk provided a significant source of trade. The wealth of Florence and Venice was largely built on textiles, both wool and silk, and other cities like Lucca in Tuscany also grew rich on the trade.[22] By the sixteenth century the manufacture of silk had developed into one of the most important industries in Italy.[23] Francis I of France was a noted patron of the arts and was considered to be France's first Renaissance monarch.[24] With strong connections to Italy he was well aware of the popularity and profitability of the silk industry. He invited Italian silk makers to create a French silk industry centred in Lyon. Many French silk weavers were Huguenots (Protestant Reformed Church of France) who, following the death of Francis I, were subject to acts of religious intolerance, culminating in the St Bartholomew's Day Massacre of 24 August 1572. Mass emigration followed with Huguenot's establishing communities in America, Great Britain, The Netherlands and South Africa, thereby contributing to the trade in ideas.[25]

THE INCENSE ROUTE

We live smelly lives. Witness the number of advertisements and commercials concerned with negating or enhancing body odour and with combating pet and cooking smells in our homes. We have long recognised that odour can affect our well-being, physical and mental. The origins of incenseuse are lost in the annuals of pre-history.[26] Presumably people were attracted to the odour emitted when certain plants were burnt; this process was refined over the millennia and the process of smouldering incense was integrated into religious practice, as a means of air

Incense coils hanging from the ceiling of the Man Mo temple, Hong Kong

purification, to assist in aromatherapy, to stimulate self-awareness and to uplift the emotional state.

    The Epic of Gilgamesh, the earliest known work of literary fiction, tells of the legendary King of Ur in Mesopotamia (modern day Iraq) and makes mention of the burning incense of Cedar wood and Myrrh to put the gods into a pleasant mood.[27] By the late fifth century BCE, Babylonia, a state in southern Mesopotamia, was a principal market for the ingredients of incense. Trade routes expanded linking the traders of the Middle East with merchants of the Ancient world where the use of incense was part of Greek and Roman culture.[28] "The trade with Arabia and India in incense and spices became increasingly important, and Greeks for the first time began to trade directly with India."[29]

SPICE ROUTE

The spice route (trade in nutmeg, cloves, mace, ginger and pepper) was primarily a series of sea journeys that ran from the Mediterranean, through the Red Sea around India and on to the Spice Islands (modern day Indonesia). The dangers were immense, from the constant threat of storm and ship wreck, to hazards of pirates. Lack of water and food, the ever present health threat of scurvy caused by a lack of vitamin C, all took their toll. The less than scrupulous commercial activities of traders and dealers along the way compounded the

challenges.[30] By the seventeenth century it was the Dutch who were dominating the trade through the powerful *Vereenigde Oost- Indische Compagnie* (VOC–the Dutch United East India Company). Indeed, this dominance lasted until the 1950s.[31]

FROM NUT TO APPLE

One of the most amazing adventures was undertaken in the seventeenth century when, on the 23 December 1616, Nathaniel Courthope sailed the Swan into the harbour of a small volcanic atoll of Run in the East Indies. Under direct instructions from King James l of England, Courthope had sailed his small vessel from London, around Africa, skirting India and navigating around the islands of Sumatra and Java before arriving at his destination. This was the journey that would have unimagined repercussions, resulting in a negotiated deal between England and The Netherlands that would shape our modern world.[32]

    The attraction of Run was the nutmeg seed "the most coveted luxury in seventeenth-century Europe, a spice held to have such powerful medicinal properties that men would risk their lives to acquire it".[33] Or, to be more precise, they would risk their lives for the fortune to be made. The mark up on the spice was around 600 per cent, ten pounds of nuts cost one English penny at source and fetched £2.10 in the English market, "A small sack full was enough to set a man up for life."[34] This scale of profit resulted in a violent confrontations between the two top trading nations of the day, the Dutch East India Company and the less structured but equally ambitious Company and Fellowship of Merchant Adventures based in London. The violence was ended by the Treaty of Breda, signed on the 18 April 1667, in which England gave up all claim to the tiny two mile long Run island in the East Indies, in exchange for a larger, somewhat desolate island with less than five thousand inhabitants,[35] but with the advantage of being closer to home. Today we know that island by the name of Manhattan.[36]

INFORMATION TRANSFER

At the start of the second millennium, thanks to the trade routes, information passed slowly between Europe and Asia. In other parts of the world the transfer of information remained very local. In what is now Mexico, the Toltec's were building massive pyramids, yet no one beyond a few weeks walk knew of their existence. It was in the year 1000 that Leif Ericsson landed in what is today Newfoundland, naming it Vinland, yet news of his 'discovery' never spread further than Scandinavia.[37] And certainly no one in your discussion group would have heard of America until those three ships of destiny, the Nina, the Pinta and the Santa Maria arrived at Lucayos (modern day Bahamas) on Friday, 12 October 1492.[38] The discovery of the New World changed the Old World forever.[39]

All cultures are living entities, they are never in a state of rest, they either grow and develop or fall into a state of atrophy. The soothsayers of our world are divided between the doom and gloom merchants who foresee a bleak outlook for humankind. They point out that our compromised environment is, according to some, beyond repair; that we are overwhelmed by tides of technology that very few understand. We face biological dangers and a world in constant partisan conflict. The more positive future forecasters, while recognising the dangers and challenges acknowledge our history of innovation and problem solving. These believe that we can steer a different course towards positively desired futures, aided by design. It would be inadvisable however, to ignore cultural roots which are covered in more detail in the final section, "Futures".

IMPERIAL JAPAN

For nearly 400 years, from around 794 to 1185, isolated *Heian* Japan was at peace, allowing the aristocracy to concentrate on the important things in life and develop a highly tuned aesthetic, celebrated in the *Pillow Book of Sei Shonganonis*.[40] She was a lady in waiting to the Empress Sadako during the last decade of the tenth century. In her book she captures the ritual and aestheticism of the Imperial court.[41] The one imported element of Chinese culture that was to have a most profound and lasting affect upon Japanese culture was the arrival of Buddhist texts

during the latter part of the sixth century (Nara period, 710–794). It was during the Heian period (794–1185) that Buddhism began to spread throughout Japan. In 1191 the monk Eisai of Kamakura introduced Rinzai Zen Buddhism which became popular among the samurai, the leading class in Japanese society. During the Kamakura Bakufu period (1192–1233) the famed samurai reached the zenith of their influence in Japan. The samurai's principle virtue, loyalty, still very much in evidence in the modern business world of Japan.

The fifteenth and sixteenth centuries are known as the Age of Civil Wars during which time samurai lords battled amongst themselves for supremacy in Japan. In 1633, during the Edo Period (1603–1867) Shogun Lemitsu initiated the policy of national seclusion (Sakoku,) banned all foreign travel (with a few exceptions) and government became increasingly insular and isolated from the rest of the 'barbarian' world. Some Asian nations were allowed to visit Japanese ports, The Netherlands was the only European nation allowed this privilege with the establishment of a trading post at Dejima in Nagasaki, all under very strict regulation and control.

The period of Seclusion in Japan lasted until 8 July 1853 when residents of *Uraga* on the outskirts of *Edo*, (modern day Tokyo) the sprawling capital of feudal Japan, were witness to the arrival of the American Commodore Perry and his small fleet of "Black Ships". Perry's fleet consisted of two frigates (the Mississippi and Susquehanna) and two sloops, with a total complement of 65 guns and a little less than 1,000 men. The steam powered vessels emitted clouds of black smoke, hence they were referred to as the Black Ships. In 1854, Commodore Perry returned to Japan to complete his mission of forcing insular Japan into the modern world.[42] The events of 1853 and 1854 constitute a pivotal moment in the modern encounter between East and West.[43] By 1868 the old administrative order of the Shoguns had been replaced by a ruling executive whose efforts to bring Japan into the nineteenth century was known as the Meiji restoration when the Shogunate lost all of its remaining political power.[44]

Nearly a century later and the Second World War was the cause of even more dramatic cultural turmoil and social realignment in Japan. Following the apocalypse of Hiroshima and Nagasaki, the general populace had to deal with many post-bomb survival realities. The entire social organisation was subject to restructuring. The immediate post-war period witnessed the emergence of a new middle class in Japan whose wealth was based not on the ownership of property or of aristocratic birth, but on their ability to produce manufactured goods that people would buy. Still the outstanding study of Japan in the emotionally testing times that followed the Second World War is the American anthropologist, Ruth Benedict's *Chrysanthemum and the Sword: Patterns of Japanese Culture*, first published in 1946.[45]

Hashimoto Sadahide, 1861, picture of Western Traders at Yokohama Transporting Merchandise, Courtesy United States Library Congress, LC-USZC4-8538.

THE PHOENIX RISES

Formulated by Einstein in 1905, $E=mc^2$, the one formula that all remember but very few understand, was to propel our civilisation into the nuclear age.[46] In 1939 while living in Princeton, Einstein heard that two German physicists, Otto Hahn and Fritz Strassman had split the uranium atom. Along with Leó Szilárd, Einstein wrote a letter expressing his well founded fears to President Franklin D Roosevelt.[47] A few years later, on 6 September 1945, close to 200,000 residents of Hiroshima were annihilated in the explosion of a single bomb that devastated the whole city in an instant.[48] The day after Hiroshima was obliterated, President Truman voiced his satisfaction with the "overwhelming success" of "the experiment".[49]

The Hiroshima bomb was also a study in media censorship. In the immediate aftermath of the bomb, the allied occupation authorities banned all mention of radiation poisoning. Reports on the realities of this unprecedented, indiscriminate, and inhumane bombing were censored. The American led occupation forces designated the horror as an item unsuitable for news coverage and imposed a strict press code. On 10 September 1945, the General Headquarters of the occupying forces issued a "Memorandum on Freedom of Speech and Press" and began censorship of the *Domei-Tsushin* News Agency, all newspapers and media outlets.[50] The outbreak of the Korean War on 25 June 1950, brought tighter restrictions on media coverage. It was not until 1952 that the press code was finally dropped and media coverage of the after effects of atomic bombing became possible.[51]

CULTURAL IDEOLOGY OF DESIGN

Understanding culture is essential to the process of design. Culture is a lens through which we view what is happening in our world. It is culture that gives meaning to an inanimate object and provides the ritual within which they are used and the values that are reflected in their form and function. A small hand made bowl becomes so much more when it is perceived as "Racku". A traditional kimono clothes its wearer in a mantle of meaning far more intense to that provided by a couture creation.[52]

There is a distinct cultural ideology of design. Cultural beliefs and values are empathetic to convention, to behavioural patterns, ethics and social aspirations. The objects we use and their design characteristics reflect and reinforce the expected behaviour of everyday life. When we travel we have to 'interpret' the designed environment—how do we eat, what implements do we use, what condiments do we use, what order do we eat things in—how do we buy a bus or subway ticket, how do we use the bathroom. In short, how do we 'live' in that culture and how does 'design' help or hinder our required actions. Design gives identifiable form to the iconic beliefs and values of a culture.

Even space has various associated meanings. When I was a student at Birmingham College of Art in England, it was fashionable to consider ourselves as Buddhist. We all wore black and read Christmas Humphreys.[53] We were fascinated by Zen but our 'understanding' was very superficial. Not for one moment did I ever suppose that I would find myself in a Zen temple. Many years latter I made my first visit to Kyoto and I made a point of going early one morning to one of the largest Zen temples in Kyoto. As it happened I was there just as they opened the temple doors and was first person to enter. I froze. In front of me was a vast *tatami* floored room and I had no idea how to proceed. My cultural heritage provided the necessary instruction for progressing through churches and chapels and the like but I was not prepared to traverse this room. Did I walk round the edge of the room, walk straight across—which was the 'appropriate' way? Luckily a monk sensing my dilemma indicated the necessary act of shoe removal and ushered me across the interior space and indicated where I should sit to witness the morning chanting. It was the interior space that was most impressive. The cognitive strategies of minimalism are hardly modern. According to Zen philosophy, the space that I was experiencing was not 'empty' but filled with endless possibilities, a view endorsed by contemporary quantum physics but that is another story, or to be more accurate, of many unending stories.

THE ROLE OF FORM

Continuing with a few more thoughts about form. In the West, there are common held beliefs concerning direction; left has certain political connotations as does right. Up is considered more desirable than down. Once again there is very little room for originality in the design of religious forms. The Christian Cathedral must have spires soaring heavenward. The Pagoda, which derived from the Indian Stupa, is orientated along more cosmic lines, radiating in all directions. Directional preferences are of little consequence when you realise that you, me, and every person on this planet are "actually spinning with the earth's rotation at 1,040 miles per hour and orbiting with the earth around the sun at 67,000 miles per hour".[54] It's all a matter of focus—and gravity!

The location of objects in our world is also subject to cultural influence. The fireplace was the very heart of the domestic environment in North America, providing a focal point for family life. All that changed in the 1950s when we had to decide where to place the television set. Some preferences have stood the test of time. In the West the church bell will still be found at the very top of the structure—partly as a continuation of medieval practice when a bell was the primary means of communal communication—partly because of applied religious overtones reflecting nearness to a god. In Buddhism, the bell is at human height. The sound of the bell interacts with the psyche, the sound

Engakuji Temple, Kamakura. The bell (2.6 metres high and 1.42 metre in diameter) is designated as a National Treasure, it was donated by Sadatoki Hojo in 1301.

waves penetrate the very being. Simon James clarifies the point:

> The mirror-like openness of the mind becomes suddenly filled with the raw 'thereness' of a thing—the morning star, the temple bell, the splash of a frog in a pond—and one finds oneself enlightened... by things.[55]

THE BUSINESS OF DESIGN

The Second World War had decimated Japan. After 1945, Japan concentrated on mastering the newly available technologies and industrial manufacturing processes that had developed during the wartime production of arms and armaments. Japanese business had to learn very quickly how the West worked and more importantly (from a standpoint of trade) how the West played. In a very short time they outpaced their mentors and became one of the leading industrial nations on Earth, a founder member of the G6 in 1975.[56]

DESIGN PROFILE: "THE WALKING MAN"

Sometime in the late 1970s, the now mature Akio Morita wanted to listen to classical music while he played tennis.[64] At about the same time, in 1978, there was organisational change in Sony's audio division; radio cassette recorders (a high profit product line) were transferred to the radio division. Each division at Sony was denominated as an independent profit centre and the tape recorder division was now eclipsed by the video division and suffered the embarrassment of losing its main profit source to a rival division. Internal competition is fierce among the various divisions at Sony. The tape division had already produced a product known as the Pressman, a small tape recorder designed to used by journalists. The divisions engineers now began to tinker with this product to see how it might be improved. The major risk that the division accepted was the general public would buy a product that did not record but only played back. Apparently the final decision to go with this concept was taken by Akio Morita himself. The first production prototype was completed on the 24 March 1979. The commercial launch of the product happened on 1 July 1979.

A ROSE IS NOT A ROSE

Initially this unique devise was only called the Walkman in Japan. The erudite Morita thought that this was an example of a typical Japanese 'loanwords' such as *depaato* (department store), *pooku choppu* (pork chops) and *biiru* (beer). He rationalised that to be grammatically correct for North America and Europe it should be called the Walking-man. On its 1980 North American debut, the TCM-600 (to give it its official model number) was dubbed the "Soundabout" and sold for $199, plus another $50 for a second set of headphones.[65] That name was already registered in Great Britain where it was called "Stowaway"; the Scandinavians objected to the illegal conation of stowaway and so it was called the "Freestyle" in Sweden. "In November, Morita telephoned

Sony from Paris and told Ohsone (Kozo Ohsone was general manager of the Tape Recorder Division) that he had decided that the product should be sold as Walkman everywhere."[66] Walkman very quickly become a generic term for a portable stereo receiver and in 1986, the term appeared in the *Oxford English Dictionary.*

PRIVATE LISTENING IN PUBLIC PLACES

The Walkman was the first product that provided a perfect fit to the demands of modern urban culture. The Walkman extends our presence—allowing us to be in more than one place and doing more than one thing at any one time, the insidious 'multi-tasking'. Travelling in a cacophonous urban environment we could now engage in an audio discourse in another world; we could use technology to both set us apart in a crowd and to define who we are. "The self sufficient individual wandering alone through the city landscape—the classic Walkman person seen so often in its advertisements, the urban nomad."[67]

Sony was the first Japanese company to produce Western-style consumer products within a social system that retained elements of the mores of traditional Japanese culture. The company was founded in 1946 by Masaru Ibuka who had run a wartime company called Japan Precision Instruments and Akio Morita, the son of a old established Sake brewing concern. The company began life in a bomb wrecked department store with a capital of about $500 and with a group of about 20 people. Initially Sony depended on imported technology, but enhanced it with a characteristically Japanese attention to detail. In 1996, Sony was voted the number one brand in America according to the annual Harris Polls "best brands" survey of American consumers, outperforming Coca-Cola, Kraft and Toyota.[57] It was an American official of the Civil Information and Education Service of the Occupation Forces who first showed this start up company a military tape recorder it had commandeered from Germany. The German conglomerate AEG had introduced ' Magnetophone' tape technology at a radio exhibition in Berlin in 1935. After the war German magnetophone technology was regarded as legitimate spoils of war and was adopted by audio related researchers in several countries.[58] (Ampex in America; EMI in Britain and Sony in Japan).

Sony produced Japans first tape recorder, the type G, in 1950.[59] It weighed a hefty 33lb and sold for a substantial $472. It was not a success, the main problem being that people did not know what to do with it. Morita bought a second hand bus and went on an educational tour of Japan—introducing, and selling the tape recorder to some of Japan's 40,000 schools as a classroom aid in foreign language instruction. This masterly display of salesmanship and the associated lesson of developing a marketing strategy, became a fundamental part of Sony business practice.

Major Japanese companies such as Sony emphasised the fundamental role played by design innovation in developing new product areas. Along with this development went, cascading, a sophisticated and innovative marketing policy. This identified a very specific market area, typically at the low end of the market, for example radios, further enhancement to the product line 'cascade' around established patterns of marketing and distribution. [60] In 1953 Sony paid $25,000 to Western Electric for a license to produce the transistor which was incorporated into the design of the TR-55 of 1955, the first mass produced transistor radio. This became Sony's first export model when Canada's General Distributors bought 50 samples. The later TR-63 was the first pocket sized radio and more than 50,000 were sold projecting Sony into a major player in the international consumer electronics market.

North American market research in the 1960s indicated that "people do not place a high value on portability of the television set".[61] In 1960 Sony introduced an 8" set which retailed at $250, nearly twice the price of a traditional 21" set. This was one of the first steps that resulted in the demise of the North American television manufacturing companies and the global dominance of the Japanese and Korean industries. It was not that Sony rejected market research, far from it; they were astute enough to realise the modifying role played in lifestyle research, by culture.[62]

Sony were to experience that being the initiator of a concept can be of prime importance, but being first also have its risks. Sony's reputed technologically advanced Betamax videocassette system, released in May 1975, was not a commercial success, the market showed an overwhelming preference for the VHS system, released by Matsushita in October 1977.[63] It was apparent that more than innovation was required.

Zen garden, *Meigetsu-in a Rinzai Zen* temple in *Kita-Kamakura*. The *karesansui*, a dry landscape gardens, also known as "rock gardens", feature of raked sand symbolising rippling water, with rocks and plants representing the mythical Buddhist Mount *Shumi* at the centre of the Universe.

GARDEN OF THE MIND

Space has always been in short supply in Japan which has resulted in a different attitude towards the use of space. A more multi-functional sensibility has evolved. The Japanese designer has learned to imply, often in very subtle ways, that which does not actually exist. Most Zen gardens are small–quiet spots for internal reflection in the chaos of modern day urban Japan. The garden is devoid of 'plants' and is made up of carefully positioned stones among racked sand. The 'garden' invites the viewer to internalise, to project an internal vision unhindered by external physical limitations, offering an alternative vision of design. (see above, "Cultural Ideology of Design").

MINDFUL FASHION

In the 1980s, Japanese fashion designers created their own alternative vision of design (see Chapter Nine). Issey Miyake was the first Japanese fashion designer to broadcast the new Japanese sensibility in fashion. The success of his designs dependent upon their ability to communicate his philosophies of life and design, while remaining respectful of the past and expressing his enthusiasms about new technologies and process of production. The designs explore the tension that exists between Western inspiration and the perpetuation of traditional Japanese values while having a global appeal.

> *As cloth is to body. Body is to spirit.*
> Laurance Wieder.[68]

Traditionally in Western clothing the fabric is cut precisely to the body shape and then sewn. The form of the garment is dictated by the natural shape of the body, and it therefore becomes a shell similar to the body shape. In creating clothes in this way the shape between the body and the garment is eliminated, the garment becomes epidermal in nature. In Japanese clothes where the cut of the garment is reduced to the minimum the relationship between the body and garment increases in importance. Changing shapes emerge as the person moved within the garment. Garments are capable of transforming a person of wisdom and insight into the shape of all things so that the power within and around may link in harmony as one being. When considering the question "What are Clothes", the noted architect Arata Isozaki observes:

> Issey Miyake has directed his attention to the co-existence of the fabric and the body... both the fabric and the body are able to assert themselves, enabling the space between them to waive, flutter, and fold with each movement of the body. The space absorbs and is absorbed. Through movement, fabric and body become one.[69]

Issey Miyake had moved to Paris in 1973. He was fascinated by the 'wrappings' of Christo, seeing connections to Japanese culture. Concerned with form and texture, with a reverence for traditional techniques and a fascination with the interaction of clothes and the body persona.[70] Miyake had personally witnessed the social confrontations in Paris during that long hot Summer of 1968. This experience laid the foundations for a fundamental shift in attitudes with the publication in 1978 of his book, *East Meets West*.[71]

Issey Miyake demonstrated a refined aesthetic which was diametrically opposed to that of the traditional fashion cognoscenti. He bypassed all traditional Western attitudes to 'fit' and 'size' by acknowledging the uniqueness of every body form and of every personality and by encouraging the built-in interaction of clothing with the body and persona encouraging a dialogue between the two. The body was not to hang clothes on but to interact with. He revitalised the fashion matrix by adding a degree of humanitarian spiritualism to the mix.[72]

Sometimes overlooked in discussions relating to the design culture is the role of economics and related government policies. These two forces combined in the seventeenth and eighteenth centuries in Britain to support the textile industry and establish Britain as the first industrial nation.[73] In the immediate aftermath of the Second World War the Marshall Plan, funded by the American government helped to re-establish the industrial base of Italy and Germany. In 2005, the Japanese government collaborated with designers in launching the first Japan Fashion Week in Paris in October, 2005.[74]

The Japanese Ministry of Economy, Trade and Industry (METI) has established the "Creative Industries Promotion Office" to promote its cultural industries around the globe.

Part of that campaign is dedicated to advancing the international profile of the Japanese fashion industry. In 2010, Mitsubishi linked with the METI to establish a project called "tokyoeye: girls/kids & tech". This is part of the "Cool Japan" campaign, a marketing initiative promoting Japanese fashion in Shanghai, the commercial hub of China.[75] The cooperative association of government, commerce and design will be a significant feature of design culture in the decades ahead.

There remains significant opportunities for the application of dedicated, insightful thinking in the design process. In 2010, Issey Miyake launched his 132 5 range developed by his Reality Lab team in collaboration with engineers and pattern makers. Theoretical math, origami, recycled plastic bottles plus an innovative design process resulted in his first line in more than a decade.

The process by which the clothing is made is groundbreaking, using a mathematical algorithm: first, a variety of three-dimensional shapes are conceived in collaboration with a computer scientist; then, these shapes are folded into two-dimensional forms with pre-set cutting lines that determine their finished shape; and finally, they are heat-pressed, to yield folded shirts, skirts, dresses etc. These clothes are significant not only for the process by which they were made but because they are also made using recycled PET products, sometimes in combination with other recycled fibers.[76]

There have been many failures in Japanese industry yet at the end of the day, just under seventy years after the near cultural annihilation of Hiroshima, Japan, practising a

Issey Miyake, Spring-Summer collection, 1989. Photo: Masaaki Miyazawa. Used with permission.

The title, 132 5, range explains the notion: one piece of fabric, a three-dimensional shape reduced to two, and the fifth dimension, which Miyake describes as the moment the garment is worn and comes to life "through the communication among people". Clothing by Reality Lab., MIYAKE DESIGN STUDIO 2010. Photo: Hiroshi Iwasaki 2010.

form of political democracy buffered by a quasi-totalitarian economy, emerged as the leading industrial force in the world. In Japan related business interests often work together for their mutual benefit to achieve common goals in a way that would be considered illegal in North America and most of Europe, where competitiveness rules rather than cooperation.[77] In Japan, loyalty still rules. Recently, Japanese market dominance in many fields has been challenged by the emerging might of a restructured China.[78]

MIDDLE KINGDOM

The Song dynasty ruled China between AD960–1279. By the late eleventh century, China had a total population of some 101 million people. It used paper-printed money, produced the most praised silk on earth, had invented the camera obscura, the water powered astronomical clock, gunpowder and the compass.[79] Writing in 1620, Francis Bacon stated in his *Novum Organum*.

> Again we should notice the force, effect, and consequences of inventions, which are nowhere more conspicuous than in those three which were unknown

to the ancients; namely, printing, gunpowder, and the compass. For these three have changed the appearance and state of the whole world; first in literature, then in warfare, and lastly in navigation: and innumerable changes have been thence derived, so that no empire, sect, or star, appears to have exercised a greater power and influence on human affairs than these mechanical discoveries.[80]

Cultural life in China existed within a Confucian code of behaviour which emphasised respect for elders and for the prevailing social structure, while remaining ever mindful of one's own responsibility to others within the existing cultural system. Confucius was a historically verifiable person, born in 551 BCE, who died in 479 BCE at the age of 72.[81] What Confucius actually looked like remains a mystery. Traditional representations of him as a bearded man wearing a gown and a ceremonial hat are based on the imagination of artists working 1,500 to 2,000 years after his death. Little is known of his life and the only work that can, with any degree of certainty, be attributed to his thoughts is the *Analects of Confucius* which were complied over a 50 year period.[82] A self made man, he undertook a 15 year journey throughout the states of China, arguing that those who govern should be chosen for what they could do rather than who they were by birth. He believed in the innate goodness of humankind and reasoned that the end of good government was the welfare of the general population.

Confucianism is an amalgam of moral, social, political, philosophical, and quasi-religious thought. Three influential components being ritual, rite and loyalty. As opposed to some other religions which externalise ritual, the Confucian code of behaviour internalises ritual. This is seen as providing an influence before any acts are undertaken. Improper acts result in internal shame, the hard to explain, 'loss of face'. Proper rites become the social norm, the appropriate mark of social correctness. Every day acts are respected for their ritualistic value. These are the routines that we all undertake everyday to get through life; (see the section on Charles and Ray Eames in Chapter Six). Successful completion of the appropriate rites results in a content and healthy society. Confucian doctrine remained influential in Chinese culture for two millennia until it was regarded as an obstacle to the modernisation of the Peoples Republic of China when the new codes of practice were contained in *The Thoughts of Mao Zedong*.[83] The current Chinese Communist Party has revised its opinion on Confucius and opened numerous Confucius Institutes around the world, including 21 in the US, ostensibly to enhance awareness of Chinese cultural heritage.

On 12 February 1912, following Sun Yat-sen's republican revolution, Henry Pu Yi (Hsian-T'ung) the last emperor of China, abdicated.[84] A provisional government was established in his place, ending 267 years of Manchu rule in China and 2,000 years of imperial rule. The unstable republic was replaced by in October 1949 by the People's Republic of China led by Mao Zedong who achieved fabled status during the preceding Long March of 1935–1936.[85] Forced by the Kuomintang to evacuate their Jiangxi province base in October 1934, the Red Armies of the Communist Party of China embarked on a 12,500km military retreat.[86] This was not a single march but a series of strategic retreats which eventually allowed for the consolidation of the remaining personal. 100,000 soldiers and party members began the march, only 28,000 reached Shaanxi province where they established a new headquarters at Yan'an. During this march Mao gained unchallenged command of the Communist Party by removing potential rivals and gained respect from the soldiers by implementing successful guerrilla tactics. The Long March is considered one of the great physical feats of endurance of the Twentieth Century. Mao and his methods polarised opinion from the very start. In 1937 the American writer Edgar Snow reported that aim of Mao and his supporters was "to shake, to arouse, the millions of rural China to their responsibilities in society; to awaken them to a belief in human rights, to combat the timidity, passiveness, and static faiths of Taoism and Confucianism... to fight for life of justice, equality, freedom, and human dignity".[87] In 1944, Theodore White, a reporter for *Time*, saw them differently as, "masters of brutality".[88]

In 1958, Mao instigated The Great Leap Forward, an economic and social plan which aimed to rapidly transform mainland China from a primarily agrarian economy dominated by peasant farmers into a modern, industrialised communist society.[89] The Great Leap Forward, and the agricultural collectivisation of 1958–1962, were disastrous, tens of millions of peasants starved to death.[90] Frank Dikötter, a professor of modern Chinese history at the University of Hong Kong estimates that Mao's Great Leap Forward cost as many as 60 million Chinese lives.[91] "Not only that: Mao also precipitated the biggest demolition of real estate, the most extensive destruction of the environment, and the biggest waste of manpower in history."[92] The Leap Forward was followed by the "Great Proletarian Cultural Revolution" (1966–1976) which was launched by Mao Zedong to halt what he perceived as a move from fundamental socialism towards capitalism.[93] Mao's decision was strongly influenced by his belief that the Soviet Union (the former role model) had abandoned socialism for a form of state controlled capitalism. Enthusiastically promoted by the state controlled information agencies the "Cultural Revolution" is now seen as having been a devastating disaster for the people of China, millions were forced into manual labour, and tens of thousands were executed. The result was massive civil unrest, and the army was sent in to control the mass disorder.[94] Mao died, aged 82, on 9 September 1976. The Cultural Revolution ended in October 1976 and China was in economic chaos. Someone had to bear the responsibility for failure. At the 1977 eleventh Party Congress, the Cultural Revolution was declared officially to have been ended with the arrest of the Gang of Four.[95]

A veteran of the Long March, Deng Xiaoping joined the Party Central Committee in 1945.[96] A rapidly-rising pragmatist, in the Cultural Revolution he was appointed by Zhou Enlai as deputy premier in 1973, but was purged from that position in 1976 after Zhou Enlai's death. When the Gang of Four were purged, Deng slowly led Mao Zedong's surviving opponents to power and began erasing the cult surrounding Mao. He was instrumental in introducing a new brand of socialist thinking and economic reform, establishing a socialist market economy. He visited New York in 1973 to address a United Nations. This first visit to America indicated to Deng how far China lagged behind in term of living standards and industrial production. It was Deng Xiaoping who opened China to the global market and created the conditions for China to become one of the fastest growing economies in the world, providing a vastly improved standard of living for many Chinese. He became the first Chinese leader to visit the United States on a return visit in 1979, meeting with President Carter at the White House. In 1986, *Time* selected Deng Xiaoping as its "Man of the Year". He resigned from his last party post in 1989, after supporting the use of suppressive military force in the upheaval of Tiananmen Square. Deng Xiaoping died in 1997 after nine years in office. During the last decade or so, China has been ruled by a collective leadership which has projected China into the forefront of industrialised nations, admittedly at significant cultural and social cost.[97]

In less than 150 years, Hong Kong was transformed from a barren island into a vibrant and dynamic metropolis, home to over seven million people, the site of the largest container port in the world, with one of the worlds finest public transportation systems and possessing a breathtaking harbourscape.[98] Great Britain acquired Hong Kong Island in 1842, the Kowloon Peninsula in 1860, and leased the New Territories in 1898.[99] The transfer of sovereignty of Hong Kong from the United Kingdom to China occurred on 1 July 1997.

In terms of design, China claims to have opened over 400 design schools over the last few years. China's policymakers, no longer content with the country's role as the 'world's factory', have been aggressively promoting the message of innovation as the key to competitiveness.[100] In 2008, the Hong Kong Polytechnic University announced the construction of a design "Innovation Tower" designed by the London based Zaha Hadid and expected to be completed by end 2011. In 2010, the Hong Kong Design Institute moved into a new facility designed by the French architecture firm, Coldefy & Associés Architectes Urbanistes. After all, architecture is a very concrete form of national propaganda. Aware of future challenges, the Faculty of Architecture at Hong Kong University has compiled a very useful list of sustainable development sources.[101]

> *A journey of a thousand miles begins with a single step.*
> The Way of Lao-tzu, Chinese philosopher. (604 BCE–531 BCE)

CHINA IS NOT ALONE

As Timothy Cheek, a historian at the University of British Columbia, explains, "Most people in China appear to accept the assumptions in this story about China's national identity, about the role of imperialism in China's history and present, and about the value of maintaining and improving this thing called China. Increasingly, moreover, China's middle classes accept the additional story in Maoism—the story of rising China: China was great, China was put down, China is rising again."[102]

Chris Patten, a former Governor of Hong Kong, now Chancellor of the University of Oxford, points out, the new found status of China should not come as any surprise; for 18 out of the past 20 centuries China has had the greatest economy in the world.[103] In 1991 the World Bank ranked Canada ninth and the USA tenth on their Gross Domestic Product list (an indicator of economic well being). China was ranked 107th. Figures for 2008 place the USA in top place followed by Japan and China now in third place. Brazil ranks eighth, Russia ninth, and India tenth.[104] Recent research figures from the UK Design Council show that the economies of Brazil, Russia, India and China now account for 35 per cent of the world's economic growth.

> India has a national design policy which aims to produce 5,000–8,000 designers a year through investment in new design centres... China has plans for its creative sector to grow by 20 per cent year on year. The country opened its first specialised design school 23 years ago: now it boasts more than 400 and a vast new design facility has opened at Guangzhou's Academy of Fine Arts to teach up to 3,000 industrial design students.[105]

In addition, Thailand, Vietnam and Turkey—which have a combined population of 230 million, are beginning to turn their attention to the role of design in their economic futures. These developments in design education are levelling the playing field. As John Thackara points out, "We are all emerging economies now. We are in a transition from mindless development which has characterised most of our careers to design mindfulness."[106] Time to think about the future of design.

FUTURES

PAST
The past is a foreign country; they do things differently there.
Leslie Poles Hartley, *The Go-Between*, 1953.

PRESENT
We are not able to operate our Spaceship Earth successfully nor for much longer unless we see it as a whole spaceship and our fate as common. It has to be everybody or nobody.
Buckminster Fuller, "World Game Series: Document One", 1970.

FUTURE
The future is a work in progress.
Maurice Barnwell, 2011.

CHAPTER TWELVE
DESIGN: THE CULTURAL DYNAMIC

In design sometimes one plus one equals three.[1]
Josef Albers.

THE GREEKS HAD A WORD FOR IT

In Greek, *synergy* means "working together". Synergy is a word that has become synonymous with creativity and yet is not easy to define within the context of design.[2] It is far more than two or more people working together for mutual benefit. It is when the combination of energies and efforts equals more than the sum of the parts, when one plus one equals three. Synergy can apply to people, working as a member of a team, combing creative resources and talent. In *The Wisdom of Crowds*, James Surowiecki maintains that groups often perform better than individuals in situations requiring problem solving, sometimes producing spectacularly superior results.[3] This synergy occurs when the performance of the group exceeds the perceived abilities of individual members—the whole is greater than the sum of the individual part—one plus one equals three. Synergy can also apply to ideas, making unusual connections across disciplines and cultures to generate new knowledge.

The Parthenon, regarded as the crowning achievement of classical Greece, was home to a 40 foot high gold and ivory statue of Athena Parthenos, the patron goddess of Athens. It was part of a complex of temples,

The temple of Athena Parthenos. Photo: Michael Korcuska.

This photograph shows the 'curve' of the Parthenon. "The peristyle columns are over ten metres tall, and incline slightly towards the centre of the building at the top (about 7 cm), while the platform upon which they rest bows on a gentle arc which brings the corners about 12 cm closer to the ground than the middle."[6]

most of which were emblazoned with vivid decoration and featured an array of representations of mortal and immortal personalities. Constructed in the fifth century BCE, it was occupied by the forces of the Ottoman Empire in 1456 and converted into a mosque. During the next 400 years or so it was subject to a variety of catastrophes, from earthquakes to artillery attacks. In 1832 when Greece regained control of Athens all traces of the medieval and Ottoman elements were destroyed. During the nineteenth century the site was looted and many of its treasures removed to foreign museums. Towards the end of the nineteenth century revitalised interest and research revealed some interesting design elements.[4]

The 'Golden Mean' mathematical reality of the Parthenon is moderated by necessary optical modifications of curvature to assure visual elegance—here are almost no straight lines or right angles in this structure.[5] Each of the individual 70,000 pieces is refined to fit in one specific place. This coming together of geometry, mathematics, aesthetics and optical illusion provides an object of 'studied harmony' that has established the Parthenon as an icon of Western culture. Much of design is like that, making connections between information that is known, utilising compromise and trade off, to design something new and innovative, that 'looks right', and fits the situation.

The degree and intensity of the design process depends upon the extent of curiosity, the level of creativity and the cultural context. In 1976, Raymond Williams, the noted cultural theorist defined culture as one of the four or five key concepts in modern social knowledge.[7] More recently, John Thackara claims that "We need to develop a combination of factual process, and cultural knowledge to manage well in today's complex world."[8] Our daily life is dependent upon things and situations that have been designed, that's the factual part—we derive meaning from those items based upon our cultural knowledge. Thinking of the near future, Pierre Vigier, of the Innovation Policy Department, European Commission, makes it clear, "What is needed is a cultural attitude towards knowledge sharing."[9] Add that observation to the defining statement of Frank Pick, that design is "intelligence made visible", and it is possible to develop an operating design mandate for the coming decade.

As we saw in Chapter One, culture can mean different things to different groups, depending upon their predisposition and focus.[10] Culture is a significant part of people's lives. It is culture that establishes the norms and conventions of life. Many of these cultural norms are the result of decades of development (the unselfconscious process) but it is possible to create new forms of behaviour very quickly (the self-conscious process) many of which are in response to new products and situations—the iPad and smartphone being current examples. The way in which we receive information, the way that we communicate, the pastimes that we engage in, even our social interactivity is driven by technology with passing reference to what has been and, hopefully, pointing the way to what may be.

Tracy Skelton and Tim Allen explain how investigations into cultural aspects of way of life can be crucial in making assessments of processes of change.

Understanding culture in a broad conceptual framework helps us interpret what things mean to different people... nuanced and sophisticated investigations into cultural aspects of ways of life can be very significant in making assessments of processes of change... we reject conceptions of culture as fixed, coherent or 'natural', and instead view it as dynamically changing over time and space—the product of ongoing human interaction. This means that we accept the term as ambiguous and suggestive rather than as an analytical precise. It reflects or encapsulates the muddles of living.[11]

Culture is composed of a wide spectrum of ideas, beliefs and customs, it is essential for designers to discover the ways in which they interact with the "muddles of living". Combined, these various aspects interpret and characterise the culture of design. Culture denotes existence, past, present and future. As explored in Chapter One, design culture is a social activity that demands creative behaviour. All forms of design activity are adaptable. The challenge is how, in an intercultural context, to promote creativity and how to encourage the generation of original forms of expression which, while being respectful of cultural differences, advance cultural vitality and engender understanding.

Writing in *Business Week*, Harry West, of the innovation consultancy, Continuum, suggests that design creativity is most active in the space between disciplines, in the synergy at the interface of the engineering approach to design and the studio based approach.[12] Unprecedented changes in forms of communication made possible by the computer and other related technologies have given new impetus to the intercultural, cross-disciplinary dialogue of design within a global context. This attitude is applicable to current design process. We adjust our lens, re-focus, or to use a more contemporary simile, we choose a matrix through which to organise our perceptions and formulate responses to new dimensions of opportunity and risk—there is always risk.[13]

In the pre-industrial period nature was seen as an inexhaustible wilderness, the impact of human presence, although noticeable had little detrimental effect, and what effect there was tended to be local. Throughout the industrial period, nature was ignored, being seen as a no more than the source of the raw material needed to power the revolution. In the post-industrial period we are having to cope with that ignorance and unthinking attitude. We are in danger of overwhelming nature to the point of extinction. Some future forecasters see similarities between now and then—with the perceived vast and inexhaustible world of nature being replaced by a much vaster, inexhaustible world of information. We cannot afford to demonstrate the same level of non-caring ignorance towards information that our predecessors did towards nature. What and how you think matters. If the sustainable design process focuses on social innovation (ONE) and emphasises the participatory role of people, to address the problems and concerns of the community, ever respectful of the cultural dynamic, (TWO) then new scenarios (THREE) may emerge in response to the problem or challenge.

HERITAGE AS A CULTURAL RESOURCE

Writing in the *Doors of Perception* website, Manzini, Ezio observes that the "dream of a well-being based on consumption is based on a promise that we now recognise as impossible to keep". He continues, "In the end, it is a heritage of knowledge, behaviour patterns and organisational forms that, seen in the light of current conditions of existence and current problems, may constitute valuable building materials for the future."[14] Do not regard cultural heritage as being out-of-date, old fashioned, or irrelevant. It provides an accurate, up-to-date cultural resource, one that can assist in the design of a sustainable future. The melding of past, present and future can generate solution that are both satisfactory from a performance point of view while remaining observant of the prevailing cultural context. (See the "Design Profile: Sustainable ECCO 9707 Bamboo Chair designed by Eric Chan"). We have a cultural disposition to the use of technology. In 1874, Christopher Shole designed the typewriter keyboard. One overriding problem was how to reduce the jamming of the type bars in the carriage. Shole's solution was the now famous QWERTY keyboard that placed machine efficiency over human efficiency.[15] Look down at your keyboard. Despite the elimination of type bars the illogical and inconvenient placement of the letters remains because of cultural custom.

As we sit here in the second decade of the twenty-first century, we have to come to terms with change on a daily basis. It becomes increasingly important for us to establish who we are and what we believe. (The personal design philosophy that we have pondered several times in the text). The old parameters of family, organised religion, national identity may no longer have the overwhelming pressure that they once did–to these we have added the world of computer mediated information and virtually discontinuous fragmented information (though iPads, smartphones, Twitter, etc.) often functioning in tandem with a social network.

Designers are participants in the creation, critique, and dissemination of culture. The designer assumes the role of mediator, balancing personal needs, with the needs of the client, and the needs of the audience. In other words, design is reflective of the context of its creation. As Penny Sparke points out, design has "a formative function within society and culture.... In this sense, design is seen as being part of a dynamic process through which culture is actually constructed, not merely reflected."[16]

We are faced with a constantly changing context. Our lifestyle is increasingly complex and the design context far more conceptual. As the context for design becomes even more abstract then it will become increasingly important for designers to ponder their individual design process and the cultural identity that that process incorporates. It is vital to formulate a clear, dynamic, yet flexible personal design philosophy. If you are in need of a little encouragement then re-read John Thackara's "Rules of Engagement" from Chapter Ten, and Dieter Rams "Ten Commandments on Design" from Chapter Seven. Then consider *Wabi-sabi*, the Zen principles of aesthetics, where everything, without exception, is constantly in flux.

Wabi sabi acknowledges three simple realities: "nothing lasts", "nothing is finished", "nothing is perfect".[17] These guiding principles have commercial application. The computer programming system, Agile, developed in 2001, is fundamental to Wiki searches.[18]

Writing in *The Skin of Culture*, Derrick De Kerckhove and Christopher Dewdney point out:

> The main role of the artist or the designer in the context of unlimited power and access is to probe history, natural and social–to cull guidelines from mankind's more successful experiments in living.[19]

Those experiments are recorded in the cultural record. Culture is not a pretentious, elitist activity of concern only to an elite minority, or the middle aged, culture is you. Cultural awareness can offer a rewarding experience, suggestive of new ways to look at the world, where very often, one plus one equals three. Design offers a form of cultural mediation in daily life, it helps us get through the day, it gives meaning to and defines our social place, it provides an identity. David Novitz claries the situation;

> Advertisement in our newspapers and on television, the gloss of our fashion magazines, the design of our motor cars and bathrooms, embody beliefs, insights, and shared knowledge that enter into and endorse the view we have of our social world.[20]

The contact that human beings have with their world is context-dependent. The future can inspire and intimidate; the past, known or imagined, is reassuring. The context of the past gives rise to nostalgia.

DÉJÀ VU IS EVERYWHERE

Many find the past more secure than the future. The past, real or imagined, is a powerful force in the design process. Referring to a past that never was, *déjà vu* shares a structure not only with fiction, but also with the ever more sophisticated effects of media technology.[21] Nostalgia generally refers to a definitive past, albeit subject to personal modification. Jonathan Woodham observes: "Nostalgia has played a significant role in the production and consumption of design throughout the twentieth century."[22] At times, our view of past culture can be distorted, *déjà vu* merges with nostalgia, in the words of *Time* critic Gerald Clarke, "Vision fades and imagination takes over."[23] The resulting images are no less powerful for this realisation–the staged raising of the American flag on *Iowa Jima* remains the most iconic image from the Second World War.[24] Conscious manipulation of the past impinges on cultural meaning. We have progressed from the heavy handed air brushing of photographs, a process so beloved by totalitarian regimes, through the hand-drawn matte extraction of *Forrest Gump*, 1994, where the embedding of false imagery produces new histories (How many believe that Gump actually meet President Kennedy?) to the sophisticated pixel manipulation of *Star Wars* and the virtual world of *Avatar*.[25]

Traditional Japanese wedding, Kama Kura, 2010.

In the world of film, production has become the first step in post-production.[26] George Lucas reveals that *Star Wars: Episode 1–The Phantom Menace*, 1999, resulted from two years of preproduction, and two years of post-production, with only 65 days of traditional on-set photography. Of the 2,200 shots, 95 per cent were digitally manipulated on a computer. With the advent of Blue-ray disc digital technology and changes in the method of digital delivery, with holographic projection on the horizon, then the process of what and how we see is being transformed—*déjà vu*, nostalgia and reality may morph into a format more in keeping with the needs of the twenty-first century.[27] The ability to manipulate past, present and future can be problematic to the design process and places the burden of social responsibility upon the shoulders of designers.

THE FUTURE IS IN YOUR HANDS

When all futures are possible, the designer needs enhanced social awareness and implicit ethical standards of practice. Cultural heritage can often provide a guide. In *Continuities in Popular Culture*, Ray Brown explains the dilemma.

When people become self-conscious, worried about their present and their future, they dig in the past for security.... Cultures that have been suppressed in the past will, when given the power, rise again. In so doing they change the status quo, driving it through the pangs of birth and rebirth through quiet or open revolution, until all have what passes for equal chance in the sun."[28]

The cult of the past may have developed as an antidote to the cult of the future, as a protection against future shock.[29] If we feel disconnected with past design we can always get a quick fix by visiting a museum, a time machine stuck in reverse, and appreciate the cultural heritage on display—pity that there is no museum of the future.[30]

The various design processes are in a state of constant change as are the associated methods of visualisation and presentation. These exciting and stimulating times are resonating with creative possibilities. Designers sensitive to the vibrations coming back from the future, operate in unknown territory, often in tandem with complex collaborative ventures with other designers and specialists from other disciplines. Designers can bring their specialist knowledge and expertise to the table, they can provide the conceptual visualisations necessary to give form to design alternatives. As Jonathan Chapman and Nick Grant point out: "Creative design practice these days is about adapting solutions found in one context for use in another."[31]

THE CULTURAL IMPERATIVE

The other vital component that design can offer is an understanding of the cultural imperative of design. Cultural knowledge is made in part by ideology which identifies the rights and responsibilities of group members, and includes the beliefs values and myths of a culture; these are the determinants required to live together. Developments in 2011 provide a very clear indication of how new technologies are affording new opportunities for cultural change, particularly in relation to social order. Cultural determinants on design include political structures and the ability to oppose the dominant power system, allowing for the development or 'counter culture'; geographic location is another ecological determinant.[32] Many cultural core beliefs are so deeply embedded in society that they are resistant to dramatic change, allowing for minor revisions that are reflective of the current cultural ethos.[33] Activities associated with life changing events such as birth, marriage and death are among the more obvious examples.

Cultural beliefs result from a form of cultural programming, and like all forms of programming, can be amended. It is culture that gives primal meaning to the process of human development. Traditionally, the term 'culture' describes a way of life of particular groups of people, nations, historic periods. In the twenty-first century the term can have a more fluid and all encompassing meaning, bypassing nationalistic ideologies and geographic location to provide an informed attitude to a distinctive way of life, an attitude shared by connecting individuals. This does not mean a rejection of tradition, rather an awareness of the diversity of traditions. In the West, we tend to view the cultural developments of the last two centuries as being the way of the world, overlooking the unbroken cultures of India, China and Japan that have a heritage stretching back over five thousand years, (see Chapter Eleven).

TWO DEGREES OF SEPARATION

Recent research has shown any two humans differ from each other by about one to two per cent of their genes.[34] We may all be genetically almost identical, yet every one of use thinks of ourselves as being an individual, and it is most obvious that there are a vast array of differences in our cultural make up. We do have commonalities, we prefer to be associated with an identifiable group, every cultural group reveres its children, we all have a very strong survival instinct, yet it is the cultural differences that make us such a diverse and fascinating species. Walk around any major urban city and you will see that some aspects of a culture can be easily adopted with varying degrees of enthusiasm and subject to the whims of fashion. This is most noticeable in restaurants where the popularity of Chinese, French, Indian, Italian, Japanese, Mexican and Thai cuisine vary with the decade. Popular magazines, websites and television shows can lend support to clothing codes that were once culture specific. This can suggest that we all enjoy a degree of cultural diversity. Core values such as ethics and morals are more resistant to change. It is essential for designers to realise that their clients, in all probability, may not share the same belief systems; the resulting design proposals should recognise this. This is not a world where our values are based on meaning derived from any single object. As Ray Eames indicated, we construct meaning from the interconnections that happen between an array of objects and possessions. That process of interconnection takes place within the context of culture.

LIFE CYCLE ANALYSIS[35]

Technology impacts culture. In a design sense, the acceptance or rejection of technological change can transform reality, sometimes beneficially, sometimes not. For far too many, the family meal (with all its connotations of togetherness, conversation, discussion, problem resolution) has been replaced by the loneliness of the TV dinner, where even reality has been transformed into a socially acceptable television show. Design can offer a sensorial interface between the physical world and the world of meaning; often that meaning is bound to cultural attitudes. We live in a world of things, too many things, many of which are discarded early in their life. Making things last longer is not the problem, making them mean more longer is. When things were crafted by hand, wear and age added value to the design. Today, when things are crafted by mind we have to find a way of achieving similar added value.

The development of ecologically friendly products which strengthen the bond between humans and their culture can be a means in reducing the environmental footprint. We take it for granted that the expensive software we have just installed will permit frequent and free updates; why does not the same attitude extend to appliances and vehicles? As Ezio Manzini points out, we no longer take care of objects, we replace them. Designers need to encourage a carrying attitude, make more things mean more for longer. There is plenty of caring evident at birth (when the product is brand new) and at old age (when it has achieved the status of "antique"), the problem are the uncaring intermediary years, when the first signs of aging appear; that first scratch, or dent, or when fashionable colours and forms change. Advances in surface chemistry which allow for modification in surface characteristics, abilities to update, all these are available to designers in their response to the challenge of extending the life of a product. It is all a matter of design, and an adaptation of cultural attitude.

The Canadian based Adbusters Foundation published their manifesto, *First Things First 2000*, an updated version of the earlier *First Things First* manifesto written and published in January 1964 following a proclamation at the Institute of Contemporary Arts in London in December 1963, by the British graphic designer Ken Garland. The Adbusters version proposes a reversal of the established norm—coercing designers to produce "more useful, lasting, and democratic forms of communication—a mindshift away from product marketing and towards the exploration and production of a new kind of meaning".[36] We have become educated in the cultural benefits associated with recycling paper, soda bottles and the like; it is about time that we gave thought to the recycling of information.

Maybe we need to adjust the romantic maxim of William Morris, "a thing of beauty is a joy forever", to the sustainable mantra "a well designed object provides satisfaction forever". We need to modify Le Corbusiers modernistic description of a house as "a machine for living in", to Ray Eames more metaphorical, frame for living, a place where magic can happen. "Much of its magic (of the Eames house) resides in the way that the trees, plants, furniture and carefully assembled objects and decorations—many bought on the Eames's extensive travels—become part of the total effect."[37] The Eames House has been understood in many ways—it is time to celebrate its cultural imperative, seeing it as a place where past, present and future coexist, where the space is brought to life by its inhabitants, a place where magic can happen, (see Chapter Six, "Utility to Populuxe").

STYLE OR SUSTAINABILITY

Products themselves do not homogenise culture into a single global entity of universal conformity; the same product can mean different things to different groups, the Vespa scooter being a case in point. Designed as a form of unisex transportation for the post-war urban streets of Italy, the cultural imperative changed the Vespa GS 160 into "the ultimate London Mod machine", a product that induced moral panic among English residents—many seeing the Vespa as a threatening machine, a product associated with the Mod invasions of the south coast resort towns in the Summer of 1964.[38] Chapter Six explored the post-war design culture in Britain and America, suggesting that Pop design promoted the consumer as someone to be catered to, for profit. The emphasis was on looking trendy rather than concern for the life of the product. Throw away was part of conspicuous consumption where life cycles were designed to be short, and where design emphasised surface over substance. Then came postmodernism which injected "meaning" into product, even if it was not always clear who determined meaning or what the meaning was. Products referenced lifestyle and social status, real or imagined.

The design culture had progressed from Mies van der Rohe's assertion that "less is more", through Robert Venturi's reformed "less is a bore", to Miss Piggy's pragmatic credo "more is more".

THE GOOD LIFE

Half a century ago, the Spanish existential philosopher José Ortega y Gasset, in his *Thoughts on Technology*, proposed that technology allows humans not just a need to live but a desire to live "a good life", one that results in a sense of "well-being", providing a meaning to life. He reasons that the primordial reality is life, not contemplation or even science but rather "staying alive". One of the instruments in that struggle being technology which he sees as one of the elements that makes human life human.[39] Technology, by design, opens up avenues of self discovery and self fulfilment. Technology extends the options available to all designers, providing for choice directed by personal conviction, attitude, morality—a choice that can be empathetic to or in conflict with the cultural ethos.

At some time in the future, technology may acquire sentient power, up until that time technology requires a human driver. That has always been the way of technology in the world; fire can cook food and destroy the home; the www can promote knowledge or pornography, as always, the choice is yours. As John Wood so eloquently explains, "At present, most designers are specialists who have been trained to delight, persuade, pamper and mollify consumers. Few see themselves as responsible professionals on a par, say, with doctors or lawyers." He suggests that such a cultural realignment "will require a shift in consciousness in which the creativity is understood as a manifold act of adaption and integration that reconciles inner realities with their surroundings, rather than emphasising self-expression, or delivering a flood of exotically innovative ideas or products".[40] It is time for more designers to respond in a more responsible way, to assist in the design of a sustainable "good life".

How, from the perspective of design, can we creatively utilise all the world knowledge in the formulation of design solutions? Considering the present conditions of our planet and the catastrophic nature of current events, we should ask ourselves what the effective role of design has been up to now. Unfortunately, the answer is only too clear. Generally speaking, design has been, and for many still is, 'part of the problem'. This is not inevitable, design can and must reverse its role and become instead 'part of the solution.'[41] Design is primarily concerned with people and their connections—with objects, the environment, but most of all with each other.

LISTEN, LEARN, ACT

Experimentation, communication, listening, flexibility, these are the touchstones of sustainable design process. What is required is a re-orientation of the design process and a reawakening of design values, some of which are part of our traditional cultural heritage.

These changes in orientation must be knowledge based, founded on research and may reflect a bottom-up infrastructure. They will explore the advances in science and technology, they will be respectful of individual knowledge, practical skills and aptitudes. Most of all, they will be based on a creative enabling attitude towards social innovation. In the nineteenth century, the Arts and Crafts Movement was a designed response to what were regarded as the inequities of industrialisation. This movement gave birth to a cottage industry approach to design (or at least to those designers who considered themselves to be reform minded.)

PEOPLE FIRST

As we accept the realities of global production and distribution, as we face up to the challenges presented by environmental degradation, enhanced by a concern for social equity and a safe, sustainable life for all of this planets inhabitants, then maybe we embrace technological and scientific advances, and change the cottage industry approach to the reality of a laptop/cell-phone industry, where designers are mediators. As Manzini indicates, the designer will function as an interpreter of cultural landscapes.[42] (And here is a linguistic challenge—we have readily embraced new words for design led technological advances such as the iPod and the portmanteau podcast (a blend of iPod and broadcast)—what we do not have are words for the new activities of the re-orientated design process, we are forced to use artificial words such as 'mediator', 'facilitator' or 'interpreter' which arrive pre-loaded with cultural meaning.) In 2008, Nokia introduced the People First concept cell phone where the design focus is on use and function rather than style and where and how people use their phones is the decisive aspect of the design. Innovations such as a zero waste charger reinforces the observations of John Thackara that "small design actions can have big effects", (see Chapter Thirteen). In this case, in the Republic of Korea for example these 'small' savings could power 70,000 homes annually. Nokia is intent on encouraging users to keep their cell phones and other devices longer, to wear them in, not out and is continuing research that will help users make more sustainable choices.[43] Research in both Europe and North America indicates that the new communication tools are helping to change patterns of communication, "the cell phone in some cases is being used as the primary computer for Latinos, serving up e-mail and the Internet, in the process bridging what has been called the digital divide that still exists for some minority and disadvantaged groups".[44]

DISABLING AND ENABLING SOLUTIONS

If mass production was the distinctive feature of the twentieth century then the twenty-first century will be the era of mass innovation where design becomes a participatory activity, focussed on achieving a good, sustainable life for all of this planets inhabitants.[45] As we have seen, the fortunate top ten per cent of Earth's population consume the majority of the physical resources of this planet. The exact figure is open to conjecture (and in need of much more research) but some commentators put this figure as high as 80 per cent. If the developed world, by design, continues to promote this pattern of un-sustainability as the desirable role model, then disaster awaits. As Ezio Manzini advises; "So what we must do is change direction. We must move in a direction where our design energies and our technological potential are focussed on rendering individuals and communities better able to work together and find a way of living better, in autonomy; or rather, to learn to live better... consuming less, far less, of our environmental resources."[46] We need to establish creative, caring design communities.

The design process is often a bottom-up approach, requiring a readjustment of the existing infrastructure and forms of governance. Ezio Manzini explains that in this 'disabled' world, design can take on enabling characteristics; "its role should be one of improving the quality of life; to act as a bridge between technical and social innovation to the point of proposing artefacts able to help people live better". He points out that "the transition towards a sustainable society is a massive social learning process" that will require "a vast capacity for listening and just as great a degree of flexibility in order to change... direction".[47]

Design comes about from an original combination of pre-existing information. The demand for the product or service is often the result of the social issues and cultural conditions of contemporary life. Satisfactory sustainable solutions will demonstrate a knowledge and respect for cultural heritage and traditions of living; an awareness of technological and scientific advances together with the skill to use them in an appropriate way; and a realisation of the pre-existing social and political constraints to the development and implementation of a creative response. Most importantly, satisfactory sustainable solutions will result from a process of listening to and engaging with, potential users. As we have seen, the real design problems are evident in all human societies from the nomadic groups and refugees of sub-Saharan Africa to the urban isolation that many inhabitants of our largest cities feel. "Today people are trying to adjust and deal with loss, loneliness, isolation, constant change, high-paced stressful jobs, single parent families, blended families and the repeated necessity of rebuilding ones social support system."[48] For many, this is the cultural context of design, not to be ignored, but responded to. In today's fragmented but connected world, it is possible for all groups to have a voice. Aided and abetted by active design intervention, all groups can be, at least in part, a source for solving their particle problem or concern.

A TIME TO ACT

The sage of communication studies, Manuel Castells make it abundantly clear, "the most fundamental form of power lies in the ability to shape the human mind. The way we feel and think determines the way we act, both individually and collectively."[49] As we sit here in the second decade of the twenty-first century, we have to come to terms with change on a daily basis; it becomes increasingly important for us to establish who we are and what we believe. The old parameters of family, organised religion, national identity may no longer have the overwhelming pressure that they once did—to these we have added the world of computer mediated information and virtually discontinuous fragmented information (though iPads, cell phones, etc.). In this brave new world designers are participants in the creation, critique, and dissemination of culture. The designer assumes the role of mediator: balancing personal need, the needs of the client, and the needs of the audience—in other words, design is reflective of the context of its creation. As Penny Sparke points out, design has "a formative function within society and culture.... In this sense, design is seen as being part of a dynamic process through which culture is actually constructed, not merely reflected."[50] In this new millennium you are faced with a constantly changing context. Our lifestyle is increasingly complex and the design context far more abstract. As the context for design becomes even more 'abstract' then it will become increasingly important for designers to ponder their individual design process and the cultural identity that that process incorporates. "The main role of the artist or the designer in the context of unlimited power and access is to probe history, natural and social—to cull guidelines from mankind's more successful experiments in living", so states Derrick De Kerckhove.[51]

Culture is not a pretentious, elitist activity of concern only to a 'cultured' minority, or the middle-aged, culture is you. Cultural awareness can offer a rewarding experience, suggestive of new ways to look at the world, where very often, one plus one equals three. So much for theory, now for an example from the real world where an innovative design process, benefitting from qualitative cultural knowledge, leads to a unique forward-looking sustainable solution, that can mean more longer.

REAL LIFE

Real life design is often an expression of balance and concept where the objective is an improvement in how people live and in the quality of life. Design comes about from an original combination of pre-existing information. The demand for the product or service is often the result of the social issues and cultural conditions of contemporary life. Satisfactory sustainable solutions will demonstrate a knowledge and respect for cultural heritage and traditions of living; an awareness of technological and scientific advances together with the skill to use them in an appropriate way; and a realisation of the pre-existing social and political constraints to the development and implementation of a creative response. Most importantly, satisfactory sustainable solutions will result from a process of listening to and engaging with, potential users;[52] (more about sustainability in Chapter Thirteen).

REAL PROBLEMS

As we have seen, the real design problems are evident in all human societies from the nomadic groups and refugees of sub-Saharan Africa to the urban isolation that many inhabitants of our largest cities feel. The psychotherapist Steve B Reed states that; "Today people are trying to adjust and deal with loss, loneliness, isolation, constant change, high-paced stressful jobs, single parent families, blended families and the repeated necessity of rebuilding ones social support system."[53] This is part of the cultural context of modern design, not to be ignored, but responded to. In today's fragmented but connected world, it is possible for all groups to have a voice. Aided and abetted by active design intervention, all groups can be, at least in part, a source for solving their particle problem or concern.

WE ARE MORE THAN CULTURE

We may see ourselves as belonging to one culture, but that does not mean that all persons within that cultural group share the same values. Any cultural group is heterogeneous by nature. Values learned in childhood become an integral part of our patterns of thought and behaviour. These values, supplemented by life experience and personal choices make us who we are and influence how we see our world, creating the lens through which we evaluate, assess, and pass judgement. These factors also influence how we respond to the multitude of cues that fill our daily lives. In *Communication Between Cultures*, the authors make it clear "how extensively your daily life is guided by culture. Factors such as family, history, religion, and cultural identity influence your decisions as to what you consider an appropriate snack: a bag of chips, a dish of hummus, or a ball of rice wrapped in seaweed."[54] Your cultural identity influences your design decisions, how you make one plus one make three. Your cultural values may also influence how you respond to the challenges ahead, including questions of sustainability.

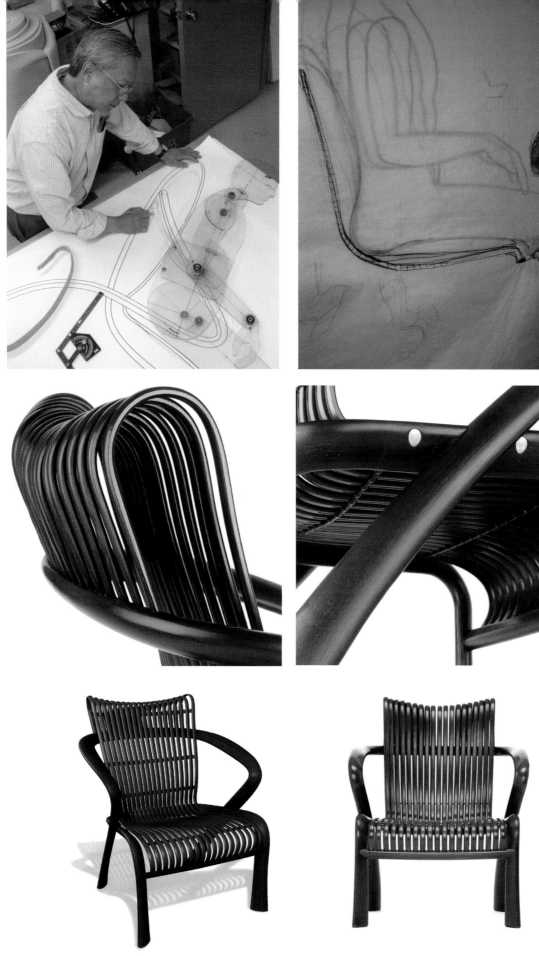

Ecco 9707, Eric Chan, 2007.

DESIGN PROFILE: SUSTAINABLE ECCO 9707 BAMBOO CHAIR DESIGNED BY ERIC CHAN

THE "RITE" PLACE TO SIT: THE ECCO 9707 CHAIR

Born in Guangzhou, Eric Chan began his design training behind the fort like facade of the Hong Kong Polytechnic University, receiving his degree in Industrial Design in 1976. Moving to America, he received a Master's Degree in 1980 from Cranbrook, noted for its illustrious furniture design alumni including Florence Knoll, Harry Bertoia and Charles and Ray Eames.

For Eric Chan design is all about balance. He sees the designer as a mediator between the manufacture and the consumer, ever mindful of technology, with a reverence for nature and respectful of cultural heritage. Eric maintains that the fundamental principles of Eastern philosophy, a sense of wellbeing, security in internal reward, appreciation of simplicity, respect for nature and honour for family values, all these have become new again in the twenty-first century. He is adamant that successful design can function and communicate across culturally defined boundaries.

More than ever, the designer's task is to mediate the balance between people and objects, poetry and logic, technology and nature. I am most interested in translating complicated technology into simple, understandable, and friendly products for people.[55]

In 2007, he joined with Herman Miller to research and develop the Ecco 9707 bamboo chair, designed to commemorate the ten year anniversary of Hong Kong's return to China. This presented Chan with the opportunity to forge an amalgam of cultural and technological forces into a calm, balanced design. His knowledge of traditional materials; his reverence for his cultural heritage, all come together in a design that incorporates elements of social responsibility with his ecological sensitivity to achieve a 'synergy' of forces into an ergonomically sound chair that is 'rite', (see Chapter Six).

The principle material is bamboo, a material that in China is revered for its honesty, endurance and resilience. The design exploits the natural flexibility and strength of the material while conforming to ergonomic requirements. The chair is manufactured in the Anji area of China renowned for bamboo production and processing while maintaining an ecological awareness. Herman Millar provided the "Super Seat" technology which improved the suspension characteristics required for consistent weight support. The design strikes a balance between heritage, modernity, technology and craftsmanship, while providing both style and comfort.

I.D. Magazine named Chan among the 40 most influential designers in the US and Business Week hailed him as "One of the new breed of ingenious American designers that is making the world take note." He has served as juror for Industrial Design Excellence Awards and for the CES Awards for Industrial Design. He was listed by Contract Magazine as among the country's ten most influential designers. In 2009, Chan received the World Technology Award from a network of peer-elected individuals and organizations from the science and technology communities. In 2010 he received the World's Outstanding Chinese Designer award. These marks of recognition bring focus to the cultural aspects of design, where often one plus one equals three.

For Eric Chan design is all about balance. He sees the designer as a mediator between the manufacture and the consumer, even mindful of technology, with a reverence for nature and respectful of cultural heritage. Eric maintains that the fundamental principles of Eastern philosophy, a sense of wellbeing, security in internal reward, appreciation of simplicity, respect for nature and honour for family values, all these have become new again in the twenty-first century. He is adamant that successful design can function and communicate across culturally defined boundaries. The Ecco 9707 chair was designed to commemorate the ten year anniversary of Hong Kong's return to China. The principle material is bamboo, a material that in China is revered for its honesty, endurance and resilience.

The Earth seen from Apollo 17. August, 2006. NASA photo ID AS17-148-2272. Earth is a water planet: three quarters of the surface covered by water, and water rich clouds fill the sky.

CHAPTER THIRTEEN
DESIGN FUTURES: QUESTIONS OF SUSTAINABILITY

In our every deliberation we must consider the impact of our decisions on the next seven generations.
From *The Great Law of the Iroquois*.[1]

50/50

The Earth is about 4.5 billion years old. 50 years is a little more than one hundredth of a millionth of Earth's age. Think of Earth's age as being one kilometre, then 50 years is about ten microns, the size of a very fine human hair.[2] 50 years ago the population of Earth was estimated at three billion, in 50 years time it is predicted to reach nine billion,[3] each one of whom will require an adequate supply of water and food. 50 years ago (the focus of Section Two, "Form") the concept of smartphones, iPads and the www would have been relegated to the field of science fiction. As we have witnessed, fiction became fact.

In December 2009, to coincide with the Copenhagen climate change summit, a common editorial calling for action from world leaders on climate change was published in 56 major newspapers in 45 countries around the world in 20 languages including Chinese, Arabic and Russian.[4] Noticeably absent being any major American newspapers. The *Miami Herald* was the sole representative of the world's second biggest polluter.[5] Today, there remain opponents to the actuality of global warming, insulated by ignorance and dogma they reject the scientific evidence. Admittedly there are a wide range of predictions as to the amount and speed of that warming process, but no sane individual can doubt that the Earth will be warmer in 50 years time. No one can doubt that this, along with population growth, will place considerable strain on water supplies and food production. In the recent past much enmity and many conflicts have been over oil. In the next 50 years they may well be over water and food, in particular rice.[6] Make no mistake, we are a hair's-breadth away from cataclysmic change. Design can, and should assist in facing up to the challenges ahead. It all begins with you.

WHAT WILL CHANGE EVERYTHING?

No one has all the answers. The following is designed to define and validate questions concerning the challenges associated with the reality of climate change. Increased communal awareness and extensive media coverage has promoted debate on climate change to the forefront of public discourse. Unfortunately, the debate has become less concerned with scientific fact and more with political stance and public relations, producing erudite reports but little action.[7] Politics aside there is a need to define the challenges ahead.

In December 2008, *Edge* asked 150 noted thinkers and social commentators, "What game-changing scientific ideas and developments do you expect to live to see?" Their forecasts ranged from artificial intelligence (Kevin Kelly, Editor-At-Large, *Wired*); through thoughts on culture (Timothy Taylor, Archaeologist, University of Bradford) and human evolution (Juan Enriquez, Founding Director, Harvard Business School's Life Sciences Project) to climate (William Calvin, Neuroscientist, University of Washington School of Medicine) and knowledge (Haim Harari, Physicist, former President, Weizmann Institute of Science). As John Brockman, the editor and publisher of *Edge*, summarised;

> Nobody ever voted for printing. Nobody ever voted for electricity. Nobody ever voted for radio, the telephone, the automobile, the airplane, television. Nobody ever voted for penicillin, antibiotics, the pill. Nobody ever voted for space travel, massively parallel computing, nuclear power, the personal computer, the Internet, email, cell phones, the Web, Google, cloning, sequencing the entire human genome. We are moving towards the redefinition of life, to the edge of creating life itself. While science may or may not be the only news, it is the news that stays news. And our politicians, our governments? Always years behind, the best they can do is play catch up.[8]

We have seen in previous chapters that sustainability is likely to be one of the most significant influences on design in the coming decades, and that the design process will make "game-changing scientific ideas and developments" intelligible and meaningful to human culture.

THE FUTURE IS SUSTAINABLE [9]

During the 1980s design acquired a 'green wash' which was largely non-effective. Today, the stakes are much higher, we can not afford a 'sustainable wash'. Most of the sustainable elements of design already exist, they are not dependent upon futuristic promises; they do acknowledge advances in technology and are respectful of existing social practices and design heritage. More significantly, they profit from the sharing of information.[10] Satisfactory sustainable design requires a creative re-think. As Chapman and Grant indicate, "Sustainable design is about criticism. Essentially, it is an edgy culture that reinvigorates design with the ethos of debate which was once the hallmark of creative practice".[11]

Today, prevailing challenges have resulted in a new wave of ecodesign practice and criticism which is concerned with a more subtle analysis of meaning and methodology and takes a fresh look at the economics and technological aspects of sustainability.[12] 'Green', 'eco' and 'sustainable' have become fairly interchangeable terms of reference. Rather than argue over linguistic variations it is more constructive to accept that public interest in environmental issues is increasing, it is going beyond the previous, simplistic notions of design and the environment. The public are better informed, designers must and should listen.[13]

Design is always a matter of asking the right question and developing an appropriate answer. In the past, design was overwhelmingly concerned with 'how'. In the very near future, 'should' will be of much greater importance. We are air breathing primates who require regular intakes of clean water and nutritious food. And yet we continue to pollute the very air we breath, the water we drink and contaminate the food we eat. As the noted anthropologist Jane Goodall asks, "we... have a highly developed intellect, so how come we're destroying our home?"[14] Whatever we do, the Earth will survive.[15] We, on the other hand, may not.

This planet is the only home we have. Protecting its biodiversity and environment are of paramount importance. There are political, technical and moral challenges to overcome.[16] Dr J Craig Venter provided an elegant summation when presenting the 2007 Richard Dimbleby Lecture on the BBC.

> Our planet is facing almost insurmountable problems, problems that governments on their own clearly can't fix. In order to survive, we need a scientifically literate society willing and able to embrace change—because our ability to provide life's essentials of food, water, shelter and energy for an expanding human population will require major advances in science and technology.[17]

Informed literacy in science and technology are essential elements in contemporary design practice and basic requirements in designing a sustainable future in the twenty-first century.

Millions of people around the world, informed by a diverse range of media on the challenges we face, are united in the belief that something must be done to protect our universal home, but what? The environmental challenges are immense and the available information complex. We are all faced by a confusing cacophony of often conflicting information, ideas and solutions.[18] 'Feel good' actions are not enough, active informed design decisions can help. Cast aside all preconceptions and oft cherished belief systems. There is truth in the old adage that if you think the same in ten years time as you think now, the only thing that it proves is that you will have stopped thinking.

A GHOST OF A CHANCE

First and foremost do your research; and make sure it is research, not a search for justification. Listen to all sides in all debates. Determine the reliability of the source, be aware to any associated bias. Think for yourself and develop your own personal, flexible and fluid opinions. Always be prepared to change your mind. Dogma in any guise is detrimental to the design process. Jacob Bronowski said it best:

> There are two parts to the human dilemma. One is a belief that the end justifies the means. That push-button philosophy, that deliberate deafness to suffering, has become a monster in the war machine. The other is the betrayal of the human spirit: the assertion of dogma that closes the mind, and turns a nation, a civilisation into a regiment of ghosts—obedient ghosts, or tortured ghosts.[19]

CO-OPERATION

Now is not the time for a sack cloth and ashes approach to design. A conscious rejection of the totality of human knowledge would be truly barbaric. It is time to accept that science, technology, manufacturing, distribution, and design, are all very much facts of life in our modern world. Answers, and there will be many, will come from a revised attitude, dependent upon a new focus and a highly developed sensibility to the role of design in the sustainable twenty-first century.

The vast majority of politically motivated advertising campaigns urging environmental awareness and instructing people to change their patterns of life are largely a complete waste of time and public money. Global corporations are often far more concerned, far more active, far more successful, in the implication of measures to counter the rate of climate change than are small to medium size companies; they have to be—partly out of a concern for market share of an increasingly informed market; partly out of recognition of the PR values; mostly because in the current global context environmental awareness is just plain good business practice that has become quantifiable in economic terms. A concerned populace is a new market segment, a new market to be catered to. My container of coffee (made with recycled material) proudly proclaims that it is "supporting sustainability" and that more than 30 per cent of its contents are "rainforest alliance certified". Such mass market assertions would have been unthinkable just a decade ago.

As we have seen in the preceding sections, human behaviour drives design innovation. As the century develops, as the challenges intensify, designers will need a revised focus, new skills, attitudes and information to bring to the table. Design has always been about cooperation, more recently the major partners in the process have been the manufacturers and the distributors. It is time to diversify and enlarge the team.

We need design to live. The text has stressed that design is a basic human activity that is practised to fulfill human needs. In today's world there are many needs to fulfill. The global population is estimated at near seven billion. Right now, almost half of all human beings on this planet live on less than $2.50 a day.[20] To quote John Thackara from the prologue, "If you find yourself designing emergency shelters for poor black people from the comfort of a Soho design studio, you are not up to speed on an important change: sustainable design means the co-design of daily life with the people who are living it."[21]

The next section is heavy on facts from what are considered reliable sources, (as indicated in the endnotes) but as mentioned previously, the onus is on you to research and assess, and then apply to your personal and professional activities.

Water, water, every where,
Nor any drop to drink.[22]

The water you use has been used several thousand times before. We already have all the water we are ever likely to have on this planet. Roughly half of all water on Earth is around four billion years old and dates back to the formation of the oceans, the other half came from outer space by way of comet and asteroid bombardment.[23]

Today, a third of the world's population (about 2.4 billion people) do not have access to proper sanitation. At least 200 million people around the world risk their health daily by eating food grown using untreated waste water, some of which may be contaminated with heavy metals and raw sewage.[24] Every year, more than 2.2 million people, mostly in developing countries, die from diseases associated with poor water and sanitary conditions. Contaminated water is the greatest single cause of human disease and death. Every 24 hours, 6,000 children die from diseases linked to lack of clean water. It is estimated that by 2025, two thirds of the world's population, that is about 5.5 billion people, will live in areas facing water shortages.[25] Dr Glen Daigger, senior vice-president of the *International Water Association*, said there was growing evidence that spending on clean water and sanitation was the single greatest contribution to reducing disease and death. "Water and sanitation is clearly a better investment than medical intervention, but it's not sexy."[26]

WATER FOOTPRINT

There is a water cost of everything we eat and drink. Copious amounts of water are often required to produce the food we eat, the liquids we drink and the plants that we utilise to produce everything from textiles to cellulosic ethanol. Often that use is 'imported' from countries already in need and often in near drought conditions.[27] We all have a water footprint.

The water footprint of a nation shows the total volume of water that is used to produce the goods and services consumed by the inhabitants of the nation. Since not all goods consumed in one particular country are produced in that country, the water footprint consists of two parts: use of domestic water resources and use of water outside the borders of the country. The water footprint includes both the water withdrawn from surface and groundwater and the use of soil water (in agricultural production).[28]

Research indicates that while many people may only drink two litres of water a day, their consumption rises dramatically to around 3,000 litres if the water needed to produce their food is taken into account.[29] The problem is that much of this scarce and valuable resource is wasted by poor design of the infrastructure.[30] The problem is that you have read these or similar facts, figures and statistics many times before and they have little impact. It is time to refocus, to ask the right questions, and to formulate appropriate answers. Nine billion people are depending on you.[31]

DEGREES OF GLOBAL WARMING

A recent report commissioned from University College London and published in *The Lancet* concludes that climate change is the biggest potential threat to global health in the twenty-first century, "devastating health consequences are anticipated with changing patterns of infections, reduced water and food security, increases in extreme climate events, and large-scale population migration".[32] In a report commissioned by Oxfam in 2009, Alex Renton states that "climate change along with poverty are the greatest threats to humanity this century".[33] A reinforcing study published in the *Proceedings of the National Academy of Science*, records that the past decade was the hottest in the northern hemisphere for at least 1,300 years. Temperatures across the world are consistently hotter than at any time since the Dark Ages.[34] Recently, the Intergovernmental Panel on Climate Change (IPCC) revised its forecast for the state of the world by 2100. It foresees sea levels rising by a metre or more, placing many low lying areas at risk of total inundation, with about 20 per cent of the world's population at risk. A recent report by the US Geological Survey predicts a one metre rise in sea levels by 2100, this would require massive defensive measures by some major cities including New York, London, Mumbai and Shanghai and would place vast areas of low lying areas such as Florida and Bangladesh at risk of being submerged, putting upwards of 600 million people at risk.[35]

By mid-century, the planet could be hotter by three degrees celsius in most areas and up to five degrees celsius in others. Deserts will spread and heat waves will become more prevalent; Ice-caps will melt and cyclones are also likely to be triggered. Change in weather patterns will intensify and become more unstable. The numbers of devastating storms will increase dramatically while snow will disappear from all but the highest mountain areas.[36]

The 2009 report from the Global Carbon Project, a network of scientists in academic institutions around the world, is even more pessimistic. It reports that between 2000 and 2008 global emissions of CO_2 rose by a staggering 29 per cent. Unchecked, this will result in a potentially catastrophic average temperatures rise across the world by up to six degrees celsius.[37]

The Antarctic region is an important regulator of global climate, it is a region that is subject to intense debate and conflicting opinions. One of the more reliable sources being that of the *British Antarctic Survey of the Natural Environment Research Council*. Their observations document an array of observable changes in the region. The report is careful to point out that an array of changes, some natural, some the result of human activity, can impact the climate. However, the report concludes "that recent warm temperatures are exceptional within the context of the last 10,000 years, making it unlikely that they can be explained by natural variability alone".[38]

Conditions in the Arctic are even more grim. "It's a highly sensitive region, and it's being profoundly affected by the changing climate. Most scientists view what's happening now in the Arctic as a harbinger of things to come."[39] *The National Geographic* reports that global warming in the Arctic is mysteriously occurring more quickly 1.2 miles (two kilometres) above the surface than at ground level. The report reiterates the proviso in the UK report, "Nobody knows how much of this change is the result of human emissions of planet-warming gases such as carbon dioxide, but it's likely that they play a role."[40] Very recently, scientists have discovered the first evidence that millions of tons of methane, a greenhouse gas which is 20 times more potent than carbon dioxide, and which has been trapped in the frozen sea bed off the northern coast of Siberia, is being released into the atmosphere as the Arctic region becomes warmer and its ice retreats.[41]

Recent surveys have shown Canada's High Arctic is undergoing irreversible change. Satellite data has revealed that the thickness of Arctic sea ice showed a dramatic decrease during the 2007 Winter.[42] Ice formations that have lasted thousands of years are breaking up. During 2008, the ice shelves have lost an area more than three times the size of Manhattan, that represents about 23 per cent of their total mass. This rate of degradation is more than ten times initial predictions. Satellite images taken in August, 2008, show that open water now stretches all the way round the Arctic, making it possible for the first time in at least 125,000 years to circumnavigate the North Pole.[43] These images provide the most important geographical information to date of the rapid progress of global warming.

The latest report from the UK Met Office's Hadley Centre, renowned for taking a cautious approach to global warming, warns that the world will have to take drastic action within two years to reduce greenhouse gas pollution if it is to avoid the worst effects of climate change. The report shows that the only hope of avoiding a global temperature rise of more than two degrees celsius is to reduce global CO_2 emissions by three per cent every year from 2010 on. Increases above two degrees celsius will likely produce both increased flooding in those areas at risk (including the Florida shoreline) and drought in many parts of the world, most noticeable in sub Saharan Africa. In an uncharacteristic forthright tone, it states that, "anyone who thinks global warming has stopped has their head in the sand".[44] Professor David Archer of Chicago University is even more forthright:

> The climatic impacts of releasing fossil fuel carbon dioxide into the atmosphere will last longer than Stonehenge, longer than time capsules, far longer than the age of human civilisation so far. Ultimate recovery takes place on timescales of hundreds of thousands of years, a geologic longevity typically associated in public perceptions with nuclear waste.[45]

The effects of CO_2 emissions will continue to exert influence on global warming for thousands of years to come. There is a need for immediate action—every day of inaction only increases the complexity of the challenge.

SMALL STEPS, BIG ACTIONS

Do not despair. We are not doomed. We need to look after our environment like any other precious resource. But we do need to act now. Designers can lead the way. The first thing to do is stop drinking bottled water—use the tap.[46] The US bottled water business in 2006 totalled roughly $15 billion, making it a very expensive, and environmentally unfriendly "lifestyle choice".[47] The next step you can take is to consider the environmental impact of every thing that you design. An environmental impact study should be an essential component of every design process, whether or not it actually appears in the brief.[48] As John Thackara points out, "small design actions can have big effects—often unexpectedly", and we need to be acutely aware of all possible consequences of our action or inaction—ignorance is not a valid excuse.[49] "Ethics and responsibility can inform design decisions without constraining the social and technical innovation we all need to do."[50] It is essential to develop a sustainable perception. It is likely that satisfactory sustainable design solutions will be the result of cooperative design, co-design of daily life with the people involved, with experts from other fields of research, with nature in mind, and conscious of advances in related areas of science and technology. The old parameters of design are no longer adequate to the challenges ahead.

THE COPENHAGEN CONSENSUS 2008

While issues of global warming are of paramount concern there are other issues of survival facing our world. The *Copenhagen Consensus* 2008 represents two years of study by more than 50 economists who have worked to find the best workable solutions to ten of the world's biggest challenges, identified as *Air pollution, Conflicts, Diseases, Education, Global Warming, Malnutrition and Hunger, Sanitation and Water, Subsidies and Trade Barriers, Terrorism, Women and Development*.[52] In May, 2008, an expert panel of eight top economists, including five Nobel Laureates, sat down to assess the research, producing a prioritised list highlighting the potential of 30 specific solutions to combat some of the biggest challenges facing the world. The list was compiled from the perspective of economic cost and benefit. Some critics have pointed out that other factors such as social justice, ecological stewardship and political acceptability are also important, but are exceptionally difficult to price.[53] The most effective and cost beneficial proposal was that put forward by Sue Horton of Wilfrid Laurier University in Canada. This proposal is to combat the malnutrition of 140 million undernourished children by providing micronutrients in capsule form at a global cost of just $60 million per year—that values the cost of protecting the life of each child at just over 40 cents a year. More importantly, according to the analysis, taking into account savings in providing healthcare and other services, this action holds yearly benefits of more than $1 billion.[54] What does this have to do with design? An oft quoted *cliché* is that 'design is problem solving'.[55] If any or all of the 30 proposals were implemented there would be major opportunities for active co-design intervention.

The last century has witnessed the continuing urbanisation of Earth's population. By the year 2050, nearly 80 per cent of the earth's population will reside in urban centres. Applying the most conservative estimates to current demographic trends, the human population will increase by about three billion people during the interim. An estimated 109 hectares of new land (about 20 per cent more land than is represented by the country of Brazil) will be needed to grow enough food to feed them.[56] Globally, food security is a key issue, with problems of distribution on par with those of production. According to the World Resources Institute, global per capita food production has been increasing substantially for the past several decades.[57] So what is the problem?

> ...a new theory is emerging among traders and economists. The same banks, hedge funds and financiers whose speculation on the global money markets caused the sub-prime mortgage crisis are thought to be causing food prices to yo-yo and inflate. The charge against them is that by taking advantage of deregulation of global commodity markets they are making billions from speculation on food and causing misery around the world.[58]

Prevailing social conditions that influence the design process are often found outside the field of design per se. Alain Findeli, makes the valid observation that the old aesthetic paradigm which was based almost "exclusively on material shapes and qualities; a code of ethics originating in a culture of business contracts and agreements; a cosmology restricted to the marketplace; a sense of history conditioned by the concept of material progress; and a sense of time limited to the cycles of fashion and technological innovations or obsolescence... there is no reason to resign ourselves to them any longer".[59] There are other parameters to consider to assist in responding to the aberrant conditions of injustice and inequality which are, unfortunately, so evident in our world. Now for a few innovative design solutions that were premised by new questions. This highly selective list moves from the personal through the communal to the national—all require a shift in focus, all require making a choice, the final example requiring a significant restructuring of accepted values.

FROM PERSONAL TO COMMUNAL

The Internet has shown that we do not need to 'own' every piece of available information, but we do need to know where to find it. A similar attitude can be applied to urban transport. Several European cities including Barcelona, Berlin, Paris and Vienna are supporting communal bike programmes.[60] A similar bike sharing scheme is planned to start in Boston in late 2010, with 2,500 bikes. The bikes in London and Boston are provided by the Canadian Bixi company which was awarded the bronze award in the 2009 International Design Excellence Award.[61] All these communal bike programmes pale by comparison with Hangzhou in China which plans to have 50,000 bikes in its scheme.[62] The interest and support for these programmes does beget the question, what other forms of beneficial service could this concept of communal use be applied to?

POWER TO THE MASSES?

One of the more innovative innovations in the automotive industry of the 1950s was the Morris/Austin Mini, designed by Alec Issigonis.[63] The Suez crisis of 1956 resulted in a reduction of 20 per cent in the UK's oil imports. Issigonis was instructed by the chairman of the British Motor Corporation (BMC), Sir Leonard Lord, to design a new range of cars suited to the constraints of the time. The resulting "Mini" with its front wheel drive, transverse mounted engine and 10" wheels came to market in 1959. In an official RAC test, an unmodified Austin Seven mini completed a three day round trip through England, Scotland and Wales, averaging an astounding 61.87 miles per gallon—that was in 1959.[64] Half a century later and there is not a car on North American roads capable of anything like this degree of fuel economy. I am left wondering if what we really need today to "encourage" a revised attitude to private/public transport is another major oil crisis!. Michael Hordeski provides a summary of the current energy conundrum. "Oil prices hovering at

Biking stations, Barcelona, London, Paris.

$100 a barrel, soaring Chinese demand, rocketing energy markets, climate destabilising carbon emissions.... Not since the energy shocks of the 1970s has the availability of energy been so important." He goes on to explain that "the two principal combustible elements in coal and petroleum are carbon and hydrogen. Of the two, hydrogen is more efficient."[65] More about hydrogen later.

GAS, ELECTRIC, HYBRID, HYDROGEN, OR AIR —THE WAY OF THE FUTURE?[66]

The electric car is over 100 years old and predates the introduction of the gasoline-powered car.[67] The English chemist Michael Faraday invented the electric motor in 1821. Experimental electric powered vehicles were developed in the 1830s in Scotland, Holland, and America.[68] Several variations of the electric car were on show at the 1893 World's Columbian Exposition in Chicago and in 1897 the first electric cabs were seen on the streets of New York. In 1908 Henry Ford introduces the mass-produced and gasoline-powered Model T, changed transportation history and began our dependence upon oil.

MILES TO GO

Less than half a century after the Exposition in Chicago, the New York Worlds Fair of 1939 witnessed the triumph of the car over public forms of transportation. True, both the train and the car featured in the Fair but it was the idea of car ownership that was to be consequential. Today, the manufacture, distribution, sales, marketing and service of private cars is, rightly or wrongly, an intrinsic part of manufacturing capitalism. What to do? The problems are complex, there are no simple answers. There is an abundance of often conflicting information on the topic. You must do your research, you must be objective; you must be highly inventive in your creative solutions relating to private versus public transportation. You need to exercise extreme caution and be very aware of managed public perceptions. The current endorsement of eco-car technology is often more motivated by PR and media hype that scientific fact. Bio fuels and hybrid vehicles are just an interim (and very profitable) solution for personal passenger transportation.[69] The problem with electric vehicles is that we are swapping one dependency for another; about three quarters of the known deposits of lithium (an essential component of the batteries) is in the Atacama Desert which is shared by Bolivia and Chile.[70]

AN ELECTRIFYING TALE

In the last half century or so, the world has become oil dependent.[71] The 2009 restructuring of the global auto industry resulted in an array of industry and government initiatives, ostensibly responding to a universal concern over the affects of CO_2 emissions on global warming. The story is complex and constantly changing. You need to maintain an objective view free from bias and constraint. All global manufactures have extensive website's lauding the capabilities and characteristics of their particular models. When accessing these sites maintain a highly cautious focus.

HYDROGEN AS A FUEL —SHOULD WE EVEN GO THERE!

Hydrogen is the most abundant element in the universe. About 93 per cent of all the atoms in the universe are hydrogen atoms.[72] On Earth things are a little different. The Earth's oceans are composed of nearly 86 per cent oxygen and close to 11 per cent hydrogen.

Hydrogen as water ($H2O$) is absolutely essential to life on earth. There is considerable debate as to whether hydrogen is truly energy efficient when the entire food chain is taken into consideration. Present mass production methods require a large input of electricity to separate hydrogen from water. Hydrogen must then be compressed, transported and stored, before it is used in a vehicle.[73] A report from Stanford University claims that, "Demonstrations of hydrogen powered vehicles have usually used compressed hydrogen gas. However, because of the low density, compressed hydrogen will not give a car as useful a range as gasoline. It may be even worse than using lead-acid batteries."[74]

UP IN THE AIR

With the advent of monster cities being home to over 20 million inhabitants, all in need of food and water, there are massive problems in need of some creative design.[75] We have, with varying degrees of success, adapted to demand by providing high-rise living for people, but have a blinkered rejection of doing the same for plants and animals. Farms in downtown New York, Hong Kong, Tokyo, Calcutta? Why not? Centrally positioned vertical farms reduce transportation costs, multiple levels of agrarian production is just one possible option for addressing the impending food crisis. But it will require a fundamental shift in cultural values.

In 2008, *Treehugger* provided a review of several high-rise farming proposals, including one proposed for a lot on Canal Street in NYC, a Center for Urban Agriculture in Seattle, a sky farm in downtown Toronto, and the vertical farm concept from Columbia University.[76] Dr Dickson Despommier, a professor of environmental health at Columbia University, is regarded as the world's leading proponent of 'vertical farming' which uses hydroponic and aeroponic crop production on an industrial scale. "It makes a lot of sense. In a way, it totally inverts the conventional wisdom of many of today's agriculturalists. Instead of using the biosphere to power the technosphere, we are using the technosphere to power the biosphere."[77] The proposed high-rise would process its own waste water and tap into the waste from other parts of the utility grid, and use the process of evapotranspiration to produce drinking water that could be returned for reuse.[78] "The quantity of food that a high-rise farm might produce is also surprising. Because the plants are grown in optimal conditions—abundant light and water, and no pests—they can yield three–four crops per year instead of one, and each crop may require no more than five vertical feet of space. This means each story of high-rise space occupying an area of one acre, for example, can literally produce 12 times as much food per year as an acre of ordinary farmland."[79]

Indoor farming is not a new concept. A wide variety of produce, including tomatoes and lettuce, herbs and spices, all have been successfully grown indoors for many years. What is required is a need to apply new attitudes to new and old technologies and to increase the scale of production from individual residents to neighbourhood communities. The need is particularly pressing in the developing world where there is an accelerating migration of people from rural areas to cities. Skyscraper farms have enormous potential to improve both the urban and rural environment in many ways. They "green" up the environment, providing more plants which assist in the conversion of carbon-dioxide in polluted urban areas. They are also a step along the path of repair to the ecosystem.

These innovative proposals use old technology—hydroponics.[80] Ancient peoples such as the Babylonians, Aztecs and Egyptians used growing techniques where nutrients were obtained from sources other than soil.[81] The earliest published work on growing plants without soil was the 1627 book, *Sylva Sylvarum*, or a *Natural History in Ten Centuries*, by Sir Francis Bacon.[82] Hydrponics received a boost in popularity during the green revolution of the 1980s'. In the twenty-first century, hydroponics features in Epcot Center's "The Land" exhibit at Disney.[83]

High rise framing requires a fundamental change in mind set, not to mention adjustments to prevailing political and economic patterns. In straight economic terms they will require substantial investment. Success of ventures exemplified above is less likely in those societies where the ownership of urban land depends upon who has the most money rather than demonstrates the most need. Banks, corporate head offices or farms—each society will make its choice, and will live by the circumstances manifest in those choices. The design challenge is to make the concept workable.[84] For example, while a purpose built structure may be prohibitively expensive could an underused inner city structure be converted into a "farm"? Then there is always the possibility of mixed use. Roof gardens could be supplemented by "farming" the lower two or three stories—providing not only a source of produce but offering the possibility of incorporating a waste water retrieval and purification process as an additional benefit. A pipe dream ? Maybe not.

FROM THE TOP DOWN

Roof top gardens present a tangential concept to be explored. With origins lost in antiquity many cultures have made use of roof tops to grow plants or more often to provide an oasis of calm in urban areas. (Two notable examples being the roof garden of the Rockefeller Center in Manhattan and Chicago City Hall.) A recent report cited by China Daily estimates that 50 per cent of the Chinese population will live in cities by 2020, with the percentage expected to increase to 75 per cent by 2050.[85] This migration from the countryside to the town has been under-way for some time now. Major metropolises such as Beijing and Shanghai are testament to the dramatic cultural

Winner of the Second International Architecture Competition for Sustainable Housing. Multi-storey Greenhouse within South Elevation, Wuhan, China. Architects, David Knafo and Tagit Klimor, Isreal.[86]

and social crisis and a loss of existing traditions that accompany this migration. These monster cities severely deplete natural resources, strain urban infrastructures and transportation systems to breaking point and add considerably to the pollution of air and the surrounding environment.

In 2007, the Israel based Knafo Klimor architectural firm won the Second International Architecture Competition for Sustainable Housing for their Agro-housing project proposed for Wuhan, China which blends urban and rural living. The programme combines a high-rise apartment complex with a vertical greenhouse which provides residents with a renewable food source. Each housing unit will have a 100 sq ft trellis on which to grow vegetables tailored to individual needs and preferences. The south-facing greenhouse was designed as a multi-storied garden for the cultivation of crops on environmentally-friendly soilless substrate, equipped with grey water drip irrigation.[87]

The challenges of urban living will become more evident as cities in the developing world continue to expand their population base. Currently there are 21 mega cities (population in excess of ten million) on Earth.

Contrary to popular belief, the world is not overpopulated. A report in *National Geographic Magazine* concludes that if all seven billion of Earths population stood shoulder to shoulder they would fill the area of Los Angeles.[88] It is not space that is the problem, it is balance. Urbanisation is endangering human survivability. The social implications of poverty, disintegration, increasing population density and inadequate infrastructures including housing need

our most urgent attention. There is an associated need to provide a balance between individual freedom and communal interaction.[89] Just how big a design challenge do you want?

SIMPLICITY VERSUS COMPLEXITY

We can be assured that the future will seem to be increasingly complex and the problems we face apparently insurmountable. In a world where complexity seems to rule we need help to navigate the maze of options. John Maeda is a graphic designer, artist, computer scientist and the founder of the Simplicity Consortium at the MIT Media Lab, currently President of the Rhode Island School of Design. His latest book offers ten laws of simplicity. Law 4, "Learn", suggests that "knowledge makes everything simpler". He observes that: "Learning occurs best when there is a desire to attain specific knowledge." He concludes:

At the core of the best rewards is this fundamental desire for freedom in thinking, living, and being. I've learned that the most complex successful product designs, whether simple, complex, rational, illogical, domestic, international, technophilic, or technophoberic, are the ones that connect deeply to the greater context of learning and life.[90]

USE YOUR BRAIN

As Maeda makes most clear—the design process is knowledge dependent. You have to have a passion for knowledge. The information needed may be practical, news of latest materials and processes. It may be business orientated, relating to markets. It may address humanitarian need or it may have a more edifying focus and address ethical concerns and personal values. Whatever is required, the motivation must be internal, you must "dare to know".

RELATE—TRANSLATE—SURPRISE!

Understand the problem; this is likely to be different from that stated in the design brief. Use what you do know in an innovative way to produce what you did not know before. Recognise that human perception is tidy, it responds to something unknown by approximating it to something already known. Picasso and Braque realised that way back at the start of the twentieth century when they introduced visually recognisable items such as letters and numbers into, what appeared at the time, to be visual chaos. They succeeded in "synthesising plausible relationships".[91] Surprise is memorable. Jonathan Ive the principal designer of the iMac, the iPad and the iPhone, utilised the surprise factor in establishing instant recognition for Apple's product range.[92] (This concept will be addressed more fully in the next chapter, "Design Orientation: Design, Creativity, and Culture").

PEOPLE MATTER

Designers all too often respond to the mantra of Raymond Loewy, "never leave well enough alone".[93] Sometimes good design is no design at all. Or, to be more precise, good design can be achieved by an improvement in service, by the implementation of available information. Less stuff more people. In 1986, the prestigious V&A in London held a remarkable forward looking exhibition featuring innovative conceptual products for the elderly.[94] New Design for Old, featured some highly original designs by prominent designers. Halmut Esslinger, president of Frog Design, offered a canopied four poster hospital bed, described as "postmodern, yet romantic". At least the "postmodern" colours of pink and blue were a lively counterpoint to drab hospital white and gray. Kenneth Grange, a founding partner of Pentagram Design, responded to shower trauma and provided a unit that was versatile and safe, ensuring a shower that was easy, pleasurable, and relaxing.

150 students entered a competition to design products "which will help elderly people stay safe and sound at home". The 'prize' entry was a potato peeler adapted for use by people with reduced dexterity. Well intentioned no doubt, but very inappropriate design. The walls of the exhibition contained information on the plight of the elderly in the UK in the 1980s, pointing out that one major concern was obtaining the recommended daily requirement of nutrients from popular and available food sources, such as the potato. Nutritionists will tell you that the most advantageous nutrients are to be found in the skin of the potato:

Potatoes are rich in several micronutrients, especially vitamin C—eaten with its skin, a single medium-sized potato of 150 g provides nearly half the daily adult requirement (100 mg). The potato is a moderate source of iron, and its high vitamin C content promotes iron absorption. It is a good source of vitamins B1, B3 and B6 and minerals such as potassium, phosphorus and magnesium, and contains folate, pantothenic acid and riboflavin. Potatoes also contain dietary antioxidants, which may play a part in preventing diseases related to ageing, and dietary fibre, which benefits health.[95] More recently, in 2004, the United States Department of Agriculture ranked the Russet potato number 17 on a list of the top 20 sources of food antioxidants, above plums, black beans, and Gala apples.[96] In this context, 'Good design' therefore would be to provide dietary information and support to encourage eating the skin of the potato rather than discarding it. Less design in this case is definitely more.

RECYCLING

We are instructed in the potential benefits of recycling—but even here, as Michael Braungart points out in *Cradle to Cradle*, we need to step with care:

> …you care about the environment. In fact, when you went shopping for a carpet recently, you deliberately chose one made from recycled polyester soda bottles. Recycled? Perhaps it would be more accurate to say 'downcycled'. Good intentions aside, your rug is made of things that were never designed with this further use in mind, and wrestling them into this form has required as much energy—and generated as much waste—as producing a new carpet…. Moreover, the recycling process may have introduced even more harmful additives than a conventional product contains, and it might be off-gassing and abrading them into your home at even higher rate.[97]

An alternative viewpoint is provided by "The State of the World 2009" from the Worldwatch Institute. The report asserts that "an economy that reconciles human aspirations with the planet's limits is eminently possible".[98] One initial step is to do more with what we produce. Recycling is among the most challenging of all current concerns. From the perspective of the World Bank, "informal waste recycling is a common way to earn income".[99] But, as a report from the Basel Action Network cautions, used computer equipment exported from the US and Europe is causing serious health and environmental damage in Africa.[100] The industrial world cannot 'recycle' its problems by exporting them to other countries, nor by treading them underfoot. What is required is far more accessible, responsible information.

Canopied four poster hospital bed, Frog Design, New Design for Old, Boilerhouse, V&A, 1986.

SOCIAL RESPONSIBILITY AND PERSONAL VALUES.

You design what you are. The cultural values that you support, or don't support, your daily input of information, in all guises, print, film, television, video, computer, iPhone—all these combine to provide you with your personal focus. "Garbage in, garbage out", is a truism developed to apply to computer usage—it is equally applicable in the development of a personal design philosophy. (And if you do not have one, you should, otherwise how to do you know what you are doing and why). Most of us are rightly concerned with the quality of the food and liquids what we digest, we have learnt the value of reading the labels. We are becoming aware of the environmental impact of the manufacture, distribution and recycling of clothing. We are beginning to realise that what is required is a similar approach to the information we arrange in our mind. We need more factual, reliable and all inclusive set of standards covering all aspects on the impact off all products, manufacturing processes and methods of distribution on the environment and society.

DESIGN FUTURES

The future is closer than you think. There are major shifts underway in demographics, in the geo-political structure, and in the cultural dynamic which will have profound effect upon your design future. The changing demographic picture was acknowledged in the last chapter alongside some of the more pressing challenges to our continued survival. Chapter Eleven "The Phoenix Rises" introduced the reality of a changing geo-political situation which will, by 2030, see India overtake China as the world's most populous country, becoming home to between four and five times as many people as the United States but on a land mass only a third as large. Yet, some argue that in reality our world is about to get much smaller.

IT'S A SMALL WORLD AFTER ALL...[101]

In 1971 Victor Papanek's seminal book *Design for the Real World: Human Ecology and Social Change* and the

1973 oil crisis, made consumers acutely aware of their dependence on oil and its by products. By the mid 1980s the 'Greenwash' had begun and the market became sensitive to the three Rs—reuse, reduce, recycle.[102] By the end of the decade designers were well versed in the necessities of reduction of materials and energy. Jeff Rubin, a Toronto-based environmentally aware economist who for nearly two decades was the chief economist for CIBC World Markets claims that the end of cheap energy will make our world much smaller. In his recent book, *Why Your World Is About To Get A Whole Lot Smaller*, he sketches out a likely scenario. He starts by explaining how cheap oil gives us access to a rather big world. He provides a case study of salmon to make his point. Caught off the coast of Norway, shipped to Hamburg or Rotterdam, transferred to another ship on route to China where it is skinned, deboned and filleted. It then will be refrozen, packaged, stowed on another container ship and sent to a supermarket in Europe or North America. Two months after it was caught, the salmon will be thawed, displayed on crushed ice under gleaming halogen lamps and sold as 'fresh'.[103] With the inevitable demise of cheap oil, our world is about to get much, much smaller.[104]

> Soon, your food is going to come from a field much closer to home, and the things you buy will probably come from a factory down the road... we must reengineer our lives to adapt to a world of growing energy scarcity. And that means learning to live using less energy...your world is about to get a lot smaller.[100]

As Rubin makes clear in his concluding chapter this development will not be restricted to food but may apply to all manufactured goods as well. Expensive oil (over 100 dollars a barrel) will bring to an end inexpensive products manufactured on the other side of the world which have become such an intrinsic part of modern consumer society. Today, as Rubin explains:

> We are in the midst of a cycle of recessions and recoveries that keeps repeating itself as the economy keeps banging up its head on oil prices.... Not only must we decouple our economy from oil but we must re-engineer our lives to adapt to a world of growing oil scarcity. And that means learning to use less energy.[105]

These changes will have a profound affect on the practice of design in the coming decades.

The immediate future is filled with an array of challenges which design alone cannot solve but design can make a difference by focussing on ethical and ecological concerns. What will be required is a revised orientation to design, creativity and culture.

CHAPTER FOURTEEN
DESIGN ORIENTATION: DESIGN, CREATIVITY AND CULTURE

I know you're out there. I can feel you now. I know that you're afraid. You're afraid of us. You're afraid of change. I don't know the future. I didn't come here to tell you how this is going to end. I came here to tell you how it's going to begin. I'm going to hang up this phone, and then I'm going to show these people what you don't want them to see. I'm going to show them a world... without you. A world without rules or controls, without borders or boundaries. A world where anything is possible. Where we go from there is a choice I leave to you.
Neo, The Matrix, 1999.

THE STORY SO FAR...

To begin this final chapter, I would like, for very personal reasons, to quote from an essay, "The Shape of Things" written by Jacob Bronowski and first published in *The Observer*, a British newspaper, in February 1952, but still very, very relevant. Bronowski was a poet, playwright, philosopher, scientist and teacher. He lectured at MIT where he was a member of the Salk Institute for Biological Studies. He was one of the most significant influences on my educational development. He died in 1974. Let me quote from Bronowski.

> A rational aesthetic must start from the conviction that art (and science too) is a normal activity of human life. All the way back to the cave paintings and the invention of the first stone tools, what has moved men either to paint or to invent was an everyday impulse. But it was an impulse in the everyday of men, not of animals....What the painter and the inventor were doing, right back in the cave, was unfolding the gift of intelligent action.[2]

As we have seen in the preceding sections, creativity (intelligent action) is one of the most defining characteristics of what it is to be human. We have used our creative abilities to design our way in the world, from stone tools to the www. The evolutionary nature

and context of design has changed. Initially, design and creativity were tools for human survival. Our prehistoric hominine ancestor, *Homo erectus*, was probably the earliest 'tool making animal'. The Achulean hand axe, dates from Lower Palaeolithic era, which lasted from around 1.65 million years ago to about 100,000 years ago.[3] William Calvin asserts that "It is the earliest hominid tool that seems "designed" in some modern sense."[4]

Many millennia later design and creativity aided and abetted territorial expansion. During the period of the early Roman Republic (509–265 BCE)[5] Roman secular architecture set the stage, providing monuments to apparent Roman invincibility.[6] Later, design was prominent in the process of colonisation, from the design of defensive structures such as castles to the naval architecture of ships of exploration and conquest.[7] In Great Britain, politically charged landscape design changed the face of medieval England.[8] In the eighteenth and nineteenth centuries, both rural and urban landscapes were transformed yet again by the new architectural forms of the industrial revolution. Patterns of work and travel were reshaped by the power of steam, applied to both modes of transportation and manufacture. It was the power of steam and the demand of market logistics that moved the factory from the hills and valleys to the centre of town. The cotton mills of Lancashire changed the clothing codes of an Empire and provided the impetus for one of the worlds major political ideologies.[9] New methods of finance were introduced, political representation was

Acheulean Hand axe, Lower Palaeolithic—approximately 500,000–200,000 years old, from the Dordogne region in South-western France, Image: Science Museum of Minnesota.[1]

expanded; all of these created new systems of social relationships, paving the way for new attitudes to design.[10] More recently design and creativity serviced the needs of a materially addicted society.

We live, as Deyan Sudjic explains in "a world drowning in objects".[11] Barely half a century ago, reflective of new, post-war cultural attitudes and values, design meant the innovation, development and manufacture of more and better things. Consumption and progress were seen as co-dependent. Design visionaries such as Raymond Loewy, Henry Dreyfus, and Norman Bel Geddes rallied around the "there's no business like big business" mantra and designed the "American way of life", a lifestyle that was to become the envy of the world and, more recently, a threat to our very survival.[12]

Some social commentators see that the developed world has evolved into one in which consumption has displaced production as the primary factor in shaping the kind of society we now live in.[13] Mike Press and Rachel Cooper observe, "Most design ideas are commercial failures, and the chief reason for failure is that these ideas fail to connect meaningfully or effectively with people's lives… the designer is not just a creator of objects but is an enabler of experiences–and it is the idea of experience that should be the starting point and focus of design."[14] Today we need new visionaries to provide sustainable visions to aim for; we need to shift our focus from things to people– we need to realign our design orientation.

THE STORY CONTINUES...

The start of the twenty-first century is stained by the after-effects of the twentieth century.

While we celebrate amazing advances in science and technology we still live in a world threatened by environmental hazards, by cities infested with social chaos, by an ever increasing divide between the rich and the poor, by continued partisan conflicts and apparent random acts of terror. We are far from civilised.[15] The future lies out there undisturbed, the only thing that we can be sure about is that the social dynamics at the end of the century will bear little resemblance to those that exist now. Many desired and required changes will come about by design. We have no choice. A recent *Living Planet* report shows that the world is facing a natural resources crisis worse than the financial crunch of 2008, and with more dire consequences. It states, quite bluntly that; "Humanity's demands exceed our planet's capacity to sustain us."[16]

The 2009 "State of the Future" report, backed by a diverse range of leading organisations such as Unesco, the World Bank, the US Army and the Rockefeller Foundation, highlights 15 Global Challenges facing humanity in the twenty-first century, it concludes that without sustainable growth, "billions of people will be condemned to poverty and much of civilisation will

collapse".[17] The report also observes that the web is the most powerful force for globalisation, democratisation, economic growth, and education in history.[18]

Ezio Manzini states that, "Transition towards sustainability requires radical change in the way we produce and consume and, more generally, in the way we live. In fact we need to learn how to live better… and at the same time, reduce our ecological footprint and improve the quality of our social fabric."[19] He calls for "a far reaching social learning process in which the most diversified forms of knowledge and organisational capabilities must be valorised in the most open and flexible way."[20] John Thackara endorses the need for revitalised attitudes to design. "Design scenarios are powerful innovation tools because they make a possible future familiar and enable the participation of potential users in conceiving and shaping what they want."[21] He explains that we need to stop designing for and begin to design with.

The current state of fragmented, instantaneous information lulls people into a false state of believing they know what is best rather than undertaking the necessary research required to understand the problem before instigating change. Increased media coverage has enhanced awareness of the challenges of achieving a sustainable world, unfortunately it has also established a hierarchy of popular solutions, some of which, such as the much heralded electric vehicles may not be the most desirable solutions, (see Chapter Thirteen "Design Futures: Questions of Sustainability"). Jonathan Chapman and Nick Gant explain: "Beyond scientifically grounded measures of ecological sustainability that proliferate the confines of design research and academia, sustainable design practice is driven largely by assumption, and preconception as to what constitutes best practice."[22]

In this exciting and challenging melee of change, new forms of social organisation will emerge, new modes of living will be established, and new methods of design practice will emerge. Bypassing the divisive attitudes of "us" and "them", you, or maybe your children, will embrace the reality of cultural diversity; communities and groups with different and often contradictory points of view and cultural values, coming together for mutual benefit will be the norm. There will be difficult choices to be made–there is no such thing as neutral action, everything that you do and do not do, every design, will have an effect. There are a multiplicity of signs and signals, varied and confusing in their message of need. Designers must make choices, often involving compromise, and construct as best they can new visions of what may be.

The real voyage of discovery consists not in seeking new landscapes but in having new eyes.
Marcel Proust, French Novelist, 1871–1922.

WE NEED TO TALK:
INTERCULTURAL COMMUNICATION[23]

This is the first human generation on this planet to be interconnected. Technology may bring us together, but cultural insensibility keeps us apart. Intercultural communication has been around ever since our ancestors first began to travel and trade. This reality is correlative to feelings of antipathy and antagonism to any group that is 'different' to our group; that has different values; that sees with different eyes and thinks different thoughts. In the past, intolerance has been tolerated and used as a pretext for conflict. Today we live in a global mobile where action in one part instantly causes reverberations through the whole. We live in a world where intolerance can be fatal, to all of us.

If we are to survive and come to terms with the challenges ahead (as outlined in Chapter Thirteen "Design Futures: Questions of Sustainability") then we will need to see with new eyes. These new visions will involve a social transition that will require wide ranging learning processes that take advantage of the most diversified forms of knowledge. Communication with all sectors of society will be essential, often talking to people previously excluded from the design dialogue. What we are witnessing is the transfer from patterns of social groups based on ethnocentric, theological, political or nationalistic values to social groups based on places or communities with shared concerns and values; social networking has come of age.[24]

We have, in earlier sections, looked at the conceptual development of new types of buildings such as high rise farms that integrate farming with water purification processes to improve the quality of life. We have seen how shared activities, such as the communal bicycle programmes, based on local need, have added a new dimension to urban centres. We have seen how poverty can, at least in part, be alleviated by micro economics and design initiatives such as the Waterloo hand pump can enhance standards of living. These initiatives make full use of local materials and skills and thereby enable local communities. We have established that many of these cases of social innovation have happened on a local and very personal scale, dependent upon local initiative– emphasising that people matter.

We know that attitudes to development and aid have to be adjusted to rid this world of ours of social injustice and ensure that all have access to the necessities of life on earth. We know from our own experiences that we are far better informed than any previous generation regarding the advantages of healthy and natural diets. We know that attitudes to ageing need radical change; new models of social interchange are urgently required; new attitudes to trade; new attitudes to product and service distribution are required. Most significantly new, or at least drastically revised, attitudes to sustainability have to be addressed. Individual and group interests will need to adjust to prevailing social and environmental concerns. Short time solutions must not be injurious to our long term survival. The physical revolutions of yesteryear need to be supplanted by revolutions of mind.

REVOLUTIONARY IDEAS:
THE LARGE HADRON COLLIDER

The design process is an affirmation that things don't have to be the way they are. Change is often the product of revolutionary ideas. Our societies and cultures can be modified, frequently through continuing research and the acquisition of knowledge. Our way of seeing the world and subsequent patterns of meaning are subject to change. The ability to change our patterns of thought is one of the great attributes of human evolution.

The Large Hadron Collider (LHC) is a particle accelerator located about 330 feet beneath the Swiss French border, near Geneva. This cathedral to science[25] sends protons on a 27 kilometre long circular collision course which will recreate conditions approximate to those one millionth of a millionth of a second after the beginning of the big bang.[26] The largest machine ever built has a gaol, "to achieve a deeper, better, truer understanding of the fundamental structure and nature of existence".[27]

Writing in the May/June 2008 issue of *Technology Review*, Nobel laureate and MIT Institute Professor, Jerome Friedman explains that these collisions should help answer some of physics' most fundamental questions, such as why do particles have mass? And are there spatial dimensions beyond the ones we know?[28] It will take time (hopefully not too long) for the cacophony of ill-informed, knee jerk opposition to the LHC to subside. Make absolutely no mistake, these developments will have fundamental and far reaching consequences for design and human culture.

Within the next decade or so it is quite likely that we will be seeing with new eyes and thinking new thoughts about the structure of our universe and our place in it. In an interview with BBC News, Professor Brian Cox, one of the LHC scientists at CERN,[29] had this to say:

> Experiment is the basis of the scientific method, without which there would be no modern world as we know it.... Without these experimental discoveries, and the subsequent deepening of our understanding of the Universe, there would be no electronics, no silicon chips or transistors, no medical imaging technology, no nuclear power stations, no X-rays or chemotherapy treatments for cancer... again an almost endless list.[30]

In response to the question, "In terms off what this could achieve for the humanity in the next 20 to 30 years, can this technology change our everyday lives within our lifetimes? Or do you see humanity waiting a little more patiently before our lives are transformed with wormhole's and quantum computing? Cox replied:

The Large Hadron Collider, September, 2008. This $8 billion experiment hopes to recreate the moments after the Big Bang by smashing protons—one of the building blocks of matter. Credit: CERN.

Let me give one positive example from history. Quantum mechanics was developed to maturity as a theory during the 1920s and by 1947 we had the first transistor. It is often said, I think with some justification, that it is extremely unlikely that transistors could have been developed without the quantum theory. Perhaps we are on the verge of a similar leap when we deepen our understanding of the sub-atomic world once again at LHC—who knows.[31]

Who knows indeed—just think where design would be without transistors—you may find it impossible to think of a pre transistor, pre-computer design age. Research at the end of 2010 recreated conditions that may have existed one millionth of a second after the big bang. Now, in your mind, go the extra two millionths of a second and tell me what is on the other side of time/space.

> *Eventually, everything connects, people, ideas, objects.*
> *The quality of the connections is the key to quality per se.*
> Charles Eames.

THE BEGINNING IS NEAR

We are addicted to speed and power. In 1965, Dr Gordon E Moore, the inventor of the integrated circuit observed that the number of transistors on an integrated circuit was doubling every two years.[32] This axiom has since been enshrined in computer lore as Moore's Law.[33] Things change. In 2004, "more transistors were produced, and at a lower cost, than grains of rice".[34] In February 2008 Intel claimed it had fabricated a chip with 2,000,000,000 transistors, provisionally named Tukwila.[35] And then there is the quantum Internet, "The promise of quantum computers is tantalisingly great: near-instantaneous problem solving, and perfectly secure data transmission." [36]

Ray Kurzweil[37] is among the most prominent and controversial of future forecasters.[38] He explains that technological change is exponential, "we won't experience 100 years of progress in the twenty-first century—it will be more like 20,000 years of progress (at today's rate)....Within a few decades, machine intelligence will surpass human intelligence, leading to the Singularity—technological change so rapid and profound it represents a rupture in the fabric of history."[39] The mathematician John Casti, director of Complexica, described as a scientific hatchery of innovation and operating from bases in Santa Fe and Vienna, supplements Kurzweil's forecast. Casti views the Singularity as representing:

> ...the end of the supremacy of *Homo sapiens* as the dominant species on planet Earth. At that point a

new species appears, and humans and machines will go their separate ways, not merge one with the other. I do not believe this necessarily implies a malevolent machine takeover; rather, machines will become increasingly uninterested in human affairs just as we are uninterested in the affairs of ants or bees. But it's more likely than not in my view that the two species will comfortably and more or less peacefully coexist—unless human interests start to interfere with those of the machines.[40]

This reinforces the comments made in 1983 by William McLaughlin of the Cal Tech Jet Propulsion Laboratory, "Judging that the current direction in machine design is not a dead end... the close of the twentieth century should bring the end of human dominance on Earth."[41] OB Hardison observes that:

Man was forced to create silicon devices when they did not exist.... In the 40 (now over 50) years of their existence, they have already evolved further than carbon life in its first two billion years."[42] He concludes, "Silicon reproduction might be hermaphroditic or androgynous.... When threatened, silicon devices will engage in active evasion.... They will be invisible.... They will be telepathetic.... Silicon life will be immortal. The farthest reaches of space will be accessible to it."[43]

Granted, all this may be a little removed from your next design challenge, but it is a indication as to how far human culture on Earth has developed in a relatively short period, and where the future may lie. It has been a fascinating ride and the best is yet to come.

FROM THEN TO NOW

About 40,000 years ago *Homo sapiens* developed and used tools and found it necessary to codify knowledge, to leave a record of what they knew to be real. In the words of Bronowski, these individuals were "unfolding the gift of intelligent action". The move from hunting and gathering to agriculture began around 12,000 years ago. The earliest cities were formed about 8,000 years ago and we began to identify periods by their material usage, with copper giving way to bronze around 6,000 years ago.

China dominated cultural development some 5,000 years ago, with writing developing in Sumeria and Egypt some 5,500 years ago. 2,000 years ago Rome ruled the world. The Roman Empire lasted for 1,200 years and some regard it as the first multinational corporation.[44] The European Renaissance was a cultural movement that developed during the fourteenth century and lasted until the seventeenth century until the onset of the industrial revolution. With the age of steam came railroads. By 1825 there were only 25 miles of public railroad open in the world. By 1875 there were 160,000 miles of track—just think for a moment the implications that that had on secular architecture and engineering, on how the countryside was transformed and how, in many cases, the positioning

of the rail station replaced the market as the town centre—trains carried goods, people and ideas—the station became a new focal point of communication. In 1879, Thomas Edison lit up our world when he created the first commercially practical incandescent lamp. The next 50 years witnessed radio, television, jet aircraft, nuclear fission and the beginnings of space travel.[45] More recently we have witnessed the onset of the computer age, genetic engineering, DNA sequencing and we are pondering the reality of dark matter and awaiting the arrival of the Singularity. Every one of the above evolutionary stages has connections with design, creativity and culture.

Your beliefs become your thoughts.
Your thoughts become your words.
Your words become your actions.
Your actions become your habits.
Your habits become your values.
Your values become your destiny.
Mahatma Gandhi (1869–1948) the political and spiritual leader of India during the move to independence, and the pre-eminent practitioner of non-violent civil disobedience.

CONNECTIONS

Your world is what you decide to make it. You can, in both your personal and professional life, maintain an open mind, demonstrate a passion for knowledge and help design human future. Conversely, you can maintain a closed dogmatic approach to design and produce yet another tape dispenser, egg cup holder or little black dress and contribute very little to design evolution. Design creativity and technological innovation are contemporaneous and synergistic. One challenge will be how humankind will associate with technological constructs such as robots and cyborgs. In some respects we are already at home with cyborgs, those self-regulating human-machine systems that operate in space.[46] How else would you describe the 800 seat Airbus 380[47] or the 330 seat Boeing 787 Dreamliner.[48]

DESIGN IS GOOD FOR YOU

As Nigel Whiteley pointed out more than a decade ago, with more than a little tinge of Ruskin, there is an established connection between a society's design and its social health. Design is very much a statement of the connections between the social, political and economic situation, reflective of the cultural ethos of the age.[50] At the experimental Mobile Experience Lab at MIT, researchers seek "to radically reinvent and creatively design connections between people, information and physical places. Using cutting-edge information and mobile technology the lab seeks to improve people's lives through the careful design of meaningful experiences."[51] Those meaningful experiences will be most beneficial to those outside the fortunate ten per cent.

Essential singularity. A technological singularity is a hypothetical event. It will occur if technological progress becomes so rapid and the growth of super-human intelligence so great that the future (after the singularity) becomes qualitatively different and harder to predict. This plot shows how approaching the essential singularity from different directions yields different behaviours. http://creativecommons.org/licenses/by-sa/3.0/.

As we have seen in the previous sections, in the not too distant past, far too much design attention has been paid to the fortunate ten per cent by pandering to the attitudes of affluence and flirtatious fashion. Speaking in 1990, Jeremy Myerson was concerned that design is "fast becoming a weapon of exclusivity, of segmentation–the means by which many desirable goods and services are put out of reach of large sections of the community".[52] More recently design has matured, thrown of the shackles that bind it to opulent privilege and become more concerned with

malnutrition than mammon, emphasising subsistence over commerce. Many designers see themselves as sustainable entrepreneurs who engage in social networking. More talk less product.

You never change things by fighting the existing reality. To change something, build a new model that makes the existing model obsolete.
Buckminster Fuller (1895–1983), architect, author, designer, environmentalist, inventor, and futurist.

TALK TO ME

In "Nomads at last", an article in *The Economist*, Andreas Kluth observes that, "wireless communication is changing the way people work, live, love and relate to places".[53] With each advance in our ability to produce, store, and access information, the amount of information available has increased exponentially. Recently, the Internet has provided an unprecedented number of people access to more information and data than at any other time in human history. Indeed, you may have access to more knowledge than all previous generations combined! Now we complain about having too much. People suffer from information overload, accompanied by increased anxiety and confusion over both the sheer volume and the apparent unstructured, chaotic storage and nature of this data. But they have learned not only to cope but to master. "According to the International Telecommunication Union, 3.3 billion people, more than half the world's population, now subscribe to a mobile-phone service so the Internet at last looks set to change the whole world."[54] According to 2009 figures, China is the largest market for cellular services with 600 million users, India is second with half a billion.[55] India is forecast to have over one billion users by 2015.[56] In our world there are five times more mobile phones than computers, which makes the mobile phone the most widely spread technology and the most common electronic device in the world–it is also one of the least sustainable with a reported 426,000 mobile phones discarded in the US every day. [57]

THE INFORMATION NOMAD

Once upon a time we were all nomads. Historically there are three kinds of nomad, the hunter-gatherer who follow the herds that represent their food supply; the pastoral nomad who moves their herds from one grazing ground to another, and the peripatetic nomad who offers their skills to the highest bidder. Our world has added two other types of nomad–the displaced who wander the streets of many of our major urban cities and the information nomad.

Around 70,000 years ago our earliest sapient ancestors left our African birthplace on foot. Approximately 1500 BCE, the Phoenicians became the first open water navigators, exploring the land locked Mediterranean sea. In 1519, the seafaring Ferdinand Magellan became the first navigator to circumnavigate the globe. The journey began in August of 1519 and was completed in September of 1522 (Magellan was killed in battle and did not complete the voyage, but 18 of his fellow sailors did). Nearly 400 years later, in 1903 we took to the air.[58] Less than half a century later, in 1949, the first round-the-world nonstop flight was completed by Captain James Gallagher and a USAF crew of 13 aboard the Lucky Lady II. The flight took 94 hours and one minute.[59]

In the early twentieth century we began to leave the physical world behind and took to the airwaves with radio and television, but most connections were local. The first email message was sent in 1971[60] and the World Wide Web was created in 1989.[61] The subsequent Internet made communication global. Now we are free to roam the world, in seconds. Kevin Kelly, a co-founder of *Wired*, foresees that "the next stage in human technological evolution is a single thinking/web/computer that is planetary in dimensions. This planetary computer will be the largest, most complex and most dependable machine we have ever built. It will also be the platform that most business and culture will run on."[62] Connections rule!

i, i, i

Ettore Sottsass domesticated the typewriter but it was Frog Design who in 1984 domesticated the computer with the introduction of the Macintosh the most successful design of the 1980s which was also the star of most successful television campaign of the era.[63] The controversial 1984 commercial was devised by Chiat/Day and directed by Ridley Scott. The introductory 60 second commercial was aired on 22 January 1984 during the third quarter of Super Bowl XVII. The cost was a staggering $800,000 and was the start of a $15 million, 100 day campaign. The commercial was viewed by 96 million people, reaching, according to AC Nielsen, 46.4 per cent of all households in America.[64] This was the defining moment when the computer was domesticated, moving from the environment of the office into the home. 14 years later, in 1998, Apple introduced the iMac, designed by Jonathan Ive, which sold over two million units in its first year. The iPod, also designed by Ive was introduced into the marketplace in November 2001, by April 2007 it had sold one hundred million units and six hundred million units by April 2010.[65] The innovative iPad sold over 300,000 units on the day of its launch in April 2010 with sales predicted to reach over the 20 million mark by the end of 2012.

> *The new media are not bridges between man and nature. They are nature.*
> Marshall McLuhan, *Understanding Media*, 1964, p. 14.

PERPETUAL CONNECTIVITY

Dr Carsten Sørensen, a noted researcher in the area of information and communication technology, based at the London School of Economics, has this to say. "Our society is transforming itself into a mobile society, where interaction itself is mobilised… but the most powerful aspect is the mobilisation of our inter-personal interaction. The mobilisation of interaction redefines our sense of time, space and context."[66] Manuel Castells, a sociologist at the Annenberg School for Communication, part of the University of Southern California, Los Angeles, concurs. "Permanent connectivity, not motion, is the critical thing."[67] For

The Cloud, Fortezza da Basso, Florence. ©2008—MIT Mobile Experience Lab ←http://mobile.mit.edu→ Massachusetts Institute of Technology ←http://mit.edu→. The Cloud is "an organic sculptural landmark that responds to human interaction and expresses context awareness using hundreds of sensors and over 15,000 individually addressable optical fibers. Constructed of carbon glass, spanning over four metres, and containing more than 65 kilometres of fiber optics, the Cloud encourages visitors to touch and interact with information in new ways, manifesting emotions and behavior through sound and a dichotomy of luminescence and darkness.

designers (and many others) one of the most critical aspects of permanent wireless connectivity is language, "and by implication thought and feeling. That major linguistic change is afoot is clear to anybody who has been around young people almost anywhere in the world. Entire subcultures now define themselves primarily or exclusively through their chosen text-messaging or instant-messaging argot."[68] (This topic was covered in more depth in Chapter Three.)

Language is the primary vehicle for thought, quintessential to the design process. As Christine Kenneally adroitly points out, "Language is the real information highway, the first virtual world. Language is the worldwide web, and everyone is logged on."[69] One challenge to open access, to bringing about a state of 'permanent connectivity', has been the market protection of some companies to lock their devices for use on a specific network. This will change.

DESIGN SCOREBOARD

As emphasised in the preceding chapters, design is an intrinsic part of the continuing evolution of our species. It is responsive to prevailing social conditions and cultural values. It is linked to global commercial life. The July 2008 issue of *Business Week* highlighted the 2008 International Design Excellence Awards (IDEAs). These annual acknowledgements provide an indication of the state of current design practice. Not surprisingly, the US held first place with 114 awards, followed by Korea with 19 and Brazil with 12. *Business Week* noted that "a strong sense of social responsibility ran through many of the winning entries". (One of its 'Gold' awards going to SizeChina for their anthropometric research project, see Chapter One, "Cosmos: Human Evolution, Cultural Evolution, and Design Evolution".)

Which countries provide the most support for design? How do countries measure up when taking into account a number of factors, including public investment in design, total number of design graduates, and number of World Intellectual Patent Office design registrations?

A consortium of British universities led by the University of Cambridge and supported by the Design Council, has produced an International Design Scoreboard which measures a country's design capability. Korea is emerging as a new design powerhouse, with other countries in East Asia displaying similar ambitions. The published rankings show the USA in first place, followed by Korea, Japan, the UK, Canada and Singapore.[70] But what of the future? Jeffrey Sachs, director of The Earth Institute, Columbia University, offers one view:

> The twenty-first century will overturn many of our basic assumptions about economic life. The twentieth century saw the end of European dominance of global politics and economics. The twenty-first century will see the end of American dominance. New powers, including China, India and Brazil, will continue to grow and their voices will be increasingly heard on the world stage.... The challenges of sustainable development—protecting the environment, stabilising the world's population, narrowing the gaps between rich and poor, and ending extreme poverty—will take centre stage.[71]

COLLECTIVE IMAGINATION

The challenges ahead will demand that all designers are extremely well informed, motivated and ever-ready to apply their creativity in the drive towards achieving a sustainable world. As we have seen in earlier chapters, creativity depends upon imagination, the ability to perceive that which does not exist. Today, imagination is under attack from data overload. At a time when we can measure everything from subatomic particle to the entirety of space and time; when we chart not only this universe but many others; when we Google any subject; when we can define all that we can see and sense and much of what we cannot; when we can describe any relationship between any one thing or event and any other, we are in danger of believing that all this data is the information that results in knowledge and wisdom.[72] What has changed is the human element. There is just too much available information for any one person to process. Rather than depend upon one individual, imagined results are now (or at least could be) the by-product of the collective imagination.

New forms of communication have resulted in what some researchers refer to as the "Wisdom of Crowds".[73] Wisdom of crowds is hardly new, at least in a design sense (see Chapter Two, "The Nature of the Design Process"). What is new is the rapidity of consensus building. New forms of communication allow for the collapse of time. We no longer require generations of trial and error to get it right—we have the Internet and Twitter. We all process information in our own individual way; the new technologies allow for ongoing links between people, all of whom will have their own unique forms of processing information. All these 'strings' of input are in a constant state of flux. The basic elements remain. A satisfactory solution is dependant upon diversity of experience and input; it recognises the uniqueness of individual input; it acknowledges the decentralisation of operation and takes full advantage of aggregation of data. It is the modern day group manifestation of Frank Pick's aphorism mentioned in the "Prologue", "Design is intelligence made visible."[74]

DESIGN MATTERS

In his recent book, *A Whole New Mind*, Daniel H Pink asserts that the last few decades have witnessed the rise and dominance of left brain thinkers, from computer programmers to contract lawyers. He suggests that the future will belong to a different type of thinker, seeing "artists, inventors, designers, story-tellers, care-givers, consolers, big picture thinkers (these) will now reap society's richest rewards and share its greatest joys".[75] As mentioned several times before, designers have the ability to imagine that which does not exist—be it product service or social environment—and by the application of design help to make the dream a reality. As Koberg and Bagnall assert, "Design is a process of making dreams come true."[76]

Over 200 years ago, Benjamin Franklin affirmed, "In this world nothing can be said to be certain, except death and taxes."[77] From our standpoint it may be appropriate to modify the two absolutes to death and design. As we have seen throughout this text, design has always been an intrinsic part of human evolution, responding to changes in social conditions and cultural values. Today, you operate in an information rich milieu that is enabled by a wide variety of sources—some, such as this book, traditional; others more modern, such as film and television, and still others wedded to the future, such as the www, the smartphone, and the iPad, the effects of which are uncertain. Devoid of political intervention these developments can be part of a democratisation of the design process. They are enabling, but are accompanied by an enhanced personal and social responsibility. (Just because you can do it, should you?)

THE "RE" WORD

Researchers such as Stuart Walker[78] prophecies that:

> ...the new design is often more enabling, more approachable, more expressive and, consequently, more engaging. Tellingly, it is often characterised by words prefixed by 're'-responding, restoring, recovering, remixing, recycling, re-using, reducing. It may even be about redemption.[79]

The last decades of the twentieth century were remarkable for their justified concern for individual rights. The first decades of the twenty-first century will need to be equally vehement about the acquisition of individual and group sensibilities. You are responsible for what and how you design.

ETHICAL ENTREPRENEURS

This is not the time for wholesale rejection of existing patterns of design. It is time for a re-examination of design education and practice. When considering how designers can best contribute to a changing design climate, the noted designer thinker, John Wood, observes that many designers feel frustrated by their design education:

> The vast majority of them are let down by an education system that fails to prepare them for the practice as ethical entrepreneurs, and sees eco-design as a passing

fad or, at best, a specialist subject area. Generally speaking, our failure to integrate specialist knowledge and skills has been an important barrier to the creation of an eco-society.... It was inexcusable that the UK government's 2005 "Cox Report on Creativity in Business" made no mention of ethics or sustainability.[80]

SUSTAINABILITY–WHEN GREEN IS NOT ENOUGH

When every label in the supermarket and store is adorned with either an 'eco' or 'sustainable' tag we are lulled into thinking that things have changed. "Given enough time it is inevitable that you will forget you are sleeping with the enemy."[81] Changing what exists is always a problem, it is much easier to stay with the *status quo*. Given the challenges ahead, we can not afford complacency, or even worse, inaction. To quote Chapman and Gant:

> The impact of sustainable design so far has been limited, and the real potential it holds has yet to be fully activated. Designers have a new purpose, and a new visionary cause to champion.... In today's competitive market, an increasing number of multinational companies see an economically viable and competitive future in eco-efficient products and processes.... As with any commercial organisation, goal oriented organisms, or eco-systems, are dependent upon diversity and pluralism to survive and prosper... progressive systems must be constructed upon a rich and diverse foundation, in order for cultural well-being to manifest within sustainable design; sustainability becomes a culture in and of itself, with values, beliefs, legends, folklore and other stories. One thing is certain—without debate, agreement and disagreement, this enriched and thriving multiculturalism in sustainable design will remain a tantalising yet unachievable utopia.[82]

We, you, must respond and take responsibility for our actions. It is time for a re-orientation of design and a re-examination of design education that will incorporate enhanced social responsibility and the implementation of improved ethical standards of design.[83] It is time to recognise the moral component in the design process.[84] Recent research indicates that "the moral sense to be the product of biologically evolved and culturally sensitive brain systems that together make up the human moral faculty".[85] Jonathan Haidt of the University of Virginia argues that our moral intuitions evolved from an affective system that generates what he calls, "hot" flashes of feeling. As Ezio Manzini points out, it is time to "learn how to navigate in the fluidity of events... with reference to the transition towards sustainability".[86] Mike Press and Rachel Cooper conclude that the need is for "design graduates who have an acute sense of changing times, a sense of self-determination and direction, who take initiative, who can 'see the world through other people's eyes' and can take a principled, responsible position in

a complex and dangerous world".[87] The enunciative Eric Chan provides a 'balanced' rational and proactive approach: "If one accepts that Americans are hard-wired consumers first and foremost, then the issue isn't how to get people to change their habits in order to become more sustainable, but how designers can change systems to fit the consumer model while still achieving sustainable practices."[88]

As stated in the "Prologue", this book has provided an inclusive, full spectrum view of design, across disciplines, across cultures and across time periods. What is evident is that changes are required to prepare for contemporary design practice. You are part of the most knowing generation ever and you face unimaginable challenges; the combination of these, along with a passion for change, should be enough to fire the creative spirit.[89] The prerequisite changes in academia and design curricula that acknowledge sustainability and the social and moral components of design are unlikely to happen unless you ask—so ask.[90]

In the last chapter we considered some of the considerable changes required of our lifestyles over the next 50 or so years if we are going to survive as a species. With population growth and depletion of natural resources; with continuing threats to national economies, food and water security, the potential exists for ongoing social unrest. I am not suggesting that design can alleviate the challenges, but it can mollify some of the underlying causes. But first we have to understand the problem.

The concept of social responsibility, the notion that an individual, group of individuals or organisations has responsibility to society, may be topical but has been around as long as humanity. Darwin, who argues the benefit of such moral responsibility to society:

> ...although a high standard of morality gives but a slight or no advantage to each individual man and his children over the other men of the same tribe, yet an advancement in the standard of morality and an increase in the number of well-endowed men will certainly give an immense advantage to one tribe over another.[91]

In the last chapter we considered the necessity for designers to develop a highly tuned sense of social responsibility. As an example we looked at the more recent pronouncement by McDonough and Braungart that places emphasis on the necessity to distinguish between eco-efficiency and eco-effectiveness. They suggest that, by design, we can use everything, including that designated as 'waste' to nourish something new—hence the title of their book, *Cradle to Cradle*, rather than the more terminal cradle to grave.[92]

Our future can sound very gloomy—but it does not have to be. We certainly face complex and interrelated challenges. The design matrix is changing. The exuberances' of Art Nouveau and Art Deco, the rational purity of post-Bauhaus design, the fun and fantasy of the 1960s, structured business approach of the 1980s and 1990s, all superseded by a growing awareness of the potential role of design in achieving a sustainable future. A future where the practising designers will have an approach to design that is directed by a well formulated personal design philosophy, bolstered by an acute moral attitude to design along with a finely tuned social awareness. As is often stated, design does not function in a vacuum—designers are part of the cultural context, the design process and the application of design involves a number of different individuals, resources and ideas. All must work together for the successful implementation of change. Sounds idealistic?

> *If you don't stretch you don't know where the edge is.*
> Sara Little Turnbull, founder and director, the Process of Change, Innovation and Design Laboratory, Stanford Graduate School of Business.

THE FUTURE BELONGS TO YOU

As we have seen time and time again in this dialogue, the future always belongs to those who are prepared. You have access to the technology that is powering change; and you know how to use it. All the world's information and misinformation and data is just a click or thumb press away. Intelligent hardware and software are beginning to emerge to guide you through what Manzini calls, "the tangled web of signals", to assist in the access, evaluation and analysis, hopefully transforming knowledge into wisdom. The one unknown is you. Do you have the passion and tenacity to become one of the new breed of navigators? Will you engage in a basic re-wiring of your brain and instruct your neurons to form new synapses and create new, creative, connections?

TAKE YOUR MIND TO THE GYM

Nancy Andreasen, Chair of Psychiatry at The University of Iowa, suggests four daily activities to encourage creative thinking; choose a new and unfamiliar area of knowledge and explore it in depth; spend some time meditating or just thinking; practise observing and describing things; and practise imagining. In *The Creative Brain*, she states that:

> We are literally remaking our brains—who we are and how we think, with all our actions, reactions, perceptions, postures, and positions-every minute of the day and every day of the week and every month and year of our entire lives.[93]

THINK ABOUT DESIGN; THINK ABOUT CREATIVITY; THINK ABOUT CULTURE. MAKE IT HAPPEN

What you do today, what you think today, will have an effect on tomorrow. Given the ever increasing life expectancy rates, your design future looks fantastic— filled with unexplored avenues and exciting possibilities. Rob Hopkins, the founder of the Transition Network, summarises: "We live in extraordinary times. Scary times.[94] Exhilarating times. Bewildering times. Yet times so pregnant with possibilities as to be unprecedented." But you will need to prepare, you will need a revised orientation to design, creativity and culture. Where you go from here is a choice I leave to you.

ENDNOTES

PROLOGUE

1 Frank Pick was Chief Executive of the London Passenger Transport Board from its creation in 1933 until 1940 and a pioneer of design management. "Design means something purposed, fit for its function, economical of material and labour, sound in form and construction. That we must seek everywhere if appearance values are to be realised. It is intelligence made visible." The quote appears in the *London Transport Third Annual Conference Proceedings*, 1938, pp. 44–45. (Thanks to Caroline Warhurst of London Transport Information Services for tracking down this oft quoted but rarely attributed remark.)

2 Kooyman, Brian Patrick, *Understanding Stone Tools and Archaeological Sites*, Albuquerque, NM: University of New Mexico Press, 2001. Dr Brian P Kooyman professor of archaeology at the University of Calgary in Alberta. In this book he explores the production, function, and context of stone tools.

3 Ehrenfeld, John, *Sustainability by Design, A Subversive Strategy for Transforming Our Consumer Culture*, New Haven, CT and London: Yale University Press, 2008. John Ehrenfeld provides a "fundamentally optimistic book about the interaction of culture, economics and technology in producing our current environmental degeneration". He covers areas that range from eco-efficiency, sustainable development and corporate social responsibility.

4 Sowell, Thomas, *Migrations and cultures: A world view*, New York: Basic Books, 1996, p. 378. Thomas Sowell is a Senior Fellow at the Hoover Institution on War, Revolution and Peace, Stanford University and a prolific writer about the history of ideas, economics and social issues. See also his more recent *Ever Wonder Why? And Other Controversial Essays*, Stanford CA: Hoover Institution, 2006.

5 Huxley, Aldous, *The Doors of Perception*, Harmondswoth: Penguin Books, 1963, p.14.

6 Spybey, Tony, "Frames of Meaning: the Rationality in Organisational Cultures", *Acta Sociologica*, vol. 27, no. 4, pp. 311–322, 1984.

7 Press, Mike, and Rachel Cooper, "Design and Consumer Culture", in *The Design Experience: The Role of Design and Designers in the Twenty-First Century*, Aldershot: Ashgate, 2003, pp. 11–34.

8 Walker Stuart, "Design Redux", in Chapman, Jonathan, Nick Grant, ed., *Designers, Visionaries + Other Stories*, London and Sterling VT: Earthscan, 2007, p. 61.

9 Carlson, David, ed., "A Check List for Sustainability", *David Report*, Issue 11, July 2009. "The David Report bulletin covers the intersection of design, culture and business life with a creative and humanistic approach." http://www.davidreport.com/File/update/360/.

10 Maeda, John, *The Laws of Simplicity. Design, Technology, Business, Life*, Cambridge MA: The MIT Press, 2006, p. 43.

11 Papanek, Victor, *Design for the Real World*, Toronto, New York, London: Bantam Books, 1971, 1973, p. 15. The introduction written by Richard Buckminster Fuller is well worth reading, pp.1–13.

12 Koberg, Don, Jim Bagnall, *The All New Universal Traveler*, Los Altos, CA: William Kaufmann, 1972, 1981, p. 16.

CHAPTER ONE

1 Thackara, John, *In the Bubble. Designing in a Complex World*, Cambridge MA: The MIT Press, 2006, p. 150.

2 Thackara, *In the Bubble. Designing in a Complex World*, p. 1.

3 The European Space Agency's Herschel space observatory has a three and a half metre diameter mirror, larger than the Hubble Space Telescope, and uses the most sensitive far-infrared telescope ever put into space, making it one of the most powerful tools to study the Universe. It is named for German-born British astronomer Frederick William Herschel who discovered infrared light over 200 years ago. http://apod.nasa.gov/apod/ap091016.html, you can follow Herschel on Twitter: http://twitter.com/esaherschel.

4 "Spiral Metamorphosis", http://www.galaxydynamics.org/spiral_metamorphosis.html. Atkinson, Nancy, "Triple Whammy: Milky Way More Massive, Spinning Faster and More Likely to Collide", *Universe Today*, 5 January, 2009. And from the National Aeronautics and Space Administration (NASA) http://www.nasa.gov/mission_pages/swift/main/index.html.

5 Rees, Martin, "What the future looks like", *The Guardian*, Tuesday 26 May, 2009. Rees, Martin, *Our Final Hour, A Scientist's Warning: How Terror, Error, and Environmental Disaster Threaten Humankind's Future In This Century–On Earth and Beyond*, New York: Basic Books, 2003. Sir Martin Rees is Astronomer Royal, Master of Trinity College, Cambridge, and President of the Royal Society.

6 For a brief, erudite and factual assessment of our universe see: Rees, Martin, "We're the 'waste' from distant stars", *The Guardian*, Thursday 1 May 2008, http://www.guardian.co.uk/science/2008/may/01/particlephysics.starsgalaxiesandplanets.

7 Rollinson, Hugh Richard, *Early Earth Systems, a geochemical approach*, Malden MA: Wiley-Blackwell, 2007, p. 1.

8 For a highly readable and informed introduction to the origin of our universe and the related time scale, see "The Law of Time and Chaos," Ray Kurzweil, *The Age of Spiritual Machines*, London: Viking Penguin, 1999, pp. 9–39. See also; Mullen, Leslie, A Question of Climate, *Astrobiology Magazine*, posted: 02/25/08. http://www.astrobio.net/index.php?option=com_news&task=detail&id=2631.

9 "Near-Earth objects and life on Earth", *Near Earth Object Program, NASA*, http://neo.jpl.nasa.gov/neo/life.html.

10 Based on research led by Kurt Konhauser, Research Chair, Geomicrobiology, University of Alberta, *Nature*, 458, pp. 750–753, 9 April, 2009. For a succinct informative review from the PBS evolution library see: http://www.pbs.org/wgbh/evolution/library/03/4/l_034_02.html. See also, Fasyovsky, David E., David B Weishampel, "Interrelationships of Vertebrates", *The Evolution and Extinction of the Dinosaurs*, Cambridge and New York: Cambridge University Press, 1996, 2005, pp. 63–85.

12 Hardison, OB, "The Curve of Evolution", *Disappearing through the Skylight: Culture and Technology in the Twentieth Century*, New York: Penguin, 1989, pp. 285–289.

13 "Dinosaurs died of cold", *Chemistry & Industry*, 2 September 2002, Issue 17, p. 5. Dinosaurs were the dominant vertebrate life form on earth for around 165 million years. Modern humans (*Homo sapiens*) have been around for about 100,000 years–which is 0.06% of the reign of the dinosaurs.

14 Silvertown, Jonathan, ed., *99% Ape: How Evolution Adds Up*, London: Natural History Museum, 2008. See also: Kurzweil, Ray, The Six Epochs, *The Singularity is Near*, New York and London: Penguin Books, 2005, pp. 14–33. Diamond, Jared, *The Third Chimpanzee*, New York: Harper Collins, 1992.

15 For "A Survey of the Biological and Cultural Evolution of *Homo habilis* and *Homo erectus*", see the excellent site created and maintained by Dr Dennis O'Neil, Behavioral Sciences Department, Palomar College, San Marcos, California http://anthro.palomar.edu/homo/homo_3.htm.

16 The research team from the Anthropological Institute, University of Zürich: Christoph PE Zollikofer, Zürich–3D skull reconstruction; Marcia S Ponce de León, Zürich–3D skull reconstruction; Elisabeth Daynès, Paris–model reconstruction (skin, eyes, hair).

17 Palmer, Douglas, *Neanderthal*, London: Channel 4 Books, Macmillan, 2000, http://www.channel4.com/history/microsites/N/neanderthal/Tattersall, Ian. *The Last Neanderthal: The Rise, Success, and Mysterious Extinction of Our Closest Human Relatives*, New York: Macmillan, 1995.

18 For an informed history and overview of all that is known about the origins and development of *Homo sapiens*, see part one: Johanson, Donald, Blake Edgar, *From Lucy to Language*, updated and expanded, New York: Simon & Schuster, 2006.

19 "The Incredible Journey Taken by Our Genes", *American Scientist*, http://www.americanscientist.org/science/pub/the-incredible-journey-taken-by-our-genes.

20 Behar, Doron M, et al, "The Genographic Project Public Participation Mitochondrial DNA Database", Plos Genetics, a peer-reviewed open-access journal published by the Public Library of Science. https://www3.nationalgeographic.com/genographic/http://www.plosgenetics.org/article/info:doi/10.1371/journal.pgen.0030104.

21 In 2009, BBC 2 produced *The Incredible Human Journey*. This series documents human origins and evolution, from our birthplace in Africa to the long migratory routes that led us to populate the most distant parts of the globe. For the accompanying book, see: Roberts, Alice, *The Incredible Human Journey*, London: Bloomsbury Publishing, 2009.

22 For comprehensive coverage of this crucial evolutionary step, see: Dawkins, Richard, *The Ancestor's Tale: A Pilgrimage to the Dawn of Evolution*, Mariner Books, 2004; Diamond, Jared, *The Third Chimpanzee: The Evolution and Future of the Human Animal*, New York: HarperPerennial, HarperCollins, 1992; Stillman, Bruce, *The Genome of Homo Sapiens*, Woodbury, NY: CSHL Press, 2003; Tattersall, Ian, *The Fossil Trail: How We Know What We Think We Know About Human Evolution*, Oxford: Oxford University Press, 1995; "*Homo sapiens*", from the Smithsonian website: http://anthropology.si.edu/HumanOrigins/ha/sap.html; For an Interactive documentary from Arizona State University. http://www.becominghuman.org/; For an informative graphic map of early human phylogeny from the National Museum of Natural History: http://anthropology.si.edu/humanorigins/ha/a_tree.html; "Early Modern *Homo sapiens*", from Behavioral Sciences Department, Palomar College, San Marcos, California http://anthro.palomar.edu/homo2/mod_homo_4.html.

23 Phillips, Helen, "The Outer Limits of the Human Brain", *New Scientist*, issue 2676, 1 October, 2008.

24 Pinker, Steven, *Blank Slate*, London and New York: Penguin Books, 2002, p. 42. For some innovative and provoking questions concerning neuroscience in the twenty-first century see: Gazzaniga, Michael S, *Social Brain: The Science of Our Moral Dilemmas*, New York: Harper Perennial, 2006. Gazzaniga introduces some of the moral predicaments raised by developments in brain science, many of which have influence on design. He does provide a note of caution, "neuroscience will never find the brain correlate of responsibility, because that is something we ascribe to humans–to people–not to brains. It is a moral value we demand of our fellow, rule-following human beings." As we will see in the last section, (*Futures*) design in the twenty-first century will have enhanced moral and ethical dimensions.

25 Robson, Davide, "Disorderly genius: How chaos drives the brain", *New Scientist*, issue 2714, 29 June 2009, pp. 34–37.

26 Locke, John, "Of Clear and Obscure, Distinct and Confused Ideas", in Locke, John, Roger Woolhouse, ed., *An Essay Concerning Human Understanding*, London: Penguin Clasics, 1998, p. 327.

27 On the evolution of the human brain see: http://genome.wellcome.ac.uk/doc%5Fwtd020880.html

28 Russell, Peter, *The Brain Book*, London: Routledge & Kegan Paul, 1979, p. 67.

29 Wrangham, Richard, *Catching Fire: How Cooking Made us Human*, New York: Basic Books, 2009. Richard Wrangham, professor of biological anthropology, Harvard University argues that the act of cooking food is an evolutionary change that underpins human development, concluding that pre-agricultural man confined to raw food would have starved.

30 Calvin, William H, *A Brief History of the Mind: From Apes to Intellect and Beyond*, Oxford and New York: Oxford University Press, 2004. The neurophysiologist William Calvin expands on the camp fire scenario in this quite remarkable book which also covers some similar evolutionary territory, including sections on the development of the 'Modern Mind'; the emergence of 'Structured Thought'; the 'creative' challenges of managing incoherence; the 'Minds Big Bang', and the 'Future of the Augmented Mind'. This is an essential read.

31 Heskett, John, *Design. A Very Short Introduction*, Oxford: Oxford University Press, 2002, p. 5–6.

32 Dusek, Val, *Philosophy of Technology: An Introduction*, Malden MA and Oxford: Blackwell, 2006, p. 118.

33 Faisal, A, Stout, D, Apel, J, Bradley, B, "The Manipulative Complexity of Lower Paleolithic Stone Toolmaking", *PLoS ONE*, 5, 11, e13718. doi:10.1371/journal.pone.0013718.

34 As quoted in, Sample, Ian, "Language and toolmaking evolved together, say researchers". This article was published on guardian.co.uk at 21.02 GMT on Wednesday 3 November 2010. A version appeared in *The Guardian* on Thursday 4 November, 2010, p. 7.

35 Curry, Andrew, "Early Tools Were Born From Fire", *Science Now*, 13 August 2009, http://news.sciencemag.org/sciencenow/2009/08/13-01.html.

36 Highmore, Ben, ed., *The Design Culture Reader*, London and New York: Routledge, 2008. This collection of essays from philosophers, media and cultural theorists, historians of design, anthropologists, cultural historians, artists and literary critics provides an extensive overview of design culture in the past, present and future.

37 Johnson, Samuel, *Rambler*, 60, Saturday 13 October, 1750.

38 Kluckhohn, Clyde, *Mirror for Man*, New York: McGraw-Hill, 1949, p.17, 23.

39 Pinker, Steven, *The Blank Slate*, London and New York: Penguin Books, 2002, p. 65.

40 *Art and Human Reality. A talk with Denis Dutton*, Introduction by Steven Pinker, http://www.edge.org/3rd_culture/dutton09/dutton09_index.html

41 Balkin, J M, *Cultural Software: A Theory of Ideology*, New Haven and London: Yale University, 1998, 2003, p.ix. Available on line at: http://www.asiaing.com/cultural-software-a-theory-of-ideology.html.

42 Sociocultural evolution is an umbrella term for theories of cultural evolution and social evolution, describing how cultures and societies have developed over time. Trigger, Bruce G, *Sociocultural Evolution*, Oxford: Blackwell, 1998, p. 13.

43 Balkin, J M, *Cultural Software: A Theory of Ideology*, New Haven and London: Yale University, 1998, 2003, p. 93.

44 Fasyovsky, David E, David B Weishampel, *The Evolution and Extinction of the Dinosaurs*, Cambridge and New York: Cambridge University Press, 1996, 2005, p. 64. Gould, Stephen Jay, *Wonderful Life: the Burgess Shale and the Nature of History*, New York: W W Norton, 1990.

45 McIntyre, Lee, *Dark Ages. The Case for a Science of Human Behavior*, Cambridge MA and London: MIT Press, 2006.

46 Collier, Paul, *The Bottom Billion: Why the Poorest Countries are Failing and What Can Be Done About It*, Oxford and New York: Oxford University Press, 2007, p. 3.

47 Negus, Keith, Michael Pickering, *Creativity, Communication and Cultural Value*, London: Sage Publications, 2004.

48 Vitruvius, Pollio, Morris Hicky Morgan, tran., *The Ten Books on Architecture*, Cambridge MA: Harvard University Press, 1914. Available on line through Project Gutenberg. http://www.gutenberg.org/etext/20239.

49 Cragoe, Carol Davidson, "The Medieval Stonemason", *British History in-depth*, http://www.bbc.co.uk/history/british/middle_ages/.

50 For some information on human anthropometrics see: http://www.roymech.co.uk/Useful_Tables/Human/Human_sizes.html, (but please note that the data is for guidance only and is not for detailed design).

51 Dreyfuss, Henry, *Designing for People*, New York: Allworth Press, 1955, 2003, pp. 26–27.

52 http://images.businessweek.com/ss/07/10/1005_asia/index_01.html.

53 http://www.sizechina.com/html/index.html http://www.youtube.com/watch?v=mSHn-_V_78U.

54 Ball, RM, 2008, *SizeChina: The world shapes up. Innovation*, Fall 2008, pp 158–161.

55 Ball R, Shu C, Xi P, Rioux M, Luximon Y, Molenbroek J, A comparison between Chinese and Caucasian head shapes, *Applied Ergonomics*, 41(6), 2010, pp. 832–9. Luximon Y, Ball R and Justice L, *The Chinese face: A 3D anthropometric analysis*, *Proceedings of the TMCE2010 Symposium*, Ancona, Italy, 2010, pp. 255–266.

56 Claude Shannon's, "A Mathematical Theory of Communication", was first published in two parts in the July and October 1948 editions of the *Bell System Technical Journal*, vol. 27, pp. 379–423 and 623–656. The paper has appeared in a number of republications since then. Shannon, Claude Elwood, Warren Weaver, *The Mathematical Theory of Communication*, Urbana: University of Illinois Press, 1949, 1998.

57 Cascio, Jamais, "Get Smarter", *The Atlantic*, July/August, 2009, http://www.theatlantic.com/magazine/archive/2009/07/get-smarter/7548/.

58 Blass, Thomas, *The Man Who Shocked The World: The Life and Legacy of Stanley Milgram*, Philadelphia: Basic Books, 2009.

59 This concept is entertainingly explored in, Vedral, Vlatko, "Social Informatics: Get Connected or Die tryin,' in *Decoding Reality. The Universe as Quantum Information*, Oxford and New York: Oxford University Press, 2010, pp. 91–109.

60 http://www.facebook.com/press/info.php?statistics.

61 Castells, Manuel, *Communication Power*, Oxford and New York: Oxford University Press, 2009, pp. 61–71.

62 Stated by Isaac Newton in a letter to Robert Hooke, dated 5 February 1676. In July 2001, Umberto Eco chose the aphorism as the title of a speech commenting upon the age-old struggle between fathers and sons. Eco, Umberto, (Alastair McEwen, trans.) "On the Shoulders of Giants", in *Turning Back the Clock. Hot Wars and Media Populism*, Orlando: Harvest Harcourt, 2007, pp. 334–354.

63 This 'model' is closer to the original metaphor as first recorded in the twelfth century and attributed to Bernard of Chartres. See: Eco, Umberto, (Alastair McEwen, trans.) "On the Shoulders of Giants," in *Turning Back the Clock. Hot Wars and Media Populism*, Orlando: Harvest Harcourt, 2007, p. 343.

64 Norman, Donald A, "The Future of Robots", in *Emotional Design: Why we love (or hate) everyday things*, New York: Basic Books, 2004, pp. 195–212. On Humanoid and Anthromorphic Robots, see the web site of the Robotics and Automation Society which has many links to current research, http://www.service-robots.org/applications/humanoids.html.

65 http://www.aldebaran-robotics.com/en, http://www.gizmag.com/nao-all-rounder-robot/13445/.

66 Thackara, John, *In the Bubble. Designing in a Complex World*, Cambridge MA: MIT Press: 2006, p.1.

67 It was John Locke who, in *An Essay Concerning Human Understanding*, 1765, proposed that it was necessary to remove humans from the restrictive nature of custom and habit and reorient their understanding to that of rational beings who are at the centre of all things. Over two thousand years earlier, Protagoras of Abdera, (c. 490–420 BCE) the fifth century Greek philosopher, had asserted that "Man is the measure of all things." Two thousand, five hundred years later, we need a reorientation of the design process to reinstate the significance of the human element.

CHAPTER TWO

1 Heskett, John, *Design: A Very Short Introduction*, Oxford: Oxford University Press, 2002, p. 2.

2 For an extensive collection of highly informative interviews by Bill Moggridge discussing the various aspects of interactive design, see: Moggridge, Bill, *Designing Interactions*, Cambridge MA: The MIT Press, 2007.

3 Kunzru, Harry, "One Year On: How Bright Does the Futurecasters' Future Look?" *Mute 19: Global Systems Meltdown*, August 2001, p. 23.

4 Jean Baudrillard is a French cultural theorist, sociologist, philosopher, political commentator, who is associated with postmodernism and post-structuralism. He taught sociology at the Université de Paris-X Nanterre, the institution that instigated the student unrest in Paris in May 1968. See Chapter Eight, "The Counter Culture: design, social protest and culture in the 1960s". Baudrillard, Jean, (Sheila Faria Glaser, trans.), *Simulacra and Simulation (The Body, In Theory: Histories of Cultural Materialism)*, Ann Arbor, MI: University of Michigan Press, 1995.

5 For an informed appraisal which highlights attributions and misconceptions see: Hanley, Richard, "Simulacra and Simulation: Baudrillard and The Matrix", http://whatisthematrix.warnerbros.com/rl_cmp/new_phil_fr_hanley2.html.

6 McAdoo, Oliver, "In the Matrix, which pill would you take, the red or the blue?", http://www.arrod.co.uk/essays/matrix.php. Yeffeth, Glenn, ed., *Taking the Red Pill: Science, Philosophy and Religion in The Matrix*, Dallas: Benbella Books, 2003.

7 Press, Mike, Rachel Cooper, "Research and the Design Process", *The Design Experience. The Role of Design and Designers in the Twenty-First Century*, Aldershot and Burlington VT: Ashgate Publishing, 2003, pp. 102–108.

8 Adams, Douglas, *The Hitchhiker's Guide to the Galaxy*, 25th Anniversary Edition, New York: Harmony Books/Crown, 2004. *The Hitchhikers Guide to the Galaxy* was broadcast on BBC Radio 4 in 1978. The first print edition appeared in 1979 and the 25th anniversary edition was published in 2004. Coincidentally, astronomers considering the weighty question of the mass of the Milky Way galaxy, have also come up with an answer which is about ten to the power of 42 kilograms. In addition, our physics can explain most of the evolution of the Universe after the so called Planck time, that is approximately 10−43 seconds after the Big Bang. That's a zero, dot, 42 zeroes, and then the figure 1. See also: "The Planck Space Telescope: Surveying the Sky", Canadian Space Agency, which includes an explanatory Qicktime video (33.4 Mb), http://www.asc-csa.gc.ca/eng/satellites/planck.asp. Given the scaremongering aimed at the Large Hadron Collider which the physics challenged see as possibly creating a black hole that will absorb the Earth, it may be worth pointing out that to go from one magnitude (the gravitational force that confined Newton's apple to earth,) to the 42/43 orders of magnitude required to create a black hole requires a massive amount of energy contained in an infinitesimally small space. Koelman, Johannes, "Shut Down the LHC? I'd rather Not Hurt a Fly," *Scientificblogging*, March 29, 2010, http://www.scientificblogging.com/hammock_physicist. Maybe the answer to the meaning of life is 42 after all!

9 Joseph Campbell and The Power of Myth with Bill Moyers PBS television series, *Mystic Fire Video*, Episode 2, Chapter 4, 2001. The Power of Myth is a book and six part television documentary originally broadcast on PBS in 1988. The documentary comprises six one-hour conversations between mythologist Joseph Campbell (1904–1987) and journalist Bill Moyers.

10 IDEO is based in Palo Alto and has eight offices around the world. The quotation was stated in a roundtable discussion which took place at the Design Council sponsored Competitiveness Summit '06 in which Bill Moggridge explains the importance of people and prototypes in the design process. For a transcript see: http://www.designcouncil.org.uk/en/Design-Council/Files/Podcast-Transcripts/Bill-Moggridge-Co-Founder-IDEO-Consulting-Associate/.

11 A statement by the economist Paul Romer, quoted in, Pinker, Steven, *The Blank Slate*, London and New York: Penguin Books, 2002, p. 238.

12 Advice given by the Queen of Hearts to Alice in *Through the Looking Glass*. Carroll, Lewis, *Alice's Adventures in Wonderland* and *Through the Looking Glass*, New York: Fine Creative Media, 1865, 1871, 2004, p. 175.

13 Wood, John, "Relative Abundance: Fuller's Discovery that the Glass is always Half Full", in Chapman, Jonathan, Nick Grant, ed., *Designers, Visionaries + Other Stories. A collection of sustainable design essays*, London and Sterling VT: Earthscan, 2007 p. 112.

14 Thackara, John, *In the Bubble. Designing in a Complex World*, Cambridge, MA and London: The MIT Press, 2006, p. 1.

15 http://www.physorg.com/news121350597.html.

16 http://www.ibm.com/ibm/ideasfromibm/us/roadrunner/20080609/index.shtml. For an up to date listing of the 500 most powerful computer systems, see: http://www.top500.org/project/introduction.

17 Hickman, Larry A, *Philosophical Tools for Technological Culture*, Bloomington and Indianapolis: Indiana University Press, 2001, p. 1.

18 Biederman, Irving, "Recognition-by-components: a theory of human image understanding", 1987, *Psychological Review*, 94, pp. 115–147. Available on line: http://geon.usc.edu/~biederman/publications/Biederman_RBC_1987.pdf. As quoted in: Norman, Donald A, *The Psychology of Everyday Things*, New York: Basic Books, 1988, p. 12.

19 Samovar, Larry A, Richard E Porter, Edwin R McDaniel, *Communication Between Cultures*, Belmont CA: Thomson/Wadsworth, 2007, p. 128.

20 Hall, Peter, "A Good Argument", *Metropolismag.com*, March 2009, http://www.metropolismag.com/story/20090318/a-good-argument. The quoted list could be compared with the "Ten Commandments on Design" offered by Dieter Rams. See Chapter Seven: "Fashion, Style and Economics: post-war reconstruction, France, Italy, and Germany".

21 Alexander, Christopher, *Notes on the Synthesis of Form*, Cambridge MA: Harvard University Press, 1964.

22 For a detailed rational concerning "goodness of fit", the "unselfconscious process", and the "self-conscious process" see: Alexander, Christopher, *Notes on the Synthesis of Form*, Cambridge MA: Harvard University Press, 1964. Regretfully this seminal book is now out of print.

23 Jacob, HE, *Six Thousand Years of Bread: Its Holy and Unholy History*, New York: Doubleday, 1944, Lyons Press, 1997. For a modern day example from the Balkans where almost all the bakers of the old Yugoslavia were Albanians, from one small corner of Kosovo, see: Thorpe, Nick, "The Balkans' bakers keep on rolling", *BBC News*, broadcast on Saturday 17 May, 2008 at 1130 BST on BBC Radio 4, http://news.bbc.co.uk/2/hi/programmes/from_our_own_correspondent/7404612.stm.

24 The Igloo, Northern Canada, from the CBC web site, includes a five minute video report, http://www.cbc.ca/sevenwonders/wonder_igloo.html. Cruickshank, Dan, "What house-builders can learn from igloos", *BBC News Magazine*, Wednesday 2 April 2008, http://news.bbc.co.uk/2/hi/uk_news/magazine/7326031.stm. For a general factual and reliable account of Early Palaeo-Eskimo culture, see *A History of the Native People of Canada*, http://www.civilization.ca/archeo/hnpc/npvol21e.html. For a step-by-step guide to building an igloo: http://www.architectureweek.com/2007/1212/building_1-3.html. For an outstanding guide to the building of a traditional igloo see"At the Spring Sea Ice Camp Part 1," from the *Netsilik Eskimo* (sic) series, a visual record dating from 1967. The commentary is in an Inuit dialect but don't let that hinder you from seeing this magnificent document to human creative design. See also: "The igloo of the innuit.—III," *Science 31*, vol. ns-2. no. 30, August 1883, pp. 259–262.

25 Papanek, Victor, *The Green Imperative: Ecology and Ethics in Design and Architecture*, London: Thames and Hudson, 1995, p. 223.

26 http://www.civilization.ca/aborig/iqqaipaa/cultur-e.html.

27 Da Cruz, Daniel, "The Black Tent", *Saudi Aramco World*, May/June 1966, pp. 26–27. http://www.saudiaramcoworld.com/issue/196603/the.black.tent.html. Faegre, Torvald, *Tents: Architecture of the Nomads*, New York: Anchor Press, 1979. Hatton, EM, *The Tent Book*, Boston: Houghton Mifflin, 1979.

28 Hilden, Joy May, "In Search of Bedouin Weavers", *Saudi Aramco World*, May/June 1988, pp. 38–40. http://www.saudiaramcoworld.com/issue/198803/in.search.of.bedouin.weavers.html.

29 Drew, Philip, *Tensile Architecture*, Boulder, CO: Westview Press, 1979. Faegre, Torvald, *Tents: Architecture of the Nomads*, Garden City, NY: Anchor/Doubleday, 1979.

30 Shills, Edward, *Tradition*, Chicago: The University of Chicago Press, 1981.

31 For an learned history of fire: Pyne, Stephen J, *Fire: A Brief History*, Seattle, WA, University of Washington Press, 2001.

32 Savery, Thomas, *The Miner's Friend; or, an engine to raise water by fire,* London: S Crouch, 1702, 1829.

33 Rolt, Lionel Thomas Caswell, Thomas Newcomen. *The Prehistory of the Steam Engine*, first edition, Dawlish, David & Charles, 1963.

34 http://www.matthewboulton2009.org/index.php/the-father-of-birmingham.

35 Matthew Boulton was a key member of the Lunar Society, a group of Birmingham area men prominent in the arts, sciences, and theology. Other members included James Watt, Erasmus Darwin, Josiah Wedgwood, and Joseph Priestley. They were called the Lunar Society because they would meet during the full moon when the extra light made the journey home easier and safer. More peripheral characters and correspondents included Richard Arkwright, (Arkwright spinning frame); the typographer John Baskerville; the ironmaster John Wilkinson; Joseph Wright of Derby, the artist of the Industrial Revolution; the architect James Wyatt, whose Fonthill Abbey was home to the gothic fantasy novel *Vathek*; the French nobleman Antoine Lavoisier regarded as the father of modern chemistry and the two Founding Fathers, Thomas Jefferson and Benjamin Franklin also had contact with the Lunar Society. As they say, "It's who you know" that counts! Schofield, Robert E, *The Lunar Society of Birmingham: A Social History of Provincial Science and Industry in Eighteenth-Century England*, London: Oxford University Press/Clarendon Press, 1963.

36 The origins of steam locomotion are still a matter of debate. Rees Cyclopaedia of 1819 states, "The application of steam-engines to driving of carriages—these are now called locomotive engines, and we may date their introduction with the patent of Messrs. Trevithick and Vivian in 1802. Mr Trevithick made a locomotive engine in South Wales in 1804, which he tried upon the railroads at Merthyr Tydfil." According to Trevithick, he chained four wagons together, loaded each with 2.5 tons of iron, besides seventy men and drew it a distance of 9.75 miles at a rate of four miles per hour. It is likely that more than one engine was produced at Merthyr and one of these may have been the one used in London in 1808, and which is reported to have reached speeds of twelve miles per hour. Richard Trevithick senior was involved in competition with James Watt in producing steam powered engines for use in Cornish mines, Both built on the pioneering work of Thomas Newcomen. For a comprehensive and well documented account see: Trevithick, Francis, *Life of Richard Trevithick*, with an account of his inventions, London and New York: E & FN Spon, 1872. Nicholas Wood, a mentor to George Stephenson took out patent 3887 in 1815 which incorporated features of Trevithick's *Catch-me-who-can*. Smiles, Samuel, *The Life of George Stephenson*, London: John Murray,1857.

37 For reports on the first rail lines, including the first fatality, see: http://www.spartacus.schoolnet.co.uk/RAliverpool.htm.

38 The Rainhill Trials, October 1829, http://www.resco.co.uk/rainhill/index.html; http://www.resco.co.uk/rainhill/.

39 From the British National Archives, "Victorian Britain? How did the railways change the lives of people in Victorian Britain?", http://www.learningcurve.gov.uk/VictorianBritain/pdf/happy.pdf.

40 George Bradshaw was an English cartographer, printer, publisher and the originator of the railway timetable. Bradshaw's Railway Companion appeared in 1840 and soon after was referenced in popular literature. In 1869 it appears in Canto IV of Lewis Carroll's long poem, *Phantasmagoria*. Even the most famous Victorian villain read Bradshaw's. In Chapter Two of Bram Stoker's, *Dracula*, 1897, Jonathan Harker recounts that in the evening, "The lamps were also lit in the study or library, and I found the Count lying on the sofa, reading, of all things in the world, an English, *Bradshaw's Guide*." Perhaps the most famous example is provided by Sir Arthur Conan Doyle when in *The Valley of Fear*, 1914–15, Sherlock Holmes observes that "the vocabulary of Bradshaw is nervous and terse, but limited."

41 Blaise, Clark, *Time Lord: Sir Sandford Fleming and the Creation of Standard Time*, London: Weidenfeld & Nicolson, 2000. See also: http://www.histori.ca/minutes/minute.do?id=10182. Currently, Canada has seven time zones, the USA four, Russia has the most at nine time zones while China has just one.

42 Urry, John, *Mobilities*, Cambridge and Malden, MA: Polity Press, 2007, p. 109.

43 Beresford Hope, Alexander James, *The English Cathedral of the Nineteenth Century*, London: John Murray, 1861, p. 128.

44 *Building News*, 29, 1875, p. 133.

45 Clark, Robert P, *Global Life Systems: Population, Food, and Disease in the Process of Globalization*, Lanham

MD: Rowman & Littlefield, 2001, p. 194. For "A Time Traveller's Guide to Victorian Britain", from Channel 4; http://www.channel4.com/history/microsites/H/history/guide19/.

46 For an examination of the early experiments with steam, electric and combustion engine cars see Rudi Volti, "Why internal combustion", *Invention & Technology Magazine*, Fall 1990, vol. 6, Issue 2, http://www.americanheritage.com/articles/magazine/it/1990/2/1990_2_42.shtml.

47 One of the oldest of all transportation records was set in 1906 when an American, Fred Marriott established a record of 127mph (204km/h) for a steam powered car. In August 2009, a team of British engineers established a new record of just under 140mph (225km/h) in a steam powered car over a measured mile at Edwards Air Force Base, California. For an update check their website. http://www.steamcar.co.uk/. Randerson, James, "New steam technology to turn car engine's waste heat into power", *The Guardian*, 27 August, 2008, http://www.guardian.co.uk/environment/2008/aug/27/alternativeenergy.energy.

48 Morris, Jan, *Pax Britannica: The Climax of an Empire*, London: Faber and Faber, 2003.

49 Binary code for the word "computer."

50 Babbage, Charles, *Passages from the Life of a Philosopher*, New York: AM Kelly, 1864, 1969, p. 40.

51 Purbrick, Louise, "The Dream Machine: Charles Babbage and his Imaginary Computers", *Journal of Design History*, 1993, 6: p. 10.

52 The Jacquard loom was invented by Joseph Marie Jacquard in 1801. Complex patterns for woven brocades could be symbolised on punched cards. These cards controlled the weaving process; weavers could programme the same loom to produce different patterns by changing the cards. Elaborate fabrics, once associated with wealth and status could now be economically mass produced for a larger market. Essinger, James, *Jacquard's Web: how a hand-loom led to the birth of the information age*, Oxford and New York: Oxford University Press, 2004.

53 As quoted in Jones, Glyn, "The Life and Times of Charles Babbage", *New Scientist*, issue 1775, 29 June 1991, p. 33.

54 Reed, David, *A Balanced Introduction to Computer Science*, Upper Saddle River, NJ: Pearson Prentice Hall, 2007, p. 99.

55 Hyman, Anthony, *Charles Babbage Pioneer of the Computer*, Princeton, NJ: Princeton University Press, 1985. Stein, Dorothy, *Ada, A Life and a Legacy*, Cambridge MA: The MIT Press,1985. Morrison, Philip, Emily Morrison, ed., *Charles Babbage and his Calculating Engines*, New York: Dover Publications,1961. Purbrick, Louise, "The Dream Machine: Charles Babbage and his Imaginary Computers", *Journal of Design History*, 1993, 6: pp. 9–23. Stein, DK, "Lady Lovelace's notes: technical text and cultural context", in P Brantlinger, *Energy and Entropy: Science and Culture in Victorian Britain*, Indiana University Press, 1989. This work contains a critical reading of Ada Lovelace's interpretation of the Analytical Engine. From Babbage himself, Babbage, C, *On the Economy of Machinery and Manufactures*, London: Charles Knight, 1835. Available on line: http://www.gutenberg.org/etext/4238. For additional information on Babbage and information on the history of information technology, see the site of the Charles Babbage Institute, University of Minnesota; http://www.cbi.umn.edu/.

56 Ceruzzi, Paul E, *A History of Modern Computing*, Cambridge MA: The MIT Press, 2003, p. 226.

57 Va Tassei, Joan M. *Digital TV over Broadband: Harvesting Bandwidth*, Oxford: Focal Press, 2001, p. 251.

58 The Three Laws of Robotics were written by Isaac Asimov, the Russian-born American author and professor of biochemistry. Asimov was a noted science fiction writer who developed rules that all positronic robots must obey. They appeared on the frontispiece of *I, Robot*, a collection of nine science fiction short stories by Isaac Asimov, first published by Gnome Press in 1950. Telotte, J P, *Replications. A Robotic History of the Science Fiction Film*, Chicago: University of Illinois Press, 1995, p. 43.

59 Elsaesser, Thomas, *Metropolis*, London: British Film Institute, 2000. Minden, Michael, Holger Bachmann, *Fritz Lang's Metropolis: Cinematic Visions of Technology and Fear*, Woodbridge: Boydell & Brewer, 2000.

60 Wiener, Norbert, *Cybernetics, or Control and Communication in the Animal and Machine*, Paris: Hermann & Cie, 1948.

61 "Come the Revolution", *Time*, 27 November, 1950.

62 The paranoid robot in *The Hitchhiker's Guide to the Galaxy* series.

63 The fastidious robot in the *Star Wars* trilogy.

64 HAL 9000 features in *2001: A Space Odyssey* as the sentient on-board computer bent on self survival (Obviously not a supporter of Asimov's).

65 Jha, Alok, "Robots, our new friends electric?", *The Guardian*, Monday, 14 April 2008, http://www.guardian.co.uk/science/2008/apr/14/sciencenews.news.

66 Merchant, Carolyn, *Radical Ecology*, New York: Routledge/Taylor and Francis, 1992, p. 7.

67 The Humanoid Robotics Group at MIT. http://www.ai.mit.edu/projects/humanoid-robotics-group/. The Humanoid Robotics Institute at Waseda University, Japan. http://www.humanoid.waseda.ac.jp/.

68 http://lirec.eu/project.

69 http://www.lirec.org/.

70 O'Connor, Fred, "Robots Will Become Part of Daily Life", *PC World*, Wednesday, 17 October 2007, http://www.pcworld.com/article/id,138569/article.html.

71 Jacobs, Susan, "House Robot Developed for Physically Impaired", *Future Health IT*, March 2008. http://www.futurehealthit.com/2008/03/house_robot_developed_for_phys.html.

72 http://robonaut.jsc.nasa.gov/default.asp.

73 The Honda humanoid robot ASIMO site: http://world.honda.com/ASIMO/. See also the home page of the Care Bots project. http://www.myu.ac.jp/~xkozima/carebots/index-eng.html

74 Toyota unveils two new robots: http://www.abry.biz/toyota-unveils-two-new-robots-110. Information also available through http://jalopnik.com.

75 http://www.technologyreview.com video/?vid=136.

76 For numerous video clips showing the advanced dexterity of this three fingered robot including high speed throwing, catching, spinning, and eye hand coordination exercises, see: http://www.k2.t.u-tokyo.ac.jp/papers/fusion_movies-e.html.

77 For a video clip of ROPID in action: http://www.robo-garage.com/en/prd/p_00/index.html.

78 Kageyama, Yuri, "Robot teacher smiles, scolds in classroom. But developers say it's not about to replace human instructors", *MSNBC*, 11 March, 2009, http://www.msnbc.msn.com/id/29634158/

79 For a video clip of the HRP-4C 'fashion robot', see: http://www.engadget.com/tag/hrp-4c.

80 The Actroid has already made her first television commercial for an insect repellent and sunscreen spray, http://www.pinktentacle.com/tag/kokoro.

81 http://www.robocup.org/.

82 Ortolani, Benito, "The Puppet Theatre", *The Japanese Theatre: From Shamanistic Ritual to Contemporary Pluralism*, Princeton NJ: Princeton University Press, 1990, 1995, pp. 208–232. The Puppet Theatre of Japan, *An Introduction to Bunraku*, The Japan Arts Council, 2004, http://www2.ntj.jac.go.jp/unesco/bunraku/en/.

83 Keene, Donald, Keizo-Kaneko, *No and Bunraku: Two Forms of Japanese Theatre*, New York: Columbia University Press, 1965–1966, 1990.

84 Ortolani, Benito, *The Japanese Theatre: From Shamanistic Ritual to Contemporary Pluralism*, p. 205.

85 This became the title of one of his most quoted books. Barthes, Roland, (Richard Howard trans.), *Empire of Signs*, New York: Hill and Wang, 1970, 1983.

86 Barthes, Roland, (David Savran trans.) "The Dolls of Bunraku", *Diacritics*, vol. 6, no. 4, Winter 1976, pp. 44–47.

87 Barthes, "The Dolls of Bunraku", p. 45.

88 Bolton, Christopher A, "From Wooden Cyborg to Celluloid Souls: Mechanical Bodies in Anime and Japanese Puppet Theater", *positions*, 10.3, 2002, pp. 729–771.

89 Bolton, Christopher A, "From Wooden Cyborg to Celluloid Souls: Mechanical Bodies in Anime and Japanese Puppet Theater", p. 729.

90 http://comipress.com/news/2007/03/10/1622.

91 Clements, Jonathan, Helen McCarthy, *The Anime Encyclopedia: A Guide to Japanese Animation Since 1917*, Berkeley, CA: Stone Bridge Press, 2006. Gravett, Paul, *Manga: Sixty Years of Japanese Comics*, London: Lawrence King, 2004. Isao, Shimizu, "Red Comic Books: The Origins of Modern Japanese Manga", in Lent, John A, *Illustrating Asia: Comics, Humor Magazines, and Picture Books*, Honolulu, Hawaii: University of Hawaii Press, 2001.

92 Napier, Susan J, "The Problem of Existence in Japanese Animation", *Proceedings of the American Philosophical Society*, vol. 149, no. 1, March, 2005, pp. 72–81, http://www.aps-pub.com/proceedings/1491/490106.pdf. East Press of Tokyo has recently released a manga version of *Das Kapital*, Karl Marx's seminal anti-capitalist magnum opus.

93 http://www.theblackmoon.com/BarefootGen/bomb.html.

94 http://www.selfmadehero.com/manga_shakespeare/index.html.

95 http://www.kyoto-seika.ac.jp/eng/3_art/manga.html.

96 Kurzweil, Ray, *The Singularity is Near*, New York, Penguin, 2005, p. 126. Kurzweil's quest is to reveal mankind's ultimate destiny and he explores many of the ideas including his concept of exponential growth, radical life expansion, and how we will transcend our biology, http://www.singularity.com/themovie/index.php.

97 See, Design21, the social design network. http://www.design21sdn.com/.

CHAPTER THREE

1 This often quoted aphorism was made by the British writer, poet and Nobel laureate Rudyard Kipling in a speech given to the Royal College of Surgeons on 14 February 1923, as reported in *The Times*, London, 15 February 1923.

2 Vedral, Vlatko, *Decoding Reality. The Universe as Quantum Information*, Oxford and New York: Oxford University Press, 2010. This quote is from the dust jacket of the book.

3 Johanson, Donald, Blake Edgar, *From Lucy to Language, (updated and expanded)*, New York: Simon & Schuster, 2006.

4 Connections between literature, culture and human evolution are many and diverse—as are the arguments of literary theorists such as Ellen Dissanayake, who focusses upon anthropological exploration of art and culture; EO Wilson who supports the idea that the sciences, the humanities, and the arts should be connected with each other; Brian Boyd, who attempts to cut through high minded jargon to reveal the simple truth that people love stories; and Denis Dutton and Joseph Carroll have made increasingly effective arguments that culture–literature and the other arts–are functionally significant features of human evolution. Tangentially connected, Raymond Williams, Dick Hebdige, and Stuart Hall emphasise the role of literature in everyday life.

5 Keen, Andrew, "Twitter at the heart of new real-time web innovation", *Telegraph*, 14 July 2009, http://twitter.com/crunchup.

6 Gestalt psychology suggests that people do not perceive the world as it is, "rather they interpret what they see in terms of their own filters (that is, they impose order and meaning on what they perceive). Meanings (significations) are different, according to each person's individual cultural and personal experiences. While the visual system is often compared to a camera, the analogy is inaccurate because a brain does more than look at pictures. It interprets them, tries to make sense of them, and considers cause and effect." http://iit.ches.ua.edu/systems/gestalt.html.

7 Trippi, Joe, *The Revolution Will Not Be Televised: Democracy, the Internet, and the Overthrow of Everything*, New York: Harper Collins, 2004, p. 84. See also: Jenkins, Henry, *Convergence Culture: Where Old and New Media Collide*, New York: New York University Press, 2006.

8 Symbol recognition is allied with the field of semiotics. From the myriad sources on semiotics, the following may be of particular interest to design students: Eco, Umberto, *A Theory of Semiotics*, Bloomington: Indiana University Press, 1976. Kim, Kyong Liong, *Caged in Our Own Signs: A Book about Semiotics*, Westport CT: Praeger/Greenwood, 1996. Noble, Ian and Russell Bestley, *Visual Research: An Introduction To Research Methodologies In Graphic Design*, Lausanne: AVA Books, 2005.

9 The home page of the Ministère de la Culture provides a detailed account: http://web.culture.fr/culture/. *Caves of Forgotten Dreams*, a quite spectacular documentary on Chauvet by Werner Herzog was released in 2010, http://www.culture.gouv.fr/culture/arcnat/chauvet/en/index.html. See also the web site of EuroPreArt, funded by the European Union, Education and Culture 2000 Programme. http://www.europreart.net/, "EuroPreArt aims to establish a lasting database of European prehistoric art documentation, to launch the base of an European institutional network devoted to this domain, and to contribute to the awareness of the diversity and richness of European Prehistoric Art, as one of the oldest artistic expression of Humankind." Not the easiest site to navigate but contains an amazing amount of well documented information and thousands of images. See also: Thurman, Judith, "First Impressions", *The New Yorker*, 23 June 2008, http://www.newyorker.com reporting/2008/06/23/080623fa_fact_thurman.

10 Gould, Stephen Jay, "Up against a wall", *Natural History*, July 1996, 105 (7), p. 16.

11 In 2006, *No. 5*, painted by Jackson Pollock in 1948 sold for US $140 million. *Woman III* by Willem de Kooning painted in 1953 sold for US $137.5 million. Also in 2006, the portrait of Adele Bloch-Bauer painted by Gustav Klimt in 1907 was sold at auction for US $135 million.

12 The emergence of cave inscriptions in Europe about 30,000 years ago is widely believed to be evidence that by this time human beings had developed sophisticated capacities for symbolisation. More recent research has

cast doubt upon this hypothesis. It may well be that the brains of our ancestors were wired differently to ours, that their pattern of neuron connections were suited to their environment, not ours. See: Humphrey, Nicholas, "Cave Art, Autism, and the Evolution of the Human Mind", *Cambridge Archaeological Journal*, 8:2, 1998, pp. 165–91.

13 Sternberg, Robert J, *Handbook of Creativity*, Cambridge: Cambridge University Press, 1999, p. 166.

14 The concept is mentioned in an interview with Umberto Eco that appeared in *Spiegel* online International, 11 November 2009. Beyer Susanne Lothar Gorris, "We Like Lists Because We Don't Want to Die." http://www.spiegel.de/international/zeitgeist/0,1518,659577,00.html.

15 For an extensive, accessible study on the synaptic architecture of the cerebral cortex see: Bruer, John T, "Neural Connections: Some you use, some you loose." www.oecd.org/dataoecd/39/25/31709587.

16 Arnheim, Rudolf, *Art and Visual Perception: a Psychology of the Creative Eye*, Berkeley and London: University of California Press, 1954, 2004.

17 Wood, Julia T, *Interpersonal Communication: Everyday Encounters*, Boston MA: Wadsworth, 2007, 2010, p. 95.

18 A contemporary example of a mnemonic device; "Neighbors actually persuaded lovely Yvonne to shut her window." Explanation: Names of the Royal Families of England (chronologically): Norman, Angevin, Plantegenet, Lancaster, York, Tudor, Stuart, Hanover, Windsor. http://www.mnemonic-device.eu/history/.

19 Nabokov, Peter, "Native History Reflected Through Things", in Trigger, Bruce G, Wilcomb E Washbum, *The Cambridge History of Native Peoples of the Americas*, vol. 1, Cambridge and New York: Cambridge University Press, 1996, pp. 38–42. For a contemporary account of mnemonics in design, see: Lidwell, William, Kritina Holden, Jill Butler, "Mnemonic Device", in *Universal Principles of Design*, Gloucester, MA: Rockport Publications, 2003, pp. 134–136.

20 Clay Tokens: The Precursors of Cuneiform, http://www.ancientscripts.com/cuneiform.html. About Cuneiform Writing: http://www.upenn.edu/museum/Games/cuneiform.html. The Cuneiform Digital Library Initiative. http://cdli.ucla.edu/ Knowledge and Power: Cuneiform script and the Sumerian and Akkadian languages, from the British Museum site: http://www.britishmuseum.org/explore/highlights/highlight_objects/me/t/tablet_recording_the_allocatio.aspx.

21 *2001: A Space Odyssey*, 1968, is remembered as a landmark, science fiction film. It was based on "The Sentinel", written in 1948 by Sir Arthur Charles Clarke. It was decided to rework the short story into a full length novel to precede the films release. Due to production delays and difficulties the film appeared before the novel on which it was based. In 1972 Clarke published *The Lost Worlds of 2001*, which details the production problems of the film and provides alternate versions of key scenes. Clarke, Arthur C, *The Lost Worlds of 2001*, London: Sidgwick and Jackson, 1972.

22 (Mitchell, Stephen, trans.) *Gilgamesh: A New English Version*, New York: Free Press, 2004, pp. 168–9.

23 For a wide-ranging selection of early writing (including the tablet from Mesopotamia) go the British museum site and enter writing in the Compass search box. http://www.thebritishmuseum.ac.uk/sitemap/sitemap.html

24 See, Robinson, Andrew, "Visible and Invisible Speech", *The Story of Writing*, London: Thames & Hudson, 1995, p. 37.

25 The Dark Ages, refers to a period in European

history that dates, from around AD476 to 1000, from the fall of the Roman Empire through the reign of Charlemagne and his successors to the first glimmer of a new age in the new millennium. Liddel, Peter, Josephine Crawley Quinn, Peter Heather, *The History of Europe: From the Dark Ages to the Renaissance: 700-1599AD*, London: Mitchell Beazley, 2006. Rubenstein, Richard E, *Aristotle's Children: How Christians, Muslims, and Jews Rediscovered Ancient Wisdom and Illuminated the Dark Ages*, Orlando: Harcourt, 2003. Asimov, Isaac, *The Dark Ages*, Boston: Houghton Mifflin, 1968.

26 For a knowledgeable and erudite assessment with connections to our current condition see: McIntyre, Lee C, *Dark Ages: The Case for a Science of Human Behavior*, Cambridge, MA: The MIT Press, 2006.

27 Harrison, Robert, *The Song of Roland*, London and New York: Penguin Putnam, 1970, 2002, p. 32.

28 Rouse, RH "Manuscript Production", in Mantello, Frank Anthony Cari, ed., *Medieval Latin: An Introduction and Bibliographic Guide*, Washington DC: The Catholic University of America Press, 1999, 2002, p. 465.

29 *The Winchester Bible*, produced between 1160 and 1175 is the largest surviving 12th-century English bible. It required the hides of 250 calves to produce the calf-skin parchment. Donovan, Claire, *The Winchester Bible*, Toronto and Buffalo: University of Toronto Press, 1993.

30 Even Charlemagne (742–814) was illiterate. He came to the throne of the Frankish kingdom in 771 and during his reign the transition from classical to early medieval civilisation was completed. Recognising the value of education he promoted a system of education for the young, insisting on a 'humane' curriculum that developed logic and science. Most noteworthy from a design view point was the establishment of Carolingian or Caroline minuscule, a script developed as a writing standard in Europe. It remained in general use until around 1200. Shlain, Leonard, *The Alphabet Versus the Goddess: The Conflict Between Word and Image*, London and New York: Penguin, 1998, p. 277. Cunningham, Lawrence S, John J Reich, "Learning in the Time of Charlemagne", in *Culture and Values: A Survey of the Humanities*, Belmont CA: Wadsworth Publishing, 2005, pp. 199–200.

31 The Buddha (Siddhartha Gautama) was a spiritual teacher in the north eastern region of the Indian sub-continent. The exact dates of his life are uncertain, the consensus among historians is that he lived c.563 BCE to 483 BCE. He did not write down a single word of his teachings, nor did any of his contemporaries leave a record of any of his thoughts. His teachings were handed down from one generation to the next by word of mouth and were not put in writing until about three centuries after his death. Monks would hence begin their discourses with the words "Thus have I heard."

32 It is claimed that the worlds oldest existing record of printing were produced during the Nara period in Japan, during the two reigns of the daughter of the Emperor Shomu. Her first reign was from 749 to 758 as the Empress Koken, then as the Empress Shotoku from 764 to 770. It was during this second reign that she ordered one million copies of a charm against smallpox be "printed". They were printed on washi, handmade Japanese paper, using Chinese wood blocks. Each sutra was situated in a small wooden three stored pagoda around 12 cm high and placed in various temples. It is unknown how many were actually produced although numerous copies have been found. Many of these charms were bilingual, being printed using both Chinese calligraphy and Sanskrit–an impressive early example of cross-cultural communication.

33 The *Vajracchedika-prjnaparamita Sutra* ("the

Diamond Sutra") is the first known printed book that is actually dated. It is a Chinese translation of a Sanskrit treatise from India on Buddhist philosophy. (And you thought that muti-culturalism was a twenty-first century phenomena.) It is thought to have been translated early in the fifth century prior to its printing in 868 AD. The translator, Kumarajiva, was of Indian and Turkish ancestry and lived in Kucha, an ancient state in eastern Turkestan. He travelled extensively in India, and later moved to China, and headed the institute of foreign languages in Xian early in the fifth century. Printing, which can arguably, be regarded as the most significant component in the development of Western civilisation was entirely non-Western in its origin. *The Diamond Sutra: The Perfection of Wisdom; Text and Commentaries Translated from Sanskrit and Chinese*, New York: Counterpoint, 2001. The Diamond Sutra is in the British Library, London and can be viewed on line. http://www.bl.uk/onlinegallery/themes/landmarks/diamondsutra.html

34 Tsien, Tsuen-Hsuin, "part one, vol.5", in Joseph Needham, *Science and Civilisation in China: Paper and Printing*, Cambridge: Cambridge University Press, 1985, pp. 201–202.

35 Christensen, Thomas, "Gutenberg and the Koreans. Did East Asian Printing Traditions Influence the European Renaissance?" http://www.rightreading.com/printing/gutenberg.asia/gutenberg-asia-2-societal-issues.html.

36 The Jikji Simche Yogol can be viewed at La Bibliotheque Nationale in Paris.

37 Most recent research is questioning this long held assumption. It is suggested that initially, Gutenberg may not have made use of re-usable moulds but may have used a much cruder system, not unlike that used by the Royal Korean Foundry, of casting the types in sand or other medium. This remains an area for more research.

38 Lester, Paul Martin, *Visual Communication: Images with Messages*, Belmont CA: Thomson Wadsworth, 2006, pp.121–129.

39 Füssel, Stephen, *Gutenberg and the Impact of Printing*, Aldershot: Ashgate Publishing, 2003, pp. 12–13.

40 For an extensive illustrated history of type which includes unlimited access to online image library with over 1000 high-resolution scans of type specimens, see: de Jong, Cees W, ed., *A visual history of fonts and graphic styles, volume 1: 1628–1900*, Köln: Taschen, 2009.

41 On the history of scripts, see http://medievalwriting.50megs.com/scripts/history1.html. From the British Library, their catalogue of illuminated manuscripts, http://www.bl.uk/catalogues/illuminatedmanuscripts/GlossA.asp. From the online research resource of the Pierpont Morgan Library. "Thousands of digital images from the Library's renowned collection of medieval and Renaissance manuscripts are now available in CORSAIR." http://corsair.morganlibrary.org/ICAIntro/ICAintroshortdesc.html.

42 For a detailed history of typefaces: Dodd, Robin, *From Gutenberg to OpenType: An Illustrated History of Type from the Earliest Letterforms to the Latest Digital Fonts*, Hartley and Marks Publisher, 2006.

43 The development of the technology of printing and the allied commercial publishing infrastructure is a complex mix of vying influences–the church, the world of business and the prevailing cultural context all exerted influence on the development of printing. For a well researched and informative exploration of the first 150 years of printing in Europe see: Pettegree, Andrew, *The Book in the Renaissance*, New Haven, CT and London: Yale University Press, 2010. Read the 450 page hard copy, the Kindle version emphasises the essential nature of 'print' by its exclusion of all the highly informative illustrations.

44 There are several versions of this phrase, the first time a form of the phrase appears in print is in James Kirke Paulding's *New Mirror for Travellers*, 1828, which contains the phrase, "A look, which said as plainly as a thousand words." Nearly a century later a faux-Chinese proverb was said to be the source in an article by Fred R Barnard in the advertising trade journal *Printers' Ink*, documenting the use of images in advertisements that appeared on the sides of streetcars. The December 8, 1921 issue carries an advertisement entitled, "One Look is Worth A Thousand Words."

45 From the vast array of material on photography and the associated changes photographic images have made in our way of looking at the world, see: Sontag, Susan, *On Photography*, New York, Picador, 1973, 2001. Savedoff, Barbara E, *Transforming Images: How Photography Complicates the Picture*, Ithaca, NY: Cornell University Press, 2000.

46 As quoted in, Briggs, Asa, Peter Burke, *A Social History of the Media: From Gutenberg to the Internet*, Cambridge, Polity, 2005, p. 133.

47 Gernsheim, Helmut, Alison Gernsheim, *History of Photography from the Camera Obscura to the Beginning Modern Era*, New York, McGraw Hill, 1955, 1969.

48 http://www.bbc.co.uk/history/historic_figures/talbot_william_henry_fox.html.

49 Barthes, Roland, Richard Howard, *Camera Lucida: Reflections on Photography*, New York: Hill and Wang, 1982. (Originally published in French as *La Chambre Claire*, Editions du Seuil, 1980.)

50 Taken at Lacock Abbey in Wiltshire, the Talbot family home. By the side of it Talbot has written "Latticed window (with the Camera Obscura) August 1835". Fox Talbot invented the first negative/positive process–any number of prints could be made from the same shot by transferring the negative image on to special paper to make a positive print.

51 On the Muybridge Collection see: http://www.kingston.gov.uk/browse/leisure/museum/museum_exhibitions/muybridge.html. Exhibition catalogue, Tate Publishing, 2010. Muybridges experimented with what he termed a "zoopraxiscope", a pioneering device for projecting motion pictures which pre-dated the film strip. It was this which inspired the fight scenes in the film *The Matrix*.

52 http://www.universalleonardo.org/trail.php?trail=541.

53 Braun, Marta, *Picturing Time: The Work of Etienne-Jules Marey (1830–1904)*, Chicago: University of Chicago Press, 1992, p. 147. This is the definitive source–this elegant and informative work provides an extensive written and visual survey, including a comprehensive bibliography of the works of Marey. There is an enlightening section on "Marey, Muybridge, and Motion Pictures". See also: http://www.ctie.monash.edu.au/hargrave/marey.html.

54 Chanan, Michael, *The Dream that Kicks: the Prehistory an Early Years of Cinema in Britain*, London: Routledge and Kegan Paul, 1980, 1996, p. 101.

55 For a selection of manipulated photographs see: "Photo Tampering Throughout History." http://www.cs.dartmouth.edu/farid/research/digitaltampering.html.

56 Plagens, Peter, "Is Photography Dead?", *Newsweek*, 1 December 2007, http://www.newsweek.com/id/73349.

57 Stephens, Mitchell, *The Rise of the Image the Fall of the Word*, Oxford and New York: Oxford University Press, 1998, p.xl. See also: Benson, Richard, *The Printed Picture*, New York: The Museum of Modern Art, 2008. The Printed Picture traces the changing technology of picture-making and offers surveys of printing techniques before the invention of photography; the photographic processes that began to appear in the early nineteenth century; the marriage

of printing and photography; and the rapidly evolving digital inventions of our time.

58 There are extensive resources that focus on the history of film. One recommended overview being: Thompson, Kristin, David Bordwell, *Film History: An Introduction*, eighth edition, New York: McGraw-Hill, 1979, 2006.

59 To see the clip: http://www.dailymotion.com/video/x1c0o_arrivalofatrain. To see ten digitised films that composed the first screening, http://www.institut-lumiere.org/english/frames.html.

60 On Japanese film see: Davis, Darrell William, *Picturing Japaneseness: Monumental Style, National Identity, Japanese Film*, New York: Columbia University Press, 1996. p. 9.

61 Chapman, James, *Past and Present: National Identity and the British Historical Film*, London: B Tauris, 2005.

62 Harris, Sue, Elizabeth Ezra, *France in Focus: Film and National Identity*, Oxford: Berg, 2000.

63 The title is a reference to Charles de Gaulle's famous declaration: "Toute ma vie, je me suis fait une certaine idée de la France." ("All my life, I have had a certain vision of France") Mémoires de Guerre, 1:1.

64 From an address at Philadelphia, 27 June 1936 by Franklin D Roosevelt. Roosevelt, Franklin D, J B S Hardman, *Rendezvous With Destiny: Addresses and Opinions of Franklin Delano Roosevelt*, Whitefish, MT: Kessinger Publishing, 2005.

65 Quart, Leonard, Albert Auster, *American Film and Society Since 1945*, Westport, Conn: Praeger/Greenwood, 2002.

66 Strasburger, Victor C, "Children, adolescent and the media: five crucial issues", (letter), *Archives of Pediatrics & Adolescent Medicine*, 153: 313, 1998. Strasburger Victor C, Barbara J Wilson, Amy B Jordan, *Children, Adolescents, and the Media*, Thousands Oaks, CA, and London: Sage, 2009.

67 Herbert, Stephen, *A History of Early TV*, London and New York: Routledge/Taylor & Francis, 2004, p. 4.

68 W1XAV Boston broadcast a portion of a CBS radio programme, *The Fox Trappers Orchestra Program*, sponsored by I J Fox Furriers, 7 December 1930. Included was what is sometimes called the first television commercial, although "commercials" were prohibited by FRC regulations. The first legitimate television commercial was a ten second spot for Bulova watches and was aired at 14:29:10 on 1 July 1941 just before a baseball game between the Brooklyn Dodgers and the Philadelphia Phillies at a cost of less than ten dollars. A thirty second, in game spot, during the 2010 super bowl cost about three million dollars.

69 http://www.zenith.com/sub_about/about_remote.html.

70 One challenge to the 515 commercial stations was to attract a daytime audience, see: Cassidy, Marsha Francis, *What Women Watched. Daytime television in the 1950s*, Austin: University of Texas Press, 2005.

71 A report from 1949, Lewis, "TV and Teen-Agers", in *Educational Screen*, reported an average weekly viewing of 23.5 hours. Luke, Carmen, *Constructing the Child Viewer*, New York: Praeger, 1990, p. 64.

72 McLuhan, Marshall, Quentin Fiore, *The Medium Is the Message: An Inventory of Effects*, Corte Madera, CA: Gingko Press, 1967, 2005. For a personalised account of McLuhan and the Centre for Culture and Technology at the University of Toronto, see: Rodgers, Bob, "In the Garden with the Guru. Adventures with Marshall McLuhan", *Literary Review of Canada*, January/February 2008, http://lrc.reviewcanada.ca/index.php?page=in-the-garden-with-the-guru.

73 According to McLuhan's son, the original title as published was the result of a typo. The proof from the printer had misprinted the "e" in message and it appeared as an "a". McLuhan is said to have thought the mistake to be supportive of the point he was trying to make in the book and decided to leave it alone. Mess-age becomes Mass-age. Unfortunately some later reprints "corrected" the error.

74 Allen, Robert Clyde, *To be Continued: Soap Operas Around the World*, London and New York: Routledge, 1995.

75 Soaps and sitcoms like *The Honeymooners*, *Lassie*, *Father Knows Best*, *The Adventures of Ozzie and Harriet*, and *I Love Lucy* featured popular characters whose lives tens of thousands of viewers watched and whose lifestyle they tried to copy.

76 Spring, Joel H, *Images of American Life: A History of Ideological Management in Schools, Movies, Radio, and Television*, Albany, NY: State University of New York, 1992, p. 160.

77 *The Clearing House, A Journal for Modern Junior and Senior High Schools*, September 1949, p. 474.

78 As quoted in Cassidy, Marsha Francis, *What Women Watched. Daytime television in the 1950s*, Austin: University of Texas Press, 2005, p. 2.

79 Exact figures are difficult to ascertain. Liebes, Tamar, James Curran, Elihu Katz, *Media, Ritual, and Identity*, London and New York: Routledge, 1998. Liebes et al report that "at present (1998) a little over one third of American homes have personal computers", p. 172. By April, 2009, it was reported that 63 per cent of adult Americans have broadband connections at home, http://www.peWinternet.org/Reports/2009/10-Home-Broadband-Adoption-2009.aspx.

80 When asked why the military decided to embed journalists with the troops in Iraq, Lt Col Rick Long of the US Marine Corps replied, "Frankly, our job is to win the war. Part of that is information warfare. So we are going to attempt to dominate the information environment." As quoted in, Kahn, Jeffery, "Postmortem: Iraq war media coverage dazzled but it also obscured", *UC Berkeley News*, 18 March 2004, http://www.berkeley.edu/news/media/releases/2004/03/18_iraqmedia.shtml.

81 As quoted in, Lester, Paul Martin, *Visual Communication: Images with Messages*, Belmont CA: Wadsworth Publishing, 2005, p. 321.

82 Bryn, Steinar, "The Coca-Cola co and the Olympic Movement - From American to Global", in Ramet, Sabrina P, Gordana Crnkovic, ed., *Kazaaam! Splat! Ploof! The American Impact on European Popular Culture, since 1945*, Oxford: Rowman & Littlefield, 2003, pp. 83–101.

83 Pendergrast, Mark, *For God, Country and Coca-Cola: The Unauthorized History of the Great American Soft Drink and the Company that Makes it*, New York: Simon & Schuster, 1998.

84 The commercial, as one of the most popular of all time, is credited with helping Coca-Cola regain its status as the preeminent soft drink in North America. http://www.thecoca-colacompany.com/heritage/pdf/cokelore/Heritage_CokeLore_HillTop.pdf. http://memory.loc.gov/ammem/ccmphtml/colaadv.html. A three part documentary series was launched in 1998, by DLI productions of Montreal, *The Cola Conquest*, http://www.dliproductions.ca/thecolaconquest/.

85 This argument is fully explored in the classic introduction to media, communication, and cultural studies: Lull, James, *Media, Communication, Culture: A Global Approach*, New York: Columbia University Press, 2000. See also the much more succinct assessment by Charles van Doren: "Mass Media and Education", *A History of Knowledge. Past, Present and Future*, New York: Ballantine Books, 1991, pp. 370–374.

86 The estimated world population in 1500 was about 400 million with approximately 100 million being in Europe. The current human population is estimated at 6.7 billion.

87 Paolo Cherchi-Usai is Adjunct Professor and Senior Curator of the Motion Picture Department, George Eastman House/International Museum of Photography and Film, Rochester, New York.

88 Cubitt, Sean, "Media, History of", Horowitz, Maryanne Cline, ed., *New Dictionary of the History of Ideas*, New York: Charles Scribner's Sons/Thomson Gale, 2004, p. 1395. The list price is $775. You can access the entry on line: http://science.jrank.org/pages/10130/Media-History-Current-Studies-in-Media-History.html.

89 Rushdie, Salman, *Haroun and the Sea of Stories*, New York: Penguin, 1990, p. 71–72.

90 For a biographic note on Sir Timothy Berners-Lee, http://www.w3.org/People/Berners-Lee/Longer.html. For his very personal website see (along with his caution about Microsoft Office) http://www.w3.org/People/Berners-Lee/ "Web in infancy, says Berners-Lee," BBC News, Wednesday, 30 April 2008. http://news.bbc.co.uk/2/hi/technology/7371660.stm.

91 Gillies, James, Robert Cailliau, *How the Web Was Born: The Story of the World Wide Web*, Oxford, Oxford University Press, 2000.

92 http://www.internetworldstats.com/stats.html.

93 Danet, Brenda, Susan C Herring, *The Multilingual Internet: Language, Culture, and Communication Online*, Oxford: Oxford University Press, 2007. This collection of 18 articles examines computer mediated information in non English speaking contexts.

94 Bruinsma, Max, "An Ideal Design is Not Yet", ten Duis, Leonie, Annelies Haase, ed., *The World Must Change*, Amsterdam: The Sandberg Instituut, 1999, p. 301.

95 Vedral, Vlatko, *Decoding Reality. The Universe as Quantum Information*, Oxford and New York: Oxford University Press, p. 3.

96 Vedral, Vlatko, *Decoding Reality. The Universe as Quantum Information*, p. 186.

97 http://discovermagazine.com/2007/jun/how-much-does-the-internet-weigh.

98 http://www.netlingo.com/emailsh.cfm.

99 Warman, Matt, "2020 vision: where will we be in a decade's time?", *Telegraph*, United Kingdom, 2 January, 2010, http://www.telegraph.co.uk/lifestyle/.

100 As reported on The Korn/Ferry Institute's Briefings on Talent & Leadership website, http://www.kornferrybriefings.com/extras/the_decade_ahead.php.

101 *Information Economy Report, 2010. ICTs, Enterprises and Poverty Alleviation*, New York and Geneva, United Nations, 2010, http://www.unctad.org/en/docs/ier2010overview_embargo2010_en.pdf.

102 Clifford, Stephanie, "New Yorker Cover Art, Painted With an iPhone", *The New York Times*, Media & Advertising, 25 May 2009, B4. http://brushesapp.com/

103 A comment attribute to Kyle Menchhofer, a district technology coordinator in St Mary's City Schools, Ohio, as reported by *Associated Press* in July, 2009, http://www.limaohio.com/news/schools-39731-add-slowly.html.

104 See, Baggott, Kate, "Literacy and Text Messaging. How will the next generation read and write?", *Technology Review*, Thursday 21 December 2006, http://www.technologyreview.com/Biztech/17927/?a=f. For "A Guide to Understanding Online Chat Acronyms & Smiley Faces", http://www.webopedia.com/quick_ref/textmessageabbreviations.asp. The NetLingo List of Acronyms & Text Message Shorthand, http://www.netlingo.com/acronyms.php.

105 Ito, Mizuko, *Personal, Portable, Pedestrian: Mobile Phones in Japanese Life*, Cambridge, MA: The MIT Press, 2005, http://www.itofisher.com/mito/archives/ito.ppp.pdf.

106 http://en.wikipedia.org/wiki/Cell_phone_novel.

107 Katayama, Lisa, "Big Books Hit Japan's Tiny Phones," Wired, 01.01.07.

108 http://twitteruse.net/.

109 The following reports are available from Nielsen online. In US, SMS Text Messaging Tops Mobile Phone Calling, *Critical Mass: The Worldwide State of the Mobile Web*, www.nielsenmobile.com/documents/CriticalMass.

110 Eco, Umberto, "The Lost Art of Handwriting", *The Guardian*, 21 September 2009, http://www.guardian.co.uk/books/2009/sep/21/umberto-eco-handwriting.

111 http://blog.twitter.com/.

112 Lenhart, Amanda, Rich Long, Scott Campbell, Kristen Purcell, "Teens and Mobile Phones", *Pew Internet & American Life Project*, 20 April 2010, http://www.peWinternet.org/.

113 Postman, Joel, *SocialCorp. Social Media Goes Corporate*, Berkeley, CA: Peachpit Press, 2009. *17 Ways You Can Use Twitter: A Guide for Beginners, Marketers and Business Owners*, http://www.doshdosh.com/ways-you-can-use-twitter/.

114 Tagg, Caroline 'wot did he say or could u not c him 4 dust? Written and Spoken Creativity in Text Messaging' in Ho, et al, eds, *Transforming Literacies and Language: Innovative Technologies, Integrated Experiences*, London and New York: Routledge, 2010, (Forthcoming).

115 Hall, Edward, T, *The Silent Language*, Westport, CT: Greenwood Press Reprint, 1959, 1980.

116 Guynn, Jessica, "Silicon Valley meetings go 'topless'", *Los Angeles Times*, 31 March 2008, as reported in, Bauerlein, Mark, "Why Gen-Y Johnny Can't Read Nonverbal Cues. An emphasis on social networking puts younger people at a face-to-face disadvantage", *The Wall Street Journal*, online journal, Friday August 28, 2009.

117 Cowen, Tyler, "Three Tweets for the Web", *The Wilson Quarterly*, Autumn, 2009.

118 Pinker, Steven, "Mind Over Mass Media", *The New York Times*, 10 June 2010.

119 This area of commercial activity is vast, growing and often overlooked in any critical assessment of current television. For details of current placements see "Product Placement News, Branded Entertainment Advances, News & Deals Updates", http://www.productplacement.biz/. For product placement 'help' for brand owners, see: http://www.brand-exposure.co.uk/. In April 2006, Broadcasting & Cable reported, "Two thirds of advertisers employ 'branded entertainment'—product placement—with the vast majority of that (80 per cent) in commercial TV programming", http://www.sourcewatch.org/index.php?title=Product_placement.

120 See, Peters, John Durham, "Introduction: The Problems of Communication", *Speaking Into the Air*, Chicago: University of Chicago Press, 2001. pp. 1–10. Peters explores communication as both historically specific and as an integral part of Western thought.

121 Saxe, Rebecca, Simon Baron-Cohen, *Theory of Mind: A Special Issue of Social Neuroscience*, Hove and Philadelphia: Psychology Press/Taylor & Francis, 2007.

122 Leith, Sam, "Grand Theft Auto, Twitter and Beowulf all demonstrate that stories will never die", Telegraph.co.uk, 24 November 2008.

123 Carlson, David, ed., "A Check List for Sustainability", *David Report*, Issue 11, July 2009. "The David Report bulletin covers the intersection of design, culture and business life with a creative and humanistic approach", http://www.davidreport.com/File/update/360/.

124 *Design Principles & Practices, Common Ground,*

http://designprinciplesandpractices.com/ideas/scope-concerns/.

125 Carroll, Lewis, *Alice's Adventures in Wonderland*, San Francisco: Chronicle Books, 1865, 2002, p. 1. *Alice's Adventures in Wonderland* tells the story of Alice and her passage into a world of fantasy populated by anthropomorphic creatures. *Through the Looking-Glass, and What Alice Found There*, 1871, is the sequel and presents a form of mirror image of Wonderland. This time Alice ponders what the world is like on the other side of a mirror, and to her surprise, is able to pass through to experience the alternate world of opposites where time runs backwards for example. The story unfolds as a game of chess and reaches an appropriate finale. "When Dodgson was in London, he met a little girl, Alice Raikes. He invited her indoors, put an orange in her right hand and asked her in which hand she was holding it. Then, he put her in front of a mirror, and asked which hand the child in the mirror was holding the orange in. Alice told him that it was in her left hand. When he asked her for an explanation, she answered: "Supposing I was on the other side of the glass, wouldn't the orange still be in my right hand?" He was delighted with her answer and decided that his new book would be about the world on the other side of the looking glass." (source: Graham, E., *Lewis Carroll and the writing of Through the Looking Glass*, as an introduction in a Penguin edition of the stories.) See, "About Through the Looking Glass and What Alice found there", http://www.alice-in-wonderland.net/alice1b.html. The most authoritative assessment of the Alice stories is; Lewis, Martin Gardner, ed., John Tenniel, illustrator, *The Annotated Alice: The Definitive Edition*, New York, W W Norton & Company, 1999. The Annotated Alice, provides a gloss which sheds light on some of the jokes contained in the text and provides details of Victorian manners and mores. Gardner decodes the wordplay and the many mathematical riddles that lie embedded in Carroll's two classic stories. Currently, there are over 166 editions of Alice in print plus numerous videos and DVD's.

126 "If a text begins with "Once upon a time," it sends out a signal that immediately enables it to select its own model reader , who must be... somebody willing to accept something that goes beyond the commonsensical and reasonable." Eco, Umberto, "Entering the Woods", in *Six Walks in the Fictional Woods*, Cambridge, MA and London: Harvard University Press, 1994, 2004, p. 9.

127 One of the four major experiments currently under study by physicists working at the Large Hadron Collider has the acronym, ALICE (A Large Ion Collider Experiment). ALICE is 26m (85ft) long, 16m (52ft) high, 16m (52ft) wide and weighs 10,000 tonnes. http://aliceinfo.cern.ch/Collaboration/index.html. In November 2010, CERN reported the first time capture of antimatter, the stuff of "Star Trek". They are suggesting that proof of extra dimensions may be possible in 2011. Currently, there is no forecast as to when we may be able to pass through the looking glass. Check their web site: http://public.web.cern.ch/public/en/lhc/lhc-en.html.

CHAPTER FOUR

1 Levi, Peter, *Edward Lear*, London: Macmillan, 1995.

2 Briggs, Asa, *The Age of Improvement, 1783-1867*, Harlow: Longman, 1959, 1999.

3 Hutchison, Elizabeth D, ed., *Dimensions of Human Behavior: Person and Environment*, Thousand Oaks, CA, and London: Sage, 2008.

4 The mathematician Roger Penrose popularised this form in the 1950s, describing it as "impossibility in its purest form". The Penrose triangle plays a major role in the drawings and works of MC Escher. Penrose,

LS, and Penrose, R, "Impossible Objects: A Special Type of Illusion", *British Journal of Psychology*, 49: 31, 1958. Much has been written on the Penrose triangle and other "impossible" forms. See: Penrose, Lionel & Roger Penrose, "Impossible Objects: A special type of visual illusion", *British Journal of Psychology*, 1958, vol. 49, pp. 31–33. Goldstein, E Bruce, "Pictorial Perception and Art", in Goldstein et al, *Blackwell Handbook of Perception*, Malden MA: Blackwell, 2001, pp. 344–379. For a revelation see "an Animation of the Penrose Triangle", by Michael Hermann, http://www.stats.uwaterloo.ca/~cgsmall/penrose.html.

5 Wallas, Graham, *The Art of Thought*, London: Jonathan Cape, 1926.

6 Plsek, Paul E ,"Working Paper: Models for the Creative Process", http://www.directedcreativity.com/pages/WPModels.html.

7 Carter, Rita, *The Brain Book*, London: Dorling Kindersley, 2009. See the section on creativity which indicates that when the brain 'relaxes' into an 'idling' mode (indicated by slow alpha waves) unusual connections are more likely to occur between thoughts, memories and existing knowledge.

8 Campbell, Donalad, T, "Blind variation and selective retention in creative thought as in other knowledge processes", *Psychological Review*, vol. 67, 1960, pp. 380–400.

9 Sawyer, Keith, *Group Genius: The Creative Power of Collaboration*, New York: Basic Books, 2008.

10 Weisberg, Robert, *Creativity: Beyond the Myth of Genius*, New York: WH Freeman, 1993. *Creativity. Understanding Innovation in Problem Solving, Science, Invention, and the Arts*, Hoboken, NJ: John Wiley, 2006.

11 For a brief but revealing discussion on creativity which considers "how conscious and unconscious brain activity can give rise to new ideas", revealing a second nature, see: Edelman, Gerald M , "Creativity", *Second Nature. Brain Science and Human Knowledge*, New Haven and London: Yale University Press, 2006, pp. 98–105.

12 Koberg, Don, Bagnall, Jim, *The Universal Traveller: A Soft-Systems Guide to Creativity, Problem-Solving, and the Process of reaching goals*, Menlo Park, CA: Thomson Crisp Learning, 1972, 2003. The original version was written over 30 years ago—this remains the most practical, understandable and explanatory account of the creative process and the allied process of conscious problem solving. In 2005 the British government instructed Sir George Cox to review the state of creativity in British business. To see the 75 page "Creativity, Design and Business Performance", http://www.berr.gov.uk/files/file13654.pdf.
To see the Cox Review of Creativity in Business: building on the UK's strengths, http://www.hm-treasury.gov.uk/independent_reviews/cox_review/coxreview_index.cfm.However, the total omission of any reference to ethics or sustainability in this report indicates the chasm between officialdom and the real world, where these two concerns will be fundamental to design in the twenty-first century.

13 Edelman, Gerald M , "Creativity", *Second Nature. Brain Science and Human Knowledge*, New Haven and London: Yale University Press, 2006, p. 104.

14 *The New Oxford English Dictionary* defines "meme" as "An element of a culture that may be considered to be passed on by non-genetic means, esp. imitation". The term "meme" was coined by Richard Dawkins in *The Selfish Gene*, Oxford: Oxford University Press, 1976. More recently Susan Blackmore has expanded that exploration in her highly original and enthralling, *The Meme Machine*, Oxford: Oxford University Press, 2000. See her home page: http://www.susanblackmore.co.uk/memetics/. The topic remains

one of intense debate, among other sources, see: Paulis, Paul B Bernard Arjan Nijstad, *Group Creativity: Innovation Through Collaboration*, Oxford and New York: Oxford University Press, 2003, p. 193. Shennan, Stephen, Genes, Memes and Human History, London: Thames & Hudson, 2002. Aunge, Robert, *The Electric Meme: A New Theory of How We Think*, New York: The Free Press, 2002. An adventurous account that proposes that memes are in fact self-replicating electrical charges in the nodes of our brains.

15 Edelman, Gerald M , "Creativity", *Second Nature. Brain Science and Human Knowledge*, New Haven and London: Yale University Press, 2006, p. 101.

16 http://www.edwarddebonofoundation.com/lateral.html.

17 http://www.edwdebono.com/debono/lateral.html. http://www.debonogroup.com/lateral_reading.html.

18 De Bono, Edward, *Children Solve Problems*, London: Penguin Books, 1972, 1984, p. 86.

19 George Kneller, Professor of Philosophy at Columbia University, http://www.gseis.ucla.edu/faculty/kellner/.

20 Koberg, Don, Jim Bagnall, *The Universal Traveller: A Soft-Systems Guide to Creativity, Problem-Solving, and the Process of reaching goals*, Menlo Park, CA: Thomson Crisp Learning, 1972, 2003, p. 10.

21 http://psy.rin.ru/eng/article/97-101.html.

22 As quoted in, Galilei, Galileo, Albert van Helden, Sidereus Nuncius, or, *The Sidereal Messenger*, Chicago and London: University of Chicago Press, 1989, p. 11.

23 Llardi, Vincent, *Renaissance Vision from Spectacles to Telescopes, (Memoirs of the American Philosophical Society series)*, Derby, PA: Diane Publishing, 2006, p. 224.

24 Garzoni, Tommaso, *La Piazza Universale di Tutte le Professiori del Mondo*, Venice, 1585.

25 Moll, G, "On the First Invention of Telescopes, collected from the notes and papers of the late Professor Van Swinden", *The Journal of the Royal Institution of Great Britain*, John Murray, vol.1, 1830–31, pp. 319–332, digitised 6 April 2007.

26 Sis, Peter, *Starry Messenger: Galileo Galilei*, New York: Farrar, Straus and Giroux (BYR), 2000.

27 McIntyre, Lee, *Dark Ages. The Case for a Science of Human Behavior*, Cambridge MA: The MIT Press, 2006, p. 75.

28 What is astonishing is the degree to which our knowledge base of the universe has increased since those first auspicious steps of Galileo. In 2008, the Sloan Digital Sky Survey, produced a three-dimensional colour map that covers a quarter of the night sky. This map reveals the position and classification of more than 200 million celestial bodies, including a million galaxies and 100,000 quasars, "The Sloan Digital Sky Survey: Asteroids to Cosmology", http://www.sdss.org/.

29 Scott, Frederick, "Paxton, Sir Joseph 1803–65", Wintle, Justin, ed., *Makers of Nineteenth Century Culture*, vol. 2, London: Routledge, 2002, p. 479.

30 Loewer, Peter H, *The Evening Garden: Flowers and Fragrance from Dusk to Dawn*, Portland: Timber Press, 2002, p. 130.

31 Previously, between 1836 and 1841, Paxton, in cooperation with the architect Decimus Burton, had designed the Great Conservatory at Chatsworth. With a length of 277 ft, a width of 123 ft and a height of 61 ft it was the largest glasshouse in the world at that time. For additional information on this quite extraordinary man and his design for the Crystal Palace, see: Auerbach, Jeffrey A, Peter H Hoffenberg eds, *Britain, the empire, and the world at the Great Exhibition of 1851*, Aldershoot and Burlington, VT: Ashgate, 2008. Auerbach, Jeffrey A, *The Great Exhibition of 1851: A Nation on Display*, New Haven, CT: Yale University Press, 1999. Colquhoun, Kate, "The Busiest Man in England: The Life of Joseph Paxton, Gardener,

Architect & Victorian Visionary", *Victorian Studies*, vol.49, no. 3, Spring 2007, pp. 541–543. Hobhouse, Hermione, *Crystal Palace and the Great Exhibition: Art, Science, and Productive Industry. A History of the Royal Commission for the Exhibition of 1851*, London and New York: Athlone, 2002. "A Grand Design: A History of the Victoria and Albert Museum", http://www.vam.ac.uk/vastatic/microsites/1159_grand_design/essay-industrial_new.html.

32 For a photographic record see : http://lartnouveau.com/belle_epoque/paris_expo_1900.html. http://www.brooklynmuseum.org/opencollection/archives/goodyear_archival_collection.

33 O Brian, Patrick, *Pablo Ruiz Picasso: A Biography*, New York and London: WW Norton, 1976, 1994, p. 124.

34 For an informative account of the nineteenth century fur trade in North America see: Buchholtz, CW, *Man in Glacier, West Glacier*, MT: Glacier National History Association, 1976, 1993.

35 Gósol is located in the park of *Cadí-Moixeró*, in Catalonia. It is home to the small Picasso Museum, which celebrates the visit by Picasso in the Summer of 1906.

36 The nineteenth century arcades of Paris had a most profound (and often overlooked) impact on the twentieth century way of seeing. This aspect of modernity is tantalisingly covered in the "fragmented" work of Walter Benjamin, http://www.wbenjamin.org/passageways.html. "The Arcades project went through many kinds of existence between 1927 and 1939. It never achieved a completed form. What remains are vast quantities of notes, images, quotes and citations; capable of being ordered and reordered in endlessly different constellations, " http://www.othervoices.org/gpeaker/Passagenwerk.php Benjamin called the project, "the theatre of all my struggles and all my ideas". http://www.hup.harvard.edu/catalog/BENARC.html.

37 http://www.moma.org/collection/conservation/demoiselles/index.html. Green, Christopher, ed., *Picasso's 'Les Demoiselles D'Avignon'*, Cambridge: Cambridge University Press, 2001. For the most detailed and intriguing account of this work see: Bohm-Duchen, Monica, "Les Demoiselles d'Avignon", in *The Private Life of a Masterpiece*, Berkeley, CA: University of California Press, 2001, pp. 178–207. For an assessment that focuses on Picasso's early life in Malaga and on his diverse cultural background, see: Staller, Natasha Elena, *A sum of destructions: Picasso's cultures & the creation of Cubism*, New Haven, CT: Yale University Press, 2001.

38 Persistence pays off, sometimes. Formulating the concept is one thing, making it work quite another. Charles Goodyear, the inventor of vulcanised rubber and Chester Carlson, inventor of the Xerox copying process, both worked for over 30 years to find a solution that worked.

39 The first nautical circumnavigation of the Earth begun in 1519. It was an attempt to prove that the coveted Spice Islands, or *Moluccas* (modern day Indonesia) were actually the property of Spain and not Portugal. Ferdinand Magellan (born in northern Portugal around 1480) set out from Spain on this exploratory voyage with five ships, the Victoria, Santiago, S Antonio, Concepeión and Trinadad. The voyage was more difficult than expected. Disease, bad weather, conflict with Portuguese ships, all handicapped the voyage. On 27 April 1521, Magellan was killed in a battle on the Philippine island of Cebu on 27 April 1521. His second in command, the Spanish Basque, Juan Sebastián Elcano, completed the journey to Spain. The 18 survivors of Ferdinand Magellan's expedition, on the sole surviving ship, the Victoria, completed the circumnavigation returning to Seville on 8 September 1522 after a journey of three years and one month. This makes Juan Sebastián Elcano the first navigator to circumnavigate the world.

40 In 1670 the Spanish priest, Pedro Cubero Sebastián undertook extensive travel in East Asia, completing an eastwards round the world trip in 1679. A considerable part of that journey was overland. He wrote the account of his adventures around the world in a very objective, detailed and interesting book, *Peregrinación del mundo* (World's peregrination), was first published in Madrid in 1680.

41 Stephenson, Charles, Ian Palmer, *Zeppelins: German Airships 1900–40*, Oxford: Osprey, 2004.

42 Slack, Charles, *Noble Obsession: Charles Goodyear, Thomas Hancock, and the Race to Unlock the Greatest Industrial Secret of the 19th Century*, New York: Hyperion, 2002. For a comprehensive overview of the history of rubber see: Loadman, John, *Tears of the Tree: The Story of Rubber–A Modern Marvel*, Oxford: Oxford University Press, 2005.

43 Kane, Robert M, "The Dirigible", in *Air Transportation*, Dubuque, IA: Kendall Hunt, 2007, pp. 36–40.

44 http://www.airforcehistory.hq.af.mil/PopTopics/ladies.html.

45 Garland, Ken, *Mr Beck's Underground Map*, London: Capital Transport Publishing, 1994.

46 http://en.wikiquote.org/wiki/Louis_Pasteur.

47 The Einstein estate did earn over $18 million in royalties in 2007. Thanks not to the famed equation but to the instantly recognisable shocked hair image of Einstein that is exploited in a range of products from the Disney owned Baby Einstein toy range to Kobe Bryant's sports shoes. The beneficiary of his estate is Jerusalem's Hebrew University.

48 The Factory was Andy Warhol's original New York City studio from 1963 to 1968, and was located on the fifth floor of 231 East 47th Street, in Midtown Manhattan.

49 David Bollier, Racine, Laurie, "Control of creativity? Fashion's secret", *Christian Science Monitor*, 9 September 2003, http://www.csmonitor.com/2003/0909/p09s01-coop.html. For a 90 page assessment of copyright in the American fashion industry, see: Raustiala, Kal, Christopher Springman, "The Piracy Paradox: Innovation and Intellectual Property in Fashion Design", *Virginia Law Review*, vol. 92, no. 8, December 2006, pp. 1687–1777.

50 For an extension of this argument see: McLeod, Kembrew, Lawrence Lessig, *Freedom of Expression, Resistance and Repression in the Age of Intellectual Property*, Minneapolis, MN: University Of Minnesota Press, 2007. This book's documentary companion DVD is available through Media Education Foundation, http://freedomofexpression.us/dvd.html.

51 Hazlitt, William, *The complete works of Michael de Montaigne: comprising his essays, letters and his journey through Germany and Italy*, Philadelphia: Willaim T Amies, 1879, p. 483. Michel Eyquem de Montaigne, 1533–1592, was one of the most influential writers of the French Renaissance. His most distinguishing literary characteristic being the practised balance of intellectual knowledge and personal story-telling.

52 Wrap the sheet with the dots on it around a cylinder. Draw a continuous line in a spiral around the cylinder, moving in one direction, and you will be able to connect all the dots.

53 Burke, James and Ornstein, Robert, *The Axemakers Gift*, New York: Putnam, 1995, p. 287.

54 Canfora, Luciano, Martin Ryle, *The Vanished Library*, Berkeley: University of California Press, 1990. MacLeod, Roy, ed., *The Library of Alexandria: Centre of Learning in the Ancient World*, London and New York, IB Tauris, 2004.

55 Two million minutes equals 33,333 hours. Allowing for a 40 hour work week this becomes 833 weeks, or 16.02 years. Even if you worked 24 hours a day, every day, it would still take you 3.805 years to search four million books. By comparison a search on Google for "Art Nouveau" produces about 11 million entries in 0.12 seconds.

56 In 2006, the worlds fastest super computer was the BlueGene/L System, a joint development of IBM and DOE's National Nuclear Security Administration (NNSA). http://www.top500.org/.

57 As quoted in, Thackara, John, *In the Bubble. Designing in a Complex World*, Cambridge MA and London: MIT Press, 2005, p. 163. The British Museum has a collection of over 13 million books, 920,000 journal and newspaper titles, 57 million patents, and three million sound recordings–an increasing number of which are available on line. http://www.bl.uk/. The European Union's digital library, Europeana, provides multilingual access in 25 languages to cultural collections across the EU. It has in excess of ten million works available, www.europeana.eu.

58 "How Much Information? 2003", http://www2.sims.berkeley.edu/research/projects/how-much-info-2003/execsum.htm.

59 Jorge Luis Borges was born on the 24 August 1899 in Buenos Aires. The concept of the universal library dates to 1939 and a nine page short story by Jorge Luis Borges, "The Library of Babel" (La biblioteca de Babel) which conceives of a universe in the form of a vast library. It first appeared in the magazine *Sur* and was later included in compilations of Borges's works. See the 1941 collection of stories *El Jardín de senderos que se bifurcan* (The Garden of Forking Paths) which was included within his much-reprinted *Ficciones*, 1944. An English language version of "The Library of Babel" appeared in *Labyrinth*, first published in 1962. Yates, Donald A James E Irby, eds, *Labyrinths*, New York: New Directions, 1962, 2007. Bell-Villada, Gene H, *Borges and His Fiction: A Guide to his Mind and Art*, Austin TX: University of Texas Press, 1999. Sassón-Henry, Perla, *Borges 2.0: From Text to Virtual Worlds*, New York: Peter Lang, 2007.

60 Bloch, William Goldbloom, *The Unimaginable Mathematics of Borge's Library of Babel*, Oxford and New York: Oxford University Press, 2008, p. 4.

61 There is debate regarding the original source of this quotation. It is most often miss attributed to E M Forster as it appears in his *Aspects of the Novel*, 1927. "Another distinguished critic has agreed with Gide–that old lady in the anecdote who was accused by her niece of being illogical. For some time she could not be brought to understand what logic was, and when she grasped its true nature she was not so much angry as contemptuous. 'Logic! Good gracious! What rubbish!' she exclaimed. 'How can I tell what I think till I see what I say?' Her nieces, educated young women, thought that she was passée; she was really more up-to-date than they were." E M Forster, *Aspects of the Novel*, Oliver Stallybrass, ed., Harmondsworth: Penguin, 1976, p. 99. The quotation also appears in Graham Wallas, *The Art of Thought*, 1926, "The little girl had the making of a poet in her who, being told to be sure of her meaning before she spoke, said, 'How can I tell what I think until I see what I say?" However, both may have been indebted to André Paul Guillaume Gide who was a French author and winner of the Nobel Prize in literature in 1947. (The Roman Catholic Church placed his works on the Index of Forbidden Books in 1952.) Unfortunately I have been unable to find the original source from amongst his voluminous productions.

62 In 1680 (more than 200 years after the death of Gutenberg) the famed philosopher and mathematician of the day, Gottfried von Leibniz suggested that

European society would fall back to a sate of barbarism if "that horrible mass of books keeps on growing". As late as 1728 Alexander Pope, considered one of the greatest English poets and regarded as the leading cultural intellectual of the eighteenth century, dismissed many "authors" of the printed word as dunces. All this sounds very reminiscent of some critics of computer mediated information.

63 Baggott, Kate, "Literacy and Text Messaging. How will the next generation read and write?" As reported in the on-line version of *Technology Review*, Thursday 21 December 2006, http://www.technologyreview.com/Biztech/17927/. See also: Bruce, B C, ed., *Literacy in the information age: Inquiries into meaning making with new technologies*, Newark, DE: International Reading Association, 2003.

64 You Know What I Mean http://www.netlingo.com/emailsh.cfm.

65 Castells, Manuel, et al, *Mobile Communication and Society. A Global Perspective*, Cambridge MA and London: The MIT Press, 2007, p. 1.

66 Castells, Manuel, et al, *Mobile Communication and Society. A Global Perspective*, p. 258.

67 http://www.webngos.org/global.php.

CHAPTER FIVE

1 Professor Bruce Archer always taught that the discipline of design was just that, a discipline, with its own requirements for systematic research and methodological rigour. He served as head of the department of design research at the Royal College of Art from 1968–1985, while also serving as a member of the Design Council. He was director of research at the RCA from 1985–1988 and was appointed as CBE in 1976. He died on 16 May 2005, aged 82. For an extensive collection of design related quotes and attributions see: http://www.designfeast.com/thoughts/default.htm.

2 For a case study from the Design Council, UK, see: http://www.designcouncil.org.uk/en/Case-Studies/All-Case-Studies/OXO-Good-Grips/.

3 Manzini, Ezio, *The Material of Invention; Materials and Design*, Cambridge, MA: The MIT Press, 1989. The text focuses upon some of the more remarkable modern materials and composites available to designers. One essential, and sometimes overlooked component of the text being the lack of distinction that Manzini applies to differentiating the 'artificial' with the natural– and essential lesson for the decades ahead.

4 Byers, David A Andrew Ugan, "Should we expect large game specialization in the late Pleistocene? An optimal foraging perspective on early Paleoindian prey choice", *Journal of Archaeological Science*,32, 2005, 1624–1640.

5 For extensive information concerning prehistoric hunting practices in North America: Davis, Leslie B, Brian OK Reeves, *Hunters of the Recent Past*, London and New York: Routledge, 1989. The cave walls at Lascaux contain over 50 images of aurochs, one of which is shown to be 5.5 metres long. These precursors to domestic cattle weighed over 1,270 kg, providing enough meet to feed the extended family for a considerable period of time. Vuure, Cis van, *Retracing the Aurochs: History, Morphology & Ecology of an Extinct Wild Ox*, Sofia and Moscow: Pensoft, 2005.

6 Hawking, Stephen, *A Stubbornly Persistent Illusion: The Essential Scientific Works of Albert Einstein*, Philadelphia, PA: Running Press Book, 2007, 2009.

7 "Has sudden climate change occurred before?" in *Climate change: evidence from the geological record*, The Geological Society, London, November 2010, http://www.geolsoc.org.uk/climatechange.

8 Straus, Lawrence Guy, *Humans at the end of the Ice Age: the archaeology of the Pleistocene-Holocene Transition*, New York: Plenum Press, 1996, p.4.

9 Bradley, Daniel G, "Genetic Hoofprints. The DNA trail leading back to the origins of today's cattle has taken some surprising turns along the way." Bradley is a lecturer in genetics and a fellow at Trinity College, Dublin. http://www.naturalhistorymag.com/master.html?http://www.naturalhistorymag.com/0203/0203_feature.html. "Pig DNA reveals farming history", from the BBC, Science and Nature site, http://news.bbc.co.uk/2/hi/science/nature/6978203.stm.

10 http://www.stonepages.com/news/archives/001919.html.

11 Emmer wheat and barley were the dominant crops of the ancient Near East, and spread in the Neolithic period into Europe and the Indian subcontinent. Emmer had a special place in ancient Egypt, where it was the only wheat cultivated in Pharaonic times. Emmer and barley were the primary ingredients in ancient Egyptian bread and beer; http://en.wikipedia.org/wiki/Emmer. For a comparison between the domestication of crops in various regions of Earth, see: Diamond, Jared, "Apples or Indians", *Guns, Germs, and Steel*, New York: Norton, 1999, pp. 131–156.

12 Chant, Colin, David C Goodman, Open University, *Pre-Industrial Cities and Technology*, London: Routledge, 1999, pp. 1–30.

13 Straus, Lawrence Guy, *Humans at the end of the Ice Age: the archaeology of the Pleistocene-Holocene Transition*, New York: Plenum Press, 1996, p. 71.

14 Gore, Rick, "The Eternal Etruscans", *National Geographic*, vol. 173, no. 6, June 1988, pp. 696–743.

15 Classically, the Iron Age is taken to begin in the 12th century BCE in the ancient Near East, (India and Iran) spreading to Greece and other areas of Europe around the sixth and eighth century BCE. The Iron Age is usually said to end in the Mediterranean with the decline of Ancient Greece and the rise of Rome, around 200 BCE. Collis, John, *The European Iron Age*, London and New York: Routledge, 1984, 1998.

16 Wickham, Chris, *Framing the Early Middle Ages: Europe and the Mediterranean, 400-800*, Oxford and New York: Oxford University Press, 2005.

17 Jay, Peter, *Road to Riches or the Wealth of Man*, London, Phoenix/Orion, 2000, p. 155.

18 Burke, James, "Credit Where It's Due", *The Day the Universe Changed*, London: British Broadcasting Corporation, 1985, pp. 163–193.

19 Horrox, Rosemary, *The Black Death*, Manchester: Manchester University Press, 1994.

20 Black, Jeremy, *Eighteenth-century Europe*, London: St Martin's Press, 1999.

21 Beales, Derek Edward Dawson, *Enlightenment and Reform in 18th-century Europe*, London: I B Tauris, 2005.

22 Wood, Gordon S, *The American Revolution*, New York and Toronto: Random House, 2002.

23 Porter, Roy, *London: A Social History*, Cambridge MA and London: Harvard University Press, 1994, 2001, p. 170.

24 Allen, Robert C, "Agriculture During the Industrial Revolution" and Bruland, Kristine, "Industrialisation and Technological Change", in Floud, Roderick, Paul A Johnson, *The Cambridge Economic History of Modern Britain*, Cambridge: Cambridge University Press, 2004, pp. 96–116 and 117–146. Hudson, Pat, "Agriculture and the Industrial Revolution" in *The Industrial Revolution*, London: Edward Arnold / Oxford University Press, 1992.

25 Pacey, Arnold, "Technology in the Industrial Revolution", in *The Maze of Ingenuity. Ideas and Idealism in the Development of Technology*, Cambridge MA and London: MIT Press, 1974, 1992, pp. 159–189.

26 Malanima, Paolo, *Pre-modern European Economy: One Thousand Years (10th–19th Centuries)*, Leiden: Brill, 2009, pp. 135–136.

27 By the late eighteenth century about 17 per cent of adult males had the right to vote. Dickinson, HT, *A Companion to Eighteenth-century Britain*, Malden MA and Oxford: Wiley-Blackwell, 2002, p. 98.

28 Bucholz, Robert, Newton Key, *Early Modern England 1485-1714: A Narrative History*, Oxford: Wiley, 2004, 2009, pp. 383–384. Mathias, Peter, *The First Industrial Nation: the Economic History of Britain 1700–1914*, London and New York: Routledge, 1969, 2001, p. 201.

29 Sharp, S Pearl, Virginia Schomp, *The Slave Trade and the Middle Passage*, Tarrytown, NY: Marshall Cavendish, 2006. Klein, Herbert S, *The Atlantic Slave Trade*, Cambridge: Cambridge University Press, 1999.

30 Thomas, Hugh, *The Slave Trade: the Story of the Atlantic Slave Trade, 1440–1870*, New York: Touchstone/Simon & Schuster, 1999. The Stone Town, Tanzania was one of the largest slave markets presided over by Arab traders until closed down by the British in 1873. Smith, David, "Zanzibar's Slave Market is a Site Made Sacred by History", *The Guardian*, London, 26 August, 2010. Larsen, Kjersti, *Where Humans and Spirits Meet: The Politics of Rituals and Identified Spirits in Zanzibar (Social Identities)*, Oxford and New York: Berghahn Books, 2008. In 2000 Stone Town was added to the UNESCO World Heritage list, http://whc.unesco.org/en/list/173.

31 On slaving and the East India company see: Keay, John, *The Honourable Company–A History of the English East India Company*, London: HarperCollins, 1991. On the East African Slave Trade: http://www.discoveringbristol.org.uk/. The records from the East India Company (and its successor India Office) are stored by the British Library in London as part of the Asia, Pacific and Africa Collection. The catalogue is searchable online in the Access to Archives catalogues. http://www.a2a.org.uk/. Some original sources are available. A Catalogue of the Library of the Hon. East-India Company complied by the East India Company Library in 1845 was digitised by the New York Public Library in September 2006. Royal African Company was established in 1672 as a slaving company set up by the Stuart family and London merchants. Between 1672 and 1689 it transported around 100,000 slaves. Its profits were increasing and so was the financial power of those in control. In 1698, the company lost its monopoly of the slave trade, and allowed all English merchants into the trade The number of slaves transported on English ships then increased dramatically. The company was dissolved in 1752. From, Itzcaribbean, the website of the Caribbean community in the UK, see: http://www.itzcaribbean.com/slavery_history.php.

32 See, "Spinning the Web. The story of the cotton industry", sponsored by the City of Manchester. http://www.spinningtheweb.org.uk/industry/. A literary portrayal of the chasm that divided the social classes and the geographic divide that existed between the industrial north and the south of England see, *North and South*, 1854, by Elizabeth Gaskell, one of most celebrated of Victorian novelists. The work originally appeared as a 22 part weekly serial (September 1854 through January 1855) in the magazine *Household Words*, which was edited by Charles Dickens.

33 Birch, Alan, "Ironworks and Ironmasters During the Industrial Revolution", in *The Economic History of the British Iron and Steel Industry, 1784–1879,* Abingdon: Routledge, 1967, 2006, pp. 57–103.

34 Dale, Richard, *The First Crash: Lessons from the South Sea Bubble*, Princeton, NJ: Princeton University Press, 2004. http://www.stock-market-crash.net/southsea.htm.

35 The income from the trade was to be secured by way of new taxes on certain commodities, including the old standbys of wine and tobacco, plus India goods, silks, and whale-fins! See: Mackay, Charles, *Extraordinary Popular Delusions and the Madness of Crowds*, Petersfield: Harriman House, 1841, 2003, p. 55. First published in 1841, this is often cited as the best book ever written about market psychology. For a detailed account of the economics of the period, see: http://people.few.eur.nl/smant/m-economics/southsea.htm.

36 Loveman, Kate, "Swift's Bites: Eighteenth-Century Raillery in Theory and Practice", in *Reading Fictions, 1660–1740*, Aldershot and Burlington VT: Ashgate Publishing, pp. 153–174.

37 "The Croppers song", from Peel, Frank, *The Rising of the Luddites Chartists and Plug Drawers* (forth edition 1895) republished by Frank Cass in 1968.

"Come cropper lads of high renown
Who love to drink good ale that's brown
And strike each haughty tyrant down
With Hatchet, pike and gun!"

"The Croppers song", in Binfield, Kevin, *Writings of the Luddites*, Baltimore, Maryland: JHU Press, 2004, p. 202.

38 "By 1811 there were over four million steam mule spindles spread over more than 50 mills in the Manchester district alone." Dickinson, HT, ed., *A Companion to Eighteenth-century Britain*, Oxford: Blackwell Publishers, 2002, p. 130. "The Steam Engine", in Mantoux, Paul, Marjorie Vernon, *The Industrial Revolution in the Eighteenth Century*, London and New York: Routledge, 1928, 2005, pp. 311–340. Pacey, Arnold, "Technology in the Industrial Revolution", *The Maze of Ingenuity*, Cambridge MA and London: MIT Press, 1974, 1992, pp. 159–189.

39 Jones, Steven E, *Against Technology: From Luddites to Neo-Luddism*, London and New York: Routledge, 2006. Explains the aims and values of the original Luddite and provides comparisons with the differing values of contemporary neo-Luddites. Sale, Kilpatrick, *Rebels Against the Future: The Luddites and Their War on the Industrial Revolution*, New York: Basic Books, 1995. A detailed account of the Luddite movement and the dehumanising aspects of modern industrial life. An alternative view is offered in the classic work by noted historian and social campaigner, Edward Palmer Thompson. Thomson, E P, *The Making of the English Working Class*, London: Victor Gollancz/Vintage, 1966. (Also see note 33 below.)

40 This is the third verse of the hymn "All things bright and beautiful", which was first published in 1848 in *Hymns for little children*, by Cecil Frances Humphreys, London: Joseph Masters, 1848. In modern versions of this hymn this verse is omitted.

41 Auerbach, Jeffrey A, *The Great Exhibition of 1851: A Nation on Display*, Yale University Press, 1999. Louise Purbrick, Louise, *The Great Exhibition of 1851*, Manchester, Manchester University Press, 2002. From the prestigious V&A, London. http://www.vam.ac.uk/collections/prints_books/great_exhibition/ BBC radio programme discussing the Great Exhibition and its impact: http://www.bbc.co.uk/radio4/history/inourtime/inourtime_20060427.shtml Contemporary Writings about the Great Exhibition. http://www.victorianweb.org.history/1851/1851bib1.html

42 The arbiter of taste in Victorian England. See: Hilton, Tim, *John Ruskin: The Later Years*, New Haven and London: Yale University Press, 2000. Quill, Sarah, *Ruskin's Stones Revisited*, Aldershot: Lund Humphries, 2000. Unrau, John, *Looking at Architecture with Ruskin*, Toronto: University of Toronto Press, 1978. See also: http://www.lancs.ac.uk/fass/ruskin/.

43 Mackail, J W, *The Life of William Morris*, London, 1899. Written by Burne-Jones's son-in-law, gives a good picture of Morris's friends and social milieu. Thompson, E P, *William Morris: Romantic to Revolutionary*, Stanford: Stanford University Press, 1955. An essential study by a social historian which places Morris in his rightful position as a founder of the Socialist/Communist movement in Britain. A revised reprint was issued in 1988. MacCarthy, Fiona, *William Morris: A Life for Our Time*, London: Faber & Faber, 1994. The definitive biography. Van der Post, Lucia, Linda Parry, *William Morris and Morris & Co.*, London: V&A, 2003. The William Morris Gallery: http://www1.walthamforest.gov.uk/wmg/home.htm.

44 The phrase was popularised by William Morris but appropriated from an epic poem, *Endymion*, composed by John Keats in 1818.

45 "The Beauty of Life", a lecture before the Birmingham Society of Arts and School of Design 19 February 1880, later published in *Hopes and Fears for Art: Five Lectures Delivered in Birmingham, London, and Nottingham, 1878–1881*, 1882.

46 Morris, William, Letter to Andreas Scheu, 15 September 1883.

47 Hounshell, David A, *From the American system to mass production, 1800-1932: The development of manufacturing technology in the United States*, Baltimore, Maryland, Md: Johns Hopkins University Press, 1984. Although mass production is associated with the onset of the twentieth century, it maybe argued that the Venice Arsenal, which in the early part of the sixteenth century, was employing 16,000 and producing close to one ship a day, was the first 'factory using mass production techniques.

48 Eyffinger, Arthur, The 1899 Hague Peace Conference: "The Parliament of Man, the Federation of the World", The Hague, Martinus Nijhoff Publishers, 1999.

49 Eco, Umberto, *Turning Back the Clock. Hot Wars and Media Populism*, New York and London: Harvest/Harcourt, 2006, p. 50.

50 From among the extensive material available on the First World War, the following are recommended. From the BBC a detailed overview with many links to more specific sites: http://www.firstworldwar.com/ http://www.bbc.co.uk/history/worldwars/wwone/ A similar site from Channel 4 "explores and dissects some of its most controversial features". http://www.channel4.com/history/microsites/F/firstworldwar/ There is an eight-part PBS series, *The Great War and the Shaping of the 20th Century*, which is supported by a website: http://www.pbs.org/greatwar/.

51 The 19th Amendment to the Constitution was passed by a narrow majority in 1919, becoming law on the 26 August 1920. This allowed women to vote in the precedential election later that year.

52 Howard, Michael, *The First World War: a Very Short Introduction*, Oxford and New York: Oxford University Press, 2002, p. 1.

53 Streissguth, Thomas, *The Roaring Twenties*, New York, Facts on File, 2001, 2007.

54 Drowne, Kathleen Morgan, Patrick Huber, *The 1920s*, Westport CT: Greenwood Publishing, 2004. Willoughby, Douglas, Susan Willoughby, "The roaring twenties", in *The USA 1917–45*, Oxford: Heinemann Educational Publishers, 2000, pp. 38–54.

55 While referencing pre war design activity I will concentrate on post-Second World War developments. I have quite consciously not covered many of the pre war movements such as Futurism, Constructivism, De Stijl and the Bauhaus. All these are well covered in other publications including: Sparke, Penny, *An Introduction to Design and Culture: 1900 to the Present*, New York: Routledge, 2004. *A Century of Design*, London: Mitchell Beazley, 1999. Woodham, Jonathan M, *Twentieth-Century Design*, Oxford and New York: Oxford University Press, 1997.

56 Cross, Gary S, *An All-consuming Century: Why Commercialism Won in Modern America*, New York: Columbia University Press, 2000.

57 The place to start is with the 12-volume encyclopaedia published to coincide with the Exposition. Exposition Internationale Des Arts Décoratifs Et Industriels Modernes–Paris 1925. You may take a re-constructed virtual tour of the Exposition: http://www.retropolis.net/exposition/ Another tour is available for the V&A: http://www.vam.ac.uk/vastatic/microsites/1157_art_deco/virtual/gallery1/paris1925.htm. An abundance of publications cover this most popular movement, see: Arwas, Victor, *Art Deco*, New York: Harry N. Abrams, 2002. This revised, well illustrated reference book, includes biographies of some of the artists and designers associated with the movement. Charlotte, Tim Benton and Ghislaine Wood, eds, *Art Deco 1910-1939*, London: Victoria and Albert Museum Publications, 2003. The catalogue from the large and luxurious exhibition of 2003 which includes nearly 40 essays on the topic. Gronberg, Tag, *Designs on Modernity: Exhibiting the City in 1920s Paris*, Manchester: Manchester University Press, 2003. A study of Paris in the 1920s which presents the 1925 Exhibition as a conscious attempt to update the image of Paris and to firmly establish Paris as "a woman's city", and as a world centre of fashion and shopping. Hillier, Bevis, *Art deco of the 20s and 30s*, London: Studio Vista, 1968 and 1973. Now somewhat dated, but it was the original book that defined and named the style. Sternau, Susan A, *Art deco: flights of artistic fancy*, New York: New Line Books, 2006. Provides an accessible general introduction with short essays on aspects of the style.

58 Richards, Charles Richard, Report of Commission appointed by the Secretary of Commerce to visit and report upon the International exposition of modern decorative and industrial art in Paris, 1925, Washington DC, US Department of Commerce, 1926.

59 Gronberg, Tag, *Designs on Modernity: Exhibiting the City in 1920s Paris*, Manchester: Manchester University Press, 1998. For an interesting review on how les grands magasins are re-inventing themselves at the start of the twenty-first century, see: http://www.francemagazine.org/articles/issue64/article52.asp?issue_id=64&article_id=52.

60 Taken from, Exposition internationale des arts décoratifs et industriels modernes: règlement, Paris, Ministère du commerce et de l'industrie, 1924.

61 To untangle the confusing and complex relationships between the state, department stores, and the various design related organisations and associations representing French furniture designers and manufactures of the period, see: Greenhalgh, Paul, "The Struggles Within French Furniture", *Modernism in Design*, London: Reaktion Books, 1990, pp. 54–82.

62 French fashion magazines featured pochoir (hand coloured) prints by artists such as George Barbier, George Lepape, Erté, and Paul Iribe. See: http://www.sil.si.edu/ondisplay/pochoir/intro.htm. Magazines included, *Art*, *Goût Beauté*, *Falbalas et fanfreluches*, *Gazette du bon ton*, *Guirlande des mois almanach* and *Modes et manières d'Aujourd'hui*.

63 The technique of veneering was perfected during the eighteenth century by craftsmen such as Jean-Henri Riesener, a French cabinetmaker of German birth who was largely responsible for the refurbishment of the French Royal Palaces and became the favourite cabinetmaker of Marie-Antoinette. He almost completely furnished her rooms at Fontainebleau. After becoming maitre ébéniste in 1768, Riesener was appointed ébéniste du roi in 1774.

64 For extensive details on the history and techniques of lacquer, see: Webb, Marianne, *Lacquer: Technology and*

Conservation: A Comprehensive Guide to the Technology and Conservation of both Asian and European Lacquer, Oxford: Butterworth-Heinemann, 2000.

65 Marchilhac, Félix, *Jean Dunand: His Life and Works*, London: Thames and Hudson, 1991.

66 FIND

67 Adam, Peter, *Eileen Gray: Architect/Designer: A Biography (Revised)*, New York: Harry N Abrams, 2000; Constant, Caroline, *Eileen Gray*, London: Phaidon, 2000; Rowlands, Penelope, *Eileen Gray*, San Francisco: Chronicle Books, 2002. From the Design Museum in London: http://www.designmuseum.org/design/eileen-gray; The National Museum of Ireland (Collins Barracks) has a permanent exhibition devoted to Eileen Gray, including personal memorabilia, lacquering tools, carpets, chairs, tables, screens, lanterns, drawings, her portfolio and reviews of her work. A newspaper article from *The Guardian*: MacCarthy, Fiona, "Future worlds", *The Guardian*, 10 September 2005. http://books.guardian.co.uk/review/story/0,12084,1565481,00.html.

68 http://www.urushi-kobo.com/process.html.

69 http://12.172.4.131/images/collection/FullSizes/07343007.jpg.

70 Allen Brooks, H, *Le Corbusier's Formative Years: Charles-Edouard Jeanneret at La Chaux-de-Fonds*, Chicago: University of Chicago Press, 1999.

71 Weber, Nicholas Fox, *Le Corbusier: A Life,* New York and Toronto: Random House, 2008, p. 77.

72 Le Corbusier, (Frederick Etchells, trans.), *Towards a New Architecture*, London: Architectural Press, 1924, 1927, p. 31.

73 Eliel, Carol S Françoise Ducros, *Tag Gronberg, L'Esprit Nouveau: Purism in Paris, 1918–1925*, New York: Harry N Abrams, 2002.

74 Hays, K Michael, *Architecture Theory Since 1968*, Cambridge, MA: MIT Press, 1998, p. 635.

75 Le Corbusier, Pierre Jeanneret, *Oeuvre Complète*, vol. 1, 1910–1929, Zurich, Les Editions d'Architecture, 1937, 1995, p. 186.

76 Thompson, James Matheson, ed., *Twentieth Century Theories of Art*, Ottawa: Carleton University Press, 1990, 1999, p. 184.

77 As quoted in, Fox Weber, Nicholas, *Le Corbusier. A Life*, New York: Alfred A Knopf, 2008, p. 296.

78 Wood, Ean, *The Josephine Baker Story*, London: Sanctuary Publishing, 2000.

79 Farès el-Dahdah, Stephen Atkinson, "The Josephine Baker House: For Loos's Pleasure", Assemblage, no. 26, April 1995, pp. 72–87.

80 http://www.kirjasto.sci.fi/lecorbu.htm.

81 There are a vast amount of sources and resources available that provide analysis and assessment of the Villa Savoye and on the life and career of Le Corbusier. For a general biography see: http://architect.architecture.sk/le-corbusier-architect/le-corbusier-architect.php. For details of his ten year association with Charlotte Perriand and on her quite amazing career (she died in 1999) see: http://www.designmuseum.org/design/charlotte-perriand. The BBC has a file on Le Corbusier, limited information but with some audio clips: http://www.bbc.co.uk/bbcfour/audiointerviews/profilepages/lecorbusierc2.shtml. For a brief, straightforward description of the Villa Savoye (free from analytical bias) see: Morel-Journel, Guillemette, *Le Corbusier's Villa Savoye*, Paris: Centre des Monuments Nationaux Monum, Éditions du patrimoine, 1998. A more extensive review is provided by Sbriglio, Jacques, (Sarah Parsons, trans.), *Le Corbusier: The Villa Savoye,* Basel, Boston and Berlin: Birkhäuser, 1999. Other informative on line sources include: Chami, Camille, "Le Corbusier and Villa Savoye Remembered", archinnovations. News and Views on the World of Architecture. http://www.

archinnovations.com/articles/editorials/le-corbusier-and-villa-savoye/; http://architypes.net/place/villa-savoye/, and for a virtual re-build (still in progress) http://archsl.wordpress.com/2007/02/21/villa-savoye-progress-report/.

82 "Brother, Can You Spare a Dime", 1931, lyrics by Yip Harburg, music by Jay Gorney is regarded as being the anthem of the Depression. *Brother, Can You Spare a Dime?* is also the title of a 1975 documentary film produced by Image Entertainment. The documentary uses newsreel footage and contemporary film clips to portray the era of the Great Depression. .

83 For a general overview of the Depression, including its global ramifications: http://en.wikipedia.org/wiki/Great_Depression. Another overview but with a specific focus on America: http://eh.net/encyclopedia/article/parker.depression, http://imdb.com/title/tt0072742/. For a literary account of the cultural ramifications of the Depression see the two essays composed in 1931 and 1932, by F Scott Fitzgerald, "Echoes of the Jazz Age" and "My Lost City", in which he described how in just two years "the most expensive orgy in history was over". Fitzgerald, F Scott, "Echoes of the Jazz Age", in Zinn, Howard, Anthony Arnove, *Voices of a People's History of the United States*, New York: Seven Stories Press, 2004, pp. 312–314.

84 Maxtone-Graham, John, *Normandie: France's legendary art deco ocean liner*, New York: WW Norton, 2007.

85 Breeze, Carla, *American Art Deco: Architecture and Regionalism*, New York: WW Norton, 2003.

86 Llewellyn Cooke, Morris, "The Early Days of the Rural Electrification Idea", *American Political Science Review*, June 1948, pp. 5–6. Nye, E David, *Electrifying America: Social Meanings of a New Technology*, 1880–1940, Cambridge MA: MIT Press, 1992.

87 As quoted in, Smith, Terry, *Making the Modern: Industry, Art, and Design in America*, Chicago: University of Chicago Press, 1993, p. 371.

88 For a personal account of the details of both the Fort Peck Dam and Louisiana Flood pictures, see: Bourke-White, Margaret, "Life Begins", Heron, Liz and Val Williams, *Illuminations: Women Writing on Photography from the 1850s to the Present*, London: IB Taurus, 1996, pp. 133–139.

89 Brinkley, Alan, *The Publisher. Henry Luce and his American Century*, New York: Knopf, 2010.

90 *Life* ceased publication in 1972. Its primary competitor as a photo intense magazine was *Look* a bi-weekly general interest magazine that ran form 1937 to 1971. When *Look* folded it donated its five miilion photograph archive to the Library of Congress.

91 Young, Nancy K, William H, Young, *The Great Depression in America: a cultural encyclopedia*, Westport CT: Greenwood Press, 2007. Cohen, Lizabeth, *A Consumers' Republic: The Politics of Mass Consumption in Postwar America*, New York: Vintage/Random House, 2004.

92 Film History of the 1903s. http://www.filmsite.org/30sintro3.html.

93 For a comprehensive and well documented review of graphic design in America from the end of the Second World War up to the 1960s, see: Meggs, Philip B "The New York School", *A History of Graphic Design*, New York: John Wiley & Sons, 1998, pp. 337–362.

94 Hardison, O B Jr, *Disappearing Through the Skylight*, New York: Penguin Books, 1989, p. 180–181.

95 Bel Geddes, *Horizons*, Boston: Dover Publications, 1932, 1977, p. 7, 22. There is also a 1972 reprint available, published by Books for Libraries Press.

96 From the vast array of available material relating to The New Deal, see: Mikkis, Sidney M, Jerome M Mileur, *The New Deal and the Triumph of Liberalism*, Amherst, MA: MIT Press, 2002. Rauchway, Eric, *The Great Depression & the New Deal: a Very Short*

Introduction, Oxford and New York: Oxford University Press, 2008.

97 Welch, Catherine A, Margaret Bourke-White: *Racing with a Dream*, Minneapolis, MN: Lerner Publishing Group, 1998. Bourke-White, Margaret, *Portrait of Myself*, New York: Simon and Schuster, 1963.

98 Tagg, John, *The Disciplinary Frame: Photographic Truths and the Capture of Meaning*, Minneapolis MA: University of Minnesota Press, 2009, pp. 102–108.

99 Jay, Peter, *Road to Riches or The Wealth of Man*, London: Phoenix, 2001, pp. 311–321.

100 Executive Committee of the Board consisted of Winthrop Aldrich (chairman of the board of Chase Manhattan Bank), Mortimer Buckner (chairman of the board of the New York Trust Company), Floyd Carlisle (chairman of the board of the Consolidated Edison Company), John J Dunnigan (majority leader of the New York State Senate), Harvey Dow Gibson (president and chairman of the board of Manufacturers Trust Company), Fiorello La Guardia (Mayor of the City of New York), Percy S Straus (president of Macy's), and other political and business leaders of note.

101 Time-Life Books, ed., *New York World's Fair, 1964/1965: Official Guide Book*, New York: Time-Life Books, 1964, 1965. New York World's Fair 1939-1940: http://websyte.com/alan/nywf.htm. The Museum of the City of New York: http://www.mcny.org/. "History of the Fair: The Design and Marketing of the Future". http://xroads.virginia.edu/~1930s/DISPLAY/39wf/history.htm. Cohen, Barbara, Steven Heller and Seymour Chwas, *Trylon and perisphere : the 1939 New York World's Fair*, New York: Abrams, 1989. Gelernter, David, 1939, *The Lost World of the Fair*, New York: Avon Books, 1995. Zim, Larry, Mel Lerner, Herbert Rolfes, *The World of Tomorrow: The 1939 New York World's Fair*, New York: Harper & Row, 1988.

102 Bernbach, William, *Book of Nations*, New York World's Fair: Winkler & Kelmans, 1939.

103 http://movies.nytimes.com/movie/32547/The-Middleton-Family-at-the-1939-New-York-World-s-Fair/overview. From the Prelinger Collection: http://www.archive.org/details/middleton_family_worlds_fair_1939.

104 While the work of this stalwart band of pioneers is of the utmost importance it is covered extensively in other publications. I have elected to minimise comment and focus on other significant influences on the design process of the time. Among the extensive available information those composed by the participants themselves are recommenced: Dreyfuss, Henry, *Designing for People*, New York: Allworth Press, 1955, 2003; Bel Geddes, Norman, *Horizons*, Boston: Dover Publications, 1932; Loewy, Raymond, *Never Leave Well Enough Alone*, Baltimore: John Hopkins University Press, 1950, 2002; Teague, Walter Dorwin, *Design This Day*, New York: Harcourt Brace, 1940. See also: Hanks, David A, Anne H Hoy, *American Streamlined Design: The World of Tomorrow*, Paris: Flammarion, 2005.

105 Cars & history: start of the aerodynamic era (1931–1933), http://www.tatra.demon.nl/cars_history_aerodynamic.htm.

106 Marchand, Roland, "The Designers go to the Fair, 1: Walter Dorwin Teague and the Professionalization of Corporate Industrial Exhibits, 1933–1940", in Doordan, Dennis P, ed., *Design History: An Anthology*, Cambridge MA: MIT Press, 1995, 2000, pp. 89–102.

107 "Best Sellers of the Week Here and Elsewhere", *New York Times* (1857-Current file); 24 April 1939; ProQuest Historical Newspapers The New York Times, 1851–2003, p. 15.

CHAPTER SIX

1 The Axis powers comprised of Germany, Italy, Japan, Hungary, Romania and Bulgaria.

2 For an authoritative assessment of post-Second World War political and economic conditions see: Jay, Peter, "False Dawns? 1945–99", *Road to Riches or The Wealth of Man*, London: Phoenix, 2001, pp. 322–366.

3 The air-raid on Dresden from the late night of the thirteenth to the early morning of the fourteenth of February 1945, saw 1,300 heavy bombers drop over 3,900 tons of high-explosive bombs and incendiary devices in four raids, destroying 13 square miles (34 km²) of the baroque city.

4 For authoritative information on the Second World War see the BBC web site: http://www.bbc.co.uk/history/worldwars/wwtwo/

5 "Dr Carrot and Potato Pete", *BBC*, h2g2, created: 1 March 2004. http://www.bbc.co.uk/dna/h2g2/ A2263529. Hammond, Richard James, *Food and Agriculture in Britain 1939–45*, Stanford: Stanford University Press, 1954, p. 54; *Food: Volume II, Studies in Administration and Control (History of the Second World War, United Kingdom Series*, London: HMSO, 1956, pp. 580–1.

6 Under the Defence of the Realm Regulations initial orders controlling the use of timber, silk, rayon, leather, wool, cotton and an array of ferrous and non-ferrous materials were introduced on 5 September 1939. Further refined quota systems followed in December, 1940. Early in 1941 further attempts were made to control raw materials, including clothing and footwear, the main quota system for domestic furniture followed in November. Price controls came in 1942 to stop gouging. In July 1942, the Advisory Committee on Utility furniture was established. An exhibition of Utility Furniture was held at the Building Centre, London, in October and the Utility Furniture catalogue went to press on 11 November, it was officially published on 1 January, 1943. The rationing of furniture was ended in June, 1948. In February 1949, a large range of garments were freed from ration restrictions. The last clothing coupons were issued in September 1948 although utility specifications remained in force until 1952.

7 Denney, Mathew, "Utility Furniture and the Myth of Utility 1943–48", in Attfield, Judy, ed., *Utility Reassessed: the Role of Ethics in the Practice of Design*, Manchester: Manchester University Press, 1999, pp. 110–124.

8 Vaizey, John et al, CC 41, *Utility Furniture and Fashion 1941–1951*, London: Geffrye Museum Trust, 1974, 1995. First published in 1974 as an illustrated catalogue to the Geffrye Museums exhibition on Utility Furniture and Fashion, this remains an invaluable guide to the movement with brief articles by Gillian Naylor, Jane Ashelford, David Mellor, and Bob Carter. See also: Briggs, Asa, *Go To It ! Working for Victory on the Home Front, 1939–1945*, London: Michael Beazley, 2000. For a comprehensive assessment of post-war British design see: Weight, Richard, *Patriots: Nation Identity in Britain, 1940–2000*, London: Macmillan, 2002. Jeremiah, David, *Architecture and Design for the Family in Britain, 1900–70*, Manchester: Manchester University Press, 2000. Massey, Anne, *The Independent Group: Modernism and Mass Culture in Britain, 1945–1959*, Manchester: Manchester University Press, 1996.

9 Ministry of Information, *Make Do and Mend*, London, Imperial War Museum, 1943, 2007.

10 Women in France had to be extremely inventive to maintain a semblance of style under the German occupation. For a revealing account see: Veillon, Dominique, Miriam Kochan (trans.), *Fashion Under the Occupation, (La Mode sous l'Occupation)*, Oxford: Berg, 2002.

11 Details on rationing and utility clothing: http://www.fashion-era.com/utility_clothing.htm.

12 "There can be no equality of sacrifice in this war. Some must lose life and limbs, others only the turn-ups on their trousers". A response to a question in the House of Commons by Hugh Dalton, President of the Board of Trade, concerning protests about austerity provisions on men's clothing. As reported in, Brown, Mike, *The 1940's Look*, Sevenoaks, Kent: Sabrestorm, 2006, p. 3. Reynolds, Helen, "The Utility Garment: its design and effect on the mass market 1942–45", in Attfield, Judy, ed., *Utility Reassessed: the Role of Ethics in the Practice of Design*, Manchester: Manchester University Press, 1999, pp. 125–142.

13 For factual information from the Imperial War Museum, London: http://www.iwm.org.uk/. For "What was life like in the second World War," see: http://www.iwm.org.uk/upload/package/20/lifeinww2/index.htm. Specific to fashion see: Sladen, Christopher, *The Conscription of Fashion: utility cloth, clothing and footwear, 1941–1952*, Aldershot: Scolar Press, 1995.

14 www.iwm.org.uk/upload/package/20/lifeinww2/wear/utility.pdf .

15 Thomas, Donald, *An Underworld at War: Spivs, Deserters, Racketeers and Civilians in the Second World War*, London: John Murray, 2004.

16 Jeremiah, David, *Architecture and Design for the Family in Britain, 1900–70*, Manchester: Manchester University Press, 2000. Stratton, Michael, Barrie Stuart Trinder, *Twentieth Century Industrial Archaeology*, London: Taylor & Francis, 2000, pp. 121–144.

17 Marcus Brumwell, the managing director of Stuart's Advertising Agency and a champion of British artists including Ben Nicholson, Edward McKnight Kauffer and Barbara Hepworth founded the DRU; Herbert Reed was the art critic; the architect was Misha Black and Milner Gray was the graphic designer; collectively they were responsible for among other things, the logo for British Rail, London's street signage system and hundreds of signs for Watney's pubs.

18 Darling, Elizabeth, *Exhibiting Britain. Display and National Identity 1946–1967*; a most valuable on line resource to the Britain Can Make It exhibition of 1946 and Expo '67, held in Montréal in 1967. http://www.vads.ac.uk/learning/designingbritain/html/esd.html. Chamberlain, Richard, Geoffrey Rayner, Annamarie Stapleton, *Austerity to Affluence: British Art & Design 1945–1962*, London: Merrell Holberton, 2003.

19 Maguire, Patrick Joseph, Jonathan M Woodham, *Design and Cultural Politics in Postwar Britain: The Britain Can Make It Exhibition of 1946*, London: Leicester University Press, 1997.

20 Robertson, Alex J, *The Bleak MidWinter*, 1947, Manchester: Manchester University Press, 1987. Cairncross, Alec, *Years of Recovery: British Economic Policy, 1945–51*, London: Methuen, 1985.

21 Clark, Paul, "Ben Bowden's 'Bicycle of the Future' 1946", Journal of Design History, vol. 5, no. 3, 1992, pp. 227–235. Published by: Oxford University Press on behalf of Design History Society. Stable URL: http://www.jstor.org/stable/1315840.

22 Clark, Paul, "Ben Bowden's 'Bicycle of the Future' 1946", p. 231.

23 Clark, Paul, "Ben Bowden's 'Bicycle of the Future' 1946".

24 "Britain Cuts the Pound", *Life*, 3 October 1949, pp. 28–32.

25 Conekin, Becky, *The Autobiography of a Nation: The 1951 Festival of Britain*, Manchester: Manchester University Press, 2003. Rennie, Paul, *Design: Festival of Britain 1951*, London: Antique Collectors' Club Ltd, 2007. http://vads.ahds.ac.uk/learning/designingbritain/html/festival.html.

26 Banham, M, and B Hillier, eds, *A Tonic to the Nation, The Festival of Britain 1951*, London: Thames and Hudson, 1976

27 Powell, P, "No Visible Means of Support", in Harwood and Power, eds, *Twentieth Century Architecture*, 81–6, p. 85.

28 Cruickshank, Dan, "The Dome of Discovery– pavilion in 1951 Festival of Britain", *Architectural Review*, January, 1995. http://findarticles.com/p/articles/mi_m3575/is_n1175_v197/ai_16565527.

29 Orwell, George, *The Lion and the Unicorn: Socialism and the English Genius*, London: Secker & Warburg, 1941.

30 Ralph, J D, "The Telekinema: Planning the Exhibition", in *British Film Institute, Films in 1951: A Special Publication on British Films and Film-Makers for the Festival of Britain*, London: Sight and Sound for the British Film Institute, 1951, p. 43.

31 Gardiner, Jullet, *From the Bomb to The Beatles*, London: Collins & Brown, 1999, pp. 48–59.

32 http://www.britishmuseum.org/ahistoryoftheworld.

33 Kennedy, Carol, *From Dynasties to Dotcoms: The Rise Fall and Reinvention of British Business in the Last 100 Years*, London: Kogan Page, 2003, p. 79.

34 Johnson, Catherine, Robert Turnock, *ITV Cultures: Independent Television Over Fifty Years*, Maidenhead: Open University Press, 2005.

35 Whitcomb, Ian, *After the Ball*, London: Limelight, 1972, 2004, pp. 226–227.

36 Abrams, M, *The Teenage Consumer*, LPE, Paper 5, London: Routledge and Kegan Paul, 1959. Available on line: http://www.questia.com/PM.qst?a=o&docId=103494554.

37 Kynaston, David, *Austerity Britain, 1945–1951*, London: Bloomsbury Publishing, 2007.

38 Akhtar, Miriam, Steve Humphries, *The Fifties And Sixties: A Lifestyle Revolution*, London: Boxtree, 2001.

39 Hewison, Robert, *The Heritage Industry: Britain in a Climate of Decline*, London: Methuen, 1987, p. 6.

40 http://news.bbc.co.uk/onthisday/hi/dates/stories/july/20/newsid_3728000/3728225.stm.

41 As quoted in, Laver, James, *A Concise History of Costume*, London: Book Club Associates, 1973, p. 114. See also: Molloy, Joseph Fitzgerald, *Royalty Restored: or London Under Charles II Volume 2*, London: Ward & Downey, 1885,

42 Kuchta, David, *The Three-Piece Suit and Modern Masculinity: England, 1550–1850*, Berkeley CA and London: University of California Press, 2002.

43 Kelly, Ian, *Beau Brummell: The Ultimate Dandy*, London: Hodder & Stoughton, 2005.

44 "Suitably Dressed", *The Economist*, 16 December 2010.

45 Chenoune, Farid (Deke Duisinberre (trans.), "Teddy Boys, Leather Boys: From Frock Coat to Jeans", in *A History of Men's Fashion*, Paris: Flammarion, 1993, pp. 229–250.

46 Steele-Perkins, Christopher, *The Teds*, London: Dewi Lewis Publishing, 1979, 2002.

47 The seminal work on the UK's post-war, music-centred, working-class subcultures, from teddy boys to mods and rockers to skinheads and Punks is: Hebdige, Dick, *Subculture: The Meaning of Style*, London: Routledge, 1979. A somewhat earlier, recently updated, informative sources being: Roszak, Theodore, *The Making of a Counter Culture, Reflections on the Technocratic Society and Its Youthful Opposition*, Berkeley, CA: University of California Press, 1969, 1995. A collection of essays covering a wide range of youth subcultures from teds and skinheads to black rastafarians: Hall, Stuart, Tony Jefferson, *Resistance Through Rituals: Youth Subcultures in Post-war Britain*, London: Routledge, 1993.

48 The date when the term "teenager" was first used to define the teen years is a matter of debate. The word makes a matter-of-fact appearance in a 1941 issue of *Reader's Digest* and very quickly fell into common parlance.

49 Barnes, 1991, p .8.

50 Hebdige, Dick, *Hiding in the Light: On Images and Things*, London: Routledge, 1988, p. 70.

51 Created by Royal charter in 1927 the British Broadcasting Corporation had a monopoly on radio broadcasting in Britain until 1973.

52 Wicke, Peter, Rachel Fogg, *Rock Music: Culture, Aesthetics and Sociology*, Cambridge and New York: Cambridge University Press, 1973, 1995.

53 Cohen, Stanley, *Folk Devils and Moral Panics: The Creation of the Mods and Rockers*, Oxford: Blackwell, 1972, 1980, p. 9. Procter James, *Stuart Hall*, London and New York: Routledge, 2004.

54 Hewitt Paolo, ed., Sean Body, ed., *The Sharper Word: A Mod Anthology*, London: Helter Skelter Publishing, 2000 (This anthology includes the Tom Wolfe essay, "The Noonday Underground"). Rawlings, Terry, *Mod: A Very British Phenomenon*, London: Omnibus Press, 2000.

55 Boni, Valerio, *Vespa*, New York: Rizzoli, 2007. Mazzanti, Davide, *Vespa*, San Francisco: Chronicle Books, 2004.

56 Wolfe, Tom, "The Noonday Underground", This essay explores the Mod scene of the mid 1960s, showing how some Mods would dance their way through their lunch break at *The Scene in Soho* (see note above).

57 Charlesworth, Chris, Ed Hanel, *The Who: The Complete Guide to Their Music*, London: Omnibus Press, 2004.

58 All tracks were written by Pete Townshend, it was recorded at "The Kitchen" in Thessally Road, Battersea, and mixed at Eel Pie Sound (aka Pete Townshend's Garage in Twickenham), http://www.quadrophenia.net/.

59 Brylcreem is still available in the UK. http://www.brylcreem.co.uk/.

60 A detailed case study of the Mods and Rockers confrontations in Britain during the mid 1960s is provided in the updated third edition of; Cohen, Stanley, *Folk Devils and Moral Panics; The Creation of the Mods and Rockers*. London and New York: Routledge, 1972, 2003. A more specific fashion focus is provided by Farrelly, Liz (Editor), Ian Mckell (Photographer), *Fashion Forever: 30 Years of Subculture*, London: imprint, 2004.

61 See a review from the *BBC* which includes some video clips of the confrontation: http://news.bbc.co.uk/onthisday/hi/dates/stories/may/18/newsid_2511000/2511245.stm.

62 Cohen, Stanley, *Folk Devils and Moral Panics; The Creation of the Mods and Rockers*, London and New York: Routledge, third edition, 1972, 2003, p. liv.

63 Hedbidge, Dick, *Subculture: The Meaning of Style*, London: Methuen, 1979, p. 18.

64 Danesi, Marcel, "Dress Codes", in *Messages, Signs, and Meanings: A Basic Textbook in Semiotics and Communication Theory*, Toronto: Canadian Scholar's Press, 2004, pp. 182–184.

65 'The Times They Are a-Changin' one of Dylan's most famous songs was released on 13 January 1964, less than two months after the assassination of John F Kennedy. A self-conscious protest song it became an immediate anthem of the age. Milton Glaser was one of the founder members of Push Pin, a Californian based studio of art associates. Glaser's 1967 poster of Bob Dylan became an iconic image of the era. This was also the time when interest in subliminal imaging entered the design debate. One of the acknowledged influences on the musical development of Dylan was Elvis Presley. If you look into the psychedelic hair of Dylan you can see the letters E.L.V.I.S.

66 Hickey, Michael, "The Korean War: An Overview", *BBC History*, accessed 15 August 2009,

http://www.bbc.co.uk/history/worldwars/coldwar/korea_hickey_01.shtml.

67 Young, William H, Nancy K Young, *The 1950s*, Westport CT: Greenwood Press, 2004, p. 3.

68 Rowsome, Frank Jr, *The Verse by the Side of the Road: The Story of the Burma-Shave Signs and Jingles*, New York: Penguin, 1965, 1990.

69 Schutts, Jeff R, "Refreshment? Coca-Colonization and the Re-Making of Postwar German Identity", in Crew, David F, *Consuming Germany in the Cold War*, Oxford and New York: Berg, 2002, pp. 121–150. Bryn, Steinar, "The Coca-Cola Co and the Olympic Movement. Global or American?". Ramet Sabrina P, Gordana P Cmkovic, ed., *Kazaam! Splat! Ploof!: the American Impact on European Popular Culture Since 1945*, Lanham MA: Rowman & Littlefield, 2003, pp. 83–101. "Italian Invasion," *Time*, 22 August 1949, p. 71. "Colonization by Coke", *Newsweek*, 12 December 1949, p. 31. Escarpit, Robert, "Mourir pour le Coca-Cola", *Le Monde*, 29 March 1950, p.1. Kuisel, Richard, *Seducing the French: The Dilemma of Americanization*, Berkeley: University of California Press, 1993, p. 64.

70 For US coverage of the Exposition, see: "The U.S. at the Fair", *Newsweek*, 51, 14 April 1958, p. 53. Hixson, Walter L, *Parting the curtain: propaganda, culture, and the Cold War, 1945–1961*, New York: St Martins Press, 1998, pp. 141–150. http://www.expo58.tk/.

71 Rogers, Mary Frances, *Barbie Culture*, Thousand Oaks, CA: Sage, 1999.

72 With theatrical references dating back to Shakespeare, the term became associated with product in the eighteenth century. The modern use is defined by the architecture critic Thomas Hine. Hine, Thomas, *Populuxe, The Look and Life of America in the '50s and '60s, from Tailfins and TV Dinners to Barbie Dolls and Fallout Shelters*, New York: Knopf, 1986.

73 American national debt increased from $73 billion in 1950 to $196 billion in 1960. Young, William H, Nancy K Young, *The 1950's*, Westport, CN: Greenwood Publishing, 2004, p. 3.

74 http://en.wikipedia.org/wiki/Walt_Disney.

75 http://www.raymondloewy.com/about/viewheadline.php?id=4257. http://www.idsa.org/webmodules/articles/anmviewer.asp?a=235.

76 Benjamin, Walter, *The Work of Art in the Age of Its Technological Reproducibility, and Other Writings on Media*, Cambridge MA: Belknap Press of Harvard University, 2008.

77 As quoted in the definitive source for information on Harley J Earl http://www.carofthecentury.com/.

78 An informative site with a vast array of information regarding GM automotive design in the 1950s. http://www.carofthecentury.com/versaille_of_industry.htm.

79 Meikle, Jeffrey L, *American Plastic: A Cultural History*, Piscataway, NJ: Rutgers University Press, 1997.

80 Programmes such as *The Ipana Troubadours*, the *Eveready Program*, the *A&P Gypsies*, *Kraft Music Hall*, *Maxwell House Showboat*, *Kodak Chorus* and the most prestigious radio programme, the *Palmolive Radio Hour*. See also: McChesney, Robert W, *Telecommunications, Mass Media, and Democracy: The Battle for the Control of U.S. Broadcasting, 1928–1935*, Oxford: Oxford University Press, 1994.

81 Newman, Kathy M, *Radio Active, Advertising and Consumer Activism, 1935–1947*, Berkeley and Los Angeles: University of California Press, 2004, p.110.

82 http://www.hfmgv.org/museum/dymaxion.aspx.

83 Buckminster Fully, R, Joachim Krausse, Claude Lichenstein, eds, *Your Private Sky. The Art of Design Science*, Baden: Lars Müller Publishers, 1999. Baldwin, J, *BuckyWorks: Buckminster Fuller's Ideas for Today*, New York: Wiley, 1996, p. 18–25.

84 Brown, Patricia Leigh, "Design Notebook: Where to Put the TV? Still no Easy Answer", *The New York Times*, 4 October, 1990.

85 Leigh Brown, Patricia, " Where to Put the TV? Still No Easy Answer", *New York Times*, 4 October 1990.

86 Miller, Douglas T, Marion Nowak, "TV's the Thing", in *The fifties: the way we really were*, New York: Doubleday, 1977, pp. 344–374.

87 "The Work of Charles and Ray Eames. A Legacy of Invention." Library of Congress/Vitra Design Museum, an exhibition held at various locations between 1999 and 2002, including Washington, New York, Saint Louis, Los Angeles, Tel Aviv, Vienna, and Berlin; http://www.loc.gov/exhibits/eames/.

88 Kirkham, Pat, *Charles and Ray Eames: Designers of the Twentieth Century*, Cambridge MA and London: MIT Press, 1995, p. 243.

89 Charles+Ray Eames, Design Museum Collection, http://designmuseum.org/design/charles-ray-eames.

90 Demetrios, Eames, "Eames Chairs. A 30 Years Flash (part 1)", in *An Eames Primer*, New York: Universe Publishing, 2002, pp. 35–47.

91 For a highly readable account of the Eames design process see: Caplan, Ralph, "Making Connections: The Designer as Universal Joint", *By Design*, New York: McGraw Hill, 1982, pp. 183–203. On Charles and Ray Eames: Albrecht, Donald, Library of Congress, Vitra Design Museum, *The Work of Charles and Ray Eames: A Legacy of Invention*, New York: Harry N Abrams in association with the Library of Congress and the Vitra Design Museum, 1997.

92 http://www.powersof10.com/index php?mod=ten_day. To view the video clip: http://www.powersof10.com/.

93 "Life in a Chinese Kite", *Architectural Forum*, September 1950. The house was featured in several magazines, including *Architectural Review*, October 1951, *Arquitectura*, Mexico, June 1952, *L'Architecture d'aujourdhui*, December 1953, *Interiors*, November 1959, *Domus*, May 1963 and *Architectural Design*, September 1966.

94 For a highly readable and perceptive assessment of the work of Charles and Ray Eames, and their design process, see: Caplan, Ralph, "Making Connections: The Designer as Universal Joint", *By Design*, New York: Fairchild, 2005.

95 Wright, Frank Lloyd, *An Organic Architecture: The Architecture of Democracy*, Cambridge, MA: MIT Press, 1939/1970, 2004.

96 de Saint-Exupéry, Antoine, Richard Howard (trans.), *The Little Prince*, Orlando, FL: Harvest Books/Harcourt, Brace, 1943, 2000, Chapter XXI.

CHAPTER SEVEN

1 Davies, Peter, *France and the Second World War: occupation, collaboration and resistance*, London: Routledge, 2001, p. 63.

2 Beevor, Antony, Artemis Cooper, *Paris After the Liberation 1944–1949*, London and New York: Penguin Books, 1994, 2004.

3 Hewitt, Nicholas, *The Cambridge Companion to Modern French Culture*, Cambridge: Cambridge University Press, 2003, p. 47.

4 Kawamura, Yuniya, "Fashion Culture in France", *The Japanese Revolution in Paris Fashion*, Oxford: Berg, 2004, pp. 21–90.

5 Cawthorne, Nigel, *The New Look: The Dior Revolution*, New Jersey: BookSales, 1998. Dior, Christian, Antonia Fraser, (trans.), *Dior by Dior: the autobiography of Christian Dior*, London, V&A, 1957, 2007. Pocha, Marie-France, *Christian Dior: The Biography*, Woodstock, NY: Overlook Press, 2008. Pocha, Marie-France, Joanne Savill, *Christian Dior: The Man Who Made the World Look New*, New York: Arcade Publishing, 1996.

6 Demornex, Jacqueline, *Lucien Lelong*, London: Thames & Hudson, 2008.

7 http://www.designmuseum.org/design/christian-dior.

8 Pochna, Marie France, "Lucky Star", in *Christian Dior: the Man Who Made the World Look New*, New York: Arcade Publishing, 1996, p. 85–98.

9 Schwarz, Benjamin, "Couture Clash", *The Atlantic Monthly*, January/February 2008, http://www.theatlantic.com/doc/200801/editors-choice.

10 Rule, Vera, "Dressed to repress", *The Independent* on Sunday, 23 September 2007. http://findarticles.com/p/articles/mi_qn4159/is_20070923/ai_n20521370.

11 Thomas, Dana, "The Sweet Smell of Success", in *Deluxe: How Luxury Lost its Lustre*, London and New York: Penguin, 2007, pp. 135–166.

12 http://www.fundinguniverse.com/company-histories/Chanel-SA-Company-History.html.

13 Karbo, Karen, Chesley McLaren, *The Gospel According to Chanel: Life Lessons from the World's Most Elegant Woman*, Guilford CT: The Globe Pequot Press, 2009, p. 215.

14 As quoted in, Downie, David, *Paris, Paris: Journey Into the City of Light*, London: Transatlantic Press, 2005, p. 93.

15 Meunier, Jacob, *On the Fast Track: French Railway Modernization and the Origins of the TGV, 1944–1983*, Westport CT: Greenwood Publishing, p. 62.

16 Beniada Frédéric, Michel Fraile, *Concorde*, Minneapolis, MN: Zenith Press, 2006.

17 Sutcliffe, Anthony, "Architecture, Planning and Design", in Hewitt, Nicholas, *The Cambridge Companion to Modern French Culture*, Cambridge: Cambridge University Press, 2003, p. 78.

18 http://www.citroenet.org.uk/passenger-cars/michelin/ds/ds-index.html.

19 http://www.usounds.com/the-citroen-ds-by-barthes. Le Wita, Beatrix, *French Bourgeois Culture*, Cambridge: Cambridge University Press, 1994. Reynolds, John, *Andre Citroen: the Man and the Motor Car*, London: Wrens Park, 1996.

20 http://www.netcarshow.com/citroen/1956-ds_19/.

21 Allemann-Ghionda, Cristina, " Dewey in postwar-Italy: The case of re-education", *Studies in Philosophy and Education*, vol. 19, no. 1–2, March 2000, pp. 53–67. John Dewey (1859–1952) was an American philosopher and teacher, see: Dewey, John, *The Quest for Certainty: A Study of the Relation of Knowledge and Action*, London: George Allen & Unwin, 1930.

22 George Catlett Marshall was awarded the Nobel Peace Prize in 1953 for his role as architect and advocate of the Marshall Plan. For the text of the lecture that precipitated the Marshall Plan, see: The "Marshall Plan" speech at Harvard University, 5 June 1947, http://www.oecd.org/document/10/0,3343,en_2649_201185_1876938_1_1_1_1,00.html.

23 Woodham, Jonathan M, *Twentieth-Century Design*, Oxford: Oxford University Press, 1997, p. 121.

24 Harper, John Lamberton, *America and the Reconstruction of Italy, 1945–1948*, Cambridge and New York: Cambridge University Press, 1986. Ellwood, D W, "The 1948 Elections in Italy: a Cold War Propaganda Battle", *Historical Journal of Film, Radio and Television*, 13:1, 1993, pp. 19–33.

25 Woodham, p. 123. See also: Andrea Branzi, C H Evans (trans.), *In The Hot House: Italian New Wave Design*, Boston: MIT Press, 1984.

26 Ellwood, David W, "The Propaganda of the Marshall Plan in Italy in a Cold War Context", in Scott-Smith, Giles, Hans Krabbendam, eds., *The Cultural Cold War in Western Europe, 1945-1960*, London, Frank Cass, 2003, p. 226.

27 Sparke, Penny, "A modern identity for a new nation: design in Italy since 1860", in *Baran'ski, Zygmunt G*, Rebecca J West, The Cambridge Companion to Modern Italian Culture, Cambridge: Cambridge University Press, 2001, pp. 265–291.

28 Ponti, Lisa Licitra, *Gio Ponti: The Complete Work, 1923-1978*, Cambridge, MA: MIT Press, 1990.

29 For a definitive case study see: Hebdige, Dick, "Objects as image: the Italian Scooter Cycle", in *Hiding in the Light: On image and Things*, London and New York: Routledge, 1989, pp. 77–115.

30 For an authoritative history of the Piaggio company and the Vespa, Mazzanti, Davide, *Vespa: Style in Motion*, San Francisco: Chronicle Books, 2004.

31 For a company profile: http://www.referenceforbusiness.com/history2/83/Piaggio-C-S-P-A.html.

32 Marinacci, Sandro, *Il Volo della Vespa: Corradino D'Ascanio, dal sogno dell'elicottero allo scooter che ha motorizzato l'Italia*, Textus, 2006.

33 *Roman Holiday* was the first American film to be shot in its entirety in Italy, thanks mainly to the fact that Paramount had assets frozen in Italy and was able to take advantage of the opportunity to film in Rome. The film received three Oscars (and was nominated for seven others): The Vespa has featured in around fifty major films from the seminal *Roman Holiday*, 1953, to *The World of Suzie Wong*, 1957, *The Talented Mr Ripley*, 1999, *The Bourne Ultimatum*, 2007, and *The Darjeeling Limited*, 2007.

34 Barnwell, Maurice, *A Context of Seats: an intuitive speculation*, Toronto: Glendon Gallery, York University, 1987.

35 Alviani, Carl, "Not Created Equal: A Long, (Loving) Plastics Primer", *Core77*. An excellent, informative and erudite overview of plastics in relation to design. Available on line from *Core77*, the industrial design web site. http://www.core77.com/reactor/03.07_plastics.asp.

36 For the definitive source see: Mateo Kries, Alexander Von Vegeaack, ed., *Joe Colombo: Inventing the Future*, Weil am Rhein: Vitra Design, 2005. For a brief biographical sketch see: http://www.designmuseum.org/design/joe-colombo.

37 Ambasz, Emilio, ed., *Italy: the New Domestic Landscape: Achievements and Problems of Italian Design*, New York: Museum of Modern Art, 1972.

38 "Domestic Disturbances", *The Architects Newspaper*, 5 June 2009. http://www.archpaper.com/e-board_rev.asp?News_ID=3460.

39 Thorpe, Ann, *The Designer's Atlas of Sustainability*, Washington, DC: Island Press, 2007, p. 130.

40 Mantle, Jonathan, *Benetton: the Family, the Business and the Brand*, New York: Pearson Education, 2000.

41 Clegg, Stewart, "Italian Fashion: the Colours of Benetton", Marceau, Jane, ed., *Reworking the World: Organisations, Technologies, and Cultures in Comparative Perspective*, Berlin and New York: Walter de Gruyter, 1992, pp. 69–74. Stone, Marilyn, A, and J B McCall, *International Strategic Marketing: A European Perspective*, London and New York: Routledge, 2004, p. 127. Rothacher, Albrecht, "United, the Benetton Way", *Corporate Cultures and Global Brands*, Singapore: World Scientific, 2004, pp. 131–144.

42 http://www.digitaljournalist.org/issue0309/lm_intro.html.

43 The following is from the Benetton Campaign History site: "The photo of the newborn baby girl, Giusy, was intended as an anthem to life, but was one of the most censured visuals in the history of Benetton ads. In the realm of advertising, traditionally occupied by pretense, the eruption of real life caused a scandal". http://press.benettongroup.com/ben_en/about/campaigns/history/.

44 For an intelligent overview of the reality campaign see: Bruinsma, Max, "Commercial art. Benetton's gospel", eye, vol. 8 no. 29, Autumn, 1998. http://maxbruinsma.nl/eye/index.html?29toscani.htm.

45 For more specific information see: Wells, Liz, "Case Study: Benetton, Toscani and the limits of advertising", *Photography: A Critical Introduction*, London and New York: Routledge, 2004, pp. 239–245. Numerous on-line resources are available including: http://www.print.duncans.tv/2007/benetton-pieta-in-aids-campaign/, http://commercial-archive.com/node/137205, http://production.investis.com/ben_en/about/campaigns/history/, http://www.creativereview.co.uk/crblog/benetton-hits-middle-age/, http://archive.salon.com/people/feature/2000/04/17/toscani_int/index.html.

46 Ollivier, Debra, "The colorful dissenter of Benetton", Salon.com. 17 April 2000, http://archive.salon.com/people/feature/2000/04/17/toscani_int/index.html.

47 For an extensive and well documented assessment of the complex issues concerning German design in the first half of the twentieth century, see: Betts, Paul, *The Authority of Everyday Objects: A Cultural History of West German Industrial Design*, Berkeley: University of California Press, 2004. For a collection of essays which address some of the cultural and social concerns of various European nations after the Second World War; Bessel, Richard, Dirk Schumann, ed., *Life After Death: Approaches to a Cultural and Social History of Europe During the 1940s and 1950s*, Cambridge: Cambridge University Press, 2003.

48 Gimbel, John, "The German Economic Jungle", in *The Origins of the Marshall Plan*, Stanford: Stanford University Press, 1976, pp. 143–166. Leffler, Melvyn P, "The Marshall Plan, Germany, and the Cold War, June 1947–June 1948, A Preponderance of Power: National Security, the Truman Administration, and the Cold War", Stanford: Stanford University Press, 1992, pp. 182–219.

49 The participation of Britain, France and Russia in this unofficial programme is without documentation. The American programmes well documented in; Lasby, Clarence G, *Project Paperclip*, New York: Atheneum, 1971.

50 Specific to the German context are: Wildt, Michael, "Continuities and Discontinuities of Consumer Mentality in West Germany in the 1950s", pp. 211–230 and Betts, Paul, "The Politics of Post-Fascist Aesthetics: 1950s West and East German Industrial Design", pp. 291–322. (See entry above.) See also: Woodham, Jonathan M, "A rational approach to design; The Hochschule für Gestaltung at Ulm: 1953-1969", *Twentieth-Century Design*, Oxford: Oxford University Press, 1997, pp. 177–180. For a brief overview of the German objects included in the V&A's Modernism exhibition of 2006, see: http://www.guardian.co.uk/travel/2006/may/21/culturaltrips.germany.observerescapesection. For information on current German Design see the newsletter of the German Design Council: http://www.german-design-council.de/index.php?id=559&L=3. For a general design history with many references to design in Germany, written by a Professor at the Academy of Art and Design in Offenbach am Main and author of numerous publications, see: Bürdek, Bernhard E, *Design: History, Theory and Practice of Product Design*, Basle: Birkhäuser/Verlag, 2005.

51 Kirsch, Karin, (trans.), *The Weissenhofsiedlung: Experimental Housing Built for the Deutscher Werkbund, Stuttgart, 1927*, New York: Rizzoli, 1989.

52 Stephenson, Charles, *Zeppelins: German Airships 1900–40*, Oxford: Osprey Publishing, 2004.

53 Swinney, G, "Kursk: the Great Soviet-German Armoured Clash". *Military History Journal*, vol. 9, no. 6, December 1994, The South African Military History Society. This online article includes a photograph of a Russian Army horse drawn field gun, with the caption," Both sides were still surprisingly reliant on horses in July 1943 employing them, amongst other tasks, to transport supplies and tow guns". http://samilitaryhistory.org/vol096gs.html.

54 Parsch, Andreas, "German Military Aircraft Designations (1933–1945) lists Westphälisch-Anhaltische Sprengstoff AG (WASAG); Schmidding; Rheinmetall-Borsig AG; Bayerische Motorenwerke GmbH (BMW); and Hellmuth Walter KG (HWK) as manufacturers' of rocket engines. http://www.designation-systems.net/non-us/germany.html#_Engines_Jet.

55 Over 2,500 drawings showing the development of the V2 are in the collection of the Public Records Office in London. See also: Dungan, Tracy D, *V-2: A Combat History of the First Ballistic Missile*, Yardley PA: Westholme Publishing, 2005. Huzel, Dieter K, *Peenemunde to Canaveral*. New York: Prentice Hall, 1962. Reuter, Claus, *The V2 and the German, Russian and American Rocket Program*.

56 Ward, Bob, *Dr. Space: the Life of Werner von Braun*, Annapolis MD: Navel Institute Press, 2005, p. 45.

57 Mowat, Farley, *My Father's Son. Memories of War and Peace*, Toronto: McClelland-Bantam, 1992, p. 367.

58 Bergaust, Erik, *Wernher von Braun: The authoritative and definitive biographical profile of the father of modern space flight*, Washington DC: National Space Institute, 1976. (The National Space Institute was a space advocacy group, founded by Wernher von Braun.) Biddle, Wayne, *Dark Side of the Moon: Wernher von Braun, the Third Reich, and the Space Race*, New York: WW Norton, 2009. Lasby, Clarence G, *Project Paperclip: German Scientists and the Cold War*, New York: Atheneum, 1971. Neufeld, Michael J, *Von Braun: Dreamer of Space, Engineer of War*, Toronto: Random House of Canada, 2008. *The Rocket and the Reich: Peenemünde and the Coming of the Ballistic Missile Era*, New York: Free Press, 1994.

59 Woodham, Jonathan M, "Germany: reconstruction and Wirtschaftswunder", *Twentieth-Century Design*, Oxford: Oxford University Press, 1997, pp. 128–131.

60 Ferdinand Porsche, the Austro-Hungarian automotive engineer, became Managing Director of Austro-Daimler in 1916 before founding the Porsche company in 1931. After designing the peoples car he went on to engineer the Tiger tank, one of the most formidable tanks of the Second World War.

61 For a unique and informative view of this of forgotten development see: "Cars & history: start of the aerodynamic era (1931–1933)", International Streamlined Tatra site: http://www.tatra.demon.nl/cars_history_aerodynamic.htm. For connections to the American Motors Gremlin model, introduced in April 1970, see: http://faculty.concord.edu/chrisz/hobby/80-AMXitems/Information/production/KammbackStory.html.

62 Price, Ryan Lee, *The Vw Beetle: A Production History of the World's Most Famous Car, 1936–1967*, New York: HP Books/Penguin, 2003, pp. 17–19.

63 Chant, Colin, "Cars, Contexts and Identities: the Volkswagen and the Trabant", Pittaway, Mark, *Globalization and Europe*, Milton Keynes: The Open University, 2003, pp. 199–248.

64 Droste, Magdalena, *Bauhaus-Archiv, Bauhaus, 1919–1933*, Berlin: Bauhaus-Archiv, Museum für Gestaltung/Taschen, 1990, 2002. Fiedler, Jeannine, Ute Ackermann, *Bauhaus*, Cologne and New York: Konemann, 2006. For the Bauhaus archive museum: http://www.bauhaus.de/english/.

65 Betts, Paul, *The Authority of Everyday Objects. A Cultural History of West German Industrial Design*, Berkeley, Los Angeles and London: University of California Press, 2004, p. 2.

66 A biography and time line from the Design Museum: http://www.designmuseum.org/design/dieter-rams. For a revealing in depth assessment of Rams and his design philosophy see the article by Marcus Fairs that appeared in *Icon*, February, 2004. http://www.iconeye.com/articles/20070322_27.

67 Belmonte, Laura A, *Selling the American way: US propaganda and the Cold War*, Philadelphia, PA: University of Pennsylvania Press, 2008, pp. 87–93. Randolph Bell, of Floating Films, created a video for the *Wall Street Journal* chronicling the American Exposition and the Moscow Kitchen Debates. Gordon, Alastair, "Wall to Wall: Kulture Vultures of the Cold War. The American National Exhibition in Moscow, 1959", *WSJ Magazine*, 22 August 2009.

68 Taylor, Frederick, *The Berlin Wall: A World Divided, 1961–1989*, New York: HarperCollins, 2008.

69 An exhibition exploring the mutual homage of Richard Hamilton and Dieter Rams opened at 72 Wigmore Street on 22 April and ran to 7 May 2005. http://www.vitsoe.com/news_exhibition_2005.php?id=79. Sudjic, Deyan, *The Language of Things: Understanding the World of Desirable Objects*, New York: WW Norton, 2009, p 171.

70 For four detailed examples of his complete design process that illustrate Rams way of thinking, see: "Four developments", in Burkhardt, François and Inez Franksen, *Design: Dieter Rams*, Berlin: Gerhardt Verlag, 1980, pp. 91–126. ISBN 3920372360/3920372344/9783920372341/3-920372-34-4 This may be very difficult to track down but it offers unique insight into a refined and effective design process.

71 A quote by Dieter Rams, reported in the *International Herald Tribune* in 2006. Rawsthorn, Alice, "Reviving Dieter Rams's pragmatism", *International Herald Tribune*, 12 November 2006, http://www.iht.com/articles/2006/11/12/features/design13.php?page=2.

72 Rawsthorn, Alice, "Does the iPhone have 'It'? Early Signs are Good", *The New York Times*, 24 June 2007.

73 Elmer-DeWitt, Philip, "How Many iPads has Apple Really Sold?" *Fortune*, 5 October 2010. http://ipod.about.com/od/glossary/qt/number-of-ipods-sold.htm.

74 http://www.vitsoe.com/ten_commandments.php. For Japanese versions: http://b.hatena.ne.jp/entrymobile/7135910. http://feed.designlinkdatabase.net/feed/outsite_89173.aspx.

CHAPTER EIGHT

1 For a photographic account of the original recording, see: Athey, Joan, *Give Peace a Chance: John and Yoko's Bed-in for Peace*, Toronto and New York: Wiley, 2009. In 2005, Paul McGrath directed a DVD, *John & Yoko: Give Peace a Song*, Canadian Broadcasting Corporation, 2005.

2 The phrase "peace for our time" has ironic overtones. It was used on the 30 September 1938, by British prime minister Neville Chamberlain, to describe the appeasement agreement reached with Hitler which gave Germany the Sudantenland of Czechoslovakia. One year later Europe would become engulfed in the Second World War.

3 Farber, David R, Beth L Bailey, *The Columbia Guide to America in the 1960s*, New York: Columbia University Press, 2001.

4 For the DAC, see the detailed account: http://archiveshub.ac.uk/search/record.html?recid=gb0532cwldac.

5 http://www.peacenews.info/issues/2448/244827.html. Westcott, Kathryn, "World's best-known protest symbol turns 50", *BBC News Magazine*, http://news.bbc.co.uk/1/hi/magazine/7292252.stm. The origin of the Peace Symbol: http://www.docspopuli.org/articles/PeaceSymbolArticle.html. Kolsbun, Ken, Michael Sweeney, *PEACE: The Biography of a Symbol*, Washington, DC: National Geographic Books, 2008. From the Campaign for Nuclear Disarmament; http://www.cnduk.org/pages/ed/cnd_sym.html. See also: http://www.designboom.com/contemporary/peace.html.

6 50 years later and the protest continues; Williams, Rachel, "5,000 take peace message to Aldermaston, 50 years on", *The Guardian*, Tuesday, 25 March 2008. http://www.guardian.co.uk/uk/2008/mar/25/antiwar.military.

7 On Liturgical colours: http://en.wikipedia.org/wiki/Liturgical_colour.

8 The Peace Museum, Bradford, "Building a Culture of Peace through a range of exhibits, lectures, theatre and film". http://www.peacemuseum.org.uk/.

9 Coulson, Clare, "50 years of the peace symbol", *The Guardian*, Friday, 22 August 2008. http://www.guardian.co.uk/world/2008/aug/22/nuclear.fashion.

10 There are opposing views concerning the nature of the explosion, see: http://www.time.com/time/magazine/article/0,9171,871556,00.html. http://www.granma.cu/ingles/2006/marzo/mierc15/12lacoubre.html.

11 Sola, Oscar, Matilde Sánchez, *Che: Images of a Revolutionary*, London: Pluto Press, 2000. Anderson, Jon Lee, *Che Guevara: A Revolutionary Life*, New York: Grove Press, 1997, 2010. Butterfield Ryan, Henry, *The Fall of Che Guevara*, Oxford and New York: Oxford University Press, 1997. Kunzle, David, *Che Guevara: Icon, Myth, and Message*, Los Angeles: University of California, 1997. Che Guevara appears on the cover and as lead story in *Time*, 8 August 1960.

12 "The Marxist Neighbor", *Time*, Monday, 20 June, 1960. http://www.time.com/time/magazine/article/0,9171,826434-3,00.html.

13 This is also the title of a visionary documentary that was released in 2006. "Revolucion: five visions reframes the Cuban revolution through the art of photography, focussing on the personal stories of five Cuban photographers whose lives and work span nearly five decades of revolution in Cuba. From Havana to Miami, photographers on both sides of the political divide reveal the Cuban people's resilient struggle for self-determination". http://www.elsuenopictures.com/.

14 Obituary, Alberto Korda, *The Telegraph*, 28 May, 2001.

15 http://news.bbc.co.uk/2/hi/americas/7028598.stm.

16 Kornbluh, Peter, "The Death of Che Guevara: Declassified", National Security Archive, Electronic Briefing Book no. 5. http://www.gwu.edu/~nsarchiv/NSAEBB/NSAEBB5/index.html.

17 Jean Lartéguy is the nom de plume of Jean Pierre Lucien Osty. "Les Guerilleros" appeared in the July 1967 issue of *Paris Match*.

18 Kornbluh, Peter, "The Death of Che Guevara: Declassified", National Security Archive, Electronic Briefing Book no. 5. http://www.gwu.edu/~nsarchiv/NSAEBB/NSAEBB5/index.html.

19 http://www.vam.ac.uk/vastatic/microsites/1541_che/.

20 http://news.bbc.co.uk/2/hi/americas/7028598.stm.

21 For a reassessment of one of the Sixties' most enduring icons: O'Hagan, Sean, "Just a pretty face?" *The Observer*, Sunday, 11 July 2004, http://film.guardian.co.uk/features/featurepages/0,,1258376,00.html.

22 Frank, Thomas, *The Conquest of Cool: Business Culture, Counterculture, and the Rise of Hip Consumerism*, Chicago: University of Chicago Press, 1997, p. 5. In this study, Thomas Frank shows how, in America, the youthful, hip, revolutionaries were joined by such unlikely allies as the advertising industry and the men's

clothing business. He explores the Pepsi Generation, recounts the Peacock Revolution, and suggests some important new questions about the culture of the 1960s.
23 For an in depth study of the soft drink industry structure and the competitive strategy of Coca-cola and Pepsi over 100 years of rivalry, see: Yoffie, David B, Yusi Wang, *Cola Wars Continue: Coke vs. Pepsi in 2006*, Harvard Business, 2006, available as electronic download, item : 9-706-447. http://doi.contentdirections.com/mr/hbsp. jsp?doi=10.1225/706447. A related tangential topic, "What happens when the world's biggest brand collides with the world's largest religion?... how brand identity is influenced by consumer perception through the struggle between Coca-Cola, icon of American culture, and rivals Qibla Cola and Mecca Cola for market share in Muslim locales". Cola wars : message in a bottle/ Videorecording, produced and directed by Arif Nurmohamed, *BBC Learning*, 2004.
24 Tedlow, Richard S, *New and Improved. The Story of Mass Marketing in America*, London: Heinemann Professional Publishing, 1990, p. 372.
25 As quoted in Whiteley, Nigel, *Reyner Banham: Historian of the Immediate Future*. Cambridge, MA: MIT Press, 2003, p. 380.
26 As quoted in Whiteley, Nigel, *Reyner Banham: Historian of the Immediate Future*, p. 384.
27 For a rational assessment of this attack on 'conventional wisdom' see: Ben-Ami, Daniel, "The midwife of miserabilism", Spiked review of books, http://www.spiked-online.com/index.php?/site/reviewofbooks_article/4363/.
28 *The Hidden Persuaders*, 1957, was followed by other best sellers, *The Waste Makers*, 1960, which dissected the strategies of planned obsolescence; *The Pyramid Climbers*, 1962, shows the futility of junior executives in their struggle for positions of power.
29 For a well researched and informative assessment see: McLaren, Carrie, "Subliminal Seduction", *Stay Free*, Issue no. 22, Spring 2004. http://www.ibiblio.org/pub/electronic-publications/stay-free/archives/22/subliminal-advertising.htm. For a more specific focus see: Kasper, Gabriele, Shoshana Blum-Kulka, "Conscious Perception versus Subliminal Influences in Learning, Interlanguage Pragmatics", Oxford: Oxford University Press, 1993, pp. 24–2.
30 McLaren, Carrie. Jason Torchinsky, *Ad Nauseam. A Survivor's Guide to American Consumer Culture*, New York: Faber and Faber, 2009, p. 226. See also "Subliminal Seduction: How Did the Uproar over Subliminal Manipulation Affect the Ad Industry?" pp. 223–246, for a documented debunking of the subliminal myth.
31 Fiske Susan T, Daniel T Gilbery, Gardner Lindzey, *Handbook of Social Psychology*, vol. 1, Hoboken NJ: Wiley, p. 401.
32 Bryan Key, Wilson, *Subliminal Seduction*, Colchester, Signet, 1974.
33 MClaren, Carrie, "Subliminal Seduction", *Stay Free*, issue no. 22. http://www.stayfreemagazine.org/archives/22/subliminal-advertising.html.
34 Richards, Barry, Jackie Botterill, Iain MacRury, *The Dynamics of Advertising*, London: Routledge, 2001, p. 62.
35 Zakia, Richard D, *Perception and Imaging*, Woburn, MA: Focal Press, 2001, p. 334. Intended as an explanation of creative photography, this work provides a more detailed account of perception in general. Dr Zakia is Professor Emeritus at the Rochester Institute of Technology.
36 Lois, George, *Covering the '60s: George Lois–The Esquire Era*, New York: Monacelli, 1996. Lois, George and Bill Pitts, *The Art of Advertising: George Lois on Mass Communication*, New York: Harry N Abrams, Inc,

1977. Hilfiger, Tommy, George Lois, *Iconic America: A Roller-Coaster Ride Through the Eye-Popping Panorama of American Pop Culture*, New York: Universe (an imprint of Rizzoli,) 2007. Meggs, Philip B, "George Lois", *A History of Graphic Design*, New York: John Wiley, 1988, pp. 359–362. For the transcript of the speech made by George Lois to the Magazine Publishers of America session of the American Magazines Conference, 18 October 2005. http://adage.com/images/random/GeorgeLois.pdf. A 1978 biography when Lois was inducted into the Art Directors Club Hall of Fame; http://www.adcglobal.org/archive/hof/1978/?id=274. For an array of sources of talks, papers, etc., from UNjobs Association of Geneva, http://unjobs.org/authors/george-lois. On being awarded the AIGA gold medal in 1998: http://www.aiga.org/content.cfm/medalist-georgelois. Lois had a show at the Philip Johnson Architecture and Design Galleries, on the third floor of the MOMA, "George Lois: The Esquire Covers", 25 April 2008–31 March 2009. http://www.artdaily.com/index.asp?int_sec=2&int_new=23534.
37 From an interview with George Lois in Metropolismag.com, 19 December 2007. http://www.metropolismag.com/cda/story.php?artid=3082.
38 Herring, George C, "Coexistence and Crises, 1953–1961", in *From Colony to Superpower*, New York: Oxford University Press, 2008, pp. 651–701.
39 In correspondence with George Lois, 3 March 2009.
40 The Museum of Modern Art Exhibitions. *George Lois: The Esquire Covers*. 25 April 2008–30 March 2009. http://www.moma.org/visit/calendar/exhibitions/72.
41 Lois, George, *The Esquire Covers @ MoMA*, New York: Assouline, 2010.
42 There are three known versions of the Martyrdom of St Sebastian by the Italian early Renaissance master Andrea Mantegna. One version dated, 1456–1459 is in Kunsthistorisches Museum, Vienna; another dated 1490 is in the Ca' d'Oro, Venice, and the third version dating from 1480 and likely to have been the inspiration for the cover, is in the collection of the Musée du Louvre, Paris.
43 The legendary account of 'M company' written by John Stack for *Esquire* magazine is available on line: http://www.esquire.com/features/vietnam-war-m-company-0365.
44 From an interview with George Lois in Metropolismag.com, 19 December 2007. http://www.metropolismag.com/cda/story.php?artid=3082.
45 Kurlansky, Mark, *1968: The Year That Rocked the World*, Toronto and New York: Random House, 2004.
46 "Waist Deep in the Big Muddy" was one of the most famous anti-Vietnam war songs. Composed by Pete Seeger it was a major hit on the college circuit, initially banned from all broadcast media, it was edited out of a Smothers Brothers Comedy Hour by CBS. Winkler, Allan M, *To Everything There is a Season, Pete Seeger and the Power of Song*, Oxford and New York: Oxford University Press, 2009, pp. 124-138. http://history.sandiego.edu/gen/snd/waistdeep.html. *The 1960s–World Events*, BBC, London. http://www.bbc.co.uk/dna/h2g2/A3768537. Also from the BBC archives, over 1,300 video clips from the 1960s. http://www.bbcmotiongallery.com/Customer/SearchResults.aspx?searchText=1960&type=Simple.
47 *The International Times* was the first counter-culture paper. *IT* covered the spread of alternative culture across the globe, from the May 1968 protests in Paris to the Black Panthers to the anti-Vietnam war movement. http://www.internationaltimes.it/.
48 Buckminster Fuller R, the American architect, author, designer, futurist, inventor, poet and visionary produced some outstanding inspirational books,

including: Fuller, Buckminster R, *Nine Chains to the Moon*, Garden City: Doubleday, 1938 (republished in 1963, 1971 and 2000). This often overlooked publication is most relevant to the current cultural context of design. Buckminster Fuller introduces the concept of ehemeralization, a process of doing more with less to allow for ever increasing standards of living and ever growing population despite finite resources. Fuller, Buckminster R, *Operating Manual for Spaceship Earth*, Carbondale: Southern Illinois University Press, 1969, republished by Lars Müller Publishers, 2008. Fuller, Buckminster, Robert Marks, *The Dymaxion World of Buckminster Fuller*, Garden City: Anchor Books, 1973. Fuller, Buckminster R, *Critical Path*, New York: St Martins Press, 1981. Considered his masterwork, a summation of his lifetimes thought and concerns. Fuller, Buckminster R, *Grunch of Giants*, New York: St Martin's Press, 1983. For an amazing collection of 42 hours of Buckminster Fuller's "Everything I Know" sessions recorded in Philadelphia in 1975. These video's are freely available to all online to use for the betterment of our world. http://www.jayhasbrouck.com/. See also the site of the Buckminster Fuller Institute; http://bfi.org/node.
49 The space odyssey explained. http://www.kubrick2001.com/.
50 For an illustrated account of Woodstock: Evans, Mike, Paul Kingsbury, eds., *Woodstock: Three Days That Rocked the World*, New York: Sterling, 2009.
51 Ali, Tariq, "Where has all the rage gone?", *The Guardian*, Saturday, 22 March 2008. http://www.guardian.co.uk/politics/2008/mar/22/vietnamwar. A lucid and factual account of the year of violence by Tariq Ali, the British-Pakistani historian, novelist, filmmaker, political campaigner, social commentator and leading demonstrator in the protest march against the Vietnam War, Grosvenor Square, London, 1968. "1968: The year of revolt". http://www.guardian.co.uk/news/1968theyearofrevolt. "1968: The year that changed the world?". Listen to the 23 minute podcast from the BBC archives, a four part series that explores the events of 1968. This series was first broadcast on *BBC Radio 4* and aired on *BBC World Service* on 1 December 2008. http://www.bbc.co.uk/worldservice/documentaries/2008/11/081125_1968_part_1.shtml.
52 For detailed account of Mario Savio, the leader of the Berkeley Free Speech Movement see: Cohen Robert, *Freedom's Orator. Mario Savio and the Radical Legacy of the 1960s*, Oxford and New York: Oxford University Press, 2010.
53 The demonstrations in Japan are often overlooked in assessments of 1968. On 21 October 1968, major rioting on the streets of Tokyo and other major cities by the Zengakuren (All-Japan Student Federation) augmented by the SOHYO (General Council of Trade Unions of Japan) was a unique happening in this very structured society. See: Nishio, Harry K, "Extraparliamentary Activities and Political Unrest in Japan", *International Journal*, vol. 24, no. 1 (Winter, 1968/1969), pp. 122–137.
54 Camus, Albert, *The Rebel (L'Homme revolte)*, New York: Vintage, 1951, p. 22.
55 Singer, Daniel, *Prelude to Revolution: France in May 1968*, Cambridge, MA: South End Press, 2002.
56 Kurlansky, Mark, *1968: The Year That Rocked the World*, Toronto and New York: Random House, 2004.
57 Lichfield, John, "Egalité! Liberté! Sexualité!: Paris, May 1968", *The Independent*, Saturday, 23 February 2008. http://www.independent.co.uk/news/europe/egalit-libert-sexualit-paris-may-1968-784703.html.
58 Although the Gaullist party won re-election, there was continued discontent with Charles de Gaulle which led to his resignation in 1969. The new government announced major reforms to the education system and

67 new universities were instigated to cater to student overload and a more democratic system of governing councils was installed.

59 Anonymous graffiti, Paris 1968, as reported in Lichfield, John, "Signs of the times: The sayings and slogans of 1968", *The Independent*, Saturday, 23 February 2008, http://www.independent.co.uk/extras/saturday-magazine/features/signs-of-the-times-the-sayings-and-slogans-of-1968-786017.html.

60 For a study on the connections between popular music and social protest, see: Peddie, Ian, *The Resisting Muse: Popular Music and Social Protest*, Aldershot and Burlington VT: Ashgate, 2006.

61 List of participating groups: Group 1: Theo Crosby, William Turnbull, Germano Facetti, Edward Wright. Group 2: Richard Hamilton, John McHale, John Voelcker. Group 3: JDH Catleugh, James Hull, Leslie Thornton. Group 4: Anthony Jackson, Sarah Jackson, Emilio Scanavino. Group 5: John Ernest, Anthony Hill, Denis Williams. Group 6: Eduardo Paolozzi, Alison and Peter Smithson, Nigel Henderson. Group 7: Victor Pasmore, Erno Goldfinger, Helen Phillips. Group 8: James Stirling, Michael Pine, Richard Matthews. Group 9: Mary Martin, John Weeks, Kenneth Martin. Group 10: Robert Adams, Frank Newby, Peter Carter, Colin St.John Wilson. Group 11: Adrian Heath, John Weeks. Group 12: Lawrence Alloway, Geoffery Holroyd, Tony del Renzio. http://www.thisistomorrow2.com/pages_gb/1956gb.html.

62 Hunt, Jeremy, "This is Tomorrow 2", www.thisistomorrow2.com/documents/. Massey, Anne, *The Independent Group: Modernism and Mass Culture in Britain, 1945–1959*, Manchester: Manchester University Press, 1996, pp. 100–120.

63 Bigham, Julia, *Pop Art Book*, London: Black Dog Publishing, 2007, p. 10.

64 Vidotto, Marco, Santiago Castán, Graham Thomson, *Alison + Peter Smithson*, Barcelona: Gustavo Gili SA, 1997.

65 Smithson, Alison, Peter Smithson, "But Today We Collect Ads", *ARK, the Journal of the Royal College of Art*, London, November 1956, p. 49–50. http://www.designmuseum.org/design/alison-peter-smithson.

66 Osterwold, Tilman, *Pop Art*, Köln: Taschen, 2003, p. 6.

67 There exist an array of excellent books, articles and web sites that provide details on the Pop art phenomenon. One on-line article that provides a factual lucid overview is: Scherman, Tony, "When Pop Turned the Art World Upside Down", *American Heritage*, February/March 2001, vol. 52, issue no. 1. http://www.americanheritage.com/articles/magazine/ah/2001/1/2001_1_68.shtml.

68 Warhol, Andy, Annette Michelson, BHD Buchloh, *Andy Warhol*, Cambridge, MA: MIT Press, 2001, p. 2.

69 On Sixties fashion and design: http://www.sixtiescity.com/Fashion/Fashion.shtm. Breward, Christopher, "The Dolly Bird: Chelsea and Kensington 1960-1970", *Fashioning London: Clothing and the Modern Metropolis*, London: Berg, 2004, pp. 151–176. For an illustrated history of rock'n'roll fashion, from the 1950s to the present: Gorman, Paul, *The Look–Adventures in Rock and Pop Fashion*, London: Adelita/Metro Media, 2006. On the pop arts in Britain: Melley, George, *Revolt in Style: The Pop Arts in Britain*, London: Allen Lane, 1970.

70 For a study of some of the fashion designers and their link with the pop culture of the 1960s, see: McRobbie, Angela, "The Fashion Girls and the Painting Boys", *British Fashion Design: Rag Trade or Image Industry?*, London and New York: Routledge, 1998, pp. 33–52.

71 Horton, Ros, Rosalind Horton, Sally Simmons, "Mary Quant", *Women Who Changed the World*, London: Quercus, 2007, pp. 170–173. Quant, Mary, *Quant by Quant*, London: Cassell, 1966. On Quant

in the context of "Swinging London", Morris, Brian, *An Introduction to Mary Quant's London*, London Museum, 1973. Gillan, Audrey, "Mary Quant quits fashion empire", *The Guardian*, Saturday, 2 December 2000. http://www.guardian.co.uk/Archive/Article/0,4273,4099577,00.html.

72 "Op art: pictures that attack the eye", *Time*, Friday, 23 October 1964; http://www.time.com/time/magazine/article/0,9171,897336-1,00.html.

73 Hulanicki, Barbara, *From A to Biba. The Autobiography of Barbara Hulanicki*, London: V&A Publications, 1983, 2007. http://www.bibacollection.co.uk/history.htm.

74 Harry, Bill, *Biba*, from the Sixties City website. http://www.sixtiescity.co.uk/Mbeat/mbfilms10.htm. *1960s Fashion and Textiles*, from the collection of the V&A, London. http://www.vam.ac.uk/collections/fashion/1960s/index.html.

75 Decharne, Max, *King's Road, The Rise and Fall of the Hippest Street in the World*, London: Weidenfeld & Nicholson, 2005. Breward, Christopher, "Chelsea and Kensington, 1960-1970", *Fashioning London*, Oxford: Berg, 2004, pp. 151–176.

76 Shirley, Ian, *Can Rock & Roll Save the World?: an Illustrated History of Music and Comics*, London: SAF Publishing, 2005, p. 45.

77 Wyman, Bill, Ray Coleman, *Stone Alone: The Story of a Rock 'n' Roll Band*, New York: Viking, 1990, p. 422.

78 On 430 Kings Road, see: http://www.jonsavage.com/Punk/430-kings-road/.

79 For press accounts of the Peacock Revolution see: "Fashion Comes to the Market", *Financial Times*, 20 May 1960, p. 10. "Peacock Revolution,", *Daily Mail*, 4 September 1965, p. 11.

80 The cover of Sgt. Pepper's was designed by Peter Blake and put together by Peter Blake and Jann Haworth, who painstakingly combed through hundreds of photos for months before the photo shoot. The photo was taken by Michael Cooper at Chelsea Manor Photographic Studios, (Flood Street, just off the Kings Road,) on 30 March 1967.... Many of the people pictured in the cover were personal heroes of The Beatles or people they admired." http://www.beatlesagain.com/btsgtppr.html. Miles, Barry, "The Pepper Sleeve", *The Beatles: A Diary*, London: Omnibus Press, 1998, p. 236. Blake, Peter, Dawn Ades, Natalie Rudd, *Peter Blake: About Collage*, Tate, 2000, pp. 21–24.

81 As quoted in, Miller, Daniel, *Consumption: Critical Concepts in the Social Sciences*, Taylor and Francis, 2001, p. 213. McDermott, Catherine, *Design: the Key Concepts*, Abingdon and New York: Routledge, 2007, pp. 127–128. Highmore, Ben, "Familiar Things", in *Ordinary Lives: Studies in the Everyday*, Abingdon and New York: Routledge, 2011, pp. 58–85.

82 Heskett, John, "Industrial Design", in Ford, Boris, ed., *The Cambridge Cultural History of Britain: Modern Britain*, vol. 9, Cambridge: Cambridge University Press, p. 312.

83 http://www.designmuseum.org/info.

84 Carson, Rachel, *Silent Spring*, New York: First Mariner, 1962, 2002.

85 Friedman, Betty, *The Feminine Mystique*, London: Gollancz, 1963.

86 Nader, Ralph, *Unsafe at any speed: the designed–in dangers of the American automobile*, New York: Grossman, 1965.

CHAPTER NINE

1 Krause, Linda, Patrice Petro, *Global Cities: cinema, architecture, and urbanism in a digital age*, Piscataway, NJ: Rutgers State University, 2003.

2 *The Memory of Tiananmen*, PBS, 1989, http://www.pbs.org/wgbh/pages/frontline/tankman/cron/.

3 The Berlin Wall had separated East and West Germany from its inception in August 1961 until it was opened up on 9 November 1989 before being demolished by the end of 1990. http://www.die-berliner-mauer.de/en/.

4 Meggs, Philip B, *A History of Graphic Design*, New York: John Wiley, 1998, p. 414.

5 Lloyd Wright, Frank, Andrew Devane, Frederick Albert Gutheim, *In the cause of architecture, Frank Lloyd Wright*, New York: McGraw-Hill, 1975, p. 23.

6 Szentes, Tamás, *The Transformation of the World Economy*, London and Tokyo: Zed Books, 1988, p. 86.

7 Organization of Arab Petroleum Exporting Countries. For detailed information see: "Arab Oil-Producing Countries and the First Oil Crisis", in Sumiya, Mikio, *A History of Japanese Trade and Industry Policy*, Oxford: Oxford University Press, 2000, p. 99.

8 "Consumer culture and postmodernity", in Sparke, Penny, *An Introduction to Design and Culture*, Abingdon and New York: Routledge, 2004, pp. 127–138. McCracken, Grant David, *Culture and Consumption*, Bloomington, IN: Indiana University Press, 1990.

9 Jencks, Charles, *The Language of Post-Modern Architecture*, New York: Rizzoli, 1977, 1984. *The New Paradigm in Architecture: the Language of Post-Modernism*, New Haven CT and London: Yale University Press, 2002.

10 "The Social Disaster of Pruitt-Igoe", in Ramroth, William G, *Planning for Disaster: How Natural and Manmade Disasters Shape the Built Environment*, New York: Kaplan, 2007, pp. 163–171. Lang, Jon T, "Case Study: Pruitt-Igoe, East St Louis, Missourir, USA: an ill fated public housing project (1950; proposal to remodel, 1956; demolished 1972)", in *Urban Design: a Typology of Procedures and Products*, Oxford and Burlington MA: Architectural Press, 2005, pp. 181–183.

11 When discussing Pruitt-Igoe, Keith Eggener makes the very valid observation that "much of the project's design was determined by the St Louis Housing Authority and the Public Housing Administration. The architects had no control over the projects isolated location, its excessive densities, the elimination of amenities, or the use of high-rise elevator buildings." Eggener, Keith, *American Architectural History*, Oxford and New York: Routledge, 2004, p. 360.

12 Jencks, Charles, *What is Post-Modernism?*, London: Academy Editions, 1996, pp. 50–54. See also: Gorman, Carma, ed., *The Industrial Design Reader*, New York: Allworth Press, 2003. This collection of over 60 readings range from "On the International Results of the Exhibition of 1851", by Henry Cole, 1852, to "Time for a Change: Design in the Post- Disciplinary Era", by Donald Norman, 1999. It includes Charles Jencks, "The Post-Modern Information World and the Rise of the Cognitariat", from 1996. An excellent collection of readings well worth finding.

13 Brownlee, David Bruce, David Gilson De Long, Kathryn B Hiesinger, Robert Venturi, Denise Scott Brown, *Out of the ordinary: Robert Venturi, Denise Scott Brown and Associates : architecture, urbanism, design*, New Haven and London: Yale University Press, 2001. This is the catalogue for an exhibition originating at the Philadelphia Museum of Art in 2001.

14 For an overview of the use of plywood in modern design, see: Ngo, Dung, Eric Pfeiffer, *Bent Ply*, New York: Princeton Architectural Press, 2003.

15 Venturi, Robert, *Complexity and Contradiction in Architecture*, New York: The Museum of Modern Art, 1966, p. 17.

16 Molloy, John, T, *Women Dress For Success*, Slough: Foulsham, 1977, 1980. Cunningham, Patricia Anne, "The Women's Dress for Success Book (1977)" in Welters,

Linda, Patricia Anne Cunningham, eds, *Twentieth-century American Fashion*, Oxford: Berg, pp. 204–5.

17 Rothwell, Roy, *Design and the Economy: the role of design and innovation in the prosperity of industrial companies*, London: The Design Council, 1983.

18 *Profit by Design*, London: National Design Council, 1974. Reissued in 1989. Keat, Russell, Nicholas Abercrombie, *Enterprise Culture*, Oxford and New York: Routledge, 1990, p. 197. In late 2009, the UK Design Council and British Chamber of Commerce (BCC) announced a new partnership to promote the 'value of design.' The objective being to offer practical help to the 100,000 businesses in the BCC network. http://www.designcouncil.org.uk/.

19 http://www.designmuseum.org/design/memphis.

20 Coffee, Kevin 'Cultural inclusion, exclusion and the formative roles of museums', Museum Management and Curatorship, 23:3, 2008, 261-279

21 Demetrios, Eames, "Eames Chairs. A 30 Years Flash (part 1)", in *An Eames Primer*, New York: Universe Publishing, 2002, pp. 35–47.

22 Demetrios, Eames, "Eames Chairs. A 30 Years Flash (part 1)", in *An Eames Primer*, p. 157.

23 Kicherer, Sibylle, *Olivetti: A Study of the Corporate Management of Design*, New York: Rizzoli, 1990. "Olivetti: a story of innovation and growth", http://www.storiaolivetti.telecomitalia.it/uk/cgi-bin/Societa/storia.asp.

24 For a biographical account of the life of this innovative designer, see: http://www.designmuseum.org/design/ettore-sottsass. See also: Labaco, Ronald T, *Ettore Sottsass: Architect & Designer*, London & New York: Merrell, 2006.

25 "Ettore Sottsass. Designer who helped to make office equipment fashionable and challenged the standard notion of tasteful interiors", *Times* online, 2 January 2008. http://www.timesonline.co.uk/tol/comment/obituaries/article3118052.ece.

26 Agerman, Johanna, "Valentine Typewriter", *ICON* 068, February, 2009. http://www.iconeye.com.

27 This period is documented by Penny Sparke in her introduction to *Ettore Sottsass: Architect&Designer*.

28 "Ettore Sottsass, Architect + Product Designer (1917–2007)", Design Museum: London. http://www.designmuseum.org/design/ettore-sottsass.

29 Radice, Barbara, *Memphis: Research, Experience, Results, Failures, and Success of New Design*, New York: Rizzoli, 1984, pp. 185–187.

30 Bürdek, Bernhard E, *Design. History, Theory and Practice of Product Design*, Basel: Birkhäuser Basel, 2005, p. 137.

31 "Ettore Sottsass, Architect + Product Designer (1917-2007)", Design Museum, London. http://www.designmuseum.org/design/ettore-sottsass.

32 This is the famous line in the 6th canto, "Les Chants de Maldoror" composed between 1868 and 1869 by Comte de Lautréamont. Considered a major influence on the modus operandi of French Symbolism, Dada, and Surrealism it was rediscovered by the Situationists and features on their "reading list."

33 Radice, Barbara, *Memphis and Fashion: Memphis, research, Experience, Results, Failures and Successes of New Design*, New York: Rizzoli, 1984, pp. 185–187. Included in, Gorman, Carma, ed., *The Industrial Design Reader*, New York: Allworth Press, 2003, pp. 204–208.

34 Rayport, Jeffrey F, "The Miracle of Memphis", *Technology Review*, 20 December 2010.

35 "Punk Music in Britain", *BBC*, h2g2, created 7 October 2002, accessed on 17 August, 2009. http://www.bbc.co.uk/dna/h2g2/A791336.

36 Taylor, Paul, *Impresario: Malcolm McLaren and the British New Wave*, Cambridge MA and New York: The New Museum of Contemporary Art, New York: MIT Press, 1988. Catalogue of the exhibition at the

New Museum of Contemporary Art, New York, 16 September–20 November, 1988.

37 For a biography of Vivienne Westwood from the V&A; http://www.vam.ac.uk/vastatic/microsites/1231_vivienne_westwood/biography1.html. And from the Design Museum: http://designmuseum.org/design/vivienne-westwood.

38 Lindner, Christopher, *Fictions of Commodity Culture: From the Victorian to the Postmodern*, Aldershot and Burlington VT: Ashgate Publishing, 203, p. 126.

39 Some informative source include: Gray, Christopher, ed., *Leaving the 20th Century: Incomplete Work of the Situationist International*, London: Rebel Press, 1974, 1998. Knabb, Ken, ed., *Situationist International Anthology*, Berkeley CA: Bureau Of Public Secrets, 2007. Iwona Blazwick, ed., *An Endless Adventure... An Endless Passion... An Endless Banquet: A Situationist Scrapbook*. London: ICA & Verso, 1989. http://www.cddc.vt.edu/sionline/notes.html. http://www.nothingness.org/SI/.

40 Lindner, Christopher, *Fictions of Commodity Culture: From the Victorian to the Postmodern*, Aldershot and Burlington VT: Ashgate Publishing, 203, p. 127. Noyer, Paul du, "One King's Road Summer", *The Independent* on Sunday, 18 August 1996.

41 As quoted in *Mail Online*, 28 August, 2008. http://www.dailymail.co.uk/home/moslive/article-1046965/Are-feeling-lucky- Punk.html#ixzz18CNh2aHV .

42 Sabin, Roger, ed., *Punk Rock: So What?*, London and New York: Routledge, 1999. Savage, Jon, *England's Dreaming*, New York: St Martin's Griffin, 1991, 2002. Josh Sims, *Rock Fashion*, London: Omnibus Press, 1999, 2002. Vermoel, Judy, Fred Vermoel, *Sex Pistols: The Inside Story*, London: Omnibus Press, 1987, http://www.rollingstone.com/artists/thesexpistols/biography.

43 Martin, Linda, Kerry Segrave, *Anti-Rock: The Opposition To Rock 'n' Roll*, Cambridge MA and New York: Da Capo Press, 1993, pp. 224–227.

44 http://editdesk.wordpress.com/2009/04/23/memorable-headline-filth-fury/.

45 Southall, Brian, *Sex Pistols: 90 Days at EMI*, London, Bobcat Books, 2007.

46 The Flour Duet between Lakmé and Mallika, is in Act one of the 1883 opera, *Lakmé*, by Léo Delibes. http://www.airodyssey.net/tvc/tvc-british.html. Since 1984, the aria had been used by composer Howard Blake to accompany British Airways commercials. http://www.howardblake.com/music/Commercials/567/British-Airways-Theme-Tune-Lakme.htm.

47 Loughran, Patrick, "Sex Pistol sends Dairy Crest butter sales soaring", *Times* Online, 3 February 2009.

48 Cowley, Jason, *The Last Game: Love, Death and Football*, London: Simon & Schuster, 2009.

49 Triggs, Teal, "Scissors and Glue: Punk Fanzines and the Creation of a DIY Aesthetic", *Journal of Design History*, vol. 19, no. 1, 2006, pp. 69–83. Perry, Mark, *Sniffin' Glue. The Essential Punk Accessory*, London: Sanctuary Publishing, 2000. Part biography of the founder, Mark Perry, who was 19 when he began producing this fanzine, part history of the fanzine, this book includes reproductions of the original issues. *Sniffin' Glue* ran for around 12 months. The first issue sold about 50 copies, the last issue in 1978 sold around 15,000 copies.

50 http://www.xulucomics.com/strangled.html.

51 As quoted in, Mulholland, Neil, *The Cultural Devolution: Art in Britain in the Late Twentieth Century*, Farnham: Ashgate, 2003, p. 65. See also: Reid, Jamie, *Up They Rise; The Incomplete Works of Jamie Reid*, London: Faber and Faber, 1987.

52 Wozencroft, Jon, *The Graphic Language of Neville Brody*, New York: Universe, 1988, 2002. For a brief

biography and 234 downloads by Brody: http://www.fontshop.com/fonts/designer/neville_brody/.

53 Heller, Steven, "Defining Style, Making i-D: An Interview with Terry Jones", *AIGA*, 15 March 2006. http://www.aiga.org/content.cfm/defining-style-making-i-d. Terry Jones, Hinterview, n.d. http://www.hintmag.com/hinterview/terryjones/terryjones1.php.

54 Kuti, John, "The Face—British Style Bible", British Council, n.d. http://www.britishcouncil.org/learnenglish-central-magazine-style-bible.htm.

55 Poynor, Rick, *No More Rules: Graphic Design and Postmodernism*, London: Laurence King Publishing, 2003.

56 The concept is well researched and documented, see: Kawamura, Yuniya, *The Japanese Revolution in Paris Fashion*, Oxford and New York: Berg, 2004, 2006. See also the various issues of the *Dress, Body, Culture* series published by Berg.

57 See, Geraldine Ranson, 1983, "Japan: The Shock of the New", in Poland, Brenda, ed., *Fashion 84*, New York: St Martin's Press, pp. 50–63.

58 See, Kawamura, Yuniya, *The Japanese Revolution in Paris Fashion*, Berg: Oxford, 2004, p.138.

59 Barnwell, Susan, "Fashion: the Cultural Interface", *Globalization of the Fashion Industry*, International Foundation of Fashion Technology Institutes, Annual Conference, Tokyo, Bunka University, 2005, p. 67.

60 In the words of Fukai Akiko, Chief Aesthetics Mentor, Kyoto Foundation for Fashion and Culture Research, "In the eyes of people outside Japan, the end result seemed to express the stoic Japanese aesthetic sense of wabi (simplicity and quietude) and sabi (solitude and withdrawal), and of jimi (unpretentiousness) as well". Akiko, Fukai, 1998, 'Black and White–A Japanese Contribution to the World of Fashion', *Nipponia*, 15 April.

61 Chiu, Edward, "Adrian Joffe: The Idea of Comme des Garçons", Hyperbeast. This excellent article includes an informative interview with Adrian Joffe, Rei Kawakubo's husband and the president of Comme des Garcons. http://hypebeast.com/2011/01/adrian-joffe-the-idea-of-comme-des-garcons/.

62 Slater, John, "Tokyo 1964", in Findling, John E, Kimberly D Pelle, *Encyclopedia of the Modern Olympic Movement*, Westport, CT: Greenwood Publishing Group, 2004, pp. 165–174.

63 Slater, John, "Tokyo 1964", in Findling, John E, Kimberly D Pelle, *Encyclopedia of the Modern Olympic Movement*, p. 167.

64 Godoy, Tiffany, Ivan Vartanian, *Style Deficit Disorder: Harajuku Street Fashion*, Tokyo, San Francisco: Chronicle Books, 2007, p. 23. Godoy, Tiffany, Ivan Vartanian, *Tokyo Street Style: Fashion in Harajuku*, London: Thames and Hudson, 2008.

65 Nanba, Koji, "Rethinking 'Shibu-Kaji", *Kwansei Gakuin Sociology Department* studies, 99, pp. 233–246. This is the English abstract. The full pdf article is only available in Japanese. http://ci.nii.ac.jp/naid/110004998464/en.

66 Raizman, David, *History of Modern Design: Graphics and Products since the Industrial Revolution*, London: Lawrence King, 2002, p. 355.

67 "The Rise of Service Design", *Core77*, 11 January 2010. http://www.core77.com/.

CHAPTER TEN

1 Doren, Charles van, *A History of Knowledge. Past, Present, and Future*, New York: Ballantine Books, 1991, p. 297.

2 Doren, Charles van, *A History of Knowledge. Past, Present, and Future*, p. 298.

3 Pacey, Arnold, "The Cathedral Builders: European Technical Achievement between 1100 and 1280", and "A Century of Invention: 1250–1350", *The Maze of Ingenuity. Ideas and Idealism in the Development of*

Technology, Cambridge MA: MIT Press, 1974, 1992, pp. 1–55.

4 Thackara, John, *In the Bubble: Designing in a Complex World*, Cambridge MA: MIT Press, 2006, p. 7.

5 Welford, Richard, Richard Starkey, *The Earthscan Reader in Business and Sustainable Development*, London: Earthscan, 2000.

6 "The Post-World War ll Golden Age of Capitalism and the Crisis of the 1970s", Gloves Off, 2006. http://www.glovesoff.org/features/gjamerica_1.html.

7 Maier, Charles S, "The Politics of productivity: foundations of American international economic policy after the Second World War", *International Organization* 31 (4), Autumn 1977.

8 Lippincott, Joshua Gordon, *Design for Business*, Chicago: Paul Theobald,1947.

9 Galbraith, John Kenneth, *The Affluent Society*, New York: Houghton Mifflin, 1958, 1998.

10 The term conspicuous consumption was introduced by Norwegian American economist and sociologist Thorstein Veblen in his 1899 book *The Theory of the Leisure Class* in which he documents the behavioural characteristic of the nouveau riche , a social class who were emerging in the late 19th century. Veblen, Thorstein, *Theory of the Leisure Class: An Economic Study in the Evolution of Institutions*. New York: Macmillan, 1899.

11 Galbraith, John Kenneth, *The Good Society: The Humane Agenda*, New York: Houghton Mifflin, 1996, p. 82.

12 http://other90.cooperhewitt.org/. In 2003, Polak was named by *Scientific American* as one of the Scientific American 50, the noted magazine's annual list recognizing outstanding acts of leadership in technology. See also: Collier, Paul, *The Bottom Billion: Why the Poorest Countries are Failing and What Can Be Done About It*, Oxford and New York: Oxford University Press, 2007.

13 http://www.d-rev.org/index.html.

14 Hamdi, Nabeel, *Small Change*, London: Earthscan, 2004.

15 http://www.doorsofperception.com/archives/2006/07/how_to_be_good.php.

16 These are four of the eight Millennium Development Goals. For a complete descriptive list see: http://www.guardian.co.uk/katine/2008/sep/25/aidanddevelopment.news2. For the *Millennium Development Goals Report*, 2008, from the United Nations: http://www.un.org/millenniumgoals/pdf/The%20Millennium%20Development%20Goals%20R eport%202008.pdf.

17 Kunzig, Robert, "Population 7 Billion", *National Geographic*, January 2011.

18 Thomas, Angharad, "Design, Poverty, and Sustainable Development", *Design Issues*, vol. 22, no. 4, Autumn 2006, pp. 54–65.

19 Polak, Paul, "Touching the Untouchables", *Out of Poverty. What Works When Traditional Approaches Fail*, January 2011. http://blog.paulpolak.com/?m=201101.

20 *Human Development Report*, 2010 report, p. 1. http://hdr.undp.org/en/mediacentre/.

21 Closing the gap in a generation: Health equity through action on the social determinants of health. *World Health Organization*, 2008. Download the full report [pdf 10.31Mb]: http://www.who.int/social_determinants/final_report/en/index.html.

22 "Global Issues. Social, Political, Economic and Environmental Issues That Affect Us All", March, 2008. http://www.globalissues.org. See also the well documented, factual and insightful "International cooperation at a crossroads. Aid, trade and security in an unequal world", in particular the sections headed "State of human development", Inequality and human development", and "Aid for the 21st Century, Human Development Report 2005, United Nations

Development Programme (UNDP), 2005. http://hdr.undp.org/en/media/hdr05_complete.pdf.

23 http://iresearch.worldbank.org/PovcalNet/jsp/index.jsp.

24 http://www.nationmaster.com/graph/eco_pov_sha_of_all_poo_peo-poverty-share-all-poor- people.

25 "2007 Human Development Report" (HDR), United Nations Development Program, 27 November 2007, p. 25. Grossberg, Lawrence, *We Gotta Get Out of this Place: popular conservatism and postmodern culture*, London and New York: Routledge, 1992, p. 313.

26 Kellner, Douglas, *Media Culture*, London and New York: Routledge, 1995, p. 263.

27 Harris, Paul, "37 million poor hidden in the land of plenty," *The Observer*, Sunday, 19 February 2006. http://www.guardian.co.uk/world/2006/feb/19/usa.paulharris.

28 French, Marilyn, *The War Against Women*, New York: Baltimore books, 1992, p. 37.

29 You can find this report and other extensive information on related areas, including *CARE USA* 2007 Annual Report on their website. http://www.careorg/about/index.asp.

30 Colander, David, *Microeconomics*, McGraw-Hill Paperback, eigth Edition, 2009. Thorpe, Ann, *The Designer's Atlas of Sustainability*, Washington DC: Island Press, 2007.

31 Polak, Paul, *Out of Poverty. What works when traditional approaches fail*. http://www.paulpolak.com/.

32 Moyo, Dambisa, "Aiding is Abetting", *Guernica*, April 2009. http://www.guernicamag.com/interviews/953/aiding_is_abetting/. Moyo, Dambisa, Niall Ferguson, *Dead Aid: Why Aid Is Not Working and How There Is a Better Way for Africa*, New York: Farrar, Straus and Giroux, 2009.

33 Yunus, Mohammad, *Creating a World Without Poverty: Social Business and the Future of Capitalism*, New York: Public Affairs, 2008. http://www.grameen-info.org/.

34 Krahe, Dialika, "How a Basic Income Program Saved a Namibian Village", *Spiegel online*, 8 October 2009, http://www.spiegel.de/international/world/0,1518,642310,00.html. BIG Coaltion Namibia. http://www.bignam.org/.

35 To obtain a first hand account of living in a deprived society see the "This is Kroo Bay" blog on the Save the Children website. "This site brings Kroo Bay, a slum in Freetown, Sierra Leone, to you. Get clicking, explore the community and meet the people. See what life's like without electricity or clean water." http://www.savethechildren.org.uk/kroobay/.

36 Lidgus, Sara, "Designing An End to Poverty", an interview with the economist Jeffrey Sachs, *Design21*, the social design network, October 2007. http://www.design21sdn.com/feature/930. For a biography see: http://www.earth.columbia.edu/articles/view/1804. For a specific example of design: "Malaria Control Calls for Mass Distribution of Insecticidal Bednets", with Awash Teklehaimanot and Chris Curtis, *The Lancet*, 21 June 2007. The bednet also features in an article in *Time*. Sachs, Jeffrey D, "The $10 Solution", *Time*, 4 January 2007. http://www.time.com/time/magazine/article/0,9171,1574152,00.html. The Earth Institute at Columbia University. http://www.earth.columbia.edu/articles/view/1795. See also: Thomas, Angharad, "Design, Poverty, and Sustainable Development", *Design Issues*, vol. 22, no. 4, Autumn 2006, pp. 54– 65.

37 Check out designmatters at the Art Center College of Design. http://www.accd-dm.org/.

38 "Education in the Developing World", Center for Global Development, December, 2006. http://www.cgdev.org/content/publications/detail/2844.

39 "Back to the drawing board. The war on education",

New Internationalist, issue 248, October 1993. http://www.newint.org/issue248/keynote.htm.

40 These figures are taken from "Education in Developing Countries", part of a report provided by the German Federal Ministry for Economic Cooperation and Development.

41 http://www.bmz.de/EN/issues/Education/hintergrund/bildungsituation/index.html. See also: "CARE Announces the Awarding of Advocacy Grants Targeting Girls Engaged in Exploitive Child Labour," June, 2008.

42 http://www.care.org/newsroom/articles/2008/06/20080612_childlabor_grants.asp. http://www.newint.org/issue287/keynote.html. http://www.histori.ca/minutes/minute.do?id=10230. For a news release from the University of Waterloo; http://newsrelease.uwaterloo.ca/news.php?id=519. From the IDRC archives: http://archive.idrc.ca/library/document/050440/.

43 The University of Malaysia is the headquarters of a worldwide network in PVC handpump technology linking 13 countries–China, India, Indonesia, Malaysia, the Philippines, Sri Lanka, Thailand, Cameroon, Egypt, Ethiopia, Kenya, Mali, and Costa Rica. The network promotes research, information-sharing and training for small businesses and community groups on all aspect of handpump technology, including manufacture, installation, maintenance, performance evaluation, financing, and community organisation. http://www.idrc.ca/en/ev-26970-201-1-DO_TOPIC.html. For detailed guide for installation, repair and maintenance https://idl-bnc.idrc.ca/dspace/handle/123456789/16654.

44 As quoted in the seminar proceeding, "Smoke in the Kitchen: Health impacts of indoor air pollution in developing countries", The United Nations Development Programme (UNDP), with support from the Intermediate Technology Development Group (ITDG), the United States Environmental Protection Agency (USEPA) and the World Health Organisation (WHO), New York, 8 February 2005. http://www.energyandenvironment.undp.org

45 Miah, Danesh, Harun Al Rashid, Man Yong Shin, "Wood fuel use in the traditional cooking stoves in the rural floodplain areas of Bangladesh: A socio-environmental perspective", *Biomass and Bioenergy*, vol. 33, no. 1, January 2009, pp. 70–78.

46 *World development report 2010: development and climate change*, Washington DC: The International Bank for Reconstruction and Development/The World Bank, 2010.

47 Elledge, Myles F et al, "Environmental Health Risk and the Use of Biomass Stoves in Sri Lanka," RTI International, October 2010, http://www.rti.org/publications/rtipress.cfm?pid=15519.

48 Global Alliance for Clean Cookstoves. http://www.unfoundation.org/our-solutions/campaigns/cookstoves/.

49 For a most readable, comprehensive, well researched and documented appraisal see: "Insight into an ageing society" and "Design for An Ageing Society", Informed Anecdotes l & ll, available from *Index 2007*, Copenhagen. http://www.indexaward.dk/2007/forside.asp. From *CABE* the British government's advisor on architecture, urban design and public space, "Homes for our old age. Independent living by design". This report features ten case studies of housing schemes for older people, each of which offers inventive design and management solutions linking home and social care. http://www.cabe.org.uk/publications/homes-for-our-old-age.

50 "Unprecedented Global Aging Examined in New Census Bureau Report Commissioned by the National Institute on Aging", *NIH News*, US Department of Health and Human Services, 20 July 2009. http://

www.nih.gov/news/health/jul2009/nia-20.htm.
www.census.gov/prod/2009pubs/p95-09-1.pdf.

51 "Paying for the Aging Revolution in China", *Future Watch*, Global Strategy Institute, July, 2004. http://www.csis.org/media/csis/pubs/0407_gsifuturewatchchinaaging.pdf. Jackson, Richard, Neil Howe, *The Graying of the Middle Kingdom*, Washington, DC: CSIS and Prudential Foundation, 2004, available on line: http://www.csis.org/index.php?option=com_csis_pubs&task=view&id=887.

52 Goodman, Roger, Sarah Harper, "Asia's position in the new global demography", Oxford Development Studies, vol. 34, no. 4, 2006. Goodman, Roger, Sarah Harper, *Ageing in Asia: Asia's Position in the New Global Demography*, London: Routledge, 2007. Goodman, Roger, *Family and Social Policy in Japan: Anthropological Approaches*, Cambridge: Cambridge University Press, 2002.

53 Chistensen, Kaare, "Ageing Populations: the Challenges Ahead", *The Lancet*, vol. 374, no. 9696, 3 October, 2009, pp. 1196–1208.

54 http://newtechmd.com/wordpress/?p=10.

55 http://culturaljapan.blogspot.com/2010/09/intelligent-toilets.html.

56 http://www.cyberdyne.jp/english/robotsuithal/index.html.

57 There is an excellent entry in PingMag which compares Harajuku with Sugamo, identifying the design distinctions in both neighbourhoods. Unfortunately PingMag has ceased operation but the archives remain accessible. "Sugamo: Top-Notch Design for Grannies", PingMag, 20 September 2007. http://pingmag.jp/2007/09/20/sugamo-for-grannies/. See also: "Playgrounds For The Elderly: Fit In An Aging Society", PingMag, 7 November 2007. http://pingmag.jp/2007/11/07/playground-equipment/. Other sources of note that report on Sugamo include: Masters, Coco, "Postcard: Tokyo", *Time*, 21 February, 2008. http://www.time.com/time/magazine/article/0,9171,1715074,00.html.

58 The information in this section is based on personal research conducted in Sugamo. We are most grateful to Masayuki Suzuki and Mariko Liliefeldt of the Toronto office of the Japan Foundation who arranged for us to meet with academics from Chuo University (Goro-maru and Masayoshi Tanishita, Department of Civil Engineering,) local government officials and members of the Merchants Association of Sugamo. A special thanks is extended to all those shop and stall owners who provided good-natured access and furnished essential local information. Thanks also and to the residents who carried out intervention into their cultural space. A more comprehensive account was presented at the *Include 2011 conference* at the Helen Hamlyn Centre, Royal College of Art, London, in 2011. http://www.hhc.rca.ac.uk.

59 Geil, William Edgar, *A Yankee on the Yangtze*, New York: Eaton and Mains, 1904. Geil was born in 1865 at Doylestown, 25 miles northeast of Philadelphia. He is very much a forgotten adventurer. He visited all 18 capital cities of China's provinces, and was, quite probably, the first individual to reconnoitre the entire 1,800 mile length of the Great Wall of China in 1908.

60 http://www.msnbc.msn.com/id/22970058/ "Deforestation: The global assault continues," World Resources Institute, 1998. http://archive.wri.org/item_detail.cfm?id=1368&section=pubs&page=pubs_content_text&z=?

61 Phillips, Tom, "Brazil: Deforestation rises sharply as farmers push into Amazon", *The Guardian*, Monday, 1 September 2008. http://www.guardian.co.uk/environment/2008/sep/01/forests.brazil.

62 For an authoritative overview of bamboo see the site of the Indonesian based, Environmental Bamboo Foundation (includes animation clips, "Grow your

own house," and "Emergency Shelter.") http://www.bamboocentral.org/index1.htm. See also: "Growing Bamboo in Georgia", University of Georgia College of Agricultural and Environmental Sciences. A most informative and detailed account of bamboo, complete with a useful bibliography. http://pubs.caes.uga.edu/caespubs/horticulture/GrowingBamboo.htm.

63 *Bamboo–The Miracle Grass*, produced in 1987 is a 21 minute film produced by the International Development Research Centre (IDRC), Canada and is available through the National Film Board of Canada (NFB). Ramanuja Rao, IV,Cherla B Sastry, "Bamboo, People and the Environment", *Proceedings of the Vth International Bamboo Workshop and the IVth International Bamboo Congress*, Ubud, Bali, Indonesia, 19–22 June, 1995. http://www.inbar.int/publication/txt/INBAR_PR_05_2.htm.

64 In 1665, the English researcher Robert Hooke was the first to describe in his book *Micrographia or some physiological descriptions of minute bodies*, the idea of producing artificial silk from a gelatinous mass.

65 The most extensive (and expensive) account of textiles from pre-history to the modern age, is: Jenkins, DT,*The Cambridge History of Western Textiles*, Cambridge: Cambridge University Press, 2003.

66 "The Song of the Shirt", Thomas Hood, first published in *Punch*, or the *London Charivari*, 16 December 1843.

67 Fletcher, Kate, "Ethically Made", *Sustainable Fashion & Textiles*, London and Sterling VA, Earthscan, 2008, pp. 41–73. Tungate, Mark, "Behind the Seams", *Fashion Brands*, London: Kogan Page, 2008, pp. 227–238. See: "Fashion Victims", *War on Want*, Corporate Accountability; http://www.waronwant.org/Fashion+Victims+13593.twl. Clean Clothes Campaign. Improving working conditions in the global garment industry. http://www.cleanclothes.org/index.htm. *The Ethical Fashion Forum* blog; http://www.ethicalfashionforum.com/8.html.

68 Engels, Friedrich, *The Condition of the Working Class in England (1845)*, London and New York: Penguin Classics, 1987. This work was first translated into English in 1886/7. A version is available free, on line, through the Gutenberg project: http://www.gutenberg.org/etext/17306.

69 As quoted in "Cotton and the Environment", *Organic Trade Association*, 2008, http://www.ota.com/organic/environment/cotton_environment.html.

70 On the water footprint of cotton from the UNESCO Institute for Water Education, http://www.waterfootprint.org/Reports/Report18.pdf.Chapagain, AK, et al, "The water footprint of cotton consumption: An assessment of the impact of worldwide consumption of cotton products on the water resources in the cotton producing countries", *Ecological Economics 60*, 2006, pp. 186–203. http://www.waterfootprint.org/Reports/Chapagain_et_al_2006_cotton.pdf.

71 http://www.waterfootprint.org/?page=files/productgallery&product=cotton.

72 You can download the London based NGO, *Environmental Justice Foundation*'s substantial and well documented report on cotton in Uzbekistan, "White Gold. The True Cost of Cotton", http://www.ejfoundation.org/pdf/white_gold_the_true_cost_of_cotton.pdf.

73 Carter, Kate, "Cotton on to Fairtrade jeans", *The Guardian*, 3 September 2008. http://www.guardian.co.uk/lifeandstyle/2008/sep/03/denim.

74 Smith, Ray A, "Shades of Green: Decoding Eco Fashion's Claims", *The Wall Street Journal*, 24 May 2008, p. 3. http://online.wsj.com/public/article/SB121158336716218711.html?mod=2_1356_leftbox.

75 Not restricted to textiles and clothing, *The New*

American Dream website helps "Americans consume responsibly, to protect the environment, enhance quality of life, and promote social justice", http://www.newdream.org/.

76 Fletcher, Kate, *Sustainable Fashion and Textiles*, London and Sterling VA: Earthscan, 2008, p. 6. For over 30 essays on fashion and sustainability see: *Future Fashion, White Papers*, New York: Earth Pledge, 2007.

77 The Danish Environmental Protection Agency provides six lifecycle assessments of textile products, Working Report, no. 24, 2007. http://www.mst.dk/English/Publications/.

78 http://www.cottoninc.com/.

79 http://www.swicofil.com/. soybeanproteinfiberproperties.html.

80 Shurtleff, William, Akiko Aoyagi, "A Special Exhibit– The History of Soy Pioneers Around the World", Unpublished Manuscript, http://www.soyinfocenter.com/HSS/henry_ford_and_employees.php.

81 Fletcher, Kate, Sustainable Fashion & Textiles, London and Sterling VA, Earthscan, 2008, p. 32–33.Bamboo: Facts behind the Fiber: http://organicclothing.blogs.com/my_weblog/2007/09/bamboo-facts-be.html. See also: "Bamboo: Processing Considerations", posted on the Green Cotton website, 2 October 2007. http://greencotton.wordpress.com/2007/10/02/bamboo-miracle-plant-vs-troublesome-fiber/. Carter, Kate, "Pandering to the green consumer", *The Guardian*, 13 August 2008. http://www.guardian.co.uk/lifeandstyle/2008/aug/13/bamboo.fabric. Browse the ethical fashion directory for more related articles from *The Guardian*.

82 This term lacks medical definition, it was 'invented' by advertises in 1953 to describe items especially cosmetics and textiles) that are claimed to cause fewer allergic reactions. http://www.cbc.ca/consumers/market/microscope/micro_2000/hypoallergenic.html.

83 The OrganicClothing.blogs.com has some entries worth referencing. http://organicclothing.blogs.com/.

84 Fletcher, Kate, "Fabric Finishing", *Sustainable Fashion & Textiles*, London and Sterling VA: Earthscan, 2008, pp. 49–57.

85 One information source is *Lift the Label on Fashion* which helps consumers understand the people behind the products in the fashion industry. http://youth.tearfund.org/lift+the+label/fashion. The European based *Clean Clothes Campaign* has similar objectives of improving working conditions in the global garment industry. http://www.cleanclothes.org/cccs.htm.

86 http://www.icebreaker.com/site/index.html.

87 http://www.wral.com/news/local/story/113994/. McNeil, Joanne, "The Afterlife of American Clothes", *Reasononline*, August/September 2008, http://www.reason.com/news/show/127435.html. *Secondband (Pepe)* is a 24 minute tri-lingual documentary about the role of used clothing. http://www.secondhandfilm.com/project.html.

88 Beer, Robert, *The Handbook of Tibetan Buddhist Symbols*, Chicago: Serindia Publications, 2003, p. 92. Kim, Chae-ung, *Polishing the diamond, enlightening the mind: reflections of a Korean Buddhist Master*, Somerville MA: Wisdom Publications, 1999, p. 19.

89 Davies, Robert, "Design for the Other 90%–Problem or Opportunity?", http://www.seeingthepossibilities.com/?p=91.

90 The "Design for the other 90%. A Revolution in Design" exhibition originated at the Cooper Hewitt, and appeared at the Walker Art Center in Minneapolis, 24 May–7 September 2008, http://other90.cooperhewitt.org/about/. For an interview in PingMag with the exhibitions curator, Cynthia E Smith: http://pingmag.jp/2007/10/24/design-for-the-other-90-percent-about-social-r esponsibility/. *The New Dynamics of Ageing* is a British based, cross-council research programme with the ultimate aim of improving quality of life of older people. http://newdynamics.group.shef.ac.uk/.

91 Damon, Anwa, "Solar Power Makes Tiny Village Beanm", CNN.com/world, 31 July 2007.

92 The Barefoot College was awarded the Sierra Club Green Energy Award for 2009, http://www.barefootcollege.org/.

93 Lal, Neeta, "Barefoot Women Light up India", *Asia Sentinel*, 3 April 2008. In 2007, Singapore based Caldecott Productions produced a 52 minute video, *The Barefoot Women Who Make Light*, which details this remarkable enterprise.

94 Lal, Basnt Kumar, *Contemporary Indian Philosophy*, Delhi: Motilal Banarsidass, 1978, 1995, pp. 154–156.

95 Ghose, Rajeshwari, "Design, Development, Culture, and Cultural Legacies in Asia", in Margolin, Victor, Richard Buchanan, ed., *The Idea of Design*, Cambridge MA: MIT Press, 1995, pp. 187–203.

96 "Swadesh: localised economics", Working Villages International, http://www.workingvillages.org/1c.html.

97 "China-India Ties to be Important in 21st Century", *The Times of India*, 21 November 2010.

98 Karon, Tony, "Why China Does Capitalism Better than the US", *Time*, Thursday, 20 January 2011, http://www.time.com/time/world/article/0,8599,2043235,00.html \l "ixzz1Cqt1OwnV" http://www.time.com/time/world/article/0,8599,2043235,00.html#ixzz1Cqt1OwnV.

99 Thakur AP Sunil Pandey, Kavita Krishamurthi, *21st Century India: View and Vision*, New Delhi: Global Vision, 2009, p. 233.

CHAPTER ELEVEN

1 Haiku (hokku) is a form of Japanese verse that consists of three phrases of five, seven, and five syllables. This haiku was likely composed in the Spring of 1676. Kyoto the old imperial capital, was replaced by Edo (now Tokyo) as the new political capital of the Tokugawa shogunate. (The Edo period, 1600–1868).

2 Smith, Julia, *Europe after Rome: A New Cultural History 500–1000*, Oxford: Oxford University Press, 2009. For a refreshingly new approach to old themes, this revitalised cultural history provides i nsight into the diversity of experience that existed in Europe after the fall of Rome. Lacey, Robert, Danny Danziger, *The Year 1000: What Life Was Like at the Turn of the First Millennium*, London: Little, Brown Book Group, 1999.

3 The most comprehensive English language reference work on Asian history and culture from the Palaeolithic era through the twentieth century is: Bowman, John Stewart, *Columbia Chronologies of Asian History and Culture*, New York: Columbia University Press, 2000. For a general introduction to the last thousand years see: Fernandez Armesto, Felipe, *Millennium: A History of the Last Thousand Years*, New York: Simon & Schuster, 1996. For an economic overview see: Jay, Peter, "Passing the Baton", in *Road to Riches or The Wealth of Man*, London: Phoenix/Orion Books, 2000, pp. 88–122. From a more 'technological perspective see: Pacey, Arnold, "An Age of Asian Technology AD700–1100", *Technology in World Civilization: A Thousand-year History*, Cambridge MA: MIT Press, 2000, pp. 1–19.

4 Thapar, Romila, *Early India: From the Origins to AD 1300*, Berkeley and Los Angeles: University of California Press, 2004. Kulke, Hermann, Dietmar Rothermund, *A History of India*, Oxford and New York: Routledge, 1986, 2004.

5 Struik, Dirk Jan, *A Concise History of Mathematics*, New York: Courier Dover, 1987, p. 67. The classic introductory text to the history of mathematics remains: Eves, Howard, *An Introduction to the History of Mathematics*, Pacific Grove, CA: Brooks Cole/Thomsin Learning, sixth edition, 1990.

6 The introduction of zero is attributed to Brahmagupta, who was the first to formalize arithmetic operations using zero in his *Brahmasphutasiddhanta*, the earliest known text to treat zero as a number in its own right, (the concept of zero may have been formulated many centuries earlier.) He used dots underneath numbers to indicate a zero. The Bakhshali Manuscript is preserved in the Bodleian Library in Oxford University. Topics treated in this manuscript include arithmetic (fractions, square roots, profit and loss, simple interest, the rule of three, and regula falsi) and algebra (simultaneous linear equations and quadratic equations), and arithmetic progressions. The Bakhshali also employs a decimal place value system with a dot for zero. The exact date of the manuscript is subject to debate, consensus seems to favour c. AD400. Hayashi, Takao "Indian Mathematics", in Flood, Gavin, *The Blackwell Companion to Hinduism*, Oxford: Basil Blackwell, 2005, pp. 360–375, 360–375. Plofker, Kim, *Mathematics in India*, Princeton: Princeton University Press, 2008, p. 151.

7 For a narrative account of the Arab Muslim conquests of the Middle East and beyond from AD632 to 750: Kennedy, Hugh, *The Great Arab Conquests: How the Spread of Islam Changed the World We Live In*, Philadelphia: Da Capo Press/Perseus, 2007. See also: Constable, Olivia Remie, *Medieval Iberia: readings from Christian, Muslim, and Jewish sources*, Philadelphia: University of Pennsylvania Press, 1997. This informative and factual text "brings together nearly one hundred original sources that testify to the peninsula's rich and sometimes volatile mix of Christians, Muslims, and Jews". Rubenstein, Richard E., *Aristotle's Children: How Christians, Muslims, and Jews Rediscovered Ancient Wisdom and Illuminated the Middle Ages*, Orlando: Houghton Mifflin Harcourt, 2004.

8 Menocal, María Rosa, "The Culture of Translation", http://www.wordswithoutborders.org/article.php?lab=Culture. Historical Evidence Regarding the Libraries of Muslim Spain: http://everything2.com/index.pl?node_id=1043514. El-Abbadi, Mostafa , *Life and fate of the ancient Library of Alexandria*, second edition, Paris: UNESCO, 1992. ISBN ISSN: 92-3-102632-1(eng).

9 Avicenna, Abd al-Wahid ibn Muhammad, Juzajani, William E Gohlman, *The Life of Ibn Sina: A Critical Edition and Annotated Translation*, Albany, NY: SUNY Press, 1974. Khan, Aisha, *Avicenna (Ibn Sina): Muslim Physician And Philosopher of the Eleventh Century*, New York: Rosen Publishing, 2006.

10 See "On Motion", from the Galileo Project, Rice University, http://galileo.rice.edu/sci/theories/on_motion.html.

11 Ede, Andrew, Lesley B Cormack, *A History of Science in Society: From Philosophy to Utility*, Peterborough, ON: Broadview Press, 2004, p. 63.

12 Nicholas J Wade, Stanley Finger (2001), "The eye as an optical instrument: from camera obscura to Helmholtz's perspective", *Perception 30* (10), pp. 1157–1177.

13 De Barry, William Theodore, ed., *Neo-Confucian Education: The Formative Stage*, Berkeley: University of California Press, 1989.

14 Miyazaki, Ichisada, *China's Examination Hell: The Civil Service Examinations of Imperial China*, New York: Weatherhill, 1976.

15 Burke, Peter, *The European Renaissance: Centres and Peripheries*, Oxford and Malden MA: Blackwell, 1998. For an assessment of the origins of the Renaissance see: Chastel, André, et al, *The Renaissance: Essays in Interpretation*, London and New York: Methuen, 1982. See also: "Studying the Renaissance with the Open University", http://www.open.ac.uk/Arts/renaissance2/index.html.

16 In 2008, the National Intelligence Council (NIC), the United States' leading intelligence organisation forecast that US dominance of world events will be at an end by 2025. The 120 page review (*Global Trends 2025: A Transformed World*) cautions that the so called triumph of western democracy will no longer be certain. "The whole international system—as constructed following the Second World War—will be revolutionised. Not only will new players—Brazil, Russia, India and China— have a seat at the international high table, they will bring new stakes and rules of the game." These emerging economies are likely to grow in influence at America's expense. The European Union will continue to suffer from internal bickering and will likely be "a hobbled giant." http://www.dni.gov/nic/NIC_2025_project.html. In recognition of this realignment of economic might, the British newspaper, *The Independent*, has made available podcasts, "Business Etiquetts in China", and "Business Etiquette in India". http://www.independent.co.uk/.

17 McNeil, William, "The Era of Chinese Predominance", *The Pursuit of Power: Technology, Armed Force, and Society since A.D. 1000*, Chicago: University of Chicago Press, 1984, pp. 24–62.

18 Whitfield, Susan, *Life Along the Silk Road*, Berkeley and Los Angeles: University of California Press, 2001. Behera, Subhakanta, "India's Encounter with the Silk Road", *Economic and Political Weekly*, vol. 37, no. 51, 21–27 December 2002, pp. 5077–5080.

19 Reid, Struan, *Cultures and Civilizations: TheSilk and Spice Routes*, Toronto: James Lorimer & Company, 1994. Intended for a junior audience, nevertheless, this work provides an informative and well documented overview.

20 See the Old World Trade Routes (OWTRAD) Project: Ciolek, T Matthew. 1999–present. *Old World Trade Routes (OWTRAD) Project*. Canberra: Asia Pacific Research Online. www.ciolek.com/owtrad.html. For an interactive map of the routes see: http://www.silkroadproject.org/silkroad/map.html. The art of producing silk cloth reached France, Spain and Italy in the twelfth century. By the nineteenth century the silk industry was an important part of the French economy. In the early part of the 19th century, Joseph Jacquard invented a loom that allowed patterns to be woven by means of punch card input. Some of Jacquard's looms were destroyed by weavers who feared unemployment. By 1812 there were 11,000 Jacquard looms working in France. See: Textile Production in Europe: Silk, 1600–1800; http://www.metmuseum.org/toah/hd/txt_s/hd_txt_s.htm. Other sources include UNESCO—an entry "silk road" in the search box will result in 76 entries. http://unesdoc.unesco.org/ulis/. "Monks and Merchants. The Silk Road: A Larger View", Asia Society: http://sites.asiasociety.org/arts/monksandmerchants/silk.htm.

21 Stockwell, Foster, *Westerners in China: A History of Exploration and Trade, Ancient Times Through the Present*, McFarland, 2003, p. 14. For a detailed account of Chinese silk, see: Vainker, S J, *Chinese Silk*, New Brunswick, NJ: Rutgers University Press, 2004.

22 Schoeser, Mary, *Silk*, New Have CT: Yale University Press, 2007, p. 36.

23 Molà, Luca, *The Silk Industry of Renaissance Venice*, Baltimore: John Hopkins University Press, 2000.

24 It was Francis I, who in 1534, sent Jacques Cartier to explore the St Lawrence River in Quebec to find "certaines iles et pays où l'on dit qu'il se doit trouver grande quantité d'or et autres riches choses", (certain islands and lands where it is said there must be great quantities of gold and other riches).

25 Benedict, Philip, *The Huguenot Population of France, 1600–1685: The Demographic Fate and Customs of a Religious Minority*, Darby, PA: Diane Publishing,

1991.Butler, Jon, *The Huguenots in America: A Refugee People in New World Society*, Cambridge, MA: Harvard University, 1983. Gwynn, Robin D, *The Huguenots of London*, Brighton: Sussex Academic Press, 1998.

26 http://en.wikipedia.org/wiki/Incense.

27 George, Andrew R, (trans. and edit), *The Babylonian Gilgamesh Epic: Critical Edition and Cuneiform Texts*, Oxford: Oxford University Press, 2003.

28 On trade between Arabia and the Empires of Rome and Asia: http://www.metmuseum.org/toah/hd/ince/hd_ince.htm. On the Incense route: http://en.wikipedia.org/wiki/Incense_Route. Retracing the incense route: http://findarticles.com/p/articles/mi_m2742/is_n220/ai_n25021751.

29 Fage, John Donnelly; et al, *The Cambridge History of Africa*, Cambridge: Cambridge University Press, 1975, p. 164.

30 Corn, Charles, Debbie Glasserman, *The Scents of Eden: A History of the Spice Trade*. New York: Kodansha America/Oxford University Press, 1999. Donkin, Robin A, *Between East and West: The Moluccas and the Traffic in Spices Up to the Arrival of Europeans*, Darby, PA: Diane Publishing Company, 2003.

31 Keay, John, *The Spice Route: A History*, Berkeley and Los Angeles: University of California Press, 2006.

32 For an extremely well researched account of this and other related journeys, see: Milton, Giles, *Nathaniel's Nutmeg, or the True and Incredible Adventures of the Spice Trader who Changed the Course of History*, London and New York: The Penguin Group, 2000.

33 Milton, Giles, *Nathaniel's Nutmeg, or the True and Incredible Adventures of the Spice Trader who Changed the Course of History*, p. 3.

34 Milton, Giles, *Nathaniel's Nutmeg, or the True and Incredible Adventures of the Spice Trader who Changed the Course of History*, p. 6. Before decimalisation in 1971, there were 20 shillings to the pound and 12 pennies to the shilling.

35 The population of Manhattan was reported to be 4,937 in 1698.

36 Rommelse, Gijs, *The Second Anglo-Dutch War (1665-1667): raison d'état, Mercantilism and Maritime Strife*, Hilversum: Uitgeverij Verloren, 2006. McNee, Tim, *New Amsterdam*, New York: Chelsea House, 2007. Shorto, Russell, *The Island at the Centre of the World*, Toronto: Random House of Canada, 2005.

37 Leif Ericson, AD970-1020, the first European to arrive in North America, http://www.scandinavica.com/culture/history/vinland.htm. A Viking settlement at L'Anse aux Meadows, in the eastern Canadian region of Terranova, is thought to date to the eleventh century.

38 Cohen, JM, *The Four Voyages of Christopher Columbus: Being His Own Log-Book, Letters and Dispatches with Connecting Narrative Drawn from the Life of the Admiral by His Son Hernando Colon and Others*, London: Penguin Classics, 1969.

39 The genetic research, made public by Spain's Centre for Scientific Research, is due to be published in the *American Journal of Physical Anthropology*. Research indicates that a woman from the North American continent probably arrived in Iceland some time around 1000AD leaving behind genes that are reflected in about 80 Icelanders today.

40 Adolphson, Mikael S, Edward Kamens, Stacie Matsumoto, eds, *Heian Japan, centers and peripheries*, Honolulu, HI: University of Hawaii Press, 2007. Whitney Hall, John, Donald H Shively, William H McCullough, *The Cambridge History of Japan*, vol. 2, *Heian Japan*, Cambridge: Cambridge University Press, 1999.

41 On aesthetic life and culture in the Heian court see: Haha, Michitsuna no, Edward Seidensticker (trans.), *The Gossamer Years: The Diary of a Noblewoman of Heian Japan*, Boston: Tuttle Publishing, 1964, 2001. Sei Sho-nagon, Ivan I Morris (trans. and ed.), *The Pillow Book of Sei Sho-nagon*, New York: Columbia University Press, 1991. The 1996 film of the same name, written and directed by Peter Greenaway tells a more modern, stylised version of the tale. As is often the case, better to read the book before seeing the film.

42 Gibney, Frank, "Introduction: Arrival of the Black Ships", in Borthwick, Mark, *Pacific Century: The Emergence of Modern Pacific Asia*, Cambridge MA: Westview/Perseus, 2007, pp. 109–116.

43 Dower, John W, "Visualizing Cultures", MIT OpenCourseWare project, http://ocw.mit.edu/ans7870/21f/21f.027j/black_ships_and_samurai/core_blackships.html. Statler, Oliver, Richard Lane (trans.), *The Black Ship Scroll: An Account of the Perry Expedition at Shimoda in 1854 and the Lively Beginnings of People-To-People Relations between Japan & America*, New York: Japan Societies of San Francisco and New York, 1963. http://www.questia.com/PM.qst?a=o&d=5958941. Walworth, Arthur, *Black Ships Off Japan the Story of Commodore Perry's Expedition*, New York: Alfred A Knopf, 1946.

44 Jansen Marius B, "The Meiji Revolution", "Building the Meiji State", "Imperial Japan", and "Meiji Culture", in *The Making of Modern Japan*, Cambridge MA: Harvard University Press, 2000, pp. 333–473.

45 Benedict, Ruth, *Chrysanthemum and the Sword: Patterns of Japanese Culture*, New York: First Mariner/Houghton, Mifflin, 1946, 2005.

46 Cox, Brian, Jeff Forshaw, *Why Does E=mc2?: (And Why Should We Care?)*, New York: De Capo Press, 2009. Bodan, David, *E=mc2: A Biography of the World's Most Famous Equation*, New York: Berkley/Penguin Group, 2004. "Eienstein's Big Idea", from *PBS* http://www.pbs.org/wgbh/nova/einstein/.

47 Issacson, Walter, *Einstein. His Life and Universe*, London: Simon & Schuster (Pocket Books), 2008, pp. 469–486. *The New Scientist* regards this work as being "readable, and highly professional; based on extensive research and thorough checking by expert physicists and historians".

48 The immediate death toll was around 14,000 with another 60,000 dying from radiation poisoning. Approximately 70 per cent of the city's buildings were destroyed.

49 Pilger, John, "The lies of Hiroshima live on, props in the war crimes of the 20th century", *The Guardian*, Wednesday, 6 August 2008. http://www.guardian.co.uk/commentisfree/2008/aug/06/secondworldwar.warcrimes.

50 Three months earlier, a pre-emptive directive had been issued on 15 May 1945, by The Office of Censorship, Washington, who gave the following confidential order to American editors and broadcasters. "Note to editors and broadcasters: (not for publication or Broadcast). Scientific experiments–The Code of Wartime Practices requests that nothing be published or broadcast about "new or secret military weapons... experiments." In extension of this highly vital precaution, you are asked not to publish or broadcast any information whatever regarding war experiments involving: Production or utilisation of atom smashing, atomic energy, atomic fission, atomic splitting, or any of their equivalents; the use for military purposes of radium or radioactive materials, heavy water, high voltage discharge equipment, cyclotrons, the following elements or any of their compounds-polonium, uranium, ytterbium, hafnium, protactinium, radium, rhenium, thorium, deuterium." Byron Price, Director, The Office of Censorship, 15 May 1945. As reported in the New York based *PM* newspaper, 8 August, 1945, http://www.typepad.com/services/trackback/6a00d83542d51e69e201157239ae26970b.

51 For archival coverage on the bombing of Hiroshima from NHK, see: http://www.nhk.or.jp/peace/english/chrono/index.html. For an eye witness account by the first Western journalist to visit Hiroshima see: Burchett, Wilfred, G, *Shadows of Hiroshima*, London: Verso, 1983. Braw, Monica, *The Atomic Bomb Suppressed: American Censorship in Occupied Japan*, Armonk, NY & London: East Gate Book, 1991. Lifton, Robert Jay, Greg Mitchell, *Hiroshima in America: Fifty Years of Denial*, New York: Putnam, 1995. All official immages of the aftermath of the bomding have 'disappeared' save for seventy four remarkable black and white photographs taken by a 19 year old marine, Joe O'Donnell. O'Donnell, Joe, *Japan 1945: a US Marine's Photographs from Ground Zero*, Vanderbuilt Press, 2008. Yosuke Yamahata was directed by the Japanese Army to record the effcets of the bomding. Jenkins, Rupert, Robert Jay Lifton, *Nagasaki Journey: The Photographs of Yosuke Yamahaya*, 10 August 1945, Darby PA: Diane Publishing, 1998. (Out of print).

52 Rudofsky, Bernard, *The Kimono Mind*, New York: Doubleday, 1965, subsequently republished in 1971 by Charles E Tuttle, Rutland VT and Tokyo. Dalby, Liza Crihfield, *Kimono: Fashioning Culture*, Seattle, WA: University of Washington Press, 2001.

53 Travers Christmas Humphreys was a prolific writer on Buddhism, responsible for around 40 books and co-author or editor of many more. He was also a British barrister, a QC, and a controversial judge at the Old Bailey. Humphreys, Christmas, *Buddhism: An Introduction and Guide*, London: Penguin, 1951, 1990.

54 Issacson, Walter, *Einstein. His Life and Universe*, London: Simon & Schuster (Pocket Books), 2008, p. 108.

55 James, Simon P, Zen Buddhism and environmental ethics, Aldershot: Ashgate, 2004, p. 43.

56 Dobson, Hugo, Japan and the G7/8, London and New York: RoutledgeCurzon, 2004.

57 http://www.sony.com/SCA/press/040709.shtml.

58 Gronow, Pekka, Llpo Saunio, "The Age of the LP", *An International History of the Recording Industry*, London and New York: Cassell, 1998, pp. 95–134.

59 http://www.sony.net/SonyInfo/CorporateInfo/History/sonyhistory-a.html.

60 Lorenz, Christopher, "Harnessing Flair: Sony", and "Appendix: How Japan 'Cascades' Through Western Markets", in *The Design Dimension. The New Competitive Weapon for Business*, Oxford and New York: Basil Blackwell, 1986, pp.79–89, 152–155.

61 Lorenz, Christopher, *The Design Dimension. The New Competitive Weapon for Business*, Oxford and New York: Basil Blackwell, 1986, p. 34.

62 Press, Mike, Rachel Cooper, *The Design Experience. The Role of Design and Designers in the Twenty-First Century*, Aldershot and Burlington VA: Ashgate, 2003, p. 111.

63 Greenberg, Joshua M, "Videophiles and Betamania: Hacking the VCR", in *From BetaMax to Blockbuster: Video Stores and the Invention of Movies on Video*, MIT Press, 2008, pp. 17–40.

64 There are many stories relating to the origin of the initial concept. See: du Gay, Paul, Stuart Hall, Linda Janes, Hugh Mackay, Keith Negus, *Doing Cultural Studies: The Story of the Sony Walkman*, London: Sage, 1997, 2003, p. 42. This book is part of a series developed by the Open University in the UK, to assist in the study of contemporary culture.

65 Popular Science, July 1980, p. 125.

66 Nathan, John, *Sony*, New York: Houghton Mifflin Harcourt, 1999, p. 154.

67 Nathan, John, *Sony*, p. 16.

68 Miyake, Issey, Shōzō Tsurumoto, ed., *Bodyworks*, Tokyo: Shogakukan, 1983, p. 52.

69 Isozaki, Arata, "What are Clothes?... A Fundamental Question", in Koike, Kazuko, ed., *Issey*

Miyake. East Meets West, Tokyo: Heibonsha, 1978, pp. 54–56.

70 As we move ever closer to virtual worlds of existence this may become a more carefully studied subject. See: Kurzweil, Ray, "Become Someone Else", in *The singularity is near: when humans transcend biology*, New York: Penguin Books, 2006, pp. 314–316.

71 Miyake, Issey, *East Meets West*, Tokyo: Heibonsha, 1978.

72 Martin, Richard, "The Kimono Mind: Reflections on Japanese Design: A Survey since 1950", *Journal of Design History*, vol. 8, no. 3, 1995, pp. 215–223. Fukai, Akiko, Japanese Design: A Survey since 1950, catalogue, Philadelphia Museum of Art, 1994.

73 http://www.greattransformations.org/21st-century-economics.

74 Kawamura, Yuniya, "Placing Tokyo on the Fashion Map. From Catwalk to Streetstyle", in Breward, Christopher, David Gilbert, eds., *Fashion World Cities*, Oxford: Berg, 2006, pp. 55–68.

75 http://www.meti.go.jp/english/press/data/20101221_01.html (English version). www.mitsubishicorp.com/jp/ja/pr/archive/2010/.../0000011523_file1.pdf. Only accessible in Japanese.

76 http://www.isseymiyake.co.jp/en/news/brand/1325isseymiyake/.

77 Traditionally, these were referred to as *Zaibatsu*, industrial and financial business conglomerates whose influence and size allowed for control over significant parts of the Japanese economy from the Meiji periods until the end of the Pacific War. The term fell out of use in Japan but was used in North America during the trade debates of the 1980s. Hane, Mikiso, *Eastern Phoenix: Japan Since 1945*, Boulder: Westview Press, 1996. For an explanation of the often opposing cultural values that underlie 'Japanese' and 'Western' business practices, see: Goodman, Roger, "Explanations for the development of the Japanese economic miracle", in Skelton, Tracey, Tim Allen, *Culture and Global Change*, London and New York: Routledge, 1999, pp. 127–136.

78 For an adroit introduction to the culture of China see: Lewis, Richard D, "The China Phenomenon", *The Cultural Imperative*, Boston: Intercultural Press, 2002, pp. 167–190.

79 Temple, Robert K G, *The Genius of China: 3,000 Years of Science, Discovery and Invention*, London: Prion, 1998. Chinese Inventions: http://sln.fi.edu/tfi/info/current/inventions.html. The extensive research and writings of Dr Joseph Needham (d.1995) are credited with recognising the impact of China's scientific and technological advances on the rest of the world. Simon Winchester provides a most readable account of Needham's work and offers related observations on the scientific heritage of China. Winchester, Simon, *Bomb, Book and Compass: Joseph Needham and the great secrets of China*, London: Viking/Penguin, 2008.

80 Bacon, Francis, *Novum Organum: True Directions Concerning the Interpretation of Nature*, Whitefish, MT: Kessinger Publishing, 1620, 2004, p. 57. Francis Bacon (22 January 1569 –April 1626) was a noted English philosopher, author and statesman who became attorney general of England in 1613.

81 Spence, Jonathan, "Chinese Vistas", *BBC*, Reith Lectures 2008, 14 May 2008, http://www.bbc.co.uk/radio4/reith2008/transcript1.shtml. Jonathan Spence is the Sterling Professor of History at Yale University. He delivered the first of four Reith lectures on 14 May at the British Library in London, and broadcast on *BBC Radio 4*.

82 Confucius, D. C. Lau (trans.), *The Analects*, London: Penguin Classics, 1979.

83 Schram, Stuart, *The Thought of Mao Tse-Tung*, Cambridge: Cambridge University Press, 1989.

84 Henry Pu Yi was born on 7 February 1906. Just before his third birthday he was instilled as the twelfth Qing Emperor of China on the 2 December, 1908. On the 12 February 1912, the Empress Dowager Longyu signed the Act of Abdication and the six year old Pu Yi was transferred with his retinue to the northern half of the Forbidden City, Peeking. He was expelled from the Forbidden City in 1914 and moved into the Japanese embassy for eighteen months before moving to the Japanese Concession in Tianjin in 1925. On the 1 March 1932 the Japanese installed Pu Yi as the ruler of Manchuria, making him Emperor in 1934. At the end of the Second World War, Pu Yi was captured by the Russians and moved to the Siberian town of Chita before being repatriated to Maoist China in 1949. He survived the Cultural Revolution and died of natural causes in Beijing on 17 October 1967. Pu Yi, Henry, *The Last Manchu: The Autobiography of Henry Pu Yi, Last Emperor of China*. New York: Skyhorse Publishing, 1967, 2010.

85 Timothy Cheek, ed., *A Critical Introduction to Mao*, Cambridge: Cambridge University Press, 2010. Chang, Jung, Jon Halliday, *Mao: the unknown story*, New York: Alfred A Knopf, 2005. Jocelyn, Ed, Andrew McEwen, Andrew, *The Long March*, London: Constable and Robinson, 2006.

86 Sun Yat-sen is revered both the People's Republic of China and the Republic of China. For an account of his life and his connections with the Kuomintang, see: Bergere, Marie-Claire, Janet Lloyd, *Sun Yat-sen*, Stanford, CA: Stanford University Press, 2000.

87 Snow, Edgar, *Red Star Over China*, New York, Random House, 1938, 1968, p. 124.

88 Mishra, Pankaj, "Staying Power: Mao and the Maoists", *The New Yorker*, New York, 20 December 2010.

89 Harms, William, "China's Great Leap Forward", *The University of Chicago Chronicle*, vol. 15, no. 13, 14 March 1996. http://chronicle.uchicago.edu/960314/china.shtml.

90 Tao Yang, Dennis, "China's Agricultural Crisis and Famine of 1959–1961: A Survey and Comparison to Soviet Famines", Palgrave MacMillan, *Comparative Economic Studies 50*, 2008, pp. 1–29.

91 Mishra, Pankaj, "Staying Power: Mao and the Maoists", *The New Yorker*, New York, 20 December 2010.

92 Dikötter, Frank, *Mao's Great Famine: The History of China's Most Devastating Catastrophe, 1958–62*, London: Bloomsbury Publishing, 2010.

93 Lynch, Michael, *Mao*, New York: Routledge, 2004. *Tang Tsou, The Cultural Revolution and Post-Mao Reforms: A Historical Perspective*, Chicago: University of Chicago Press, 1986. Harding, Harry, *China's Second Revolution: Reform After Mao*, Washington, DC: Brookings Institution Press, 1987.

94 The savagery of the Cultural Revolution is explained in detail, in an authoritative account by Roderick MacFarquhar and Michael Schoenhals, *Mao's Last Revolution*, Cambridge MA: Belknap Press/Harvard University Press, 2006.

95 The so called Gang of Four consisted of Jiang Qing, Mao's last wife and her close associates Zhang Chunqiao, Yao Wenyuan, and Wang Hongwen.Masi, Edoarda, translated by Adrienne Foulke, *China Winter: Workers, Mandarins, and the Purge of the Gang of Four*, New York: Dutton/Penguin, 1982.

96 Evans, Richard, *Deng Xiaoping and the Making of Modern China*, New York: Viking, 1997. Spence, Jonathan, "Deng Xiaoping. The Maoist who reinvented himself, transformed a nation, and changed the world". 60 Years of Asian Heroes, Time Asia, 2006. http://www.time.com/time/asia/2006/heroes/nb_deng.html.

97 Fenby, Jonathan, *The Penguin History of Modern China: The Fall and Rise of a Great Power, 1850-2008*, London: Allen Lane, 2008. Fenby is a former editor of both *the Observer* and the *South China Morning Post*. George Walden "His book is a miracle of thoroughness, truthfulness and readability–the perfect primer for a time when China is about to enter all our lives". http://www.telegraph.co.uk/arts/main.jhtml?xml=/arts/2008/05/25/bofen125.xml.

98 Tsang, Steve, Steve Yui-Sang Tsang, *A Modern History of Hong Kong*, New York: IB Taurus, 2004.

99 "Hong Kong's territory was acquired from three separate treaties: the Treaty of Nanking in 1842, the Treaty of Beijing in 1860, and The Convention for the Extension of Hong Kong Territory in 1898, which gave the United Kingdom the control of Hong Kong Island, Kowloon (area south of Boundary Street), and the New Territories (area north of Boundary Street and south of the Shenzhen River, and outlying islands), respectively. Although Hong Kong Island and Kowloon had been ceded to the United Kingdom in perpetuity, the control on the New Territories was a 99-year lease." http://en.wikipedia.org/wiki/Transfer_of_the_sovereignty_of_Hong_Kong.

100 In China, both government and the private sector support and promote design. The Hong Kong Design Centre forges links between designers and the world of business, offers support to local designers through the provision of research, case studies and best practice guidelines. It provides emerging designers with 'incubator' space to develop their studio and business skills and sponsors various design awards, including the annual, "The World's Chinese Designer Award," recent recipients include the fashion designer Vivienne Tam, 2005, and Chelsia Lau, 2006, a design director at Ford.

101 http://www.arch.hku.hk/research/BEER/sustain.htm.

102 Timothy Cheek, ed., *A Critical Introduction to Mao*, Cambridge: Cambridge University Press, 2010, p. 20.

103 Patten, Chris, "Who's afraid of big bad China? Why?", *The Times*, 13 May 2008. Lord Patten of Barnes is Chancellor of the University of Oxford and a former Governor of Hong Kong. http://www.timesonline.co.uk/tol/comment/columnists/guest_contributors/article3918802.ece.

104 http://web.worldbank.org/.

105 http://www.dexigner.com/jump/directory/15. See also the *Business Week* podcast on China's exploding design scene by New School Provost Tim Marshall, previously dean of Parsons School of Design. http://www.businessweek.com/mediacenter/qt/podcasts/innovation/iotw_marshall_102609.m p3 For more information on The New School, http://www.newschool.edu/admin/provost/.

106 John Thackara is the founder and programme director of Dott (Design of the time) "Dott is about creating demand for new and more sustainable ways to live." http://www.dott07.com/.

CHAPTER TWELVE

1 1 + 1 = 3 was used as the cover illustration to the 1992 reprint of Henri Bergson's *The Creative Mind: An Introduction to Metaphysics*. This collection of essays and lectures concerning the nature of intuition was first published in 1946. Henri-Louis Bergson was a French philosopher who was very influential during the first half of the twentieth century. In 1927 he was awarded the Nobel Prize in Literature. In 1914 all of Bergson's writings were placed upon the list of books devout Catholics were forbidden to read.

2 For examples of visual-verbal synergy, see: Meggs, Philip B, *Type & Image: The Language of Graphic Design*, New York, Wiley, 1992, pp. 64–67.

3 Surowiecki, James, *The Wisdom of Crowds*, New York: Doubleday, 2004.

4 http://www.ancient-greece.org/architecture/parthenon2.html.

5 Neils, Jenifer, ed., *The Parthenon: from Antiquity to the Present*, Cambridge: Cambridge University Press, 2005.
6 Hadingham, Evan, "Unlocking the Mysteries of the Parthenon", *Smithsonian*, February 2008. http://www.smithsonianmag.com/history-archaeology/parthenon.html. See the transcript of the Nova television programme, "Secrets of the Parthenon", first broadcast 29 January 2008. http://www.pbs.org/wgbh/nova/transcripts/3502_partheno.html.
7 Williams has updated and revised this work, see: Williams, Raymond, *Keywords, A Vocabulary of Culture and Society*, Oxford and New York: Oxford University Press, 1976, 1983.
8 Thackara, John, *In the Bubble. Designing in a Complex World*, Cambridge MA: MIT Press, 2006, p. 136.
9 The Innovation policy department, European Commission, hosts *iScience*, which brings together academics, institutions and industry to map out the goals and strategies of European research into information and communication science and technology. http://iscience.blogactiv.eu/about/.
10 For a listing of over 300 definitions of culture from a wide array of disciplines, see: Baldwin, John R, et al, *Redefining Culture: Perspectives Across the Disciplines*, Mahwah, NJ: Lawrence Erlbaum, 2008.
11 Skelton, Tracey, Tim Allen, *Culture and Global Change*, London: Routledge, 1999, p. 4.
12 West, Harry, "The Cross-Discipline Design Imperative", *Business Week*, 4 October 2007. The article provides a link to a video produced by Continuum which discusses design education–well worth seeing.
13 Jerrard, Robert N, Nick Barnes, Adele Reid, "Design, Risk and New Product Development in Five Small Creative Companies", *International Journal of Design*, vol. 2, no. 1, 2008. http://www.ijdesign.org/ojs/index.php/IJDesign/article/view/218/145.
14 Manzini, Ezio, "Enabling platforms for creative communities", *Doors of Perception*, 18 January 2005. http://doors8delhi.doorsofperception.com/presentationspdf/manzini.html.
15 Menzies, Heather, *Whose Brave New World?: the Information Highway and the New Economy*, Toronto: Between the Lines, 1996, 2001, p. 27. Rehrer, Darryl, "The Typewriter", *Popular Mechanics*, August 1996, pp. 56–59.
16 Sparke, Penny, *An Introduction to Design and Culture*, London: Routledge, 2004, p. 4.
17 Leonard Koren, *Wabi-Sabi: For Artists, Designers, Poets & Philosophers*, Berkeley CA: Imperfect Publishing, 1994, 2008. http://c2.com/cgi/wiki?WabiSabi. Juniper, Andrew, *Wabisabi: the Japanese Art of Impermanence*, Boston: Tuttle Publishing, 2003.
18 Dingsoyr, Torgeir, Tore Dyba, Nils Brede Moe, *Agile Software Development: Current Research and Future Directions*, London and New York: Springer, 2007.
19 De Kerckhove, Derrick, Christopher Dewdney, *The Skin of Culture*, London, Kogan Page, 1997, p. 167.
20 Novitz, David, "Art, Culture, and Identity", Muller, Adam, ed., *Concepts of Culture: Art, Politics, and Society*, Calgary: University of Calgary Press, 2005.
21 Krapp, Peter, *Déjà Vu*, Minneapolis, MN: University of Minnesota Press, 2004.
22 Woodham, Jonathan M, *Twentieth Century Design*, Oxford and New York: Oxford University Press, 1997, p. 205.
23 Clarke, Gerald, "The meaning of nostalgia", *Time*, 3 May 1971. http://www.time.com/time/magazine/article/0,9171,876989-2,00.html.
24 Hariman, Robert, John Louis Lucaites, "Flag Raisings at Iwo Jima and Ground Zero", *No Caption Needed*, Chicago: University of Chicago Press, 2007, pp. 93–136. Povich, Shirley, *All Those Mornings...*

at the Post, New York: Public Affairs, 2006, p. 115. Brennen, Bonnie, Hanno Hardt, *Picturing the Past*, Champaign, IL: University of Illinios Press, 1999, pp. 143–144.
25 Prince Stephen, "New Lies", Turner, Graeme, *The Film Culture Reader*, London: Routledge, 2002, pp. 115–128. The article originally appeared in *Film Quarterly*, 49 (3), Spring 1996, pp. 27–37.
26 Manovich, Lev, *The Language of New Media*, Cambridge, MA: MIT Press, 2001, p. 303.
27 From the Department of State's Bureau of International Information Programs, see: Ascher, Steven, "The Digital Revolution", http://usinfo.state.gov/journals/itsv/0607/ijse/ascher.htm.
28 Brown, Ray Broadus, Ronald J Ambrosetti, ed., *Continuities in Popular Culture*, Bowling Green, OH: Bowling Green State University Popular Press, 1993, p. 2.
29 Alvin Toffler coined the term "future shock" in 1965 article in *Horizon* "to describe the shattering stress and disorientation that we induce in individuals by subjecting them to too much change in too short a time". Toffler, Alvin, *Future Shock*, Mattituck, NY: Ameroen, 1970, p. 4.
30 The closest we have to a museum of the future is the Miraikan Museum (National Museum of Emerging Science and Innovation) in Koto-ku, Tokyo. The stated aim of the museum is to "link people directly with the new wisdom of the twenty-first century." http://www.miraikan.jst.go.jp/index_e.html.
31 Chapman, Jonathan, Nick Grant, *Designers, Visionaries and Other Stories*, London and Sterling VA: Eartscan, 2007.
32 These divisions are based on the work of M R Solomon; Solomon, M R, *Consumer Behaviour*, Needham Heights, MA: Allyn and Bacon, 1994.
33 The basic premise offered by Lewis is that "cultural core beliefs are so deeply embedded that they will resist most forms of infiltration or erosion." Lewis, Richard D, *The Cultural Imperative*, Boston: Intercultural Press, 2002. For an overview of Islam and culture with a focus on Muslim American culture, see: Umar Faruq Abd-Allah, "Islam and the Cultural Imperative", *A Nawawi Foundation Paper*, available on line: http://www.nawawi.org/downloads/article3.pdf.
34 http://www.bbc.co.uk/pressoffice/pressreleases/stories/2007/12_december/05/dimbleby.shtml. Groff, Linda, "Future Evolution of Humanity", *Journal of Futures Studies*, August 2007, vol. 12 no. 1, pp. 61–80. http://www.jfs.tku.edu.tw/12-1/A04.pdf.
35 From the Higher Education Academy in the UK, see: Arnold, Chris, "Environmental Materials", available on line: http://www.materials.ac.uk/guides/environmental.asp.
36 *First Things First 2000*, a design manifesto published jointly by 33 signatories in: *Adbusters*, the *AIGA journal*, *Blueprint*, *Emigre*, *Eye*, *Form*, *Items* in fall 1999/Spring 2000. http://www.xs4all.nl/~maxb/ftf2000.htm. Rampley, Matthew, *Exploring Visual Culture: Definitions, Concepts, Contexts*, Edinburgh: Edinburgh University Press, 2005. The book comments on the role of Adbusters and references the manifesto (p. 63). It adopts a cross-disciplinary perspective on visual culture, referencing various field of media and forms of expression, including architecture, fashion, and product design.
37 Weston, Richard, *Plans, Sections and Elevations*, London: Laurence King, 2004, p. 90.
38 Rawlings, Terry, *Mod*, London: Omnibus Press, 2000, p. 136. In 2008, Piaggio, the manufacturer of the iconic Vespa PX, ceased production because the two-stroke 125cc manual transmission scooter fails to meet European emission standards. Contexts change.
39 As quoted in an assessment of José Ortega y Grasset on the *BookRags* website; http://www.bookrags.com/

research/ortega-y-gasset-jos-este-0001_0003_0/.
Ortega y Grasset, José, "Thoughts on Technology", in Mitcham-Mackey, eds, *Philosophy and Technology*, Boston: D Reidel, 1981, pp. 290–313. "Towards a Philosophy of Technology", *Technology and Culture 7*, no. 3, Summer 1966, pp. 301–390.
40 Wood, John, "Relative Abundance", Chapman, Jonathan, Nick Grant, *Designers, Visionaries and Other Stories*, London and Sterling VA: Eartscan, 2007, pp. 96–115. The 'synergy-of-synergies' map is well worth noting.
41 Manzini, Ezio, "The Scenario of a Multi-local Society: Creative Communities, Active Networks and Enabling Solutions", in Chapman, Jonathan, ed., Nick Gant, ed., *Designers Visionaries + Other Stories. A collection of sustainable design essays*, London and Sterling VA: Earthscan, 2007, p. 77.
42 Manzini, Ezio, "The Company as a Cultural Operator", *ICSID News*, 5 August 1992, 1–2.
43 As featured on Homegrown, the umbrella project that works towards the most sustainable, ethical, and desirable communication solutions for Nokia. The site is maintained by Raphael Grignani. http://grignani.org/thoughts/tag/nokia/. See also, "Conversation with Raphael Grignani of Nokia Design about Homegrown", *Putting People First*, 24 June 2008. http://www.experientia.com/blog/. *Putting People First* is a "non-commercial experience design gateway is developed as a public service to all those interested in the broader field of experience design and user-centred design." It is sponsored by an Italian based experience design company Experientia.
44 "Recent immigrants driving advanced mobile phone use, both in Europe and in the US," *Putting People First*, 4 May 2008. http://www.experientia.com/blog/. See also the website of The Pew Research Center, a nonpartisan "fact tank" that provides information on the issues, attitudes and trends shaping America and the world. http://www.peWinternet.org/About-Us/Our-Mission.aspx.
45 This argument is based on an observation made by Charles Leadbeater in an article entitled, "Design your own revolution", which appeared in *The Observer*, Sunday, 19 June 2005, on p. 15 of the Focus section. Charles Leadbeater is an associate of the UK Design Council. See his article, "Welcome to We-think: mass innovation, not mass production", available on his blog. http://www.wethinkthebook.net/book/home.aspx.
46 Manzini, Ezio, "Enabling platforms for creative communities", *Doors of Perception*, 18 January 2005. http://doors8delhi.doorsofperception.com/presentationspdf/manzini.html.
47 Manzini, Ezio, F Jegou, *Sustainable Everyday. Scenarios of urban life*, Milano: Edizioni Ambiente, 2003. Manzini, Ezio, "Enabling solutions, social innovation and design for sustainability", accessible on line from his blog: http://www.sustainable-everyday.net/manzini/.
48 Reed, Steve B, "Alone in the Crowd", Dallas Counseling and Psychotherapy site: http://www.psychotherapy-center.com/how_to_overcome_urban_isolation.html.
49 Castells, Manuel, *Communication Power*, Oxford and New York: Oxford University Press, 2009, p. 3.
50 Sparke, Penny, *An Introduction to Design and Culture*, London: Routledge, 2004, p. 4.
51 De Kerckhove, Derrick, Christopher Dewdney, *The Skin of Culture*, London: Kogan Page, 1997, p. 167.
52 A good place to start is the *Sustainable Everyday Project* site. *SEP* is an independent network funded by public research projects and organisation of events. http://www.sustainable-everyday.net/SEPhome/home.html.
53 Reed, Steve B, "Alone in the crowd", Dallas Counselling and Psychotherapy website: http://www.

psychotherapy-center.com/how_to_overcome_urban_isolation.html.

54 Samovar, Larry, A, et al, "Shaping Interpretations of Reality: Cultural Values", in *Communication Between Cultures*, seventh edition, Boston MA: Wadsworth, 2010, pp. 184.

55 http://www.hermanmiller.com.br/our-business/research-and-design/design-biographies/eric- chan/.

CHAPTER THIRTEEN

1 Hauptman, Laurence M, *Seven Generations of Iroquois Leadership: The Six Nations Since 1800* (Iroquois and Their Neighbors), Syracuse, NY: Syracuse University Press, 2008.

2 1x10^-8 km (kilometres) is roughly equivalent to a typical cotton fibre width (ten micron), human hair varies from 20 to 100 microns.

3 "World Population Prospects: The 2008 Revision", *Population Newsletter*, no. 87, United Nations Department of Economic and Social Affairs, June 2009.

4 http://www.guardian.co.uk/commentisfree/2009/dec/06/copenhagen-editorial.

5 *The Garbage Project & :The Archaeology of Us.* http://traumwerk.stanford.edu:3455/17/174. Rogers, Heather, *Gone Tomorrow: The Hidden Life Of Garbage*, New Press, 2005.

6 Mulvey, Stephen, "Averting a Perfect Storm of Shortages", *BBC*, 24 August 2009. http://news.bbc.co.uk/2/hi/science/nature/8213884.stm. Blain, Loz, "Four Crucial Resources That May Run Out in Your Lifetime", *Gizmag.com*, 27 August 2009. This article poses the question, "Can the Earth sustain 9 billion people?" Well find out in the next 50 years". The four crucial resources are seen as being, oil; food; water, and fish. http://www.gizmag.com/four-crucial-resources-running-out/12630/.

7 For an extensive scientific evaluation see the Analysis Paper; Tol, Richard S J, "An Analysis of Mitigation as a Response to Climate Change", Copenhagen Consensus Centre, Denmark, 14 August 2009. http://fixtheclimate.com/.

8 Edge.org is the web publication of Edge Foundation. The mandate of Edge Foundation is to promote inquiry into and discussion of intellectual, philosophical, artistic, and literary issues, as well as to work for the intellectual and social achievement of society. "To arrive at the edge of the world's knowledge, seek out the most complex and sophisticated minds, put them in a room together, and have them ask each other the questions they are asking themselves". http://www.edge.org/q2009/q09_index.html.

9 Among the more outstanding recent publications on the subject of sustainability are: Assadourian, Erik et al, *State of the World 2010: Transforming Cultures*, New York and London: WW Norton, 2010. http://www.worldwatch.org/sow10. Brand, Stewart, *Whole Earth Discipline: An Ecopragmatist Manifesto*, New York: Viking/Penguin, 2009. Chapman, Jonathan, ed., Nick Gant, ed., *Designers Visionaries + Other Stories. A collection of sustainable design essays*, London and Sterling VA, Earthscan, 2007. Edwards, Andrés R, *The Sustainability Revolution*, Gabriola Island, BC: New Society, 2005. Fletcher, Kate, *Sustainable Fashion & Textiles*, London and Sterling VA: Earthscan, 2008. Shedroff, Nathan, *Design is the Problem. The Future of Design Must be Sustainable*, Brooklyn: Rosenfeld Media, 2009. Thorpe, Ann, *The Designer's Atlas of Sustainability*, Washington DC: Island Press, 2007.One of the most valuable sites on th subject is *The Sustainable Everyday Project* that "proposes an open web platform to stimulate social conversation on possible sustainable futures…" http://www.sustainable-everyday.net/SEPhome/home.

html. Be sure to check the DESIS09 links. DESIS is a network of design schools, companies and non-profit organisations that support design for social innovation and sustainability The business orientated The Natural Step, works "to accelerate global sustainability by guiding companies, communities and governments onto an ecologically, socially and economically sustainable path. More than 70 people in eleven countries work with an international network of sustainability experts, scientists ,universities, and businesses to create solutions, innovative models and tools that will lead the transition to a sustainable future." http://www.naturalstep.org. The economic reality of sustainability is explored in Sachs, Jeffrey, *Common Wealth: Economics for a Crowded Planet*, London and New York: Penguin Press, 2008. And in case you are sufficiently motivated to undertake an International Masters Programme, "Strategic Leadership towards Sustainability", at the Blekinge Institute of Technology in Sweden, http://www.bth.se/ste/tmslm.nsf/. And if you looking for a job in the sustainable field then check out GoodWork "Canada's green job site. www.goodworkcanada.ca

10 Manzini, Ezio, Stuart Walker, Barry Wylant, eds., *Enabling Solutions for Sustainable Living*, Calgary: University of Calgary Press, 2008.

11 Chapman, Jonathan, Nick Grant, *Designers, Visionaries + Other Stories. A collection of sustainable design essays*, London and Sterling VA: Earthscan, 2007, p. 4–5. "GoodGuide provides the world's largest and most reliable source of information on the health, environmental, and social impacts of the products in your home." http://www.goodguide.com/.

12 For a very extensive, well researched and documented report see: Murphy, Joseph, ed., *Governing Technology for Sustainability*, London and Sterling VA, Earthscan, 2007. Available on line: http://oro.open.ac.uk/4026/1/GST_proof.pdf.

13 One place to start is the recent book by Victor Papanek which explores the relationships between design, ecology and ethics. Papanek, Victor, *The Green Imperative*, London: Thames and Hudson, 1995.

14 "Jane Goodall spreading conservation message in Adelaide", *City Messenger*, 1 October 2008. See also: the Jane Goodall Institute, http://www.janegoodall.org.

15 The Gaia hypothesis is an ecological hypothesis proposing that the biosphere and the physical components of the Earth are coupled to form a complex, interacting, self-regulating system. Gribbin, John, Mary Gribbin, *James Lovelock: In Search of Gai*, Princeton, NJ: Princeton University Press, 2009. Harding, Stephan, *Animate Earth* (2nd edition), Totnes: Green Books, 2009. Lovelock, James, *The Vanishing Face of Gaia: A Final Warning*, New York: Basic Books, 2009. Lovelock, James, *The Revenge of Gaia: Why the Earth Is Fighting Back–and How We Can Still Save Humanity*. Santa Barbara, CA: Allen Lane, 2006. Lovelock, James, *Gaia: A New Look at Life on Earth*, Oxford & New York: Oxford University Press, 2000. Schneider, Stephen H, James R Miller, Eileen Crist, Penelope J Boston, eds., *Scientists Debate Gaia: The Next Century*, Cambridge MA and London: MIT Press, 2004. Volk, Taylor, *The Earth's Biosphere: Evolution, Dynamics, and Change*, Cambridge, MA: MIT Press, 2003.

16 Amstutz, Mark P, *International Ethics: Concepts, Theories, and Cases in Global Politics*, Oxford: Rowman & Littlefield, 2005, p. 198.

17 Dr J Craig Venter, "A DNA-Driven World", The Richard Dimbleby Lecture 2007, broadcast on Tuesday 4 December 2007. A quite brilliant lecture that ranges over many current concerns–highly recommended. http://www.bbc.co.uk/pressoffice/pressreleases/stories/2007/12_december/05/dimbleby.shtml. See also: "More than Six Million New Genes, Thousands of New Protein Families, and

Incredible Degree of Microbial Diversity Discovered from First Phase of Sorcerer II Global Ocean Sampling Expedition", available from the J Craig Venter Institute (JCVI). http://www.jcvi.org. In 2008 Venter was named as a visiting scholar at Harvard University's Origins of Life Initiative. http://harvardscience.harvard.edu/foundations/articles/j-craig-venter-named-visiting-scholar.

18 Climate Debate Daily claims to foster a new way to understand disputes about global warming by offering both calls to action and dissenting voices. http://climatedebatedaily.com/. Other informative sites include Grist, which exists "to tell the untold stories, spotlight trends before they become trendy, and engage the apathetic." http://gristmill.grist.org/. The "Environment" blog on Digg is worth checking http://digg.com/environment. From the *New York Times* http://dotearth.blogs.nytimes.com/. For a British perspective on environmental challenges, from *The Guardian Unlimited*, http://blogs.guardian.co.uk/climatechange/. *The New Scientist* has continually updated special report available on-line, http://environment.newscientist.com/channel/earth/climate-change/. *The Natural Resources Defense Council* provides extensive information (in English and Spanish) including a monthly newsletter and informative annual reports. http://www.nrdc.org/about/default.asp.

19 Bronowski, Jacob, *The Ascent of Man*, London: BBC Publications, 1973, pp. 370–374.

20 Shah, Anup, "Poverty Facts and Stats", *Global Issues*, http://www.globalissues.org/article/26/poverty-facts-and-stats.

21 A quote by John Thackara in his foreword to: Chapman, Jonathan, Nick Grant, *Designers, Visionaries and Other Stories*, London and Sterling VA: Earthscan, 2007. This is an anthology of articles by many of the leading proponents of enhanced environmental awareness and practice, including Ezio Manzini, John Thackara, Kate Fletcher, Alastair Fuad-Luke, Stuart Walker and John Wood. A must read.

22 A quotation from *The Rime of the Ancient Mariner*, Samuel Taylor Coleridge, 1797–1799.

23 The exact proportions are still a matter of research. For more information on the basic concept see: Gleick, Peter H, et al, "The Origins of Water on Earth, The World's Water 2008-2009: The Biennial Report on Freshwater Resources", Washington, DC: Island Press, 2009, p. 5. Ward, Peter Douglas, Donald Brownlee, "Finish Work", *Rare earth: Why Complex Life is Uncommon in the Universe*, New York: Springer-Verlag, 2000, pp. 52–54.

24 See the working papers produced by the UN supported International Water Management Institute of Sri Lanka. http://www.iwmi.cgiar.org/. Kinver, Mark, "Wastewater fears for urban farms", *BBC News*, 18 August 2008. http://news.bbc.co.uk/2/hi/science/nature/7563295.stm.

25 These figures are taken from the 2002 fact sheet, "Water: A Matter of Life and Death", published by the United Nations Department of Public Information. http://www.un.org/events/water/factsheet.pdf. http://www.wateraidamerica.org/.

26 Jowit, Juliette, "Environment: Huge increase in spending on water urged to avert global catastrophe", *The Guardian*, Thursday, 11 September 2008, p. 25, http://www.guardian.co.uk/environment/2008/sep/11/water.climatechange. "Go against the flow", Editorial, *The Guardian*, Wednesday 20 August 2008, p. 30, http://www.guardian.co.uk/commentisfree/2008/aug/20/water.food.

27 See the volumes of water needed for a cup of coffee, a kilo of beef, a slice of bread and more, http://www.guardian.co.uk/environment/gallery/2008/aug/19/

water.food?picture=336718185 .

28 "The USA appears to have an average water footprint of 2480m3/cap/yr, while China has an average footprint of 700m3/cap/yr. The global average water footprint is 1240m3/cap/yr. The four major direct factors determining the water footprint of a country are: volume of consumption (related to the gross national income); consumption pattern (e.g. high versus low meat consumption); climate (growth conditions); and agricultural practice (water use efficiency)". http://www.waterfootprint.org. Hoekstra, AY, A K Chapagain, "Water footprints of nations: Water use by people as a function of their consumption pattern", Water Resour Manage, 2007, http://www.waterfootprint.org/Reports/Hoekstra_and_Chapagain_2007.pdf.

29 "Running Dry", *The Economist*, 18 September 2008.

30 As cited in "Running Dry," *The Economist*, September 18, 2008. See also the extensive and fully documented website of the International Water Management Institute. http://www.iwmi.cgiar.org/ Molden, David, Water for Food. Water for Life, London and Sterling VA, Earthscan, 2007.

31 "By 2050 or so, the world population is expected to reach nine billion, essentially adding two China's to the number of people alive today. Those billions will be seeking food, water and other resources on a planet where, scientists say, humans are already shaping climate and web of life." http://dotearth.blogs.nytimes.com/.

32 "A Commission on climate change", *The Lancet*, vol. 373, no. 9676, 16 May 2009, pp. 1659–1734.

33 Renton, Alex, "Our ship is sinking: We must act now", Oxfam, 8 September 2009, http://www.oxfam. org.uk/applications/blogs/pressoffice/?p=6868. See also: "Suffering the Science. Climate change, people, and poverty", "Oxfam Briefing Paper 130", 6 July 2009.

34 Kates, Robert W, Thomas M Parris, "Long term trends and a sustainability transition, Proceedings of the National Academy of Sciences of the United States of America", 8 July 2003, vol. 100, no. 14, p. 8062–8067. (See the section, "Atmosphere.") http://www. pnas.org/content/100/14/8062.full?sid=1c5da84c-db50-4d8e-84ea-61e7d3e8586c. See also: Archer, David, *The Long Thaw: How Humans Are Changing the Next 100,000 Years of Earth's Climate*, Princeton, NJ: Princeton University Press, 2008. "Univ. of Chicago geophysicist Archer has perfectly pitched answers to the most basic questions about global warming while providing a sound basis for understanding the complex issues frequently misrepresented by global warming skeptics." Gavin Schmidt, Gavin, *Climate Change: Picturing the Science*, New York: W W Norton, 2009. Fagan, Brian, *The Great Warming, Climate Change and the Rise and Fall of Civilizations*, New York: Bloomsbury Press, 2008.

35 Recent updates can be obtained from the USGS website, http://www.usgs.gov/.

36 The Geneva based IPCC was awarded the 2007 Nobel Peace Prize. Their website offers extensive and reliable information on climate change. http://www.ipcc.ch/.

37 The Global Carbon Project, http://www. globalcarbonproject.org/.

38 http://www.antarctica.ac.uk/bas_research/our_views/climate_change.php. For updated information from the US National Snow and Ice Data Center, see: http://www.nsidc.org/.

39 http://www.nrdc.org/globalwarming/qthinice.asp.

40 Lovett, Richard A, "Arctic Warming Faster Above Ground Level, Study Finds", *National Geographic News*, 2 January 2008. http://news. nationalgeographic.com/news/2008/01/080102-arctic-warming.html.

41 Connor, Steve, Exclusive: The methane time bomb", *The Independent*, 23 September 2008. The preliminary findings of the International Siberian Shelf Study 2008, being prepared for publication by the American Geophysical Union, are being overseen by Igor Semiletov of the Far-Eastern branch of the Russian Academy of Sciences. http://www.independent. co.uk/news/science/exclusive-the-methane-time-bomb-938932.html.

42 Giles, Katharine A, et al, "Antarctic sea ice elevation from satellite radar altimetry", *Geophysical Research Letters*, vol. 35, L03503, 5 February 2008.

43 Vidal, John, "Arctic sea ice at second lowest extent ever recorded. The area of ice at least five years old has fallen by more than half since 1985 and the Northwest and Northeast Passages are now navigable by sea", This article was first published on guardian. co.uk on Thursday, 18 September 2008. http:// www.guardian.co.uk/environment/2008/sep/18/ poles.endangeredhabitats. See also: Paterson, Tony, "A triumph for man, a disaster for mankind", *The Independent*, Saturday, 12 September 2009.

44 "Global warming goes on", UK Met Office, 2008. http://www.metoffice.gov.uk/research/ hadleycentre/.

45 Archer, David, *The Long Thaw: How Humans Are Changing the Next 100,000 Years of Earth's Climate*, Princeton, NJ: Princeton University Press, 2008.

46 Royte, Elizabeth, *Bottlemania: How Water Went on Sale and Why We Bought It*, New York: Bloomsbury Press, 2008. For an edited extract see: http://www. guardian.co.uk/lifeandstyle/2008/aug/23/bottled. water.tap. For a global perspective on water supplies see: "Water for the Ages,"blog; http://waterfortheages. wordpress.com/. For a reliable guide to public water systems in the United States see: *Water on tap what you need to know*, United States Environmental Protection Agency, Darby, PA: Diane Publishing, 2004. Datson, Trevor, "Coca-Cola Admits That Dasani is Nothing But Tap Water", Reuters, Thursday, 4 March 2004. From the US Food and Drug Administration, *Consumer magazine*, July-August 2002, http:// www.commondreams.org/headlines04/0304-04. htm. Editorial, "In Praise of Tap Water", *The New York Times*, 1 August 2007, http://www.fda.gov/ FDAC/features/2002/402_h2o.html. "Take Back the Tap", Food & Water Watch, Washington, DC, 2007. http://www.foodandwaterwatch.org/water/ pubs/reports/take-back-the-tap. http://www.nytimes. com/2007/08/01/opinion/01wed2.html. "Bottled water boycotts: Back-to-the-Tap Movement Gains Momentum", from the Earth Policy Institute. http:// www.earth-policy.org/Updates/2007/Update68_ data.htm. In 2009, Bundanoon, a rural town in New South Wales, Australia claims to have been the first community in the world to have an extensive ban on the sale of bottled water, http://news.bbc.co.uk/2/hi/ asia-pacific/8141569.stm.

47 Byron, Katy, "Pepsi says Aquafina is tap water", CNNMoney.com, 27 July 2007, http://money.cnn. com/2007/07/27/news/companies/pepsi_coke/.

48 Bhan, Niti, "Ecodesign, Ecolabels and the Environment: How Europe is redesigning our footprint on earth", *Core77*, August, 2008. http://www.core77. com/reactor/08.07_ecodesign.asp. The Designers Accord is a global coalition of designers, educators, researchers, engineers, and corporate leaders, working together to create positive environmental and social impact. http://www.designersaccord.org/. The British based Industrial Design Consultancy has developed a Life Cycle Assessment Calculator. It is a free, easy-to-use tool that claims to be able to estimate the carbon footprint and embodied energy of any product. http:// www.lcacalculator.com/. An Environmental impact study can benefit the environment and serve as positive value to the client. See for example how Apple computer makes full PR use of elements of their design impact study. http://www.apple.com/environment/.

49 Thackara, John, *In the Bubble. Designing in a Complex World*, Cambridge MA: MIT Press, 2006, p. 7.

50 Thackara, John, *In the Bubble. Designing in a Complex World*, p. 7.

51 http://www.grida.no/climate/vitalafrica/ english/27.htm.

52 http://www.copenhagenconsensus.com.

53 Henderson, Mark, "An Introduction to the Copenhagen Consensus 2008", *Timesonline*, 24 May 2008, http://www.timesonline.co.uk/tol/news/ environment/article3993299.ece.

54 http://www.copenhagenconsensus.com/Default. aspx?ID=788.

55 An alternative view, that while design involves problem solving, "it is not only and not mainly problem solving" is justified and explained in: Visser, Willemien, *The Cognitive Artifacts of Designing*, Abingdon and New York: Routledge, 2006, p. 221.

56 The Vertical Farm Project, Columbia University, http://verticalfarm.com/. Dr Dickson Despommier's Vertical Farming website provides a valuable resource which brings you the state of the art and future ideas around the vertical farming theme, http://verticalfarm. com/NewsUpdates.aspx. "The high-rise future of food production", from ecoGizmo website: http://www. gizmag.com/go/7500/.

57 "Agriculture and Food–Agricultural Production Indicies: Food Production per capita index", Food and Agriculture Organisation of the United Nations (FAO), 2006, www.foa.org.

58 Vidal, John, "Food Speculation: People Die From Hunger While Banks Make a Killing on Food", Globaldevelopment, *The Guardian*, 23 January 2011.

59 Findeli, Alain, "Rethinking Design Education for the 21st Century: Theoretical, Methodological, and Ethical Discussion", *Design Issues*, vol. 17, no. 1, Winter, 2001, pp. 5–17.

60 In Paris, during 2007, over 20,000 bicycles were available for short term rental from over 1,400 self service docking stations positioned throughout the city. In Barcelona, Bicing offers 3,000 bicycles for rent at over 120 stations. One associated design postscript has been developed in the Netherlands by Studio HiMom, the Heklucht hand pump is incorporated into the durable stainless steel bike stand. The pump was the winner of the Dutch Design Award 2006 (Product–Public Space category). Montreal is the first city in North America to experiment with a communal bike programme, it has 2,400 Bixi bikes for rent at $1 per half-hour, from 300 stations scattered around town. Tech savy users can use an apps on their iPhone's, which using a global positioning system (GPS) can locate the Bixi station closest to the user and indicate how many bikes are available at each station.

61 http://www.idsa.org/IDEA2009/gallery/award_ details.asp?ID=15.

62 http://www.china.org.cn/china/life/2009-05/01/content_17706931_2.htm. http://en.ce.cn/ Life/society/200905/01/t20090501_18968509. shtml. http://bike-sharing.blogspot.com/2009/03/ bike-sharing-in-hangzhou-china.html.

63 Wood, Jonathan, *Alec Issigonis: The Man Who Made the Mini*, Derby: Breedon Books, 2005, http:// designmuseum.org/design/alec-issigonis.

64 http://www.uniquecarsandparts.com.au/car_info_ mini_1959.htm.

65 Hordeski, Michael F, *Alternative Fuels: the Future of Hydrogen*, Lilburn, GA: The Fairmont Press, 2008.

66 "Alternative Fuels and Advanced Vehicles Data Center", U.S. Department of Energy, http://www. afdc.energy.gov/afdc/.

67 "Timeline: Life & Death of the Electric Car", *PBS*,

http://www.pbs.org/now/shows/223/electric-car-timeline.html.

68 Anderson, Judy, Curtis D, Anderson, *Electric and Hybrid Cars: a History*, Jefferson, NC: McFarland, 2005. Mom, Gijs, "The First Generation (1881–1902)", in *The Electric Vehicle: Technology and Expectations in the Automobile Age*, Baltimore, MA: The John Hopkins University Press, 2004, pp. 17–100.

69 For a review of 13 models currently on the market: http://greenterrafirma.com/electric-plugin-vehicles.html. Wynn, Gerrard, "Electric Cars Win Hype, Staying Power Questioned", Reuters, Monday, 5 April 2010.

70 Rothkopf, David J, "The Great Lithium Game", in "Is a Green World a Safer World?", Foreign Policy, 27 August 2009, http://www.foreignpolicy.com.Regaldo, Antonio, "The Lithium Rush. In the Bolivian Andes lies a vast salt flat that may shape the future of transportation", *Technology Review*, January/February, 2010, http://www.technologyreview.com/energy/24058/.

71 Heinberg, Richard, *The Party's Over: Oil, War and the Fate of Industrial Societies*, Gabriola Island, BC: New Society, 2005. Roberts, Paul, *The End of Oil. On the Edge of a Perilous New World*, New York: First Mariner/Houghton Mifflin, 2005.

72 http://www.boc.ebcnet.co.uk/hydrogen/properties/index.html.

73 Hoffmann, Peter, *Tomorrow's Energy. Hydrogen, Fuel Cells, and the Prospects for a Cleaner Planet*, Boston: MIT Press, 2002.

74 "Hydrogen", http://www-formal.stanford.edu/jmc/progress/hydrogen.html.

75 There are very confusing statistics regarding the size of cities. The largest cities in the world ranked by population show Tokyo with a populace of 33.2 million but with a density of 4,750 per sq Km. New York is shown with a population of 17.8 million but with a low density figure of 2,050. By contrast, the most densely populated cities are Bombay (29,650) and Calcutta 23,900). http://www.citymayors.com/statistics/largest-cities-population-125.html.

76 http://www.treehugger.com/files/2008/04/vertical-diagonal-farm-in-new-york.php.

77 Ring, Ed, "Skyscraper Farms", *ECOworld*, 14 November 2007. http://ecoworld.com/blog/2007/11/14/skyscraper-farms/. For a subterranean application of the concept, see "The Subterranean Farms of Tokyo", posted on the *Prune* blogspot, 12 February 2008, http://pruned.blogspot.com/2008/02/subterranean-farms-of-tokyo.html.

78 http://en.wikipedia.org/wiki/Evapotranspiration.

79 Ring, Ed, "Skyscraper Farms", *ECOworld*, 14b November 2007, http://ecoworld.com/blog/2007/11/14/skyscraper-farms/.

80 Hydroponics is a technology for growing plants in nutrient solutions (water containing fertilisers) with or without the use of an artificial medium (sand, gravel, vermiculite, rockwool, perlite, peatmoss. coir, or sawdust) to provide mechanical support, http://en.wikipedia.org/wiki/Hydroponics. The Crop Physiology Laboratory at Utah State University is one of the oldest established academic research centres in North America that focus on the use of controlled environments in agriculture. For more than 20 years it has received funding from NASA to study the challenges associated with growing food crops in bioregenerative life support systems in space. http://www.usu.edu/cpl/research_hydroponics.htm. For a selection of growers guides from Controlled Environment Agriculture (CEA), at Cornell. http://www.cornellcea.com/handbook_home.htm.

81 Resh, Howard M, *Hydroponic Food Production*, sixth edition, Long Island City: Newconcept Press, 2006, p. 25.

82 Bacon, Francis, *Sylva Sylvarum: Or a Natural History in Ten Centuries*, Whitefish, MT: Kessinger Publishing, 1627, 1997, p. 66.

83 See the 2008 report of the World Congress on Ecological Sustainability: http://www.wcoes.org/2008/06/disneys-hydroponic-approach-to.html.

84 For one attempt, see GROW housing, proposed by Canadian architect, Gordon Graff and available on line: http://www.growhousingtoronto.com/ght-Report.pdf.

85 http://www.chinadaily.com.cn/china/2010-05/12/content_9840240.htm.

86 http://www.knafoklimor.co.il/living-steel/index.html.

87 See the booklet, *Houses of Steel*, published by Living Steel in 2009 and available online: http://www.kkarc.com/Publications.aspx?pubID=17. Living Steel is a global collaboration of companies to develop and stimulate the use of steel in innovative and more sustainable residential construction.

88 http://ngm.nationalgeographic.com/7-billion.

89 Urban World: Urban Sustainable Mobility, vol. 2, no. 5, Geneva, UN: Habitat for a Better Urban Future, December 2010, http://www.unchs.org/pmss/listItemDetails.aspx?publicationID=3075.

90 Maeda, John, *The Laws of Simplicity, Design, Technology, Business, Life*, Cambridge MA: MIT Press, 2006, pp. 33–43, http://lawsofsimplicity.com.

91 Maeda, John, *The Laws of Simplicity, Design, Technology, Business, Life*, p. 39.

92 For a biography: http://www.jonathanive.com/biography/. Hirschmann, Kris, *Innovators. Jonathan Ive: Designer of the iPod*, Farmington Hills, MI: KidHaven Press/Gale, 2007. Intended for a junior audience, nevertheless, it provides a detailed biography of Jonathan Ive on "the gestalt of the iPod", see Maeda, John, *The Laws of Simplicity, Design, Technology, Business, Life*, Cambridge MA: MIT Press, 2006, pp. 17–21.

93 Loewy, Raymond, *Never Leave Well Enough Alone*, Baltimore, MD: The Johns Hopkins University Press, 1951, 2002.

94 "New Designs for Old: An exhibition of new products designed to help older people stay independent at home", a Boilerhouse Project, V&A, London, 29 May to 3 July 1986.

95 http://www.potato2008.org/en/potato/factsheets.html.

96 http://www.sciencedaily.com/releases/2004/06/040617080908.htm.

97 Braungart, Michael, *Cradle to Cradle: Remaking the Way We Make the World*, New York: North Point Press, 2002, p. 4.

98 *State of the World: Into a Warming World*, Worldwatch Institute, Washington DC: WW Norton, New York, 2009, p. 119.

99 Medina, Martin, "The Informal recycling sector in developing countries", *GridLines*, no. 44, October 2008, http://www.ppiaf.org/documents/gridlines/44informal_recycling_sectors.pdf.

100 "The Digital Dump: Exporting RE-Use and Abuse to Africa", Basel Action Network, October 24, 2005,http://www.ban.org/BANreports/10-24-05/index.htm. Royte, Elizabeth, *Garbage Land: On the Secret Trail of Trash*, New York: Back Bay Books/Little Brown, 2006.

101 "It's a Small World" theme song and children's ride originated at the Pepsi Pavilion at the 1964/1965 New York World's Fair. In 1966, after the fair closed, the ride was transferred to Disneyland. The catch phrase has been used in many situations ranging from a tag line at the 2009 Copenhagen Design Week to an editorial heading in *The Progressive Economics*, 9 September 2009.

102 Bruno, Kenny, Jed Greer, *The Greenpeace Book of Greenwash*, Washington DC: Greenpeace, 1992. See also the Greenpeace site: http://www.greenpeace.org/international/en/.

103 Rubin, Jeff, *Why Your World Is About to Get a Whole Lot Smaller*, Toronto and New York: Random House, 2009, p. 3.

104 Rubin, Jeff, *Why Your World Is About to Get a Whole Lot Smaller*, pp. 23–24.

105 http://www.treehugger.com/files/2009/06/why-your-world-is-about-to-get-smaller.php.

CHAPTER FOURTEEN

1 "The Acheulean handaxe industry is significant because it marks a conceptual shift in the making of stone tools which could be linked to cognitive development in Homo Erectus and early *Homo Sapiens*", http://www.smm.org/buzz/museum/object/2004_10_acheulean_handaxe.

2 The essay was included in his more widely read publication, *The Ascent of Man*, Boston: Little Brown, 1974. Other of his books worthy of attention include: *The Origins of Knowledge and Imagination*, Yale University Press, 1979.

3 Scarre, ed., *The Human Past*, London: Thames and Hudson, 2005, p. 110.

4 Calvin, William H, "Rediscovery and the cognitive aspects of toolmaking: Lessons from the handaxe", *Behavioral and Brain Sciences*, vol. 25, no. 3, pp. 403–404. http://williamcalvin.com/2002/BBS-Wynn.htm.

5 "Territorial Expansion of the Roman World", available on line from the University of Calgary: http://www.ucalgary.ca/applied_history/tutor/firsteuro/roman.html. Bispham, Edward, ed., *Roman Europe. 1000BC–AD400*, Oxford and New York: Oxford University Press, 2008. This publication provides eighy essays that explore Iron Age Europe, Roman society, warfare and the army, economy and trade, religions, and the cultural implications of Roman conquest.

6 Jones, Mark Wilson, *Principles of Roman Architecture*, New Haven & London: Yale University Press, 2003. An exploration of how the architects of ancient Rome approached design, dealt with the principles of architecture and the practicalities of construction as they engaged in the creative process. Even the Romans architects had to come to terms with the design conflicts between ideals and the physical realities of construction.

7 Hattendorf, John B, Richard W Unger, eds, *War at sea in the Middle Ages and the Renaissance*, Woodbridge: The Boydell Press, 2003.

8 Lilley, Keith d, "Urban landscapes and the cultural politics of territorial control in Anglo-Norman England", *Landscape Research*, vol. 24, no. 1, March 1999, p. 5–23.

9 For an authoritative source on the Lancashire cotton industry see: "Cotton Times–understanding the industrial revolution," http://www.cottontimes.co.uk/. For a brief annotated bibliography of fifteen sources on the British textile industry: http://www.questia.com/library/economics-and-business/british-textile-industry.jsp. For a recent "appreciation" of the political connections with modern day parallels, see: Hunt, Tristram, "Groundhog capitalism. As Marx and Engels found in Victorian Britain, predicting revolutions can be a frustrating business", *The Guardian*, Saturday, 20 September 2008, Comment and debate section, p. 36. http://www.guardian.co.uk/business/2008/sep/20/creditcrunch.marketturmoil.

10 Brief but accurate summations of many associated developments can be found on the history pages of the *BBC* site–see: "Industrial Revolution", "Technology and Innovation" and "Daily Life", http://www.bbc.co.uk/history/british/victorians/. For more derailed accounts of the cultural context of the Industrial Revolution, see the collection of readings used in the foundation course in Humanities at The

Open University. Christopher Harvie, Christopher, Graham Martin, Aaron Scharf, eds, *Industrialisation and Culture, 1830–1914*, London: Open University Press/Macmillan, 1970, 1976. For information on urbanisation in America from US census of 1790 which reported 5 per cent of the population living in urban areas, to 1990, when 75 per cent of the American population lived in urban areas, see: Roberts, Gerrylynn K, Philip Steadman, *American Cities & Technology*, New York: Routledge, 1999.

11 Sudjic, Deyan, *The Language of Things*, New York: WW Norton and Company, 2009, p. 7.

12 Hauffe, Thomas, *Design. A Concise History*, London: Laurence King, 1998, p. 111.

13 Ransome, Paul, *Work, Consumption and Culture*, London: Sage, 2005, p. 1.

14 Press, Mike, Rachel Cooper, *The Design Experience. The Role of Design and Designers in the Twenty-First Century*, Aldershot and Burlington VA: Ashgate, 2003, p. 69.

15 Mendenhall, Mark E, Torsten M Kühlmann, Günter K Stahl, *Developing Global Business Leaders*, Westport CT: Greenwood Publishing/Quorum Books, 2001, p. 74.

16 The Living Planet Report, "is the world's leading, science-based analysis on the health of our only planet and the impact of human activity". http://wwf.panda.org/about_our_earth/all_publications/living_planet_report/.

17 http://www.millennium-project.org/millennium/challenges.html.

18 Owen, Jonathan, "The planet's future: Climate change 'will cause civilisation to collapse', *The Independent on Sunday*, 17 July 2009.

19 Manzini, Ezio, "Creative Communities in a Network Society", in Cornelis, Jan, Marleen Wynants, ed., *Brave New Interfaces*, Brussels: ASP/VUBPRESS, 2008, pp. 89–99.

20 Manzini, Ezio, "Creative Communities in a Network Society", in Cornelis, Jan, Marleen Wynants, ed., *Brave New Interfaces*, p. 90.

21 Thackara, John, *In the Bubble. Designing in a Complex World*, Cambridge MA: MIT Press, 2006, p. 219.

22 Chapman, Jonathan and Nick Gant, eds, *Designers Visionaries + Other Stories. A collection of sustainable design essays*, London and Sterling VA: Earthscan, 2007, p. 138.

23 The premier text on inter-cultural communication being: Samovar, Larry A, Richard E Porter, Edwin R McDaniel, *Communication Between Cultures*, (seventh edition), Boston: Wadsworth, 2010.

24 Mobile-enabled social change: http://www.kiwanja.net/. "Since 2003, kiwanja.net has been helping empower local, national and international non-profit organisations to make better use of information and communications technology in their work."

25 For a most readable, factual summation, see: Anderson, Kurt, "The Genesis 2.0 Project", *Vanity Fair*, January 2010, http://www.vanityfair.com/culture/features/2010/01/hadron-collider-201001?

26 "At full power, trillions of protons will race around the LHC accelerator ring 11,245 times a second, travelling at 99.99 per cent the speed of light. It is capable of engineering 600 million collisions every second. When two beams of protons collide, they will generate temperatures more than 100,000 times hotter than the heart of the sun, concentrated within a miniscule space. The data recorded by the LHC's big experiments will fill around 100,000 dual-layer DVDs each year. Tens of thousands of computers around the world have been harnessed in a computing network called "The Grid" that will hold the information. At 7:06 am EDT (12.06pm BST,) 30 March 2010, detectors at the lab's Large Hadron Collider (LHC) recorded the accelerator's first proton-on-proton collisions at energy levels roughly 3.5 times higher than those in previous experiments. The event marks the beginning of what researchers expect to be a historic 18- to 24-month science run. That energy level corresponds to energies present when the universe was only one ten-billionth of a second old". This of course begs the question—What's on the other side of time? "Factbox: Five facts about CERN's Large Hadron Collider", Reuters, 20 March 2010, http://www.reuters.com/article/idUSTRE62T1KT20100330. See also: Bryson, Bill, "Bill Bryson's Notes from a Large Hadron Collider", *Times* online, 5 November 2009. A most informative and readable account of the scientists who are hoping to unlock the secrets of the Universe". http://www.timesonline.co.uk/tol/news/science/eureka/article6899505.ece. In November 2010, researchers at the LHC successfully reproduced conditions a millionth of a second after the Big Bang. Alleyne, Richard, "Start of the Universe: mini Big Bang Recreated", *The Telegraph*, 8 November, 2010.

27 Anderson, Kurt, "The Genesis 2.0 Project", *Vanity Fair*, January 2010, http://www.vanityfair.com/culture/features/2010/01/hadron-collider-201001?

28 Friedman, Jerome, "The New Collider: The large hadron collider may solve nature's great mysteries", *Technology Review*, May/June 2008. These and other challenges to modern physics are addressed by Anil Ananthaswamy consultant editor of *New Scientist* in his recent and most readable book: Ananthaswamy, Anil, *The Edge of Physics*, New York, Houghton Mifflin, 2010.

29 For the CERN (European Organization for Nuclear Research) homepage: http://public.web.cern.ch/public/.

30 "Big Bang experiment starts well", an interview with Professor Brian Cox, one of the LHC scientists at Cern, *BBC News*, Saturday, 6 September 2008, http://news.bbc.co.uk/2/hi/uk_news/7598996.stm. Bourzac, Katherine, "The Making of a New Collider", *Technology Review*, May/June 2008, http://www.technologyreview.com/Infotech/20588/?a=f.

31 http://news.bbc.co.uk/2/hi/uk_news/7598996.stm.

32 Moore, Gordon E, "Cramming more components onto integrated circuits", *Electronics*, vol. 38, no. 8, 19 April 1965.

33 http://www.technologyreview.com/computing/21901/?a=f.

34 Jones, Terril Yue, "A Law of Continuing Returns", *Los Angeles Times*, Business section, 17 April 2005, http://articles.latimes.com/2005/apr/17/business/fi-silicon17.

35 World's First two-Billion Transistor Microprocessor, Intel / Technology / Architecture and Silicon Technology, 2007. Includes a webcast featuring Gordon Moore, http://www.intel.com/technology/architecture-silicon/2billion.htm?iid=SEARCH.

36 Greene, Kate, "Toward a Quantum Internet. A quantum logic gate in an optical fiber could lay the foundation for a quantum computer network", *Technology Review*, 15 April 2008, http://www.technologyreview.com/Infotech/20565/?nlid=1004&a=f. Cringley, Robert X, "Parallel Universe. In an effort to move forward, Intel dusts off old supercomputing technology", *Technology Review*, January/February, 2009, http://www.technologyreview.com/computing/21806/?a=f.

37 For a brief biography and list of achievements see: http://www.kurzweiltech.com/aboutray.html. For a video of the 80 minute presentation Kurzeil made at the 2007 Killer App Expo in Fort Wayne see: http://www.technologyevangelist.com/2007/05/killer_app_expo_ray.html.

38 Kurzweil expands his rational. "In line with my earlier predictions, supercomputers will achieve one human brain capacity by 2010, and personal computers will do so by around 2020.... By 2050, $1000 of computing will equal the processing power of all human brains on Earth.... One of the principal assumptions underlying the expectation of the Singularity is the ability of nonbiological mediums to emulate the richness, subtlety, and depth of human thinking.... By human levels I include all the diverse and subtle ways in which humans are intelligent, including musical and artistic aptitude, creativity, physically moving through the world, and understanding and responding appropriately to emotion". http://www.kurzweilai.net/articles/art0134.html.

39 Kurzweil, Ray, "The Law of Accelerating Returns", in Teuscher, Christof, Dan Hofstader, *Alan Turning*, Springer, 2004, pp. 381–416. Kurzweil, Ray, *The Singularity is Near. When Humans Transcend Biology*, London and New York: Penguin Books, 2005.

40 John Casti is Senior Research Scholar, the International Institute for Applied Systems Analysis, in Laxenburg, Austria and cofounder of the Kenos Circle, a Vienna-based society for exploration of the future. This quote appears in part of IEEE Spectrum's Special report: the singularity, June 2008. http://www.spectrum.ieee.org/jun08/6277. See also: IEEE Spectrum online, IEEE is the world's largest professional technology association. http://www.spectrum.ieee.org/singularity.

41 McLaughlin, William I, "Human Evolution in the Age of the Intelligent Machine", *Leonardo*, vol. 17, no. 4, 1984, pp. 277–287.

42 O B Hardison, *Disappearing Through the Skylight. Culture and Technology in the Twentieth Century*, London and New York: Penguin Books, 1990, p. 337.

43 O B Hardison, *Disappearing Through the Skylight. Culture and Technology in the Twentieth Century*, pp. 346–348.

44 Bing, Stanley, *Rome, Inc: The Rise and Fall of the First Multinational Corporation*, New York: WW Norton, 2006.

45 The first human spaceflight was Vostok 1 on 12 April 1961, aboard which Soviet cosmonaut Yuri Gagarin made one orbit circumnavigation of the Earth.

46 The concept first appeared in print in 1960. Clynes, Manfred E, Nathan S Kline, "Cyborgs and Space", *Astronautics*, September 1960, pp. 29–33, http://www.scribd.com/doc/2962194/Cyborgs-and-Space-Clynes-Kline.

47 http://www.airbus.com/en/aircraftfamilies/a380/.

48 http://www.boeing.com/commercial/index.html.

49 "Wireless technologies and mobile media change the way people communicate and interact, modify the dynamics of accessing and sharing knowledge, as well as alter notions of place and space. The Mobile Experience Lab, with a multidisciplinary approach, aims to understand peoples experiences using wireless communication technologies, exploring the impact of mobile media on communities, societies, and space." http://design.mit.edu/research.

50 Nigel Whiteley, *Design for Society*, London: Reaktion Books, 1993, 1998.

51 http://mobile.mit.edu/.

52 Jeremy Myerson, "Designing for Public Good", *DesignWeek*, 27 July 1990, p. 13.

53 *The Economist* produced a special report, "Nomads at Last", on mobile communication. The report offers an engaging and thoughtful appraisal by Andreas Kluth of mobile communication technology. It addresses such topics as the joys and drawbacks of being able to work from anywhere, family ties, love in cyberspace, mobility and location, the political, healthcare and environmental ramifications of nomadic monitoring, and the evolution of Homo mobilis. Kluth, Andreas, "Nomads at last", *The Economist*, special report, April, 2008, http://www.economist.com/specialreports/displaystory.cfm?story_id=10950394. For a contact list of 26 academic theorists and researchers in the field of mobile communication studies from Rutgers School of Communication, Information and Library Studies;

http://www.scils.rutgers.edu/ci/cmcs/theorists/.

54 Ibid.

55 For the latest figures check the site of the Telecom Regulatory Authority of India, http://www.trai.gov.in/Default.asp.

56 http://theindependent-bd.com/details.php?nid=150547.

57 Gartrell, Andrew et al, *Asia Design Journal 2010*, Design for Social Innovation, http://grignani.org/thoughts/tag/nokia/.

58 Orville and Wilbur Wright were the two Americans who are generally credited with inventing and building the world's first successful aeroplane and making the first controlled, powered and sustained heavier-than-air human flight on 17 December 1903.

59 The Boeing B-50A Superfortress flew around the world nonstop from Ft Worth. It was refuelled four times in air. The circumnavigation was completed on 2 March 1949. The aircraft flew 37,743 km (23,452 miles) at an average speed of 398 km/h (249 mph).

60 http://openmap.bbn.com/~tomlinso/ray/firstemailframe.html.

61 Berners-Lee, Tim, Mark Fischetti, *Weaving the Web*, San Francisco: Harper Collins, 1999.

62 Detailed information on the envisaged One Machine and many other tantalisingly engaging topics can be found on Kevin Kelly's website, http://www.kk.org.

63 Linzmayer, Owen W, *Apple Confidential 2.0: The Definitive History of the World's Most Colorful Company*, San Francisco, CA: No Starch Press, 2004.

64 Linzmayer, Owen W, *Apple Confidential 2.0: The Definitive History of the World's Most Colorful Company*, p. 113.

65 http://www.apple.com/pr/library/2007/04/09ipod.html. Levy, Steven, *The Perfect Thing: How the iPod Shuffles Commerce, Culture, and Coolness*, New York: Simon & Schuster, 2006.

66 Sørensen, Carsten, "Digital nomads and mobile services". This article was written for receiver. It is based on research documented in the conference paper "Mobile Services–functional diversity and overload" by C Sørensen, L Mathiassen and M Kakihara, 2002, http://www.vodafone.com/flash/receiver/06/articles/pdf/06.pdf. Dr Sørensen has also produced an informative guide to writing an article. Read it: http://personal.lse.ac.uk/SORENSEC/attachments/ThisIsStillNotAnArticlePre0.pdf.

67 Castells, Manuel, et al, "The Mobile Communication Society. A cross-cultural analysis of available evidence on the social uses of wireless communication technology", a research report prepared for the *International Workshop on Wireless Communication Policies and Prospects: A Global Perspective*, held at the Annenberg School for Communication, University of Southern California, Los Angeles, 8 and 9 October 2004. This extensive (327 page) report includes sections on the statistical diffusion of mobile technology, its social use and differentiation, a study of the mobile youth culture in a cross-cultural perspective, and the language of wireless communication. The final appendix concerns non-standard orthographic forms in SMS language, pp.310-327, http://arnic.info/workshop04/MCS.pdf. See also The mobility@lse unit which researches contemporary issues related to the development and use of mobile and ubiquitous information technology, http://mobility.lse.ac.uk/news.html.

68 Kluth, Andreas, "Nomads at last", *The Economist*, special report, April, 2008, http://www.economist.com/specialreports/displaystory.cfm?story_id=10950394.

69 Kenneally, Christine, *The First Word. The Search for the Origins of Language*, New York: Penguin Group, 2007, p. 3.

70 You can download a PDF copy of the full 92 page report: http://www.designcouncil.org.uk/en/About-Design/Research/International-Design-Research/.

71 Sachs, Jeffrey, *Common Wealth: Economics for a Crowded Planet*, London and New York: Penguin Press, 2008, p. 3.

72 The classic definition of wisdom being the knowledge needed to live a good life. "Excellence and knowledge", in Meyer, Susan Sauvé, *Ancient Ethics*, London and New York: Routledge, 2008, pp. 14–17.

73 Surowiecki, James, *The Wisdom of Crowds: Why the many are Smarter than the few and how Collective Wisdom Shapes Business, Economies, Societies and Nations*, New York: Random House, 2004. See also the Internet entrepreneurial focussed, Silver, Aaron David, *Smart Start-ups: How Entrepreneurs and Corporations Can Profit by Starting Online Communities*, John Wiley and Sons, 2007.

74 Frank Pick was Chief Executive of the London Passenger Transport Board from its creation in 1933 until 1940. "Design means something purposed, fit for its function, economical of material and labour, sound in form and construction. That we must seek everywhere if appearance values are to be realised. It is intelligence made visible". The quote appears in *the London Transport Third Annual Conference Proceedings*, 1938, pp. 44–45. (Thanks to Caroline Warhurst of London Transport Information Services for tracking down this oft quoted but rarely attributed quotation.)

75 Pink, Daniel H, *A Whole New Mind*, New York: Riverhead Books/Penguin Group, 2005, p. 1.

76 Koberg, Don, Jim Bagnall, *The All New Universal Traveler*, Los Altos CA: William Kaufmann, 1972, 1981, back cover.

77 Benjamin Franklin (1706–90) used this phrase in a letter to Jean-Baptiste Leroy, 1789, which was re-printed in *The Works of Benjamin Franklin*, 1817.

78 Professor Stuart Walker, a former member of the Faculty of Environmental Design at the University of Calgary is Co-Director of the creative research lab ImaginationLancaster, Lancaster University which offers post-graduate programmes in Sustainability, Innovation and Design. He has written extensively on sustainable design and serves as an advisor to the UK's 'Design for the 21st Century' initiative. http://imagination.lancaster.ac.uk/.

79 Walker, Stuart, "Design Redux", in Chapman, Jonathan, Nick Grant, Designers, *Visionaries + Other Stories*, London and Sterling VT: Earthscan, 2007, p. 57.

80 Wood, John, "Relative Abundance", in Chapman, Jonathan, Nick Grant, *Designers, Visionaries + Other Stories*, London and Sterling VT: Earthscan, 2007, pp. 101–102.

81 Wood, John, "Relative Abundance", in Chapman, Jonathan, Nick Grant, *Designers, Visionaries + Other Stories*, London & Sterling VT: Earthscan, 2007, p. 99.

82 Chapman, Jonathan, Nick Grant, *Designers, Visionaries + Other Stories*, London and Sterling VT: Earthscan, 2007, p. 140. See also the site of the World Watch Institute whose objective is to help "create a safer, more sustainable world today". They have an array of well researched, well documented publications. http://www.worldwatch.org/.

83 Longstaff, Simon, "Ethics: can you afford not to have them?" This article discusses the role of ethics in modern business practice. The article is available online from the Australian based St James Ethics Centre. http://www.ethics.org.au/.

84 In the post industrial age in may be worth while to consider observations made in the pre-industrial age. It was not the famous *Wealth of Nations*, but a work on ethics and human nature called *The Theory of Moral Sentiments*, published in 1759, which made the Scottish economist Adam Smith's career. Interconnections

between systems and societies; the effect of far-away disasters, principles of selfishness and comments on materialism make this work worthy of consulting. Wen Jiabao, the Chinese premier, claims to be motivated by Adam Smith's pronouncements, http://www.fmprc.gov.cn/eng/zxxx/t535971.htm. In her recent publication, social scientist Riane Eisler charts the development of economics from Adam Smith to the present day, concluding that "the real wealth of nations consists of the contributions of people and our natural environment". Eisler sets out six foundations for a caring economic system. Eisler, Riane, *The Real Wealth of Nations*, San Francisco: Berrett-Koehler, 2007. *The United Nations 1990 Human Development Report* begins with the pronouncement that "People are the real wealth of a nation". http://hdr.undp.org/en/reports/global/hdr1990/.

85 Jones, Dan, "The emerging moral psychology", *Prospect*, April, 2008, no. 145.

86 Manzini, Ezio, Stuart Walker, Barry Wylant, eds., *Enabling Solutions for Sustainable Living*, Calgary: University of Calgary Press, 2008.

87 Press, Mike, Rachel Cooper, *The Design Experience. The Role of Design and Designers in the Twenty-First Century*, Aldershot and Burlington VA: Ashgate, 2003, p. 5.

88 Carey, Peter, "Eric Chan: Everyday Meaningful Use", *Office Insight*, 22 March 2010, pp. 3–5, www.eccoid.com/DOCS/EricChan_EverydayMeaningfulUse.pdf.

89 Twenge, Jean M, "Applying Our Knowledge: The Future of Business and the Future of the Young", *Generation Me: Why Today's Young Americans Are More Confident, Assertive, Entitled and More Miserable Than Ever Before*, New York: Free Press/Simon & Schuster, 2006, pp. 212–242.

90 Among the subject areas that are likely to have an impact on the design process over the next two decades are: Life Cycle Analysis; Ethnography; Human Cantered Product Development; Ethics, and Sustainability.

91 Darwin, Charles, Joseph Carroll, ed., *On the Origin of Species*, Peterborough, Ontario, Broadview Press, 1859, 2003, p. 537.

92 McDonough, William, Michael Braungart, *Cradle to Cradle: Remaking The Way We Make Things*, New York: North Point Press, 2002.

93 Andreasen, Nancy C, *The Creative Brain: The Science of Genius*, New York: Plume Book, 2006. Small, Gary, *iBrain: Surviving the Technological Alteration of the Modern Mind*, New York: Harper Collins, 2008. "Learning: It's a Memory Thing. Neurons make a hookup", *The Why Files*, University of Wisconsin, 2003, http://whyfiles.org/184make_memory/4.html.

94 Hopkins, Rob, "Forward", in Chamberlin, Shaun, Rob Hopkins, *The Transition Timeline: For a Local, Resilient Future*, Totnes: Chelsea Green Publishing, 2009, p. 10.

FURTHER READING

History teaches everything including the future.
Alphonse de Lamartine, (1790–1869)

THE NEXT THREE TO READ:
van Doren, Charles, *A History of Knowledge. Past, Present, and Future*, New York: Ballantine, 1991. Knowledge of the past provides the sphere of influence for future actions. This concise, clear and engaging account of humankind is a good place to start.

Hardison, OB, *Disappearing Through the Skylight. Culture and Technology in the Twentieth Century*, New York: Penguin, 1989. A cross-disciplinary and fascinating account of where we have come from and where we are going. Many examples from and connections to the creative world of art, architecture and design.

Thackara, John, *In the Bubble. Designing in a Complex World*, Cambridge MA: Mit Press, 2006. Essential reading for all involved in design.

**THREE GEMS—
SMALL IN FORMAT, VAST IN POTENTIAL:**
As we have seen in this book, design is first and foremost about mind set. These three small format books could be at least mind changing if not life changing.

Edelman, Gerald M, *Second Nature: brain science and human knowledge*, New Haven: Yale University Press, 2006. Using plain language, this Nobel laureate describes the role that the brain plays in knowledge acquisition and creativity.

Maeda, John, *The Laws of Simplicity*, Cambridge MA: MIT Press, 2006. Graphic designer, visual artist, computer scientist, and a former professor in MIT's Media Lab, and currently President of the Rhode Island School of Design, Maeda tell us "Simplicity is about subtracting the obvious, and adding the meaningful."

McIntyre, Lee, *Dark Ages. The Case for a Science of Human Behaviour*, Cambridge, MA: MIT Press, 2006. Most of the design challenges ahead have social and cultural ramifications. This is a call for the application of scientific method to social science.

DESIGN, CREATIVITY, AND CULTURE:
This list makes no claims as to being a comprehensive listing of all available thinking on the subject, rather it is a highly selective shortlist of sources that I have found to be of particular use and interest.

DESIGN AND CREATIVITY:
Chapman, Jonathan, Nick Grant, *Designers, Visionaries + Other Stories. A Collection of Sustainable Design Essays*, London: Earthscan, 2007.

Cornelis, Jan, Marleen Wynants, ed., *Brave New Interfaces*, Brussels: ASP/VUBPRESS, 2008.

Design for the Other 90%, New York: Cooper-Hewitt National Design Museum, Smithsonian Institution, 2007.

Fletcher, Kate, *Sustainable Fashion & Textiles*, London & Sterling VA: Earthscan, 2008.

Heskett, John, *Design. A Very Short Introduction*, Oxford: Oxford University Press, 2002.

Kelley, Tom, Jonathan Littman, *The Art of Innovation*, New York: Doubleday/Random House, 2001.

Merholz, Peter, Todd Wilkens, Brandon Schauer, David Verba, *Subject To Change: Creating Great Products & Services for an Uncertain World. Adaptive Path on Design*, Sebastopol, CA: O'Reilly, 2008.

Moggridge, Bill, *Designing Interactions*, Cambridge MA: MIT Press, 2007.

Norman, Donald A, *The Psychology of Everyday Things*, (1988) reissued as *The Design of Everyday Things*, New York: Basic Books, 2002, and *Living With Complexity*, Cambridge MA: MIT Press, 2010.

Press, Mike, Rachel Cooper, *The Role of Design and Designers in the Twenty-First Century*, Aldershot and Burlington VT: Ashgate, 2003.

Sparke, Penny, *An Introduction to Design and Culture: 1900 to the Present*, New York: Routledge, 2004.

Woodham, Jonathan M, *Twentieth Century Design*, Oxford: Oxford University Press, 1997.

CULTURE:
Castells, Manuel, Mireia Fernández-Ardèvol, Jack Linchuan Qiu, Araba Sey, *Mobile Communication and Society. A Global Perspective*, Cambridge MA: MIT Press, 2007.

Eco, Umberto, *Turning Back the Clock. Hot Wars and Media Populism*, Orlando: Houghton Miffin Harcourt, 2007.

Friedman, Thomas L, *The World is Flat. A Brief History of the Twenty-First Century*, New York: Farrar, Straus and Giroux, 2006.

Kellner, Douglas, *Cultural Studies, Identity and Politics Between the Modern and the Postmodern*, London: Routledge, 1995.

Kurzweil, Ray, *The Age of Spiritual Machines*, New York: Viking, 1999. *The Singularity is Near*, London and New York, Penguin, 2005.

Lewis, Richard D, *The Cultural Imperative. Global Trends in the 21st Century*, London: Nicholas Brealey, 2003.

Verdal, Vlatko, *Decoding Reality. The Universe as Quantum Information*, Oxford: Oxford University Press, 2010.

INDEX

BIOGRAPHY

Maurice Barnwell received his design education in Birmigham and in Toronto. He has worked and taught in the UK, Hong Kong and Canada. In February 1991 he founded Idforum, the first computer newsgroup dedicated to the world of industrial design. His teaching career covers two decades and includes courses concerned with the History of Design; History of Communication Design; Image, Text and Ideas; The Cultural Controls of Design; Design in Society; Design Creativity and Research in Design. Maurice is a well-travelled speaker and has presented conferences in Europe, Asia and North America. His current research is focused on the changing nature of design.

ACKNOWLEDGEMENTS

Some time in the late 1950s as a bemused youngster I wandered into Kings Heath public library in Birmingham. The mature librarian took the time to introduce me to the library system showed me how to use the card index (it was a long time ago!) and revealed the magic of cross-referencing. Much more important was that she encouraged in me a love of learning which has never diminished. Regretfully I never knew her name, but I would like to say a very belated, "thank you".

I have been most fortunate to have the support and friendship of many people, all of whom have helped in one way or another in the development of this book—although I hasten to add that all the mistakes are mine. A sincere thanks to, Michael Farr, Paul D Fleck, Don Newgren, Akinori Ogimura, Andy Tomcik, Arthur Wiley and to all those hundreds of students whose bright enquiring minds often surprised, energised and taught me new things.

This project would never have seen the light of day without the help and support of the editorial and design departments at Black Dog Publishing. In particular my thanks go to Duncan McCorquodale for his support and to Anna Stratigakis for her design management. I would also like to acknowledge the initial design concepts of Toronto based Frank Maidens. The book would not have been possible without the loving support of Susan, my friend and partner for over 40 years—thank you all.

Toronto, April 2011

COLOPHON

© 2011 Black Dog Publishing Limited and the author.
All rights reserved.

Black Dog Publishing Limited
10A Acton Street
London
WC1X 9NG

t. +44 (0)207 713 5097
f. +44 (0)207 713 8682
e. info@blackdogonline.com
www.blackdogonline.com

All opinions expressed within this publication are those of
the author and not necessarily of the publisher.

Designed by Anna Stratigakis at Black Dog Publishing.

British Library Cataloguing-in-Publication Data.
A CIP record for this book is available from
The British Library.

ISBN 978 1 907317 40 8

Black Dog Publishing is an environmentally responsible
company. *Design, Creativity and Culture* is printed on FSC
accredited paper.

Printed in China.

architecture art design
fashion history photography
theory and things

**black dog
publishing**

www.blackdogonline.com   london uk